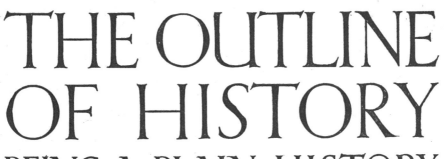

THE OUTLINE OF HISTORY

BEING A PLAIN HISTORY OF LIFE AND MANKIND

BY H. G. WELLS

Written with the advice and
: editorial help of :
Mr Ernest Barker
Sir H. H. Johnston
Sir E. Ray Lankester
and Professor Gilbert
Murray:

VOLUME TWO

LONDON
GEORGE NEWNES LIMITED
SOUTHAMPTON ST. STRAND W.C.2

XXXI

SEVEN CENTURIES IN ASIA

(Circa 50 B.C. to A.D. 650)

§ 1

IN the preceding two chapters we have concentrated our attention chiefly on the collapse in the comparatively short space of four centuries of the political and social order of the western part of the great Roman Empire of Cæsar and Trajan.

Justinian the Great. We have dwelt upon the completeness of that collapse. To any intelligent and public-spirited mind living in the time and under the circumstances of St. Benedict or Cassiodorus, it must have seemed, indeed, as if the light of civilization was waning and near extinction. But with the longer views a study of universal history gives us, we can view those centuries of shadow as a phase, and probably a necessary phase, in the onward march of social and political ideas and understandings. And if, during that time, a dark sense of calamity rested upon Western Europe, we must remember that over large portions of the world there was no retrogression.

With their Western prepossessions European writers are much too prone to underrate the tenacity of the Eastern empire that centred upon Constantinople. This empire embodied a tradition much more ancient than that of Rome. If the reader will look at the map we have given of its extent in the sixth century, and if he will reflect that its official language had then become Greek, he will realize that what we are dealing with here is only nominally a branch of the Roman Empire ; it is really the Hellenic Empire of which Herodotus dreamt and which Alexander the Great founded. True it called itself Roman and its people "Romans," and to this day modern Greek is called "Romaic." True also that Constantine the Great knew no Greek and that Justinian's accent was bad. These superficialities of name and form cannot alter the fact that the empire was in reality Hellenic, with a past of six centuries at the time of Constantine the Great, and that while the real Roman Empire crumpled up completely

in four centuries, this Hellenic "Roman Empire" held out for more than eleven, from 312, the beginning of the reign of Constantine the Great, to 1453, when Constantinople fell to the Ottoman Turks.

And while we have had to tell of something like a complete social collapse in the west, there were no such equivalent breakdowns in the east. Towns and cities flourished, the country-side was well cultivated, trade went on. For many centuries Constantinople was the greatest and richest city in the world. We will not trouble ourselves here with the names and follies, the crimes and intrigues, of its tale of emperors. As with most monarchs of great states, they did not guide their empire ; they were carried by it. We have already dealt at some length with Constantine the Great (312-337), we have mentioned Theodosius the Great (379-395), who for a little while reunited the empire, and Justinian I (527-565).[1] Presently we shall tell something of Heraclius (610-641). Justinian, like Constantine, may have had Slav blood in his veins. He was a man of great ambition and great organizing power, and he had the good fortune to be married to a woman of equal or greater ability, the Empress Theodora, who had in her youth been an actress of doubtful reputation. But his ambitious attempts to restore the ancient greatness of the empire probably overtaxed its resources. As we have told, he reconquered the African province from the Vandals and most of Italy from the Goths. He also recovered the South of Spain. He built the great and beautiful church of Saint Sophia in Constantinople, founded a university, and codified the law.[2] But against this we must

---

[1] See Holmes' *Justinian and Theodora.*—E. B.

[2] Great importance is attached to this task by historians, including one of the editors of this history. We are told that the essential contribution of Rome to the inheritance of mankind is the idea of society founded on *law*, and that this exploit of Justinian was the crown of the gift. The writer is ill-equipped to estimate the peculiar value of Roman legalism to man-

Photo: Alinari.

JUSTINIAN AND HIS COURT.
Mosaic at Ravenna.

set his closing of the schools of Athens. Meanwhile a great plague swept the world, and at his death this renewed and expanded empire of his crumpled up again like a blown-out bladder. The greater part of his Italian conquests was lost to the Lombards. Italy was indeed at that time almost a desert; the Lombard historians assert they came into an empty country. The Avars and Slavs struck down from the Danube country towards the Adriatic, Slav populations establishing themselves in what is now Serbia, Croatia, and Dalmatia, to become the Yugo-Slavs of to-day. Moreover, a great and exhausting struggle began with the Sassanid Empire in Persia.

kind. Existing law seems to him to be based upon a confused foundation of conventions, arbitrary assumptions, and working fictions about human relationship, and to be a very impracticable and antiquated system indeed; he is persuaded that a time will come when the whole theory and practice of law will be recast in the light of a well-developed science of social psychology in accordance with a scientific conception of human society as one developing organization and in definite relationship to a system of moral and intellectual education. He contemplates the law and lawyers of to-day with a temperamental lack of appreciation. This may have made him negligent of Justinian and unjust to Rome as a whole.

But before we say anything of this struggle, in which the Persians thrice came near to taking Constantinople, and which was decided by a great Persian defeat at Nineveh (627), it is necessary to sketch very briefly the history of Persia from the Parthian days.

§ 2

We have already drawn a comparison between the brief four centuries of Roman imperialism and the obstinate vitality of the imperialism of the Euphrates-Tigris country. We have glanced very transitorily at the Hellenized Bactrian and Seleucid monarchies that flourished in the eastern half of Alexander's area of conquest for three centuries, and told how the Parthians came down into Mesopotamia in the last century B.C. We have described the battle of Carrhæ and the end of Crassus. Thereafter for two centuries and a half the Parthian dynasty of the Arsacids ruled in the east and the Roman in the west, with Armenia and Syria between them, and the boundaries shifted east and west as either side grew stronger. We have marked the utmost eastward extension of the Roman

The Sassanid Empire in Persia.

Empire under Trajan (see map to chap. xxix., § 3), and we have noted that about the same time the Indo-Scythians (chap. xxix., § 4) poured down into India.

In 227 occurred a revolution, and the Arsacid dynasty gave way to a more vigorous line, the Sassanid, a national Persian line under Ardashir I. In one respect the empire of Ardashir I presented a curious parallelism with that of Constantine the Great a hundred years later. Ardashir attempted to consolidate it by insisting upon religious unity, and adopted as the state religion the old Persian faith of Zoroaster, of which we shall have more to say later.

This new Sassanid Empire immediately became aggressive, and under Sapor I, the son and successor of Ardashir, took Antioch. We have already noted how the Emperor Valerian was defeated (260) and taken prisoner. But as Sapor was retiring from a victorious march into Asia Minor, he was fallen upon and defeated by Odenathus, the Arab king of a great desert-trading centre, Palmyra.

For a brief time under Odenathus, and then under his widow Zenobia, Palmyra was a considerable state, wedged between the two empires. Then it fell to the Emperor Aurelian, who carried off Zenobia in chains to grace his triumph at Rome (272).

We will not attempt to trace the fluctuating fortunes of the Sassanids during the next three centuries. Throughout that time war between Persia and the empire of

Constantinople wasted Asia Minor like a fever. Christianity spread widely and was persecuted, for after the Christianization of Rome the Persian monarch remained the only god-monarch on earth, and he saw in Christianity merely the propaganda of his Byzantine rival. Constantinople became the protector of the Christians and Persia of the Zoroastrians; in a treaty of 422, the one empire agreed to tolerate Zoroastrianism and the other Christianity. In 483, the Christians of the east split off from the Orthodox church and became the Nestorian church; which, as we have already noted, spread its missionaries far and wide throughout Central and Eastern Asia. This separation from Europe, since it freed the Christian bishops of the east from the rule of the Byzantine patriarchs, and so lifted from the Nestorian church the suspicion of political disloyalty, led to a complete toleration of Christianity in Persia. With Chosroes I (531-579) came a last period of Sassanid vigour. He was the contemporary and parallel of Justinian. He reformed taxation, restored the orthodox Zoroastrianism, extended his power into Southern Arabia (Yemen), which he rescued from the rule of Abyssinian Christians, pushed his northern frontier into Western Turkestan, and carried on a series of wars with Justinian. His reputation as an enlightened ruler stood so high, that when Justinian closed the schools of Athens, the last Greek philosophers betook themselves to his court. They

JUSTINIAN'S CHURCH OF ST. SOPHIA AT CONSTANTINOPLE.

Photo : Major W. J. P. Rodd.

CHOSROES II ON HIS WAR-HORSE.
A rock carving at Takht-i-Bostan.

sought in him the philosopher king—that mirage which, as we have noted, Confucius and Plato had sought in their day. The philosophers found the atmosphere of orthodox Zoroastrianism even less to their taste than orthodox Christianity, and in 549 Chosroes had the kindness to insert a clause in an armistice with Justinian, permitting their return to Greece, and ensuring that they should not be molested for their pagan philosophy or their transitory pro-Persian behaviour.

It is in connection with Chosroes that we hear now of a new Hunnish people in Central Asia, the Turks, who are, we learn, first in alliance with him and then with Constantinople.

Chosroes II (590-628), the grandson of Chosroes I, experienced extraordinary fluctuations of fortune. At the outset of his career he achieved astonishing successes against the empire of Constantinople. Three times (in 608, 615, and 627) his armies reached Chalcedon, which is over against Constantinople ; he took

Antioch, Damascus, and Jerusalem (614), and from Jerusalem he carried off a cross, said to be the true cross on which Jesus was crucified, to his capital Ctesiphon. (But some of this or some other true cross had already got to Rome. It had been brought from Jerusalem, it was said, by the "Empress Helena," the idealized and canonized mother of Constantine, a story for which Gibbon displayed small respect.[1]) In 619 Chosroes II conquered that facile country, Egypt. This career of conquest was at last arrested by the Emperor Heraclius (610), who set about restoring the ruined military power of Constantinople. For some time Heraclius avoided a great battle while he gathered his forces. He took the field in good earnest in 623. The Persians experienced a series of defeats culminating in the battle of Nineveh (617) ; but neither side had the strength for the complete defeat of the other. At the end of

[1] *The Decline and Fall of the Roman Empire*, chap. xxiii.

the struggle there was still an undefeated Persian army upon the Bosphorus, although there were victorious Byzantine forces in Mesopotamia. In 628 Chosroes II was deposed and murdered by his son. An indecisive peace was concluded between the two exhausted empires a year or so later, restoring their old boundaries ; and the true cross was sent back to Heraclius, who replaced it in Jerusalem with much pomp and ceremony.

§ 3

So we give briefly the leading events in the history of the **The Decay of Syria under the Sassanids.** Persian as of the Byzantine Empire. What is more interesting for us and less easy to give are the changes that went on in the lives of the general population of those great empires during that time. The present writer can find little of a definite character about the great pestilences that we know swept the world in the second and sixth centuries of this era. Certainly they depleted population, and probably they disorganized social order in these regions just as much as we know they did in the Roman and Chinese empires.

The late Sir Mark Sykes, whose untimely death in Paris during the influenza epidemic of 1919 was an irreparable loss to Great Britain, wrote in *The Caliph's Last Heritage* a vivid review of the general life of Nearer Asia during the period we are considering. In the opening centuries of the present era, he says : " the direction of military administration and imperial finance became entirely divorced in men's minds from practical government ; and notwithstanding the vilest tyranny of sots, drunkards, tyrants, lunatics, savages, and abandoned women, who from time to time held the reins of government, Mesopotamia, Babylonia, and Syria contained enormous populations, huge canals and dykes were kept in repair,

and commerce and architecture flourished, in spite of a perpetual procession of hostile armies and a continual changing of the nationality of the governor. Each peasant's interest was centred in his ruling town ; each citizen's interest was in the progress and prosperity of his city ; and the advent of an enemy's army may have sometimes been looked on even with

The EASTERN EMPIRE and the SASSANIDS

satisfaction, if his victory was assured and the payment of his contracts a matter of certainty.

" A raid from the north,[1] on the other hand, must have been a matter for dread. Then the villagers had need to take refuge behind the walls of the cities, from whence they could descry the smoke which told of the wreck and damage caused by the nomads. So long, however, as the canals were not destroyed (and indeed they were built with such solidity and caution that their safety was assured), no irreparable damage could be effected. . . .

" In Armenia and Pontus the condition of life was quite otherwise. These were mountain districts, containing fierce tribes headed by powerful native nobility under recognized ruling kings, while in the valleys and plains the peaceful cultivator provided the necessary economic resources. . . . Cilicia and Cappadocia

[1] Turanians from Turkestan or Avars from the Caucasus.

were now thoroughly subject to Greek influence, and contained numerous wealthy and highly civilized towns, besides possessing a considerable merchant marine. Passing from Cilicia to the Hellespont, the whole Mediterranean coast was crowded with wealthy cities and Greek colonies, entirely cosmopolitan in thought and speech, with those municipal and local ambitions which seem natural to the Grecian character. The Grecian Zone extended from Caria to the Bosphorus, and followed the coast as far as Sinope on the Black Sea, where it gradually faded away.

"Syria was broken up into a curious quilt-

which even now command our admiration. . . . Bending in towards Galilee we find the wondrous cities of Gerasa and Philadelphia (Amman) connected by solid roads of masonry and furnished with gigantic aqueducts. . . . Syria is still so rich in ruins and remains of the period that it is not difficult to picture to oneself the nature of its civilization. The arts of Greece, imported long before, had been developed into magnificence that bordered on vulgarity. The richness of ornamentation, the lavish expense, the flaunting wealth, all tell that the tastes of the voluptuous and artistic Semites were then as now. I have stood in the colonnades of Palmyra and I have dined in the Hotel Cecil, and, save that the latter is built of iron, daubed with sham wood, sham stucco, sham gold, sham velvet, and sham stone, the effect is identical. In Syria there were slaves in sufficient quantity to make real buildings, but the artistic spirit is as debased as anything made by machinery. Over against the cities the village folk must have dwelt pretty much as they do now, in houses of mud and dry stone wall; while out in the distant pastures the Bedouin tended their flocks in freedom under the rule of the Nabatean kings of their own race, or performed the

Cities of ASIA MINOR, SYRIA & MESOPOTAMIA during the first centuries of the Christian Era....

Trade routes ----
Mountains shaded vertically.

like pattern of principalities and municipal kingdoms; beginning with the almost barbarous states of Commagene and Edessa (Urfa) in the north. South of these stood Bambyce, with its huge temples and priestly governors. Towards the coast a dense population in villages and towns clustered around the independent cities of Antioch, Apamea, and Emesa (Homs); while out in the wilderness the great Semitic merchant city of Palmyra was gaining wealth and greatness as the neutral trading-ground between Parthia and Rome. Between the Lebanon and Anti-Lebanon we find, at the height of its glory, Heliopolis (Baalbek), the battered fragments of

office of guardians and agents of the great trading caravans.

"Beyond the herdsmen lay the parching deserts, which acted as the impenetrable barrier and defence of the Parthian Empire behind the Euphrates, where stood the great cities of Ctesiphon, Seleucia, Hatra, Nisibin, Harran, and hundreds more whose very names are forgotten. These great townships subsisted on the enormous cereal wealth of Mesopotamia, watered as it then was by canals, whose makers' names were even then already lost in the mists of antiquity. Babylon and Nineveh had passed away; the successors of Persia and Macedon

Photo: H. J. Shepstone.
VIEW OF PALMYRA FROM THE GRAND COLONNADE, SHOWING THE (LATER) CASTLE IN THE DISTANCE.

had given place to Parthia; but the people and the cultivation were the same as when Cyrus the Conqueror had first subdued the land. The language of many of the towns was Greek, and the cultured citizens of Seleucia might criticize the philosophies and tragedies of Athens; but the millions of the agricultural population knew possibly no more of these things than does many an Essex peasant of to-day know of what passes in the metropolis."

Compare with this the state of affairs at the end of the seventh century.

"Syria was now an impoverished and stricken land, and her great cities, though still populated, must have been encumbered with ruins which the public funds were not sufficient to remove. Damascus and Jerusalem themselves had not recovered from the effects of long and terrible sieges; Amman and Gerash had declined into wretched villages under the sway and lordship of the Bedouin. The Hauran, perhaps, still showed signs of the prosperity for which it had been noted in the days of Trajan; but the wretched buildings and rude inscriptions of this date all point to a sad and depressing decline. Out in the desert, Palmyra stood empty and desolate save for a garrison in the castle. On the coasts and in the Lebanon a shadow of the former business and wealth was still to be seen; but in the north, ruin, desolation, and abandonment must have been the common state of the country, which had been raided with unfailing regularity for one hundred years and had been held by an enemy for fifteen. Agriculture must have declined, and the population notably decreased through the plagues and distresses from which it had suffered.

"Cappadocia had insensibly sunk into barbarism; and the great basilicas and cities, which the rude countrymen could neither repair nor restore, had been levelled with the ground. The Anatolian peninsula had been ploughed and harrowed by the Persian armies; the great cities had been plundered and sacked."

§ 4

It was while Heraclius was engaged in restoring order in this already desolated Syria after the death of Chosroes II, **The First Message from Islam.** and before the final peace with Persia, that a strange message was brought to him. The bearer had ridden over to the imperial outpost at Bostra in the wilderness south of Damascus. The letter was in Arabic, the obscure Semitic language of the nomadic peoples of the southern desert; and probably only an interpretation reached him— presumably with deprecatory notes by the interpreter.

It was an odd, florid challenge from someone who called himself "Muhammad[1] the Prophet of God." This Muhammad, it appeared, called upon Heraclius to acknowledge the one true God and to serve him. Nothing else was definite in the document.

There is no record of the reception of this missive, and presumably it went unanswered. The emperor probably shrugged his shoulders, and was faintly amused at the incident.

But at Ctesiphon they knew more about this Muhammad. He was said to be a tiresome false prophet, who had incited Yemen, the rich province of Southern Arabia, to rebel against the King of Kings. Kavadh was much occupied with affairs. He had deposed and murdered his father Chosroes II, and he was attempting to reorganize the Persian military forces. To him also came a message identical with that sent to Heraclius. The thing angered him. He tore up the letter, flung the fragments at the envoy, and bade him begone.

When this was told to the sender far away in the squalid little town of Medina, he was very angry. "Even so, O Lord!" he cried; "rend Thou his kingdom from him." (A.D. 628.)

§ 5

But before we go on to tell of the rise of Islam in the world, it will be well to complete our survey of the condition of Asia in the dawn of the seventh century. And a word or so is due to religious developments in the Persian community during the Sassanid period.

Zoroaster and Mani.

---

[1] The appearance of this name in our *Outline* produced a violent conflict of opinion between the writer and Sir H. H. Johnston upon the question of spelling. The writer clung for a time to Mohammed, the form adopted in the *Encyclopædia Britannica*. "There is no *o* and there is no *e* in the Arab alphabet," Sir Harry wrote. "The word is *Muhammad*, meaning 'the praiser,' from *hamada*, 'he praised.' Why should we go on spelling this name wrong because the eighteenth-century writers would not take the trouble to find the right pronunciation?" Moreover, *Mohammed* is only one of a multitude of unrighteous variations. So *Muhammad* has it.

From the days of Cyrus onward Zoroastrianism had prevailed over the ancient gods of Nineveh and Babylon. Zoroaster (the Greek spelling of the Iranian, "Zarathustra"), like Buddha, was an Aryan. We know nothing of the age in which he lived; some authorities make him as early as 1,000 B.C., others make him contemporary with Buddha or Confucius; and as little of his place of birth or his exact nationality. His teachings are preserved to us in the Zend Avesta, but here, since they no longer play any great part in the world's affairs, we cannot deal with them in any detail. The opposition of a good god, Ormuzd, the god of light, truth, frankness, and the sun, and a bad god, Ahriman, god of secrecy, cunning, diplomacy, darkness, and night, formed a very central part of his religion. As we find it in history, it is already surrounded by a ceremonial and sacerdotal system; it has no images, but it has priests, temples, and altars, on which burn a sacred fire and at which sacrificial ceremonies are performed. Among other distinctive features is its prohibition of either the burning or the burial of the dead. The Parsees of India, the last surviving Zoroastrians, still lay their dead out within certain open towers, the Towers of Silence, to which the vultures come.

Under the Sassanid kings from Ardashir onward (227), this religion was the official religion; its head was the second person in the state next to the king, and the king in quite the ancient fashion was supposed to be divine or semi-divine and upon terms of peculiar intimacy with Ormuzd.

But the religious fermentation of the world did not leave the supremacy of Zoroastrianism undisputed in the Persian Empire. Not only was there a great eastward diffusion of Christianity, to which we have already given notice, but new sects arose in Persia, incorporating the novel ideas of the time. One early variant or branch of Zoroastrianism, Mithraism, we have already named.[2] It had spread into Europe by the first century B.C., after the eastern campaigns of Pompey the Great. It became enormously popular with the soldiers and common people, and, until the time of Constantine the Great, continued to be a serious rival to

---

[2] There is a good account of Mithraism in C. Bigg's *The Church's Task in the Roman Empire.*—E. B.

Christianity. Indeed, one of his successors, the Emperor Julian (361-363), known in Christian history as "Julian the Apostate," made a belated attempt to substitute it for the accepted faith.[1] Mithras was a god of light, "proceeding" from Ormuzd and miraculously born, in much the same way that the second person in the Christian Trinity proceeds from the first. Of this branch of the Zoroastrian stem we need say no more now. In the third century A.D., however, another religion, Manichæism, arose, which deserves some notice now.

Photo: Anderson.

JULIAN THE APOSTATE.

a conflict of light and darkness, Ormuzd was God and Ahriman Satan. But how man was created, how he fell from light into darkness, how he is being disentangled and redeemed from the darkness, and of the part played by Jesus in this strange mixture of religions we cannot explain here even if we would. Our interest with the system here is historical and not theological.

But of the utmost historical interest is the fact that Mani not only went about Iran preaching these new and to him these finally satisfying ideas of his, but into Tur-

Mani, the founder of Manichæism, was born the son of a good family of Ecbatana, the old Medean capital (A.D. 216). He was educated at Ctesiphon. His father was some sort of religious sectary, and he was brought up in an atmosphere of religious discussion. There came to him that persuasion that he at last had the complete light, which is the moving power of all religious initiators. He was impelled to proclaim his doctrine. In A.D. 242, at the accession of Sapor I, the second Sassanid monarch, he began his teaching.

It is characteristic of the way in which men's minds were moving in those days that his teaching included a sort of theocrasia. He was not, he declared, proclaiming anything new. The great religious founders before him had all been right: Moses, Zoroaster, Buddha, Jesus Christ—all had been true prophets, but to him it was appointed to clarify and crown their imperfect and confused teaching. This he did in Zoroastrian language. He explains the perplexities and contradictions of life as

kestan, into India, and over the passes into China. This freedom of travel is to be noted. It is interesting also because it brings before us the fact that Turkestan was no longer a country of dangerous nomads, but a country in which cities were flourishing and men had the education and leisure for theological argument. The ideas of Mani spread eastward and westward with great rapidity, and they were a most fruitful rootstock of heresies throughout the entire Christian world for nearly a thousand years.

Somewhen about A.D. 270 Mani came back to Ctesiphon and made many converts. This brought him into conflict with the official religion and the priesthood. In 277 the reigning monarch had him crucified and his body, for some unknown reason, flayed, and there began a fierce persecution of his adherents. Nevertheless, Manichæism held its own in Persia with Nestorian Christianity and orthodox Zoroastrianism (Mazdaism) for some centuries.

§ 6

It becomes fairly evident that in the fifth and sixth centuries A.D. not merely Persia, but

---

[1] Julian was not so much a Mithraist as a syncretist. See Alice Gardner, *Julian the Apostate.*—E. B.

Hunnish Peoples in Central Asia and India. the regions that are now Turkestan and Afghanistan were far more advanced in civilization than were the French and English of that time. The obscurity of the history of these regions has been lifted in the last two decades chiefly through the energy and ability of German explorers, and a very considerable literature written in languages of the Turkish group has been discovered. These extant manuscripts date from the seventh century onward. The alphabet is an adaptation of the Syrian, introduced by Manichæan missionaries, and many of the MSS. discovered—parchments have been found in windows in the place of glass—are as beautifully written as any Benedictine production. Mixed up with a very

Photo: Major W. J. P. Rodd.
ARCH OF CTESIPHON. EXTERIOR VIEW, SHOWING METHOD OF CONSTRUCTION OF OUTER ARCHES.

extensive Manichæan literature are translations of the Christian scriptures and Buddhistic writings. Much of this early Turkish material still awaits examination.

Everything points to the conclusion that those centuries which were centuries of disaster and retrogression in Europe were comparatively an age of progress in Middle Asia eastward into China.

A steady westward drift to the north of the Caspian of Hunnish peoples, who were now called Tartars and Turks, was still going on in the sixth century, but it must be thought of as an overflow rather than as a migration of whole peoples. The world from the Danube to the Chinese frontiers was still largely a nomadic world, with towns and cities growing up upon the chief trade routes. There is very little for

Photo: A. B. W. Holland.
THE ARCH OF CTESIPHON, NEAR BAGDAD.

us to tell of the constant clash of the Turkish peoples of Western Turkestan with the Persians to the south of them, the age-long bickering of Turanian and Iranian. We hear nothing of any great northward marches of the Persians, but there were great and memorable raids to the south both by the Turanians to the east and the Alans to the west of the Caspian before the big series of movements of the third and fourth century westward that carried the Alans and Huns into the heart of Europe. There was

India in the footsteps of their kinsmen about the year 470, about a quarter of a century after the death of Attila. They did not migrate into India; they went to and fro, looting in India and returning with their loot to their own country, just as later the Huns established themselves in the great plain of the Danube and raided all Europe.

The history of India during these seven centuries we are now reviewing is punctuated by these two invasions of the Yue-Chi, the Indo-

Photo: Major W. J. P. Rodd.

REMAINS OF AN OLD ZOROASTRIAN TEMPLE AT KANGAVAH, PERSIA.

a nomadic drift to the east of Persia and southward through Afghanistan towards India, as well as this drift to the north-west. These streams of nomads flowed by Persia on either side. We have already mentioned the Yue-Chi (chap. xxix., § 4), who finally descended into India as the Indo-Scythians in the second century. A backward, still nomadic section of these Yue-chi remained in Central Asia, and became numerous upon the steppes of Turkestan, as the Ephthalites or White Huns. After being a nuisance and a danger to the Persians for three centuries, they finally began raiding into

Scythians who, as we have said, wiped out the last traces of Hellenic rule, and the Ephthalites. Before the former of these, the Indo-Scythians, a wave of uprooted populations, the Sakas, had been pushed; so that altogether India experienced three waves of barbaric invasion, about A.D. 100, about A.D. 120, and about A.D. 470. But only the second of these invasions was a permanent conquest and settlement. The Indo-Scythians made their headquarters on the North-west Frontier and set up a dynasty, the Kushan dynasty, who ruled most of North India as far east as Benares.

The chief among these Kushan monarchs was Kanishka (date unknown), who added to North India Kashgar, Yarkand, and Khotan. Like Asoka, he was a great and vigorous promoter of Buddhism, and these conquests, this great empire of the North-west Frontier, must have brought India into close and frequent relations with China and Tibet.

We will not trouble to record here the divisions and coalescences of power in India, nor the dynasties that followed the Kushans, because these things signify very little to us from our present point of view. Sometimes all India was a patchwork quilt of states; sometimes such empires as that of the Guptas prevailed over great areas. These things made little difference in the ideas, the religion, and the ordinary way of life of the Indian peoples. Brahminism held its own against Buddhism, and the two religions prospered side by side. The mass of the population was living then very much as it lives to-day; dressing, cultivating, and building its houses in much the same fashion.

The irruption of the Ephthalites is memorable not so much because of its permanent effects as because of the atrocities perpetrated by the invaders. These Ephthalites

Reproduced by permission from the Report of the Archæological Survey of India, 1911-1912.

REMAINS OF A STATUE OF KANISHKA FOUND IN THE CENTRAL PROVINCES. HIS TYPICAL TARTAR QUILTED BOOTS ARE TO BE NOTED.

very closely resembled the Huns of Attila in their barbarism; they merely raided, they produced no such dynasty as the Kushan monarchy; and their chiefs retained their headquarters in Western Turkestan. Mihiragula, their most capable leader, has been called the Attila of India. One of his favourite amusements, we are told, was the expensive one of rolling elephants down precipitous places in order to watch their sufferings. His abominations roused his Indian tributary princes to revolt, and he was overthrown (528). But the final ending of the Ephthalite raids into India was effected not by Indians, but by the destruction of their central establishment on the Oxus (565) by the growing power of the Turks, working in alliance with the Persians. After this break-up, the Ephthalites dissolved very rapidly and completely into the surrounding populations, much as the European Huns did after the death of Attila a hundred years earlier. Nomads without central grazing lands must disperse; there is nothing else for it. Some of the chief Rajput clans of to-day in Rajputana in North India are descended, it is said, from these White Huns.[1]

[1] The Ephthalites on the Oxus produced a coinage in silver and copper

An Ephthalite Coin .....

§ 7

During these seven centuries which saw the beginning and the end of the emperors in Rome,

The Great Age of China. and the complete breakdown and recasting of the social, economic, political, and religious life of Europe, the history of China is one of comparative social stability. While the Western world, after its first disastrous attempts to bring in autocracy as a corrective to plutocracy, was beginning again amidst the debris of its social order, China was continuing steadfastly upon the conservative lines that Confucius had emphasized. She had set-backs, pestilences, invasions, great civil wars, and commotions, but the seventh century saw the vast dominions that had been nominally unified by Shi Hwang Ti nine hundred years before, populous, prosperous, and consolidated, the same faiths and the same institutions wearing well and serving an increasing multitude of mankind. From its early beginnings in Kan-su from which it had spread down the Hwang-ho valley and invaded that of the Yang-tse-kiang, the Chinese civilization had now spread over an area much greater than all Europe or than the empire of Trajan at its utmost extent. And its unity was far more real than any unity the Roman Empire could boast ; it had a common culture, a common script, common religions, a common body of ideas.

As the compiler of this history sits among

The **CHINESE EMPIRE** under the **TANG** Dynasty (greatest extent)
[Superimposed—The Roman Empire at its greatest extent, under Trajan]

his books, he searches for some striking social novelty to set against the universal change of ideas, habits, customs, that was going on in the west. Prominent among his notes is the word " tea." China began to drink tea in the sixth century A.D. Chinese poets were writing delightful poems about the effects of the first cup and the second cup and the third cup, and so on. The importance of that fact measures the contrast of east and west. While the west was reconstructing fundamentally, the east was elaborating. Already before the Christian Era, China was producing beautiful paintings. In the second, third, and fourth centuries some of the most lovely landscapes were painted that have ever been done by mankind. There was also a great production of beautiful vases and carvings. Everywhere fine buildings and decoration increased. Printing from wood blocks began about the same time as tea-drinking. The seventh century also saw a great outbreak of poetry.

These things suggest a world of peaceful progress. But in certain matters China was intensely conservative. Throughout this period she was making no changes in her elaborate, beautiful, but tedious, clumsy, and inflexible script.[1] All the world to the west of her was

consisting of three denominations : heavy silver, light silver, and copper. Thirteen specimens are known to survive, the light silver denomination being represented by two specimens in the British Museum and one at Petrograd, until I was fortunate enough to add two to their number by a *trouvaille* in Oxford Street.—P. G.

Our illustration shows one of these two coins. It may have been struck in India in some state under Ephthalite dominion. Its interest for us lies in the figure it gives of a Hun horseman. He seems to wear a feather head-dress, reminding one of a Red Indian or a Moscow hotel porter, and his leg gear suggests an American cow-boy. Note his great quiver of arrows.—H. G. W.

---

[1] The printed characters have remained unchanged, but a cursive script was developing and has developed for ordinary writing and correspondence.—L. Y. C.

ARRIVAL OF A CHIEF AT THE GATE OF A TOWN.
Stone relief, Han dynasty (first century A.D.), British Museum

getting on with developments of the swift and simple invention, the Mediterranean alphabet ; all the alphabets of India and Central Asia are derived from that ; but China remained content with a method of writing that takes long years to learn, and so is inaccessible to the vast majority of her people. And, what may or may not have been one of the clues to her stability, she was developing no general coinage. The cash and credit system of the Western world, at once efficient and dangerous, had not strained her economic life. Not that the monetary idea was unknown. For small transactions the various provinces were using perforated zinc and brass "cash," but for larger there was nothing but stamped ingots of silver. This great empire was still carrying on most of its business on a basis of barter like that which prevailed in Babylon in the days of the Aramean merchants. And so it con-

tinued to do to the dawn of the twentieth century.

We have seen how in the Roman republic economic and social order was destroyed by the too great fluidity of property that money brought about. Money became abstract, and lost touch with the real values it was supposed to represent. Individuals and communities got preposterously into debt, and the world was saddled by a class of rich men who were creditors, men who did not handle and administer any real wealth, but who had the power to call up money. No development of "finance" occurred to the same extent in China. Wealth in China remained real and visible. And China had no need for any Licinian law, nor for a Tiberius Gracchus. The idea of property in China did not extend far beyond tangible things. There was no slavery. The occupier and user of the land was in most

THE LADY FONG (FIRST CENTURY B.C.) THROWING HERSELF BEFORE AN ESCAPED BEAR TO SAVE
THE LIFE OF THE EMPEROR.
Scene from the scroll painting by Ku K'ai-chih (fourth century A.D.) in the British Museum.

instances practically the owner of it, subject to a land tax. There was a certain amount of small scale landlordism, but no great estates. Landless men worked for wages paid mostly in kind—as they were in ancient Babylon.

The government that spent the land tax of this great industrious community, whose chief ideals were politeness and the correct observance of precedent, was of far less importance to its internal life than to the peoples upon its borders. We have already noted the long rule of the Han dynasty. A division of the empire followed, and a phase known as the "Three Kingdom Period." The fourth century saw a dynasty of more or less civilized Huns established as rulers in the province of Shen-si. This Hunnish kingdom included not merely the north of China, but great areas of Siberia; its dynasty absorbed the Chinese civilization, and its influence carried Chinese trade and knowledge to the Arctic circle. These Huns melted at last into the general population. There were two centuries more of political confusion, but by no means devastating political confusion; which ended in a sort of unification under the Suy dynasty in 590. Under a Suy monarch the Lu-chu isles were annexed to China, and there was a phase of great literary activity. The number of volumes at this time in the imperial library was increased, we are told, to 54,000. The dawn of the seventh century saw the beginning of the great Tang dynasty, which was to endure for three centuries. With the accession (627) of the second emperor of this dynasty, Tai-tsung, we may conclude this chapter of Chinese history.

The dominions of this emperor Tai-tsung extended southward into Annam and westward to the Caspian sea. His southern frontier in that direction marched with that of Persia.

CHRIST WITH NESTORIAN PRIESTS.
From a painting by a Chinese artist of the seventh century (Tang dynasty). From *Chinese Pictorial Art*, by Prof. H. A. Giles.

His northern ran along the Altai from the Kirghis steppe, north of the desert of Gobi. But it did not include Corea, which was conquered and made tributary by his son. This Tang dynasty civilized and incorporated into the Chinese race the whole of the southward population, and just as the Chinese of the north call themselves the "men of Han," so the Chinese of the south call themselves the "men of Tang." The law was codified, the literary examination system was revised, and a complete and accurate edition of all the Chinese classics was produced. To the court of Tai-tsung came an embassy from Byzantium, and, what is more significant, from Persia came a company of Nestorian missionaries (631). These latter Tai-tsung received with great respect; he heard them state the chief articles of their creed, and ordered the Christian scriptures to be translated into Chinese for his further examination. In 638 he announced that he found the new religion entirely satisfactory, and that it might be preached within the empire. He also allowed the building of a church and the foundation of a monastery.

A still more remarkable embassy also came to the court of Tai-tsung in the year 628, three years earlier than the Nestorians. This was a party of Arabs, who came by sea to Canton in a trading vessel from Yanbu, the port of Medina in Arabia. (Incidentally it is interesting to know that there were such vessels engaged in an east and west trade at this time.) These Arabs had been sent by that Muhammad we have already mentioned, who styled himself "The Prophet of God," and the message they brought to Tai-tsung was probably identical with the summons which was sent in the same year to the Byzantine emperor Heraclius and to Kavadh in Ctesiphon. But the

Chinese monarach neither neglected the message as Heraclius did, nor insulted the envoys after the fashion of the parricide Kavadh. He received them well, expressed great interest in their theological views, and assisted them, it is said, to build a mosque for the Arab traders in Canton—a mosque which survives to this day. It is one of the oldest mosques in the world.

§ 8

The urbanity, the culture, and the power of China at the dawn of the seventh century A.D.

Intellectual Fetters of China. are in so vivid a contrast with the decay, disorder, and divisions of the Western world, as at once to raise some of the most interesting questions in the history of civilization. Why did not China keep this great lead ? Why does she not to this day dominate the world culturally and politically ?

For a long time she certainly did keep ahead. It is only a thousand years later in the sixteenth and seventeenth centuries, with the discovery of America, the spread of printed books and education in the west, and the dawn of modern scientific discovery, that we can say with confidence that the Western world began to pull ahead of China. Under the Tang rule, and then again under the Sung dynasty (960-1279), and again during the period of the Mings (1358-1644), China presented a spectacle of prosperity, happiness, culture, and artistic and intellectual activity far in front of any contemporary state. And seeing that she achieved so much, why did she not achieve more ? Chinese shipping was upon the seas, and there was a considerable overseas trade during that time; China knew very early of the mariner's compass. Why did the Chinese never discover America or Australia ? There was much isolated observation, ingenuity, and invention. The Chinese knew of gunpowder in the sixth century,[1] they used coal and gas heating centuries before these things were used in Europe; their bridge-building, their hydraulic engineering was admirable ; the knowledge of materials shown in their enamel and lacquer ware is very great. Why did they never organize the system of record and co-operation in inquiry that has given the world modern science. And why, in spite of their general training in

[1] Helmolt.

good manners and self-restraint, did intellectual education never soak down into the general mass of the population ? Why are the masses of China to-day, and why have they always been, in spite of an exceptionally high level of natural intelligence, illiterate ?

It is customary to meet such questions with rather platitudinous answers. We are told that the Chinaman is the most conservative of human beings, that, in contrast with the European races, his mind is twisted round towards the past, that he is the willing slave of etiquette and precedent to a degree inconceivable to Western minds. He is represented as having a mentality so distinct that one might almost expect to find a difference in brain structure to explain it. The appeals of Confucius to the wisdom of the ancients are always quoted to clinch this suggestion.

If, however, we examine this generalization more closely, it dissolves into thin air. The superior intellectual initiative, the liberal enterprise, the experimental disposition that is supposed to characterize the Western mind, is manifest in the history of that mind only during certain phases and under exceptional circumstances. For the rest, the Western world displays itself as traditional and conservative as China. And, on the other hand, the Chinese mind has, under conditions of stimulus, shown itself quite as inventive and versatile as the European, and the very kindred Japanese mind even more so. For, take the case of the Greeks, the whole swing of their mental vigour falls into the period between the sixth century B.C. and the decay of the Alexandrian Museum under the later Ptolemies in the second century B.C. There were Greeks before that time and Greeks since, but a history of a thousand years of the Byzantine Empire showed the Hellenic world at least as intellectually stagnant as China. Then we have already drawn attention to the comparative sterility of the Italian mind during the Roman period and its abundant fertility since the Renaissance of learning. The English mind again had a phase of brightness in the seventh and eighth centuries, and it did not shine again until the fifteenth. Again the mind of the Arabs, as we shall presently tell, blazed out like a star for half a dozen generations after the appearance of Islam, having never achieved anything of importance before or since. On the other hand, there was always a great deal of scattered inventiveness in China, and the progress of Chinese art witnesses to new movements and vigorous innovations. We exaggerate the reverence of the Chinese for their fathers; parricide was a far commoner crime among the Chinese emperors than it was even among the rulers of Persia. Moreover, there have been several liberalizing movements in China, several recorded struggles against the " ancient ways."

It has already been suggested that phases of real intellectual progress in any community seem to be connected with the existence of a detached class of men, sufficiently free not to be obliged to toil or worry exhaustively about mundane needs, and not rich and powerful enough to be tempted into extravagances of lust, display, or cruelty. They must have a sense of security, but not a conceit of superiority. This class, we have further insinuated, must be able to talk freely and communicate easily. It must not be watched for heresy or persecuted for any ideas it may express. Such a happy state of affairs certainly prevailed in Greece during its best days. A class of intelligent, free gentlefolk is indeed evident in history whenever there is a record of bold philosophy or effective scientific advances.

In the days of Tang and Sung and Ming there must have been an abundance of pleasantly circumstanced people in China of just the class that supplied most of the young men of the Academy at Athens, or the bright intelligences of Renaissance Italy, or the members of the London Royal Society, that mother society of modern science ; and yet China did not produce in these periods of opportunity any such large beginnings of recorded and analysed fact.

If we reject the idea that there is some profound racial difference between China and the West which makes the Chinese by nature conservative and the West by nature progressive, then we are forced to look for the operating cause of this difference in progressiveness in some other direction. Many people are disposed to find that operating cause which has, in spite of her original advantages, retarded China so greatly during the last four or five centuries, in the imprisonment of the Chinese mind in a

script and in an idiom of thought so elaborate and so difficult that the mental energy of the country has been largely consumed in acquiring it. This view deserves examination.

We have already given an account in chap. xviii. of the peculiarities of Chinese writing and of the Chinese language. The Japanese writing is derived from the Chinese, and consists of a more rapidly written system of forms. A

MODEL OF A CHINESE HOUSE, PLACED ON TWO BRICKS.
From a tomb, Han dynasty (first and second centuries A.D.), British Museum.

great number of these forms are ideograms taken over from the Chinese and used exactly as the Chinese ideograms are used, but also a number of signs are used to express syllables ; there is a Japanese syllabary after the fashion of the Sumerian syllabary we have described in chap. xviii. The Japanese writing remains a clumsy system, as clumsy as cuneiform, though not so clumsy as Chinese ; and there has been a movement in Japan to adopt a Western alphabet. Korea long ago went a step farther and developed a true alphabet from the same Chinese origins. With these exceptions all the great writing systems now in use in the world are based on the Mediterranean alphabets, and are beyond comparison more easily learnt and mastered than the Chinese. This means that while other peoples learn merely a comparatively simple and straightforward method of setting down the language with which they are familiar, the Chinaman has to master a great multitude of complex word signs and word groups. He must not simply learn the signs, but the established grouping of those signs to represent various meanings. He must familiarize himself, therefore, with a number of exemplary classical works. Consequently in China, while you will find great numbers of people who know the significance of certain frequent and familiar characters, you discover only a few whose knowledge is sufficiently extensive to grasp the meaning of a newspaper paragraph, and still fewer who can read any subtlety of intention or fine shades of meaning. In a lesser degree this is true also of Japan. No doubt European readers, especially of such word-rich languages as English or Russian, vary greatly among themselves in regard to the extent of books they can understand and how far they understand them; their power varies according to their vocabularies; but the corresponding levels of understanding among the Chinese represent a far greater expenditure of time and labour upon their attainment. A mandarin's education in China is practically learning to read. A man who can read and write well in China is a specialist, and we are told of the Emperor Tai-Tsung of the Tang dynasty as one of his glories that " he himself knew how to write."

And it may be that the consequent preoccupation of the educated class during its most susceptible years upon the Chinese classics gave them a bias in favour of this traditional learning upon which they had spent so much time and energy. Few men who have toiled to build up any system of knowledge in their minds will willingly scrap it in favour of something strange and new; this disposition is as characteristic of the West as of the East; it is shown as markedly by the scholars of the British and American universities as by any Chinese mandarins, and the British at the present time, in spite of the great and manifest advantages in popular education and national propaganda

the change would give them, refuse to make any move from their present barbaric orthography towards a phonetic alphabet and spelling. The peculiarities of the Chinese script, and the educational system arising out of that script, must have acted age after age as an invincible filter that favoured the plastic and scholarly mind as against the restive and originating type, and kept the latter out of positions of influence and authority. There is much that is plausible in this explanation.

There have been several attempts to simplify the Chinese writing and to adopt an alphabetical system. In the early days of Buddhism in China, when there was a considerable amount of translation from Sanscrit, Indian influences came near to achieving this end; two Chinese alphabets were indeed invented, and each had some little use. But what hindered the general adoption of these, and what stands in the way of any phonetic system of Chinese writing to-day, is this, that while the literary script and phraseology is the same from one end of China to the other, the spoken language of the common people, both in pronunciation and in its familiar idioms, varies so widely that men from one province may be incomprehensible to men from another. There is, however, a "standard Chinese," a rather bookish spoken idiom, which is generally understood by educated people; and it is upon the possibility of applying an alphabetical system of writing to this standard Chinese that the hopes of modern educational reformers in China are based at the present time. For fresh attempts are now being made to release the Chinese mind from this ancient entanglement.

The very success and early prosperity and general contentment of China in the past must have worked to justify in that land all the natural self-complacency and conservatism of mankind. No animal will change when its conditions are "good enough" for present survival, and in this matter man is still an animal. Until the nineteenth century, for more than two thousand years, there was really nothing in the history of China that could cause any serious doubts in the mind of a Chinaman of the general superiority of his own civilization to that of the rest of the world, and there was no reason apparent therefore for any alteration. China produced a profusion of beautiful art, some delightful poetry, astonishing cookery, and thousands of millions of glowingly pleasant lives generation after generation. Her ships followed her marvellous inland waterways, and put to sea but rarely, and then only to India or Borneo as their utmost adventure. (Until the sixteenth century we must remember European seamen never sailed out into the Atlantic Ocean. The Norse discovery of America, the Phœnician circumnavigation of Africa, were exceptional feats.) And these things were attained without any such general boredom, servitude, indignity, and misery as underlay the rule of the rich in the Roman Empire. There was much poverty, much discontent, but it was not massed poverty, it was not a necessary popular discontent. For a thousand years the

Chinese system, though it creaked and swayed at times, seemed proof against decay. Dynastic changes there were, rebellions, phases of disorder, famines, pestilences ; two great invasions that set foreign dynasties upon the throne of the Son of Heaven, but no such shock as to revolutionize the order of the daily round. The emperors and dynasties might come and go ; the mandarins, the examinations, the classics, and the traditions and habitual life remained. China's civilization had already reached its fullest development in the seventh century A.D., and though it continued to spread slowly and steadily into Annam, into Cambodia, into Siam, into Tibet, into Nepal, Korea, Mongolia, and Manchuria, there is henceforth little more than such geographical progress to record of it in this history for a thousand years.[1]

---

[1] The reason for the stationariness of China goes, we think, deeper than a script. China has formed a social-economic system which (1) cannot be transplanted, and (2) cannot be changed without tremendous effort. She lives by agriculture—rice-growing. (There is some tea among the foot hills, but it has to grow *with* rice to support the population.) Towns exist—on the edge of the rice-fields, for their needs. The town is dependent on the country, not as elsewhere, country on town. There are small properties ; all the hands are wanted, and can be absorbed, in old ancestral agricultural jobs. A state of small peasants, tilling, tilling, tilling, has no source of initiative towards change. If coal is to be mined in the future, and China industrialized, then a society that has not fundamentally changed for thousands of years may be changed. China is like an Egypt or Sumeria, so big that the nomads—those terrible agents of change—beat on its mass in vain. What the nomads have not done, modern industrialism may do.—J. L. M. and E. B.

L. C. B. disagrees with these two historians in his analysis of the Chinese problem. He writes as follows :

"In order to answer the question—why China achieved so much under the T'ang, Sung, and Ming dynasties, and thereafter failed to achieve more, it is necessary to consider what were the principal factors of culture and progress under these dynasties, and how they came to be extinguished.

"From the earliest times there have always been two widely differing types of Chinese mind—the Northern or Confucian, and the Southern or Taoist. As Mr. Okakura has pointed out, the Yangtse-Kiang and the Hoang-Ho rivers are respectively, from the point of view of thought and culture, the Mediterranean and the Baltic of China. Taoism was the idealism of the south, Confucianism the practice of the north. Both stood for adjustment ; but the adjustment of Confucius was the adjustment of the individual in his social and ceremonial relations to others, while that of

Lao-tse was the adjustment of the individual soul in its relation to the Infinite. The history of China is bound up with the struggle of those two forces, culminating in the practically complete defeat of Taoism after centuries of ebb and flow. Chu Hsi, A.D. 1130–1200, was the later St. Paul of modern Confucianism. During the T'ang, Sung, and Ming dynasties China was temporarily united, and free play was allowed to the thought of both schools. Each played its part and each reacted upon the other, to the great benefit of the Empire. Yet both systems carried within them the seeds of decay. Taoism, divorced from the affairs of everyday life and the education of the people, lost itself in art, literature, and mythology. Confucianism added layer after layer of hard shell about the inert organism of social life. The end was finally reached in 1421 under the Mings with the transference of the capital from Nanking to Peking, and the dominance of the Confucian party who had brought it about. Only in the later Ming period does the great solitary figure of Wang Yang Ming arise. His central doctrine that thought and learning are of small value unless translated into action had little immediate effect in China, but it fell upon Japanese soil, quickened the drooping Samurai spirit, and reached maturity with the Russo-Japanese war and the advance of modern Japan.

"The imprisonment of the Chinese mind in the ancient script is merely one aspect of Confucianism in its bondage to the past. The statement of J. L. M. and E. B. that China is a nation of peasants is incomprehensible to me. There has always been a great urban industrialism and a great commerce. 'The Chinese,' as Dyer Ball says, ' are pre-eminently a trading race. . . . Nor has the trade of China been simply a modern affair. From remote antiquity the Chinese have been true to their commercial instincts, and have not only been the civilizers of Eastern Asia, supplying them with their letters and literature ' [and artistic products], ' but they have also provided for their more

§ 9[1]

In the year 629, the year after the arrival of Muhammad's envoys at Canton and thirty odd years after the landing of Pope Gregory's missionaries in England, a certain learned and devout Buddhist named Yuan Chwang started out from Singan, Tai-Tsung's capital, upon a great journey to India. He was away sixteen years, he returned in 645, and he wrote an account of his travels which is treasured as a Chinese classic. One or two points about his experi-

The Travels of Yuan Chwang.

YUAN CHWANG'S route from China to India, 629-645 A.D.

ences are to be noted here because they contribute to our general review of the state of the world in the seventh century A.D.

Yuan Chwang was as eager for marvels and as credulous as Herodotus, and without the latter writer's fine sense of history; he could never pass a monument or ruin without learning some fabulous story about it; Chinese ideas of the dignity of literature perhaps prevented him from telling us much detail of how he travelled, who were his attendants, how he was lodged, or what he ate and how he paid his expenses—details precious to the historian;

material wants, and received in exchange the commodities which they required from the neighbouring nations.' Trade with India was developed to a great extent in the ninth century A.D."

This interesting question is also discussed very ably and interestingly in Hubbard's *The Fate of Empires*.

[1] See Watters' *Travels of Yuan Chwang* and Beal's *Life of Hiuen Tsiang* (= Yuan Chwang).

nevertheless, he gives us a series of illuminating flashes upon China, Central Asia, and India in the period now under consideration.

His journey was an enormous one. He went and came back by way of the Pamirs. He went by the northern route, crossing the desert of Gobi, passing along the southern slopes of the Thian Shan, skirting the great deep blue lake of Issik Kul, and so to Tashkend and Samarkand, and then more or less in the footsteps of Alexander the Great southward to the Khyber Pass and Peshawur. He returned by the southern route, crossing the Pamirs from Afghanistan to Kashgar, and so along the line of retreat the Yue Chi had followed in the reverse direction seven centuries before, and by Yarkand, along the slopes of the Kuen Lun to rejoin his former route near the desert end of the Great Wall. Each route involved some hard mountaineering. His journeyings in India are untraceable; he was there fourteen years, and he went all over the peninsula from Nepal to Ceylon.

At that time there was an imperial edict forbidding foreign travel, so that Yuan Chwang started from Singan like an escaping criminal. There was a pursuit to prevent him carrying out his project. How he bought a lean red-coloured horse that knew the desert paths from a strange greybeard, how he dodged a frontier guard-house with the help of a "foreign person" who made him a bridge of brushwood lower down the river, how he crossed the desert guided by the bones of men and cattle, how he saw a mirage, and how twice he narrowly escaped being shot by arrows when he was getting water near the watch-towers on the desert track, the reader will find in the *Life*. He lost his way in the desert of Gobi, and for four nights and five days he had no water; when he was in the mountains among the glaciers, twelve of his party were frozen to death. All this is in the *Life*; he tells little of it in his own account of his travels.

He shows us the Turks, this new development of the Hun tradition, in possession not only of what is now Turkestan, but all along the northern route. He mentions many cities and considerable cultivation. He is entertained by various rulers, allies of or more or less nominally tributaries to China, and among others by the Khan of the Turks, a magnificent person in green satin, with his long hair tied with silk.

" The gold embroidery of this grand tent shone with a dazzling splendour ; the ministers of the presence in attendance sat on mats in long rows on either side all dressed in magnificent brocade robes, while the rest of the retinue on duty stood behind. You saw that although it was a case of a frontier ruler, yet there was an air of distinction and elegance. The Khan came out from his tent about thirty paces to meet Yuan-chwang, who after a courteous greeting entered the tent. . . . After a short interval envoys from China and Kao-chang were admitted and presented their despatches and credentials, which the Khan perused. He was much elated, and caused the envoys to be seated ; then he ordered wine and music for himself and them and grape-syrup for the pilgrim. Hereupon all pledged each other, and the filling and draining of the winecups made a din and bustle, while the mingled music of various instruments rose loud : although the airs were the popular strains of foreigners, yet they pleased the senses and exhilarated the mental faculties. After a little, piles of roasted beef and mutton were served for the others, and lawful food, such as cakes, milk, candy, honey, and grapes, for the pilgrim. After the entertainment, grape-syrup was again served, and the Khan invited Yuan Chwang to improve the occasion, whereupon the pilgrim expounded the doctrines of the ' ten virtues,' compassion for animal life, and the paramitas and emancipation. The Khan, raising his hands, bowed and gladly believed and accepted the teaching."

Yuan Chwang's account of Samarkand[1] is of a large and prosperous city, " a great commercial entrepôt, the country about it very fertile, abounding in trees and flowers and yielding many fine horses. Its inhabitants were skilful craftsmen, smart and energetic."

At that time we must remember there was hardly such a thing as a town in Anglo-Saxon England.

As his narrative approached his experiences in India, however, the pious and learned pilgrim in Yuan Chwang got the better of the traveller, and the book becomes congested with monstrous stories of incredible miracles.[2] Nevertheless, we get an impression of houses, clothing, and the like, closely resembling those of the India of to-day. Then as now the kaleidoscopic variety of an Indian crowd contrasted with the blue uniformity of the multitude in China. In the time of Buddha it is doubtful if there were reading and writing in India ; now reading and writing were quite common accomplishments. Yuan Chwang gives an interesting account of a great Buddhist university at Nalanda, where ruins have quite recently been discovered and excavated. Nalanda and Taxilla seem to have been considerable educational centres as early as the opening of the schools of Athens. The caste system Yung Chwang found fully established in spite of Buddha, and the Brahmins were now altogether in the ascendant. He names the four main castes we have mentioned in chap. xx., § 4 (Q.V.), but his account of their functions is rather different. The Sudras, he says, were the tillers of the soil. Indian writers say that their function was to wait upon the three " twice born " castes above them.

But, as we have already intimated, Yuan Chwang's account of Indian realities is swamped by his accumulation of legends and pious inventions. For these he had come, and in these he rejoiced. The rest, as we shall see, was a task that had been set him. The faith of Buddha which in the days of Asoka, and even so late as Kaniska, was still pure enough to be a noble inspiration, we now discover absolutely lost in a wilderness of preposterous rubbish, a philosophy of endless Buddhas, tales of manifestations and marvels like a Christmas pantomime, immaculate conceptions by six-tusked elephants, charitable princes giving themselves up to be eaten by starving tigresses, temples built over a sacred nail-paring and the like. We cannot give such stories here ; if the reader likes that sort of thing, he must go to the publications of the Royal Asiatic Society or the India

---

[1] There is some little doubt about this identification. See Watters.

[2] The *British Encyclopædia* article (Hsuan Tsang) is full and good on his Indian travels.

Society, where he will find a delirium of such imaginations. And in competition with this Buddhism, intellectually undermined as it now was and smothered in gilded decoration, Brahminism was everywhere gaining ground again, as Yung Chwang notes with regret.

Side by side with these evidences of a vast intellectual decay in India we may note the repeated appearance in Yuan Chwang's narrative of ruined and deserted cities. Much of the country was still suffering from the ravages of the Ephthalites and the consequent disorders. Again and again we find such passages as this : " he went north-east through a great forest, the road being a narrow, dangerous path, with wild buffalo and wild elephants, and robbers and hunters always in wait to kill travellers, and emerging from the forest he reached the country of Kou-shih-na-ka-lo (Kúsinagara). The city walls were in ruins, and the towns and villages were deserted. The brick foundations of the " old city " (that is, the city which had been the capital) were above ten *li* in circuit ; there were very few inhabitants, the interior of the city being a wild waste." This ruin was, however, by no means universal ; there is at least as much mention of crowded cities and villages and busy cultivations.

The *Life* tells of many hardships upon the return journey : he fell among robbers ; the great elephant that was carrying the bulk of his possessions was drowned ; he had much difficulty in getting fresh transport. Here we cannot deal with these adventures.

The return of Yuan Chwang to Singan, the Chinese capital, was, we gather, a triumph. Advance couriers must have told of his coming. There was a public holiday ; the streets were decorated by gay banners and made glad with music. He was escorted into the city with great pomp and ceremony. Twenty horses were needed to carry the spoils of his travels ; he had brought with him hundreds of Buddhist books written in Sanskrit, and made of trimmed leaves of palm and birch bark strung together in layers ; he had many images great and small of Buddha, in gold, silver, crystal, and sandalwood ; he had holy pictures, and no less than one hundred and fifty well authenticated true relics of Buddha. Yuan Chwang was presented to the emperor, who treated him as a personal friend, took him into the palace, and questioned him day by day about the wonders of these strange lands in which he had stayed so long. But while the emperor asked about India, the pilgrim was disposed only to talk about Buddhism.

Buddhist writers thought very highly of Tai-Tsung because of his reception of Yung Chwang (645). But so did the Moslem historians because of that mosque at Canton, and so did the Christian writers because of the Nestorian envoys (631).

The subsequent history of Yuan Chwang contains two incidents that throw light upon the mental workings of this great monarch, Tai Tsung, who was probably quite as much a Moslem as he was a Christian or a Buddhist. The trouble about all religious specialists is that they know too much about their own religion and how it differs from others ; the advantage, or disadvantage, of such creative statesmen as Tai Tsung and Constantine the Great is that they know comparatively little of such matters. Evidently the fundamental good of all these religions seemed to Tai Tsung to be much the same fundamental good. So it was natural to him to propose that Yung Chwang should now give up the religious life and come into his foreign office, a proposal that Yung Chwang would not entertain for a moment. The emperor then insisted at least upon a written account of the travels, and so got this classic we treasure. And finally Tai Tsung proposed to this highly saturated Buddhist that he should now use his knowledge of Sanscrit in translating the works of the great Chinese teacher Lao-tse, so as to make them available for Indian readers. It seemed, no doubt, to the emperor a fair return and a useful service to the fundamental good that lies beneath all religions. On the whole, he thought Lao-tse might very well rank with or even a little above Buddha, and therefore that if his work was put before the Brahmins, they would receive it gladly. In much the same spirit Constantine the Great had done his utmost to make Arius and Athanasius settle down amicably together. But naturally enough this suggestion was repulsed by Yuan Chwang. He retired to a monastery and spent the rest of his years translating as much as he could of

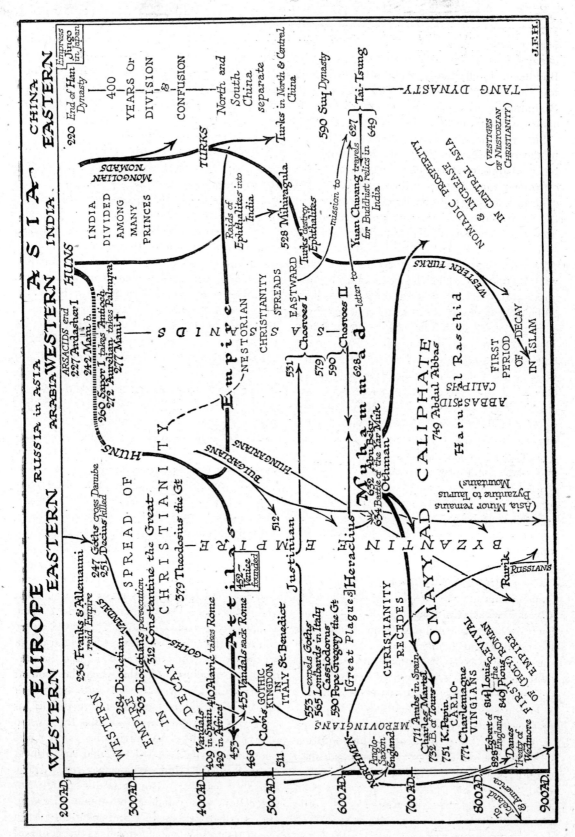

TIME CHART

EUROPE | ASIA | CHINA
WESTERN | EASTERN | RUSSIA in ASIA | ARABIA | WESTERN ASIA | INDIA | EASTERN

the Buddhist literature he had brought with him into elegant Chinese writing.

CHRONOLOGICAL TABLE

Since the last three chapters have been parallel chapters covering the same period, it will perhaps help the reader to keep his idea of the order of events clear and assist him in his grasp upon this period, if we give here a chronological table of the chief events between 50 B.C. and the year A.D. 650, and also a diagram of what we may call the chief time masses of that period.

B.C.

50. Rome recovering from Carrhæ (53). Parthians in Persia.
China and much of Central Asia under the Han dynasty.
Huns drifting westward.
48. Cæsar defeats Pompey at Pharsalus.
44. Cæsar assassinated.

31. Battle of Actium.
27. Augustus Cæsar Princeps.

4. True date of birth of Jesus of Nazareth.

A.D. Christian Era begins.
6. Province of Mœsia established.
9. Province of Pannonia established. Imperial boundary carried to the Danube.
14. Augustus dies. Tiberius emperor.

30. Jesus of Nazareth crucified.
37. Caligula succeeds Tiberius.
41. Claudius (the first emperor of the legions) made emperor by pretorian guard after murder of Caligula.

54. Nero succeeds Claudius.
61. Boadicea massacres Roman garrison in Britain.
68. Suicide of Nero. Galba. Otho. Vitellus.
69. Vespasian begins the so-called Flavian dynasty.

79. Titus succeeds Vespasian.
81. Domitian.
84. North Britain annexed.

A.D.
96. Nerva begins the so-called dynasty of the Antonines.
98. Trajan succeeds Nerva.
102. Pan Chau on the Caspian Sea. (Indo-Scythians invading North India.)

117. Hadrian succeeds Trajan. Roman Empire at its greatest extent.

138. Antoninus Pius succeeds Hadrian.
(The Indo-Scythians at this time are destroying the last traces of Hellenic rule in India.)

150. [About this time Kanishka reigned in India, Kashgar, Yarkand, and Kotan.]

161. Marcus Aurelius succeeds Antoninus Pius.
164. Great plague begins, and lasts to the death of M. Aurelius (180). This also devastated all Asia.

180. Death of Marcus Aurelius.
(Nearly a century of war and disorder begins in the Roman Empire.)

220. End of the Han dynasty. Beginning of four hundred years of division in China.
227. Ardashir I (first Sassanid shah) puts an end to Arsacid line in Persia.

242. Mani begins his teaching.
247. Goths cross Danube in a great raid.
251. Great victory of Goths. Emperor Decius killed.
260. Sapor I, the second Sassanid shah, takes Antioch, captures the Emperor Valerian, and is cut up on his return from Asia Minor by Odenathus of Palmyra.
269. The Emperor Claudius defeats the Goths at Nish.
270. Aurelian becomes emperor.
272. Zenobia carried captive to Rome. End of the brief glories of Palmyra.
275. Probus succeeds Aurelian.
276. Goths in Pontus. The Emperor Probus forces back Franks and Alemanni.

A.D.

277. Mani is crucified in Persia.
284. Diocletian becomes emperor.

303. Diocletian persecutes the Christians.

311. Galerius abandons the persecution of the Christians.

312. Constantine the Great becomes emperor.
313. Constantine presides over a Christian Council at Arles.

321. Fresh Gothic raids driven back.
323. Constantine presides over the Council of Nicæa. The Nicene Creed.

337. Vandals driven by Goths obtain leave to settle in Pannonia.
Constantine is baptized on his death-bed.

354. St. Augustine born.
361–3. Julian the Apostate attempts to substitute Mithraism for Christianity.

379. Theodosius the Great (a Spaniard) emperor.

390. The statue of Serapis at Alexandria broken up.
392. Theodosius the Great is emperor of east and west.
395. Theodosius the Great dies. Honorius and Arcadius re-divide the empire with Stilicho and Alaric as their masters and protectors.

410. The Visigoths under Alaric capture Rome.

425. Vandals settling in south of Spain. Huns in Pannonia, Goths in Dalmatia. Visigoths and Suevi in Portugal and North Spain. English invading Britain.
429. Vandals under Genseric invade Africa.

439. Vandals take Carthage.

448. Priscus visits Attila.
451. Attila raids Gaul and is defeated by Franks, Alemanni, and Romans at Troyes.
453. Death of Attila.

A.D.

455. Vandals sack Rome.

470. Ephthalites' raid into India.
476. Odoacer, king of a medley of Teutonic tribes, informs Constantinople that there is no emperor in the West. End of the Western Empire.

480. St. Benedict born.
481. Clovis in France.
483. Nestorian church breaks away from the Orthodox Christian church.

493. Theodoric, the Ostrogoth, conquers Italy and becomes King of Italy, but is nominally subject to Constantinople.

(Gothic kings in Italy. Goths settle on special confiscated lands as a garrison.)

527. Justinian emperor.
528. Mihiragula, the (Ephthalite) Attila of India, overthrown.
529. Justinian closes the schools at Athens, which had flourished nearly a thousand years. Belisarius (Justinian's general) takes Naples.

531. Chosroes I begins to reign.

543. Great plague in Constantinople.
544. St. Benedict dies.

553. Goths expelled from Italy by Justinian. Cassiodorus founds a monastery.

565. Justinian dies. The Lombards conquer most of North Italy (leaving Ravenna and Rome Byzantine). The Turks break up the Ephthalites in Western Turkestan.

570. Muhammad born.
579. Chosroes I dies.
(The Lombards prevail in Italy.)
590. Plague raging in Rome. (Gregory the Great—Gregory I—and the vision of St. Angelo.) Chosroes II begins to reign.

610. Heraclius begins to reign.
619. Chosroes II holds Egypt, Jerusalem, Damascus, and has armies on Hellespont. Tang dynasty begins in China.

A.D.

622. The Hegira.

623. Battle of Badr.

627. Great Persian defeat at Nineveh by Heraclius. The Meccan Allies besiege Medina. Tai Tsung becomes Emperor of China.

628. Kavadh II murders and succeeds his father, Chosroes II.

Muhammad writes letters to all the rulers of the earth.

629. Yuan Chwang starts for India. Muhammad enters Mecca.

631. Tai Tsung receives Nestorian missionaries.

A.D.

632. Muhammad dies. Abu Bekr Caliph.

634. Battle of the Yarmuk. Moslems take Syria. Omar second Caliph.

637. Battle of Kadessia.

638. Jerusalem surrenders to Omar.

642. Heraclius dies.

643. Othman third Caliph.

645. Yuan Chwang returns to Singan.

655. Defeat of the Byzantine fleet by the Moslems.

656. Othman is murdered at Medina.

XXXII

MUHAMMAD AND ISLAM[1]

§ 1

WE have already described how in A.D. 628 the courts of Heraclius, of Kavadh, and of Tai Tsung were visited by Arab envoys sent from a certain Muhammad, "The Prophet of God," at the small trading town of Medina in Arabia. We must tell now who this prophet was who had arisen among the nomads and traders of the Arabian desert.

Arabia before Muhammad.

From time immemorial Arabia, except for the fertile strip of the Yemen to the south, had been a land of nomads, the headquarters and land of origin of the Semitic peoples. From Arabia at various times waves of these nomads had drifted north, east, and west into the early civilizations of Egypt, the Mediterranean coast, and Mesopotamia. We have noted in this history how the Sumerians were swamped and overcome by such Semitic waves, how the Semitic Phœnicians and Canaanites established themselves along the eastern shores of the Mediterranean, how the Babylonians and Assyrians were settled Semitic peoples, how the Hyksos conquered Egypt, how the Arameans established themselves in Syria with Damascus as their capital, and how the Hebrews partially conquered their " Promised Land." At some unknown date the Chaldeans drifted in from Eastern Arabia and settled in the old southern Sumerian lands. With each invasion first this and then that section of the Semitic peoples comes into history. But each of such swarmings still leaves a tribal nucleus behind to supply fresh invasions in the future.

The history of the more highly organized empires of the horse and iron period, the empires of roads and writing, shows Arabia thrust like a wedge between Egypt, Palestine, and the Euphrates Tigris country, and still a reservoir of nomadic tribes who raid and trade and exact tribute for the immunity and protection of caravans. There are temporary and flimsy subjugations. Egypt, Persia, Macedonia, Rome, Syria, Constantinople, and again Persia claim some unreal suzerainty in turn over Arabia, profess some unsubstantial protection. Under Trajan there was a Roman province of " Arabia," which included the then fertile region of the Hauran and extended as far as Petra. Now and then some Arab chief and his trading city rises to temporary splendour. Such was that Odenathus of Palmyra, whose brief career we have noted in chap. xxxi, § 2, and another such transitory desert city whose ruins still astonish the traveller was Baalbek.

After the destruction of Palmyra, the desert Arabs began to be spoken of in the Roman and Persian records as Saracens.

[1] See Margoliouth's *Mahommedanism* and his *Life of Mahomet.*—E. B.

In the time of Chosroes II, Persia claimed a certain ascendancy over Arabia, and maintained officials and tax collectors in the Yemen. Before that time the Yemen had been under the rule of the Abyssinian Christians for some years, and before that for seven centuries it had had native princes professing, be it noted, the Jewish faith.

Until the opening of the seventh century A.D. there were no signs of any unwonted or dangerous energy in the Arabian deserts. The life of the country was going on as it had gone on for long generations. Wherever there were fertile patches, wherever, that is, there was a spring or a well, a scanty agricultural population subsisted, living in walled towns because of the Bedouin who wandered with their sheep, cattle, and horses over the desert. Upon the main caravan routes the chief towns rose to a certain second-rate prosperity, and chief among them were Medina and Mecca.[1] In the beginning of the seventh century Medina was a town of about 15,000 inhabitants all told; Mecca may have had twenty or twenty-five thousand. Medina was a comparatively well-watered town, and possessed abundant date groves; its inhabitants were Yemenites, from the fertile land to the south. Mecca was a town of a different character, built about a spring of water with a bitter taste, and inhabited by recently settled Bedouin.

Mecca was not merely nor primarily a trading centre; it was a place of pilgrimage. Among the Arab tribes there had long existed a sort of Amphictyony (see chap. xxii., § 1) centering upon Mecca and certain other sanctuaries; there were months of truce to war and blood feuds, and customs of protection and hospitality for the pilgrim. In addition there had grown up an Olympic element in these gatherings; the Arabs were discovering possibilities of beauty in their language, and there were recitations of war poetry and love songs. The sheiks of the tribes, under a " king of the Poets,"

[1] Should be spelt Mădina and Măkka.—H. H. J.

sat in judgment, and awarded prizes; the prize songs were sung through all Arabia.

The Kaaba, the sanctuary at Mecca, was of very ancient date. It was a small square temple of black stones, which had for its corner-stone a meteorite. This meteorite was regarded as a god, and all the little tribal gods of Arabia were under his protection. The permanent inhabitants of Mecca were a tribe of Bedouin who had seized this temple and constituted

Map of ARABIA and adjacent countries

themselves its guardians. To them there came in the months of truce a great incourse of people, who marched about the Kaaba ceremonially, bowed themselves, and kissed the stone, and also engaged in trade and poetical recitations. The Meccans profited much from these visitors.

All of this is very reminiscent of the religious and political state of affairs in Greece fourteen centuries earlier. But the paganism of these more primitive Arabs was already being assailed from several directions. There had been a great proselyting of Arabs during the period of the Maccabeans and Herods in Judea; and, as we have already noted, the Yemen had been in succession under the rule of Jews (Arab proselytes to Judaism, i.e.), Christians, and Zoroastrians. It is evident that there must

Photo : E. N. A.   MEDINA : A PANORAMA OF THE CITY.

have been plenty of religious discussion during the pilgrimage fairs at Mecca and the like centres. Naturally enough Mecca was a stronghold of the old pagan cult which gave it its importance and prosperity ; Medina, on the other hand, had Jewish proclivities, and there were Jewish settlements near by. It was inevitable that Mecca and Medina should be in a state of rivalry and bickering feud.

§ 2

It was in Mecca about the year A.D. 570 that Muhammad, the founder of Islam, was born.

Life of Muhammad to the Hegira.
He was born in considerable poverty, and even by the standards of the desert he was uneducated ; it is doubtful if he ever learnt to write. He was for some years a shepherd's boy ; then he became the servant of a certain Kadija, the widow of a rich merchant. Probably he had to look after her camels or help in her trading operations ; and he is said to have travelled with caravans to the Yemen and to Syria. He does not seem to have been a very useful trader, but he had the good fortune to find favour in the lady's eyes, and she married him, to the great annoyance of her family. He was then only twenty-five years old. It is uncertain if his wife was much older, though tradition declares she was forty. After the marriage he probably made no more long journeys. There were several children, one of whom was named Abd Manif—that is to say, the servant of the Meccan god Manif, which demonstrates that at that time Muhammad had made no religious discoveries.

Until he was forty he did indeed live a particularly undistinguished life in Mecca, as the husband of a prosperous wife. There may be some ground for the supposition that he became partner in a business in agricultural produce. To anyone visiting Mecca about A.D. 600 he would probably have seemed something of a loafer, a rather shy, good-looking individual, sitting about and listening to talk, a poor poet, and an altogether second-rate man.

About his internal life we can only speculate. Imaginative writers have supposed that he had great spiritual struggles, that he went out into the desert in agonies of doubt and divine desire. " In the silence of the desert night, in the bright heat of noontide desert day, he, as do all men, had known and felt himself alone yet not in solitude, for the desert is of God, and in the desert no man may deny Him." [1] Maybe that was so, but there is no evidence of any such desert trips. Yet he was certainly thinking deeply of the things about him. Possibly he had seen Christian churches in Syria ; almost certainly he knew much of the Jews and their religion, and he heard their scorn for this black stone of the Kaaba that ruled over the three hundred odd tribal gods of Arabia. He saw the pilgrimage crowds, and noted the threads of insincerity and superstition in the paganism of the town. It oppressed his mind. The Jews had perhaps converted him to a belief in the One True God, without his knowing what had happened to him.

At last he could keep these feelings to himself no longer. When he was forty he began to talk about the reality of God, at first apparently only to his wife and a few intimates. He produced certain verses, which he declared had been revealed to him by an angel. They involved an assertion of the unity of God and some acceptable generalizations about righteousness. He also insisted upon a future life, the fear of hell for the negligent and evil, and the reservation of paradise for the believer in the One God.

Except for his claim to be a new prophet, there does not seem to have been anything very new about these doctrines at the time, but this was seditious teaching for Mecca, which partly subsisted upon its polytheistic cult, and which was therefore holding on to idols when all the rest of the world was giving them up. Like Mani, Muhammad claimed that the prophets before him, and especially Jesus and Abraham, had been divine teachers, but that he crowned and completed their teaching. Buddhism, however, he did not name, probably because he had never heard of Buddha. Desert Arabia was in a theological backwater.

For some years the new religion was the secret of a small group of simple people, Kadija, the prophet's wife, Ali, an adopted son, Zeid, a slave, and Abu Bekr,[2] a friend and admirer. For some years it was an obscure sect in a few households of Mecca, a mere scowl and muttering at idolatry, so obscure and unimportant that the leading men of the town did not trouble about it in the least. Then it gathered strength. Muhammad began to preach more openly, to teach the doctrine of a future life, and to

[1] Mark Sykes.
[2] Should be Abu Bakr (= Father of Blessedness).— H. H. J.

Photo : H. J. Shepstone.

A BIRD'S-EYE VIEW OF MECCA, THE RELIGIOUS CAPITAL OF ISLAM.

Photo : H. J. Shepstone.
PILGRIMS FROM THE FOUR CORNERS OF THE EARTH PROSTRATING THEMSELVES BEFORE THE KAABA,
THE MOSLEM HOLY OF HOLIES AT MECCA.

threaten idolaters and unbelievers with hell fire. He seems to have preached with considerable effect. It appeared to many that he was aiming at a sort of dictatorship in Mecca, and drawing many susceptible and discontented people to his side; and an attempt was made to discourage and suppress the new movement.

Mecca was a place of pilgrimage and a sanctuary; no blood could be shed within its walls; nevertheless, things were made extremely disagreeable for the followers of the new teacher. Boycott and confiscation were used against them. Some were driven to take refuge in Christian Abyssinia. But the Prophet himself went unscathed because he was well connected, and his opponents did not want to begin a blood feud. We cannot follow the fluctuations of the struggle here, but it is necessary to note one perplexing incident in the new prophet's career, which, says Sir Mark Sykes, "proves him to have been an Arab of the Arabs." After all his insistence upon the oneness of God, he wavered. He came into the courtyard of the Kaaba, and declared that the gods and goddesses of Mecca might, after all, be real, might be a species of saints with a power of intercession.

His recantation was received with enthusiasm, but he had no sooner made it than he repented, and his repentance shows that he had indeed the fear of God in him. His lapse from honesty proves him honest. He did all he could to repair the evil he had done. He said that the devil had possessed his tongue, and denounced idolatry again with renewed vigour. The struggle against the antiquated deities, after a brief interval of peace, was renewed again more grimly, and with no further hope of reconciliation.

For a time the old interests had the upper hand. At the end of ten years of prophesying, Muhammad found himself a man of fifty, and altogether unsuccessful in Mecca. Kadija, his first wife, was dead, and several of his chief supporters had also recently died. He sought a refuge at the neighbouring town of Tayf, but Tayf drove him out with stones and abuse. Then, when the world looked darkest to him, opportunity opened before him. He found he had been weighed and approved in an unexpected quarter. The city of Medina was much torn by internal dissension, and many of its people, during the time of pilgrimage to Mecca, had been attracted by Muhammad's teaching. Probably the numerous Jews in Medina had shaken the ancient idolatry of the people. An invitation was sent to him to come and rule in the name of his God in Medina.

He did not go at once. He parleyed for two years, sending a disciple to preach in Medina and destroy the idols there. Then he began sending such followers as he had in Mecca to Medina to await his coming there; he did not want to trust himself to unknown adherents in a strange city. This exodus of the faithful continued, until at last only he and Abu Bekr remained.

In spite of the character of Mecca as a sanctuary, he was very nearly murdered there. The elders of the town evidently knew of what was going on in Medina, and they realized the danger to them if this seditious prophet presently found himself master of a town on their main caravan route to Syria. Custom must bow to imperative necessity, they thought; and they decided that, blood feud or no blood feud, Muhammad must die. They arranged that he should be murdered in his bed; and in order to share the guilt of this breach of sanctuary, they appointed a committee to do this, representing every family in the city except Muhammad's own. But Muhammad had already prepared his flight; and when in the night they rushed into his room, they found Ali, his adopted son, sleeping or feigning sleep on his bed.

The flight (the Hegira [1]) was an adventurous one, the pursuit was pressed hard. Expert desert trackers sought for the spoor to the north of the town, but Muhammad and Abu Bekr had gone south to certain caves where camels and provisions were hidden, and thence he made a great detour to Medina. There he and his faithful companion arrived, and were received with great enthusiasm on September 20, 622. It was the end of his probation and the beginning of his power. [2]

[1] Should be spelt and pronounced Hijra.—H. H. J.
[2] From the year of this flight (= Hegira) from Mecca through the desert to Medina, the Moslem world dates its era. By adding 622 if a date is between September and the New Year, or 623 if it is between the New Year and September, A.H. can be converted, therefore, into A.D.

§ 3

Until the Hegira, until he was fifty-one, the character of the founder of Islam is a matter of speculation and dispute. Thereafter he is in the light. We discover a man of great imaginative power but tortuous in the Arab fashion, and with most of the virtues and defects of the Bedouin.

Muhammad becomes a Fighting Prophet.

The opening of his reign was "very Bedouin." The rule of the One God of all the earth, as it was interpreted by Muhammad, began with a series of raids—which for more than a year were invariably unsuccessful—upon the caravans of Mecca. Then came a grave scandal, the breaking of the ancient customary truce of the Arab Amphictyony in the sacred month of Rahab. A party of Moslems, in this season of profound peace, treacherously attacked a small caravan and killed a man. It was their only success, and they did it by the order of the Prophet.

Presently came a battle. A force of seven hundred men had come out from Mecca to convoy home another caravan, and they encountered a large raiding party of three hundred. There was a fight, the battle of Badr, and the Meccans got the worst of it. They lost about fifty or sixty killed and as many wounded. Muhammad returned in triumph to Medina, and was inspired by Allah and this success to order the assassination of a number of his opponents among the Jews in the town who had treated his prophetic claims with a disagreeable levity.

But Mecca resolved to avenge Badr, and at the battle of Uhud, near Medina, inflicted an indecisive defeat upon the Prophet's followers. Muhammad was knocked down and nearly killed, and there was much running away among his followers. The Meccans, however, did not push their advantage and enter Medina.

For some time all the energies of the Prophet were concentrated upon rallying his followers, who were evidently much dispirited. The Koran records the chastened feelings of those days. "The *suras* of the Koran," says Sir Mark Sykes, "which are attributed to this period, excel nearly all the others in their majesty and sublime confidence." Here, for the judgment of the reader, is an example of these majestic utterances, from the recent orthodox translation by the Maulvi Muhammad Ali.[1]

"Oh, you who believe! If you obey those who disbelieve, they will turn you back upon your heels, so you will turn back losers.

"Nay! Allah is your Patron, and He is the best of the helpers.

"We will cast terror into the hearts of those who disbelieve, because they set up with Allah that for which He has sent down no authority, and their abode is the fire; and evil is the abode of the unjust.

"And certainly Allah made good to you his promise, when you slew them by His permission, until when you became weak-hearted and disputed about the affair and disobeyed after He had shown you that which you loved; of you were some who desired this world, and of you were some who desired the hereafter; then He turned you away from them that He might try you; and He has certainly pardoned you, and Allah is Gracious to the believers.

"When you ran off precipitately, and did not wait for anyone, and the Apostle was calling you from your rear, so He gave you another sorrow instead of your sorrow, so that you might not grieve at what had escaped you, nor at what befell you; and Allah is aware of what you do.

"Then after sorrow he sent down security upon you, a calm coming upon a party of you, and there was another party whom their own souls had rendered anxious; they entertained about Allah thoughts of ignorance quite unjustly, saying: We have no hand in this affair. Say, surely the affair is wholly in the hands of Allah. They conceal within their souls what they would not reveal to you. They say: Had we any hand in the affair, we would not have been slain here. Say: had you remained in your houses, those for whom slaughter was ordained would certainly have gone forth to the places where they would be slain, and that Allah might test what was in your breasts and that He might purge what was in your hearts; and Allah knows what is in the breasts.

"As for those of you who turned back on the day when the two armies met, only the devil sought to cause them to make a slip on account of some deeds they had done, and certainly Allah has pardoned them; surely Allah is Forgiving, Forbearing."

Inconclusive hostilities continued for some years, and at last Mecca made a crowning effort to stamp out for good and all the growing power of Medina. A mixed force of no less than 10,000

[1] Published by the *Islamic Review*.

men was scraped together, an enormous force for the time and country. It was, of course, an entirely undisciplined force of footmen, horsemen, and camel riders, and it was prepared for nothing but the usual desert scrimmage. Bows, spears, and swords were its only weapons. When at last it arrived amid a vast cloud of dust, in sight of the hovels and houses of Medina, instead of a smaller force of the same kind drawn up for battle, as it had expected, it found a new and entirely disconcerting phenomenon, a trench and a wall. Assisted by a Persian convert, Muhammad had entrenched himself in Medina!

This trench struck the Bedouin miscellany as one of the most unsportsmanlike things that had ever been known in the history of the world. They rode about the place. They shouted their opinion of the whole business to the besieged. They discharged a few arrows, and at last encamped to argue about this amazing outrage. They could arrive at no decision. Muhammad would not come out; the rains began to fall, the tents of the allies got wet and the cooking difficult, views became divergent and tempers gave way, and at last this great host dwindled again into its constituent parts without ever having given battle (627). The bands dispersed north, east, and south, became clouds of dust, and ceased to matter. Near Medina was a castle of Jews, against whom Muhammad was already incensed because of their disrespect for his theology. They had shown a disposition to side with the probable victor in this last struggle, and Muhammad now fell upon them, slew all the men, nine hundred of them, and enslaved the women and children. Possibly many of their late allies were among the bidders for these slaves. Never again after this quaint failure did Mecca make an effective rally against Muhammad, and one by one its leading men came over to his side.

We need not follow the windings of the truce and the treaty that finally extended the rule of the Prophet to Mecca. The gist of the agreement was that the faithful should turn towards Mecca when they prayed instead of turning towards Jerusalem as they had hitherto done, and that Mecca should be the pilgrimage centre of the new faith. So long as the pil-

THE CALIPH OMAR RIDES TO JERUSALEM.

417]

A RELIGIOUS PROCESSION PASSING THROUGH THE STREETS OF MEDINA.

grimage continued, the men of Mecca, it would seem, did not care very much whether the crowd assembled in the name of one god or many. Muhammad was getting more and more hopeless of any extensive conversion of the Jews and Christians, and he was ceasing to press his idea that all these faiths really worshipped the same One God. Allah was becoming more and more his own special God, tethered now by this treaty to the meteoric stone of the Kaaba, and less and less the father of all mankind. Already the Prophet had betrayed a disposition to make a deal with Mecca, and at last it was effected. The lordship of Mecca was well worth the concession. Of comings and goings and a final conflict we need not tell. In 629 Muhammad came to the town as its master. The image of Manif, the god after whom he had once named his son, was smashed under his feet as he entered the Kaaba.

Thereafter his power extended, there were battles, treacheries, massacres ; but on the whole he prevailed, until he was master of all

Arabia ; and when he was master of all Arabia in 632, at the age of sixty-two, he died.

Throughout the concluding eleven years of his life after the Hegira, there is little to distinguish the general conduct of Muhammad from that of any other welder of peoples into a monarchy. The chief difference is his use of a religion of his own creation as his cement. He was diplomatic, treacherous, ruthless, or compromising as the occasion required and as any other Arab king might have been in his place ; and there was singularly little spirituality in his kingship. Nor was his domestic life during his time of power and freedom one of exceptional edification. Until the death of Khadija, when he was fifty, he seems to have been the honest husband of one wife ; but then, as many men do in their declining years, he developed a disagreeably strong interest in women.

He married two wives after the death of Khadija, one being the young Ayesha, who became and remained his favourite and most influential partner ; and subsequently a number of other women, wives and concubines, were added to his establishment. This led to much trouble and confusion, and in spite of many special and very helpful revelations on the part of Allah, these complications still require much explanation and argument from the faithful. There was, for example, a scandal about Ayesha ; she was left behind on one occasion when the howdah and the camel went on, while she was looking for her necklace among the bushes ; and so Allah had to intervene with some heat and denounce her slanderers. Allah also had to speak very plainly about the general craving among this household of women for " this world's life and its ornature " and for " finery." Then there was much discussion because the Prophet first married his young cousin Zainib to his adopted son Zaid, and afterwards, " when Zaid had accomplished his want of her," the Prophet took her and married her—but, as the inspired book makes clear, only in order to show the difference between an adopted and a real son. " We gave her to you as a wife, so that there should be no difficulty for the believers in respect of the wives of their adopted sons, when they have accomplished their want of them, and Allah's command shall be performed." Yet surely a simple statement in the Koran should have sufficed without this excessively practical demonstration. There was, moreover, a mutiny in the harem on account of the undue favours shown by the Prophet to an Egyptian concubine who had borne him a boy, a boy for whom he had a great affection, since none of Khadija's sons had survived. These domestic troubles mingle inextricably with our impression of the Prophet's personality. One of his wives was a Jewess, Safiyya, whom he had married on the evening of the battle in which her husband had been captured and executed. He viewed the captured women at the end of the day, and she found favour in his eyes and was taken to his tent.

These are salient facts in these last eleven years of Muhammad's career. Because he, too, founded a great religion, there are those who write of this evidently lustful and rather shifty leader as though he were a man to put beside Jesus of Nazareth or Gautama or even Mani. But it is surely manifest that he was a being of a commoner clay ; he was vain, egotistical, tyrannous, and a self-deceiver ; and it would throw all our history out of proportion if, out of an insincere deference to the possible Moslem reader, we were to present him in any other light.

Yet unless we balance it, this insistence upon his vanity, egotism, self-deception, and hot desire does not complete the justice of the case. We must not swing across from the repudiation of the extravagant pretensions of the faithful to an equally extravagant condemnation. Can a man who has no good qualities hold a friend ? Because those who knew Muhammad best believed in him most. Khadija for all her days believed in him—but she may have been a fond woman. Abu Bekr is a better witness, and he never wavered in his devotion. Abu Bekr believed in the Prophet, and it is very hard for anyone who reads the history of these times not to believe in Abu Bekr. Ali again risked his life for the Prophet in his darkest days. Muhammad was no impostor, at any rate, though at times his vanity made him behave as though Allah was at his beck and call, and as if his thoughts were necessarily God's thoughts. And if his bloodstained passion with Safiyya amazes and disgusts our modern minds, his love for little Ibrahim, the son of Mary the Egyptian, and his passionate grief when the child died, reinstate him in the fellowship of all those who have known love and loss.

He smoothed the earth over the little grave with his own hands. " This eases the afflicted heart," he said. " Though it neither profits nor injures the dead, yet is it a comfort to the living."

§ 4

But the personal quality of Muhammad is one thing and the quality of Islam, the religion he *The* founded, is quite another. Muhammad *Teachings* was not pitted against Jesus or Mani, *of Islam.* and his relative stature is only a very secondary question for us ; it is Islam which was pitted against the corrupted Christianity of the seventh century and against the decaying tradition of the Zoroastrian Magi with which the historian has the greater concern. And whether it was through its Prophet or whether it was in spite of its Prophet, and through certain accidents in its origin and certain qualities of the desert from which it sprang, there can be no denying that Islam possesses many fine and noble attributes. It is not always through sublime persons that great things come into human life. It is the folly of the simple disciple which demands miraculous frippery on the majesty of truth and immaculate conceptions for righteousness.

A year before his death, at the end of the tenth year of the

Photo: Underwood & Underwood.

OFFERING A SHEEP FOR A BRASS POT IN THE BAZAAR AT BAGDAD.

"Ye people: Hearken to my words; for I know not whether, after this year, I shall ever be amongst you here again. Your lives and property are sacred and inviolable amongst one another until the end of time.

"The Lord hath ordained to every man the share of his inheritance; a testament is not lawful to the prejudice of heirs.

"The child belongeth to the parent; and the violator of wedlock shall be stoned.

"Whoever

Hegira, Muhammad made his last pilgrimage from Medina to Mecca. He made then a great sermon to his people, of which the tradition is as follows. There are, of course, disputes as to the authenticity of the words, but there can be no dispute that the world of Islam, a world still of three hundred million people, receives them to this day as its rule of life, and to a great extent observes it. The reader will note that the first paragraph sweeps away all plunder and blood feuds among the followers of Islam. The last makes the believing Negro the equal of the Caliph. They may not be sublime words, as certain utterances of Jesus of Nazareth are sublime; but they established in the world a great tradition of dignified fair dealing, they breathe a spirit of generosity, and they are human and workable. They created a society more free from widespread cruelty and social oppression than any society had ever been in the world before.

claimeth falsely another for his father, or another for his master, the curse of God and the angels and of all mankind shall rest upon him.

"Ye people! Ye have rights demandable of your wives, and they have rights demandable of you. Upon them it is incumbent not to violate their conjugal faith nor commit any act of open impropriety; which things if they do, ye have authority to shut them up in separate apartments and to beat them with stripes, yet not severely. But if they refrain therefrom, clothe them and feed them suitably. And treat your women well, for they are with you as captives and prisoners; they have not power over anything as regards themselves. And ye have verily taken them on the security of God, and have made their persons lawful unto you by the words of God.

"And your slaves, see that ye feed them with such food as ye eat yourselves, and clothe them with the stuff ye wear. And if they commit a fault which ye are not inclined to forgive, then sell them, for they are the servants of the Lord, and are not to be tormented.

" Ye people ! hearken to my speech and comprehend the same. Know that every Moslem is the brother of every other Moslem. All of you are on the same equality."

This insistence upon kindliness and consideration in the daily life is one of the main virtues of Islam, but it is not the only one. Equally important is the uncompromising monotheism, void of any Jewish exclusiveness, which is sustained by the Koran. Islam from the outset was fairly proof against the theological elaborations that have perplexed and divided Christianity and smothered the spirit of Jesus. And its third source of strength has been in the meticulous prescription of methods of prayer and worship, and its clear statement of the limited and conventional significance of the importance ascribed to Mecca. All sacrifice was barred to the faithful ; no loophole was left for the sacrificial priest of the old dispensation to come back into the new faith. It was not simply a new faith, a purely prophetic religion, as the religion of Jesus was in the time of Jesus,

or the religion of Gautama in the lifetime of Gautama, but it was so stated as to remain so. Islam to this day has learned doctors, teachers, and preachers ; but it has no priests.

It was full of the spirit of kindliness, generosity, and brotherhood ; it was a simple and understandable religion ; it was instinct with the chivalrous sentiment of the desert ; and it made its appeal straight to the commonest instincts in the composition of ordinary men. Against it were pitted Judaism, which had made a racial hoard of God ; Christianity talking and preaching endlessly now of trinities, doctrines, and heresies no ordinary man could make head or tail of ; and Mazdaism, the cult of the Zoroastrian Magi, who had inspired the crucifixion of Mani. The bulk of the people to whom the challenge of Islam came did not trouble very much whether Muhammad was lustful or not, or whether he had done some shifty and questionable things ; what appealed to them was that this God, Allah, he preached, was by the test of the conscience in their hearts a God of righteousness, and that the honest acceptance of his doctrine and method opened the door wide in a world of uncertainty,

Photo : American Colony, Jerusalem.

GENERAL VIEW OF DAMASCUS, SHOWING THE MINARET OF THE GREAT MOSQUE.

treachery, and intolerable divisions to a great and increasing brotherhood of trustworthy men on earth, and to a paradise not of perpetual exercises in praise and worship, in which saints, priests, and anointed kings were still to have the upper places, but of equal fellowship and simple and understandable delights such as their souls craved for. Without any ambiguous symbolism, without any darkening of altars or chanting of priests, Muhammad had brought home those attractive doctrines to the hearts of mankind.

§ 5

The true embodiment of the spirit of Islam was not **The Caliphs Abu Bekr and Omar.** Muhammad, but his close friend and supporter Abu Bekr. There can be little doubt that if Muhammad was the mind and imagination of primitive Islam, Abu Bekr was its conscience and its will. Throughout their life together it was Muhammad who said the thing, but it was Abu Bekr who believed the thing. When Muhammad wavered, Abu Bekr sustained him. Abu Bekr was a man without doubts, his beliefs cut down to acts cleanly as a sharp knife cuts. We may feel sure that Abu Bekr would never have temporized about the minor gods of Mecca, or needed inspirations from Allah to explain his private life. When in the eleventh year of the Hegira (632) the Prophet sickened of a fever and died, it was Abu Bekr who succeeded him as Caliph and leader of the people (Kalifa = Successor), and it was the unflinching confidence of Abu Bekr in the righteousness of Allah which prevented a split between Medina and Mecca, which stamped down a widespread insurrection of the Bedouin against taxation for the common

cause, and carried out a great plundering raid into Syria that the dead Prophet had projected. And then Abu Bekr, with that faith which moves mountains, set himself simply and sanely to organize the subjugation of the whole world to Allah—with little armies of 3,000 or 4,000

Photo: American Colony, Jerusalem.

A TYPICAL STREET IN DAMASCUS.

Arabs—according to those letters the Prophet had written from Medina in 628 to all the monarchs of the world.

And the attempt came near to succeeding. Had there been in Islam a score of men, younger men to carry on his work, of Abu Bekr's quality, it would certainly have succeeded. It came near to succeeding because Arabia was now a centre of faith and will, and because nowhere else in the world until China was reached, unless it was upon the steppes of Russia or Turkestan, tary prince, whose capital was at Hira. Arab influence was strong in such cities as Damascus, where Christian Arab gentlemen would read and recite the latest poetry from the desert competitors. There was thus a great amount of easily assimilable material ready at hand for Islam.

And the military campaigns that now began were among the most brilliant in the world's history. Arabia had suddenly become a garden of fine men. The name of Khalid stands out as the brightest star in a constellation of able and devoted Moslem generals. Whenever he commanded he was victorious, and when the jealousy of the second Caliph, Omar, degraded him unjustly and inexcusably.[1] he made no ado, but served Allah cheerfully and well as a subordinate to those over whom he had ruled. We cannot trace the story of this warfare here; the Arab armies struck simultaneously at Byzantine Syria and the Persian frontier city of Hira, and everywhere they offered a choice of three alternatives; either pay tribute, or confess the true God and join us, or die. They encountered armies, large and disciplined but spiritless armies, and defeated them. And nowhere was there such a thing as a popular resistance. The people of the populous irrigation lands of Mesopotamia cared not a jot whether they paid taxes to Byzantium or Persepolis or to Medina; and of the two, Arabs or Persian court, the Arabs, the Arabs of the great years, were manifestly the cleaner people, more just and more merciful. The Christian Arabs joined the invaders very readily and so did many Jews. Just as in the west, so now in

was there another community of free-spirited men with any power of belief in their rulers and leaders. The head of the Byzantine Empire, Heraclius, the conqueror of Chosroes II, was past his prime and suffering from dropsy, and his empire was exhausted by the long Persian war. Nor had he at any time displayed such exceptional ability as the new occasion demanded. The motley of people under his rule knew little of him and cared less. Persia was at the lowest depths of monarchist degradation, the parricide Kavadh II had died after a reign of a few months, and a series of dynastic intrigues and romantic murders enlivened the palace but weakened the country. The war between Persia and the Byzantine Empire was only formally concluded about the time of the beginning of Abu Bekr's rule. Both sides had made great use of Arab auxiliaries; over Syria a number of towns and settlements of Christianized Arabs were scattered who professed a baseless loyalty to Constantinople; the Persian marches between Mesopotamia and the desert were under the control of an Arab tribu-

---

[1] But Schurtz, see footnote, p. 425, says that the private life of the gallant Khalid was a scandal to the faithful. He committed adultery, a serious offence in a world of polygamy.

the east, an invasion became a social revolution. But here it was also a religious revolution with a new and distinctive mental vitality.

It was Khalid who fought the decisive battle (634) with the army of Heraclius upon the banks of the Yarmuk, a tributary of the Jordan. The legions, as ever, were without proper cavalry; for seven centuries the ghost of old Crassus had haunted the east in vain; the imperial armies relied upon Christian Arab auxiliaries, and these deserted to the Moslems as the armies joined issue. A great parade of priests, sacred banners, pictures, and holy relics was made by the Byzantine host, and it was further sustained by the chanting of monks. But there was no magic in the relics and little conviction about the chanting. On the Arab side the Emirs and sheiks harangued the troops, and after the ancient Arab fashion the shrill voices of women in the rear encouraged their men. The Moslem ranks were full of believers before whom shone victory or paradise. The battle was never in doubt after the defection of the irregular cavalry. An attempt to retreat dissolved into a rout and became a massacre. The Byzantine army had fought with its back to the river, which was presently choked with its dead.

Thereafter Heraclius slowly relinquished all Syria, which he had so lately won back from the Persians, to his new antagonists. Damascus soon fell, and a year later the Moslems entered Antioch. For a time they had to abandon it again to a last effort from Constantinople, but they re-entered it for good under Khalid.

Meanwhile on the eastern front, after a swift initial success which gave them Hira, the Persian resistance stiffened. The dynastic struggle had ended at last in the coming of a king of kings, and a general of ability had been found in Rustam. He gave battle at Kadessia (637). His army was just such another composite host as Darius had led into Thrace or Alexander defeated at Issus; it was a medley of levies. He had thirty-three war elephants, and he sat on a golden throne upon a raised platform behind the Persian ranks, surveying the battle, which throne will remind the reader of Herodotus, the Hellespont, and Salamis more than a thousand years before. The battle lasted three days; each day the Arabs attacked and the Persian host held its ground until night-fall called a truce. On the third day the Arabs received reinforcements, and towards the evening the Persians attempted to bring the struggle to an end by a charge of elephants. At first the huge beasts carried all before them; then one was wounded painfully and became uncontrollable, rushing up and down between the armies. Its panic affected the others, and for a time both armies remained dumfounded in the red light of sunset, watching the frantic

Photo: American Colony, Jerusalem.

THE MOSQUE OF OMAR, JERUSALEM.
(Justinian's Church.)

efforts of these grey, squealing monsters to escape from the tormenting masses of armed men that hemmed them in. It was by the merest chance that at last they broke through the Persian and not through the Arab array, and that it was the Arabs who were able to charge home upon the resulting confusion. The twilight darkened to night, but this time the armies did not separate. All through the night the Arabs smote in the name of Allah, and pressed upon the shattered and retreating Persians. Dawn broke upon the vestiges of Rustam's army in flight far beyond the litter of the battle-field. Its path was marked by scattered weapons and war material, abandoned transport, and the dead and dying. The platform and the golden throne were broken down, and Rustam lay dead among a heap of dead men. . . .

Already in 634 Abu Bekr had died and given place to Omar, the Prophet's brother-in-law, as Caliph ; and it was under Omar (634–643) that the main conquests of the Moslem occurred. The Byzantine Empire was pushed out of Syria altogether, Armenia was overrun, all Mesopotamia was conquered and Persia beyond the rivers. Egypt passed almost passively from Greek

Photo: H. J. Shepstone.
SHRINE AT HUR, NEAR KERBELA.
Typical Moslem architecture.

came the six-hundred-mile journey with only one attendant ; he was mounted on a camel, and a bag of barley, another of dates, a water-skin, and a wooden platter were his provision for the journey. He was met outside the city by his chief captains, robed splendidly in silks and with richly caparisoned horses. At this amazing sight the old man was overcome with rage. He slipped down from his saddle, scrabbled up dirt and stones with his hands, and pelted these fine gentlemen, shouting abuse. What was this insult ? What did this finery mean ? Where were his warriors ? Where were the desert men ? He

to Arab ; in a few years the Semitic race, in the name of God and His Prophet, had recovered nearly all the dominions it had lost to the Aryan Persian a thousand years before. Jerusalem fell early, making a treaty without standing a siege, and so the True Cross which had been carried off by the Persians a dozen years before, and elaborately restored by Heraclius, passed once more out of the rule of Christians. But it was still in Christian hands ; the Christians were to be tolerated, paying only a poll tax ; and all the churches and all the relics were left in their possession.

Jerusalem made a peculiar condition for its surrender. The city would give itself only to the Caliph Omar in person. Hitherto he had been in Medina organizing armies and controlling the general campaign. He came to Jerusalem (638), and the manner of his coming shows how swiftly the vigour and simplicity of the first Moslem onset was being sapped by success. He

would not let these popinjays escort him. He went on with his attendant, and the smart Emirs rode afar off—well out of range of his stones. He met the Patriarch of Jerusalem, who had apparently taken over the city from its Byzantine rulers, alone. With the Patriarch he got on very well. They went round the Holy Places together, and Omar, now a little appeased, made sly jokes at the expense of his too magnificent followers.

Equally indicative of the tendencies of the time is Omar's letter ordering one of his governors who had built himself a palace at Kufa, to demolish it again.

"They tell me," he wrote, "you would imitate the palace of Chosroes, [1] and that you would even use the gates that once were his. Will you also have guards and porters at those gates, as Chosroes had ? Will you keep the faithful afar off and deny audience to the poor ?

[1] At Ctesiphon.

Would you depart from the custom of our Prophet. and be as magnificent as those Persian emperors, and descend to hell even as they have done ? " [1]

§ 6

Abu Bekr and Omar I are the two master figures in the history of Islam. It is not within **The Great Days of the Omayyads.** our scope here to describe the wars by which in a hundred and twenty-five years Islam spread itself from the Indus to the Atlantic and Spain, and from Kashgar on the borders of China to Upper Egypt. Two maps must suffice to show the limits to

the better. Islam prevailed because it was the best social and political order the times could offer. It prevailed because everywhere it found politically apathetic peoples, robbed, oppressed, bullied, uneducated, and unorganized, and it found selfish and unsound governments out of touch with any people at all. It was the broadest, freshest, and cleanest political idea that had yet come into actual activity in the world, and it offered better terms than any other to the mass of mankind. The capitalistic and slave-holding system of the Roman Empire and the literature and culture and social tradition of Europe had altogether decayed

The GROWTH of the MOSLEM POWER in 25 years

Moslem Empire at the death of Muhammad, 632 ..
at the death of Othman, 656 ....

which the vigorous impulse of the new faith carried the Arab idea and the Arabic scriptures, before worldliness, the old trading and plundering spirit, and the glamour of the silk robe had completely recovered their paralysing sway over the Arab intelligence and will. The reader will note how the great tide swept over the footsteps of Yuan Chwang, and how easily in Africa the easy conquests of the Vandals were repeated in the reverse direction. And if the reader entertains any delusions about a fine civilization, either Persian, Roman, Hellenic, or Egyptian, being submerged by this flood, the sooner he dismisses such ideas

[1] Paraphrased from Schurtz in Helmolt's *History of the World.*

and broken down before Islam arose ; it was only when mankind lost faith in the sincerity of its representatives that Islam too began to decay.

The larger part of its energy spent itself in conquering and assimilating Persia and Turkestan; its most vigorous thrusts were northwardly from Persia and westwardly through Egypt. Had it concentrated its first vigour upon the Byzantine Empire, there can be little doubt that by the eighth century it would have taken Constantinople and come through into Europe as easily as it reached the Pamirs. The Caliph Moawiya, it is true, besieged the capital for seven years (672 to 678), and Suleiman in 717 and 718 ; but the pressure was not

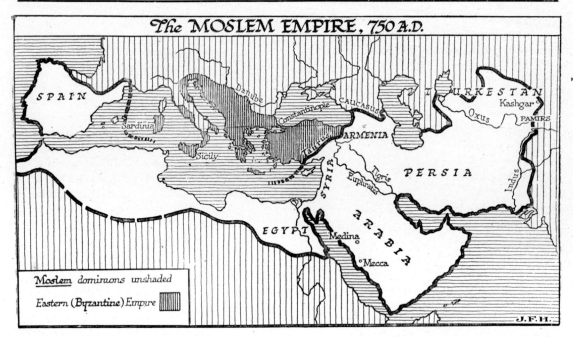

sustained, and for three or four centuries longer the Byzantine Empire remained the crazy bulwark of Europe. In the newly Christianized or still pagan Avars, Bulgars, Serbs, Slavs, and Saxons, Islam would certainly have found as ready converts as it did in the Turks of Central Asia. And though, instead of insisting upon Constantinople, it first came round into Europe by the circuitous route of Africa and Spain, it was only in France, at the end of a vast line of communications from Arabia, that it encountered a power sufficiently vigorous to arrest its advance.

From the outset the Bedouin aristocrats of Mecca dominated the new empire. Abu Bekr, the first Caliph, was in an informal shouting way elected at Medina, and so were Omar I and Othman, the third Caliph, but all three were Meccans of good family. They were not men of Medina. And though Abu Bekr and Omar were men of stark simplicity and righteousness Othman was of a baser quality, a man quite in the vein of those silk robes, to whom conquest was not conquest for Allah, but for Arabia, and especially for Mecca in Arabia, and more particularly for himself and for the Meccans and for his family, the Omayyads. He was a worthy man, who stood out for his country and his town and his " people." He was no early convert as his two predecessors had been ; he

had joined the Prophet for reasons of policy in fair give and take. With his accession the Caliph ceases to be a strange man of fire and wonder, and becomes an Oriental monarch like many Oriental monarchs before and since, a fairly good monarch by Eastern standards as yet, but nothing more.

The rule and death of Othman brought out the consequences of Muhammad's weaknesses as clearly as the lives of Abu Bekr and Omar had witnessed to the divine fire in his teaching. Muhammad had been politic at times when Abu Bekr would have been firm, and the new element of aristocratic greediness that came in with Othman was one fruit of those politic moments. And the legacy of that carelessly compiled harem of the Prophet, the family complications and jealousies which had lurked in the background of Moslem affairs during the rule of the first two Caliphs, was now coming out into the light of day. Ali, who was the nephew, the adopted son, and the son-in-law of the Prophet— he was the husband of the Prophet's daughter Fatima—had always considered himself the rightful Caliph. His claims formed an undertow to the resentment of Medina and of the rival families of Mecca against the advancement of the Omayyads. But Ayesha, the favourite wife of the Prophet, had always been jealous of Fatima and hostile to Ali. She supported

Othman. . . . The splendid opening of the story of Islam collapses suddenly into this squalid dispute and bickering of heirs and widows.

In 656 Othman, an old man of eighty, was stoned in the streets of Medina by a mob, chased to his house, and murdered; and Ali became at last Caliph, only to be murdered in his turn (661). In one of the battles in this civil war, Ayesha, now a gallant, mischievous old lady, distinguished herself by leading a charge, mounted on a camel. She was taken prisoner and treated well.

While the armies of Islam were advancing triumphantly to the conquest of the world, this sickness of civil war smote at its head. What was the rule of Allah in the world to Ayesha when she could score off the detested Fatima, and what heed were the Omayyads and the partisans of Ali likely to take of the unity of mankind when they had a good hot feud of this sort to entertain them, with the caliphate as a prize? The world of Islam was rent in twain by the spites, greeds, and partisan silliness of a handful of men and women in Medina. That quarrel still lives. To this day one main division of the Moslem, the Shiites, maintain the hereditary right of Ali to be Caliph *as an article of faith!* They prevail in Persia and India. But an equally important section, the Sunnites, with whom it is difficult for a disinterested observer not to agree, deny this peculiar addendum to Muhammad's simple creed. So far as we can gather at this length of time, Ali was an entirely commonplace individual.

To watch this schism creeping across the brave beginnings of Islam is like watching a case of softening of the brain. To the copious literature of the subject we must refer the reader who wishes to learn how Hasan, the son of Ali, was poisoned by his wife, and how Husein, his brother, was killed. We do but name them here because they still afford a large section of mankind scope for sentimental partisanship and mutual annoyance. They are the two chief Shiite martyrs. Amidst the coming and going of their conflicts the old Kaaba at Mecca was burnt down, and naturally there began endless disputation whether it should be rebuilt in exactly its ancient form or on a much larger scale.

In this and the preceding sections we have seen once more the inevitable struggle of this newest and latest unifying impulse in the world's affairs against the everyday worldliness of mankind, and we have seen also how from the first the complicated household of Muhammad was like an evil legacy to the new faith. But as this history now degenerates into the normal crimes and intrigues of an Oriental dynasty, the student of history will realize a third fundamental weakness in the world reforms of Muhammad. He was an illiterate Arab, ignorant of history, totally ignorant of all the political experiences of Rome and Greece, and almost as ignorant of the real history of Judea; and he left his followers with no scheme for a stable government embodying and concentrating the general will of the faithful, and no effective form to express the very real spirit of democracy (using the word in its modern sense) that pervades the essential teaching of Islam. His own rule was unlimited autocracy, and autocratic Islam has remained. Politically Islam was not an advance, but a retrogression from the traditional freedoms and customary laws of the desert. The breach of the pilgrims' truce that led to the battle of Badr is the blackest mark against early Islam. Nominally Allah is its chief ruler—but practically its master has always been whatever man was vigorous and unscrupulous enough to snatch and hold the Caliphate—and, subject to revolts and assassinations, its final law has been that man's will.

For a time, after the death of Ali, the Omayyad family was in the ascendant, and for nearly a century they gave rulers to Islam.

The Arab historians are so occupied with the dynastic squabbles and crimes of the time, that it is difficult to trace the external history of the period. We find Moslem shipping upon the seas defeating the Byzantine fleet in a great sea fight off the coast of Lycia (A.D. 655), but how the Moslem acquired this victorious fleet thus early we do not clearly know. It was probably chiefly Egyptian. For some years Islam certainly controlled the Eastern Mediterranean, and in 662 and again in 672, during the reign of Muawiya (662–680), the first great Omayyad Caliph, made two sea attacks upon Constantinople. They had to be sea attacks because Islam, so long as it was under Arab rule, never surmounted the barrier of the Taurus Mountains. During the same period the Moslems were also pressing their conquests further and further into Central Asia. While Islam was already decaying at its centre, it was yet making great hosts of new adherents and awakening a new spirit among the hitherto divided and aimless Turkish peoples. Medina was no longer a possible centre for its vast enterprises in Asia, Africa, and the Mediterranean, and so Damascus became the usual capital of the Omayyad Caliphs.

Chief among these, as for a time the clouds of dynastic intrigue clear, are Abdal Malik (685–705) and Walid I (705–715), under whom the Omayyad line rose to the climax of its successes. The western boundary was carried to the Pyrenees, while to the east the domains of the Caliph marched with China. The son of Walid, Suleiman (715), carried out a second series of Moslem attacks upon Constantinople which his father had planned and proposed. As with the Caliph Muawiya half a century before, the approach was by sea—for Asia Minor, as we have just noted, was still unconquered—and the shipping was drawn chiefly from Egypt. The emperor, a usurper, Leo the Isaurian, displayed extraordinary skill and obstinacy in the defence; he burnt most of the Moslem shipping in a brilliant sortie, cut up the troops they had landed upon the Asiatic side of the Bosphorus, and after a campaign in Europe of two years (717–718), a winter of unexampled severity completed their defeat.

From this point onward the glory of the Omayyad line declines. The first tremendous impulse of Islam was now spent. There was no further expansion and a manifest decline in religious zeal. Islam had made millions of converts, and had digested those millions very imperfectly. Cities, nations, whole sects and races, Arab pagans, Jews, Christians, Manichæans, Zoroastrians, Turanian pagans, had been swallowed up into this new vast empire of Muhammad's successors. It has hitherto been the common characteristic of all the great unifying religious initiators of the world, the common oversight, that they have accepted the moral and theological ideals to which the first appeal was made, as though they were universal ideals. Muhammad's appeal, for example, was to the traditional chivalry and underlying monotheistic feelings of the intelligent Arabs of his time. These things were latent in the mind and conscience of Mecca and Medina; he did but call them forth. Then, as the new teaching spread and stereotyped itself, it had to work on a continually more uncongenial basis, it had to grow in soil that distorted and perverted it. Its sole text-book was the Koran. To minds untuned to the melodies of Arabic, this book seemed to be, as it seems to many European minds to-day, a mixture of fine-spirited rhetoric with—to put it plainly—formless and unintelligent gabble. Countless converts missed the real thing in it altogether. To that we must ascribe the readiness of the Persian and Indian sections of the faith to join the Shiite schism upon a quarrel that they could at least understand and feel. And to the same attempt to square the new stuff with old prepossessions was due such extravagant theology as presently disputed whether the Koran was and always had been co-existent with God.[1] We should be stupefied by the preposterousness of this idea if we did not recognize in it at once the well-meaning attempt of some learned Christian convert to Islamize his belief that " In the beginning was the Word, and the Word was with God, and the Word was God."[2]

None of the great unifying religious initiators of the world hitherto seems to have been accompanied by any understanding of the vast educational task, the vast work of lucid and varied exposition and intellectual organization involved in its propositions. They all present the same history of a rapid spreading, like a little water poured over a great area, and then of superficiality and corruption.

In a little while we hear stories of an Omayyad Caliph, Walid II (743–744), who mocked at the Koran, ate pork, drank wine, and did not pray. Those stories may have been true or they may have been circulated for political reasons. There began a puritan reaction in Mecca and Medina against the levity and luxury of Damascus. Another great Arab family, the Abbas family, the Abbasids, a thoroughly wicked family, had long been scheming for power, and was making capital of the general discontent.

[1] Mark Sykes.   [2] St. John's Gospel, chap. i. 1.

The feud of the Omayyads and the Abbasids was older than Islam; it had been going on before Muhammad was born. These Abbasids took up the tradition of the Shiite " martyrs," Ali and his sons Hasan and Husein, and identified themselves with it. The banner of the Omayyads was white; the Abbasid adopted a black banner, black in mourning for Hasan and Husein, black because black is more impressive than any colour; moreover, the Abbasids declared that all the Caliphs after Ali were usurpers. In 749 they accomplished a carefully prepared revolution, and the last of the Omayyad Caliphs was hunted down and slain in Egypt. Abul Abbas was the first of the Abbasid Caliphs, and he began his reign by collecting into one prison every living male of the Omayyad line upon whom he could lay hands and causing them all to be massacred. Their bodies were heaped together, a leathern carpet was spread over them, and on this gruesome table Abul Abbas and his councillors feasted.[1] Moreover, the tombs of the Omayyad Caliphs were rifled, and their bones burnt and scattered to the four winds of heaven. So the grievances of Ali were avenged at last, and the Omayyad line passed out of history.

There was, it is interesting to note, a rising on behalf of the Omayyads in Khorasan which was assisted by the Chinese Emperor.

§ 7

But the descendants of Ali were not destined to share in this triumph for long. The Abbasids

The Decay of Islam under the Abbasids.

were adventurers and rulers of an older school than Islam. Now that the tradition of Ali had served its purpose, the next proceeding of the new Caliph was to hunt down and slaughter the surviving members of his family, the descendants of Ali and Fatima.

[1] Thus Sykes. But Skrine and Ross say only that seventy members of the Omayyad family were invited to a feast under promise of amnesty, and then massacred by the attendants. Gibbon gives eighty victims, and tells his story thus: " Four score of the Omayyads, who had yielded to the faith or clemency of their foes, were invited to a banquet at Damascus. The laws of hospitality were violated by a promiscuous massacre; the board was spread over their fallen bodies; and the festivity of their guests was enlivened by the music of their dying groans." History is not yet an exact science.

Clearly the old traditions of Sassanid Persia and of Persia before the Greeks were returning to the world. With the accession of the Abbasids the control of the sea departed from the Caliph, and with it went Spain and North Africa, in which, under an Omayyad survivor in the former case, independent Moslem states now arose. The centre of gravity of Islam shifted across the desert from Damascus to Mesopotamia. Mansur, the successor of Abul Abbas, built himself a new capital at Baghdad near the ruins of Ctesiphon, the former Sassanid capital. Turks and Persians as well as Arabs became Emirs, and the army was reorganized upon Sassanid lines. Medina and Mecca were now only of importance as pilgrimage centres, to which the faithful turned to pray. But because it was a fine language, and because it was the language of the Koran, Arabic continued to spread until presently it had replaced Greek and become the language of educated men throughout the whole Moslem world.

Of the Abbasid monarchs after Abul Abbas we need tell little here. A bickering war went on year by year in Asia Minor in which neither Byzantium nor Baghdad made any permanent gains, though once or twice the Moslem raided as far as the Bosphorus. A false prophet Mokanna, who said he was God, had a brief but troublesome career. There were plots, there were insurrections; they lie flat and colourless now in the histories like dead flowers in an old book. One other Abbasid Caliph only need be named, and that quite as much for his legendary as for his real importance, Haroun-al-Raschid[2] (786–809). He was not only the Caliph of an outwardly prosperous empire in the world of reality, but he was also the Caliph of an undying empire in the deathless world of fiction, he was the Haroun-al-Raschid of the *Arabian Nights*.

Sir Mark Sykes[3] gives an account of the reality of his empire from which we will quote certain passages. He says: " The Imperial Court was polished, luxurious, and unlimitedly wealthy; the capital, Baghdad, a gigantic mercantile city surrounding a huge administrative fortress, wherein every department of state had a properly regulated and well-ordered public

[2] Harun-ar-Rashid = Aaron the Just.—H. J.
[3] *The Caliph's Last Heritage.*

Photo: H. J. Shepstone.

THE BRIDGE OF BOATS AT BAGHDAD.

office ; where schools and colleges abounded ; whither philosophers, students, doctors, poets, and theologians flocked from all parts of the civilized globe. . . . The provincial capitals were embellished with vast public buildings, and linked together by an effective and rapid service of posts and caravans ; the frontiers were secure and well garrisoned, the army loyal, efficient, and brave ; the governors and ministers honest and forbearing. The empire stretched with equal strength and unimpaired control from the Cilician gates to Aden, and from Egypt to Central Asia. Christians, Pagans, Jews, as well as Moslems, were employed in the government service. Usurpers, rebellious generals, and false prophets seemed to have vanished from the Moslem dominions. Traffic and wealth had taken the place of revolution and famine. . . . Pestilence and disease were met by Imperial hospitals and government physicians. . . . In government business the rough-and-ready methods of Arabian administration had given place to a complicated system of Divans, initiated partly from the Roman, but chiefly taken from the Persian system of government. Posts, Finance, Privy Seal, Crown Lands, Justice, and Military affairs were each administered by separate bureaux in the hands of ministers and officials ; an army of clerks, scribes, writers, and accountants swarmed into these offices and gradually swept the whole power of the government into their own hands by separating the Commander of the Faithful from any direct intercourse with his subjects. The Imperial Palace and the entourage were equally based on Roman and Persian precedents. Eunuchs, closely veiled ' harems ' of women, guards, spies, go-betweens, jesters, poets, and dwarfs clustered around the person of the Commander of the Faithful, each, in his degree, endeavouring to gain the royal favour and indirectly distracting the royal mind from affairs of business and state. Meanwhile the mercantile trade of the East poured gold into Baghdad, and supplemented the other enormous stream of money derived from the contributions of plunder and loot despatched to the capital by the commanders of the victorious raiding forces which harried Asia Minor, India, and Turkestan. The seemingly unending supply of Turkish slaves and Byzantine specie added to the richness of the revenues of Irak, and, combined with the vast commercial traffic of which Baghdad was the centre, produced a large and powerful moneyed class, composed of the sons of generals, officials, landed proprietors, royal favourites, merchants, and the like, who encouraged the arts, literature, philosophy, and poetry as the mood took them, building palaces for themselves, vying with each other in the luxury of their entertainments, suborning poets to sound their praises, dabbling in philosophy, supporting various schools of thought, endowing charities, and, in fact, behaving as the wealthy have always behaved in all ages.

" I have said that the Abbasid Empire in the days of Haroun-al-Raschid was weak and feeble to a degree, and perhaps the reader will consider this a foolish proposition when he takes into consideration that I have described the Empire as orderly, the administration definite and settled, the army efficient, and wealth abundant. The reason I make the suggestion is that the Abbasid Empire had lost touch with everything original and vital in Islam, and was constructed entirely by the reunion of the fragments of the empires Islam had destroyed. There was nothing in the empire which appealed to the higher instincts of the leaders of the people ; the holy war had degenerated into a systematic acquisition of plunder. The Caliph had become a luxurious Emperor or King of Kings ; the administration had changed from a patriarchal system to a bureaucracy. The wealthier classes were rapidly losing all faith in the religion of the state ; speculative philosophy and high living were taking the place of Koranic orthodoxy and Arabian simplicity. The solitary bond which could have held the empire together, the sternness and plainness of the Moslem faith, was completely neglected by both the Caliph and his advisers. . . . Haroun-al-Raschid himself was a winebibber, and his palace was decorated with graven images of birds and beasts and men. . . .

" For a moment we stand amazed at the greatness of the Abbasid dominion ; then suddenly we realize that it is but as a fair husk enclosing the dust and ashes of dead civilizations."

Haroun-al-Raschid died in 809. At his death his great empire fell immediately into civil war and confusion, and the next great event of unusual importance in this region of the world comes two hundred years later when the Turks, under the chiefs of the great family of the Seljuks, poured southward out of Turkestan, and not only conquered the empire of Baghdad, but Asia Minor also. Coming from the northeast as they did, they were able to outflank the great barrier of the Taurus Mountains, which had hitherto held back the Moslems. They were still much the same people as those of whom Yuan Chwang gave us a glimpse four hundred years earlier, but now they were Moslems, and Moslems of the primitive type, men whom Abu Bekr would have welcomed to Islam. They caused a great revival of vigour in Islam, and they turned the minds of the Moslem world once more in the direction of a religious war against Christendom. For there had been a sort of truce between these two great religions after the cessation of the Moslem advance and the decline of the Omayyads. Such warfare as had gone on between Christianity and Islam had been rather border-bickering than sustained war. It became only a bitter fanatical struggle again in the eleventh century.

§ 8

But before we go on to tell of the Turks and the Crusaders, the great wars that began between Christendom and Islam, and which have left a quite insane intolerance between these great systems right down to the present time, it is necessary to give a little more attention to the intellectual life of the Arabic-speaking world which was now spreading more and more widely over the regions which Hellenism had once dominated. For some generations before Muhammad, the Arab mind had been, as it were, smouldering, it had been producing poetry and much religious discussion ; under the stimulus of the national and racial successes it presently blazed out with a brilliance second only to that of the Greeks during their best period. From a new angle and with a fresh vigour it took up that systematic development of positive knowledge which the Greeks had begun and relin-

The Intellectual Life of Arab Islam.

quished. It revived the human pursuit of science. If the Greek was the father, then the Arab was the foster-father of the scientific method of dealing with reality, that is to say, by absolute frankness, the utmost simplicity of statement and explanation, exact record, and exhaustive criticism. Through the Arabs it was and not by the Latin route that the modern world received that gift of light and power.

Their conquests brought the Arabs into contact with the Greek literary tradition, not at first directly, but through the Syrian translations of the Greek writers. The Nestorian Christians, the Christians to the east of orthodoxy, seem to have been much more intelligent and active-minded than the court theologians of Byzantium, and at a much higher level of general education than the Latin-speaking Christians of the west. They had been tolerated during the latter days of the Sassanids, and they were tolerated by Islam until the ascendancy of the Turks in the eleventh century. They had preserved much of the Hellenic medical science, and had even added to it. In the Omayyad times most of the physicians in the Caliph's dominions were Nestorians, and no doubt many learned Nestorians professed Islam without any serious compunction or any great change in their work and thoughts. They had preserved much of Aristotle both in Greek and in Syrian translations. They had a considerable mathematical literature. Their equipment makes the contemporary resources of Saint Benedict or Cassiodorus seem very pitiful. To these Nestorian teachers came the fresh Arab mind out of the desert, keen and curious, and learnt much and improved upon its teaching.

But the Nestorians were not the only teachers available for the Arabs. Throughout all the rich cities of the east the kindred Jews were scattered with their own distinctive literature and tradition, and the Arab and the Jewish mind reacted upon one another to a common benefit. The Arab was informed and the Jew sharpened to a keener edge. The Jews have never been pedants in the matter of their language ; we have already noted that a thousand years before Islam they spoke Greek in Hellenized Alexandria, and now all over this new Moslem world they were speaking and writing Arabic. Some of the greatest of Jewish literature was written in Arabic, the religious writings of Maimonides for example. Indeed, it is difficult to say in the case of this Arabic culture where the Jew ends and the Arab begins, so important and essential were its Jewish factors.

Moreover, there was a third source of inspiration, more particularly in mathematical science, to which at present it is difficult to do justice, India. There can be little doubt that the Arab mind during its best period was in effective contact with Sanskrit literature and with Indian ideas, and that it derived much from this source.

The distinctive activities of the Arab mind were already manifest under the Omayyads. though it was during the Abbasid time that it made its best display. History is the beginning and core of all sound philosophy and all great literature, and the first Arab writers of distinction were historians, biographers, and quasi-historical poets. Romantic fiction and the short story followed as a reading public developed, willing to be amused. And as reading ceased to be a special accomplishment, and became necessary to every man of affairs and to every youth of breeding, came the systematic growth of an educational system and an educational literature. By the ninth and tenth centuries there are not only grammars, but great lexicons, and a mass of philological learning in Islam.

And a century or so in advance of the west, there grew up in the Moslem world at a number of centres, at Basra, at Kufa, at Baghdad and Cairo, and at Cordoba, out of what were at first religious schools dependent upon mosques, a series of great universities. The light of these universities shone far beyond the Moslem world, and drew students to them from east and west. At Cordoba in particular there were great numbers of Christian students, and the influence of Arab philosophy coming by way of Spain upon the universities of Paris, Oxford, and North Italy and upon Western European thought generally, was very considerable indeed. The name of Averroes (Ibn-rushd), of Cordoba (1126–1198), stands out as that of the culminating influence of Arab philosophy upon European thought. He developed the teachings of Aristotle upon lines that made a sharp division

HIC WILLELM: HIC WILLELM VENIT BAGIAS VBI HAROL

DEDIT: HAROLDO ARMA

REVERSVS: EST AD ANGLICAM: TERRAM: ET

PORTIONS OF THE BAYEUX TAPESTRY SHOWING NORMAN SHIPPING, ARMS, AND EQUIPMENT.

between religious and scientific truth, and so prepared the way for the liberation of scientific research from the theological dogmatism that restrained it both under Christianity and under Islam. Another great name is that of Avicenna (Ibn-sinā), the Prince of Physicians (980–1037), who was born at the other end of the Arabic world at Bokhara, and who travelled in Khorasan. . . . The book-copying industry flourished at Alexandria, Damascus, Cairo, and Baghdad, and about the year 970 .

Photo: Anderson.

THE ALHAMBRA, GRANADA, THE CULMINATING TRIUMPH OF ARABIC ARCHITECTURE IN SPAIN (Thirteenth Century).

there were twenty-seven free schools open in Cordoba for the education of the poor.

"In mathematics," say Thatcher and Schwill,[1] "the Arabs built on the foundations of the Greek mathematicians. The origin of the so-called Arabic numerals is obscure. Under Theodoric the Great, Boethius made use of certain signs which were in part very like the nine digits which we now use. One of the pupils of Gerbert also used signs which were still more like ours, but the zero was unknown till the twelfth century, when it was invented by an Arab mathematician named Muhammad-Ibn-Musa, who also was the first to use the decimal notation, and who gave the digits the value of position. In geometry the Arabs did not add much to Euclid, but algebra is practically their creation; also they developed spherical trigonometry, inventing the sine, tangent, and cotangent. In physics they invented the pendulum, and produced work on optics. They made progress in the science of astronomy.

[1] *A General History of Europe.*

28

They built several observatories, and constructed many astronomical instruments which are still in use. They calculated the angle of the ecliptic and the precession of the equinoxes. Their knowledge of astronomy was undoubtedly considerable.

"In medicine they made great advances over the work of the Greeks. They studied physiology and hygiene, and their *materia medica* was practically the same as ours to-day. Many of their methods of treatment are still in use among us. Their surgeons understood the use of anæsthetics, and performed some of the most difficult operations known. At the time when in Europe the practice of medicine was forbidden by the Church, which expected cures to be effected by religious rites performed by the clergy, the Arabs had a real science of medicine. In chemistry they made a good beginning. They discovered many new substances and compounds, such as alcohol, potassium, nitrate of silver, corrosive sublimate, and nitric and sulphuric acid. . . . In manufactures they outdid the world in variety and beauty of design and perfection of workmanship. They worked in all the metals—gold, silver, copper, bronze, iron, and steel. In textile fabrics they have never been surpassed. They made glass and pottery of the finest quality. They knew the secrets of dyeing, and they manufactured paper. They had many processes of dressing leather, and their work was famous throughout Europe. They made tinctures, essences, and syrups. They made sugar from the cane, and grew many fine kinds of wine. They practised farming in a scientific way, and had good systems of irrigation. They knew the value of fertilizers, and adapted their crops to the quality of the ground. They excelled in horticulture, knowing how to graft and how to produce new varieties of fruit and flowers. They introduced into the west many trees and plants from the east, and wrote scientific treatises on farming."

One item in this account must be underlined here because of its importance in the intellectual life of mankind, the manufacture of paper. This the Arabs seem to have learnt from the Chinese by way of Central Asia. The Europeans acquired it from the Arabs. Until that time books had to be written upon parchment or papyrus, and after the Arab conquest of Egypt Europe was cut off from the

Photo: Anderson.

THE ALHAMBRA, GRANADA.

papyrus supply. Until paper became abundant, the art of printing was of little use, and newspapers and popular education by means of books was impossible. This was probably a much more important factor in the relative backwardness of Europe during the dark ages than historians seem disposed to admit. . . .

And all this mental life went on in the Moslem world in spite of a very considerable amount of political disorder. From first to last the Arabs never grappled with the problem, the still unsolved problem, of the stable progressive state ; everywhere their form of government was absolutist and subject to the convulsions,

changes, intrigues, and murders that have always characterized the extremer forms of monarchy. But for some centuries, beneath the crimes and rivalries of courts and camps, the spirit of Islam did preserve a certain general decency and restraint in life ; the Byzantine Empire was impotent to shatter this civilization, and the Turkish danger in the north-east gathered strength only very slowly. Until the Turk fell upon it, the intellectual life of Islam continued. Perhaps it secretly flattered itself that it would always be able to go on in spite of the thread of violence and unreason in its political direction. Hitherto in all countries that has been the characteristic attitude of science and literature. The intellectual man has been loth to come to grips with the forcible man. He has generally been something of a courtier and time server. Possibly he has never yet been quite sure of himself. Hitherto men of reason and knowledge have never had the assurance and courage of the religious fanatic. But there can be little doubt that they have accumulated settled convictions and gathered confidence during the last few centuries ; they have slowly found a means to power through the development of popular education and popular literature, and to-day they are far more disposed to say things plainly and to claim a dominating voice in the organization of human affairs than they have ever been before in the world's history.

XXXIII

CHRISTENDOM AND THE CRUSADES

§ 1

LET us turn again now from this intellectual renaissance in the cradle of the ancient civilizations to the affairs of the Western world. We have described the complete economic, social, and political break up of the Roman imperial system in the west, the confusion and darkness that followed in the sixth and seventh centuries, and the struggles of such men as Cassiodorus to keep alight the flame of human learning amidst these windy confusions. For a time it would be idle to write of states and rulers. Smaller or greater adventurers seized a castle or a country-side and ruled an uncertain area. The British Islands, for instance, were split up amidst a multitude of rulers; numerous Keltic chiefs in Ireland and Scotland and Wales and Cornwall fought and prevailed over and succumbed to each other; the English invaders were also divided into a number of fluctuating "kingdoms," Kent, Wessex, Essex, Sussex, Mercia, Northumbria, and

The Western World at its Lowest Ebb.

East Anglia, which were constantly at war with one another. So it was over most of the Western world. Here a bishop would be the monarch, as Gregory the Great was in Rome; here a town or a group of towns would be under the rule of the duke or prince of this or that. Amidst the vast ruins of the city of Rome half-independent families of quasi-noble adventurers and their retainers maintained themselves. The Pope kept a sort of general predominance there, but he was sometimes more than balanced by a "Duke of Rome." The great arena of the Colosseum had been made into a privately owned castle, and so too had the vast circular tomb of the Emperor Hadrian; and the adventurers who had possession of these strongholds and their partisans waylaid each other and fought and bickered in the ruinous streets of the once imperial city. The tomb of Hadrian was known after the days of Gregory the Great as the Castle of St. Angelo, the Castle of the Holy Angel, because when he was crossing the bridge over the Tiber on his way to St. Peter's

Photo: Anderson

CASTLE OF ST. ANGELO, ROME.

to pray against the great pestilence which was devastating the city, he had had a vision of a great angel standing over the dark mass of the mausoleum and sheathing a sword, and he had known then that his prayers would be answered. This Castle of St. Angelo played a very important part in Roman affairs during this age of disorder.

Spain was in much the same state of political fragmentation as Italy or France or Britain ; and in Spain the old feud of Carthaginian and Roman was still continued in the bitter hostility of their descendants and heirs, the Jew and the Christian. So that when the power of the Caliph had swept along the North African coast to the Straits of Gibraltar, it found in the Spanish Jews ready helpers in its invasion of Europe. A Moslem army of Arabs and of Berbers, the nomadic Hamitic people of the African desert and mountain hinterland who had been converted to Islam, crossed and defeated the West Goths in a great battle in 711. In a few years the whole country was in their possession.

In 720 Islam had reached the Pyrenees, and had pushed round their eastern end into France ; and for a time it seemed that the faith was likely to subjugate Gaul as easily as it had subjugated the Spanish peninsula. But presently it struck against something hard, a new kingdom of the Franks, which had been consolidating itself for some two centuries in the Rhineland and North France.

§ 2

But before we go on to tell of the kingdom of the Franks that formed the western bulwark (as Byzantium formed the eastern) of Christendom against the faith of Muhammad, it may be well to devote a section to that system of political relationships in Europe that was growing up out of the necessities of the time and the temperament and traditions of the Teutonic peoples, the feudal system. The fundamental factor of the feudal system was the advantage of a free alliance between weaker and stronger in the universal mêlée, by which the former secured protection and the latter service and enhanced strength. In a world from which effective government had gone, this was the only method

The Feudal System.

by which any sort of security was possible for the generality of mankind. The freeman or the weak lordling of a petty territory linked himself to some more powerful lord. The protection of that lord (or the danger of his hostility) became more considerable with every such accession. So very rapidly there went on this process of political crystallization in the confused and lawless sea into which the Western Empire had liquefied.

This process speedily took on technical forms and laws of its own. In such a country as Gaul it was already well in progress in the days of insecurity *before* the barbarian tribes broke into the empire as conquerors. The Franks when they came into Gaul brought with them an institution, which we have already noted in the case of the Macedonians, and which was probably of very wide distribution among the Nordic people, the gathering about the chief or war king of a body of young men of good family, the companions or *comitatus*, his counts or captains. It was natural in the case of invading peoples that the relations of a weak lord to a strong lord should take on the relations of a count to his king, and that a conquering chief should divide seized and confiscated estates among his companions. From the side of the decaying empire there came to feudalism the idea of the grouping for mutual protection of men and estates ; from the Teutonic side came the notions of knightly association, devotion, and personal service. The former was the economic side of the institution, the latter the chivalrous.

The analogy of the aggregation of feudal groupings with crystallization is a very close one. As the historian watches the whirling and eddying confusion of the fourth and fifth century in Western Europe, he begins to perceive the appearance of these pyramidal growths, which jostle against one another, branch, dissolve again, or coalesce. " We use the term ' feudal system ' for convenience sake, but with a degree of impropriety if it conveys the meaning ' systematic.' Feudalism in its most flourishing age was anything but systematic. It was confusion roughly organized. Great diversity prevailed everywhere, and we should not be surprised to find some different fact or custom in every lordship. Anglo-Norman feudalism attained a logical completeness and a uniformity of practice which, in the feudal age proper, can hardly be found elsewhere through so large a territory. . . .

" The foundation of the feudal relationship proper was the fief, which was usually land, but might be any desirable thing, as an office, a revenue in money or kind, the right to collect a toll, or operate a mill. In return for the fief, the man became the vassal of his lord ; he knelt before him, and, with his hands between his lord's hands, promised him fealty and service. . . . The faithful performance of all the duties he had assumed in homage constituted the vassal's right and title to his fief. So long as they were fulfilled, he, and his heir after him, held the fief as his property, practically and in relation to all under-tenants as if he were the owner. In the ceremony of homage and investiture, which is the creative contract of feudalism, the obligations assumed by the two parties were, as a rule, not specified in exact terms. They were determined by local custom. . . . In many points of detail the vassal's services differed widely in different parts of the feudal world. We may say, however, that they fall into two classes, general and specific. The general included all that might come under the idea of loyalty, seeking the lord's interests, keeping his secrets, betraying the plans of his enemies, protecting his family, etc. The specific services are capable of more definite statement, and they usually received exact definition in custom and sometimes in written documents. The most characteristic

of these was the military service, which included appearance in the field on summons with a certain force, often armed in a specified way, and remaining a specified length of time. It often included also the duty of guarding the lord's castle, and of holding one's own castle subject to the plans of the lord for the defence of his fief. . . .

" Theoretically regarded, feudalism covered Europe with a network of these fiefs, rising in graded ranks one above the other from the smallest, the knight's fee, at the bottom, to the king at the top, who was the supreme landowner, or who held the kingdom from God. . . ." [1]

But this was the theory that was superimposed upon the established facts. The reality of feudalism was its voluntary co-operation.

" The feudal state was one in which, as it has been said, private law had usurped the place of public law. Public duty had become private obligation."

[1] *Encyclopædia Britannica*, article "Feudalism," by Professor G. B. Adams.

Map of EUROPE about 500 A.D.

§ 3

We have already mentioned various kingdoms of the barbarian tribes who set up a more or less flimsy dominion over this or that area amidst the debris of the empire, the kingdoms of the Suevi and West Goths in Spain, the East-Gothic kingdom in Italy, and the Italian Lombard kingdom which succeeded the Goths after Justinian had expelled the latter and

The Frankish Kingdom of the Mero-vingians.

divided them. A more serious split arose, however, through the Latinization of the Western Franks, who occupied Romanized Gaul and who learnt to speak the corrupt Latin of the subject population, while the Franks of the Rhineland retained their Low German speech. At a low level of civilization, differences in language cause very powerful political strains. For a hundred and fifty years the Frankish world was split in two, Neustria, the nucleus of France, speaking a Latinish speech, which became at last the French language we know, and Austrasia, the Rhineland, which remained German.[1]

We will not tell here of the decay of the dynasty, the Merovingian dynasty, founded by Clovis ; nor how in Austrasia a certain court official, the Mayor of the Palace, gradually became the king *de facto* and used the real king as a puppet. The position of Mayor of the Palace also became hereditary in the seventh century, and in 687 a certain Pepin of Heristhal, the Austrasian Mayor of the Palace, had conquered Neustria and reunited all the Franks. He was followed in 714 by his son, Charles Martel, who also bore no higher title than mayor of the palace. (His poor little Merovingian kings do not matter in the slightest degree to us here.) It was this Charles Martel who stopped the Moslems. They had pushed as far as Tours when he met them, and in a great battle between that place and Poitiers (732) utterly defeated them and

Area more or less under FRANKISH dominion in the time of CHARLES MARTEL

after the great pestilence had devastated Italy. The Frankish kingdom was another such barbarian power which arose first in what is now Belgium, and which spread southward to the Loire, but it developed far more strength and solidarity than any of the others. It was the first real state to emerge from the universal wreckage. It became at last a wide and vigorous political reality, and from it are derived two great powers of modern Europe, France and the German Empire.

Its founder was Clovis (481–511), who began as a small king in Belgium and ended with his southern frontiers nearly at the Pyrenees. He divided his kingdom among his four sons, but the Franks retained a tradition of unity in spite of this division, and for a time fraternal wars for a single control united rather than

[1] The Franks differed from the Swabians and South Germans, and came much nearer the Anglo-Saxons in that they spoke a " Low German " and not a " High German " dialect. Their language resembled platt-deutsch and Anglo-Saxon, and was the direct parent of Dutch and Flemish. In fact, the Franks where they were not Latinized became Flemings and " Dutch-men " of South Holland (North Holland is still Friesisch —i.e. Anglo-Saxon). The " French " which the Latinized Franks and Burgundians spoke in the seventh to the tenth centuries was remarkably like the Ru-mansch language of Switzerland, judging from the vestiges that remain in old documents.—H. H. J.

broke their spirit. Thereafter the Pyrenees remained their utmost boundary; they came no further into Western Europe.

Charles Martel divided his power between two sons, but one resigned and went into a monastery, leaving his brother Pepin sole ruler. This Pepin it was who finally extinguished the descendants of Clovis. He sent to the Pope to ask who was the true king of the Franks, the man who held the power or the man who wore the crown; and the Pope, who was in need of a supporter, decided in favour of the Mayor of the Palace. So Pepin was chosen king at a gathering of the Frankish nobles in the Merovingian capital Soissons, and anointed and crowned. That was in 751. The Franco-Germany he united was consolidated by his son Charlemagne. It held together until the death of his grandson Louis (840), and then France and Germany broke away again—to the great injury of mankind. It was not a difference of race or temperament, it was a difference of language and tradition that split these Frankish peoples asunder.

That old separation of Neustria and Austrasia still works out in bitter consequences. In 1916 the ancient conflict of Neustria and Austrasia had broken out into war once more. In the August of that year the present writer visited Soissons, and crossed the temporary wooden bridge that had been built by the English after the Battle of the Aisne from the main part of the town to the suburb of Saint Médard. Canvas screens protected passengers upon the bridge from the observation of the German sharpshooters who were sniping from their trenches down the curve of the river. He went with his guides across a field and along by the wall of an orchard in which a German shell exploded as he passed. So he reached the battered buildings that stand upon the site of the ancient abbey of St. Médard, in which the last Merovingian was deposed and Pepin the Short was crowned in his stead. Beneath these ancient buildings there were great crypts, very useful as dug-outs—for the German advanced lines were not more than a couple of hundred yards away. The sturdy French soldier lads were cooking and resting in these shelters, and lying down to sleep among the stone coffins that had held the bones of their Merovingian kings.

§ 4

The populations over which Charles Martel and King Pepin ruled were at very different

The Christianization of the Western Barbarians. levels of civilization in different districts. To the west and south the bulk of the people consisted of Latinized and Christian Kelts; in the central regions these rulers had to deal with such more or less Christianized Germans as the Franks and Burgundians and Alemanni; to the north-east were still pagan Frisians and Saxons; to the east were the Bavarians, recently Christianized through the activities of St. Boniface; and to the east of them again

RUINS OF THE ABBEY OF ST. MÉDARD, SOISSONS.

pagan Slavs and Avars. The "Paganism" of the Germans and Slavs was very similar to the primitive religion of the Greeks; it was a manly religion in which temple, priest, and sacrifices played a small part, and its gods were like men, a kind of "school prefects" of more powerful beings who interfered impulsively and irregularly in human affairs. The Germans had a Jupiter in Odin, a Mars in Thor, a Venus in Freya, and so on. Throughout the seventh and eighth centuries a steady process of conversion to Christianity went on amidst these German and Slavonic tribes.

Photo: Frith.

ST. MARTIN'S CHURCH, CANTERBURY, ONE OF THE OLDEST CHRISTIAN CHURCHES IN ENGLAND.

It will be interesting to English-speaking readers to note that the most zealous and successful missionaries among the Saxons and Frisians came from England. Christianity was twice planted in the British Isles. It was already there while Britain was a part of the Roman Empire ; a martyr, St. Alban, gave his name to the town of St. Albans, and nearly every visitor to Canterbury has also visited little old St. Martin's church, which was used during the Roman times. From Britain, as we have already noted, Christianity spread beyond the imperial boundaries into Ireland— the chief missionary was St. Patrick—and there was a vigorous monastic movement with which are connected the names of St. Columba and the religious settlements of Iona. Then in the fifth and sixth centuries came the fierce and pagan English, and they cut off the early Church of Ireland from the main body of Christianity. In the seventh century Christian missionaries were converting the English, both in the north from Ireland and in the south from Rome. The Rome mission was sent by Pope Gregory the Great just at the close of the

sixth century. The story goes that he saw English boys for sale in the Roman slave market, though it is a little difficult to understand how they got there. They were very fair and good-looking. In answer to his inquiries, he was told that they were Angles. "Not Angles, but Angels," said he, "had they but the gospel."

The mission worked through the seventh century. Before that century was over, most of the English were Christians ; though Mercia, the central English kingdom, held out stoutly against the priests and for the ancient faith and ways. And there was a swift progress in learning upon the part of these new converts. The monasteries of the kingdom of Northumbria in the north of England became a centre of light and learning. Theodore of Tarsus was one of the earliest archbishops of Canterbury (669–690). "While Greek was utterly unknown in the west of Europe, it was mastered by some of the pupils of Theodore. The monasteries contained many monks who were excellent scholars. Most famous of all was Bede, known as the Venerable Bede (673–735), a monk of

Jarrow (on Tyne). He had for his pupils the six hundred monks of that monastery, besides the many strangers who came to hear him. He gradually mastered all the learning of his day, and left at his death forty-five volumes of his writings, the most important of which are "The Ecclesiastical History of the English" and his translation of the Gospel of John into English. His writings were widely known and used throughout Europe. He reckoned all dates from the birth of Christ, and through his works the use of Christian chronology became common in Europe. Owing to the large number of monasteries and monks in Northumbria, that part of England was for a time far in advance of the south in civilization."[1]

In the seventh and eighth centuries we find the English missionaries active upon the eastern frontiers of the Frankish kingdom. Chief among these was St. Boniface (680–755), who was born at Crediton, in Devonshire, who converted the Frisians, Thuringians, Hessians, and who was martyred in Holland.

Both in England and on the Continent the ascendant rulers seized upon Christianity as a unifying force to cement their conquests. Christianity became a banner for aggressive chiefs—as it did in Uganda in Africa in the bloody days before that country was annexed to the British Empire. After Pepin, who died in 768, came two sons, Charles and another, who divided his kingdom; but the brother of Charles died in 771, and Charles then became sole king (771–814) of the growing realm of the Franks. This Charles is known in history as Charles the Great, or Charlemagne. As in the case of Alexander the Great and Julius Cæsar, posterity has enormously exaggerated his memory.

[1] *A General History of Europe*, Thatcher and Schwill.

ENGLAND in 640 A.D.

He made his wars of aggression definitely religious wars. All the world of North-western Europe, which is now Great Britain, France, Germany, Denmark, and Norway and Sweden, was in the ninth century an arena of bitter conflict between the old faith and the new. Whole nations were converted to Christianity by the sword just as Islam in Arabia, Central Asia, and Africa had converted whole nations a century or so before.

With fire and sword Charlemagne preached the Gospel of the Cross to the Saxons, Bohemians, and as far as the Danube into what is now Hungary; he carried the same teaching down the Adriatic Coast through what is now Dalmatia, and drove the Moslems back from the Pyrenees as far as Barcelona.

Moreover, he it was who sheltered Egbert, an exile from Wessex, in England, and assisted him presently to establish himself as King in Wessex (802). Egbert subdued the Britons in Cornwall, as Charlemagne conquered the Britons of Brittany, and, by a series of wars, which he continued after the death of his Frankish patron, made himself at last the first King of all England (828).

But the attacks of Charlemagne upon the last strongholds of paganism provoked a vigorous

ENGLAND
at the
Treaty of Wedmore
878
Alfred's kingdom...

J.F.H.

reaction on the part of the unconverted. The Christianized English had retained very little of the seamanship that had brought them from the mainland, and the Franks had not yet become seamen. As the Christian propaganda of Charlemagne swept towards the shores of the North and Baltic Seas, the pagans were driven to the sea. They retaliated for the Christian persecutions with plundering raids and expeditions against the northern coasts of France

and against Christian England. These pagan Saxons and English of the mainland and their kindred from Denmark and Norway are the Danes and Northmen of our national histories. They were also called Vikings [1] by the English, which means "creek-men," because they first appeared in the creeks of Eastern England and about the Thames mouth. They came in long black galleys, making little use of sails.

Most of our information about these wars and invasions of the pagan Vikings is derived from Christian sources, and so we have abundant information of the massacres and atrocities of their raids and very little about the cruelties inflicted upon their pagan brethren, the Saxons, at the hands of Charlemagne. Their animus against the cross and against monks and nuns was extreme. They delighted in the burning of monasteries and nunneries and the slaughter of their inmates.

Throughout the period between the fifth and the ninth centuries these Vikings or Northmen were learning seamanship, becoming bolder, and ranging further. They braved the northern seas until the icy shores of Greenland were a familiar haunt, and by the ninth century they had settlements (of which Europe in general knew nothing) in America. In the tenth and eleventh century many of their sagas began to be written down in Iceland. They saw the world in terms of valiant adventure. They assailed the walrus, the bear, and the whale. In their imaginations, a great and rich city to the south, a sort of confusion of Rome and Byzantium, loomed large. They called it "Micklegarth." The magnetism of Micklegarth was to draw the descendants of these Northmen down into the Mediterranean by two routes, by the west and also across Russia from the Baltic, as we shall tell later.

So long as Charlemagne and Egbert lived, the Vikings were no more than raiders; but as the ninth century wore on, these raids developed

[1] N.B.—Vik-ings, not Vi-kings. Vik = creek.

into organized invasions. In several districts of England the hold of Christianity was by no means firm as yet. In Mercia in particular the pagan Northmen found sympathy and help. By 886 the Danes had conquered a fair part of England, and the English king, Alfred the Great, had recognized their rule over their conquests, the Dane-law, in the pact he made with Guthrum their leader. A little later, in 912, another expedition under Rolf the Ganger established itself upon the coast of France in the region that was known henceforth as Normandy (= Northman-dy). But of how there was presently a fresh conquest of England by the Danes, and how finally the Duke of Normandy became King of England, we cannot tell at any length. There were very small racial and social differences between Angle, Saxon, Jute, Dane, or Norman; and though these changes loom large in the imaginations of the English, they are seen to be very slight rufflings indeed of the stream of history when we measure them by the standards of a greater world. The issue between Christianity and paganism vanished presently from the struggle. By the Treaty of Wedmore the Danes agreed to be baptized if they were assured of their conquests; and the descendants of Rolf in Normandy were not merely Christianized, but they learnt to speak French from the more civilized people about them, forgetting their own Norse tongue. Of much greater significance in the history of mankind are the relations of Charlemagne with his neighbours to the south and east, and to the imperial tradition.

§ 5

Through Charlemagne the tradition of the Roman Cæsar was revived in Europe.[1] The Roman Empire was dead and decaying; the Byzantine Empire was far gone in decay; but the education and mentality of Europe had sunken to a level at which new creative political ideas were probably impossible. In all Europe there survived not a tithe of the speculative vigour that we find in the Athenian literature of the fifth century B.C. There was no power to postulate a new occasion or to conceive and organize

Charlemagne becomes Emperor of the West.

[1] *Vide* Stubbs' *History of Germany in the Middle Ages,* and Bryce's *Holy Roman Empire.*

a novel political method. Official Christianity had long overlaid and accustomed itself to ignore those strange teachings of Jesus of Nazareth from which it had arisen. The Roman Church, clinging tenaciously to its possession of the title of *pontifex maximus,* had long since abandoned its appointed task of achieving the Kingdom of Heaven. It was preoccupied with the revival of Roman ascendancy on earth, which it conceived of as its inheritance. It had become a political body, using the faith and needs of simple men to forward its schemes. Europe drifted towards a dreary imitation and revival of the misconceived failures of the past. For eleven centuries from Charlemagne onwards, " Emperors " and " Cæsars " of this line and that come and go in the history of Europe like fancies in a disordered mind. We shall have to tell of a great process of mental growth in Europe, of enlarged horizons and accumulating power, but it was a process that went on independently of, and in spite of, the political forms of the time, until at last it shattered those forms altogether. Europe during those eleven centuries of the imitation Cæsars which began with Charlemagne, and which closed only in the monstrous bloodshed of 1914–1918, has been like a busy factory owned by a somnambulist, who is sometimes quite unimportant and sometimes disastrously in the way. Or rather than a somnambulist, let us say by a corpse that magically simulates a kind of life. The Roman Empire staggers, sprawls, is thrust off the stage, and reappears, and—if we may carry the image one step further—it is the Church of Rome which plays the part of the magician and keeps this corpse alive.

And throughout the whole period there is always a struggle going on for the control of the corpse between the spiritual and various temporal powers. We have already noted the spirit of St. Augustine's *City of God.* It was a book which we know Charlemagne read, or had read to him—for his literary accomplishments are rather questionable. He conceived of this Christian Empire as being ruled and maintained in its orthodoxy by some such great Cæsar as himself. He was to rule even the Pope. But at Rome the view taken of the revived empire differed a little from that. There the view taken was that the Christian Cæsar must be

EUROPE at the death of CHARLEMAGNE — 814.

anointed and guided by the Pope—who would even have the power to excommunicate and depose him. Even in the time of Charlemagne this divergence of view was apparent. In the following centuries it became acute.

The idea of the empire dawned only very gradually upon the mind of Charlemagne. At first he was simply the ruler of his father's kingdom of the Franks, and his powers were fully occupied in struggles with the Saxons and Bavarians, and with the Slavs to the east of them, with the Moslem in Spain, and with various insurrections in his own dominions. And as the result of a quarrel with the King of Lombardy, his father-in-law, he conquered Lombardy and North Italy. We have noted the establishment of the Lombards in North Italy about 570 after the great pestilence, and after the overthrow of the East Gothic kings by Justinian. These Lombards had always been a danger and a fear to the Popes, and there had been an alliance between Pope and Frankish

King against them in the time of Pepin. Now Charlemagne completely subjugated Lombardy (774), sent his father-in-law to a monastery, and carried his conquests beyond the present north-eastern boundaries of Italy into Dalmatia in 776. In 781 he caused one of his sons, Pepin, who did not outlive him, to be crowned King of Italy in Rome.

There was a new Pope, Leo III, in 795, who seems from the first to have resolved to make Charlemagne emperor. Hitherto the court at Byzantium had possessed a certain indefinite authority over the Pope. Strong emperors like Justinian had bullied the Popes and obliged them to come to Constantinople; weak emperors had annoyed them ineffectively. The idea of a breach, both secular and religious, with Constantinople had long been entertained at the Lateran,[1] and in the Frankish power there seemed to be just the support that was

[1] The Lateran was the earlier palace of the Popes in Rome. Later they occupied the Vatican.

necessary if Constantinople was to be defied. So at his accession Leo III sent the keys of the tomb of St. Peter and a banner to Charlemagne as the symbols of his sovereignty in Rome as King of Italy. Very soon the Pope had to appeal to the protection he had chosen. He was unpopular in Rome ; he was attacked and ill-treated in the streets during a procession, and obliged to fly to Germany (799). Eginhard says his eyes were gouged out and his tongue cut off ; he seems, however, to have had both eyes and tongue again a year later. Charlemagne brought him back and reinstated him (800).

Then occurred a very important scene. On Christmas Day, in the year 800, as Charles was rising from prayer in the Church of St. Peter, the Pope, who had everything in readiness, clapped a crown upon his head and hailed him Cæsar and Augustus. There was great popular applause. But Eginhard, the friend and biographer of Charlemagne, says that the new emperor was by no means pleased by this coup of Pope Leo's. If he had known this was to happen, he said, " he would not have entered the church, great festival though it was." No doubt he had been thinking and talking of making himself emperor, but he had evidently not intended that the Pope should make him emperor. He had had some idea of marrying the Empress Irene, who at that time reigned in Constantinople, and so becoming monarch of both Eastern and Western Empires. He was now obliged to accept the title in the manner that Leo III had adopted as a gift from the Pope, and in a way that estranged Constantinople and secured the separation of Rome from the Byzantine Church.

At first Byzantium was unwilling to recognize the imperial title of Charlemagne. But in 810 a great disaster fell upon the Byzantine Empire. The pagan Bulgarians, under their Prince Krum (802–814), defeated and destroyed the armies of the Emperor Nicephorus, whose skull became a drinking-cup for Krum. The greater part of the Balkan peninsula was conquered by these people. (The Bulgarian and the English nations thus became established as political unities almost simultaneously.) After this misfortune Byzantium was in no position to dispute this revival of the empire in the West, and in 812 Charlemagne was formally recognized by Byzantine envoys as Emperor and Augustus.

So the Empire of Rome, which had died at the hands of Odoacer in 476, rose again in 800 as the "Holy Roman Empire." While its physical strength lay north of the Alps, the centre of its idea was Rome. It was therefore from the beginning a divided thing of uncertain power, a claim and an argument rather than a necessary reality. The German sword was always clattering over the Alps into Italy, and missions and legates toiling over in the reverse direction. But the Germans could never hold Italy permanently, because they could not stand the malaria that the ruined, neglected, undrained country fostered. And in Rome, as well as in several other of the cities of Italy, there smouldered a more ancient tradition, the tradition of the aristocratic republic, hostile to both Emperor and Pope.

§ 6

In spite of the fact that we have a life of him written by his contemporary, Eginhard,[1] the character and personality of Charlemagne are difficult to visualize. Eginhard lacks vividness ; he tells many particulars, but not the particulars that make a man live again in the record. Charlemagne, he says, was a tall man, with a rather feeble voice ; and he had bright eyes and a long nose. " The top of his head was round," whatever that may mean, and his hair was " white." He had a thick, rather short neck, and " his belly too prominent." He wore a tunic with a silver border, and gartered hose. He had a blue cloak, and was always girt with his sword, hilt and belt being of gold and silver. He was evidently a man of great activity, one imagines him moving quickly, and his numerous love affairs did not interfere at all with his incessant military and political labours. He had numerous wives and mistresses. He took much exercise, was fond of pomp and religious ceremonies, and gave generously. He was a man of very miscellaneous activity and great intellectual enterprise, and with a self-confidence that is rather suggestive of William II, the ex-German Emperor, the last, perhaps for ever,

The Personality of Charlemagne.

[1] Eginhard's *Life of Karl the Great.* (Glaister.)

of this series of imitation Cæsars in Europe which Charlemagne began.

The mental life that Eginhard records of him is interesting, because it not only gives glimpses of a curious character, but serves as a sample of the intellectuality of the time. He could read probably; at meals he "listened to music or reading," but we are told that he had not acquired the art of writing; "he used to keep his writing-book and tablets under his pillow, that when he had leisure he might practise his hand in forming letters, but he made little progress in an art begun too late in life," he had, however, a real respect for learning and a real desire for knowledge, and he did his utmost to attract men of learning to his court. Among others who came was Alcuin, a learned Englishman. All those

CHARLEMAGNE AND HIS WIFE, AFTER AN ILLUMINATED PAINTING.
This is the nearest approach to a trustworthy portrait we can find.

learned men were, of course, clergymen, there were no other learned men, and naturally they gave a strongly clerical tinge to the information they imparted to their master. At his court, which was usually at Aix-la-Chapelle or Mayence, he maintained in the winter months a curious institution called his "school," in which he and his erudite associates affected to lay aside all thoughts of worldly position, assumed names taken from the classical writers or from Holy Writ, and discoursed upon theology and literature. Charlemagne himself was "David." He developed a considerable knowledge of theology, and it is to him that

we must ascribe the addition of the words *filioque* to the Nicene Creed (see chap. xxx., § 8), an addition that finally split the Latin and Greek Churches asunder. But it is more than doubtful if he had any such separation in mind. He wanted to add a word or so to the creed, just as the Emperor William II wanted to write operas and paint pictures,[1] and he took up what was originally a Spanish innovation.

Of his organization of his empire there is little to be said here. He was far too restless and busy to consider the quality of his successor or the condition of political stability, and the most noteworthy thing in this relationship is that he particularly schooled his son and successor, Louis the Pious (814–840), to take the crown from the altar and *crown himself*. But Louis the Pious was far too pious to adhere to those instructions when the Pope made an objection.

The legislation of Charlemagne was greatly coloured by Bible reading; he knew his Bible well, as the times went; and it is characteristic of him that after he had been crowned emperor he required every male subject above the age of twelve to renew his oath of allegiance, and to undertake to be not simply a good subject,

[1] The addition was discreetly opposed by Leo III. "In the correspondence between them the Pope assumes the liberality of a statesman and the prince descends to the prejudice and passions of a priest."— Gibbon, chap. lx.

but a good Christian. To refuse baptism or to retract after baptism was a crime punishable by death. He did much to encourage architecture, and imported many Italian architects, chiefly from Ravenna, to whom we owe that pleasant Byzantine style that still at Worms and Cologne and elsewhere delights the tourist in the Rhineland.[1] He founded a number of cathedrals and monastic schools, did much to encourage the study of classical Latin, and was a distinguished amateur of church music. The possibility of his talking Latin and understanding Greek is open to discussion; probably he talked French-Latin. Frankish, however, was his habitual tongue. He made a collection of old German songs and tales, but these were destroyed by his successor Louis the Pious on account of their paganism.

He corresponded with Haroun-al-Raschid, the Abbasid Caliph at Baghdad, who was not perhaps the less friendly to him on account of his vigorous handling of the Omayyad Arabs in Spain. Gibbon supposes that this "public correspondence was founded on vanity," and that "their remote situation left no room for a competition of interest." But with the Byzantine Empire between them in the East, and the independent caliphate of Spain in the West, and a common danger in the Turks of the great plains, they had three very excellent reasons for cordiality. Haroun-al-Raschid, says Gibbon, sent him by his ambassadors a splendid tent, a water clock, an elephant, and the keys of the Holy Sepulchre. The last item suggests that Charlemagne was to some extent regarded by the Saracen monarch as the protector of the Christians and Christian properties in his dominions. Some historians declare explicitly that there was a treaty to that effect. [2]

§ 7

The Empire of Charlemagne did not outlive his son and successor, Louis the Pious. It

[1] The Byzantine style in Gaul is, I fancy, much earlier than Charlemagne, and goes back to the 4th century or earlier. See Rivoira's *History of Lombard Architecture*, or T. G. Jackson's *History of Gothic Architecture.*—E. B.

[2] See L. Bréhier, *L'Église et l'Orient au Moyen Age.*

RELIEF FROM THE SHRINE OF CHARLEMAGNE, AIX-LA-CHAPELLE, SHOWING THE EMPEROR DEDICATING THE CATHEDRAL TO THE VIRGIN.

fell apart into its main constituents. The Latinized Keltic and Frankish population of

The French and the Germans become distinct. Gaul begins now to be recognizable as France, though this France was broken up into a number of dukedoms and principalities, often with no more than a nominal unity; the German-speaking peoples between the Rhine and the Slavs to the east similarly begin to develop an even more fragmentary beginning of Germany. When at length a real emperor reappears in Western Europe (962), he is not a Frank, but a Saxon; the conquered in Germany have become the masters.

It is impossible here to trace the events of the ninth and tenth centuries in any detail, the alliances, the treacheries, the claims and acquisitions. Everywhere there was lawlessness, war, and a struggle for power. In 987 the nominal kingdom of France passed from the hands of the Carlovingians, the last descendants of Charlemagne, into the hands of Hugh Capet, who founded a new dynasty. Most of his alleged subordinates were in fact independent, and willing to make war on the king at the slightest provocation. The dominions of the Duke of Normandy, for example, were more extensive and more powerful than the patrimony of Hugh Capet. Almost the only unity of this France over which the king exercised a nominal authority lay in the common resolution of its great provinces to resist incorporation in any empire dominated either by a German ruler or by the Pope. Apart from the simple organization dictated by that common will, France was a mosaic of practically independent nobles. It was an era of castle-building and fortification, and what was called " private war " throughout all Europe.

The state of Rome in the tenth century is almost indescribable. The decay of the Empire of Charlemagne left the Pope without a protector, threatened by Byzantium and the Saracens (who had taken Sicily), and face to face with the unruly nobles of Rome. Among the most powerful of these were two women, Theodora and Marozia, mother and daughter,[1] who in succession held the Castle of St. Angelo (§ 1), which Theophylact, the patrician husband of

[1] Gibbon mentions a second Theodora, the sister of Marozia.

Theodora, had seized with most of the temporal power of the Pope; these two women were as bold, unscrupulous, and dissolute as any male prince of the time could have been, and they are abused by historians as though they were ten times worse. Marozia seized and imprisoned Pope John X (928), who speedily died under her care. She subsequently made her illegitimate son pope, under the title of John XI. After him her grandson, John XII, filled the chair of St. Peter. Gibbon's account of the manners and morals of John XII takes refuge at last beneath a veil of Latin footnotes. This Pope, John XII, was finally degraded by the new German Emperor Otto, who came over the Alps and down into Italy to be crowned in 962.[2]

This new line of Saxon emperors, which thus comes into prominence, sprang from a certain Henry the Fowler, who was elected King of Germany by an assembly of German nobles, princes and prelates in 919. In 936 he was succeeded as King by his son Otto I, surnamed the Great, who was also elected to be his successor at Aix-la-Chapelle, and who finally descended upon Rome at the invitation of John XII, to be crowned emperor in 962. His subsequent degradation of John was forced upon him by that pope's treachery. With his assumption of the imperial dignity, Otto I did not so much overcome Rome as restore the ancient tussle of Pope and Emperor for ascendancy to something like decency and dignity again. Otto I was followed by Otto II (973–983), and he again by a third Otto (983–1002).[3]

[2] This period is a tangled one. The authority is Gregorovius, *History of the City of Rome in the Middle Ages* (an excellent general book from A.D. 400 to 1527), vol. iii. of the Eng. trans., p. 249 *seq.* John X owed the tiara to his mistress, the elder Theodora, but he was " the foremost statesman of his age " (Gregorovius, p. 259). He fell in 928 owing to Marozia. John XI became Pope in 931 (after two Popes had intervened in the period 928–931) ; he was Marozia's son, possibly by Pope Sergius III. John XII did not come at once after John XI., who died in 936 ; there were several Popes in between ; and he became Pope in 955.—E. B.

[3] There were three dynasties of emperors in the early middle ages :

Saxon : Otto I (962) to Henry II, ending 1024.

Salian : Conrad II to Henry V, ending about 1125.

Hohenstaufen : Conrad III to Frederic II, ending in 1250.

The Hohenstaufens were Swabian in origin. Then came the Habsburgs with Rudolph I in 1273, who lasted until 1918.

CONTEMPORARY PORTRAIT OF SALADIN.

About A.D. 1180. Reproduced by permission from "The Miniature Painting and Painters of Persia,
India and Turkey," by F. R. Martin. (Bernard Quaritch Ltd.) From a miniature in a MS. in the
possession of the author.

The struggle between the Emperor and the Pope for ascendancy over the Holy Roman Empire plays a large part in the history of the early Middle Ages, and we shall have presently to sketch its chief phases. Though the church never sank quite to the level of John XII again, nevertheless the story fluctuates through phases of great violence, confusion, and intrigue. Yet the outer history of Christendom is not the whole history of Christendom. That the Lateran was as cunning, foolish, and criminal as most other contemporary courts has to be recorded ; but, if we are to keep due proportions in this history, it must not be unduly emphasized. We must remember that through all those ages, leaving profound consequences, but leaving no conspicuous records and scars upon the historian's page, countless men and women were touched by that Spirit of Jesus which still lived and lives still at the core of Christianity, that they led lives that were on the whole gracious and helpful, and that they did unselfish and devoted deeds. Through those ages such lives cleared the air and made a better world possible. Just as in the Moslem world the Spirit of Islam generation by generation produced its crop of courage, integrity, and kindliness.

§ 8

While the Holy Roman Empire and the kingdoms of France and England were thus appearing amidst the extreme political fragmentation of the civilization of Western Europe, both that civilization and the Byzantine Empire were being subjected to a threefold attack: from the Saracen powers, from the Northmen, and, more slowly developed and most formidable of all, from a new westward-thrust of the Turkish peoples through South Russia, and also by way of Armenia and the Empire of Bagdad from Central Asia.

The Normans, the Saracens, the Hungarians, and the Seljuk Turks.

After the overthrow of the Omayyads by the Abbasid dynasty, the strength of the Saracenic impulse against Europe diminished. Islam was no longer united. Spain was under a separate Omayyad Caliph, North Africa, though nominally subject to the Abbasids, was really independent, and presently (969) Egypt became a separate power with a Shiite Caliph of its own, a pretender claiming descent from Ali and

29

Fatima (the Fatimite Caliphate). These Egyptian Fatimites, the green flag Moslems, were fanatics in comparison with the Abbasids, and did much to embitter the genial relations of Islam and Christianity. They took Jerusalem, and interfered with the Christian access to the Holy Sepulchre. On the other side of the shrunken Abbasid domain there was also a Shiite kingdom in Persia. The chief Saracen conquest in the ninth century was Sicily ; but this was not overrun in the grand old style in a year or so, but subjugated tediously through a long century, and with many set-backs. The Spanish Saracens disputed in Sicily with the Saracens from Africa. In Spain the Saracens were giving ground before a renascent Christian effort. Nevertheless the Byzantine Empire and Western Christendom were still so weak upon the Mediterranean Sea, that the Saracen raiders and pirates from North Africa were able to raid almost unchallenged in South Italy and the Greek Islands.

But now a new force was appearing in the Mediterranean. We have already remarked that the Roman Empire never extended itself to the shores of the Baltic Sea, nor had ever the vigour to push itself into Denmark. The Nordic Aryan peoples of these neglected regions learnt much from the empire that was unable to subdue them ; as we have already noted in § 4, they developed the art of shipbuilding and became bold seamen ; they spread across the North Sea to the west, and across the Baltic and up the Russian rivers into the very heart of what is now Russia. One of their earliest settlements in Russia was Novgorod the Great. There is the same trouble and confusion for the student of history with these northern tribes as there is with the Scythians of classical times, and with the Hunnish Turkish peoples of Eastern and Central Asia. They appear under a great variety of names, they change and intermingle. In the case of Britain, for example, the Angles, the Saxons, and Jutes conquered most of what is now England in the fifth and sixth centuries ; the Danes, a second wave of practically the same people, followed in the eighth and ninth ; and in 1013 a Danish King, Canute, reigned in England, and not only over England, but over Denmark and Norway. For a time, under Canute and his sons, it seemed possible that a great confederation of the Northmen might have established itself. Then in 1066 a third wave of the same people flowed over England from the "Norman" state in France, where the Northmen had been settled since the days of Rolf the Ganger (912), and where they had learnt to speak French. William, Duke of Normandy, became the William the Conqueror (1066) of English history. Practically, from

FRANCE IN THE TIME OF HUGH CAPET AFTER A.D. 987.

the standpoint of universal history, all these peoples were the same people, waves of one Nordic stock. These waves were not only flowing westward, but eastward. Already we have noted (chap. xxix, § 4) a very interesting earlier movement of the same peoples under the name of Goths from the Baltic to the Black Sea. We have traced the splitting of these Goths into the Ostrogoths and the Visigoths, and the adventurous wanderings that ended at last in the Ostrogoth kingdom in Italy and the

Visigoth states in Spain. In the ninth century a second movement of the Northmen across Russia was going on at the same time that their establishments in England and their dukedom of Normandy were coming into existence. The population of South Scotland, England, East Ireland, Flanders, Normandy, and the Russias have more elements in common than we are accustomed to recognize. All are fundamentally Gothic and Nordic peoples. These "Russian" Norsemen travelled in the summer-time, using the river routes that abounded in Russia; they carried their ships by portages from the northward-running rivers to those flowing southward. They appeared as pirates, raiders, and traders both upon the Caspian and the Black Sea. The Arabic chroniclers note their apparition upon the Caspian, and give them the name of Russians. They raided Persia, and threatened Constantinople with a great fleet of small craft (in 865, 904, 941 and 1043).[1] One of these Northmen, Rurik (*circa* 850), established himself as the ruler of Novgorod and Kief, and laid the foundations of modern Russia. The fighting qualities of the Russian Vikings were speedily appreciated at Constantinople; the Greeks called them Varangians, and an imperial Varangian body-guard was formed. After the conquest of England by the Normans (1066), a number of Danes and English were driven into exile and joined these Russian Varangians, apparently finding few obstacles to intercourse in their speech and habits.

Meanwhile the Normans from Normandy

[1] These dates are from Gibbon. Beazley gives 865, 904-7, 935, 944, 971-2. (*History of Russia*, Clarendon Press.)

were also finding their way into the Mediterranean from the West. They came first as mercenaries, and later as independent invaders; and they came, mainly, not, it is to be noted, by sea, but in scattered bands by land. They came through the Rhineland and Italy partly in the search for warlike employment and loot, partly as pilgrims. For the ninth and tenth centuries saw a great development of pilgrimage. These Normans, as they grew powerful, discovered themselves such rapacious and vigorous robbers that they forced the Eastern emperor and the Pope into a feeble and ineffective alliance against them (1053). They defeated and captured and were pardoned by the Pope; they established themselves in Calabria and South Italy, conquered Sicily from the Saracens (1060–1090), and under Robert Guiscard, who had entered Italy as a pilgrim adventurer and began his career as a brigand in Calabria, threatened the Byzantine Empire itself (1081). His army, which contained a contingent of Sicilian Moslems, crossed from Brindisi to Epirus in the reverse direction to that in which Pyrrhus had crossed to attack the Roman Republic, thirteen centuries before (275 B.C.). He laid siege to the Byzantine stronghold of Durazzo.

NOTE THAT THIS MAP (972) IS NEARLY CONTEMPORARY WITH THE ONE OF FRANCE ABOUT A.D. 987.

and sack Rome (1084); and Gibbon notes with quiet satisfaction the presence of a large contingent of Sicilian Moslems among the looters. There were in the twelfth century three other Norman attacks upon the Eastern power, one by the son of Robert Guiscard, and the two others directly from Sicily by sea. . . .

But neither the Saracens nor the Normans pounded quite so heavily against the old empire at Byzantium or against the Holy Roman Empire, the vamped-up Roman Empire of the West, as did the double thrust from the Turanian centres in Central Asia, of which we must

Robert captured Durazzo (1082), but the pressure of affairs in Italy recalled him, and ultimately put an end to this first Norman attack upon the Empire of Byzantium, leaving the way open for the rule of a comparatively vigorous Comnenian dynasty (1081–1204). In Italy, amidst conflicts too complex for us to tell here, it fell to Robert Guiscard to besiege

THE COMING OF THE SELJUKS.

now tell. We have already noted (chap. xxix, § 5) the westward movement of the Avars, and the Turkish Magyars who followed in their track. From the days of Pepin I onward, the Frankish power and its successors in Germany were in conflict with these Eastern raiders along all the Eastern borderlands. Charlemagne held and punished them, and established some sort of overlordship as far east as the Carpathians; but amidst the enfeeblement that followed his death, these peoples, more or less blended now in the accounts under the name of Hungarians, led by the Magyars, re-established their complete freedom again, and raided yearly, often as far as the Rhine. They destroyed, Gibbon notes, the monastery of St. Gall in Switzerland, and the town of Bremen. Their great raiding period was between 900 and 950. Their biggest effort, through Germany right into France, thence over the Alps and home again by North Italy, was in 938-9.

Thrust southward by these disturbances, and by others to be presently noted, the Bulgarians, as we have told in § 5, established themselves under Krum, between the Danube and Constantinople. Originally a Turkish people, the Bulgarians, since their first appearance in the east of Russia, had become by repeated admixture almost entirely Slavonic in race and language. For some time after their establishment in Bulgaria they remained pagan. Their king, Boris (852–884), entertained Moslem envoys, and seems to have contemplated an adhesion to Islam, but finally he married a Byzantine princess, and handed himself and his people over to the Christian faith.

The Hungarians were drubbed into a certain respect for civilization by Henry the Fowler, the elected King of Germany, and Otto the First, the first Saxon emperor, in the tenth century. But they did not decide to adopt Christianity until about A.D. 1000. Though they were Christianized, they retained their own Turko-Finnic language (Magyar), and they retain it to this day.

Bulgarians and Hungarians do not, however, exhaust the catalogue of the peoples whose westward movements embodied the Turkish thrust across South Russia. Behind the Hungarians and Bulgarians thrust the Khazars, a Turkish people, with whom were mingled a very considerable proportion of Jews who had been expelled from Constantinople, and who had mixed with them and made many proselytes. To these Jewish Khazars are to be ascribed the great settlements of Jews in Poland and Russia.[1] Behind the Khazars again, and overrunning them, were the Petschenegs (or Patzinaks), a savage Turkish people who are first heard of in the ninth century, and who were destined to dissolve and vanish as the kindred Huns did five centuries before. And while the trend of all these peoples was westward, we have, when we are thinking of the present population of these South Russian regions, to remember also the coming and going of the Northmen between the Baltic and the Black Sea, who interwove with the Turkish migrants like warp and woof, and bear in mind also that there was a considerable Slavonic population, the heirs and descendants

[1] "A Turkish people whose leaders had adopted Judaism," says Harold Williams.

of Scythians, Sarmatians, and the like, already established in these restless, lawless, but fertile areas. All these races mixed with and reacted upon one another. The universal prevalence of Slavonic languages, except in Hungary, shows that the population remained predominantly Slav. And in what is now Rumania, for all the passage of peoples, and in spite of conquest after conquest, the tradition and inheritance of the Roman provinces of Dacia and Mœsia Inferior still kept a Latin speech and memory alive.

But this direct thrust of the Turkish peoples against Christendom to the north of the Black Sea was, in the end, not nearly so important as their indirect thrust south of it through the empire of the Caliph. We cannot deal here with the tribes and dissensions of the Turkish peoples of Turkestan, nor with the particular causes that brought to the fore the tribes under the rule of the Seljuk clan. In the eleventh century these Seljuk Turks broke with irresistible force not in one army, but in a group of armies, and under two brothers, into the decaying fragments of the Moslem Empire. For Islam had long ceased to be one empire. The orthodox Sunnite Abbasid rule had shrunken to what was once Babylonia ; and even in Bagdad the Caliph was the mere creature of his Turkish palace guards. A sort of mayor of the palace, a Turk, was the real ruler. East of the Caliph, in Persia, and west of him in Palestine, Syria, and Egypt, were Shiite heretics. The Seljuk Turks were orthodox Sunnites ; they now swept down upon and conquered the Shiite rulers and upstarts, and established themselves as the protectors of the Bagdad Caliph, taking over the temporal powers of the mayor of the palace. Very early they conquered Armenia from the Greeks, and then, breaking the bounds that had restrained the power of Islam for four centuries, they swept on to the conquest of Asia Minor, almost to the gates of Constantinople. The mountain barrier of Cilicia that had held the Moslem so long had been turned by the conquest of Armenia from the north-east. Under Alp Arslan, who had united all the Seljuk power in his own hands, the Turks utterly smashed the Byzantine army at the battle of Manzikert, or Melasgird (1071). The effect of this battle upon people's imagina-

tions was very great. Islam, which had appeared far gone in decay, which had been divided religiously and politically, was suddenly discovered to have risen again, and it was the secure old Byzantine Empire that seemed on the brink of dissolution. The loss of Asia Minor was very swift. The Seljuks established themselves at Iconium (Konia), in what is now Anatolia. In a little while they were in possession of the fortress of Nicæa over against the capital.

§ 9

We have already told of the attack of the Normans upon the Byzantine Empire from the west, and of the battle of Durazzo (1081) ; and we have noted that Constantinople had still vivid memories of the Russian sea raids (1043). Bulgaria, it is true, had been tamed, but there was heavy and uncertain warfare going on with the Petschenegs. North and west, the emperor's hands were full. This swift advance of the Turks into country that had been so long securely Byzantine must have seemed like the approach of final disaster. The Eastern Emperor, Michael VII, under the pressure of these convergent dangers, took a step that probably seemed both to himself and to Rome of the utmost political significance. He appealed to the Pope, Gregory VII, for assistance. His appeal was repeated still more urgently by his successor Alexius Comnenus to Pope Urban II.

How Constantinople appealed to Rome.

To the counsellors of Rome this must have presented itself as a supreme opportunity for the assertion of the headship of the Pope over the entire Christian world.

In this history we have traced the growth of this idea of a religious government of Christendom—and through Christendom of mankind—and we have shown how naturally, and how necessarily, because of the tradition of world empire, it found a centre at Rome. The Pope of Rome was the only Western patriarch ; he was the religious head of a vast region in which the ruling tongue was Latin ; the other patriarchs of the Orthodox Church spoke Greek, and so were inaudible throughout his domains ; and the two words, *Filioque*, which had been

TOMBS OF CRUSADERS (EXETER CATHEDRAL).

added to the Latin creed (see chap. xxx, § 8, and chap. xxxiii, § 6), had split off the Byzantine Christians by one of those impalpable and elusive doctrinal points upon which there is no reconcilation. (The final rupture was in 1054.) The life of the Lateran changed in its quality with every occupant of the chair of St. Peter: sometimes papal Rome was a den of corruption and uncleanness, as it had been in the days of John XII; sometimes it was pervaded by the influence of widely thinking and nobly thinking men. But behind the Pope was the assembly of the cardinals, priests, and a great number of highly educated officials, who never, even in the darkest and wildest days, lost sight altogether of the very grand idea of a divine world dominion, of a peace of Christ throughout the earth that St. Augustine had expressed. Through all the Middle Ages that idea was the guiding influence in Rome. For a time, perhaps, mean minds would prevail there, and in the affairs of the world Rome would play the part of a greedy, treacherous, and insanely cunning old woman; followed a phase of masculine and quite worldly astuteness perhaps,

or a phase of exaltation. Came an interlude of fanaticism or pedantry, when all the pressure was upon exact doctrine. Or there was a moral collapse, and the Lateran became the throne of some sensuous or æsthetic autocrat, ready to sell every hope or honour the church could give for money to spend upon pleasure or display. Yet, on the whole, the papal ship kept its course, and came presently into the wind again.

In this period to which we have now come, the period of the eleventh century, we discover a Rome dominated by the personality of an exceptionally great statesman, Hildebrand, who occupied various official positions under a succession of Popes, and finally became Pope himself under the name of Gregory VII (1073–1085). We find that under his influence, vice, sloth, and corruption have been swept out of the church, that the method of electing the Popes has been reformed, and that a great struggle has been waged with the Emperor upon the manifestly vital question of " investitures," the question whether Pope or temporal monarch should have the decisive voice in the appointment of the bishops in their domains. Hitherto the Roman clergy had been able to marry; but now, to detach them effectually from the world and to make them more completely the instruments of the church, celibacy was imposed upon all priests. . . .[1]

Gregory VII had been prevented by his struggle over the investitures from any effectual answer to the first appeal from Byzantium; but he had left a worthy successor in Urban II (1087–1099); and when the letter of Alexius came to hand, Urban seized at once upon the opportunity it afforded for drawing together all the thoughts and forces of Western Europe into one passion and purpose. Thereby he might hope to end the private warfare that prevailed, and find a proper outlet for the immense energy of the Normans. He saw, too, an opportunity of thrusting the Byzantine power and Church aside, and extending the influence of the Latin Church over Syria, Palestine, and Egypt. The envoys of Alexius were heard at a church council, hastily summoned at Piacenza (= Placentia), and next year (1095) at Clermont, Urban held a second great council, in which all the slowly gathered strength of the Church was organized for a universal war propaganda against the Moslems. Private war, all war among Christians, was to cease until the infidel had been swept back and the site of the Holy Sepulchre was again in Christian hands.

The fervour of the response enables us to understand the great work of creative organization that had been done in Western Europe in the previous five centuries. In the beginning of the seventh century we saw Western Europe as a chaos of social and political fragments, with no common idea nor hope, a system shattered almost to a dust of self-seeking individuals. Now in the dawn of the eleventh century there is everywhere a common belief, a linking idea, to which men may devote themselves, and by which they can co-operate together in a universal enterprise. We realize that, in spite of much weakness and intellectual and moral unsoundness, to this extent the Christian Church has *worked*. We are able to

[1] For the development of the papacy, see H. W. C. Davis, *Mediæval Europe*.

measure the evil phases of tenth-century Rome, the scandals, the filthiness, the murders and violence, at their proper value by the scale of this fact. No doubt also all over Christendom there had been many lazy, evil, and foolish priests; but it is manifest that this task of teaching and co-ordination that had been accomplished could have been accomplished only through a great multitude of right-living priests and monks and nuns. A new and greater amphictyony, the amphictyony of Christendom, had come into the world, and it had been built by thousands of anonymous, faithful lives.

And this response to the appeal of Urban the Second was not confined only to what we should call educated people. It was not simply knights and princes who were willing to go upon this crusade. Side by side with the figure of Urban we must put the figure of Peter the Hermit, a type novel to Europe, albeit a little reminiscent of the Hebrew prophets. This man appeared preaching the crusade to the common people. He told a story—whether truthful or untruthful hardly matters in this connection—of his pilgrimage to Jerusalem, of the wanton destruction at the Holy Sepulchre by the Seljuk Turks, who took it in 1073, and of the exactions, brutalities, and deliberate cruelties practised upon the Christian pilgrims to the Holy Places. Barefooted, clad in a coarse garment, riding on an ass, and bearing a huge cross, this man travelled about France and Germany, and everywhere harangued vast crowds in church or street or market-place. . . .

Here for the first time we discover Europe with an idea and a soul! Here is a universal response of indignation at the story of a remote wrong, a swift understanding of a common cause for rich and poor alike. You cannot imagine this thing happening in the Empire of Augustus Cæsar, or indeed in any previous state in the world's history. Something of the kind might perhaps have been possible in the far smaller world of Hellas, or in Arabia before Islam. But this movement affected nations, kingdoms, tongues, and peoples. It is clear that we are dealing with something new that has come into the world, a new clear connection of the common interest with the consciousness of the common man.

§ 10

From the very first this flaming enthusiasm was mixed with baser elements. There was the cold and calculated scheme of the free and ambitious Latin Church to subdue and replace the emperor-ruled Byzantine Church; there was the free-booting instinct of the Normans, who were tearing Italy to pieces, which turned readily enough to a new and richer world of plunder; and there was something in the multitude who now turned their faces east, something deeper

The Crusades.

famine from the Scheldt to Bohemia, and there was great social disorganization. " No wonder," says Mr. Ernest Barker, " that a stream of emigration set towards the East, such as would in modern times flow towards a newly discovered goldfield—a stream carrying in its turbid waters much refuse, tramps and bank-rupts, camp-followers and hucksters, fugitive monks and escaped villeins, and marked by the same motley grouping, the same fever of life, the same alternations of affluence and beggary, which mark the rush for a goldfield to-day."

But these were secondary contributory causes. The fact of predominant interest to the historian of mankind is this *will to crusade* suddenly revealed as a new mass possibility in human affairs.

The story of the crusades abounds in such romantic and picturesque detail that the writer of an Outline of History must ride his pen upon the curb through this alluring field. The first forces to move eastward were great crowds of undisciplined people rather than armies, and they sought to make their way by the valley of the Danube, and thence southward to Constantinople. This was the " people's crusade "; never before in the whole history of the world had there been such a spectacle as these masses of practically leaderless people moved by an idea. It was a very crude idea. When they got among foreigners, they do not seem to have realized that they were not already among the infidel. Two great mobs, the advance guard of the expedition, committed such excesses in Hungary, where the language must have been incomprehensible to them, as to provoke the Hungarians to destroy them. They were massacred. A third host began with a great pogrom of the Jews in the Rhineland—for the Christian blood was up—and this multitude was also dispersed in Hungary. Two other hosts under Peter got through and reached Constan-

Map to illustrate the FIRST CRUSADE

States set up by the Crusaders...
Eastern Empire...
Seljuks.....
Route of Crusaders

than love in the human composition, namely, fear-born hate, that the impassioned appeals of the propagandists and the exaggeration of the horrors and cruelties of the infidel had fanned into flame. And there were still other forces; the intolerant Seljuks and the intolerant Fatimites lay now an impassable barrier across the eastward trade of Genoa and Venice that had hitherto flowed through Bagdad and Aleppo, or through Egypt. They must force open these closed channels, unless Constantinople and the Black Sea route were to monopolize Eastern trade altogether. Moreover, in 1094 and 1095 there had been a pestilence and tinople, to the astonishment and dismay of the Emperor Alexius. They looted and committed outrages as they came, and at last he shipped them across the Bosphorus, to be massacred rather than defeated by the Seljuks (1096).

This first unhappy appearance of the "people" as people in modern European history was followed in 1097 by the organized forces of the First Crusade. They came by diverse routes from France, Normandy, Flanders, England, Southern Italy and Sicily, and the will and power of them were the Normans. They crossed the Bosphorus and captured Nicæa, which Alexius snatched away from them before they could loot it. They then went on by much the same route as Alexander the Great, through the Cilician Gates, leaving the Turks in Konia unconquered, past the battle-field of the Issus, and so to Antioch, which they took after nearly a year's siege. Then they defeated a great relieving army from Mosul. A large part of the Crusaders remained in Antioch, a smaller force under Godfrey of Bouillon (in Belgium) went on to Jerusalem. "After a little more than a month's siege, the city was finally captured (July 15). The slaughter was terrible; the blood of the conquered ran down the streets, until men splashed in blood as they rode. At nightfall, 'sobbing for excess of joy,' the crusaders came to the Sepulchre from their treading of the winepress, and put their blood-stained hands together in prayer. So, on that day of July, the First Crusade came to an end." [1]

The authority of the Patriarch of Jerusalem was at once seized upon by the Latin clergy with the expedition, and the Orthodox Christians found themselves in rather a worse case under Latin rule than under the Turk. There were already Latin principalities established at Antioch and Edessa, and there began a struggle for ascendancy between these various courts and kings, and an unsuccessful attempt to make Jerusalem a property of the Pope. These are complications beyond our present scope.

Let us quote, however, a characteristic passage from Gibbon:—

"In a style less grave than that of history, I should perhaps compare the Emperor Alexius to the jackal, who is said to follow the steps

[1] E. Barker, art. "Crusades," *Encyclopædia Britannica.*

and to devour the leavings of the lion. Whatever had been his fears and toils in the passage of the First Crusade, they were amply recompensed by the subsequent benefits which he derived from the exploits of the Franks. His dexterity and vigilance secured their first conquest of Nicæa, and from this threatening station the Turks were compelled to evacuate the neighbourhood of Constantinople. While the Crusaders, with blind valour, advanced into the midland countries of Asia, the crafty Greek improved the favourable occasion when the emirs of the sea coast were recalled to the standard of the Sultan. The Turks were driven from the isles of Rhodes and Chios; the cities of Ephesus and Smyrna, of Sardes, Philadelphia, and Laodicea were restored to the empire, which Alexius enlarged from the Hellespont to the banks of the Mæander and the rocky shores of Pamphylia. The churches resumed their splendour; the towns were rebuilt and fortified; and the desert country was peopled with colonies of Christians, who were gently removed from the more distant and dangerous frontier. In these paternal cares we may forgive Alexius, if we forget the deliverance of the holy sepulchre; but, by the Latins, he was stigmatized with the foul reproach of treason and desertion. They had sworn fidelity and obedience to his throne; but *he* had promised to assist their enterprise in person, or at least, with his troops and treasures; his base retreat dissolved their obligations; and the sword, which had been the instrument of their victory, was the pledge and title of their just independence. It does not appear that the emperor attempted to revive his obsolete claims over the kingdom of Jerusalem, but the borders of Cilicia and Syria were more recent in his possession and more accessible to his arms. The great army of the Crusaders was annihilated or dispersed; the principality of Antioch was left without a head, by the surprise and captivity of Bohemond; his ransom had oppressed him with a heavy debt; and his Norman followers were insufficient to repel the hostilities of the Greeks and Turks. In this distress, Bohemond embraced a magnanimous resolution, of leaving the defence of Antioch to his kinsman, the faithful Tancred; of arming the West against the Byzantine

Empire, and of executing the design which he inherited from the lessons and example of his father Guiscard. His embarkation was clandestine ; and if we may credit a tale of the Princess Anna, he passed the hostile sea closely secreted in a coffin. (Anna Comnena adds, that to complete the imitation, he was shut up with a dead cock ; and condescends to wonder how the barbarian could endure the confinement and putrefaction. This absurd tale is unknown to the Latins.) But his reception in France

Photo: American Colony, Jerusalem.
TOMB OF SALADIN, DAMASCUS.

was dignified by the public applause and his marriage with the king's daughter ; his return was glorious, since the bravest spirits of the age enlisted under his veteran command ; and he repassed the Adriatic at the head of five thousand horse and forty thousand foot, assembled from the most remote climates of Europe. The strength of Durazzo and prudence of Alexius, the progress of famine and approach of winter, eluded his ambitious hopes ; and the venal confederates were seduced from his standard. A treaty of peace suspended the fears of the Greeks."

We have dealt thus lengthily with the First Crusade, because it displays completely the quality of all these expeditions. The reality of the struggle between the Latin and the Byzantine system became more and more nakedly apparent. In 1101 came reinforcements, in which the fleet of the mercantile republics of Venice and Genoa played a prominent part, and the power of the kingdom of Jerusalem was extended. The year 1147 saw a Second Crusade, in which both the Emperor Conrad III and King Louis of France participated. It was a much more stately and far less successful and enthusiastic expedition than its predecessor. It had been provoked by the fall of Edessa to the Moslems in 1144. One large division of Germans, instead of going to the Holy Land, attacked and subjugated the still pagan Wends east of the Elbe. This, the Pope agreed, counted as crusading, and so did the capture of Lisbon, and the foundation of the Christian kingdom of Portugal by the Flemish and English contingents.

In 1169 a Kurdish adventurer, named Saladin, became ruler of Egypt, in which country the Shiite heresy had now fallen before a Sunnite revival. This Saladin reunited the efforts of Egypt and Bagdad, and preached a Jehad, a Holy War, a counter-crusade, of all the Moslems against the Christians. This Jehad excited almost as much feeling in Islam as the First Crusade had done in Christendom. It was now a case of crusader against crusader ; and in 1187 Jerusalem was retaken. This provoked the Third Crusade (1189). This also was a grand affair, planned jointly by the Emperor Frederick I (known better as Frederick Barbarossa), the King of France, and the King of England (who at that time owned many of the fairest French provinces). The papacy played a secondary part in this expedition ; it was in one of its phases of enfeeblement, and the crusade was the most courtly, chivalrous, and romantic of all. Religious bitterness was mitigated by the idea of knightly gallantry, which obsessed both Saladin and Richard I (1189–1199) of England (Cœur-de-Lion), and the lover of romance may very well turn to the romances about this period for its flavour. The crusade saved the principality of Antioch for a time, but failed to retake Jerusalem. The Christians, however, remained in possession of the sea coast of Palestine.

Photo: Anderson.

ST. MARK'S, VENICE. BUILT CHIEFLY DURING THE ELEVENTH AND TWELFTH CENTURIES BY LOMBARD AND ORIENTAL ARTIFICERS.

By the time of the Third Crusade, the magic and wonder had gone out of these movements altogether. The common people had found them out. Men went, but only kings and nobles straggled back ; and that often only after heavy taxation for a ransom. The idea of the crusades was cheapened by their too frequent and trivial use. Whenever the Pope quarrelled with anyone now, he called for a crusade, until the word ceased to mean anything but an attempt to give flavour to an unpalatable civil war. There was a crusade against the heretics in the south of France, one against John (King of England), one against the Emperor Frederick II. The Popes did not understand the necessity of dignity to the papacy. They had achieved a moral ascendancy in Christendom. Forthwith they began to fritter it away. They not only cheapened the idea of the crusades, but they made their tremendous power of excommunication, of putting people outside all the sacraments, hopes, and comforts of religion, ridiculous by using it in mere disputes of policy. Frederick II was not only crusaded against, but excommuni-

cated—without visible injury. He was excommunicated again in 1239, and a third time in 1245.[1]

The bulk of the Fourth Crusade never reached the Holy Land at all. It started from Venice (1202), captured Zara, encamped at Constantinople (1203), and finally, in 1204, stormed the city. It was frankly a combined attack on the Byzantine Empire. Venice took much of the coasts and islands of the empire, and a Latin, Baldwin of Flanders, was set up as emperor in Constantinople. The Latin and Greek Churches were declared to be reunited, and Latin emperors ruled as conquerors in Constantinople from 1204 to 1261.

In 1212 occurred a dreadful thing, a children's crusade. An excitement that could no longer affect sane adults was spread among the children in the south of France and in the Rhone valley. A crowd of many thousands of French boys marched to Marseilles ; they were

[1] Technically only twice, the excommunication of 1245 was a renewal by Innocent IV of that of 1239.— E. B.

then lured on board ship by slave traders, who sold them into slavery in Egypt. The Rhineland children tramped into Italy, many perishing by the way, and there dispersed. Pope Innocent III made great capital out of this strange business. " The very children put us to shame," he said ; and sought to whip up enthusiasm for a Fifth Crusade. This crusade aimed at the conquest of Egypt, because Jerusalem was now held by the Egyptian Sultan ; its remnants returned in 1221, after an inglorious evacuation of its one capture, Damietta, with the Jerusalem vestiges of the True Cross as a sort of consolation concession on the part of the victor. We have already noted the earlier adventures of this venerable relic before the days of Muhammad in chap. xxxi, § 2, when it was carried off by Chosroes II to Ctesiphon, and recovered by the Emperor Heraclius. Fragments of the True Cross, however, had always been in Rome at the

Photo: Anderson.
INTERIOR OF ST. MARK'S, VENICE.

church of S. Croce-in-Gerusalemme, since the days of the Empress Helena (the mother of Constantine the Great) to whom, says the legend, its hiding-place had been revealed in a vision during her pilgrimage to the Holy Land.[1]

The Sixth Crusade (1229) was a crusade bordering upon absurdity. The Emperor Frederick II had promised to go upon a crusade, and evaded his vow. He had made a false start and returned. He was probably bored by the mere idea of a crusade. But the vow had been part of the bargain by which he secured the support of Pope Innocent III in his election as emperor. He busied himself in reorganizing the government of his Sicilian kingdom, though he had given the Pope to understand that he would relinquish those possessions if he became emperor ; and the Pope was anxious to stop this process of consolidation by sending him to the Holy Land. The Pope did not want Frederick II, or any German emperor at all in Italy, because he himself wished to rule Italy. As Frederick II remained evasive, Gregory IX excommunicated him, proclaimed a crusade against him, and invaded his dominions in Italy (1228). Whereupon the Emperor sailed with an army to the Holy Land. There he had a meeting with the Sultan of Egypt (the Emperor spoke six languages freely, including Arabic) ; and it would seem these two gentlemen, both of sceptical opinions, exchanged views of a congenial sort, discussed the Pope in a worldly spirit, debated the Mongolian rush westward, which threatened them both alike, and agreed finally to a commercial convention, and the surrender of a

[1] " The custody of the *True Cross*, which on Easter Sunday was solemnly exposed to the people, was entrusted to the Bishop of Jerusalem ; and he alone might gratify the curious devotion of the pilgrims, by the gift of small pieces, which they enchased in gold or gems, and carried away in triumph to their respective countries. But, as this gainful branch of commerce must soon have been annihilated, it was found convenient to suppose that the marvellous wood possessed a secret power of vegetation, and that its substance, though continually diminished, still remained entire and unimpaired."—Gibbon.

part of the kingdom of Jerusalem to Frederick. This indeed was a new sort of crusade, a crusade by private treaty. As this astonishing crusader had been excommunicated, he had to indulge in a purely secular coronation in Jerusalem, taking the crown from the altar with his own hand, in a church from which all the clergy had gone. Probably there was no one to show him the Holy Places ; indeed these were presently all put under an interdict by the Patriarch of Jerusalem and locked up ; manifestly the affair differed altogether in spirit from the red onslaught of the First Crusade. It had not even the kindly sociability of the Caliph Omar's visit six hundred years before. Frederick II rode out of Jerusalem almost alone, returned from this unromantic success to Italy, put his affairs there in order very rapidly, chased the papal armies out of his possessions, and obliged the Pope to give him absolution from his excommunication (1230). This Sixth Crusade was indeed not only the *reductio ad absurdum* of crusades, but of papal excommunications. Of this Frederick II we shall tell more in a later section, because he was very typical of certain new forces that were coming into European affairs.

The Christians lost Jerusalem again in 1244 ; it was taken from them very easily by the Sultan of Egypt when they attempted an intrigue against him. This provoked the Seventh Crusade, the Crusade of St. Louis, King of France (Louis IX), who was taken prisoner in Egypt and ransomed in 1250. Not until 1918, when it fell to a mixed force of French, British, and Indian troops, did Jerusalem slip once more from the Moslem grasp. . . .

One more crusade remains to be noted, an expedition to Tunis by this same Louis IX, who died of fever there.

§ 11

The essential interest of the crusades for the historian of mankind lies in the wave of emotion, **The Crusades a Test of Christianity.** of unifying feeling, that animated the first. Thereafter these expeditions became more and more an established process, and less and less vital events. The First Crusade was an occurrence like the discovery of America ; the later ones were more and more like a trip across the Atlantic. In the eleventh century, the idea of the crusade must have been like a strange and wonderful light in the sky ; in the thirteenth one can imagine honest burghers saying in tones of protest, " What ! *another* crusade ! " The experience of St. Louis in Egypt is not like a fresh experience for mankind ; it is much more like a round of golf over some well-known links, a round that was dogged by misfortune. It is an insignificant series of events. The interest of life had shifted to other directions.

The beginning of the crusades displays all Europe saturated by a naïve Christianity, and ready to follow the leading of the Pope trustfully and simply. The scandals of the Lateran during its evil days, with which we are all so familiar now, were practically unknown outside Rome. And Gregory VII and Urban II had redeemed all that. But intellectually and morally their successors at the Lateran and the Vatican[1] were not equal to their opportunities. The strength of the papacy lay in the faith men had in it, and it used that faith so carelessly as to enfeeble it. Rome has always had too much of the shrewdness of the priest and too little of the power of the prophet. So that while the eleventh century was a century of ignorant and confiding men, the thirteenth was an age of knowing and disillusioned men. It was a far more civilized and profoundly sceptical world.

The bishops, priests, and the monastic institutions of Latin Christendom before the days of Gregory VII had been perhaps rather loosely linked together and very variable in quality ; but it is clear that they were, as a rule, intensely intimate with the people among whom they found themselves, and with much of the spirit of Jesus still alive in them ; they were trusted, and they had enormous power *within the conscience of their followers*. The church, in comparison with its later state, was more in the hands of local laymen and the local ruler ; it lacked its later universality. The energetic bracing up of the church organization by Gre-

---

[1] The Popes inhabited the palace of the Lateran until 1305, when a French Pope set up the papal court at Avignon. When the Pope returned to Rome in 1377 the Lateran was almost in ruins, and the palace of the Vatican became the seat of the papal court. It was, among other advantages, much nearer to the papal stronghold, the Castle of San Angelo.

gory VII, which was designed to increase the central power of Rome, broke many subtle filaments between priest and monastery on the one hand, and the country-side about them on the other. Men of faith and wisdom believe in growth and their fellow men; but priests, even such priests as Gregory VII, believe in the false " efficiency " of an imposed discipline. The squabble over investitures made every prince in Christendom suspicious of the bishops as agents of a foreign power; this suspicion filtered down to the parishes. The political enterprises of the papacy necessitated an increasing demand for money. Already in the thirteenth century it was being said everywhere that the priests were not good men, that they were always hunting for money.

In the days of ignorance there had been an extraordinary willingness to believe the Catholic priesthood good and wise. Relatively it was better and wiser in those days. Great powers beyond her spiritual functions had been entrusted to the church, and very extraordinary freedoms. Of this confidence the fullest advantage had been taken. In the Middle Ages the church had become a state within the state. It had its own law courts. Cases involving not merely priests, but monks, students, crusaders, widows, orphans, and the helpless, were reserved for the clerical courts; and whenever the rites or rules of the church were involved, there the church claimed jurisdiction over such matters as wills, marriages, oaths, and of course over heresy, sorcery, and blasphemy. There were numerous clerical prisons in which offenders might pine all their lives. The Pope was the supreme law-giver of Christendom, and his court at Rome the final and decisive court of appeal. And the church levied taxes; it had not only vast properties and a great income from fees, but it imposed a tax of a tenth, the tithe, upon its subjects. It did not call for this as a pious benefaction; it demanded it as a right. The clergy, on the other hand, were now claiming exemption from lay taxation.

This attempt to trade upon their peculiar prestige and evade their share in fiscal burdens was certainly one very considerable factor in the growing dissatisfaction with the clergy. Apart from any question of justice, it was impolitic. It made taxes seem ten times more burthensome to those who had to pay. It made everyone feel the immunities of the church. And a still more extravagant and unwise claim made by the church was the claim to the power of *dispensation*. The Pope might in many instances set aside the laws of the church in individual cases; he might allow cousins to marry, permit a man to have two wives, or release anyone from a vow. But to do such things is to admit that the laws affected are not based upon necessity and an inherent righteousness; that they are in fact restrictive and vexatious. The law-giver, of all beings, most owes the law allegiance. He of all men should behave as though the law compelled him. But it is the universal weakness of mankind that what we are given to administer we presently imagine we own.

§ 12

The Emperor Frederick II is a very convenient example of the sort of doubter and rebel the thirteenth century could produce. It may be interesting to tell a little of this intelligent and cynical man. He was the son of the German Emperor, Henry VI, and grandson of Frederick Barbarossa, and his mother was the daughter of Roger I, the Norman King of Sicily. He inherited this kingdom in 1198, when he was four years old; his mother was his guardian for six months, and when she died, Pope Innocent III (1198 to 1216) became regent and guardian. He seems to have had an exceptionally good and remarkably mixed education, and his accomplishments earned him the flattering title of *Stupor mundi*, the amazement of the world. The result of getting an Arabic view of Christianity, and a Christian view of Islam, was to make him believe that all religions were impostures, a view held perhaps by many a stifled observer in the Age of Faith. But he talked about his views; his blasphemies and heresies are on record. Growing up under the arrogant rule of Innocent III, who never seems to have realized that his ward had grown up, he developed a slightly humorous evasiveness. It was the papal policy to prevent any fresh coalescence of the power of Germany and Italy, and it was equally Frederick's determination to get whatever he could. When presently

The Emperor Frederick II.

opportunity offered him the imperial crown of Germany, he secured the Pope's support by agreeing, if he were elected, to relinquish his possessions in Sicily and South Italy, and to put down heresy in Germany. For Innocent III was one of the great persecuting Popes, an able, grasping, and aggressive man. (For a Pope, he was exceptionally young. He became Pope at thirty-seven.) It was Innocent who had preached a cruel crusade against the heretics in the south of France, a crusade that presently became a looting expedition beyond his control. So soon as Frederick was elected emperor (1211),[1] Innocent pressed for the performance of the vows and promises he had wrung from his dutiful ward. The clergy were to be freed from lay jurisdiction and from taxation, and exemplary cruelties were to be practised upon the heretics. None of which things Frederick did. As we have already told, he would not even relinquish Sicily. He liked Sicily as a place of residence better than he liked Germany.

Innocent III died baffled in 1216, and his successor, Honorius III, effected nothing. Honorius was succeeded by Gregory IX (1227), who evidently came to the papal throne with a nervous resolution to master this perplexing young man. He excommunicated him at once for failing to start upon his crusade, which was now twelve years overdue; and he denounced his vices, heresies, and general offences in a public letter (1227). To this Frederick replied in a far abler document addressed to all the princes of Europe, a document of extreme importance in history, because it is the first clear statement of the issue between the pretensions of the Pope to be absolute ruler of all Christendom, and the claims of the secular

Photo: Rischgitz Collection.

TYPICAL CRUSADER.

William Mareshal the elder, 1st Earl of Pembroke, Regent of England. Effigy in the Temple Church.

rulers.[2] This conflict had always been smouldering; it had broken out here in one form, and there in another; but now Frederick put it in clear general terms upon which men could combine together.

Having delivered this blow, he departed upon the pacific crusade of which we have already told. In 1239, Gregory IX was excommunicating him for a second time, and renewing that warfare of public abuse in which the papacy had already suffered severely. The controversy was revived after Gregory IX was dead, when Innocent IV was Pope; and again a devastating letter, which men were bound to remember, was written by Frederick against the church. He denounced the pride and irreligion of the clergy, and ascribed all the corruptions of the time to their pride and wealth. He proposed to his fellow princes a general confiscation of church property—for the good of the church. It was a suggestion that never afterwards left the imaginations of the European princes.

We will not go on to tell of his last years or of the disaster at Parma, due to his carelessness, which cast a shadow of failure over his end. The particular events of his life are far less significant than its general atmosphere. It is possible to piece together something of his court life in Sicily. He is described towards the end of his life as "red, bald, and short-sighted"; but his features were good and pleasing. He was luxurious in his way of living, and fond of beautiful things. He is described as licentious. But it is clear that his mind was not satisfied by religious scepticism, and that he was a man of very effectual curiosity and inquiry. He gathered Jewish and Moslem as well as Christian philosophers at his court, and he did much to

---

[1] He was crowned emperor in 1220 by Honorius III, the successor of Innocent.

[2] Some authorities deny his authorship of this letter. See A. L. Smith's *Church and State in the Middle Ages.*

irrigate the Italian mind with Saracenic influences. Through him Arabic numerals and algebra were introduced to Christian students, and among other philosophers at his court was Michael Scott, who translated much of Aristotle and the commentaries thereon of the great Arab philosopher Averroes (of Cordoba). In 1224 Frederick founded the University of Naples, and he enlarged and enriched the great medical school at Salerno University, the most ancient of universities. He also founded a zoological garden. He has left a book on hawking, which shows him to have been an acute observer of the habits of birds, and he was one of the first Italians to write Italian verse. Italian poetry was indeed born at his court. He has been called by an able writer, " the first of the moderns," and the phrase expresses aptly the unprejudiced detachment of his intellectual side. His was an all-round originality. During a gold shortage he introduced and made a success of a coinage of stamped leather, bearing his promise to pay in gold, a sort of leather bank-note issue.[1]

In spite of the torrent of abuse and calumny in which Frederick was drenched, he left a profound impression upon the popular imagination. He is still remembered in South Italy almost as vividly as is Napoleon I by the peasants of France ; he is the " Gran Federigo." And German scholars declare[2] that, in spite of Frederick's manifest dislike for Germany, it is he, and not Frederick I, Frederick Barbarossa, to whom that German legend originally attached —that legend which represents a great monarch slumbering in a deep cavern, his beard grown round a stone table, against a day of awakening when the world will be restored by him from an extremity of disorder to peace. Afterwards, it seems, the story was transferred to the Crusader Barbarossa, the grandfather of Frederick II.

A difficult child was Frederick II for Mother Church, and he was only the precursor of many such difficult children. The princes and edu-

cated gentlemen throughout Europe read his letters and discussed them. The more enterprising university students found, marked, and digested the Arabic Aristotle he had made accessible to them in Latin. Salerno cast a baleful light upon Rome. All sorts of men must have been impressed by the futility of the excommunications and interdicts that were levelled at Frederick.

§ 13[3]

We have said that Innocent III never seemed to realize that his ward, Frederick II, was growing up. It is equally true that the papacy never seemed to realize that Europe was growing up. It is impossible for an intelligent modern student of history not to sympathize with the underlying idea of the papal policy, with the idea of one universal rule of righteousness keeping the peace of the earth, and not to recognize the many elements of nobility that entered into the Lateran policy. Sooner or later mankind must come to one universal peace, unless our race is to be destroyed by the increasing power of its own destructive inventions ; and that universal peace must needs take the form of a government, that is to say a law-sustaining organization, in the best sense of the word religious ; a government ruling men through the educated co-ordination of their minds in a common conception of human history and human destiny.

Defects and Limitations of the Papacy.

The papacy we must now recognize as the first clearly conscious attempt to provide such a government in the world. We cannot too earnestly examine its deficiences and inadequacies, for every lesson we can draw from them is necessarily of the greatest value to us in forming our ideas of our own international relationships. We have tried to suggest the main factors in the breakdown of the Roman Republic, and it now behoves us to attempt a diagnosis of the failure of the Roman Church to secure and organize the good will of mankind.

The first thing that will strike the student is the intermittence of the efforts of the church to establish the world City of God. The policy

[1] Perhaps parchment rather than leather. Such promises on parchment were also used by the Carthaginians. Was Frederick's money an inheritance from an old tradition living on in Sicily since Carthaginian times ?—E. B.

[2] *Encyclopædia Britannica,* art. " Frederick II."

[3] In relation to this section, see the chapter on the "Unity of the Middle Ages" in F. S. Marvin's *Unity of Western Civilization.*

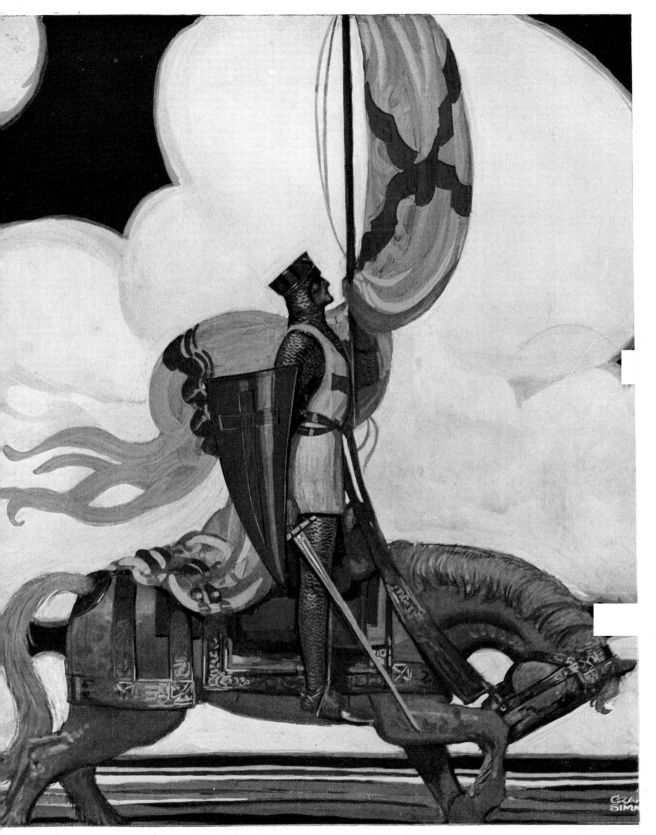

THE IDEAL OF THE CRUSADES.

of the church was not whole-heartedly and continuously set upon that end. It was only now and then that some fine personality or some group of fine personalities dominated it in that direction. The Kingdom of God that Jesus of Nazareth had preached was overlaid, as we have explained, almost from the beginning by the doctrines and ceremonial traditions of an earlier age, and of an intellectually inferior type. Christianity almost from its commencement ceased to be purely prophetic and creative. It entangled itself with archaic traditions of human sacrifice, with Mithraic blood-cleansing, with priestcraft as ancient as human society, and with elaborate doctrines about the structure of the divinity. The gory forefinger of the Etruscan pontifex maximus emphasized the teachings of Jesus of Nazareth; the mental complexity of the Alexandrian Greek entangled them. In the inevitable jangle of these incompatibles the church had become dogmatic. In despair of other solutions to its intellectual discords it had resorted to arbitrary authority. Its priests and bishops were more and more men moulded to creeds and dogmas and set procedures; by the time they became cardinals or popes they were usually oldish men, habituated to a politic struggle for immediate ends and no longer capable of world-wide views. They no longer wanted to see the Kingdom of God established in the hearts of men—they had forgotten about that; they wanted to see the power of the church, which was their own power, dominating men. They were prepared to bargain even with the hates and fears and lusts in men's hearts to ensure that power. And it was just because many of them probably doubted secretly of the entire soundness of their vast and elaborate doctrinal fabric, that they would brook no discussion of it. They were intolerant of questions or dissent, not because they were sure of their faith, but because they were not. They wanted conformity for reasons of policy. By the thirteenth century the church was evidently already morbidly anxious about the gnawing doubts that might presently lay the whole structure of its pretensions in ruins. It had no serenity of soul. It was hunting everywhere for heretics as timid old ladies are said to look under beds and in cupboards for burglars before retiring for the night.

30

We have already mentioned (chap. xxxi, § 5) the Persian Mani, who was crucified and flayed in the year 277. His way of representing the struggle between good and evil was as a struggle between a power of light which was, as it were, in rebellion against a power of darkness inherent in the universe. All these profound mysteries are necessarily represented by symbols and poetic expressions, and the ideas of Mani still find a response in many intellectual temperaments to-day. One may hear Manichæan doctrines from many Christian pulpits. But the orthodox Catholic symbol was a different one. These Manichæan ideas had spread very widely in Europe, and particularly in Bulgaria and the south of France. In the south of France the people who held them were called the Cathars or Albigenses. Their ideas jarred so little with the essentials of Christianity, that they believed themselves to be devout Christians. As a body they lived lives of conspicuous virtue and purity in a violent, undisciplined, and vicious age. But they questioned the doctrinal soundness of Rome and the orthodox interpretation of the Bible. They thought Jesus was a rebel against the cruelty of the God of the Old Testament, and not his harmonious son. Closely associated with the Albigenses were the Waldenses, the followers of a man called Waldo, who seems to have been quite soundly Catholic in his theology, but equally offensive to the church because he denounced the riches and luxury of the clergy. This was enough for the Lateran, and so we have the spectacle of Innocent III preaching a crusade against these unfortunate sectaries, and permitting the enlistment of every wandering scoundrel at loose ends to carry fire and sword and rape and every conceivable outrage among the most peaceful subjects of the King of France. The accounts of the cruelties and abominations of this crusade are far more terrible to read than any account of Christian martyrdoms by the pagans, and they have the added horror of being indisputably true.

This black and pitiless intolerance was an evil spirit to be mixed into the project of a rule of God on earth. This was a spirit entirely counter to that of Jesus of Nazareth. We do not hear of his smacking the faces or wringing the wrists of recalcitrant or unresponsive disciples. But the Popes during their centuries of power were always raging against the slightest reflection upon the intellectual sufficiency of the church.

And the intolerance of the church was not confined to religious matters. The shrewd, pompous, irascible, and rather malignant old men who manifestly constituted a dominant majority in the councils of the church, resented any knowledge but their own knowledge, and distrusted any thought at all that they did not correct and control. They set themselves to restrain science, of which they were evidently jealous. Any mental activity but their own struck them as being insolent. Later on they were to have a great struggle upon the question of the earth's position in space, and whether it moved round the sun or not. This was really not the business of the church at all. She might very well have left to reason the things that are reason's, but she seems to have been impelled by an inner necessity to estrange the intellectual conscience in men.

Had this intolerance sprung from a real intensity of conviction it would have been bad enough, but it was accompanied by a scarcely disguised contempt for the intelligence and mental dignity of the common man that makes it far less acceptable to our modern judgments, and which no doubt made it far less acceptable to the free spirits of the time. We have told quite dispassionately the policy of the Roman church towards her troubled sister in the East. Many of the tools and expedients she used were abominable. In her treatment of her own people a streak of real cynicism is visible. She destroyed her prestige by disregarding her own teaching of righteousness. Of dispensations we have already spoken (§ 11). Her crowning folly in the sixteenth century was the sale of *indulgences*, whereby the sufferings of the soul in purgatory could be commuted for a money payment. But the spirit that led at last to this shameless and, as it proved, disastrous proceeding, was already very evident in the twelfth and thirteenth centuries.

Long before the seed of criticism that Frederick II had sown had germinated in men's minds and produced its inevitable crop of rebellion, there was apparent a strong feeling in Christendom that all was not well with the spiritual atmosphere. There began movements, movements that nowadays we should call " revivalist," within the church, that implied rather than uttered a criticism of the sufficiency of her existing methods and organization. Men sought fresh forms of righteous living outside the monasteries and priesthood. One notable figure is that of St. Francis of Assisi (1181–1226). We cannot tell here in any detail of how this pleasant young gentleman gave up all the amenities and ease of his life and went forth to seek God ; the opening of the story is not unlike the early experiences of Gautama Buddha. He had a sudden conversion in the midst of a life of pleasure, and, taking a vow of extreme poverty, he gave himself up to an imitation of the life of Christ, and to the service of the sick and wretched, and more particularly to the service of the lepers, who then abounded in Italy. He was joined by great multitudes of disciples, and so the first Friars of the Franciscan Order came into existence. An order of women devotees was set up beside the original confraternity, and in addition great numbers of men and women were brought into less formal association. He preached, unmolested by the Moslems, be it noted, in Egypt and Palestine, though the Fifth Crusade was then in progress. His relations with the church are still a matter for discussion.[1] His work had been sanctioned by Pope Innocent III, but while he was in the East there was a reconstitution of his order, intensifying its discipline and substituting authority for responsive impulse, and as a consequence of these changes he resigned its headship. To the end he clung passionately to the ideal of poverty, but he was hardly dead before the order was holding property through trustees and building a great church and monastery to his memory at Assisi. The disciplines of the order that were applied after his death to his immediate associates are scarcely to be distinguished from a persecution ; several of the more conspicuous zealots for simplicity were scourged, others were imprisoned, one was killed while attempting to escape, and Brother Bernard, the " first disciple," passed a year in the woods and hills, hunted like a wild beast.

[1] See Paul Sabatier's *Vie de S. François d'Assise* (English trans. by Houghton).

This struggle within the Franciscan Order is a very interesting one, because it foreshadows the great troubles that were coming to Christendom. All through the thirteenth century a section of the Franciscans were straining at the rule of the church, and in 1318 four of them were burnt alive at Marseilles as incorrigible heretics. There seems to have been little difference between the teaching and spirit of St. Francis and that of Waldo in the twelfth century, the founder of the murdered sect of Waldenses. Both were passionately enthusiastic for the spirit of Jesus of Nazareth. But while Waldo rebelled against the church, St. Francis did his best to be a good child of the church, and

Photo: Mansell.
ST. FRANCIS OF ASSISI.
By Luca della Robbia.

his comment on the spirit of official Christianity was only implicit. But both were instances of an outbreak of conscience against authority and the ordinary procedure of the church. And it is plain that in the second instance, as in the first, the church scented rebellion.

A very different character to St. Francis was the Spaniard St. Dominic (1170–1221), who was, of all things, orthodox. He had a passion for the argumentative conversion of heretics, and he was commissioned by Pope Innocent III to go and preach to the Albigenses. His work went on side by side with the fighting and massacres of the crusade ; whom Dominic could not convert, Innocent's crusaders slew ; yet his very activities and the recognition and encouragement of his order by the Pope witness to the rising tide of discussion, and to the persuasion even of the papacy that force was no remedy. In several respects the development of the Black Friars or Dominicans—the Franciscans were the Grey Friars—shows the Roman church at the parting of the ways, committing itself more and more deeply to organized dogma, and so to a hopeless conflict with the quickening intelligence and courage

of mankind. She whose one duty was to lead, chose to compel. The last discourse of St. Dominic to the heretics he had sought to convert is preserved to us. It is a signpost in history. It betrays the fatal exasperation of a man who has lost his faith in the power of truth because *his* truth has not prevailed. " For many years," he said, " I have exhorted you in vain, with gentleness, preaching, praying, and weeping. But according to the proverb of my country, ' where blessing can accomplish nothing, blows may avail.' We shall rouse against you princes and prelates, who, alas ! will arm nations and kingdoms against this land . . . and thus blows will avail where blessings and gentleness have been powerless."[1]

The thirteenth century saw the development of a new institution in the church, the papal Inquisition. Before this time it had been customary for the Pope to make occasional inquests or inquiries into heresy in this region or that, but now Innocent III saw in the new order of the Dominicans a powerful instrument of suppression. The Inquisition was organized as a standing inquiry under their direction, and with fire and torment the church set itself, through this instrument, to assail and weaken the human conscience in which its sole hope of world dominion resided. Before the thirteenth century the penalty of death had been inflicted but rarely upon heretics and unbelievers. Now in a hundred market-places in Europe the dignitaries of the church watched the blackened bodies of its antagonists, for the most part poor and insignificant people, burn and sink pitifully, and their own great mission to mankind burn and sink with them into dust and ashes.

The beginnings of the Franciscans and the Dominicans were but two among many of the new forces that were arising in Christendom,

[1] *Encyclopædia Britannica*, art. "Dominic."

either to help or shatter the church, as its own wisdom might decide. Those two orders the church did assimilate and use, though with a little violence in the case of the former. But other forces were more frankly disobedient and critical. A century and a half later came Wycliffe (1320-1384). He was a learned doctor at Oxford ; for a time he was Master of Balliol ; and he held various livings in the church. Quite late in his life he began a series of outspoken criticisms of the corruption of the clergy and the unwisdom of the church. He organized a number of poor priests, the Wycliffites, to spread his ideas throughout England; and in order that people should judge between the church and himself, he translated the Bible into English. He was a more learned and far abler man than either St. Francis or St. Dominic. He had supporters in high places and a great following among the people ; and though Rome raged against him, and ordered his imprisonment, he died a free man, still administering the Sacraments as parish priest of Lutterworth. But the black and ancient spirit that was leading the Catholic church to its destruction would not let his bones rest in his grave. By a decree of the Council of Constance in 1415, his remains were ordered to be dug up and burnt, an order which was carried out at the command of Pope Martin V by Bishop Fleming in 1428. This desecration was not the act of some isolated fanatic ; it was the official act of the church.

§ 14

The history of the papacy is confusing to the general reader because of the multitude and abundance of the Popes. They mostly began to reign as old men, and their reigns were short, averaging less than two years each. But certain of the Popes stand out and supply convenient handles for the student to grasp. Such were Gregory I (590-604) the Great, the first monkish Pope, the friend of Benedict, the sender of the English mission. Other noteworthy Popes are Leo III (795-816), who crowned Charlemagne, the scandalous Popes John XI (931-936) and John XII (955-963), which latter was deposed by the Emperor Otto I, and the great Hildebrand, who ended his days as Pope Gregory VII

A List of Leading Popes.

(1073-1085), and who did so much by establishing the celibacy of the clergy, and insisting upon the supremacy of the church over kings and princes, to centralize the power of the church in Rome. The next Pope but one after Gregory VII was Urban II (1087-1099), the Pope of the First Crusade. The period from the time of Gregory VII onward for a century and a half, was the great period of ambition and effort for the church. There was a real sustained attempt to unite all Christendom under a purified and reorganized church.

The setting up of Latin kingdoms in Syria and the Holy Land, in religious communion with Rome, after the First Crusade, marked the opening stage of a conquest of Eastern Christianity by Rome that reached its climax during the Latin rule in Constantinople (1204-1261).

In 1176, at Venice, the Emperor Frederick Barbarossa (Frederick I) knelt to the Pope Alexander III, recognized his spiritual supremacy, and swore fealty to him. But after the death of Alexander III, in 1181, the peculiar weakness of the papacy, its liability to fall to old and enfeebled men, became manifest. Five Popes tottered to the Lateran to die within the space of ten years. Only with Innocent III (1198-1216) did another vigorous Pope take up the great policy of the City of God.

Under Innocent III, the guardian of that Emperor Frederick II, whose career we have already studied in §§ 10 and 12, and the five Popes who followed him, the Pope of Rome came nearer to being the monarch of a united Christendom than he had ever been before, and was ever to be again. The empire was weakened by internal dissensions, Constantinople was in Latin hands, from Bulgaria to Ireland and from Norway to Sicily and Jerusalem the Pope was supreme. Yet this supremacy was more apparent than real. For, as we have seen, while in the time of Urban the power of faith was strong in all Christian Europe, in the time of Innocent III the papacy had lost its hold upon the hearts of princes, and the faith and conscience of the common people was turning against a merely political and aggressive church.

The church in the thirteenth century was extending its legal power in the world, and losing its grip upon men's consciences. It was becoming less persuasive and more violent. No intelligent man can tell of this process, or read of this process of failure without very mingled feelings. The church had sheltered and formed a new Europe throughout the long ages of European darkness and chaos; it had been the matrix in which the new civilization had been cast. But this new-formed civilization was impelled to grow

Photo: Brogi.

ST. DOMINIC AND ST. FRANCIS.
By Andrea della Robbia.

and Rudolf of Habsburg was elected first Habsburg Emperor (1273), the policy of the Lateran began to fluctuate between France and Germany, veering about with the sympathies of each successive Pope. In the East in 1261 the Greeks recaptured Constantinople from the Latin emperors, and the founder of the new Greek dynasty, Michael Palæologus, Michael VIII, after some unreal tentatives of reconciliation with the Pope,

by its own inherent vitality, and the church lacked sufficient power of growth and accommodation. The time was fast approaching when this matrix was to be broken.

The first striking intimation of the decay of the living and sustaining forces of the papacy appeared when presently the Popes came into conflict with the growing power of the French king. During the lifetime of the Emperor Frederick II, Germany fell into disunion, and the French king began to play the rôle of guard, supporter, and rival to the Pope that had hitherto fallen to the Hohenstaufen emperors. A series of Popes pursued the policy of supporting the French monarchs. French princes were established in the kingdom of Sicily and Naples, with the support and approval of Rome, and the French kings saw before them the possibility of restoring and ruling the Empire of Charlemagne. When, however, the German interregnum after the death of Frederick II, the last of the Hohenstaufens, came to an end

broke away from the Roman communion altogether, and with that, and the fall of the Latin kingdoms in Asia, the eastward ascendancy of the Popes came to an end.

In 1294 Boniface VIII became Pope. He was an Italian, hostile to the French, and full of a sense of the great traditions and mission of Rome. For a time he carried things with a high hand. In 1300 he held a jubilee, and a vast multitude of pilgrims assembled in Rome. "So great was the influx of money into the papal treasury, that two assistants were kept busy with rakes collecting the offerings that were deposited at the tomb of St. Peter."[1] But this festival was a delusive triumph. It is easier to raise a host of excursionists than a band of crusaders. Boniface came into conflict with the French king in 1302, and in 1303, as he was about to pronounce sentence of excommunication against that monarch, he was

[1] J. H. Robinson.

surprised and arrested in his own ancestral palace, at Anagni, by Guillaume de Nogaret. This agent from the French king forced an entrance into the palace, made his way into the bedroom of the frightened Pope—he was lying in bed with a cross in his hands—and heaped threats and insults upon him. The Pope was liberated a day or so later by the townspeople, and returned to Rome; but there he was seized upon and again made prisoner by the Orsini family, and in a few weeks' time the shocked and disillusioned old man died a prisoner in their hands.

The people of Anagni did resent the first outrage, and rose against Nogaret to liberate Boniface, but then Anagni was the Pope's native town. The important point to note is that the French king, in this rough treatment of the head of Christendom, was acting with the full approval of his people; he had summoned a council of the Three Estates of France (lords, church, and commons) and gained their consent before proceeding to extremities. Neither in Italy, Germany, nor England was there the slightest general manifestation of disapproval at this free handling of the sovereign pontiff. The idea of Christendom had decayed until all its power over the minds of men had gone.

Throughout the fourteenth century the papacy did nothing to recover its moral sway. The next Pope elected, Clement V, was a Frenchman, the choice of King Philip of France. He never came to Rome. He set up his court in the town of Avignon, which then belonged not to France, but to the Papal See, though embedded in French territory, and there his successors remained until 1377, when Pope Gregory XI returned to the Vatican palace in Rome. But Gregory XI did not take the sympathies of the whole church with him. Many of the cardinals were of French origin, and their habits and associations were rooted deep at Avignon. When in 1378 Gregory XI died, and an Italian, Urban VI, was elected, these dissentient cardinals declared the election invalid, and elected another Pope, the anti-Pope, Clement VII. This split is called the Great Schism. The Popes remained in Rome, and all the anti-French powers, the Emperor, the King of England, Hungary, Poland, and the North

of Europe were loyal to them. The anti-Popes, on the other hand, continued in Avignon, and were supported by the King of France, his ally the King of Scotland, Spain, Portugal, and various German princes. Each Pope excommunicated and cursed the adherents of his rival, so that by one standard or another all Christendom was damned during this time (1378-1417). The lamentable effect of this split upon the solidarity of Christendom it is impossible to exaggerate. Is it any marvel that such men as Wycliffe began to teach men to think on their own account when the fountain of truth thus squirted against itself? In 1417 the Great Schism was healed at the Council of Constance, the same council that dug up and burnt Wycliffe's bones, and which, as we shall tell later, caused the burning of John Huss; at this council, Pope and anti-Pope resigned or were swept aside, and Martin V became the sole Pope of a formally reunited but spiritually very badly strained Christendom.

How later on the Council of Basle (1437) led to a fresh schism, and to further anti-Popes, we cannot relate here.

Such, briefly, is the story of the great centuries of papal ascendancy and papal decline. It is the story of the failure to achieve the very noble and splendid idea of a unified and religious world. We have pointed out in the previous section how greatly the inheritance of a complex dogmatic theology encumbered the church in this its ambitious adventure. It had too much theology, and not enough religion. But it may not be idle to point out here how much the individual insufficiency of the Popes also contributed to the collapse of its scheme and dignity. There was no such level of education in the world as to provide a succession of cardinals and popes with the breadth of knowledge and outlook needed for the task they had undertaken; they were not sufficiently educated for their task, and only a few, by sheer force of genius, transcended that defect. And, as we have already pointed out, they were, when at last they got to power, too old to use it. Before they could grasp the situation they had to control, most of them were dead. It would be interesting to speculate how far it would have tilted the balance in favour of the church if the cardinals had retired at fifty, and if no one could have been elected Pope after fifty-five. This would have lengthened the average reign of each Pope, and enormously increased the continuity of the policy of the church. And it is perhaps possible that a more perfect system of selecting the cardinals, who were the electors and counsellors of the Pope, might have been devised. The rules and ways by which men reach power are of very great importance in human affairs. The psychology of the ruler is a science that has still to be properly studied. We have seen the Roman Republic wrecked, and here we see the church failing in its world mission very largely through ineffective electoral methods.

Book VII

THE MONGOL EMPIRES OF THE LAND WAYS AND THE NEW EMPIRES OF THE SEA WAYS

XXXIV

THE GREAT EMPIRE OF JENGIS KHAN AND HIS SUCCESSORS

(The Age of the Land Ways)

§ 1

WE have to tell now of the last and greatest of all the raids of nomadism upon the civilizations of the East and West. We have traced in this history the development side by side of these two ways of living, and we have pointed out that as the civilizations grew more extensive and better organized, the arms, the mobility, and the intelligence of the nomads also improved. The nomad was not simply an uncivilized man, he was a man specialized and specializing along his own line. From the very beginning of history the nomad and the settled people have been in reaction. We have told of the Semitic and Elamite raids upon Sumeria ; we have seen the Western empire smashed by the nomads of the great plains and Persia conquered and Byzantium shaken by the nomads of Arabia. Whenever civilization seems to be choking amidst its weeds of wealth and debt and servitude, when its faiths seem rotting into cynicism and its powers

Asia at the End of the Twelfth Century.

of further growth are hopelessly entangled in effete formulæ, the nomad drives in like a plough to break up the festering stagnation and release the world to new beginnings. The Mongol aggression, which began with the thirteenth century, was the greatest, and so far it has been the last, of all these destructive reploughings of human association.

From entire obscurity the Mongols came very suddenly into history towards the close of the twelfth century. They appeared in the country to the north of China, in the land of origin of the Huns and Turks, and they were manifestly of the same strain as these peoples. They were gathered together under a chief, with whose name we will not tax the memory of the reader ; under his son Jengis Khan their power grew with extraordinary swiftness.

The reader will already have an idea of the gradual breaking up of the original unity of Islam. In the beginning of the thirteenth century there were a number of separate and discordant Moslem states in Western Asia.

Map of
EUROPE and ASIA
about 1200 A.D.

KIN EMPIRE

SUNG EMPIRE

HSIA EMPIRE

Oldest Settlements of the Mongols

l. Baikal

Early power of JENGIS KHAN

Old Karakorum

MONGOLIA

Uigurs

TIBET

Dravidian kingdoms

Tartar Peoples

RUSSIA

Pr. or REP. of NOVGOROD

KHIVAN (Kharismian) EMPIRE

K. of NORWAY

K. of SWEDEN

ARABIA

K. of DENMARK

K. of ENGLAND

PRUSSIA

POLAND

LITHUANIA

Pr. of KIEFF

SELJUKS

The Caliphate

Successors of SALADIN

K. of HUNGARY

BULGARIA

SERBIA

BYZANTINE EMPIRE

CYPRUS

THE EMPIRE

APULIA

SICILY

K. of FRANCE

English domination

NAVARRE

ARAGON

CASTILE

K. of LEON

K. of CASTILE

K. of PORTUGAL

Moslem Kingdoms

J.F.H.

472

There was Egypt (with Palestine and much of Syria) under the successors of Saladin, there was the Seljuk power in Asia Minor, there was still an Abbasid caliphate in Bagdad, and to the east of this again there had grown up a very considerable empire, the Kharismian empire, that of the Turkish princes from Khiva who had conquered a number of fragmentary Seljuk principalities and reigned from the Ganges valley to the Tigris. They had but an insecure hold on the Persian and Indian populations.

The state of the Chinese civilization was equally inviting to an enterprising invader. One last glimpse of China in this history was in the seventh century during the opening years of the Tang dynasty, when that shrewd and able emperor Tai-tsung was weighing the respective merits of Nestorian Christianity, Islam, Buddhism, and the teachings of Lao-tse, and on the whole inclining to the opinion that Lao-tse was as good a teacher as any. We have described his reception of the traveller Yuan Chwang. Tai-tsung tolerated all religions, but several of his successors conducted a pitiless persecution of the Buddhist faith; it flourished in spite of these persecutions, and its monasteries played a somewhat analogous part in at first sustaining learning and afterwards retarding it, that the Christian monastic organization did in the West. By the tenth century the great Tang dynasty was in an extreme state of decay; the usual degenerative process through a series of voluptuaries and incapables had gone on, and China broke up again politically into a variable number of contending states, "The age of the Ten States," an age of confusion that lasted through the first half of the tenth century. Then arose a dynasty, the Northern Sung (960—1127), which established a sort of unity, but which was in constant struggle with a number of Hunnish peoples from the north who were pressing down the eastern coast. For a time one of these peoples, the Khitan, prevailed. In the twelfth century these people had been subjugated and had given place to another Hunnish empire, the empire of the Kin, with its capital at Pekin and its southern boundary south of Hwang-ho. The Sung empire shrank before this Kin empire. In 1138 the capital was shifted from Nankin, which was now too close to the northern frontier, to the city of Han Chau on the coast. From 1127 onward to 1295, the Sung dynasty is known as the Southern Sung. To the north-west of its territories there was now the Tartar empire of the Hsia; to the north, the Kin empire, both states in which the Chinese population was under rulers in whom nomadic traditions were still strong. So that here on the east also the main masses of Asiatic mankind were under uncongenial rulers and ready to accept, if not to welcome, the arrival of a conqueror.

Northern India we have already noted was also a conquered country at the opening of the thirteenth century. It was at first a part of the Khivan empire, but in 1206 an adventurous ruler, Kutub, who had been a slave and who had risen as a slave to be governor of the Indian province, set up a separate Moslem state of Hindustan in Delhi. Brahminism had long since ousted Buddhism from India, but the converts to Islam were still but a small ruling minority in the land.

Such was the political state of Asia when Jengis Khan began to consolidate his power among the nomads in the country between Lakes Balkash and Baikal in the beginning of the thirteenth century.

§ 2

The career of conquest of Jengis Khan and his immediate successors astounded the world, and probably astounded no one more than these Mongol Khans themselves.

The Mongols were in the twelfth century a tribe subject to those Kin who had conquered North-east China. They were a **The Rise and Victories of the Mongols.** horde of nomadic horsemen living in tents, and subsisting mainly upon mare's milk products and meat. Their occupations were pasturage and hunting, varied by war. They drifted northward as the snows melted for summer pasture, and southward to winter pasture after the custom of the steppes. Their military education began with a successful insurrection against the Kin. The empire of Kin had the resources of half China behind it, and in the struggle the Mongols learnt very much of the military science of the Chinese. By the end of the twelfth century they were already a fighting tribe of exceptional quality.

The opening years of the career of Jengis were spent in developing his military machine, in assimilating the Mongols and the associated tribes about them into one organized army. His first considerable extension of power was westward, when the Tartar Kirghis and the Uigurs (who were the Tartar people of the Tarim basin) were not so much conquered as induced to join his organization. He then attacked the Kin empire and took Pekin (1214). The Khitan people, who had been so recently subdued by the Kin, threw in their fortunes with his, and were of very great help to him. The settled Chinese population went on sowing and reaping and trading during this change of masters without lending its weight to either side.

We have already mentioned the very recent Kharismian empire of Turkestan, Persia and North India. This empire extended eastward to Kashgar, and it must have seemed one of the most progressive and hopeful empires of the time. Jengis Khan, while still engaged in this war with the Kin empire, sent envoys to Kharismia. They were put to death, an almost incredible stupidity. The Kharismian government, to use the political jargon of to-day, had decided not to " recognize " Jengis Khan, and took this spirited course with him. Thereupon (1218) the great host of horsemen that Jengis Khan had consolidated and disciplined swept over the Pamirs and down into Turkestan. It was well armed, and probably it had some guns and gunpowder for siege work—for the Chinese were certainly using gunpowder at this time, and the Mongols learnt its use from them. Kashgar, Khokand, Bokhara fell and then Samarkand, the capital of the Kharismian empire. Thereafter nothing held the Mongols in the Kharismian territories. They swept westward to the Caspian, and southward as far as Lahore. To the north of the Caspian a Mongol army encountered a Russian force from Kieff. There was a series of battles, in which the Russian armies were finally defeated and the Grand Duke of Kieff taken prisoner. So it was the Mongols appeared on the northern shores of the Black Sea. A panic swept Constantinople, which set itself to reconstruct its fortifications. Meanwhile other armies were engaged in the conquest of the empire of the

Hsia in China. This was annexed, and only the southern part of the Kin empire remained unsubdued. In 1227 Jengis Khan died in the midst of a career of triumph. His empire reached already from the Pacific to the Dnieper. And it was an empire still vigorously expanding.

Like all the empires founded by nomads, it was, to begin with, purely a military and administrative empire, a framework rather than a rule. It centred on the personality of the monarch, and its relations with the mass of the populations over which it ruled was simply one of taxation for the maintenance of the horde. But Jengis

CLAY STATUETTE OF A CHINESE HORSEMAN FROM TOMBS OF THE T'ANG DYNASTY (SEVENTH TO TENTH CENTURIES A.D.). (BRITISH MUSEUM.)

Khan had called to his aid a very able and experienced administrator of the Kin empire, who was learned in all the traditions and science of the Chinese. This statesman, Yeliu Chutsai, was able to carry on the affairs of the Mongols long after the death of Jengis Khan, and there can be little doubt that he is one of the great political heroes of history. He tempered the barbaric ferocity of his masters, and saved innumerable cities and works of art from destruction. He collected archives and inscriptions, and when he was accused of corruption, his sole wealth was found to consist of documents and a few musical instruments. To him perhaps quite as much as to Jengis is the

The EMPIRE of JENGIS KHAN at his death (1227)

efficiency of the Mongol military machine to be ascribed. Under Jengis, we may note further, we find the completest religious toleration established across the entire breadth of Asia.

At the death of Jengis the capital of the new empire was still in the great barbaric town of Karakorum in Mongolia. There an assembly of Mongol leaders elected Ogdai Khan, the son of Jengis, as his successor. The war against the vestiges of the Kin empire was prosecuted until Kin was altogether subdued (1234). The Chinese empire to the south under the Sung dynasty helped the Mongols in this task, so destroying their own bulwark against the universal conquerors. The Mongol hosts then swept right across Asia to Russia (1235), an amazing march. Kieff was destroyed in 1240, and nearly all Russia became tributary to the Mongols. Poland was ravaged, and a mixed army of Poles and Germans was annihilated at the battle of Liegnitz in Lower Silesia in 1241. The Emperor Frederick II does not seem to have made any great efforts to stay the advancing tide.

"It is only recently," says Bury, in his notes to Gibbon's *Decline and Fall of the Roman Empire*, "that European history has begun to understand that the successes of the Mongol army which overran Poland and occupied Hungary in the spring of A.D. 1241 were won by consummate strategy and were not due to a mere overwhelming superiority of numbers. But this fact has not yet become a matter of common knowledge; the vulgar opinion which represents the Tartars as a wild horde carrying all before them solely by their multitude, and galloping through Eastern Europe without a strategic plan, rushing at all obstacles and overcoming them by mere weight, still prevails. . . .

"It was wonderful how punctually and effectually the arrangements of the commander were carried out in operations extending from the Lower Vistula to Transylvania. Such a campaign was quite beyond the power of any European army of the time, and it was beyond the vision of any European commander. There was no general in Europe, from Frederick II downward, who was not a tiro in strategy compared to Subutai. It should also be noticed that the Mongols embarked upon the enterprise with full knowledge of the political situation of

Hungary and the condition of Poland—they had taken care to inform themselves by a well-organized system of spies ; on the other hand, the Hungarians and Christian powers, like childish barbarians, knew hardly anything about their enemies."

But though the Mongols were victorious at Liegnitz, they did not continue their drive westward. They were getting into woodlands and hilly country, which did not suit their tactics ; and so they turned southward and prepared to settle in Hungary, massacring or assimilating the kindred Magyar, even as these had previously massacred and assimilated the mixed Scythians and Avars and Huns before them. From the Hungarian plain they would probably have made raids west and south as the Hungarians had done in the ninth century, the Avars in the seventh and eighth, and the Huns in the fifth. But in Asia the Mongols were fighting a stiff war of conquest against the Sung, and they were also raiding Persia and Asia Minor ; Ogdai died suddenly, and in 1242 there was trouble about the succession, and recalled by this, the undefeated hosts of Mongols began to pour back across Hungary and Rumania towards the east.

To the great relief of Europe the dynastic troubles at Karakorum lasted for some years, and this vast new empire showed signs of splitting up. Mangu Khan became the Great Khan in 1251, and he nominated his brother Kublai Khan as Governor-General of China. Slowly but surely the entire Sung empire was subjugated, and as it was subjugated the eastern Mongols became more and more Chinese in their culture and methods. Tibet was invaded and devastated by Mangu, and Persia and Syria invaded in good earnest. Another brother of Mangu, Hulagu, was in command of this latter war. He turned his arms against the caliphate and captured Bagdad, in which city he perpetrated a massacre of the entire population. Bagdad was still the religious capital of Islam, and the Mongols had become bitterly hostile to the Moslems. This hostility exacerbated the natural discord of nomad and townsman. In 1259 Mangu died, and in 1260— for it took the best part of a year for the Mongol leaders to gather from the extremities of this vast empire, from Hungary and Syria and

Scind and China—Kublai was elected Great Khan. He was already deeply interested in Chinese affairs ; he made his capital Pekin instead of Karakorum, and Persia, Syria, and Asia Minor became virtually independent under his brother Hulagu, while the hordes of Mongols in Russia and Asia next to Russia, and various smaller Mongol groups in Turkestan became also practically separate. Kublai died in 1294, and with his death even the titular supremacy of the Great Khan disappeared.

At the death of Kublai there was a main Mongol empire, with Pekin as its capital, including all China and Mongolia ; there was a second great Mongol empire, that of Kipchak in Russia ; there was a third in Persia, that founded by Hulagu, the Ilkhan empire, to which the Seljuk Turks in Asia Minor were tributary ; there was a Siberian state between Kipchak and Mongolia ; and another separate state " Great Turkey " in Turkestan. It is particularly remarkable that India beyond the Punjab was never invaded by the Mongols during this period, and that an army under the Sultan of Egypt completely defeated Ketboga, Hulagu's general, in Palestine (1260), and stopped them from ever entering Africa. By 1260 the impulse of Mongol conquest had already passed its zenith. Thereafter the Mongol story is one of division and decay.

The Mongol dynasty that Kublai Khan had founded in China, the Yuan dynasty, lasted from 1280 until 1368. Later on a recrudescence of Mongolian energy in Western Asia was destined to create a still more enduring monarchy in India.

§ 3

Now this story of Mongolian conquests is surely the most remarkable in all history. The conquests of Alexander the Great cannot compare with them in extent. And their effect in diffusing and broadening men's ideas, though such things are more difficult to estimate, is at least comparable to the spread of the Hellenic civilization which is associated with Alexander's adventure. For a time all Asia and Western Europe enjoyed an open intercourse ; all the roads were temporarily open, and representatives of every nation appeared at the court of Karakorum.

The Travels of Marco Polo.

The barriers between Europe and Asia set up by the religious feud of Christianity and Islam were lowered. Great hopes were entertained by the papacy for the conversion of the Mongols to Christianity. Their only religion so far had been Shamanism, a primitive paganism. Envoys of the Pope, Buddhist priests from India, Parisian and Italian and Chinese artificers, Byzantine and Armenian merchants, mingled with Arab officials and Persian and Indian astronomers and mathematicians at the Mongol court. We hear too much in history of the campaigns and massacres of the Mongols, and not enough of their indubitable curiosity and zest for learning. Not perhaps as an originative people, but as transmitters of knowledge and method their influence upon the world's history has been enormous. And everything one can learn of the vague and romantic personalities of Jengis or Kublai tends to confirm the impression that these men were built upon a larger scale, and were at least as understanding and creative monarchs as either that flamboyant but egotistical figure Alexander the Great, or that raiser of political ghosts, that energetic but illiterate theologian, Charlemagne.

The missionary enterprises of the papacy in Mongolia ended in failure. Christianity was losing its persuasive power. The Mongols had no prejudice against Christianity; they evidently preferred it at first to Islam; but the missions that came to them were manifestly using the power in the great teachings of Jesus to advance the vast claims of the Pope to world dominion. Christianity so vitiated was not good enough for the Mongol mind. To make the empire of the Mongols part of the kingdom of God might have appealed to them; but not to make it a fief of a group of French and Italian priests, whose claims were as gigantic as their powers and outlook were feeble, who were now the creatures of the Emperor of Germany, now the nominees of the King of France, and now the victims of their own petty spites and vanities. In 1269 Kublai Khan sent a mission to the Pope with the evident intention of finding some common mode of action with Western Christendom. He asked that a hundred men of learning and ability should be sent to his court to establish an understanding. His mission found the Western world popeless, and engaged in one of those disputes about the

MONGOL States about 1280 A.D. & MARCO POLO'S travels.

Marco Polo's route ——→   homeward ·-·-·-·   0   500   1000   2000 Miles

J.F.H.

succession that are so frequent in the history of the papacy. For two years there was no pope at all. When at last a pope was appointed, he dispatched two Dominican friars to convert the greatest power in Asia to his rule ! Those worthy men were appalled by the length and hardship of the journey before them, and found an early excuse for abandoning the expedition.

But this abortive mission was only one of a number of attempts to communicate, and always they were feeble and feeble-spirited attempts, with nothing of the conquering fire of the earlier Christian missions. Innocent IV had already sent some Dominicans to Karakorum, and Saint Louis of France had also dispatched missionaries and relics by way of Persia ; Mangu Khan had numerous Nestorian Christians at his court, and subsequent papal envoys actually reached Pekin. We hear of the appointment of various legates and bishops to the East, but many of these seem to have lost themselves and perhaps their lives before they reached China. There was a papal legate in Pekin in 1346, but he seems to have been a mere papal diplomatist. With the downfall of the Mongolian (Yuan) dynasty (1368), the dwindling opportunity of the Christian missions passed altogether. The house of Yuan was followed by that of Ming, a strongly nationalist Chinese dynasty, at first very hostile to all foreigners. There may have been a massacre of the Christian missions. Until the later days of the Mings (1644) little more is heard of Christianity, whether Nestorian or Catholic, in China. Then a fresh and rather more successful attempt to propagate Catholic Christianity in China was made by the Jesuits, but this second missionary wave reached China by the sea.

Photo : Anderson.

MARCO POLO.
By Titian.

In the year 1298 a naval battle occurred between the Genoese and the Venetians, in which the latter were defeated. Among the 7,000 prisoners taken by the Genoese was a Venetian gentleman named Marco Polo, who had been a great traveller, and who was very generally believed by his neighbours to be given to exaggeration. He had taken part in that first mission to Kublai Khan, and had gone on when the two Dominicans turned back. While this Marco Polo was a prisoner in Genoa, he beguiled his tedium by talking of his travels to a certain writer named Rusticiano, who wrote them down. We will not enter here into the vexed question of the exact authenticity of Rusticiano's story—we do not certainly know in what language it was written—but there can be no doubt of the general truth of this remarkable narrative, which became enormously popular in the fourteenth and fifteenth centuries with all men of active intelligence. *The Travels of Marco Polo* is one of the great books of history. It opens this world of the thirteenth century, this century which saw the reign of Frederick II and the beginnings of the Inquisition, to our imaginations as no mere historian's chronicle can do. It led directly to the discovery of America.

It begins by telling of the journey of Marco's father, Nicolo Polo, and uncle, Maffeo Polo, to China. These two were Venetian merchants of standing, living in Constantinople, and somewhen about 1260 they went to the Crimea and thence to Kazan ; from that place they journeyed to Bokhara, and at Bokhara they fell in with a party of envoys from Kublai Khan in China to his brother Hulagu in Persia. These envoys pressed them to come on to the Great Khan, who at that time had never seen men of the "Latin" peoples. They went on; and it is clear they made a very favourable impression upon Kublai, and interested him greatly in the civilization of Christendom. They were made the bearers of that request for a hundred teachers and learned men, "intelligent men acquainted with the Seven Arts, able to enter into controversy and able clearly to prove to idolators and other kinds of folk that the Law of Christ was best," to which we have just alluded. But when they returned Christendom was in a phase of confusion, and it was only after a delay of two years that they got their authorization to start for China again in the company of those two faint-hearted Dominicans. They took with them young Marco, and it is due to his presence and the boredom of his subsequent captivity at Genoa that this most interesting experience has been preserved to us.

The three Polos started by way of Palestine and not by the Crimea, as in the previous expedition. They had with them a gold tablet and other indications from the Great Khan that must have greatly facilitated their journey. The Great Khan had asked for some oil from the lamp that burns in the Holy Sepulchre at Jerusalem; and so thither they first went, and then by way of Cilicia into Armenia. They went thus far north because the Sultan of Egypt was raiding the Ilkhan domains at this time. Thence they came by way of Mesopotamia to Ormuz on the Persian Gulf, as if they contemplated a sea voyage. At Ormuz they met merchants from India. For some reason they did not take ship, but instead turned northward through the Persian deserts, and so by way of Balkh over the Pamir to Kashgar, and by way of Kotan and the Lob Nor (so following in the footsteps of Yuan Chwang) into the Hwangho valley and on to Pekin. Pekin, Polo calls "Cambulac"; Northern China, "Cathay" (= Khitan); and Southern China of the former Sung dynasty, "Manzi." At Pekin was the Great Khan, and they were hospitably entertained. Marco particularly pleased Kublai; he was young and clever, and it is clear he had mastered the Tartar language very thoroughly. He was given an official position and sent on several missions, chiefly in South-west China. The tale he had to tell

of vast stretches of smiling and prosperous country, "all the way excellent hosteleries for travellers," and "fine vineyards, fields and gardens," of "many abbeys" of Buddhist monks, of manufactures of "cloth of silk and gold and many fine taffetas," a "constant succession of cities and boroughs," and so on, first roused the incredulity and then fired the imagination of all Europe. He told of Burmah, and of its great armies with hundreds of elephants, and how these animals were defeated by the Mongol bowmen, and also of the Mongol conquest of Pegu. He told of Japan, and greatly exaggerated the amount of gold in that country. And, still more wonderful, he told of Christians and Christian rulers in China, and of a certain "Prester John," John the Priest, who was the "king" of a Christian people. Those people he had not seen. Apparently they were a tribe of Nestorian Tartars in Mongolia. An understandable excitement probably made Rusticiano over-emphasize what must have seemed to him the greatest marvel of the whole story, and Prester John became one of the most stimulating legends of the fourteenth and fifteenth centuries. It encouraged European enterprise enormously to think that far away in China was a community of their co-religionists, presumably ready to welcome and assist them. For three years Marco ruled the city of Yang-chow as governor, and he probably impressed the Chinese inhabitants as being very little more of a foreigner than any Tartar would have been. He may also have been sent on a mission to India. Chinese records mention a certain Polo attached to the imperial council in 1277, a very valuable confirmation of the general truth of the Polo story.

The Polos had taken about three and a half years to get to China. They stayed there upwards of sixteen. Then they began to feel homesick. They were the protégés of Kublai, and possibly they felt that his favours roused a certain envy that might have disagreeable results after his death. They sought his permission to return. For a time he refused it, and then an opportunity occurred. Argon, the Ilkhan monarch of Persia, the grandson of Hulagu, Kublai's brother, had lost his Mongol wife, and on her death-bed had promised not to wed any other woman but a Mongol of her own tribe. He sent ambassadors to Pekin, and a suitable princess was selected, a girl of seventeen. To spare her the fatigues of the caravan route, it was decided to send her by sea with a suitable escort. The " Barons " in charge of her asked for the company of the Polos because these latter were experienced travellers and sage men, and the Polos snatched at this opportunity of getting homeward. The expedition sailed from some port on the east of South China ; they stayed long in Sumatra and South India, and they reached Persia after a voyage of two years. They delivered the young lady safely to Argon's successor—for Argon was dead—and she married Argon's son. The Polos then went by Tabriz to Trebizond, sailed to Constantinople, and got back to Venice about 1295. It is related that the returned travellers, dressed in Tartar garb, were refused admission to their own house. It was some time before they could establish their identity. Many people who admitted that, were still inclined to look askance at them as shabby wanderers ; and, in order to dispel such doubts, they gave a great feast, and when it was at its height they had their old padded suits brought to them, dismissed the servants, and then ripped open these garments, whereupon an incredible display of " rubies, sapphires, carbuncles, emeralds, and diamonds " poured out before the dazzled company. Even after this, Marco's accounts of the size and population of China were received with much furtive mockery. The wits nicknamed him *Il Milione*, because he was always talking of millions of people and millions of ducats.

Such was the story that raised eyebrows first in Venice and then throughout the Western world. The European literature, and especially the European romance of the fifteenth century, echoes with the names in Marco Polo's story, with Cathay and Cambulac and the like.

§ 4

These travels of Marco Polo were only the beginning of a very considerable intercourse. That intercourse was to bring many

The Ottoman Turks and Constantinople. revolutionary ideas and many revolutionary things to Europe, including a greatly extended use of paper and printing from blocks, the almost equally revolutionary use of gunpowder in warfare, and the mariner's compass which was to release the European shipping from navigation by coasting. The popular imagination has always been disposed to ascribe every such striking result to Marco Polo. He has become the type and symbol for all such interchanges. As a matter of fact, there is no evidence that he had any share in these three importations. There were many mute Marco Polos who never met their Rusticianos, and history has not preserved their names. Before we go on, however, to describe the great widening of the mental horizons of Europe that was now beginning, and to which this book of travels was to contribute very materially, it will be convenient first to note a curious side consequence of the great Mongol conquests, the appearance of the Ottoman Turks upon the Dardanelles, and next to state in general terms the breaking up and development of the several parts of the empire of Jengis Khan.

The Ottoman Turks were a little band of fugitives who fled south-westerly before the first invasion of Western Turkestan by Jengis. They made their long way from Central Asia, over deserts and mountains and through alien populations, seeking some new lands in which they might settle. " A small band of alien herdsmen," says Sir Mark Sykes, " wandering unchecked through crusades and countercrusades, principalities, empires, and states. Where they camped, how they moved and preserved their flocks and herds, where they found pasture, how they made their peace with the various chiefs through whose territories they passed, are questions which one may well ask in wonder."

They found a resting-place at last and kindred and congenial neighbours on the table-lands of Asia Minor among the Seljuk Turks. Most of this country, the modern Anatolia, was now largely Turkish in speech and Moslem in religion, except that there was a considerable proportion of Greeks, Jews, and Armenians in the town populations. No doubt the various strains of Hittite, Phrygian, Trojan, Lydian, Ionian Greek, Cimmerian, Galatian, and Italian (from the Pergamus times) still flowed in the blood of the people, but they had long since forgotten these ancestral elements. They were

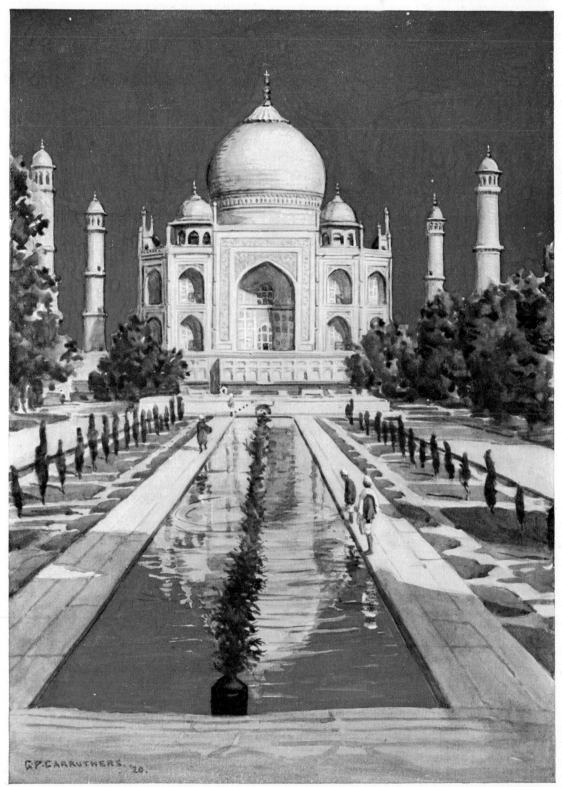

THE TAJ MAHAL, AGRA.

The Taj, the last resting-place of Shah Jehan and his beloved wife, is acknowledged to be the most perfect building in the world. It is constructed of white marble, and is said to have taken 20,000 men, employed incessantly, seventeen years to build.

indeed much the same blend of ancient Mediterranean dark-whites, Nordic Aryans, Semites and Mongolians as were the inhabitants of the Balkan peninsula, but they believed themselves to be a pure Turanian race, and altogether superior to the Christians on the other side of the Bosphorus.

Gradually the Ottoman Turks became important, and at last dominant among the small principalities into which the Seljuk empire, the empire of " Roum," had fallen. Their relations with the dwindling empire of Constantinople remained for some centuries tolerantly hostile. They made no attack upon the Bosphorus, but they got a footing in Europe at the Dardanelles, and, using this route, the route of Xerxes and not the route of Darius, they pushed their way steadily into Macedonia, Epirus, Illyria, Yugo-Slavia, and Bulgaria. In the Serbs (Yugo-Slavs) and Bulgarians the Turks found people very like themselves in culture and, though neither side recognized it, probably very similar in racial admixture, with a little less of the dark Mediterranean and Mongolian strains than the Turks and a trifle more of the Nordic element. But these Balkan peoples were Christians, and bitterly divided among themselves. The Turks on the other hand spoke one language; they had a greater sense of unity, they had the Moslem habits of temperance and frugality, and they were on the whole better soldiers. They converted what they could of the conquered people to Islam; the Christians they disarmed, and conferred upon them the monopoly of tax-paying. Gradually the Ottoman princes consolidated an empire that reached from the Taurus mountains in the east to Hungary and Roumania in the west. Adrianople became their chief city. They surrounded the shrunken empire of Constantinople on every side.

The Ottomans organized a standing military force, the Janissaries, rather on the lines of the Mamelukes who dominated Egypt. " These troops were formed of levies of Christian youths to the extent of one thousand per annum, who were affiliated to the Bektashi order of dervishes, and though at first not obliged to embrace Islam, were one and all strongly imbued with the mystic and fraternal ideas of the confraternity to which they were attached. Highly paid, well disciplined, a close and jealous secret society, the Janissaries provided the newly formed Ottoman state with a patriotic force of trained infantry soldiers, which, in an age of light cavalry and hired companies of mercenaries, was an invaluable asset. . . .[1]

" The relations between the Ottoman Sultans and the Emperors has been singular in the

The OTTOMAN EMPIRE before 1453.

annals of Moslem and Christian states. The Turks had been involved in the family and dynastic quarrels of the Imperial City, were bound by ties of blood to the ruling families, frequently supplied troops for the defence of Constantinople, and on occasion hired parts of its garrison to assist them in their various campaigns; the sons of the Emperors and Byzantine statesmen even accompanied the Turkish forces in the field, yet the Ottomans never ceased to annex Imperial territories and cities both in Asia and Thrace. This curious intercourse between the House of Osman and the Imperial government had a profound effect on both institutions; the Greeks grew more

[1] Sir Mark Sykes, *The Caliphs' Last Heritage.*

31

and more debased and demoralized by the shifts and tricks that their military weakness obliged them to adopt towards their neighbours, the Turks were corrupted by the alien atmosphere of intrigue and treachery which crept into their domestic life. Fratricide and parricide, the two crimes which most frequently stained the annals of the Imperial Palace, eventually formed a part of the policy of the Ottoman dynasty. One of the sons of Murad I embarked on an intrigue with Andronicus, the son of the Greek Emperor, to murder their respective fathers. . . .

" The Byzantine found it more easy to negotiate with the Ottoman Pasha than with the Pope. For years the Turks and Byzantines had intermarried, and hunted in couples in strange by-paths of diplomacy. The Ottoman had played the Bulgar and the Serb of Europe against the Emperor, just as the Emperor had played the Asiatic Amir against the Sultan ; the Greek and Turkish Royal Princes had mutually agreed to hold each other's rivals as prisoners and hostages ; in fact, Turk and

Byzantine policy had so intertwined that it is difficult to say whether the Turks regarded the Greeks as their allies, enemies, or subjects, or whether the Greeks looked upon the Turks as their tyrants, destroyers, or protectors. . . ." [1]

It was in 1453, under the Ottoman Sultan, Muhammad II, that Constantinople at last fell to the Moslems. He attacked it from the European side, and with a great power of artillery. The Greek Emperor was killed, and there was much looting and massacre. The great church of Saint Sophia which Justinian the Great had built (532) was plundered of its treasures and turned at once into a mosque. This event sent a wave of excitement throughout Europe, and an attempt was made to organize a crusade, but the days of the crusades were past.

Says Sir Mark Sykes : " To the Turks the capture of Constantinople was a crowning mercy and yet a fatal blow. Constantinople had been the tutor and polisher of the Turks. So long as the Ottomans could draw science, learning, philosophy, art, and tolerance from

[1] Sir Mark Sykes, *The Caliphs' Last Heritage.*

a living fountain of civilization in the heart of their dominions, so long had the Ottomans not only brute force, but intellectual power. So long as the Ottoman Empire had in Constantinople a free port, a market, a centre of world finance, a pool of gold, an exchange, so long did the Ottomans never lack for money and financial support. Muhammad was a great statesman, the moment he entered Constantinople he endeavoured to stay the damage his ambition had done ; he supported the patriarch, he conciliated the Greeks, he did all he could to continue Constantinople the city of the Emperors . . . but the fatal step had been taken, Constantinople as the city of the Sultans was Constantinople no more ; the markets died away, the culture and civilization fled, the complex finance faded from sight ; and the Turks had lost their governors and their support. On the other hand, the corruptions of Byzantium remained, the bureaucracy, the eunuchs, the palace guards, the spies, the bribers, go-betweens—all these the Ottomans took over, and all these survived in luxuriant life. The Turks, in taking Stambul, let slip a treasure and gained a pestilence. . . ."

Muhammad's ambition was not sated by the capture of Constantinople. He set his eyes also upon Rome. He captured and looted the Italian town of Otranto, and it is probable that a very vigorous and perhaps successful attempt to conquer Italy—for the peninsula

Photo : H. J. Shepstone.
INTERIOR OF THE MOSQUE OF ST. SOPHIA, SHOWING THE ARABIC INSCRIPTIONS THAT COVER ITS ORIGINAL MOSAIC.
Note the Nubràle (place of prayer) which faces Mecca.

was divided against itself—was averted only by his death (1481). His sons engaged in fratricidal strife. Under Bayezid II (1481—1512), his successor, war was carried into Poland, and most of Greece was conquered. Selim (1512—1520), the son of Bayezid, extended the Ottoman power over Armenia and conquered Egypt. In Egypt, the last Abbasid Caliph was living under the protection of the Mameluke Sultan—for the Fatimite caliphate was a thing of the past. Selim bought the title of Caliph from this last degenerate Abbasid, and acquired the sacred banner and other relics of the Prophet. So the Ottoman Sultan became also Caliph of all Islam. Selim was followed by Suleiman the Magnificent (1520—1566), who conquered Bagdad in the east and the greater part of Hungary in the west, and very nearly captured Vienna. His fleets also took Algiers, and inflicted a number of reverses upon the Venetians. In most of his warfare with the empire he was in alliance with the French. Under him the Ottoman power reached its zenith.

§ 5

Let us now very briefly run over the subsequent development of the main masses of the empire of the Great Khan. In no case did Christianity succeed in capturing the imagination of these Mongol states. Christianity was

Why the Mongols were not Christianized.

in a phase of moral and intellectual insolvency, without any collective faith, energy, or honour; we have told of the wretched brace of timid Dominicans which was the Pope's reply to the appeal of Kublai Khan, and we have noted the general failure of the overland missions of the thirteenth and fourteenth centuries. That apostolic passion that could win whole nations to the Kingdom of Heaven was dead in the church.

In 1305, as we have told, the Pope became the kept pontiff of the French king. All the craft and policy of the Popes of the thirteenth century to oust the Emperor from Italy had only served to let in the French to replace him. From 1305 to 1377 the Popes remained at Avignon; and such slight missionary effort as they made was merely a part of the strategy of Western European politics.[1] In 1377 the Pope Gregory XI did indeed re-enter Rome and die there, but the French cardinals split off from the others at the election of his successor, and two Popes were elected, one at Avignon and one at Rome. This split, the Great Schism, lasted from 1378 to 1418. Each Pope cursed the other, and put all his supporters under an interdict. Such was the state of Christianity, and such were now the custodians of the teachings of Jesus of Nazareth. All Asia was white unto harvest, but there was no effort to reap it.

When at last the church was reunited and missionary energy returned with the foundation of the order of the Jesuits, the days of opportunity were over. The possibility of a worldwide moral unification of East and West through Christianity had passed away. The Mongols in China and Central Asia turned to Buddhism; in South Russia, Western Turkestan, and the Ilkhan Empire they embraced Islam.

§ 5A

In China the Mongols were already saturated with Chinese civilization by the time of Kublai. **Kublai Khan founds the Yuan Dynasty.** After 1280 the Chinese annals treat Kublai as a Chinese monarch, the founder of the Yuan dynasty (1280 —1368). This Mongol dynasty was finally overthrown by a Chinese nationalist movement which set up the Ming dynasty

[1] But see Pastor, *History of the Popes*, Vol. I.

(1368—1644), a cultivated and artistic line of emperors, ruling until a northern people, the Manchus, who were the same as the Kin whom Jengis had overthrown, conquered China and established a dynasty which gave way only to a native republican form of government in 1912.

It was the Manchus who obliged the Chinese to wear pig-tails as a mark of submission. The pigtailed Chinaman is quite a recent, and now a vanished figure in history.

§ 5B

In the Pamirs, in much of Eastern and Western Turkestan, and to the north, the **The Mongols revert to Tribalism.** Mongols dropped back towards the tribal conditions from which they had been lifted by Jengis. It is possible to trace the dwindling succession of many of the small Khans who became independent during this period, almost down to the present time. The Kalmuks in the seventeenth and eighteenth centuries founded a considerable empire, but dynastic troubles broke it up before it had extended its power beyond Central Asia. The Chinese recovered Eastern Turkestan from them about 1757.

Tibet became more and more closely linked with China, and became the great home of Buddhism and Buddhist monasticism.

Over most of the area of Western Central Asia and Persia and Mesopotamia, the ancient distinction of nomad and settled population remains to this day. The townsmen despise and cheat the nomads, the nomads ill-treat and despise the townsfolk.

§ 5C

The Mongols of the great realm of Kipchak remained nomadic, and grazed their stock **The Kipchak Empire and the Tsar of Muscovy.** across the wide plains of South Russia and Western Asia adjacent to Russia. They became not very devout Moslems, retaining many traces of their earlier barbaric Shamanism. Their chief Khan was the Khan of the Golden Horde. To the west, over large tracts of open country, and more particularly in what is now known as Ukrainia, the old Scythian population, Slavs with a Mongol admixture, reverted to a similar nomadic life. These Christian nomads, the Cossacks, formed a sort of frontier screen against the Tartars, and their free and adventurous life was so attractive to the peasants of Poland and Lithuania that severe laws had to be passed to prevent a vast migration from the ploughlands to the steppes. The serf-owning landlords of Poland regarded the Cossacks with considerable hostility on this account, and war was as frequent between the Polish chivalry and the Cossacks as it was between the latter and the Tartars.[1]

In the empire of Kipchak, as in Turkestan almost up to the present time, while the nomads roamed over wide areas, a number of towns and cultivated regions sustained a settled population which usually paid tribute to the nomad Khan. In such towns as Kieff, Moscow, and the like, the pre-Mongol, Christian town life went on under Russian dukes or Tartar governors, who collected the tribute for the Khan of the Golden Horde. The Grand Duke of Moscow gained the confidence of the Khan, and gradually, under his authority, obtained an ascendancy over many of his fellow tributaries. In the fifteenth century, under Ivan III, Ivan the Great (1462—1505), Moscow threw off its Mongol allegiance and refused to pay tribute any longer. Ivan assumed the title of Tsar (Cæsar again!) as the equivalent of Great Khan, and took possession of the Byzantine double-headed eagle for his arms. He claimed to be the heir to Byzantium because of his marriage (1472) with Zoe Palæologus of the imperial line. This Tsardom of Moscow assailed and subjugated the ancient Northman trading republic of Novgorod to the north, and so the foundations of the modern Russian Empire were laid and a link with the mercantile life of the Baltic established. Although the ruler of Moscow called himself Tsar, his tradition was in many respects Tartar rather than European; he was autocratic after the unlimited Asiatic pattern, and the form of Christianity he affected was the Eastern, court-ruled, "orthodox" form, which had reached Russia long before the Mongol conquest, by means of Bulgarian missionaries from Constantinople.

[1] See Beazley, Forbes and Birkett's *Russia* for a fuller account of the Cossacks, and also see later chap. xxxvi, § 10.

To the west of the domains of Kipchak, outside the range of Mongol rule, a second centre of Slav consolidation had been set up during the tenth and eleventh centuries in Poland. The Mongol wave had washed over Poland, but had never subjugated it. Poland was not "orthodox," but Roman Catholic in religion; it used the Latin alphabet instead of the strange Russian letters, and its monarch never assumed an absolute independence of the Emperor. Poland was in fact in its origins an outlying part of Christendom and of the Holy Roman Empire; Russia never was anything of the sort.

§ 5D

The nature and development of the empire of the Ilkhans in Persia, Mesopotamia, and Syria is perhaps the most interesting of all the stories of these Mongol powers, *Timurlane.* because in this region nomadism really did attempt, and really did to a very considerable degree succeed in its attempt to stamp a settled civilized system out of existence. When Jengis Khan first invaded China, we are told that there was a serious discussion among the Mongol chiefs whether all the towns and settled populations should not be destroyed. To these simple practitioners of the open-air life the settled populations seemed corrupt, crowded, vicious, effeminate, dangerous, and incomprehensible; a detestable human efflorescence upon what would otherwise have been good pasture. They had no use whatever for the towns. The early Franks and the Anglo-Saxon conquerors of South Britain had much the same feeling towards townsmen. But it was only under Hulagu in Mesopotamia that these ideas seem to have been embodied in a deliberate policy. The Mongols here did not only burn and massacre; they destroyed the irrigation system that had endured for at least eight thousand years, and with that the mother civilization of all the Western world came to an end. Since the days of the priest-kings of Sumeria there had been a continuous cultivation in these fertile regions, an accumulation of tradition, a great population, a succession of busy cities, Eridu, Nippur, Babylon, Nineveh, Ctesiphon, Bagdad. Now the fertility ceased. Mesopotamia became a land of ruins and desolation, through which great waters ran to waste, or overflowed their banks to make malarious swamps. Later on Mosul and Bagdad revived feebly as second-rate towns. . . .

But for the defeat and death of Hulagu's general Kitboga in Palestine (1260), the same fate might have overtaken Egypt. But Egypt was now a Turkish sultanate; it was dominated by a body of soldiers, the Mamelukes, whose ranks, like those of their imitators, the Janissaries of the Ottoman Empire, were recruited and kept vigorous by the purchase and training of boy slaves. A capable Sultan such men

savage school, and he created an empire of desolation from North India to Syria. Pyramids of skulls were his particular architectural fancy; after the storming of Ispahan he made one of 70,000. His ambition was to restore the empire of Jengis Khan as he conceived it, a project in which he completely failed. He spread destruction far and wide; the Ottoman Turks—it was before the taking of Constantinople and their days of greatness—and Egypt paid him tribute; the Punjab he devastated; and Delhi surrendered to him. After Delhi had surrendered, however, he made a frightful massacre of its inhabitants. At

The EMPIRE of TIMURLANE

would obey; a weak or evil one they would replace. Under this ascendancy Egypt remained an independent power until 1517, when it fell to the Ottoman Turks.

The first destructive vigour of Hulagu's Mongols soon subsided, but in the fifteenth century a last tornado of nomadism arose in Western Turkestan under the leadership of a certain Timur the Lame, or Timurlane. He was descended in the female line from Jengis Khan. He established himself in Samarkand, and spread his authority over Kipchak (Turkestan to South Russia), Siberia, and southward as far as the Indus. He assumed the title of Great Khan in 1369. He was a nomad of the

the time of his death (1405) very little remained to witness to his power but a name of horror, ruins and desolated countries, and a shrunken and impoverished domain in Persia.

The dynasty founded by Timur in Persia was extinguished by another Turkoman horde fifty years later.

§ 5E [1]

In 1505 a small Turkoman chieftain, Baber, **The Mongol** a descendant of Timur and there- **Empire of** fore of Jengis, was forced after some **India.** years of warfare and some temporary successes—for a time he held Samarkand—

[1] See Malleson's *Akbar*, in the *Rulers of India* series.

to fly with a few followers over the Hindu Kush to Afghanistan. There his band increased, and he made himself master of Cabul. He assembled an army, accumulated guns, and then laid claim to the Punjab, because Timur had conquered it a hundred and seven years before. He pushed his successes beyond the Punjab. India was in a state of division, and quite ready to welcome any capable invader who promised peace and order. After various fluctuations of fortune Baber met the Sultan of Delhi at Panipat (1525), ten miles north of that town, and though he had but 25,000 men, provided, however, with guns, against a thousand elephants and four times as many men—the numbers, by the by, are his own estimate—he gained a complete victory. He ceased to call himself King of Cabul, and assumed the title of Emperor of Hindustan. "This," he wrote, "is quite a different world from our countries." It was finer, more fertile, altogether richer. He conquered as far as Bengal, but his untimely death in 1530 checked the tide of Mongol conquest for a quarter of a century, and it was only after the accession of his grandson Akbar that it flowed again. Akbar subjugated all India as far as Berar, and his great-grandson Aurungzeb (1658—1707) was practically master of the entire peninsula. This great dynasty of Baber (1526—1530), Humayun (1530—1556), Akbar (1556—1605), Jehangir (1605—1628), Shah Jehan (1628—1658), and Aurungzeb (1658—1707), in which son succeeded father for six generations, this "Mogul (= Mongol) dynasty,"[1] marks the most splendid age that had hitherto dawned upon India. Akbar, next perhaps to Asoka, was one of the greatest of Indian monarchs, and one of the few royal figures that approach the stature of great men.

To Akbar it is necessary to give the same distinctive attention that we have shown to Charlemagne or Constantine the Great. He is one of the hinges of history. Much of his work of consolidation and organization in India survives to this day. It was taken over and continued by the British when they became the

[1] "Mogul" is our crude rendering of the Arabic spelling Mughal, which itself was a corruption of Mongol, the Arabic alphabet having no symbol for ng.—H. H. J.

successors of the Mogul emperors. The British monarch, indeed, now uses as his Indian title the title of the Mogul emperors, *Kaisar-i-Hind*. All the other great administrations of the descendants of Jengis Khan, in Russia, throughout Western and Central Asia and in China, have long since dissolved away and given place to other forms of government. Their governments were indeed little more than taxing governments; a system of revenue-collecting to feed the central establishment of the ruler, like the Golden Horde in South Russia or the imperial city at Karakorum or Pekin. The life and ideas of the people they left alone,

Photo: *Underwood & Underwood.*
TOMB OF AKBAR, SIKANDARAH, INDIA.

careless how they lived—so long as they paid. So it was that after centuries of subjugation, a Christian Moscow and Kieff, a Shiite Persia, and a thoroughly Chinese China rose again from their Mongol submergence. But Akbar made a new India. He gave the princes and ruling classes of India some inklings at least of a common interest. If India is now anything more than a sort of rag-bag of incoherent states and races, a prey to every casual raider from the north, it is very largely due to him.

His distinctive quality was his openness of mind. He set himself to make every sort of able man in India, whatever his race or religion, available for the public work of Indian life. His instinct was the true stateman's instinct for synthesis. His empire was to be neither a Moslem nor a Mongol one, nor was it to be Rajput or Aryan, or Dravidian, or Hindu, or high or low caste ; it was to be *Indian*. "During the years of his training he enjoyed many opportunities of noting the good qualities, the fidelity, the devotion, often the nobility of soul, of those Hindu princes, whom, because they were followers of Brahma, his Moslem courtiers devoted mentally to eternal torments. He noted that these men, and men who thought like them, constituted the vast majority of his subjects. He noted, further, of many of them, and those the most trustworthy, that though they had apparently much to gain from a worldly point of view by embracing the religion of the court, they held fast to their own. His reflective mind, therefore, was unwilling from the outset to accept the theory that because he, the conqueror, the ruler, happened to be born a Muhammadan, therefore Muhammadanism was true for all mankind. Gradually his thoughts found words in the utterance : 'Why should I claim to guide men before I myself am guided'? and, as he listened to other doctrines and other creeds, his honest doubts became confirmed, and, noting daily the bitter narrowness of sectarianism, no matter of what form of religion, he became more and more wedded to the principle of toleration for all."

"The son of a fugitive emperor," says Dr. Emil Schmit, "born in the desert, brought up in nominal confinement, he had known the bitter side of life from his youth up. Fortune had given him a powerful frame, which he trained to support the extremities of exertion. Physical exercise was with him a passion ; he was devoted to the chase, and especially to the fierce excitement of catching the wild horse or elephant or slaying the dangerous tiger. On one occasion, when it was necessary to dissuade the Raja of Jodhpore to abandon his intention of forcing the widow of his deceased son to mount the funeral pyre, Akbar rode two hundred and twenty miles in two days. In battle he displayed the utmost bravery. He led his troops in person during the dangerous part of a campaign, leaving to his generals the lighter task of finishing the war. In every victory he displayed humanity to the conquered, and decisively opposed any exhibition of cruelty. Free from all those prejudices which separate society and create dissension, tolerant to men of other beliefs, impartial to men of other races, whether Hindu or Dravidian, he was a man obviously marked out to weld the conflicting elements of his kingdom into a strong and prosperous whole.

"In all seriousness he devoted himself to the work of peace. Moderate in all pleasures, needing but little sleep and accustomed to divide his time with the utmost accuracy, he found leisure to devote himself to science and art after the completion of his State duties. The famous personages and scholars who adorned the capital he had built for himself at Fatepur-Sikri were at the same time his friends ; every Thursday evening a circle of these was collected for intellectual conversation and philosophical discussion. His closest friends were two highly talented brothers, Faizi and Abul Fazl, the sons of a learned free-thinker. The elder of these was a famous scholar in Hindu literature ; with his help, and under his direction, Akbar had the most important of the Sanskrit works translated into Persian. Fazl, on the other hand, who was an especially close friend of Akbar, was a general, a statesman, and an organizer, and to his activity Akbar's kingdom chiefly owed the solidarity of its internal organization." [1]

(Such was the quality of the circle that used to meet in the palaces of Fatehpur-Sikri, buildings which still stand in the Indian sunlight—but empty now and desolate. Fatehpur-Sikri, like the city of Ambar, is now a dead city. A few years ago the child of a British official was killed by a panther in one of its silent streets.)

All this that we have quoted reveals a pre-eminent monarch. But Akbar, like all men, great or petty, lived within the limitations of his period and its circle of ideas. And a Turkoman, ruling in India, was necessarily ignorant of much that Europe had been painfully learning for a thousand years. He knew nothing of the growth of a popular consciousness in Europe, and little or nothing of the wide

[1] Dr. Schmit in Helmolt's *History of the World*.

enough under the circumstances the nomadic peoples were always supplying the civilizations with fresh rulers and new aristocracies. That is the rhythm of all early history. It was only after thousands of years of cyclic changes between refreshment by nomadic conquest, civilization, decadence, and fresh conquest that the present process of a mutual blending of " civilized " and " free " tendencies into a new type of community, that now demands our attention and which is the substance of contemporary history, began.

We have traced in this history the slow development of larger and larger " civilized " human communities from the days of such a Palæolithic family tribe as that described in Chapter IX. We have seen how the advantages and necessities of cultivation, the fear of tribal gods, the ideas of the priest-king and the god-king, played their part in consolidating continually larger and more powerful societies in regions of maximum fertility. We have watched the interplay of priest, who was usually native, and monarch, who was usually a conqueror, in these early civilizations, the development of a written tradition and its escape from priestly control, and the appearance of novel forces, at first apparently incidental and secondary, which we have called the free intelligence and the free conscience of mankind. We have seen the rulers of the primitive civilizations of the river valleys widening their area and extending their sway, and simultaneously over the less fertile areas of the earth we have seen mere tribal savagery develop into a more and more united and politically competent nomadism. Steadily and divergently mankind pursued one or other of these two lines. For long ages all the civilizations grew and developed along monarchist lines, upon lines of absolute monarchy, and in every monarchy and dynasty we have watched, as if it were a necessary process, efficiency and energy give way to pomp, indolence, and decay, and finally succumb to some fresher lineage from the desert or the steppe. The story of the early cultivating civilizations and their temples and courts and cities bulks large in human history, but it is well to remember that the scene of that story was never more than a very small part of the land surface of the globe. Over the greater

part of the earth until quite recently, until the last two thousand years, the hardier, less numerous tribal peoples of forest and parkland and the nomadic peoples of the seasonal grasslands maintained and developed their own ways of life.

The primitive civilizations were, we may say, " communities of obedience " ; obedience to god-kings or kings under gods was their cement ; the nomadic tendency on the other hand has always been towards a different type of association which we shall here call a " community of will." In a wandering, fighting community the individual must be at once self-reliant and disciplined. The chiefs of such communities must be chiefs who are followed, not masters who compel. This community of will is traceable throughout the entire history of mankind ; everywhere we find the original disposition of all the nomads alike, Nordic, Semitic, or Mongolian, was individually more *willing* and more *erect* than that of the settled folk. The Nordic peoples came into Italy and Greece under leader kings ; they did not bring any systematic temple cults with them, they found such things in the conquered lands and adapted as they adopted them. The Greeks and Latins lapsed very easily again into republics, and so did the Aryans in India. There was a tradition of election also in the early Frankish and German kingdoms.[1] The early Caliphs were elected, the Judges of Israel and the " kings " of Carthage and Tyre were elected, and so was the Great Khan of the Mongols until Kublai became a Chinese monarch. . . . Equally constant in the settled lands do we find the opposite idea, the idea of a non-elective divinity in kings and of their natural and inherent right to rule. . . . As our history has developed we have noted the appearance of new and complicating elements in the story of human societies ; we have seen that nomad turned go-between,

[1] The early Frankish and other German kings were not elective. They were hereditary ; but as there was no primogeniture, there was either partition among the sons, or a struggle to decide which son or relative should succeed. In such a struggle the nobles might take part, and this might mean some form of election. But heredity is the thing: *reges ex nobilitate sumunt,* says Tacitus: the king must have the nobility of being Woden-born, or he cannot be king. The genealogies of our early Saxon kings all go back to Woden, and George V is Woden-born.—E. B.

the trader, appear, and we have noted the growing importance of shipping in the world. It seems as inevitable that voyaging should make men free in their minds as that settlement within a narrow horizon should make men timid and servile. . . . But in spite of all such complications, the broad antagonism between the method of obedience and the method of will runs through history down into our own times. To this day their reconciliation is incomplete.

Civilization even in its most servile forms has always offered much that is enormously attractive, convenient, and congenial to mankind; but something restless and untamed in our race has striven continually to convert civilization from its original reliance upon unparticipating obedience into a community of participating wills. And to the lurking nomadism in our blood, and particularly in the blood of monarchs and aristocracies, we must ascribe also that incessant urgency towards a wider range that forces every state to extend its boundaries if it can, and to spread its interests to the ends of the earth. The power of nomadic restlessness that tends to bring all the earth under one rule, seems to be identical with the spirit that makes most of us chafe under direction and restraint, and seek to participate in whatever government we tolerate. And this natural, this temperamental struggle of mankind to reconcile civilization with freedom has been kept alive age after age by the military and political impotence of every " community of obedience " that has ever existed. Obedience, once men are broken to it, can be easily captured and transferred; witness the passive rôle of Egypt, Mesopotamia, and India, the original and typical lands of submission, the " cradles of civilization," as they have passed from one lordship to another. A servile civilization is a standing invitation to predatory free men. But on the other hand a " community of will " necessitates a fusion of intractable materials; it is a far harder community to bring about, and still more difficult to maintain. The story of Alexander the Great displays the community of will of the Macedonian captains gradually dissolving before his demand that they should worship him. The incident of the murder of Clitus is quite typical of the struggle between

the free and the servile tradition that went on whenever a new conqueror from the open lands and the open air found himself installed in the palace of an ancient monarchy.

In the case of the Roman Republic, history tells of the first big community of will in the world's history, the first free community much larger than a city, and how it weakened with growth and spent itself upon success until at last it gave way to a monarchy of the ancient type, and decayed swiftly into one of the feeblest communities of servitude that ever collapsed before a handful of invaders. We have given some attention in this book to the factors in that decay, because they are of primary importance in human history. One of the most evident was the want of any wide organization of education to base the ordinary citizens' minds upon the idea of service and obligation to the republic, to keep them *willing*, that is; another was the absence of any medium of general information to keep their activities in harmony, to enable them to *will* as one body. The community of will is limited in size by the limitations set upon the possibilities of a community of knowledge. The concentration of property in a few hands and the replacement of free workers by slaves were rendered possible by the decay of public spirit and the confusion of the public intelligence that resulted from these limitations. There was, moreover, no efficient religious idea behind the Roman state; the dark Etruscan liver-peering cult of Rome was as little adapted to the political needs of a great community as the very similar Shamanism of the Mongols. It is in the fact that both Christianity and Islam, in their distinctive ways, did at least promise to supply, for the first time in human experience, this patent gap in the Roman republican system as well as in the nomadic system, to give a common moral education for a mass of people, and to supply them with a common history of the past and a common idea of a human purpose and destiny, that their enormous historical importance lies. Aristotle, as we have noted, had set a limit to the ideal community of a few thousand citizens, because he could not conceive how a larger multitude could be held together by a common idea. He had had no experience of any sort of education beyond the tutorial methods of his time. Greek education was almost purely *viva-voce* education; it could reach therefore only to a limited aristocracy. Both the Christian church and Islam demonstrated the unsoundness of Aristotle's limitation. We may think they did their task of education in their vast fields of opportunity crudely or badly, but the point of interest to us is that they did it at all. Both sustained almost world-wide propagandas of idea and inspiration. Both relied successfully upon the power of the written word to link great multitudes of diverse men together in common enterprises. By the eleventh century, as we have seen, the idea of Christendom had been imposed upon all the vast warring miscellany of the smashed and pulverized Western empire, and upon Europe far beyonds its limits, as a uniting and inspiring idea. It had made a shallow but effective community of will over an unprecedented area and out of an unprecedented multitude of human beings. Only one other thing at all like this had ever happened to any great section of mankind before, and that was the idea of a community of good behaviour that the *literati* had spread throughout China.[1]

The Catholic Church provided what the Roman Republic had lacked, a system of popular teaching, a number of universities and methods of intellectual inter-communication. By this achievement it opened the way to the new possibilities of human government that now become apparent in this Outline, possibilities that are still being apprehended and worked out in the world in which we are living. Hitherto the government of states had been either authoritative, under some uncriticized and unchallenged combination of priest and monarch, or it had been a democracy, uneducated and uninformed, degenerating with any considerable increase of size, as Rome and Athens did, into a mere rule by mob and politician. But by the thirteenth century the first intimations had already dawned of an ideal of government which is still making its way to realization, the modern ideal, the ideal

of a world-wide *educational government*, in which the ordinary man is neither the slave of an absolute monarch nor of a demagogue-ruled state, but an informed, inspired, and consulted part of his community. It is upon the word educational that stress must be laid, and upon the idea that information must precede consultation. It is in the practical realization of this idea[2] that education is a collective function and not a private affair that one essential distinction of the " modern state " from any of its precursors lies. The modern citizen, men are coming to realize, must be informed first and then consulted.

Photo: Mansell.

CLOTH HALL, YPRES, WHICH PRIOR TO THE GREAT WAR WAS ONE OF THE FINEST MONUMENTS OF GOTHIC ART IN FLANDERS.

Before he can vote he must hear the evidence; before he can decide he must know. It is not by setting up polling booths, but by setting up schools and making literature and knowledge and news universally accessible that the way is opened from servitude and confusion to that willingly co-operative state which is the modern ideal. Votes in themselves are worthless things. Men had votes in Italy in the time of the Gracchi. Their votes did not help them. Until a man has education, a vote is a useless and dangerous thing for him to possess. The ideal community towards which we move is not a community of will simply; it is *a community of knowledge and will*, replacing *a community of faith and*

[1] But the Jews were already holding their community together by systematic education at least as early as the beginning of the Christian era.

[2] The Greeks had this idea.—E. B.

obedience. Education is the adapter which will make the nomadic spirit of freedom and self-reliance compatible with the co-operations and wealth and security of civilization.

§ 2

But though it is certain that the Catholic Church, through its propagandas, its popular appeals, its schools and universities, opened up the prospect of the modern educational state in Europe, it is equally certain that the Catholic Church never intended to do anything of the sort. It did not send out knowledge with its blessing ; it let it loose inadvertently. It was not the Roman Republic whose heir the Church esteemed itself, but the Roman Emperor. Its conception of education was not release, not an invitation to participate, but the subjugation of minds. Two of the greatest educators of the Middle Ages were indeed not churchmen at all, but monarchs and statesmen, Charlemagne and Alfred the Great of England, who made use of the church organization. But it was the church that had provided the organization. Church and monarchs in their mutual grapple for power were both calling to their aid the thoughts of the common man. In response to these conflicting appeals appeared the common man, the unofficial outside independent man, thinking for himself.

Europe begins to think for itself.

Already in the thirteenth century we have seen Pope Gregory IX and the Emperor Frederick II engaging in a violent public controversy. Already then there was a sense that a new arbitrator greater than pope or monarchy had come into the world, that there were readers and a public opinion. The exodus of the Popes to Avignon, and the divisions and disorders of the Papacy during the fourteenth century, stimulated this free judgment upon authority throughout Europe enormously.

At first the current criticism upon the church concerned only moral and material things. The wealth and luxury of the higher clergy and the heavy papal taxation were the chief grounds of complaint. And the earlier attempts to restore Christian simplicity, the foundation of the Franciscans for example, were not movements of separation, but movements of revival. Only later did a deeper and more distinctive criticism develop which attacked the central fact of the church's teaching and the justification of priestly importance, namely, the sacrifice of the mass.

We have sketched in broad outlines the early beginnings of Christianity, and we have shown how rapidly that difficult and austere conception of the Kingdom of God, which was the central idea of the teachings of Jesus of Nazareth, was overlaid by a revival of the ancient sacrificial idea, a doctrine more difficult indeed to grasp, but easier to reconcile with the habits and dispositions and acquiescences of everyday life in the Near East. We have noted how a sort of theocrasia went on between Christianity and Judaism and the cult of the Serapeum and Mithraism and other competing cults, by which the Mithraist Sunday, the Jewish idea of blood as a religious essential, the Alexandrian importance of the Mother of God, the shaven and fasting priest, self-tormenting asceticism, and many other matters of belief and ritual and practice, became grafted upon the developing religion. These adaptations, no doubt, made the new teaching much more understandable and acceptable in Egypt and Syria and the like. They were things in the way of thought of the dark-white Mediterranean race ; they were congenial to that type. But as we have shown in our story of Muhammad, these acquisitions did not make Christianity more acceptable to the Arab nomads ; to them these features made it disgusting. And so too, the robed and shaven monk and nun and priest seem to have roused something like an instinctive hostility in the Nordic barbarians of the North and West. We have noted the peculiar bias of the early Anglo-Saxons and Northmen against the monks and nuns. They seem to have felt that the lives and habits of these devotees were queer and unnatural.

The clash between what we may call the " dark-white " factors and the newer elements in Christianity was no doubt intensified by Pope Gregory VII's imposition of celibacy upon the Catholic priests in the eleventh century. The East had known religious celibates for thousands of years ; in the West they were

Photo: Mansell.

HÔTEL DE CLUNY, PARIS, ONE OF THE MOST INTERESTING EXAMPLES STILL EXISTING OF A
PRIVATE RESIDENCE OF THE FIFTEENTH CENTURY.

regarded with the profoundest scepticism and suspicion.[1]

And now in the thirteenth and fourteenth centuries, as the lay mind of the Nordic peoples began to acquire learning, to read and write and express itself, and as it came into touch with the stimulating activities of the Arab mind, we find a much more formidable criticism of Catholicism beginning, an intellectual attack upon the priest as priest, and upon the ceremony

of the mass as the central fact of the religious life, coupled with a demand for a return to the personal teachings of Jesus as recorded in the Gospels.

We have already mentioned the career of the Englishman Wycliffe (c. 1320—1384), and how he translated the Bible into English in order to set up a counter authority to that of the Pope. He denounced the doctrines of the church about the mass as disastrous error, and particularly the teaching that the consecrated bread eaten in that ceremony becomes in some magical way the actual body of Christ. We will not pursue the question of transubstantiation, as this process of the mystical change of the elements in the sacrament is called, into its intricacies. These are matters for the theological specialist. But it will be obvious that any doctrine, such as the Catholic doctrine, which makes the consecration of the elements in the sacrament a miraculous process performed by the priest, and only to

---

[1] I do not think this is just. The Anglo-Saxons were not anti-monastic. They were converted by Benedictine monks in 600 ; just after 700 they sent out monks to convert Germany ; about 960, under Dunstan and Edgar, they experienced a monastic revival. The Normans after 1066 introduced the Cluniac and Cistercian orders, and spread monasticism, while the earlier Northmen, after 900, were quite favourable to the Church in England.

Note that Gregory's imposition of celibacy on the clergy *was* accepted, and willingly accepted, by the contemporary lay world. William the Conqueror, through Archbishop Lanfranc, enforced celibacy in England.—E. B.

32

be performed by the priest, and which makes the sacrament the central necessity of the religious system, enhances the importance of the priestly order enormously. On the other hand, the view, which was the typical " Protestant " view, that this sacrament is a mere eating of bread and drinking of wine as a personal remembrance of Jesus of Nazareth, does away at last with any particular need for a consecrated priest at all. Wycliffe himself did not go to this extremity ; he was a priest, and he remained a priest to the end of his life, but his doctrine raised a question that carried men far beyond his positions. From the point of view of the historian, the struggle against Rome that Wycliffe opened became very speedily a struggle of what one may call rational or layman's religion making its appeal to the free intelligence and the free conscience in mankind, against authoritative, traditional, ceremonial, and priestly religion. The ultimate tendency of this complicated struggle was to strip Christianity as bare as Islam of every vestige of ancient priestcraft, to revert to the Bible documents as authority, and to recover, if possible, the primordial teachings of Jesus. Most of its issues are still undecided among Christians to this day.[1]

Wycliffe's writings had nowhere more influence than in Bohemia. About 1396 a learned Czech, John Huss, delivered a series of lectures in the university of Prague based upon the doctrines of the great Oxford teacher. Huss became rector of the university, and his teachings roused the church to excommunicate him (1412). This was at the time of the Great Schism, just before the Council of Constance (1414—1418) gathered to discuss the scandalous disorder of the church. We have already told (chap. xxxiii, § 13) how the schism was ended by the election of Martin V. The council aspired to reunite Christendom completely. But the methods by which it sought this reunion jar with our modern consciences. Wycliffe's bones were condemned to be burnt. Huss was decoyed to Constance under promise of a safe conduct, and he was then put upon his trial for heresy. He was ordered to recant certain of his opinions. He replied that he could not recant until he was convinced of his error. He was told that it was his duty to recant if his superiors required it of him, whether he was convinced or not. He refused to accept this view. In spite of the Emperor's safe conduct, he was burnt alive (1415), a martyr not for any specific doctrine, but for the free intelligence and free conscience of mankind.

It would be impossible to put the issue between priest and anti-priest more clearly than it was put at this trial of John Huss, nor to demonstrate more completely the evil spirit in priestcraft. A colleague of Huss, Jerome of Prague, was burnt in the following year.

These outrages were followed by an insurrection of the Hussites in Bohemia (1419), the first of a series of religious wars that marked the breaking-up of Christendom. In 1420 the Pope, Martin V, issued a bull proclaiming a crusade " for the destruction of the Wycliffites, Hussites, and all other heretics in Bohemia," and attracted by this invitation the unemployed soldiers of fortune and all the drifting blackguardism of Europe converged upon that valiant country. They found in Bohemia, under its great leader Ziska, more hardship and less loot than crusaders were disposed to face. The Hussites were conducting their affairs upon extreme democratic lines, and the whole country was aflame with enthusiasm. The crusaders beleaguered Prague, but failed to take it, and they experienced a series of reverses that ended in their retreat from Bohemia. A second crusade (1421) was no more successful. Two other crusades failed. Then unhappily the Hussites fell into internal dissensions. Encouraged by this, a fifth crusade (1431) crossed the frontier under Frederick, Margrave of Brandenburg.

The army of these crusaders, according to the lowest estimates, consisted of 90,000 infantry and 40,000 horsemen. Attacking Bohemia from the west, they first laid siege to the town of Tachov, but failing to capture the strongly fortified city, they stormed the little town of Most, and here, as well as in the surrounding country, committed the most horrible atrocities on a population a large part of which was

---

[1] Wycliffe believed in a real presence—but he held that it was spiritual and not substantial. The host was two things—bread, and at the same time a spiritual Christ. This is not the "memorial" view.—E. B.

entirely innocent of any form of theology whatever. The crusaders, advancing by slow marches, penetrated further into Bohemia, till they reached the neighbourhood of the town of Domazlice (Tauss). " It was at three o'clock on August 14th, 1431, that the crusaders, who were encamped in the plain between Domazlice and Horsuv Tyn, received the news that the Hussites, under the leadership of Prokop the Great, were approaching. Though the Bohemians were still four miles off, the rattle of their war-wagons and the song, ' All ye warriors of God,' which their whole host was chanting, could already be heard." The enthusiasm of the crusaders evaporated with astounding rapidity. Lutzow [1] describes how the papal representative and the Duke of Saxony ascended a convenient hill to inspect the battlefield. It was, they discovered, not going to be a battlefield. The German camp was in utter confusion. Horsemen were streaming off in every direction, and the clatter of empty wagons being driven off almost drowned the sound of that terrible singing. The crusaders were abandoning even their loot. Came a message from the Margrave of Brandenburg advising flight ; there was no holding any of their troops. They were dangerous now only to their own side, and the papal representative spent an unpleasant night hiding from them in the forest. . . . So ended the Bohemian crusade.

In 1434 civil war again broke out among the Hussites, in which the extreme and most valiant section was defeated, and in 1436 an agreement was patched up between the Council of Basle and the moderate Hussites, in which the Bohemian church was allowed to retain certain distinctions from the general Catholic practice, which held good until the German Reformation in the sixteenth century.

§ 3

The split among the Hussites was largely due to the drift of the extremer section towards a primitive communism, which alarmed the wealthier and more influential Czech noblemen. Similar tendencies had already appeared among the English Wycliffites. They seem to

The Great Plague and the Dawn of Communism.

[1] Lutzow's *Bohemia*.

follow naturally enough upon the doctrines of equal human brotherhood that emerge whenever there is an attempt to reach back to the fundamentals of Christianity.

The development of such ideas had been greatly stimulated by a stupendous misfortune that had swept the world and laid bare the foundations of society, a pestilence of unheard-of virulence. It was called the Black Death, and it came nearer to the extirpation of mankind than any other evil has ever done. It was far more deadly than the plague of Pericles, or the plague of Marcus Aurelius, or the plague waves of the time of Justinian and Gregory the Great that paved the way for the Lombards in Italy. It arose in China, where, the Chinese records say, thirteen million people perished. In China the social disorganization led to a neglect of the river embankments, and great floods devastated the crowded agricultural lands. It came through Central Asia, and by way of the Crimea and a Genoese ship to Genoa and Western Europe. It passed by Armenia to Asia Minor, Egypt, and North Africa. It reached England in 1348. Two-thirds of the students at Oxford died, we are told ; it is estimated that between a quarter and a half of the whole population of England perished at this time. Throughout all Europe there was as great a mortality. Hecker estimates the total as twenty-five million dead.

Never was there so clear a warning to mankind to seek knowledge and cease from bickering, to unite against the dark powers of nature. All the massacres of Hulagu and Timur were as nothing to this. " Its ravages," says J. R. Green, " were fiercest in the greater towns, where filthy and undrained streets afforded a constant haunt to leprosy and fever. In the burial-ground which the piety of Sir Walter Manny purchased for the citizens of London, a spot whose site was afterwards marked by the Charter House, more than fifty thousand corpses are said to have been interred. Thousands of people perished at Norwich, while in Bristol the living were hardly able to bury the dead. But the Black Death fell on the villages almost as fiercely as on the towns. More than one-half of the priests of Yorkshire are known to have perished ; in the diocese of Norwich two-thirds of the parishes changed their incumbents. The whole organization of labour was thrown out of gear. The scarcity of hands made it difficult for the minor tenants to perform the services due for their lands, and only a temporary abandonment of half the rent by the landowners induced the farmers to refrain from the abandonment of their farms. For a time cultivation became impossible. 'The sheep and cattle strayed through the fields and corn,' says a contemporary, 'and there were none left who could drive them.'"

It was from these distresses that the peasant wars of the fourteenth century sprang. There was a great shortage of labour and a great shortage of goods, and the rich abbots and monastic cultivators who owned so much of the land, and the nobles and rich merchants, were too ignorant of economic laws to understand that they must not press upon the toilers in this time of general distress. They saw their property deteriorating, their lands going out of cultivation, and they made violent statutes to compel men to work without any rise in wages, and to prevent their straying in search of better employment. Naturally enough this provoked "a new revolt against the whole system of social inequality which had till then passed unquestioned as the divine order of the world. The cry of the poor found a terrible utterance in the words of 'a mad priest of Kent,' as the courtly Froissart calls him, who for twenty years (1360—1381) found audience for his sermons, in defiance of interdict and im-

prisonment, in the stout yeomen who gathered in the Kentish churchyards. 'Mad,' as the landowners called him, it was in the preaching of John Ball that England first listened to a declaration of natural equality and the rights of man. 'Good people,' cried the preacher, 'things will never go well in England so long as goods be not in common, and so long as there be villeins and gentlemen. By what right are they whom we call lords greater folk than we? On what grounds have they deserved it? Why do they hold us in serfage? If we all came of the same father and mother, of Adam and Eve, how can they say or prove that they are better than we, if it be not that they make us gain for them by our toil what they spend in their pride? They are clothed in velvet and warm in their furs and their ermines, while we are covered with rags. They have wine and spices and fair bread; and we oat-cake and straw, and water to drink. They have leisure and fine houses; we have pain and labour, the rain and the wind in the fields. And yet it is of us and of our toil that these men hold their state.' A spirit fatal to the whole system of the Middle Ages breathed in the popular rhyme which condensed the levelling doctrine of John Ball: 'When Adam delved and Eve span, who was then the gentleman?'"[1]

[1] The seeds of conflict which grew up into the Peasants' Revolt of 1381 were sown upon ground which is strangely familiar to any writer in 1920. A European catastrophe had reduced production and consequently increased the earnings of workers and traders. Rural wages had risen by 48 per cent. in

SCENES OF PEASANT LIFE, FROM THE LOUTERELL PSALTER.

Wat Tyler, the leader of the English insurgents, was assassinated by the Mayor of London in the presence of the young King Richard II (1381), and his movement collapsed. The communist side of the Hussite movement was a part of the same system of disturbance. A little earlier than the English outbreak had occurred the French " Jacquerie " (1358), in which the French peasants had risen, burnt châteaux, and devastated the country-side. A century later the same urgency was to sweep Germany into a series of bloody Peasant Wars. These began late in the fifteenth century. Economic and religious disturbance mingled in the case of Germany even more plainly than in England. One conspicuous phase of these German troubles was the Anabaptist outbreak. The sect of the Anabaptists appeared in Wittenberg in 1521 under three " prophets," and broke out into insurrection in 1525. Between 1532 and 1535 the insurgents held the town of Münster in Westphalia, and did their utmost to realize their ideas of a religious communism. They were besieged by the Bishop of Münster, and under the distresses of the siege a sort of insanity ran rife in the town ; cannibalism is said to have occurred, and a certain John of Leyden seized power, proclaimed himself the successor of King David, and followed that monarch's evil example by practising polygamy. After the surrender of the city the victorious bishop had the Anabaptist leaders tortured very horribly and executed in the market-place, their mutilated bodies being hung in cages from a church tower to witness to all the world that decency and order were now restored in Münster. . . .

England, when an unwise executive endeavoured to enforce in the Ordinance and Statute of Labourers (1350–51) a return to the pre-plague wages and prices of 1346, and aimed a blow in the Statute of 1378 against labour combinations. The villeins were driven to desperation by the loss of their recent increase of comfort, and the outbreak came, as Froissart saw it from the angle of the Court, " all through the too great comfort of the commonalty." Other ingredients which entered into the outbreak were the resentment felt by the new working class at the restrictions imposed on its right to combine, the objection of the lower clergy to papal taxes, and a frank dislike of foreigners and landlords. There was no touch of Wycliffe's influence in the rising. It was at its feeblest in Leicestershire, and it murdered one of the only other liberal churchmen in England.—P. G.

These upheavals of the common labouring men of the Western European countries in the fourteenth and fifteenth centuries were more serious and sustained than anything that had ever happened in history before. The nearest previous approach to them were certain communistic Muhammadan movements in Persia. There was a peasant revolt in Normandy about A.D. 1000, and there were revolts of peasants (Bagaudæ) in the later Roman Empire, but these were not nearly so formidable. They show a new spirit growing in human affairs, a spirit altogether different from the unquestioning apathy of the serfs and peasants in the original regions of civilization or from the anarchist hopelessness of the serf and slave labour of the Roman capitalists. All these early insurrections of the workers that we have mentioned were suppressed with much cruelty, but the movement itself was never completely stamped out. From that time to this there has been a spirit of revolt in the lower levels of the pyramid of civilization. There have been phases of insurrection, phases of repression, phases of compromise and comparative pacification ; but from that time until this, the struggle has never wholly ceased. We shall see it flaring out during the French Revolution at the end of the eighteenth century, insurgent again in the middle and at the opening of the last quarter of the nineteenth century, and achieving vast proportions in the world of to-day. The socialist movement of the nineteenth century was only one version of that continuing revolt.

In many countries, in France and Germany and Russia, for example, this labour movement has assumed at times an attitude hostile to Christianity, but there can be little doubt that this steady and, on the whole, growing pressure of the common man in the West against a life of toil and subservience is closely associated with Christian teaching. The church and the Christian missionary may not have intended to spread equalitarian doctrines, but behind the church was the unquenchable personality of Jesus of Nazareth, and even in spite of himself the Christian preacher brought the seeds of freedom and responsibility with him, and sooner or later they shot up where he had been.

This steady and growing upheaval of "Labour," its development of a consciousness of itself as a class and of a definite claim upon the world at large, quite as much as the presence of schools and universities, quite as much as abundant printed books and a developing and expanding process of scientific research, mark off our present type of civilization, the "modern

There after ben conteyned & declared the x comandementes of the lawe which god wrote with his propre fyngre/& delyuerid them to Moyses the prophete for to preche to the peple for to holde & kepe capitulo

primo

For to haue & to come vnto the knowlech of the x comandementes of the lawe. the which euery creature resonable is holden to kepe for to haue lyf pardurable · is to wete that syth the creacõn of thumayn creature four lawes haue ben ¶ The first lawe is called the lawe of nature. Which is none other thynge but knowlege of good & euyl by the which we knowe that/ which we ouzt trñue we after reason.& also that which we ouzt to flee. that is to do to other that which we wold after rayson shold be doon to vs. & not to do to other that / whiche we wold after reason shold not be doon to vs.& this lawe gaf god to man & to woman in hys creacõn.& that same lawe euery creature resonable ought to kepe.& by ygnoraũce he shal not be excused/ syth they haue vnderstõdyng of reason¶ The ij lawe cometh of the coupl to as trope the lawe of nature aforsayd.& that is said lawe of conscuppscence whiche was put in the creature resonable by the

Photo: Rischgitz Collection.
A PAGE FROM THE "RYAL BOOK," BY CAXTON.

civilization," from any pre-existing state of human society, and mark it, for all its incidental successes, as a thing unfinished and transitory. It is an embryo or it is something doomed to die. It may be able to solve this complex problem of co-ordinated toil and happiness, and so adjust itself to the needs of the human soul, or it may fail and end in a catastrophe as the Roman system did. It may be the opening phase of some more balanced and satisfying

order of society, or it may be a system destined to disruption and replacement by some differently conceived method of human association. Like its predecessor, our present civilization may be no more than one of those crops farmers sow to improve their land by the fixation of nitrogen from the air ; it may have grown only that, accumulating certain traditions, it may be ploughed into the soil again for better things to follow. Such questions as these are the practical realities of history, and in all that follows we shall find them becoming clearer and more important, until in our last chapter we shall end, as all our days and years end, with a recapitulation of our hopes and fears—and a note of interrogation.

§ 4

The development of free discussion in Europe during this age of fermentation was enormously stimulated by the appearance of printed books. It was the introduction of paper from the East that made practicable the long latent method of printing. It is still difficult to assign the honour of priority in the use of the simple expedient of printing for multiplying books. It is a trivial question that has been preposterously debated.[1] Apparently the glory, such as it is, belongs to Holland. In Haarlem, one Coster was printing from movable type somewhen before 1446. Gutenberg was printing at Mainz about the same time. There were printers in Italy by 1465, and Caxton set up his press in Westminster in 1477. But long before this time there had been a partial use of printing. Manuscripts as early as the twelfth century display initial letters that may have been printed from wooden stamps.

How Paper liberated the Human Mind.

Far more important is the question of the manufacture of paper. It is scarcely too much to say that paper made the revival of Europe possible. Paper originated in China, where its use probably goes back to the second century B.C. In 751 the Chinese made an attack upon the Arab Moslems in Samarkand ; they were repulsed, and among the prisoners taken

[1] See article "Typography" in the *Encyclo. Brit.*

from them were some skilled paper-makers, from whom the art was learnt. Arabic paper manuscripts from the ninth century onward still exist. The manufacture entered Christendom either through Greece or by the capture of Moorish paper-mills during the Christian reconquest of Spain. But under the Christian Spanish the product deteriorated sadly. Good paper was not made in Christian Europe until near the end of the thirteenth century, and then it was Italy which led the world. Only by the fourteenth century did the manufacture reach Germany, and not until the end of that century was it abundant and cheap enough for the printing of books to be a practicable business proposition. Thereupon printing followed naturally and necessarily, and the intellectual life of the world entered upon a new and far more vigorous phase. It ceased to be a little trickle from mind to mind; it became a broad flood, in which thousands and presently scores and hundreds of thousands of minds participated.

One immediate result of this achievement of printing was the appearance of an abundance of Bibles in the world. Another was a cheapening of school-books. The knowledge of reading spread swiftly. There was not only a great increase of books in the world, but the books that were now made were plainer to read and so easier to understand. Instead of toiling at a crabbed text and then thinking over its significance, readers now could think unimpeded as they read. With this increase in the facility of reading, the reading public grew. The book ceased to be a highly decorated toy or a scholar's mystery. People began to write books to be read as well as looked at by ordinary people. With the fourteenth century the real history of the European literatures begins. We find a rapid development of standard Italian, standard English, standard French, standard Spanish, and standard German.[1] These languages became literary languages; they were tried over, polished by use, and made exact and vigorous. They became

[1] Standard Italian dates from Dante (1300); standard English from Chaucer and Wycliffe (1380); standard German from Luther (1520).—E. B.

at last as capable of the burden of philosophical discussion as Greek or Latin.

§ 5

Here we devote a section to certain elementary statements about the movement in men's religious ideas during the fifteenth and sixteenth centuries. They are a necessary introduction to the political history of the seventeenth and eighteenth centuries that follows in Chapter XXXVI.

Protestantism of the Princes and Protestantism of the Peoples.

PAGE FROM GUTENBERG'S ("MAZARIN") BIBLE, ONE OF THE EARLIEST LARGE BOOKS PRINTED FROM METAL TYPES.

We have to distinguish clearly between two entirely different systems of opposition to the Catholic church. They intermingled very confusingly. The church was losing its hold upon the consciences of princes and rich and able people; it was also losing the faith and confidence of common people. The effect of its decline of spiritual power upon the former class was to make them resent its interference, its moral restrictions, its claims to overlordship, its claims to tax, and to dissolve allegiances. They ceased to respect its power and its property. This insubordination of princes and rulers was going on throughout the Middle Ages, but it was only when in the sixteenth century the church began to side openly with its old antagonist the Emperor, when it offered him its support and accepted his help in its campaign against heresy, that princes began to think seriously of breaking away from the Roman communion and setting up fragments of a church. And they would never have done so if they had not perceived that the hold of the church upon the masses of mankind had relaxed.

The revolt of the princes was essentially an irreligious revolt against the world-rule of the church. The Emperor Frederick II, with his epistles to his fellow princes, was its forerunner. The revolt of the people against the church, on the other hand, was as essentially religious. They objected not to the church's power, but to its weaknesses. They wanted a deeply righteous and fearless church to help them and organize them against the wickedness of powerful men. Their movements against the church, within it and without, were movements not for release from a religious control, but for a fuller and more abundant religious control. They did not want less religious control, but more—but they wanted to be assured that it was religious. They objected to the Pope not because he was the religious head of the world, but because he was not; because he was a wealthy earthly prince when he ought to have been their spiritual leader.

The contest in Europe from the fourteenth century onward therefore was a three-cornered contest. The princes wanted to use the popular forces against the Pope, but not to let those forces grow too powerful for their own power and glory. For a long time the church went from prince to prince for an ally without realizing that the lost ally it needed to recover was popular veneration.

Because of this triple aspect of the mental and moral conflicts that were going on in the fourteenth and fifteenth and sixteenth centuries, the series of ensuing changes, those changes that are known collectively in history as the Reformation, took on a threefold aspect. There was the Reformation according to the princes, who wanted to stop the flow of money to Rome and to seize the moral authority, the educational power, and the material possessions of the church within their dominions. There was the Reformation according to the people, who sought to make Christianity a power against unrighteousness, and particularly against the unrighteousness of the rich and powerful. And finally there was the Reformation within the church, of which St. Francis of Assisi was the precursor, which sought to restore the goodness of the church and, through its goodness, to restore its power.

The Reformation according to the princes took the form of a replacement of the Pope by the prince as the head of the religion and the controller of the consciences of his people. The princes had no idea and no intention of letting free the judgments of their subjects, more particularly with the object-lessons of the Hussites and the Anabaptists before their eyes ; they sought to establish national churches dependent upon the throne. As England, Scotland, Sweden, Norway, Denmark, North Germany, and Bohemia broke away from the Roman communion, the princes and other ministers showed the utmost solicitude to keep the movement well under control. Just as much reformation as would sever the link with Rome they permitted ; anything beyond that, any dangerous break towards the primitive teachings of Jesus or the crude direct interpretation of the Bible, they resisted. The Established Church of England is one of the most typical and successful of the resulting compromises. It is still sacramental and sacerdotal ; but its organization centres in the Court and the Lord Chancellor, and though subversive views may, and do, break out in the lower and less prosperous ranks of its priesthood, it is impossible for them to struggle up to any position of influence and authority.

The Reformation according to the common man was very different in spirit from the Princely Reformation. We have already told something of the popular attempts at Reformation in Bohemia and Germany. The wide spiritual upheavals of the time were at once more honest, more confused, more enduring, and less immediately successful than the reforms of the princes. Very few religious-spirited men had the daring to break away or the effrontery to confess that they had broken away from all authoritative teaching, and that they were now relying entirely upon their own minds and consciences. That required a very high intellectual courage. The general drift of the common man in this period in Europe was to set up his new acquisition, the Bible, as a counter authority to the church. This was particularly the case with the great leader of German Protestantism, Martin Luther (1483—1546). All over Germany, and indeed all over Western Europe, there were now men spelling over the black-letter pages of the newly translated and printed Bible, over the Book of Leviticus and the Song of Solomon and the Revelation of St. John the Divine—strange and perplexing books—quite as much as over the simple and inspiring record of Jesus in the Gospels. Naturally they produced strange views and grotesque interpretations. It is surprising that they were not stranger and grotesquer. But the human reason is an obstinate thing, and will criticize and select in spite of its own resolutions. The bulk of these new Bible students took what their consciences approved from the Bible and ignored its riddles and contradictions. All over Europe, wherever the new Protestant churches of the princes were set up, a living and very active residuum of Protestants remained who declined to have their religion made over for them in this fashion. These were the Nonconformists, a medley of sects, having nothing in common but their resistance to authoritative religion, whether of the Pope or the State.[1] Most, but not all

Photo: Rischgitz Collection.

MARTIN LUTHER.

(After the portrait by Holbein.)

of these Nonconformists held to the Bible as a divinely inspired and authoritative guide. This was a strategic rather than an abiding position, and the modern drift of Nonconformity has been onward away from this original Bibliolatry towards a mitigated and sentimentalized recognition of the bare teachings of Jesus of Nazareth. Beyond the range of Nonconformity, beyond the range of professed Christianity at all, there is also now a great and growing mass of equalitarian belief and altruistic impulse in the modern civilizations, which certainly owes, as we have already asserted, its spirit to Christianity, which began to appear in Europe as the church lost its grip upon the general mind.[2]

Let us say a word now of the third phase of the Reformation process, the Reformation within the church. This was already beginning in the twelfth and thirteenth centuries with the appearance of the Black and Grey Friars (chap. xxxiii., § 13). In the sixteenth century, and when it was most needed, came a fresh impetus of the same

[1] But Nonconformity was stamped out in Germany. See § 11b of this chapter.

[2] " If I were writing a history of democracy," comments E. B., " I should deal first with democracy in religion, which is Calvinism, founded by a great Frenchman at Geneva, and then with democracy in politics, which is the French Revolution, inaugurated by another great Frenchman at Geneva, Rousseau. (The parallel of these two is striking—both typical exponents of the French genius, in its ardent logic and its apostolic fervour which gives in a burning lava to the world the findings of its logic.) It is noticeable in England how democracy in religion (Presbyterianism, which is simply Calvinism, plus Independency or Congregationalism) leads straight under the Stuarts to the English democratic ideas of the seventeenth century. I do not think the democratic element in Protestantism is sufficiently appreciated in the text. Even Luther, in the early days of 1520, could write *The Freedom of a Christian Man* and champion the priesthood of each believer and his direct access to his Maker. Luther, it is true, changed by 1525, and became a monarchist, the apostle of a state religion, under a godly prince who was *summus episcopus.*

kind. This was the foundation of the Society of the Jesuits by Inigo Lopez de Recalde, better known to the world of to-day as Saint Ignatius of Loyola.

Ignatius began his career as a very tough and gallant young Spaniard. He was clever and dexterous and in-spired by a passion for pluck, hardihood, and rather showy glory. His love affairs were free and picturesque. In 1521 the French took the town of Pampeluna in Spain from the Emperor Charles V, and Ignatius was one of the defenders. His legs were smashed by a cannon-ball, and he was taken prisoner. One leg was badly set and had to be broken again, and these painful and complex operations nearly cost him his life. He received the last sacraments. In the night, thereafter, he began to mend, and presently he was convalescent and facing the prospect of a life in which he would perhaps always be a cripple. His thoughts turned to the adventure of religion. Sometimes he would think of a

Photo: Rischgitz Collection.

LOYOLA.

certain great lady, and how, in spite of his broken state, he might yet win her admiration by some amazing deed; and sometimes he would think of being in some especial and personal way the Knight of Christ. In the midst of these confusions, one night as he lay awake, he tells us, a new great lady claimed his attention; he had a vision of the Blessed Virgin Mary carrying the Infant Christ in her arms. "Immediately a loathing seized him for the former deeds of his life." He resolved to give up all further thoughts of earthly women, and to lead a life of absolute chastity and devotion to the Mother of God. He projected great pilgrim-ages and a monastic life.

His final method of taking his vows marks him the countryman of Don Quixote. He had regained his strength, and he was riding out into the world rather aimlessly, a penniless soldier of fortune with little but his arms and the mule on which he rode, when he fell into company with a Moor. They went on to-gether and talked, and presently disputed about religion. The Moor was the better educated man; he had the best of the argument, he said offensive things about the Virgin Mary that were difficult to answer, and he parted triumphantly from Ignatius. The young Knight of our Lady was boiling with shame and indignation. He hesitated whether he should go after the Moor and kill him or pursue the pilgrimage he had in mind. At a fork in the road he left things to his mule, which spared the Moor. He came to the Benedictine Abbey of Manresa near Montserrat, and here he imitated that peerless hero of the mediæval romance, Amadis de Gaul, and kept an all-night vigil before the Altar of the Blessed Virgin. He presented his mule to the abbey, he gave his worldly clothes to a beggar, he laid his sword and dagger upon the altar, and

Anglicanism was from the first a monarchist religion, under a Henry VIII who was *supremum caput*. But if Lutheranism became, and Anglicanism was from the first, a religion of the State, Calvinism was always the religion of resistance to the State—in Holland and in Scotland most especially. The Reformation thus produced two opposite effects in politics; so far as it was Lutheran and Anglican, it was monarchist; so far as it was Calvinistic, it was democratic. It is at first sight curious, but it is really quite natural, that the Catholics of the counter-reformation should also have been democratic. The Catholics could not admit the control of the monarch in the sphere of religion any more than the Calvinist; and here, as in other things (*e.g.* in the claim to possession of infallible truth), the Catholic priest and the Calvinistic presbyter were agreed. Filmer, an exponent of Anglican monarchism, expresses this well when he says, in speaking of the doctrine of a social contract, that 'Cardinal Bellarmine and Calvin both look asquint this way.' For the doctrine of a social contract was the democratic doctrine put forward by Catholics and Calvinists in opposition to the Lutheran and Anglican doctrine of divine right."

clothed himself in a rough sackcloth garment and hempen shoes. He then took himself to a neighbouring hospice and gave himself up to scourgings and austerities. For a whole week he fasted absolutely. Thence he went on a pilgrimage to the Holy Land.

For some years he wandered, consumed with the idea of founding a new order of religious knighthood, but not knowing clearly how to set about this enterprise. He became more and more aware of his own illiteracy, and the Inquisition, which was beginning to take an interest in his proceedings, forbade him to attempt to teach others until he had spent at least four years in study. So much cruelty and intolerance is laid at the door of the Inquisition that it is pleasant to record that in its handling of this heady, imaginative young enthusiast it showed itself both sympathetic and sane. It recognized his vigour and possible uses ; it saw the dangers of his ignorance. He studied at Salamanca and Paris, among other places. He was ordained a priest in 1538, and a year later his long-dreamt-of order was founded under the military title of the " Company of Jesus." Like the Salvation Army of modern England, it made the most direct attempt to bring the generous tradition of military organization and discipline to the service of religion.

This Ignatius of Loyola who founded the order of Jesuits was a man of forty-seven ; he was a very different man, much wiser and steadier, than the rather absurd young man who had aped Amadis de Gaul and kept vigil in the abbey of Manresa ; and the missionary and educational organization he now created and placed at the disposal of the Pope was one of the most powerful instruments the church had ever handled. These men gave themselves freely and wholly to be used by the church. It was the Order of the Jesuits which carried Christianity to China again after the downfall of the Ming Dynasty, and Jesuits were the chief Christian missionaries in India and North America. To their civilizing work among the Indians in South America we shall prese tly allude. But their main achievement lay in raising the standard of Catholic education. Their schools became and remained for a long times the best schools in Christendom. Says Lord Verulam (= Sir Francis Bacon) : " As for the pedagogic part . . . consult the schools of the Jesuits, for nothing better has been put in practice." They raised the level of intelligence, they quickened the conscience of all Catholic Europe, they stimulated Protestant Europe to competitive educational efforts. . . . Some day it may be we shall see a new order of Jesuits, vowed not to the service of the Pope, but to the service of mankind.

And concurrently with this great wave of educational effort, the tone and quality of the church was also greatly improved by the clarification of doctrine and the reforms in organization and discipline that were made by the Council of Trent. This council met intermittently either at Trent or Bologna between the years 1545 and 1563, and its work was at least as important as the energy of the Jesuits in arresting the crimes and blunders that were causing state after state to fall away from the Roman communion. The change wrought by the Reformation within the Church of Rome was as great as the change wrought in the Protestant churches that detached themselves from the mother body. There are henceforth no more open scandals or schisms to record. But if anything, there has been an intensification of doctrinal narrowness, and such phases of imaginative vigour as are represented by Gregory the Great, or by the group of Popes associated with Gregory VII and Urban II, or by the group that began with Innocent III, no longer enliven the sober and pedestrian narrative. The world war of 1914—1918 was a unique opportunity for the Papacy ; the occasion was manifest for some clear strong voice proclaiming the universal obligation to righteousness, the brotherhood of men, the claims of human welfare over patriotic passion. No such moral lead was given. The Papacy seemed to be balancing its traditional reliance upon the faithful Habsburgs against its quarrel with republican France.

§ 6

The reader must not suppose that the de-
The structive criticism of the Catholic
Reawakening Church and of Catholic Christian-
of Science. ity, and the printing and study of
the Bible, were the only or even the most

important of the intellectual activities of the fourteenth and fifteenth centuries. That was merely the popular and most conspicuous aspect of the intellectual revival of the time. Behind this conspicuous and popular awakening to thought and discussion, other less immediately striking but ultimately more important mental developments were in progress. Of the trend of these developments we must now give some brief indications. They had begun long before books were printed, but it was printing that released them from obscurity.

We have already told something of the first appearance of the free intelligence, the spirit of inquiry and plain statement, in human affairs. One name is central in the record of that first attempt at systematic knowledge, the name of Aristotle. We have noted also the brief phase of scientific work at Alexandria. From that time onward the complicated economic and political and religious conflicts of Europe and Western Asia impeded further intellectual progress. These regions, as we have seen, fell for long ages under the sway of the Oriental type of monarchy and of Oriental religious traditions. Rome tried and abandoned a slave-system of industry. The first great capitalistic system developed and fell into chaos through its own inherent rottenness. Europe relapsed into universal insecurity. The Semite rose against the Aryan, and replaced Hellenic civilization throughout Western Asia and Egypt by an Arabic culture. All Western Asia and half of Europe fell under Mongolian rule. It is only in the twelfth and thirteenth centuries that we find the Nordic intelligence struggling through again to expression.

We then find in the growing universities of Paris, Oxford, and Bologna an increasing amount of philosophical discussion going on. In form it is chiefly a discussion of logical questions. As the basis of this discussion we find part of the teachings of Aristotle, not the whole mass of writings he left behind him, but his logic only. Later on his work became better known through the Latin translations of the Arabic edition annotated by Averroes.[1] Except for these translations of

Aristotle, very little of the Greek philosophical literature was read in Western Europe until the fifteenth century. The creative Plato— as distinguished from the scientific Aristotle— was almost unknown. Some neo-Platonic writers were known, but neo-Platonism had much the same relation to Plato that Christian Science has to Christ or science.[2]

It has been the practice of recent writers to decry the philosophical discussion of the mediæval " schoolmen" as tedious and futile. It was nothing of the sort. It had to assume a severely technical form because the dignitaries of the church, ignorant and intolerant, were on the watch for heresy. It lacked the sweet clearness, therefore, of fearless thought. It often hinted what it dared not say. But it dealt with fundamentally important things, it was a long and necessary struggle to clear up and correct certain inherent defects of the human mind, and many people to-day blunder dangerously through their neglect of the issues the schoolmen discussed.

[1] Aristotle's *Organon,* or logic, had always been in part known to the West and was known as a whole after about 1130. In the thirteenth century the rest of his writings became known, in two ways. One way was that of direct translation from the Greek into Latin : it was in this way that St. Thomas Aquinas knew the *Ethics* and the *Politics* (the latter translated about 1260 by William of Moerbeke, Archbishop of Corinth in the Latin Empire of Constantinople started under Baldwin of Flanders in 1204, and a Fleming himself). The other way was that of indirect translation, that is to say, of translations of Arabic paraphrases of, or commentaries on, the works of Aristotle, such as had been made by Averroes and by Avicenna before him. It was Aristotle's *Physics* and (I think) *Metaphysics* that first became known in this way. In this latter way the West received a version of Aristotle which, like Bottom the Weaver, was strangely " translated." Sometimes translations were made direct from Arabic into Latin ; sometimes they were made first into Hebrew, and then new translations were made from Hebrew into Latin. As the Arabic version of Aristotle was not always itself direct, but sometimes made from Syriac versions of the Greek, confusion became confounded. The Latin translations of the Arabic Aristotle sometimes contained not translation, but *transliteration* of Arabic words or sentences ; and Roger Bacon very naturally objected to their unintelligibility. What is more, Aristotle's views, as well as his words, were transmogrified in the process. But the important thing is that for Aristotle's *Organon, Ethics* and *Politics* there were direct translations from the Greek. (See Sandys' *History of Classical Scholarship* and Renan's *Averroes et l'Averroisme.*)—E. B.

[2] This is too harsh. It is much more Platonic than you make out. See Dean Inge's two volumes on the subject, recently published.—E. B.

There is a natural tendency in the human mind to exaggerate the differences and resemblances upon which classification is based, to suppose that things called by different names are altogether different, and that things called by the same name are practically identical. This tendency to exaggerate classification produces a thousand evils and injustices. In the sphere of race or nationality, for example, a "European" will often treat an "Asiatic" almost as if he were a different animal, while he will be disposed to regard another "European" as necessarily as virtuous and charming as himself. He will, as a matter of course, take sides with Europeans against Asiatics. But, as the reader of this history must realize, there is no such difference as the opposition of these names implies. It is a phantom difference created by two names. . . .

The main mediæval controversy was between the "Realists" and the "Nominalists," and it is necessary to warn the reader that the word "Realist" in mediæval discussion has a meaning almost diametrically opposed to "Realist" as it is used in the jargon of modern criticism. The modern "Realist" is one who insists on materialist details; the mediæval "Realist" was far nearer what nowadays we should call an Idealist, and his contempt for incidental detail was profound. The Realists outdid the vulgar tendency to exaggerate the significance of class. They held that there

Photo: Rischgitz Collection.

RHEIMS CATHEDRAL.

A superb example of the Gothic cathedrals built during the thirteenth and fourteenth centuries.

was something in a name, in a common noun that is, that was essentially real. For example, they held there was a typical "European," an ideal European, who was far more real than any individual European. Every European was, as it were, a failure, a departure, a flawed specimen of this profounder reality. On the other hand the Nominalist held that the only realities in the case were the individual Europeans, that the name "European" was merely a name and nothing more than a name applied to all these instances.

Nothing is quite so difficult as the compression of philosophical controversies, which are by their nature voluminous and various and tinted by the mental colours of a variety of minds. With the difference of Realist and Nominalist stated baldly as we have stated it here, the modern reader unaccustomed to philosophical discussion may be disposed to leap at once to the side of the Nominalist. But the matter is not so simple that it can be covered by one instance, and here we have purposely chosen an extreme instance. Names and classifications differ in their value and reality. While it is absurd to suppose that there can be much depth of class difference between men called Thomas and men called William, or that there is an ideal and quintessential Thomas or William, yet on the other hand there may be much profounder differences between a white man and a Hottentot, and still more between *Homo sapiens* and *Homo neanderthalensis*. While again the distinction between the class of pets and the class of useful animals is dependent upon very slight differences of habit and application, the difference of a cat and dog is so profound that the microscope can trace it in a drop of blood or a single hair. When this aspect of the question is considered, it becomes understandable how Nominalism had ultimately to abandon the idea that names were as insignificant as labels, and how, out of a revised and amended Nominalism, there grew up that systematic attempt to find the *true*, the most significant and fruitful, classification of things and substances which is called Scientific Research.

And it will be almost as evident that while the tendency of Realism, which is the natural tendency of every untutored mind, was towards dogma, harsh divisions, harsh judgments, and uncompromising attitudes, the tendency of earlier and later Nominalism was towards qualified statements, towards an examination of individual instances, and towards inquiry and experiment and scepticism. And it may not surprise the reader to learn that the philosophy of the Catholic Church was essentially a Realist philosophy.[1]

So while in the market-place and the ways of the common life men were questioning the morals and righteousness of the clergy, the good faith and propriety of their celibacy, and the justice of papal taxation; while in theological circles their minds were set upon the question of transubstantiation, the question of the divinity or not of the bread and wine in the mass, in studies and lecture-rooms a wider-reaching criticism of the methods of thought upon which the very fundamentals of Catholic teaching rested was in progress. We cannot attempt here to gauge the significance in this process of such names as Peter Abelard (1079—1142), Albertus Magnus (1193—

1280), and Thomas Aquinas (1225—1274). These men sought to reconstruct Catholicism on a sounder system of reasoning. Chief among their critics and successors were Duns Scotus (? —1308), an Oxford Franciscan and, to judge by his sedulous thought and deliberate subtleties, a Scotchman, and Occam, an Englishman (? —1347). Both these latter, like Averroes (see chap. xxxii., § 8), made a definite distinction between theological and philosophical truth; they placed theology on a pinnacle, but they placed it where it could no longer obstruct research; Duns Scotus declared that it was impossible to prove by reasoning the existence of God or of the Trinity or the credibility of the Act of Creation; Occam was still more insistent upon this separation—which manifestly released scientific inquiry from dogmatic control. A later generation, benefiting by the freedoms towards which these pioneers worked, and knowing not the sources of its freedom, had the ingratitude to use the name of Scotus as a term for stupidity, and so we have our English word "Dunce." Says Professor Pringle Pattison,[2] "Occam, who is still a Scholastic, gives us the Scholastic justification of the spirit which had already taken hold upon Roger Bacon, and which was to enter upon its rights in the fifteenth and sixteenth centuries."

Standing apart by himself because of his distinctive genius is this Roger Bacon (about 1210 to about 1293), who was also English. He was a Franciscan of Oxford, and a very typical Englishman indeed, irritable, hasty, honest, and shrewd. He was two centuries ahead of his world. Says H. O. Taylor of him [3]:

"The career of Bacon was an intellectual tragedy, conforming to the old principles of tragic art: that the hero's character shall be large and noble, but not flawless, inasmuch as the fatal consummation must issue from character, and not happen through chance. He died an old man, as in his youth, so in his age, a devotee of tangible knowledge. His pursuit of a knowledge which was not altogether learning had been obstructed by the Order of which he was an unhappy and re-

[1] I do not agree with this paragraph. In the first sentence things are alleged about Realism which are not justified. It was the philosophy of the priests and most humane thinkers of the Middle Ages, of St. Anselm and of John Wycliffe. Nor is it true that Realism was the philosophy of the church. It was, in the early Middle Ages; but after Occam (1330) Nominalism triumphed, and was the philosophy of the church till the Reformation. Luther denounced Nominalism.—E. B.

[2] *Encyclopædia Britannica*, article "Scholasticism."
[3] *The Medieval Mind*, by Henry Osborn Taylor.

bellious member ; quite as fatally his achievement was deformed from within by the principles which he accepted from his time. But he was responsible for his acceptance of current opinions ; and as his views roused the distrust of his brother Friars, his intractable temper drew their hostility (of which we know very little) on his head. Persuasiveness and tact were needed by one who would impress such novel views as his upon his fellows, or, in the thirteenth century, escape persecution for their divulgence. Bacon attacked dead and living worthies, tactlessly, fatuously, and unfairly. Of his life scarcely anything is known, save from his allusions to himself and others ; and these are insufficient for the construction of even a slight consecutive narrative. Born; studied at Oxford ; went to Paris, studied, experimented ; is at Oxford again, and a Franciscan ; studies, teaches, becomes suspect to his Order, is sent back to Paris, kept under surveillance, receives a letter from the Pope, writes, writes, writes—his three best-known works ; is again in trouble, confined for many years, released, and dead, so very dead, body and fame alike, until partly unearthed after five centuries."

The bulk of these " three best-known works " is a hotly phrased and sometimes quite abusive, but entirely just attack on the ignorance of the times, combined with a wealth of suggestions for the increase of knowledge. In his passionate insistence upon the need of experiment and of collecting knowledge, the spirit of Aristotle lives again in him. " Experiment, experiment," that is the burthen of Roger Bacon. Yet of Aristotle himself Roger Bacon fell foul. He fell foul of him because men, instead of facing facts boldly, sat in rooms and pored over bad Latin translations of the master. " If I had my way," he wrote, in his intemperate fashion, " I should burn all the books of Aristotle, for the study of them can only lead to a loss of time, produce error, and increase ignorance," a sentiment that Aristotle would probably have echoed could he have returned to a world in which his works were not so much read as worshipped— and that, as Roger Bacon showed, in the most abominable translations.

Throughout his books, a little disguised by the necessity of seeming to square it all with orthodoxy for fear of the prison and worse, Roger Bacon shouted to mankind, " Cease to be ruled by dogmas and authorities; *look at the world !* " Four chief sources of ignorance he denounced; respect for authority, custom, the sense of the ignorant crowd, and the vain proud unteachableness of our dispositions. Overcome but these, and a world of power would open to men :—

" Machines for navigating are possible without rowers, so that great ships suited to river or ocean, guided by one man, may be borne with greater speed than if they were full of men. Likewise cars may be made so that without a draught animal they may be moved *cum impetu*

Photo: Mansell.

HÔTEL DE VILLE, BRUGES.

" Among the monuments of the later Gothic period are the beautiful town-halls of Flemish cities, which rose confronting the churches . . . as if to symbolise the growth of a new power, that of the civic laity."—REINACH.

inæstimabili, as we deem the scythed chariots to have been from which antiquity fought. And flying machines are possible, so that a man may sit in the middle turning some device by which artificial wings may beat the air in the manner of a flying bird."

Occam, Roger Bacon, these are the early precursors of a great movement in Europe away from "Realism" towards reality. For a time the older influences fought against the naturalism of the new Nominalists. In 1339 Occam's books were put under a ban and Nominalism solemnly condemned. As late as 1473 an attempt was made to bind teachers of Paris by an oath to teach Realism.[1] It was only in the sixteenth century with the printing of books and the increase of intelligence that the movement from absolutism towards experiment became massive, and that one investigator began to co-operate with another.

Throughout the thirteenth and fourteenth centuries experimenting with material things was on the increase, items of knowledge were being won by men, but there was no inter-related advance. The work was done in a detached, furtive, and inglorious manner. A tradition of isolated investigation came into Europe from the Arabs, and a considerable amount of private and secretive research was carried on by the alchemists, for whom modern writers are a little too apt with their contempt. These alchemists were in close touch with the glass and metal workers and with the herbalists and medicine-makers of the times; they pried into many secrets of nature, but they were obsessed by "practical" ideas; they sought not knowledge, but power; they wanted to find out how to manufacture gold from cheaper materials, how to make men immortal by the elixir of life, and such-like vulgar dreams. Incidentally in their researches they learnt much about poisons, dyes, metallurgy, and the like; they discovered various refractory substances, and worked their way towards clear glass and so to lenses and optical instruments; but as scientific men tell us continually, and as "practical" men still refuse to learn, it is only when knowledge is sought for her own sake that she gives rich and unexpected gifts in any abundance to her servants. The world of to-day is still much more disposed to spend money on technical research than on pure science. Half the men in our scientific laboratories still dream of patents and secret processes. We live to-day largely in the age of the alchemists, for all our sneers at their memory. The "business man" of to-day still thinks of research as a sort of alchemy.

Closely associated with the alchemists were the astrologers, who were also a "practical" race. They studied the stars—to tell fortunes. They lacked that broader faith and understanding which induces men simply to study the stars.

Not until the fifteenth century did the ideas which Roger Bacon first expressed begin to produce their first-fruits in new knowledge and a widening outlook. Then suddenly, as the sixteenth century dawned, and as the world recovered from the storm of social trouble that had followed the pestilences of the fourteenth century, Western Europe broke out into a galaxy of names that outshine the utmost scientific reputations of the best age of Greece. Nearly every nation contributed, the reader will note, for science knows no nationality.

One of the earliest and most splendid in this constellation is the Florentine, Leonardo da Vinci (1452—1519), a man with an almost miraculous vision for reality. He was a naturalist, an anatomist, an engineer, as well as a very great artist. He was the first modern to realize the true nature of fossils,[2] he made note-books of observations that still amaze us,

[1] This gives a wrong impression about Nominalism, that it was banned in the fourteenth and fifteenth centuries. The contrary is the case. The attempt of 1339 came to nothing ; that of 1473 was belated and unsuccessful. Except Wycliffe, there is no considerable thinker of these centuries, so far as I know, who is not Nominalist. The triumph of Nominalism was no unmixed benefit. Its insistence on study of the individual was indeed favourable to natural science ; and Harnack says that it led to good work in psychology. But its nescience about Universals led to obscurantism in theology. Wycliffe as a Realist could hold that God acted *secundum rationes exemplares*, by certain and known universal rules ; the Nominalists reduced God to inscrutable omnipotence. They went on to add that He could therefore only be known at all by the miraculous intervention of the mass through the priesthood. Their scepticism about Universals thus overleapt itself, and fell on the other side, into obscurantist ecclesiasticism.—E. B.

[2] *Cp.* chap. ii, § 1, towards the end.

INTERIOR OF ST. PETER'S, ROME.

he was convinced of the practicability of mechanical flight. Another great name is that of Copernicus, a Dane (1473—1543), who made the first clear analysis of the movements of the heavenly bodies and showed that the earth moves round the sun. Tycho Brahe (1546—1601), of Prague, rejected this latter belief, but his observations of celestial movements were of the utmost value to his successors, and especially to the German, Kepler (1571—1630). Galileo Galilei (1564—1642) was the founder of the science of dynamics. Before his time it was believed that a weight a hundred times greater than another would fall a hundred times as fast. Galileo denied this. Instead of arguing about it

Photo : Rischgitz Collection.

GALILEO.

like a scholar and a gentleman, he put it to the coarse test of experiment by dropping two unequal weights from an upper gallery of the leaning tower at Pisa—to the horror of all erudite men. He made what was almost the first telescope, and he developed the astronomical views of Copernicus; but the church, still struggling gallantly against the light, decided that to believe that the earth was smaller and inferior to the sun made man and Christianity of no account, and diminished the importance of the Pope; so Galileo, under threats of dire punishment, when he was an old man of sixty-nine, was made to recant this view and put the earth back in its place as the immovable centre of the universe. He knelt before ten cardinals in scarlet, an assembly august enough to overawe truth itself, while he amended the creation he had disarranged. The story has it that as he rose from his knees, after repeating his recantation, he muttered, "*Eppur si muove*"—"it moves nevertheless."

Newton (1642—1727) was born in the year

33

of Galileo's death. By his discovery of the law of gravitation he completed the clear vision of the starry universe that we have to-day. But Newton carries us into the eighteenth century. He carries us too far for the present chapter. Among the earlier names, that of Dr. Gilbert (1540—1603), of Colchester, is pre-eminent. Roger Bacon had preached experiment, Gilbert was one of the first to practise it. There can be little doubt that his work, which was chiefly upon magnetism, helped to form the ideas of Francis Bacon, Lord Verulam (1561—1626), Lord Chancellor to James I of England. This Francis Bacon has been called the "Father of Experimental Philosophy," but his share in the development of scientific work has been made far too much of.[1] He was, says Sir R. A. Gregory, "not the founder, but the apostle" of the scientific method. His greatest service to science was a fantastic book, *The New Atlantis*. "In his *New Atlantis*, Francis Bacon planned in somewhat fanciful language a palace of invention, a great temple of science, where the pursuit of knowledge in all its branches was to be organized on principles of the highest efficiency."

From this Utopian dream arose the Royal Society of London, which received a Royal Charter from Charles II of England in 1662. The essential use and virtue of this society was and is *publication*. Its formation marks a definite step from isolated inquiry towards co-operative work, from the secret and solitary investigations of the alchemist to the frank report and open discussion which is the life of the modern scientific process. For the true scientific method is this: to trust no statements without verification, to test all

[1] See Gregory's *Discovery*, chap. vi.

things as rigorously as possible, to keep no secrets, to attempt no monopolies, to give out one's best modestly and plainly, serving no other end but knowledge.

The long-slumbering science of anatomy was revived by Harvey (1578—1657), who demonstrated the circulation of the blood. . . . Presently the Dutchman, Leeuwenhoek (1632—1723) brought the first crude microscope to bear upon the hidden minutiæ of life.

These are but some of the brightest stars amidst that increasing multitude of men who have from the fifteenth century to our own time, with more and more collective power and vigour, lit up our vision of the universe, and increased our power over the conditions of our lives.

§ 7

We have dealt thus fully with the beginnings of science in the Middle Ages because of its ultimate importance in human affairs. In the long run, Roger Bacon is of more significance to mankind than any monarch of his time. But the contemporary world, for the most part, knew nothing of this smouldering activity in studies and lecture-rooms and alchemists' laboratories that was presently to alter all the conditions of life. The church did indeed take notice of what was afoot, but only because of the disregard of her conclusive decisions. She had decided that the earth was the very centre of God's creation, and that the Pope was the divinely appointed ruler of the earth. Men's ideas on these essential points, she insisted, must not be disturbed by any contrary teaching. So soon, however, as she had compelled Galileo to say that the world did not move she was satisfied ; she does not seem to have realized how ominous it was for her that, after all, the earth did move.

The New Growth of European Towns.

Very great social as well as intellectual developments were in progress in Western Europe throughout this period of the later Middle Ages. But the human mind apprehends events far more vividly than changes ; and men for the most part, then as now, kept on in their own traditions in spite of the shifting scene about them.

In an outline such as this it is impossible to crowd in the clustering events of history that do not clearly show the main process of human development, however bright and picturesque they may be. We have to record the steady growth of towns and cities, the reviving power of trade and money, the gradual re-establishment of law and custom, the extension of security, the supersession of private warfare that went on in Western Europe in the period between the First Crusade and the sixteenth century. Of much that looms large in our national histories we cannot tell anything. We have no space for the story of the repeated attempts of the English kings to conquer Scotland and set themselves up as kings of France, nor of how the Norman English established themselves insecurely in Ireland (twelfth century), and how Wales was linked to the English crown (1282). All through the Middle Ages the struggle of England with Scotland and France was in progress ; there were times when it seemed that Scotland was finally subjugated and when the English king held far more land in France than its titular sovereign. In the English histories this struggle with France is too often represented as a single-handed and almost successful attempt to conquer France. In reality it was a joint enterprise undertaken in concert with the powerful French vassal state of Burgundy to conquer and divide the patrimony of Hugh Capet.[1] Of the English rout by the Scotch at Bannockburn (1314), and of William Wallace and Robert the Bruce, the Scottish national heroes, of the battles of Crecy (1346) and Poitiers (1356) and Agincourt (1415) in France, which shine like stars in the English imagination, little battles in which sturdy bowmen through some sunny hours made a great havoc among French knights in armour, of the Black Prince and Henry V of England, and of how a peasant girl, Joan of Arc, the Maid of Orleans, drove the English out of her country again (1429—1430), this history relates nothing. For every country has such cherished national events. They are the ornamental tapestry of history, and no part of the building. Rajputana or Poland, Russia, Spain, Persia, and China can

[1] Not from 1340–1360, under Edward III, but later under Henry V, 1413–1422.—E. B.

Edward had Flemish and Bavarian allies.—H. G. W.

Principal EUROPEAN TRADE ROUTES of the 14th Cent.y

Land routes ———
Sea routes :—
  Venetian ----V----
  Genoese   ----G----
  Hansa   ----H----

all match or outdo the utmost romance of Western Europe, with equally adventurous knights and equally valiant princesses and equally stout fights against the odds. Nor can we tell how Louis XI of France (1461—1483), the son of Joan of Arc's Charles VII, brought Burgundy to heel and laid the foundations of a centralized French monarchy. It signifies more that in the thirteenth and fourteenth centuries, gunpowder, that Mongol gift, came to Europe, so that the kings (Louis XI included) and the law, relying upon the support of the growing towns, were able to batter down the castles of the half-independent robber knights and barons of the earlier Middle Ages and consolidate a more centralized power. The fighting nobles and knights of the barbaric period disappear slowly from history during these centuries; the Crusades consumed them, such dynastic wars as the English Wars of the Roses killed them off, the arrows from the English longbow pierced them and stuck out

a yard behind, infantry so armed swept them from the stricken field; they became reconciled to trade and changed their nature. They disappeared in everything but a titular sense from the west and south of Europe before they disappeared from Germany. The knight in Germany remained a professional fighting man into the sixteenth century.

Between the eleventh and the fifteenth centuries in Western Europe, and particularly in France and England, there sprang up like flowers a multitude of very distinctive and beautiful buildings, cathedrals, abbeys, and the like, the Gothic architecture. This lovely efflorescence marks the appearance of a body of craftsmen closely linked in its beginnings to the church. In Italy and Spain too the world was beginning to build freely and beautifully again. At first it was the wealth of the church that provided most of these buildings; then kings and merchants also began to build.

From the twelfth century onward, with the increase of trade, there was a great revival of town life throughout Europe. Prominent among these towns were Venice, with its dependents Ragusa and Corfu, Genoa, Verona, Bologna, Pisa, Florence, Naples, Milan, Marseilles, Lisbon, Barcelona, Narbonne, Tours, Orleans, Bordeaux, Paris, Ghent, Bruges, Boulogne, London, Oxford, Cambridge, Southampton, Dover, Antwerp, Hamburg, Bremen, Cologne, Mayence, Nuremberg, Munich, Leipzig, Magdeburg, Breslau, Stettin, Dantzig, Königsberg, Riga, Pskof, Novgorod, Wisby, and Bergen.

" A West German town, between 1400 and 1500,[1] embodied all the achievements of progress at that time, although from a modern standpoint much seems wanting. . . . The streets were mostly narrow and irregularly built, the houses chiefly of wood, while almost every burgher kept his cattle in the house, and the herd of swine which was driven every morning by the town herdsman to the pasture-ground formed an inevitable part of city life.[2] In Frankfort-on-Main it was unlawful after 1481 to keep swine in the Altstadt, but in the Neustadt and in Sachsenhausen this custom remained as a matter of course. It was only in 1645, after a corresponding attempt in 1556 had failed, that the swine-pens in the inner town were pulled down at Leipzig. The rich burghers, who occasionally took part in the great trading companies, were conspicuously wealthy landowners, and had extensive courtyards with large barns inside the town walls. The most opulent of them owned those splendid patrician houses which we still admire even to-day. But even in the older towns most houses of the fifteenth century have disappeared; only here and there a building with open timber-work and overhanging storeys, as in Bacharach or Miltenburg, reminds us of the style of architecture then customary in the houses of burghers. The great bulk of the inferior population, who lived on mendicancy, or got a livelihood by the exercise of the inferior industries, inhabited squalid hovels outside the town; the town wall was often the only

[1] From Dr. Tille in Helmolt's *History of the World.*
[2] Charles Dickens in his *American Notes* mentions swine in Broadway, New York, in the middle nineteenth century.

support for these wretched buildings. The internal fittings of the houses, even amongst the wealthy population, were very defective according to modern ideas; the Gothic style was as little suitable for the petty details of objects of luxury as it was splendidly adapted for the building of churches and town halls. The influence of the Renaissance added much to the comfort of the house.

" The fourteenth and fifteenth centuries saw the building of numerous Gothic town churches and town halls throughout Europe which still in many cases serve their original purpose. The power and prosperity of the towns find their best expression in these and in the fortifications, with their strong towers and gateways. Every picture of a town of the sixteenth or later centuries shows conspicuously these latter erections for the protection and honour of the town. The town did many things which in our time are done by the State. Social problems were taken up by town administration or the corresponding municipal organization. The regulation of trade was the concern of the guilds in agreement with the council, the care of the poor belonged to the church, while the council looked after the protection of the town walls and the very necessary fire brigades. The council, mindful of its social duties, superintended the filling of the municipal granaries, in order to have supplies in years of scarcity. Such store-houses were erected in almost every town during the fifteenth century. Tariffs of prices for the sale of all wares, high enough to enable every artisan to make a good livelihood, and to give the purchaser a guarantee for the quality of the wares, were maintained. The town was also the chief capitalist; as a seller of annuities on lives and inheritances it was a banker, and enjoyed unlimited credit. In return it obtained means for the construction of fortifications or for such occasions as the acquisition of sovereign rights from the hand of an impecunious prince."

For the most part these European towns were independent or quasi-independent aristocratic republics. Most admitted a vague overlordship on the part of the church, or of the emperor or of a king. Others were parts of kingdoms, or even the capitals of dukes or kings. In such cases their internal freedom was maintained by a royal or imperial charter. In England the Royal City of Westminster on the Thames stood cheek by jowl with the walled City of London, into which the King came only with ceremony and permission. The entirely free Venetian republic ruled an empire of dependent islands and trading ports, rather after the fashion of the Athenian republic. Genoa also stood alone. The Germanic towns of the Baltic and North Sea from Riga to Middleburgh in Holland, Dortmund, and Cologne were loosely allied in a confederation, the confederation of the Hansa towns under the leadership of Hamburg, Bremen, and Lubeck, a confederation which was still more loosely attached to the Empire. This confederation, which included over seventy towns in all, and which had depôts in Novgorod, Bergen, London, and Bruges, did much to keep the northern seas clean of piracy, that curse of the Mediterranean and of the Eastern seas. The Eastern Empire throughout its last phase, from the Ottoman conquest of its European hinterland in the fourteenth and early fifteenth centuries until its fall in 1453, was practically only the trading town of Constantinople, a town state like Genoa or Venice, except that it was encumbered by a corrupt imperial court.

Photo: E. N. A.

AMIENS CATHEDRAL—THE WEST FRONT.

The fullest and most splendid developments of this city life of the later Middle Ages occurred in Italy. After the end of the Hohenstaufen line in the thirteenth century, the hold of the Holy Roman Empire upon North and Central Italy weakened, although, as we shall tell, German Emperors were still crowned as kings and emperors in Italy up to the time of Charles V (*circ.* 1530). There arose a number of quasi-independent city states to the north of Rome, the papal capital. South Italy and Sicily, however, remained under foreign dominion. Genoa and her rival, Venice, were the great trading seaports of this time; their noble palaces, their lordly paintings, still win our admiration. Milan, at the foot of the St. Gothard pass, revived to wealth and power. Inland was Florence, a trading and financial centre which, under the almost monarchical rule of the Medici family in the fifteenth century, enjoyed a " second Periclean age." But already before the time of these cultivated Medici " bosses," Florence had produced much beautiful art. Giotto's tower (Giotto, born 1266, died 1337) and the glorious Duomo (by Brunellesco, born 1377, died 1446) already existed. Towards the end of the fourteenth century Florence became the centre of the rediscovery, restoration, and imitation of antique art (the " Renaissance " in its narrower sense). Artistic productions, unlike philosophical thought and scientific discovery, are the ornaments and expression rather than the creative substance of history, and here we cannot attempt to trace the development of the art of Filippo Lippi, Botticelli, Donatello (died 1466), Leonardo da Vinci (died 1579), Michelangelo (1475—1564), and Raphael (died 1520). Of the scientific speculation of Leonardo we have already had occasion to speak.

COLUMBUS.

§ 8

In 1453, as we have related, Constantinople fell. Throughout the next century the Turkish pressure upon Europe was heavy and continuous. The boundary line between Mongol and Aryan, which had lain somewhere east of the Pamirs in the days of Pericles, had receded now to Hungary. Constantinople had long been a mere island of Christians in a Turk-ruled Balkan peninsula. Its fall did much to interrupt the trade with the East.

America comes into History.

Of the two rival cities of the Mediterranean, Venice was generally on much better terms with the Turks than Genoa. Every intelligent Genoese sailor fretted at the trading monopoly of Venice, and tried to invent some way of getting through it or round it. And there were now new peoples taking to the sea trade, and disposed to look for new ways to the old markets because the ancient routes were closed to them. The Portuguese, for example, were developing an Atlantic coasting trade. The Atlantic was waking up again after a vast period of neglect that dated from the Roman murder of Carthage. It is rather a delicate matter to decide whether the Western European was pushing out into the Atlantic or whether he was being pushed out into it by the Turk, who lorded it in the Mediterranean until the Battle of Lepanto (1571). The Venetian and Genoese ships were creeping round to Antwerp, and the Hansa town seamen were coming south and extending their range. And there were considerable developments of seamanship and shipbuilding in progress. The Mediterranean, as we have noted (Chapter XVII) is a sea for galleys and coasting. But upon the Atlantic Ocean and the North Sea winds are more prevalent, seas run higher, the shore is often a danger rather than a refuge. The high seas called for the sailing ship, and in the fourteenth and fifteenth centuries it appears keeping its course by the compass and the stars.

By the thirteenth century the Hansa merchants were already sailing regularly from Bergen across the grey cold seas to the Northmen in Iceland. In Iceland men knew of Greenland, and adventurous voyagers had long ago found a further land beyond, Vinland, where the climate was pleasant and where men could settle if they chose to cut themselves off from the rest of human kind. This Vinland was either Nova Scotia or, what is more probable, New England.

All over Europe in the fifteenth century merchants and sailors were speculating about new ways to the East. The Portuguese, unaware that Pharaoh Necho had solved the problem ages ago, were asking whether it was not possible to go round to India by the coast of Africa. Their ships followed in the course that Hanno took to Cape Verde (1445). They put out to sea to the west and found the Canary Isles, Madeira, and the Azores.[1] That was a

[1] In these maritime adventures in the Eastern Atlantic and the West African coast the Portuguese were preceded in the thirteenth, fourteenth, and early fifteenth centuries by Normans, Catalonians, and Genoese. See Raymond Beazley, *History of Exploration in the Middle Ages.*—H. H. J.

Map of the World to show the CHIEF VOYAGES of EXPLORATION (to 1522)

Columbus' (outward) voyages — 1492, 1493, 1498, 1502 — are numbered 1 to 4.

Coasts visited by European navigators up to 1522 (the year of the return of Magellan's expedition)

fairly long stride across the Atlantic. In 1486 a Portuguese, Diaz, reported that he had rounded the south of Africa. . . .

A certain Genoese, Christopher Columbus, began to think more and more of what is to us a very obvious and natural enterprise, but which strained the imagination of the fifteenth century to the utmost, a voyage due west across the Atlantic. At that time nobody knew of the existence of America as a separate continent. Columbus knew that the world was a sphere, but he underestimated its size ; the travels of Marco Polo had given him an exaggerated idea of the extent of Asia, and he supposed therefore that Japan, with its reputation for a great wealth of gold, lay across the Atlantic in about the position of Mexico. He had made various voyages in the Atlantic ; he had been to Iceland and perhaps heard of Vinland, which must have greatly encouraged these ideas of his, and this project of sailing into the sunset became the ruling purpose of his life. He was a penniless man, some accounts say he was a bankrupt, and his only way of securing a ship was to get someone to entrust him with a command. He went first to King John II of Portugal, who listened to him, made difficulties, and then arranged for an expedition to start without his knowledge, a purely Portuguese expedition. This highly diplomatic attempt to steal a march on an original man failed, as it deserved to fail; the crew became mutinous, the captain lost heart and returned (1483). Columbus then went to the Court of Spain.

At first he could get no ship and no powers. Spain was assailing Granada, the last foothold of the Moslems in Western Europe. Most of Spain had been recovered by the Christians between the eleventh and the thirteenth centuries; then had come a pause; and now all Spain, united by the marriage of Ferdinand of Aragon and Isabella of Castile, was setting itself to the completion of the Christian conquest. Despairing of Spanish help, Columbus sent his brother Bartholomew to Henry VII of England, but the adventure did not attract that canny monarch. Finally in 1492 Granada fell, and then, helped by some merchants of the town of Palos, Columbus got his ships, three ships, of which only one, the *Santa Maria*, of 100 tons burthen, was decked. The two other were open boats of half that tonnage.

The little expedition—it numbered altogether eighty-eight men!—went south to the Canaries, and then stood out across the unknown seas, in beautiful weather and with a helpful wind.

The story of that momentous voyage of two months and nine days must be read in detail to be appreciated. The crew was full of doubts and fears; they might, they feared, sail on for ever. They were comforted by seeing some birds, and later on by finding a pole worked with tools, and a branch with strange berries. At ten o'clock, on the night of October 11th, 1492, Columbus saw a light ahead; the next morning land was sighted, and, while the day was still young, Columbus landed on the shores of the New World, richly apparelled and bearing the royal banner of Spain. . . .

Early in 1493 Columbus returned to Europe. He brought gold, cotton, strange beasts and birds, and two wild-eyed painted Indians to be baptized. He had not found Japan, it was thought, but India. The islands he had found were called therefore the West Indies. The same year he sailed again with a great expedition of seventeen ships and fifteen thousand men, with the express permission of the Pope to take possession of these new lands for the Spanish crown. . . .

We cannot tell of his experiences as Governor of this Spanish colony, nor how he was superseded and put in chains. In a little while a swarm of Spanish adventurers were exploring the new lands. But it is interesting to note that Columbus died ignorant of the fact that he had discovered a new continent. He believed to the day of his death that he had sailed round the world to Asia.

The news of his discoveries caused a great excitement throughout Western Europe. It spurred the Portuguese to fresh attempts to reach India by the South African route. In 1498, Vasco da Gama sailed from Lisbon to Zanzibar, and thence, with an Arab pilot, he struck across the Indian Ocean to Calicut in India. In 1515 there were Portuguese ships in Java and the Moluccas. In 1519 a Portuguese sailor, Magellan, in the employment of the Spanish King, coasted to the south of South America, passed through the dark and forbidding Magellan's straits, and so came into the Pacific Ocean, which had already been sighted by Spanish explorers who had crossed the Isthmus of Panama.

Magellan's expedition continued across the Pacific Ocean westward. This was a far more heroic voyage than that of Columbus; for *eight and ninety days* Magellan sailed unflinchingly over that vast, empty ocean, sighting nothing but two little desert islands. The crews were rotten with scurvy; there was little water and that bad, and putrid biscuit to eat. Rats were hunted eagerly; cowhide was gnawed and sawdust devoured to stay the pangs of hunger. In this state the expedition reached the Ladrones. They discovered the Philippines, and here Magellan was killed in a fight with the natives. Several other captains were murdered. Five ships had started with Magellan in August 1519 and two hundred and eighty men; in July 1522 the *Vittoria*, with a remnant of one and thirty men aboard, returned up the Atlantic to her anchorage near the mole of Seville, in the river Guadalquivir—the first ship that ever circumnavigated this planet.[1]

The English and French and Dutch and the sailors of the Hansa towns came rather later into this new adventure of exploration. They

[1] See Guillemard's *Ferdinand Magellan*.

had not the same keen interest in the Eastern trade. And when they did come in, their first efforts were directed to sailing round the north of America as Magellan had sailed round the south, and to sailing round the north of Asia as Vasco da Gama had sailed round the south of Africa. Both these enterprises were doomed to failure by the nature of things. Both in America and the East, Spain and Portugal had half a century's start of England and France and Holland. And Germany never started. The King of Spain was Emperor of Germany in those crucial years, and the Pope had given the monopoly of America to Spain, and not simply to Spain, but to the kingdom of Castile. This must have restrained both Germany and Holland at first from American adventures. The Hansa towns were quasi-independent; they had no monarch behind them to support them, and no unity among themselves for so big an enterprise as oceanic exploration. It was the misfortune of Germany, and perhaps of the world, that, as we will presently tell, a storm of warfare exhausted her when all the Western powers were going to this newly opened school of trade and administration upon the high seas.

THE LANDING OF COLUMBUS ON *ESPANIOLA*.
(From a contemporary pamphlet, printed at Basle, 1494.)

Slowly throughout the sixteenth century the immense good fortune of Castile unfolded itself before the dazzled eyes of Europe. She had found a new world, abounding in gold and silver and wonderful possibilities of settlement. It was all hers, because the Pope had said so. The Court of Rome, in an access of magnificence, had divided this new world of strange lands which was now opening out to the European imagination, between the Spanish, who were to have everything west of a line 370 leagues west of the Cape Verde islands, and the Portu-

guese, to whom everything east of this line was given.

At first the only people encountered by the Spaniards in America were savages of a Mongoloid type. Many of these savages were cannibals. It is a misfortune for science that the first Europeans to reach America were these rather incurious Spaniards, without any scientific passion, thirsty for gold, and full of the blind bigotry of a recent religious war. They made few intelligent observations of the native methods and ideas of these primordial people. They slaughtered them, they robbed them, they enslaved them, and baptized them; but they made small note of the customs and motives that changed and vanished under their assault. They were as destructive and reckless as the British in Tasmania, who shot the last Palæolithic men at sight, and put out poisoned meat for them to find.

Great areas of the American interior were prairie land, whose nomadic tribes subsisted upon vast herds of the now practically extinct bison. In their manner of life, in their painted garments and their free use of paint, in their general physical characters, these prairie Indians showed remarkable resemblances to the Later Palæolithic men of the Solutrian age in Europe. But they had no horses. They seem to have made no very great advance from that primordial state, which was probably the state in which their ancestors had reached America. They had, however, a knowledge of metals, and most notably a free use of native copper, but no knowledge of iron. As the Spaniards penetrated into the continent, they found and they attacked, plundered, and destroyed two separate civilized systems that had developed in America, perhaps quite independently of the civilized systems of the Old World. One of them was the Aztec civilization of Mexico; the other, that of Peru. They had arisen out of the heliolithic sub-civilization that had drifted across the Pacific from its region of origin round and about the Mediterranean. We have already noted one or two points of interest in these unique developments. Along their own lines these civilized peoples had reached to a state of affairs roughly parallel with the culture of pre-dynastic Egypt or the early Sumerian cities.

idea of sin and the need for bloody propitiations.[1]

The Aztec civilization was destroyed by an expedition under Cortez. He had eleven ships, four hundred Europeans, two hundred Indians, sixteen horses, and fourteen guns. But in Yucatan he picked up a stray Spaniard who had been a captive with the Indians for some years, and who had more or less learnt various Indian languages, and knew that the Aztec rule was deeply resented by many of its subjects. It was in alliance with these that Cortez advanced over the mountains into the valley of Mexico (1519). How he entered Mexico, how its monarch, Montezuma, was killed by his own people for favouring the Spaniards, how Cortez was besieged in Mexico, and escaped with the loss of his guns and horses, and how after a terrible retreat to the coast he was able to return and subjugate the whole land, is a romantic and picturesque story which we cannot even attempt to tell here. The population of Mexico to this day is largely of native blood, but Spanish has replaced the native languages, and such culture as exists is Catholic and Spanish.

The still more curious Peruvian state fell a victim to another adventurer, Pizarro. He sailed from the Isthmus of Panama in 1530, with an expedition of a hundred and sixty-eight Spaniards. Like Cortez in Mexico, he availed himself of native dissensions to secure possession of the doomed state. Like Cortez, too, who had made a captive and tool of Montezuma, he seized the Inca of Peru by treachery, and attempted to rule in his name. Here again we cannot do justice to the tangle of subsequent events, the ill-planned insurrections of the natives, the arrival of Spanish reinforcements from Mexico, and the reduction of the state to a Spanish province. Nor can we tell

MEXICO and PERU

Before the Aztecs and the Peruvians there had been still earlier civilized beginnings which had either been destroyed by their successors, or which had failed and relapsed of their own accord.

The Aztecs seem to have been a conquering, less civilized people dominating a more civilized community, as the Aryans dominated Greece and North India. Their religion was a primitive, complex, and cruel system, in which human sacrifices and ceremonial cannibalism played a large part. Their minds were haunted by the

[1] For an interesting account of these American civilizations, see L. Spence, *The Civilization of Ancient Mexico* and *Myths of Mexico and Peru*.

much more of the swift spread of Spanish adventurers over the rest of America, outside the Portuguese reservation of Brazil. To begin with each story is nearly always a story of adventurers and of cruelty and loot. The Spaniards ill-treated the natives, they quarrelled among themselves, the law and order of Spain were months and years away from them ; it was only very slowly that the phase of violence and conquest passed into a phase of government and settlement. But long before there was much order in America, a steady stream of gold and silver began to flow across the Atlantic to the Spanish government and people.

After the first violent treasure hunt came plantation and the working of mines. With that arose the earliest labour difficulty in the New World. At first the Indians were enslaved with much brutality and injustice ; but to the honour of the Spaniards this did not go uncriticized. The natives found champions, and very valiant champions, in the Dominican Order and in a secular priest Las Casas, who was for a time a planter and slave-owner in Cuba until his conscience smote him. An importation of negro slaves from West Africa also began quite early in the sixteenth century. After some retrogression, Mexico, Brazil, and Spanish South America began to develop into great slave-holding, wealth-producing lands. . . .

We cannot tell here, as we would like to do, of the fine civilizing work done in South America, and more especially among the natives, by the Franciscans, and presently by the Jesuits, who came into America in the latter half of the sixteenth century (after 1549). . . .[1]

So it was that Spain rose to a temporary power and prominence in the world's affairs. It was a very sudden and very memorable rise. From the eleventh century this infertile and corrugated peninsula had been divided against itself, its Christian population had sustained a perpetual conflict with the Moors ; then by what seems like an accident it achieved unity just in time to reap the first harvest of benefit from the discovery of America. Before that time Spain had always been a poor country ; it is a poor country to-day, almost its only wealth lies in its mines. For a century, however, through its monopoly of the gold and

[1] See Cunninghame Graham's *A Vanished Arcadia*.

silver of America, it dominated the world. The east and centre of Europe were still overshadowed by the Turk and Mongol ; the discovery of America was itself a consequence of the Turkish conquests ; very largely through the Mongolian inventions of compass and paper, and under the stimulus of travel in Asia and of the growing knowledge of Eastern Asiatic wealth and civilization, came this astonishing blazing up of the mental, physical, and social energies of the "Atlantic fringe." For close in the wake of Portugal and Spain came France and England, and presently Holland, each in its turn taking up the rôle of expansion and empire overseas. The centre of interest for European history which once lay in the Levant shifts now from the Alps and the Mediterranean Sea to the Atlantic. For some centuries the Turkish Empire and Central Asia and China are relatively neglected by the limelight of the European historian. Nevertheless, these central regions of the world remain central, and their welfare and participation is necessary to the permanent peace of mankind.

§ 9

And now let us consider the political consequences of this vast release and expansion of European ideas in the fourteenth and fifteenth centuries with the new development of science, the exploration of the world, the great dissemination of knowledge through paper and printing, and the spread of a new craving for freedom and equality. How was it affecting the mentality of the courts and kings that directed the formal affairs of mankind ? We have already shown how the hold of the Catholic church upon the consciences of men was weakening at this time. Only the Spaniards, fresh from a long and finally successful religious war against Islam, had any great enthusiasm left for the church. The Turkish conquests and the expansion of the known world robbed the Roman Empire of its former prestige of universality. The old mental and moral framework of Europe was breaking up. What was happening to the dukes, princes, and kings of the old dispensation during this age of change ?

In England, as we shall tell later, very subtle and interesting tendencies were leading towards

What Machiavelli thought of the World.

a new method in government, the method of Parliament, that was to spread later on over nearly all the world. But of these tendencies the world at large was as yet practically unconscious in the sixteenth century.

Few monarchs have left us intimate diaries ; to be a monarch and to be frank are incompatible feats ; monarchy is itself necessarily a pose. The historian is obliged to speculate about the contents of the head that wears a crown as best he can. No doubt regal psychology has varied with the ages. We have, however, the writings of a very able man of this period who set himself to study and expound the arts of kingcraft as they were understood in the later fifteenth century. This was the celebrated Florentine, Niccolo Machiavelli (1469—1527). He was of good birth and reasonable fortune, and he had entered the public employment of the republic by the time he was twenty-five. For eighteen years he was in the Florentine diplomatic service ; he was engaged upon a number of embassies, and in 1500 he was sent to France to deal with the French king. From 1502 to 1512 he was the right-hand man of the gonfalonier (the life president) of Florence, Soderini. Machiavelli reorganized the Florentine army, wrote speeches for the gonfalonier, was indeed the ruling intelligence in Florentine affairs. When Soderini, who had leant upon the French, was overthrown by the Medici family whom the Spanish supported, Machiavelli, though he tried to transfer his services to the victors, was tortured on the rack and expelled. He took up his quarters in a villa near San Casciano twelve miles or so from Florence, and there entertained himself partly by collecting and writing salacious stories to a friend in Rome, and partly by writing books about Italian politics in which he could no longer play a part. Just as we owe Marco Polo's book of travels to his imprisonment, so we owe Machiavelli's *Prince*, his *Florentine History*, and the *Art of War* to his downfall and the boredom of San Casciano.

The enduring value of these books lies in the clear idea they give us of the quality and limitations of the ruling minds of this age. Their atmosphere was his atmosphere. If he brought an exceptionally keen intelligence to their business, that merely throws it into a brighter light.

His susceptible mind had been greatly impressed by the cunning, cruelty, audacity, and ambition of Cæsar Borgia, the Duke of Valentino, in whose camp he had spent some months as an envoy. In his *Prince* he idealized this dazzling person. Cæsar Borgia (1476—1507), the reader must understand, was the son of Pope Alexander VI, Alexander Borgia (1492—1503). The reader will perhaps be startled at the idea of a Pope having a son, but this, we must remember, was a pre-reformation Pope. The Papacy at this time was in a mood of moral relaxation, and though Alexander was, as a priest, pledged to live unmarried, this did not hinder him from living openly with a sort of unmarried wife, and devoting the resources of Christendom to the advancement of his family. Cæsar was a youth of spirit even for the times in which he lived ; he had early caused his elder brother to be murdered, and also the husband of his sister, Lucrezia. He had indeed betrayed and murdered a number of people. With his father's assistance he had become duke of a wide area of Central Italy when Machiavelli visited him. He had shown little or no military ability, but considerable dexterity and administrative power. His magnificence was of the most temporary sort. When presently his father died, it collapsed like a pricked bladder. Its unsoundness was not evident to Machiavelli.[1] Our chief interest in Cæsar Borgia is that he realized Machiavelli's highest ideals of a superb and successful prince.

Much has been written to show that Machiavelli had wide and noble intentions behind his political writings, but all such attempts to ennoble him will leave the sceptical reader who insists on reading the lines instead of reading imaginary things between the lines of Machiavelli's work, cold towards him. This man manifestly had no belief in any righteousness at all, no belief in a God ruling over the world or in a God in men's hearts, no understanding of the power of conscience in men. Not for him were Utopian visions of world-wide human order, or attempts to realize the *City of God*. Such things he did not want. It seemed to him that to get power, to gratify one's desires

[1] Machiavelli examines the causes of Cæsar's collapse, but he holds that it was due to *fortuna*, against which Cæsar's *virtù* could not prevail.—E. B.

Photo: Photochrom Co., Ltd.
FLORENCE ; BRUNELLESCO'S DUOMO AND GIOTTO'S CAMPANILE (p. 517).

and sensibilities and hates, to swagger triumphantly in the world, must be the crown of human desire. Only a prince could fully realize such a life. Some streak of timidity or his sense of the poorness of his personal claims had evidently made him abandon such dreams for himself ; but at least he might hope to serve a prince, to live close to the glory, to share the plunder and the lust and the gratified malice. He might even make himself indispensable ! He set himself, therefore, to become an " expert " in prince-craft. He assisted Soderini to fail. When he was racked and rejected by the Medicis, and had no further hopes of being even a successful court parasite, he wrote these handbooks of cunning to show what a clever servant some prince had lost. His ruling thought, his great contribution to political literature, was that the moral obligations upon ordinary men cannot bind princes.[1]

There is a disposition to ascribe the virtue of patriotism to Machiavelli because he suggested that Italy, which was weak and divided—she had been invaded by the Turks and saved from conquest only by the death of the Sultan Muhammad, and she was being fought over by the French and Spanish as though she was something inanimate—might be united and strong ; but he saw in that possibility only a great opportunity for a prince. And he advocated a national army only because he saw the Italian method of carrying on war by hiring bands of foreign mercenaries was a hopeless one. At any time such troops might go over to a better paymaster or decide to plunder the state they protected. He had been deeply impressed by the victories of the Swiss over the Milanese, but he never fathomed the secret of the free spirit that made those victories possible. The Florentine militia he created was a complete failure. He was a man born blind to the qualities that make peoples free and nations great.

Yet this morally blind man was living in a

---

[1] E. B. writes as follows : " I think better of Machiavelli than you do, and especially on two points. (1) He raises a real issue—whether, when a crisis besets the State, the ruler is not bound to abandon the rules of private morality, if by doing so he can preserve the State. If he abandons those rules, he does *wrong*—and Machiavelli admits that—but, at the same time, as the agent and organ of the State, he does *right* by preserving it, so far, at any rate, as it is right that it should be preserved. This is a real issue, which one cannot simply dismiss. *E.g.*, all war is wrong, by the rules of private morality, because it is killing ; but it may have a qualified and conditioned rightness if it is necessary to preserve the State, and if the State, as a scheme of good life, ought to be preserved. (2) Machiavelli did believe in the people. He only exalts the *new* prince, who arises to restore order and security in a troubled State. In normal times he believes that the people is a good judge of men : that ' better than many fortresses is not to be hated by the people ' ; that the trite proverb, ' He who founds himself on the people founds himself on mud,' is untrue, except as applied to demagogues."

little world of morally blind men. It is clear that his style of thought was the style of thought of the courts of his time. Behind the princes of the new states that had grown up out of the wreckage of the empire and the failure of the church, there were everywhere chancellors and secretaries and trusted ministers of the Machiavellian type. Cromwell, for instance, the minister of Henry VIII of England after his breach with Rome, regarded Machiavelli's *Prince* as the quintessence of political wisdom. When the princes were themselves sufficiently clever they too were Machiavellian. They were scheming

became frankly republican in 1499. As early as the thirteenth century, the peasant farmers of three valleys round about the Lake of Lucerne took it into their heads that they would dispense with an overlord and manage their own affairs in their own fashion. Their chief trouble came from the claims of a noble family of the Aar valley, the Habsburg family. In 1245 the men of Schwyz burnt the castle of New Habsburg which had been set up near Lucerne to overawe them ; its ruins are still to be seen there.

This Habsburg family was a growing and acquisitive one ; it had lands and possessions throughout Germany ; and in 1273, after the extinction of the Hohenstaufen house, Rudolf of Habsburg was elected Emperor of Germany, a distinction that became at last practically hereditary in his family. None the less, the men of Uri, Schwyz, and Unterwalden did not mean to be ruled by any Habsburg ; they formed an Everlasting League in 1291, and they held their own among the mountains from that time onward to this day, first as free members of the empire and

SWITZERLAND, showing principal Passes and Routes

The Everlasting League, 1291
Frontiers of the Confederation, 16th Cent'y
Mountains above 6000 feet

then as an absolutely independent confederation. Of the heroic legend of William Tell we have no space to tell here, nor have we room in which to trace the gradual extension of the confederation to its present boundaries. Romansh, Italian, and French-speaking valleys were presently added to this valiant little republican group. The red cross flag of Geneva has become the symbol of international humanity in the midst of warfare. The bright and thriving cities of Switzerland have been a refuge for free men from a score of tyrannies.

to outdo one another, to rob weaker contemporaries, to destroy rivals, so that they might for a brief interval swagger. They had little or no vision of any scheme of human destinies greater than this game they played against one another.

§ 10

It is interesting to note that this Swiss infantry which had so impressed Machiavelli **The Republic of Switzerland.** was no part of the princely system of Europe. At the very centre of the European system there had arisen a little confederation of free states, the Swiss Confederation, which after some centuries of nominal adhesion to the Holy Roman Empire,

§ 11A

Most of the figures that stand out in history,

The Life of the Emperor Charles V. do so through some exceptional personal quality, good or bad, that makes them more significant than their fellows. But there was born at Ghent in Belgium in 1500 a man of commonplace abilities and melancholy temperament, the son of a mentally defective mother who had been married for reasons of state, who was, through no fault of his own, to become the focus of the accumulating stresses of Europe. The historian must give him a quite unmerited and accidental prominence side by side with such marked individualities as Alexander and Charlemagne and Frederick II. This was the Emperor Charles V. For a time he had an air of being the greatest monarch in Europe since Charlemagne. Both he and his illusory greatness were the results of the matrimonial statecraft of his grandfather the Emperor Maximilian I (born 1459, died 1519).

Some families have fought, others have intrigued their way to world power; the Habsburgs married their way. Maximilian began his career with the inheritance of the Habsburgs, Austria, Styria, part of Alsace and other districts; he married—the lady's name scarcely matters to us—the Netherlands and Burgundy. Most of Burgundy slipped from him after his first wife's death, but the Netherlands he held. Then he tried unsuccessfully to marry Brittany. He became Emperor in succession to his father, Frederick III, in 1493, and married the duchy of Milan. Finally he married his son to the weak-minded daughter of Ferdinand and Isabella, the Ferdinand and Isabella of Columbus, who not only reigned over a freshly united Spain, and over Sardinia and the kingdom of the Two Sicilies, but by virtue of the papal gifts to Castile, over all America west of Brazil. So it was that Charles, his grandson, inherited most of the American continent and between a third and a half of what the Turks had left of Europe. The father of Charles died in 1506, and Maximilian did his best to secure his grandson's election to the imperial throne.

Charles succeeded to the Netherlands in 1506; he became practically king of the Spanish dominions, his mother being imbecile, when his grandfather Ferdinand died in 1516; and his grandfather Maximilian dying in 1519,

he was in 1520 elected Emperor at the still comparatively tender age of twenty.

His election as Emperor was opposed by the young and brilliant French King, Francis I, who had succeeded to the French throne in 1515 at the age of twenty-one. The candidature of Francis was supported by Leo X (1513), who also requires from us the epithet brilliant. It was indeed an age of brilliant monarchs. It was the age of Baber in India (1526—1530) and Suleiman in Turkey (1520). Both Leo and Francis dreaded the concentration of so much power in the hands of one man as the election of Charles threatened. The only other monarch who seemed to matter in Europe was Henry VIII, who had become King of England in 1509 at the age of eighteen. He also offered himself as a candidate for the empire, and the imaginative English reader may amuse himself by working out the possible consequences of such an election. There was much scope for diplomacy in this triangle of kings. Charles on his way from Spain to Germany visited England and secured the support of Henry against Francis by bribing his minister, Cardinal Wolsey. Henry also made a great parade of friendship with Francis, there were feasting, tournaments, and suchlike antiquated gallantries in France, in a courtly picnic known to historians as the Field of the Cloth of Gold (1520). Knighthood was becoming a picturesque affectation in the sixteenth century. The Emperor Maximilian I is still called "the last of the knights" by German historians.

The election of Charles was secured, it is to be noted, by a vast amount of bribery. He had as his chief supporters and creditors the great German business house of the Fuggers. That large treatment of money and credit which we call finance, which had gone out of European political life with the collapse of the Roman Empire, was now coming back to power. This appearance of the Fuggers, whose houses and palaces outshone those of the emperors, marks the upward movement of forces that had begun two or three centuries earlier in Cahors in France and in Florence and other Italian towns. Money, public debts, and social unrest and discontent, re-enter upon the miniature stage of this *Outline*. Charles V was not so much a Habsburg as a Fugger emperor.

For a time this fair, not very intelligent-looking young man with the thick upper lip and a long, clumsy chin—features which still afflict his descendants—was largely a puppet in the hands of his ministers. Able servants after the order of Machiavelli guided him at first in the arts of kingship. Then in a slow but effectual way he began to assert himself. He was confronted at the very outset of his reign in Germany with the perplexing dissensions of Christendom. The revolt against the papal rule which had been going on since the days of Huss and Wycliffe had been recently exasperated by a new and unusually cynical selling of indulgences to raise money for the completion of St. Peter's at Rome. A monk named Luther, who had been consecrated as a priest, who had taken to reading the Bible, and who, while visiting Rome on the business of his order, had been much shocked by the levity and worldly splendour of the Papacy, had come forward against these papal expedients at Wittenberg (1517), offering disputation and propounding certain theses. An important controversy ensued. At first Luther carried on this controversy in Latin, but presently took to German, and speedily had the people in a ferment. Charles found this dispute raging when he came from Spain to Germany. He summoned an assembly or "diet" of the empire at Worms on the Rhine. To this, Luther, who had been asked to recant his views by Pope Leo X, and who had refused to do so, was summoned. He came, and, entirely in the spirit of Huss, refused to recant unless he was convinced of his error by logical argument or the authority of Scripture. But his protectors among the princes were too powerful for him to suffer the fate of John Huss.

Here was a perplexing situation for the young Emperor. There is reason to suppose that he was inclined at first to support Luther against the Pope. Leo X had opposed the election of Charles, and was friendly with his rival, Francis I. But Charles V was not a good Machiavellian, and he had acquired in

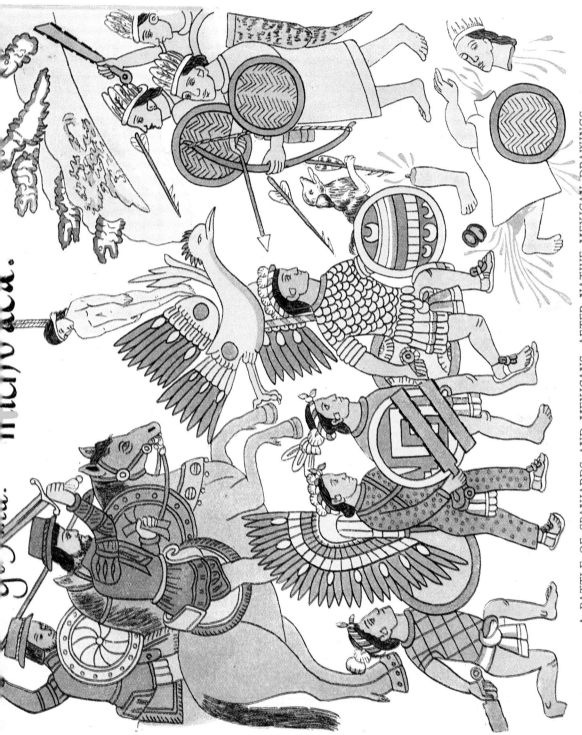

A BATTLE OF SPANIARDS AND MEXICANS, AFTER NATIVE MEXICAN DRAWINGS.

This drawing shows the Spaniards with their native allies and their war-dogs. The symbols of the native chiefs (the bird and the fish) float over them. A Spaniard has written on the name of the Spanish leader Guzman and of Michuacan, the district of the fight. An Indian traitor has been hung. Note the odd similarity in manner between this and the Bayeux tapestry already figured in this *Outline*.

Photo: *Rischgitz Collection.*
FRANCIS I.
(By Titian.)

Photo: *Rischgitz Collection.*
HENRY VIII.
(By Holbein.)

Photo: *Rischgitz Collection.*
THE EMPEROR CHARLES V.
(By Titian.)

Spain a considerable religious sincerity. He decided against Luther. Many of the German princes, and especially the Elector of Saxony, sided with the reformer. Luther went into hiding under the protection of the Saxon Elector, and Charles found himself in the presence of the opening rift that was to split Christendom into two contending camps.

Close upon these disturbances, and probably connected with them, came a widespread peasants' revolt throughout Germany. This outbreak frightened Luther very effectually. He was shocked by its excesses, and from that time forth the Reformation he advocated ceased to be a Reformation according to the people and became a Reformation according to the princes. He lost his confidence in that free judgment for which he had stood up so manfully.

Meanwhile Charles realized that his great empire was in very serious danger both from the west and from the east. On the west of him was his spirited rival, Francis I; to the east was the Turk in Hungary, in alliance with Francis and clamouring for certain arrears of tribute from the Austrian dominions. Charles had the money and army of Spain at his disposal, but it was extremely difficult to get any effective support in money from Germany. His grandfather had developed a German infantry on the Swiss model, very much upon the lines expounded in Machiavelli's *Art of War*, but these troops had to be paid and his imperial subsidies had to be supplemented by unsecured borrowings, which were finally to bring his supporters, the Fuggers, to ruin.

On the whole, Charles, in alliance with Henry VIII, was successful against Francis I and the Turk. Their chief battlefield was North Italy; the generalship was dull on both sides; their advances and retreats depended chiefly on the arrival of reinforcements. The German army invaded France, failed to take Marseilles, fell back into Italy, lost Milan, and was besieged in Pavia. Francis I made a long and unsuccessful siege of Pavia, was caught by fresh German forces, defeated, wounded, and taken prisoner. He sent back a message to his queen that all was "lost but honour," made a humiliating peace, and broke it as soon as he was liberated, so that even the salvage of honour was but temporary. Henry VIII and the Pope, in obedience to the rules of Machiavellian strategy, now went over to the side of France in order to prevent Charles becoming too powerful. The German troops in Milan, under the Constable of Bourbon, being unpaid, forced rather than followed their commander into a raid upon Rome. They stormed the city and pillaged it (1527). The Pope took refuge in the Castle of San Angelo while the looting and slaughter went on. He bought off the German troops at last by the payment of four hundred thousand ducats. Ten years of such stupid and confused fighting impoverished all Europe and left the Emperor in possession of Milan. In 1530 he was crowned by the Pope—he was the last German Emperor to be crowned by the Pope—at Bologna. One thinks of the rather dull-looking blonde face, with its long lip and chin, bearing the solemn expression of one who endures a doubtful though probably honourable ceremony.

34

Meanwhile the Turks were making great headway in Hungary. They had defeated and killed the King of Hungary in 1526, they held Buda-Pesth, and in 1529, as we have already noted, Suleiman the Magnificent very nearly took Vienna. The Emperor was greatly concerned by these advances, and did his utmost to drive back the Turks, but he found the greatest difficulty in getting the German princes to unite even with this formidable

place of a great campaign to recover Hungary for Christendom Charles had to turn his mind to the gathering internal struggle in Germany. Of that struggle he saw only the opening war. It was a struggle, a sanguinary irrational bickering of princes for ascendancy, now flaming into war and destruction, now sinking back to intrigues and diplomacies; it was a snake's sack of Machiavellian policies, that was to go on writhing incurably right into the nineteenth century, and to waste and desolate Central Europe again and again.

The Emperor never seems to have grasped the true forces at work in these gathering troubles. He was for his time and station an exceptionally worthy man, and he seems to have taken the religious dissensions that were tearing Europe into warring fragments as genuine theological differences. He gathered diets and councils in futile attempts at reconciliation. Formulæ and confessions were tried over. The student of German history must struggle with the details of the Religious Peace of Nuremberg, the settlement at the diet of Ratisbon, the Interim of Augsburg, and the like. Here we do but mention them as details in the worried life of this culminating emperor. As a matter of fact, hardly one of the multifarious princes and rulers in Europe seems to have been acting in good faith. The widespread religious trouble of the world, the desire of the common people for truth and social righteousness, the spreading knowledge of the time, all those things were merely counters in the imaginations of princely diplomacy. Henry

Photo: Mansell.

GHENT. HÔTEL DE VILLE.

enemy upon their very borders. Francis I remained implacable for a time, and there was a new French war; but in 1538 Charles won his rival over to a more friendly attitude by ravaging the south of France. Francis and Charles then formed an alliance against the Turk, but the Protestant princes, the German princes who were resolved to break away from Rome, had formed a league, the Schmalkaldic League (named after the little town of Schmalkalden in Hesse, at which its constitution was arranged) against the Emperor, and in the

VIII of England, who had begun his career with a book written against heresy, and who had been rewarded by the Pope with the title of " Defender of the Faith," being anxious to divorce his first wife in favour of an animated young lady named Anne Boleyn, and wishing also to turn against the Emperor in favour of Francis I and to loot the vast wealth of the church in England, joined the company of Protestant princes in 1530. Sweden, Denmark, and Norway had already gone over to the Protestant side.

The German religious war began in 1546, a few months after the death of Martin Luther. We need not trouble about the incidents of the campaign. The Protestant Saxon army was badly beaten at Lochau. By something very like a breach of faith Philip of Hesse, the Emperor's chief remaining antagonist, was caught and imprisoned, and the Turks were bought off by the payment of an annual tribute. In 1547, to the great relief of the Emperor, Francis I died. So by 1547 Charles got to a kind of settlement, and made his last efforts to effect peace where there was no peace. In 1552 all Germany was at war again, only a precipitate flight from Innsbruck saved Charles from capture, and in 1552, with the Treaty of Passau, came another unstable equilibrium. Charles was now utterly weary of the cares and splendours of empire; he had never had a very sound constitution, he was naturally indolent, and he was suffering greatly from gout. He abdicated. He made over all his sovereign rights in Germany to his brother Ferdinand, and Spain and the Netherlands he resigned to his son Philip. He then retired to a monastery at Yuste, among the oak and chestnut forests in the hills to the north of the Tagus valley, and there he died in 1558.

Much has been written in a sentimental vein of this retirement, this renunciation of the world by this tired majestic Titan, world-weary, seeking in an austere solitude his peace with God. But his retreat was neither solitary nor austere; he had with him nearly a hundred and fifty attendants; his establishment had all the indulgences without the fatigues of a court, and Philip II was a dutiful son to whom his father's advice was a command. As for his austerities, let Prescott witness: " In the almost daily correspondence between Quixada, or Gaztelu, and the Secretary of State at Valladolid, there is scarcely a letter that does not turn more or less on the Emperor's eating or his illness. The one seems naturally to follow, like a running commentary, on the other. It is rare that such topics have formed the burden of communications with the department of state. It must have been no easy matter for the secretary to preserve his gravity in the perusal of despatches in which politics and gastronomy were so strangely mixed together.

The courier from Valladolid to Lisbon was ordered to make a detour, so as to take Jarandilla in his route, and bring supplies for the royal table. On Thursdays he was to bring fish to serve for the *jour maigre* that was to follow. The trout in the neighbourhood Charles thought too small; so others, of a larger size, were to be sent from Valladolid. Fish of every kind was to his taste, as, indeed, was anything that in its nature or habits at all approached to fish. Eels, frogs, oysters, occupied an important place in the royal bill of fare. Potted fish, especially anchovies, found great favour with him; and he regretted that he had not brought a better supply of these from the Low Countries. On an eel-pasty he particularly doted." . . .[1]

In 1554 Charles had obtained a bull from Pope Julius III granting him a dispensation from fasting, and allowing him to break his fast early in the morning even when he was to take the sacrament.

" That Charles was not altogether unmindful of his wearing apparel in Yuste, may be inferred from the fact that his wardrobe contained no less than sixteen robes of silk and velvet, lined with ermine, or eider down, or the soft hair of the Barbary goat. As to the furniture and upholstery of his apartments, how little reliance is to be placed on the reports so carelessly circulated about these may be gathered from a single glance at the inventory of his effects, prepared by Quixada and Gaztelu soon after their master's death. Among the items we find carpets from Turkey and Alcarez, canopies of velvet and other stuffs, hangings of fine black cloth, which since his mother's death he had always chosen for his own bedroom; while the remaining apartments were provided with no less than twenty-five suits of tapestry, from the looms of Flanders, richly embroidered with figures of animals and with landscapes. . . . Among the different pieces of plate we find some of pure gold, and others especially noted for their curious workmanship; and as this was an age in which the art of working the precious metals was carried to the highest perfection, we cannot doubt that some of the finest specimens had come into the

[1] Prescott's Appendix to Robertson's *History of Charles V.*

Emperor's possession. The whole amount of plate was estimated at between twelve and thirteen thousand ounces in weight." . . .[1]

Charles had never acquired the habit of reading, but he would be read aloud to at meals after the fashion of Charlemagne, and would make what one narrator describes as a "sweet and heavenly commentary." He also amused himself with mechanical toys, by listening to music or sermons, and by attending to the imperial business that still came drifting in to him. The death of the Empress, to whom he was greatly attached, had turned his mind towards religion, which in his case took a punctilious and ceremonial form; every Friday in Lent he scourged himself with the rest of the monks with such good will as to draw blood. These exercises and the gout released a bigotry in Charles that had been hitherto restrained by considerations of policy. The appearance of Protestant teaching close at hand in Valladolid roused him to fury. "Tell the grand inquisitor and his council from me, to be at their posts, and to lay the axe at the root of the evil before it spreads further." . . . He expressed a doubt whether it would not be well, in so black an affair, to dispense with the ordinary course of justice, and to show no mercy; "lest the criminal, if pardoned, should have the opportunity of repeating his crime." He recommended, as an example, his own mode of proceeding in the Netherlands, "where all who remained obstinate in their

[1] Prescott.

Photo: Anderson.

LORENZO DE' MEDICI.
(The statue by Michelangelo in the Medici Chapel, Florence.)

errors were burned alive, and those who were admitted to penitence were beheaded."

Among the chief pleasures of the Catholic monarch between meals during this time of retirement were funeral services. He not only attended every actual funeral that was celebrated at Yuste, but he had services conducted for the absent dead, he held a funeral service in memory of his wife on the anniversary of her death, and finally he celebrated his own obsequies. "The chapel was hung with black, and the blaze of hundreds of wax-lights was scarcely sufficient to dispel the darkness. The brethren in their conventual dress, and all the Emperor's household clad in deep mourning, gathered round a huge catafalque, shrouded also in black, which had been raised in the centre of the chapel. The service for the burial of the dead was then performed; and, amidst the dismal wail of the monks, the prayers ascended for the departed spirit, that it might be received into the mansions of the blessed. The sorrowful attendants were melted to tears, as the image of their master's death was presented to their minds—or they were touched, it may be, with compassion by this pitiable display of weakness. Charles, muffled in a dark mantle, and bearing a lighted candle in his hand, mingled with his household, the spectator of his own obsequies; and the doleful ceremony was concluded by his placing the taper in the hands of the priest, in sign of his surrendering up his soul to the Almighty."

Other accounts make Charles wear a shroud and lie in the coffin, remaining there alone until the last mourner had left the chapel.

Within two months of this masquerade he was dead. And the greatness of the Holy Roman Empire died with him. The Holy Roman Empire struggled on indeed to the days of Napoleon, but as an invalid and dying thing.

§ 11B

Ferdinand, the brother of Charles V, took over his abandoned work and met the German **Protestants** princes at the diet of Augsburg in **if the Prince** 1555. Again there was an attempt **wills it.** to establish a religious peace. Nothing could better show the quality of that attempted settlement and the blindness of the princes and statesmen concerned in it, to the deeper and broader processes of the time, than the form that settlement took. The recognition of religious freedom was to apply to the states and not to individual citizens; *cujus regio ejus religio, " the confession of the subject was to be dependent on that of the territorial lord."*

§ 11C

We have given as much attention as we have done to the writings of Machiavelli and to the **The** personality of Charles V because **Intellectual** they throw a flood of light upon **Undertow.** the antagonisms of the next period in our history. This present chapter has told the story of a vast expansion of human horizons and of a great increase and distribution of knowledge; we have seen the conscience of common men awakening and intimations of a new and profounder social justice spreading throughout the general body of the Western civilization. But this process of light and thought was leaving courts and the political life of the world untouched. There is little in Machiavelli that might not have been written by some clever secretary in the court of Chosroes I or Shi-Hwang-Ti—or even of Sargon I or Pepi. While the world in everything else was moving forward, in political ideas, in ideas about the relationship of state to state and of sovereign to citizen, it was standing still. Nay, it was falling back. For the great idea of the Catholic Church as the world City

VENICE. THE DOGE'S PALACE.

of God had been destroyed in men's minds by the church itself, and the dream of a world imperialism had, in the person of Charles V, been carried in effigy through Europe to limbo. Politically the world seemed falling back towards personal monarchy of the Assyrian or Macedonian pattern.

It is not that the newly awakened intellectual energies of ¹Western European men were too absorbed in theological restatement, in scientific investigations, in exploration and mercantile development, to give a thought to the claims and responsibilities of rulers. Not only were common men drawing ideas of a theocratic or republican or communistic character from the now accessible Bible, but the renewed study of the Greek classics was bringing the creative and fertilizing spirit of Plato to bear upon the Western mind. In England Sir Thomas More produced a quaint imitation of Plato's *Republic* in his *Utopia*, setting out a sort of autocratic communism. In Naples, a century later, a certain friar Campanella was equally bold in his *City of the Sun*. But such discussions were having no immediate effect upon political arrangements. Compared with the massiveness of the task, these books do indeed seem poetical and scholarly and flimsy. (Yet later on the *Utopia* was to bear fruit in the English Poor Laws.) The intellectual and moral development of the Western mind and this drift towards Machiavellian monarchy in Europe were for a time going on concurrently in the same world, but they were going on almost independently. The statesmen still schemed and manœuvred as if nothing changed in the world but frontiers, and as if nothing grew but the power of wary and fortunate kings. It was only in the seventeenth and eighteenth centuries that these two streams of tendency, the stream of general ideas and the drift of traditional and egoistic monarchial diplomacy, interfered and came into conflict.

Chronological Table.

We will now draw together into a chronological table another nine centuries of history, from the time of the Caliph Omar to the death of Charles V.

650. Othman, the Third Caliph, is reigning in Medina, Tai Tsung of the Tang Dynasty dies this year in Singan, Constans II, the grandson of Heraclius, is emperor in Constantinople, Merovingian kings reign in Austrasia and Neustria, Christian missionaries are active in England.

655. Moslems defeat Byzantine fleet.

656. Othman murdered at Medina.

661. Ali murdered.

662. Moawija Caliph. (First of the Omayyad caliphs.)

668. The Caliph Moawija attacks Constantinople by sea—Theodore of Tarsus becomes Archbishop of Canterbury.

675. Last of the sea attacks by Moawija on Constantinople.

687. Pepin of Hersthal as mayor of the palace, reunites Austrasia and Neustria.

711. Moslem army invades Spain from Africa.

714. Charles Martel mayor of the palace.

715. The domains of the Caliph Walid I extend from the Pyrenees to China.

717—18. Suleiman, son and successor of Walid, fails to take Constantinople. The Omayyad line passes its climax.

732. Charles Martel defeats the Moslems near Poitiers.

735. Death of the Venerable Bede.

743. Walid II Caliph. The unbelieving Caliph.

749. Overthrow of the Omayyads. Abdul Abbas, the first Abbasid Caliph. Spain remains Omayyad. Beginning of the break-up of the Arab Empire.

751. Pepin crowned King of the French.

755. Martyrdom of St. Boniface.

768. Pepin dies.

771. Charlemagne sole king.

774. Charlemagne conquers Lombardy.

776. Charlemagne in Dalmatia.

786. Haroun al Raschid Abbasid Caliph in Bagdad (to 809).

795. Leo III becomes Pope (to 816).
800. Leo crowns Charlemagne Emperor of the West.
802. Egbert, formerly an English refugee at the court of Charlemagne, establishes himself as King of Wessex.
810. Krum of Bulgaria defeats and kills the Emperor Nicephorus.
814. Charlemagne dies, Louis the Pious succeeds him.
828. Egbert becomes first King of England.
843. Louis the Pious dies, and the Carlovingian Empire goes to pieces. Until 962 there is no regular succession of Holy Roman Emperors, though the title appears intermittently.
850. About this time Rurik (a Northman) becomes ruler of Novgorod and Kieff.
852. Boris first Christian King of Bulgaria (to 884).
865. The fleet of the Russians (Northmen) threatens Constantinople.
886. The Treaty of Alfred of England and Guthrum the Dane, establishing the Danes in the Danelaw.
904. Russian (Northman) fleet off Constantinople.
912. Rolf the Ganger establishes himself in Normandy.
919. Henry the Fowler elected King of Germany.
928. Marozia imprisons Pope John X.
931. John XI Pope (to 936).
936. Otto I becomes King of Germany in succession to his father, Henry the Fowler.
941. Russian fleet again threatens Constantinople.
955. John XII Pope.
960. Northern Sung Dynasty begins in China.

962. Otto I, King of Germany, is crowned Emperor (first Saxon Emperor) by John XII.
963. Otto deposes John XII.
969. Separate Fatimite Caliphate set up in Egypt.
973. Otto II.
983. Otto III.
987. Hugh Capet becomes King of France. End of the Carlovingian line of French kings.
1013. Canute becomes King of England, Denmark, and Norway.
1037. Avicenna of Bokhara, the Prince of Physicians, dies.
1043. Russian fleet threatens Constantinople.
1066. Conquest of England by William Duke of Normandy.
1071. Revival of Islam under the Seljuk Turks. Battle of Melasgird.
1073. Hildebrand becomes Pope (Gregory VII) to 1085.
1082. Robert Guiscard captures Durazzo.
1084. Robert Guiscard sacks Rome.
1087—99. Urban II Pope.
1094. Pestilence.
1095. Urban II at Clermont summons the First Crusade.
1096. Massacre of the People's Crusade.
1099. Godfrey of Bouillon captures Jerusalem. Paschal II Pope (to 1118).
1138. Kin Empire flourishes. Sung capital shifted from Nankin to Hang Chau.
1147. The Second Crusade. Foundation of the Christian Kingdom of Portugal.
1169. Saladin Sultan of Egypt.

1176. Frederick Barbarossa acknowledges supremacy of the Pope (Alexander III) at Venice.

1187. Saladin captures Jerusalem.
1189. The Third Crusade.

1198. Averroes of Cordoba, the Arab philosopher, dies. Innocent III Pope (to 1216). Frederick II (aged four), King of Sicily, becomes his ward.
1202. The Fourth Crusade attacks the Eastern Empire.
1204. Capture of Constantinople by the Latins.
1206. Kutub founds Moslem state at Delhi.

1212. The Children's Crusade.
1214. Jengis Khan takes Pekin.
1216. Honorius III Pope.
1218. Jengis Khan invades Kharismia.
1221. Failure and return of the Fifth Crusade. St. Dominic dies (the Dominicans).
1226. St. Francis of Assisi dies. (The Franciscans.)
1227. Jengis Khan dies, Khan from the Caspian to the Pacific, and is succeeded by Ogdai Khan.
1227. Gregory IX Pope.
1228. Frederick II embarks upon the Sixth Crusade, and acquires Jerusalem.
1234. Mongols complete conquest of the Kin Empire with the help of the Sung Empire.
1239. Frederick II excommunicated for the second time.
1240. Mongols destroy Kieff. Russia tributary to the Mongols.
1241. Mongol victory at Liegnitz in Silesia.
1244. The Egyptian Sultan recaptures Jerusalem. This leads to the Seventh Crusade.
1245. Frederick II re-excommunicated. The men of Schwyz burn the castle of New Habsburg.
1250. St. Louis of France ransomed. Frederick II, the last Hohenstaufen Emperor, dies. German interregnum until 1273.
1251. Mangu Khan becomes Great Khan. Kublai Khan is governor of China.
1258. Hulagu Khan takes and destroys Bagdad.
1260. Kublai Khan becomes Great Khan. Ketboga defeated in Palestine.

1261. The Greeks recapture Constantinople from the Latins.

1269. Kublai Khan sends a message of inquiry to the Pope by the older Polos.
1271. Marco Polo starts upon his travels.
1273. Rudolf of Habsburg elected Emperor. The Swiss form their Everlasting League.

1280. Kublai Khan founds the Yuan Dynasty in China.

1292. Death of Kublai Khan.
1293. Roger Bacon, the prophet of experimental science, dies.
1294. Boniface VIII Pope (to 1303).
1295. Marco Polo returns to Venice.

1303. Death of Pope Boniface VIII after the outrage of Anagni by Guillaume de Nogaret.
1305. Clement V Pope. The papal court set up at Avignon.
1308. Duns Scotus dies.

1318. Four Franciscans burnt for heresy at Marseilles.

1347. Occam dies.
1348. The Great Plague, the Black Death.

1358. The Jacquerie in France.
1360. In China the Mongol (Yuan) Dynasty falls, and is succeeded by the Ming Dynasty (to 1644).
1367. Timurlane assumes the title of Great Khan.

1377. Pope Gregory XI returns to Rome.
1378. The Great Schism. Urban VI in Rome, Clement VII at Avignon.
1381. Peasant revolt in England. Wat Tyler murdered in the presence of King Richard II.
1384. Wycliffe dies.

1398 Huss preaches Wycliffism at Prague.
1405. Death of Timurlane.

1414—18. The Council of Constance. Huss is burnt (1415).

1417. The Great Schism ends, Martin V Pope.

1420. The Hussites rebel. Martin V preaches a crusade against them.

1431. The Catholic Crusaders dissolve before the Hussites at Domazlice. The Council of Basle meets.

1436. The Hussites come to terms with the church.

1439. Council of Basle creates a fresh schism in the church.

1445. Discovery of Cape Verde by the Portuguese.

1446. First printed books (Coster in Haarlem).

1449. End of the Council of Basle.

1453. Ottoman Turks under Muhammad II take Constantinople.

1480. Ivan III Grand Duke of Moscow throws off the Mongol allegiance.

1481. Death of the Sultan Muhammad II while preparing for the conquest of Italy. Bayazid II Turkish Sultan (to 1512).

1486. Diaz rounds the Cape of Good Hope.

1492. Columbus crosses the Atlantic to America. Alexander Borgia, Alexander VI, Pope (to 1503).

1493. Maximilian I becomes Emperor.

1498. Vasco da Gama sails round the Cape to India.

1499. Switzerland becomes an independent republic.

1500. Charles V born.

1509. Henry VIII King of England.

1512. Selim Sultan (to 1520). He buys the title of Caliph. Fall of Soderini (and Machiavelli) in Florence.

1513. Leo X Pope.

1515. Francis I King of France.

1517. Selim annexes Egypt. Luther propounds his theses at Wittenberg.

1519. Leonardo da Vinci dies. Magellan's expedition starts to sail round the world. Cortez enters Mexico city.

1520. Suleiman the Magnificent Sultan (to 1566), who ruled from Bagdad to Hungary. Charles V Emperor.

1521. Luther at the Diet of Worms. Loyola wounded at Pampeluna.

1525. Baber wins the battle of Panipat, captures Delhi, and founds the Mogul Empire.

1527. The German troops in Italy, under the Constable of Bourbon, take and pillage Rome.

1529. Suleiman besieges Vienna.

1530. Pizarro invades Peru. Charles V crowned by the Pope. Henry VIII begins his quarrel with the Papacy.

1532. The Anabaptists seize Münster.

1535. Fall of the Anabaptist rule in Münster.

1539. The Company of Jesus is founded.

1543. Copernicus dies.

1545. The Council of Trent (to 1563) assembles to put the church in order.

1546. Martin Luther dies.

1547. Francis I dies.

1549. First Jesuit missions arrive in South America.

1552. Treaty of Passau. Temporary pacification of Germany.

1556. Charles V abdicates. Akbar Great Mogul (to 1605). Ignatius of Loyola dies.

1558. Death of Charles V.

(Here our chronology ends for the present, but it will round off one or two topics if we add a few later dates.)

1601. Tycho Brahe dies.

1603. Dr. Gilbert dies.

1626. Sir Francis Bacon (Lord Verulam) dies.

1630. Kepler dies.

1642. Galileo dies. Newton born.

1657. Harvey dies.

1662. The Royal Society founded.

1683. Vienna besieged by the Turks for the last time, and rescued by Polish cavalry.

Book VIII
THE AGE OF THE GREAT POWERS

XXXVI
PRINCES, PARLIAMENTS, AND POWERS

§ 1

IN the preceding chapter we have traced the beginnings of a new civilization, the civilization of the " modern " type which becomes at the present time world-wide. It is still a vast unformed thing, still only in the opening phases of growth and development to-day. We have seen the mediæval ideas of the Holy Roman Empire and of the Roman Church, as forms of universal law and order, fade in its dawn. They fade out, as if it were necessary in order that these ideas of one law and one order for all men should be redrawn on world-wide lines. And while in nearly every other field of human interest there was advance, the effacement of these general political ideas of the church and empire led back for a time in things political towards merely personal monarchy and monarchist nationalism of the Macedonian type. There came an interregnum, as it were, in the consolidation of human affairs, a phase of the type the Chinese annalists would call an " Age of Confusion." This interregnum has lasted as long as that between the fall of the Western Empire and the crowning of Charlemagne in Rome. We are living in it to-day. It may be drawing to its close ; we cannot tell yet. The old leading ideas had broken down, a medley of new and untried projects and suggestions perplexed men's minds and actions, and meanwhile the world at large had to fall back for leadership upon the ancient tradition of an individual prince. There was no new way clearly apparent for men to follow, and the prince was there.

Princes and Foreign Policy.

All over the world the close of the sixteenth century saw monarchy prevailing and tending towards absolutism. Germany and Italy were patchworks of autocratic princely dominions, Spain was practically autocratic, the throne had never been so powerful in England, and as the seventeenth century drew on, the French monarchy gradually became the greatest and most consolidated power in Europe. The phases and fluctuations of its ascent we cannot record here.

At every court there were groups of ministers and secretaries who played a Machiavellian game against their foreign rivals. Foreign policy is the natural employment of courts and monarchies. Foreign offices are, so to speak, the leading characters in all the histories of the seventeenth and eighteenth centuries. They kept Europe in a fever of wars. And wars were becoming expensive. Armies were no longer untrained levies, no longer assemblies of feudal knights who brought their own horses and weapons and retainers with them ; they needed more and more artillery ; they consisted of paid troops who insisted on their pay ; they were professional and slow and elaborate, conducting long sieges, necessitating elaborate fortifications. War expenditure increased everywhere and called for more and more taxation. And here it was that these monarchies of the sixteenth and seventeenth centuries came into conflict with new and shapeless forces of freedom in the community. In practice the princes found they were not masters of their subjects' lives or property. They found an inconvenient resistance to the taxation that was necessary if their diplomatic aggressions and alliances were to continue. Finance became an unpleasant spectre in every council chamber. In theory the monarch owned his country. James I of England (1603) declared that " As it is atheism and blasphemy to dispute what God can do ; so it is presumption and high contempt in a subject to dispute what a king can do, or say that a king cannot do this or that." In practice, however, he found, and his son Charles I (1625) was to find still more effectually, that there were in his dominions a great number of landlords and merchants, substantial and intelligent persons, who set a very definite limit to the calls and occasions of the monarch and his ministers. They were prepared to tolerate his rule if they themselves might also be monarchs of their lands and businesses and trades and what not. But not otherwise.

Everywhere in Europe there was a parallel development. Beneath the kings and princes there were these lesser monarchs, the private owners, noblemen, wealthy citizens and the like, who were now offering the sovereign prince much the same resistance that the kings and princes of Germany had offered the Emperor. They wanted to limit taxation so far as it pressed upon themselves, and to be free in their own houses and estates. And the spread of books and reading and intercommunication

Photo: Rischgitz Collection.
KING CHARLES THE FIRST.
(From the portrait by Van Dyck in the Dresden Gallery.)

was enabling these smaller monarchs, these monarchs of ownership, to develop such a community of ideas and such a solidarity of resistance as had been possible at no previous stage in the world's history. Everywhere they were disposed to resist the prince, but it was not everywhere that they found the same facilities for an organized resistance. The economic circumstances and the political traditions of the Netherlands and England made those countries the first to bring this antagonism of monarchy and private ownership to an issue.[1]

At first this seventeenth-century "public," this public of property owners, cared very little for foreign policy. They did not perceive at first how it affected them. They did not want to be bothered with it ; it was, they conceded, the affair of kings and princes.[2] They made no attempt therefore to control foreign entanglements. But it was with the direct consequences of these entanglements that they quarrelled ; they objected to heavy taxation, to interference with trade, to arbitrary imprisonment, and to the control of consciences by the monarch. It was upon these questions that they joined issue with the Crown.

§ 2

The open struggle of the private property owner against the aggressions of the "Prince" behistory" is always tempting, but men's souls have always mattered more than their pockets. Englishmen fought Charles I for the sake of free consciences rather than for the sake of free pockets. This is a large issue, on which much could be written ; but I feel sure that religion came first in our Civil War.—E. B.

The English Republic.

I do not agree. Loth as I am to differ from E. B., I can find no evidence of any religious issue as important as the issue of taxation either in the English Civil War or the American War of Independence.—H. G. W.

I did not mention the Americans. I will surrender them to H. G. W.—E. B.

[1] It was private *conscience*, rather than private property, that quarrelled with and limited princes. The Puritan Revolution in England (1640—1660) *was* a puritan revolution—it sprang from the religious motive first and foremost. The economic motive was secondary. The "economic interpretation of

[2] Englishmen did try to control the foreign policy of James I, because it involved questions of religion, and because their primary concern was religious. They wanted foreign policy to be directed to the militant defence of Protestantism. James I, a good internationalist (in his way), and at any rate a lover of peace, wanted to secure European peace by diplomacy—and failed to do so. His parliaments, and all seventeenth-century parliaments, were vitally interested in foreign policy.—E. B.

gins in England far back in the twelfth century.[1] The phase in this struggle that we have to study now is the phase that opened with the attempts of Henry VII and VIII and their successors, Edward VI, Mary and Elizabeth, to make the government of England a " personal monarchy " of the continental type. It became more acute when, by dynastic accidents, James, King of Scotland, became James I, King of both Scotland and England (1603), and began to talk in the manner we have already quoted of his " divine right " to do as he pleased. But never had the path of English monarchy been a smooth one. In all the monarchies of the Northmen and Germanic invaders of the empire there had been

Photo : Rischgitz Collection.
CROMWELL.

a tradition of a popular assembly of influential and representative men to preserve their general liberties, and in none was it more living than in England France had her tradition of the assembly of the Three Estates, Spain her Cortes, but the English assembly was peculiar in two respects ; that it had behind it a documentary declaration of certain elementary and universal rights, and that it contained elected " Knights of the Shire," as well as elected burghers from the towns. The French and Spanish assemblies had the latter, but not the former element.

These two features gave the English Parliament a peculiar strength in its struggle with the Throne. The document in question was *Magna Carta*, the Great Charter, a declaration which was forced from King John (1199—1216), the brother and successor of Richard Cœur de Lion (1189—99) after a revolt of the Barons in 1215. It rehearsed a number of fundamental rights that made England a legal

and not a regal state. It rejected the power of the king to control the personal property and liberty of every sort of citizen—save with the consent of that man's equals.

The presence of the elected shire representatives in the English Parliament, the second peculiarity of the British situation, came about from very simple and apparently innocuous beginnings. From the shires, or county divisions, knights seem to have been summoned to the national council to testify to the taxable capacity of their districts. They were sent up by the minor gentry, freeholders and village elders of their districts as early as 1254, two knights from each shire. This idea inspired Simon de Montfort,[2] who was in rebellion against Henry III, the successor of John, to summon to the national council two knights from each shire and two citizens from each city or borough. Edward I, the successor to Henry III, continued this practice because it seemed a convenient way of getting into financial touch with the growing towns. At first there was considerable reluctance on the parts of the knights and townsmen to attend Parliament, but gradually the power they possessed of linking the redress of grievances with the granting of subsidies was realized. Quite early, if not from the first, these representatives of the general property owners in town and country, the Commons, sat and debated apart from the great Lords and Bishops. So there grew up in England a representative assembly, the Commons, beside an episcopal and patrician one, the Lords. There was no profound and fundamental difference between the personnel of the two assemblies ; many of

---

[1] A very good general history of Great Britain, too little known as yet, is A. D. Innes' *History of the British Nation* (1912).

[2] N.B.—Not the same Simon de Montfort as the leader of the crusades against the Albigenses, but his son.

the knights of the shire were substantial men who might be as wealthy and influential as peers and also the sons and brothers of peers, but on the whole the Commons was the more plebeian assembly. From the first these two assemblies, and especially the Commons, displayed a disposition to claim the entire power of taxation in the land. Gradually they extended their purview of grievances to a criticism of all the affairs of the realm. We will not follow the fluctuations of the power and prestige of the English Parliament through the time of the Tudor monarchs (*i.e.*, Henry VII and VIII, Edward VI, Mary and Elizabeth), but it will be manifest from what has been said that when at last James Stuart made his open claim to autocracy, the English merchants, peers, and private gentlemen found themselves with a seasoned and honoured traditional means of resisting him such as no other people in Europe possessed.

Another peculiarity of the English political conflict was its comparative detachment from the great struggle between Catholic and Protestant that was now being waged all over Europe. There were, it is true, very distinct religious issues mixed up in the English struggle, but upon its main lines it was a political struggle of King against the Parliament embodying the class of private-property-owning citizens. Both Crown and people were formally reformed and Protestant. It is true that many people on the latter side were Protestants of a Bible-respecting, non-sacerdotal type, representing the reformation according to the peoples, and that the king was the nominal head of a special sacerdotal and sacramental church, the established Church of England, representing the reformation according to the princes, but this antagonism never completely obscured the essentials of the conflict.

Photo : Rischgitz Collection.

CROMWELL STATUE.

(By Hamo Thornycroft, outside the Houses of Parliament.)

The struggle of King and Parliament had already reached an acute phase before the death of James I (1625), but only in the reign of his son Charles I did it culminate in civil war. Charles did exactly what one might have expected a king to do in such a position, in view of the lack of Parliamentary control over foreign policy; he embroiled the country in a conflict with both Spain and France, and then came to the country for supplies in the hope that patriotic feeling would over-ride the normal dislike to giving him money. When Parliament refused supplies, he demanded loans from various subjects, and attempted similar illegal exactions. This produced from Parliament in 1628 a very memorable document, the *Petition of Right*, citing the Great Charter and rehearsing the legal limitations upon the power of the English king, denying his right to levy charges upon, or to imprison, or punish anyone, or to quarter soldiers on the people, without due process of law. The Petition of Right stated the case of the English Parliament. The disposition to " state a case " has always been a very marked English characteristic. When President Wilson, during the

Great War of 1914—18, prefaced each step in his policy by a " Note," he was walking in the most respectable traditions of the English. Charles dealt with this Parliament with a high hand, he dismissed it in 1629, and for eleven years he summoned no Parliament. He levied money illegally, but not enough for his purpose ; and realizing that the church could be used as an instrument of obedience, he made Laud, an aggressive high churchman, very much of a priest and a very strong believer in " divine right," Archbishop of Canterbury, and so head of the Church of England.

In 1638 Charles tried to extend the half-Protestant, half-Catholic characteristics of the Church of England to his other kingdom of Scotland, where the secession from catholicism had been more complete, and where a non-sacerdotal, non-sacramental form of Christianity, Presbyterianism, had been established as the national church. The Scotch revolted, and the English levies Charles raised to fight them mutinied. Insolvency, at all times the natural result of a " spirited " foreign policy, was close at hand. Charles, without money or trustworthy troops, had to summon a Parliament at last in 1640. This Parliament, the Short Parliament, he dismissed in the same year ; he tried a Council of Peers at York (1640), and then, in the November of that year, summoned his last Parliament.

This body, the Long Parliament, assembled in the mood for conflict. It seized Laud, the Archbishop of Canterbury, and charged him with treason. It published a " Grand Remonstrance," which was a long and full statement of its case against Charles. It provided by a bill for a meeting of Parliament at least once in three years, whether the King summoned it or no. It prosecuted the King's chief ministers who had helped him to reign for so long without Parliament, and in particular the Earl of Strafford. To save Strafford the King plotted for a sudden seizure of London by the army. This was discovered, and the Bill for Strafford's condemnation was hurried on in the midst of a vast popular excitement. Charles I, who was probably one of the meanest and most treacherous occupants the English throne has ever known, was frightened by the London crowds. Before Strafford could die

by due legal process, it was necessary for the King to give his assent. Charles gave it—and Strafford was beheaded. Meanwhile the King was plotting and looking for help in strange quarters—from the Catholic Irish, from treasonable Scotchmen. Finally he resorted to a forcible-feeble display of violence. He went down to the Houses of Parliament to arrest five of his most active opponents. He entered the House of Commons and took the Speaker's chair. He was prepared with some bold speech about treason, but when he saw the places of his five antagonists vacant, he was baffled, confused, and spoke in broken sentences. He learnt that they had departed from his royal city of Westminster and taken refuge in the city of London (see chap. xxxv, § 7). London defied him. A week later the Five Members were escorted back in triumph to the Parliament House in Westminster by the Trained Bands of London, and the King, to avoid the noise and hostility of the occasion, left Whitehall for Windsor.

Both parties then prepared openly for war.

The King was the traditional head of the army, and the habit of obedience in soldiers is to the King. The Parliament had the greater resources. The King set up his standard at Nottingham on the eve of a dark and stormy August day in 1642. There followed a long and obstinate civil war, the King holding Oxford, the Parliament, London. Success swayed from side to side, but the King could never close on London nor Parliament take Oxford. Each antagonist was weakened by moderate adherents who " did not want to go too far." There emerged among the Parliamentary commanders a certain Oliver Cromwell, who had raised a small troop of horse and who rose to the position of general. Lord Warwick, his contemporary, describes him as a plain man, in a cloth suit " made by an ill country tailor." He was no mere fighting soldier, but a military organizer ; he realized the inferior quality of many of the Parliamentary forces, and set himself to remedy it. The Cavaliers of the King had the picturesque tradition of chivalry and loyalty on their side ; Parliament was something new and difficult—without any comparable traditions. " Your troops are most of them old decayed serving men and tapsters," said Cromwell. "Do you think that the spirits of such base and mean fellows will ever be able to encounter gentlemen that have honour and courage and resolution in them?" But there is something better and stronger than picturesque chivalry in the world, religious enthusiasm. He set himself to get together a "godly" regiment. They were to be earnest, sober-living men. Above all, they were to be men of strong convictions. He disregarded all social traditions, and drew his officers from every class. "I had rather have a plain, russet-coated captain *that knows what he fights for and loves what he knows*, than what you call a gentleman and is nothing else." England discovered a new force, the Ironsides, in its midst, in which footmen, draymen, and ships' captains held high command, side by side with men of family. They became the type on which the Parliament sought to reconstruct its entire army. The Ironsides were the backbone of this " New Model." From Marston Moor to Naseby these men swept the Cavaliers before them. The King was at last a captive in the hands of Parliament.

There were still attempts at settlement that would have left the King a sort of king, but Charles was a man doomed to tragic issues, incessantly scheming, " so false a man that he is not to be trusted." The English were drifting towards a situation new in the world's history, in which a monarch should be formally tried for treason to his people and condemned.

Most revolutions are precipitated, as this English one was, by the excesses of the ruler, and by attempts at strength and firmness beyond the compass of the law; and most revolutions swing by a kind of necessity towards an extremer conclusion than is warranted by the original quarrel. The English revolution was no exception. The English are by nature a compromising and even a vacillating people, and probably the great majority of them still wanted the King to be King and the people to be free, and all the lions and lambs to lie down together in peace and liberty. But the army of the New Model could not go back. There would have been scant mercy for these draymen and footmen who had ridden down the King's gentlemen if the King came back. When Parliament began to treat again with this regal trickster, the New Model intervened; Colonel Pride turned out eighty members from the House of Commons who favoured the King, and the illegal residue, the Rump Parliament, then put the King on trial.

But indeed the King was already doomed. The House of Lords rejected the ordinance for the trial, and the Rump then proclaimed "that the People are under God, the original of all just power," and that "the Commons of England . . . have the supreme power in this nation," and—assuming that it was itself the Commons—proceeded with the trial. The King was condemned as a "tyrant, traitor, murderer, and enemy of his country." He was taken one January morning in 1649 to a scaffold erected outside the windows of his own banqueting-room at Whitehall. There he was beheaded. He died with piety and a certain noble self-pity—eight years after the execution of Strafford, and after six and a half years of a destructive civil war which had been caused almost entirely by his own lawlessness.

LIGHT HORSEMAN OF THE CROMWELL PERIOD.

This was indeed a great and terrifying thing that Parliament had done. The like of it had never been heard of in the world before. Kings had killed each other times enough; parricide, fratricide, assassination, those are the privileged expedients of princes; but that a section of the people should rise up, try its king solemnly and deliberately for disloyalty, mischief, and treachery, and condemn and kill him, sent horror through every court in Europe. The Rump Parliament had gone beyond the ideas and conscience of its time. It was as if a committee of jungle deer had taken and killed a tiger—a crime against nature. The Tsar of Russia chased the English envoy from his court. France and Holland committed acts of open hostility. England, confused and conscience-stricken at her own sacrilege, stood isolated before the world.

But for a time the personal quality of Oliver Cromwell and the discipline and strength of the army he had created maintained England in the republican course she had taken. The Irish Catholics had made a massacre of the Protestant English in Ireland, and now Cromwell suppressed the Irish insurrection with great vigour. Except for certain friars at the storm of Drogheda, none but men with arms in their hands were killed by his troops ; but the atrocities of the massacre were fresh in his mind, no quarter was given in battle, and so his memory still rankles in the minds of the Irish. For the Irish are more subtle than the English, and they resent being killed because they have begun killing. They take it ill. After Ireland came Scotland, where Cromwell shattered a Royalist army at his " crowning mercy," the Battle of Dunbar (1650). Then he turned his attention to Holland, which country had rashly seized upon the divisions among the English as an excuse for the injury of a trade rival. The Dutch were then the rulers of the sea, and the English fleet fought against odds ; but after a series of obstinate sea fights the Dutch were driven from the British seas and the English took their place as the ascendant naval power. Dutch and French ships must dip their flags to them. An English fleet went into the Mediterranean—the first English naval force to enter those waters ; it put right various grievances of the English shippers with Tuscany and Malta, and bombarded the pirate nest of Algiers and destroyed the pirate fleet—which in the lax days of Charles had been wont to come right up to the coasts of Cornwall and Devon to intercept ships and carry off slaves to Africa. The strong arm of England also intervened to protect the Protestants in the south of France, who were being hunted to death by the Duke of Savoy. France, Sweden, Denmark, all found it wiser to overcome their first distaste for regicide and allied themselves with England. Came a war with

Spain, and the great English Admiral Blake destroyed the Spanish Plate Fleet at Teneriffe in an action of almost incredible daring. He engaged land batteries. He was the first man " that brought ships to contemn castles on the shore." (He died in 1657, and was buried in Westminster Abbey, but after the restoration of the monarchy his bones were dug out by the order of Charles II, and removed to St. Margaret's, Westminster.) Such was the figure that England cut in the eyes of the world during her brief republican days.

On September 3rd, 1658, Cromwell died in the midst of a great storm that did not fail to impress the superstitious. Once his strong hand lay still, England fell away from this premature attempt to realize a righteous commonweal of free men. In 1660 Charles II, the son of Charles the " Martyr," was welcomed back to England with all those manifestations of personal loyalty dear to the English heart, and the country relaxed from its military and naval efficiency as a sleeper might wake and stretch and yawn after too intense a dream. The Puritans were done with. " Merrie England " was herself again, and in 1667 the Dutch, once more masters of the sea, sailed up the Thames to Gravesend and burnt an English fleet in the Medway. " On the night when our ships were burnt by the Dutch," says Pepys, in his diary, " the King did sup with my Lady Castelmaine, and there they were all mad, hunting a poor moth." Charles, from the date of his return, 1660, took control of the foreign affairs of the state, and in 1670 concluded a secret treaty with Louis XIV of France by which he undertook to subordinate entirely English foreign policy to that of France for an annual pension of £100,000. Dunkirk, which Cromwell had taken, had already been sold back to France. The King was a great sportsman ; he had the true English love for watching horse races, and the great racing centre at Newmarket is perhaps his most characteristic monument.

While Charles lived, his easy humour enabled him to retain the British crown, but he did so by wariness and compromise, and when in 1685 he was succeeded by his brother James II, who was a devout Catholic, and too dull to recognize the hidden limitation of the monarchy

in Britain, the old issue between Parliament and Crown became acute. James set himself to force his country into a religious reunion with Rome. In 1688 he was in flight to France. But this time the great lords and merchants and gentlemen were too circumspect to let this revolt against the King fling them into the hands of a second Pride or a second Cromwell. They had already called in another king, William, Prince of Orange, to replace James. The change was made rapidly. There was no civil war—except in Ireland—and no release of the deeper revolutionary forces of the country.

Of William's claim to the throne, or rather of his wife Mary's claim, we cannot tell here, its interest is purely technical ; nor how William III and Mary ruled, nor how, after the widower William had reigned alone for a time, the throne passed on to Mary's sister Anne (1702—14). Anne seems to have thought favourably of a restoration of the Stuart line, but the Lords and the Commons, who now dominated English affairs, preferred a less competent king. Some sort of claim could be made out for the Elector of Hanover, who became King of England as George I (1714—27). He was entirely German, he could speak no English, and he brought a swarm of German women and German attendants to the English court ; a dullness, a tarnish, came over the intellectual life of the land with his coming, the poetry, painting, architecture, and imaginative litera-ture of later eighteenth-century England is immeasurably below that of the seventeenth century,[1] but this isolation of the court from English life was his conclusive recommendation to the great landowners and the commercial interests who chiefly brought him over. England entered upon a phase which Lord Beaconsfield has called the " Venetian oligarchy " stage ; the supreme power resided in Parliament, dominated now by the Lords, for the art of bribery and a study of the methods of working elections carried to a high pitch by

Sir Robert Walpole had robbed the House of Commons of its original freedom and vigour. By ingenious devices the parliamentary vote was restricted to a shrinking number of electors, old towns with little or no population would return one or two members (old Sarum had one non-resident voter, no population, and two members), while newer populous centres had no representation at all. And by insisting upon a high property qualification for members, the chance of the Commons speaking in common accents of vulgar needs was still more restricted. George I was followed by the very similar George II (1727—60), and it was only at his death that England had again a king who had been born in England, and one who could speak English fairly well, his grandson George III. On this monarch's attempt to recover some of the larger powers of monarchy we shall have something to say in a later section.

Such briefly is the story of the struggle in England during the seventeenth and eighteenth centuries between the three main factors in the problem of the " modern state " ; between the crown, the private property owners, and that vague power, still blind and ignorant, the power of the quite common people. This latter factor appears as yet only at moments when the country is most deeply stirred ; then it sinks back into the depths. But the end of the story, thus far, is a very complete triumph of the British private property owner over the dreams and schemes of Machiavellian absolutism. With the Hanoverian Dynasty, England became—as the *Times* recently styled her—a " crowned republic." She had worked out a new method of government, Parliamentary government, recalling in many ways the Senate and Popular Assembly of Rome, but more steadfast and efficient because of its use, however restricted, of the representative method. Her assembly at Westminster was to become the " Mother of Parliaments " throughout the world. Towards the crown the English Parliament has held and still holds much the relation of the mayor of the palace to the Merovingian kings. The king is conceived of as ceremonial and irresponsible, a living symbol of the royal and imperial system. But much power remains latent in the tradition and prestige of the crown, and the succession of the four Hanoverian

[1] But Sir Joshua Reynolds, Hogarth, Gray, Gibbon, for instance !—G. M.

And the golden age of the great cabinet makers !
—P. G.

Exactly ! Culture taking refuge in the portraits, libraries, and households of a few rich people. No national culture in the court, nor among the commonalty : a steady decay.—H. G. W.

Georges, William IV (1830), Victoria (1837), Edward VII (1901), and the present king, George V (1910), is of a quite different strain from the feeble and short-lived Merovingian monarchs. In the affairs of the church, the military and naval organizations, and the foreign office, these sovereigns have all in various degrees exercised an influence which is none the less important because it is indefinable.

§ 3

The breaking away of the Netherlands from absolutist monarchy was on the face of it much more of a religious and national affair and much less economic and social than the English parliamentary

The Dutch Republic.

revolution. In the twelfth century all the Lower Rhine country was divided up among a number of small rulers, and the population was a Low German one on a Celtic basis, mixed with subsequent Danish ingredients very similar to the English admixture. The south-eastern fringe of it spoke French dialects ; the bulk, Frisian, Dutch, and other Low German languages. The Netherlands figured largely in the crusades. Godfrey of Bouillon, who took Jerusalem (First Crusade), was a Belgian ; and the founder of the so-called Latin Dynasty of emperors in Constantinople (Fourth Crusade) was Baldwin of Flanders. (They were called Latin emperors because they were on the side of the Latin church.) In the thirteenth and fourteenth centuries considerable towns grew up in the Netherlands ; Ghent, Bruges, Ypres, Utrecht, Leiden, Haarlem, and so forth ; and these towns developed quasi-independent municipal governments and a class of educated townsmen. We will not trouble the reader with the dynastic accidents that linked the affairs of the Netherlands with Burgundy (Eastern France), and which finally

Photo : Rischgitz Collection.
WILLIAM THE SILENT.

made their overlordship the inheritance of the Emperor Charles V.

It was under Charles that the Protestant doctrines that now prevailed in Germany spread into the Netherlands. Charles persecuted with some vigour, but in 1556, as we have told, he handed over the task to his son Philip (Philip II). Philip's spirited foreign policy—he was carrying on a war with France—presently became a second source of trouble between himself and the Netherlandish noblemen and townsmen, because he had to come to them for supplies. The great nobles, led by William the Silent, Prince of Orange, and the Counts of Egmont and Hoorn, made themselves the heads of a popular resistance, in which it is now impossible to disentangle the objection to taxation from the objection to religious persecution. The great nobles were not at first Protestants. They became Protestants as the struggle grew in bitterness. The people were often bitterly Protestant.

Philip was resolved to rule both the property and consciences of his Netherlanders. He sent picked Spanish troops into the country, and he made governor-general a nobleman named Alva, one of those ruthless " strong " men who wreck governments and monarchies. For a time he ruled the land with a hand of iron, but the hand of iron begets a soul of iron in the body it grips, and in 1567—about eighty years, that is, before the English civil war— the Netherlands were in open revolt. Alva murdered, sacked, and massacred—in vain. Counts Egmont and Hoorn were executed. William the Silent became the great leader of the Dutch, a king de facto. For a long time, and with many complications, the struggle for liberty continued, and through it all it is noteworthy that the rebels continued to cling to

Photo: Rischgitz Collection.
VELAZQUEZ'S FAMOUS PICTURE OF THE SURRENDER OF BREDA BY THE DUTCH TO THE SPANIARDS (1625).

the plea that Philip II was their king—if only he would be a reasonable and limited king. But the idea of limited monarchy was distasteful to the crowned heads of Europe at that time, and at last Philip drove the United Provinces, for which we now use the name of Holland, to the republican form of government. Holland, be it noted—not all the Netherlands; the Southern Netherlands, Belgium as we now call that country, remained at the end of the struggle a Spanish possession and Catholic.

The siege of Alkmaar (1573), as Motley[1] describes it, may be taken as a sample of that long and hideous conflict between the little Dutch people and the still vast resources of Catholic Imperialism.

"'If I take Alkmaar,' Alva wrote to Philip, 'I am resolved not to leave a single

[1] *Rise of the Dutch Republic.*

creature alive; the knife shall be put to every throat.' . . .

"And now, with the dismantled and desolate Haarlem before their eyes, a prophetic phantom, perhaps, of their own imminent fate, did the handful of people shut up within Alkmaar prepare for the worst. Their main hope lay in the friendly sea. The vast sluices called the Zyp, through which the inundation of the whole northern province could be very soon effected, were but a few miles distant. By opening these gates, and by piercing a few dykes, the ocean might be made to fight for them. To obtain this result, however, the consent of the inhabitants was requisite, as the destruction of all the standing crops would be inevitable. The city was so closely invested, that it was a matter of life and death to venture forth, and it was difficult, therefore, to find an envoy for this hazardous mission. At last, a carpenter in the city, Peter Van der Mey by name, undertook the adventure. . . .

" Affairs soon approached a crisis within the beleaguered city. Daily skirmishes, without decisive results, had taken place outside the walls. At last, on the 18th of September, after a steady cannonade of nearly twelve hours, Don Frederick, at three in the afternoon, ordered an assault. Notwithstanding his seven months' experience at Haarlem, he still believed it certain that he should carry Alkmaar by storm. The attack took place at once upon the Frisian gate and upon the red tower on the opposite side. Two choice regiments, recently arrived from Lombardy, led the onset, rending the air with their shouts and confident of an easy victory. They were sustained by what seemed an overwhelming force of disciplined troops. Yet never, even in the recent history of Haarlem, had an attack been received by more dauntless breasts. Every living man was on the walls. The storming parties were assailed with cannon, with musketry, with pistols. Boiling water, pitch and oil, molten lead, and unslaked lime were poured upon them every moment. Hundreds of tarred and burning hoops were skilfully quoited around the necks of the soldiers, who struggled in vain to extricate themselves from these fiery ruffs, while as fast as any of the invaders planted foot upon the breach, they were confronted face to face with sword and dagger by the burghers, who hurled them headlong into the moat below.

" Thrice was the attack renewed with ever-increasing rage—thrice repulsed with unflinching fortitude. The storm continued four hours long. During all that period not one of the defenders left his post, till he dropped from it dead or wounded. . . . The trumpet of recall was sounded, and the Spaniards, utterly discomfited, retired from the walls, leaving at least one thousand dead in the trenches, while only thirteen burghers and twenty-four of the garrison lost their lives. . . . Ensign Solis, who had mounted the breach for an instant, and miraculously escaped with life, after having been hurled from the battlements, reported that he had seen ' neither helmet nor harness ' as he looked down into the city : only some plain-looking people, generally dressed like fishermen. Yet these plain-looking fishermen had defeated the veterans of Alva. . . .

" Meantime, as Governor Sonoy had opened many of the dykes, the land in the neighbourhood of the camp was becoming plashy, although as yet the threatened inundation had not taken place. The soldiers were already very uncomfortable and very refractory. The carpenter-envoy had not been idle. . . ."

He returned with despatches for the city. By accident or contrivance he lost these despatches as he made his way into the town, so that they fell into Alva's hands. They contained a definite promise from the Duke of Orange to flood the country so as to drown the whole Spanish army. Incidentally this would also have drowned most of the Dutch harvest and cattle. But Alva, when he had read these documents, did not wait for the opening of any more sluices. Presently the stout men of Alkmaar, cheering and jeering, watched the Spaniards breaking camp. . . .

The form assumed by the government of Holland was a patrician republic under the headship of the house of Orange. The States-General was far less representative of the whole body of citizens than was the English Parliament even in its " Venetian " days. Though the worst of the struggle was over after Alkmaar, Holland was not effectively independent until 1609, and its independence was only fully and completely recognized by the treaty of Westphalia in 1648. We have given this account of the origin of free Holland *after* our account of the English revolution because it was less representative of the essential triangle of forces in the developing modern state, and because it was complicated by the merely patriotic element of insurrection against the Spanish foreigner. But though we have told of it later, the reader must remember it came to its climax in the time of Queen Elizabeth of England, half a century earlier than the English civil war. As Motley says, the Dutch, the English, and the American revolution, of which latter we have presently to tell, " form but a single chapter in the great volume of human fate."

§ 4

Upon no part of Europe did the collapse of the idea of a unified Christendom bring more disas-

Central EUROPE after the Peace of Westphalia, 1648.

Boundary of the Empire ━━━	Free Towns, thus: •Cologne	Swedish territory.... French ″ .... Austrian Habsburgs..	Spanish Habsburgs Brandenburg (Prussia)....

trous consequences than to Germany. Naturally one would have supposed that the Emperor, being by origin a German,
both in the case of the earlier lines
and in the case of the Habsburgs,
would have developed into the
national monarch of a united German-speaking
state. It was the accidental misfortune of Germany that her Emperors never remained German. Frederick II, the last Hohenstaufen, was,
as we have seen, a half-Orientalized Sicilian; the
Habsburgs, by marriage and inclination, became in the person of Charles V, first Burgun-
dian and then Spanish in spirit. After the
death of Charles V, his brother Ferdinand took
Austria and the empire, and his son Philip II
took Spain, the Netherlands, and South Italy;
but the Austrian line, obstinately Catholic,
holding its patrimony mostly on the eastern

The Break-up and Disorders of Germany.

frontiers, deeply entangled therefore with
Hungarian affairs and paying tribute, as
Ferdinand and his two successors did, to the
Turk, retained no grip upon the North Germans
with their disposition towards Protestantism,
their Baltic and westward affinities, and their
ignorance of or indifference to the Turkish
danger.

The sovereign princes, dukes, electors, prince-
bishops and the like, whose domains cut up
the map of the Germany of the Middle Ages
into a crazy patchwork, were really not the
equivalents of the kings of England and France.
They were rather on the level of the great
land-owning dukes and peers of France and
England. Until 1701 none of them had the
title of "King." Many of their dominions
were less both in size and value than the larger
estates of the British nobility. The German

Diet was like the States-General or like a parliament without the presence of elected representatives. So that the great civil war in Germany that presently broke out, the Thirty Years' War (1618—48) was in its essential nature much more closely akin to the civil war in England (1643—49) and to the war of the Fronde (1648—53), the league of feudal nobles against the crown in France, than appears upon the surface. In all these cases the crown was either Catholic or disposed to become Catholic, and the recalcitrant nobles found their individualistic disposition tending

the struggle. Finally, the French monarchy, triumphant now over its own nobles, although it was Catholic, came in on the Protestant side with the evident intention of taking the place of the Habsburgs as the imperial line.

The prolongation of the war, and the fact that it was not fought along a determined frontier, but all over an empire of patches, Protestant here, Catholic there, made it one of the most cruel and destructive that Europe had known since the days of the barbarian raids. Its peculiar mischief lay not in the fighting, but in the concomitants of the fighting. It came at

Photo: Rischgitz Collection.
INFANTRY SOLDIERS OF THE SEVENTEENTH CENTURY—TIME OF THE THIRTY YEARS' WAR.

to a Protestant formula. But while in England and Holland the Protestant nobles and rich merchants ultimately triumphed and in France the success of the crown was even more complete, in Germany neither was the Emperor strong enough, nor had the Protestant princes a sufficient unity and organization among themselves to secure a conclusive triumph. It ended there in a torn-up Germany. Moreover, the German issue was complicated by the fact that various non-German peoples, the Protestant Bohemians and the Protestant Swedes (who had a new Protestant monarchy which had arisen under Gustava Vasa as a direct result of the Reformation) were entangled in

a time when military tactics had developed to a point that rendered ordinary levies useless against trained professional infantry. Volley firing with muskets at a range of a few score yards had abolished the individualistic knight in armour, but the charge of disciplined masses of cavalry could still disperse any infantry that had not been drilled into a mechanical rigidity. The infantry with their muzzle-loading muskets could not keep up a steady enough fire to wither determined cavalry before it charged home. They had, therefore, to meet the shock standing or kneeling behind a bristling wall of pikes or bayonets. For this they needed great discipline and experience.

Iron cannon were still of small size and not very abundant, and they did not play a decisive part as yet in warfare. They could " plough lanes" in infantry, but they could not easily smash and scatter it if it was sturdy and well drilled. War under these conditions was entirely in the hands of seasoned professional soldiers, and the question of their pay was as important a one to the generals of that time as the question of food or munitions. As the long struggle dragged on from phase to phase, and the financial distress of the land increased, the commanders of both sides were forced to fall back upon the looting of towns and villages, both for supply and to make up the arrears of their soldiers' pay. The soldiers became, therefore, more and more mere brigands living on the country, and the Thirty Years' War set up a tradition of looting as a legitimate operation in warfare and of outrage as a soldiers' privilege that has tainted the good name of Germany right down to the Great War of 1914. The earlier chapters of Defoe's *Memoirs of a Cavalier*, with its vivid description of the massacre and burning of Magdeburg, will give the reader a far better idea of the warfare of this time than any formal history. So harried was the land that the farmers ceased from cultivation, what snatch crops could be harvested were hidden away, and great crowds of starving women and children became camp followers of the armies, and supplied a thievish tail to the rougher plundering. At the close of the struggle all Germany was ruined and desolate. Central Europe did not fully recover from these robberies and devastations for a century.

Here we can but name Tilly and Wallenstein, the great plunder captains on the Habsburg side, and Gustavus Adolphus, the King of Sweden, the Lion of the North, the champion of the Protestants, whose dream was to make the Baltic Sea a " Swedish Lake." Gustavus Adolphus was killed in his decisive victory over Wallenstein at Lützen (1632), and Wallenstein was murdered in 1634. In 1648 the princes and diplomatists gathered amidst the havoc they had made to patch up the affairs of Central Europe at the Peace of Westphalia. By that peace the power of the Emperor was reduced to a shadow, and the acquisition of Alsace brought France up to the Rhine. And one

German prince, the Hohenzollern Elector of Brandenburg, acquired so much territory as to become the greatest German power next to the Emperor, a power that presently (1701) became the kingdom of Prussia. The Treaty also recognized two long accomplished facts, the separation from the empire and the complete independence of both Holland and Switzerland.

§ 5

We have opened this chapter with the stories of two countries, Britain and the Netherlands, in which the resistance of the private citizen to this new type of monarchy, the Machiavellian monarchy, that was arising out of the moral collapse of Christendom, succeeded. But in France, Russia, in many states of Germany and of Italy—Saxony and Tuscany e.g.— personal monarchy was not so restrained and overthrown; it established itself indeed as the ruling European system during the seventeenth and eighteenth centuries.

The Splendours of Grand Monarchy in Europe.

(In Poland conditions were peculiar, and they will be dealt with in a later section.)

In France there had been no Magna Carta, and there was no tradition of parliamentary rule. There was the same opposition of interests between the crown on the one hand and the landlords and merchants on the other, but the latter had no recognized and traditional gathering-place, and no dignified method of unity. They formed oppositions to the crown, they made leagues of resistance—such was the " Fronde," which was struggling against the young King Louis XIV and his great minister Mazarin, while Charles I was fighting for his life in England—but ultimately (1652), after a civil war, they were conclusively defeated; and while in England after the establishment of the Hanoverians the House of Lords and their subservient Commons ruled the country, in France, after 1652, the court entirely dominated the aristocracy. Cardinal Mazarin was himself building upon a foundation that Cardinal Richelieu, the contemporary of King James I of England, had prepared for him. After the time of Mazarin we hear of no great French nobles unless they are at court as court servants and officials. They have been tamed—but at a price, the price of throwing the burthen of

Photo : Rischgitz Collection.

THE PALACE OF VERSAILLES.

taxation upon the voiceless mass of the common people. From many taxes both the clergy and the nobility—everyone indeed who bore a title—were exempt. In the end this injustice became intolerable, but for a while the French monarchy flourished like the Psalmist's green bay tree. By the opening of the eighteenth century English writers are already calling attention to the misery of the French lower classes and the comparative prosperity, *at that time*, of the English poor.

On such terms of unrighteousness what we may call " Grand Monarchy" established itself in France. Louis XIV, styled the Grand Monarque, reigned for the unparalleled length of seventy-two years (1643—1715), and set a pattern for all the kings of Europe. At first he was guided by his Machiavellian minister, Cardinal Mazarin; after the death of the Cardinal he himself in his own proper person became the ideal " Prince." He was, within his limitations, an exceptionally capable king; his ambition was stronger than his baser passions, and he guided his country towards bankruptcy through the complication of a spirited foreign policy, with an elaborate dignity that still extorts our admiration. His immediate desire was to consolidate and extend France to the Rhine and Pyrenees, and to absorb the Spanish Netherlands; his remoter view saw the French kings as the possible successors of Charlemagne in a recast Holy Roman Empire. He made bribery a state method almost more important than warfare.

Photo : Rischgitz Collection.

THE FAMOUS HALL OF MIRRORS AT VERSAILLES.

Charles II of England was in his pay, and so were most of the Polish nobility, presently to be described. His money, or rather the money of the tax-paying classes in France, went everywhere. But his prevailing occupation was splendour. His great palace at Versailles, with its salons, its corridors, its mirrors, its terraces and fountains and parks and prospects, was the envy and admiration of the world. He provoked a universal imitation. Every king and princelet in Europe was building his own Versailles as much beyond his means as his subjects and credits would permit. Everywhere the nobility rebuilt or extended their châteaux to the new pattern. A great industry of beautiful and elaborate fabrics and furnishings developed. The luxurious arts flourished everywhere; sculpture in alabaster, faience, gilt woodwork, metal work, stamped leather, much music, magnificent painting, beautiful

printing and bindings, fine cookery, fine vintages. Amidst the mirrors and fine furniture went a strange race of " gentlemen " in vast powdered wigs, silks and laces, poised upon high red heels, supported by amazing canes ; and still more wonderful " ladies," under towers of powdered hair and wearing vast expansions of silk and satin sustained on wire. Through it all postured the great Louis, the sun of his world, unaware of the meagre and sulky and bitter faces that watched him from those lower darknesses to which his sunshine did not penetrate.

We cannot give here at any length the story of the wars and doings of this monarch. In many ways Voltaire's *Siècle de Louis XIV* is still the best and most wholesome account. He created a French navy fit to face the English and Dutch ; a very considerable achievement. But because his intelligence did not rise above the lure of that Fata Morgana, that crack in the political wits of Europe, the dream of a world-wide Holy Roman Empire, he drifted in his later years to the propitiation of the Papacy, which had hitherto been hostile to him. He set himself against those spirits of independence and disunion, the Protestant princes, and he made war against Protestantism in France. Great numbers of his most sober and valuable subjects were driven abroad by his religious persecutions, taking arts and industries with them. The English silk manufacture, for instance, was founded by French Protestants. Under his rule were carried out the " dragonnades," a peculiarly malignant and effectual form of persecution. Rough soldiers were quartered in the houses of the Protestants, and were free to disorder the life of their hosts and insult their womankind as they thought fit. Men yielded to that sort of pressure who would not have yielded to rack and fire. The education of the next generation of Protestants was broken up, and the parents had to give Catholic instruction or none. They gave it, no doubt, with a sneer and an intonation that destroyed all faith in it. While more tolerant countries became mainly sincerely Catholic or sincerely Protestant, the persecuting countries, like France and Spain and Italy, so destroyed honest Protestant teaching that these peoples became mainly Catholic believers or Catholic atheists, ready to break out into blank atheism whenever the opportunity offered. The next reign, that of Louis XV, was the age of that supreme mocker, Voltaire (1694—1778), an age in which everybody in French society conformed to the Roman church and hardly anyone believed in it.

It was part—and an excellent part—of the pose of Grand Monarchy to patronise literature and the sciences. Louis XIV set up an academy of sciences in rivalry with the English Royal Society of Charles II and the similar association at Florence. He decorated his court with poets, playwrights, philosophers, and scientific men. If the scientific process got little inspiration from this patronage, it did at any rate acquire resources for experiment and publication, and a certain prestige in the eyes of the vulgar.

Louis XV was the great-grandson of Louis XIV, and an incompetent imitator of his predecessor's magnificence. He posed as a king, but his ruling passion was that common obsession of our kind, the pursuit of women, tempered by a superstitious fear of hell. How such women as the Duchess of Châteauroux, Madame de Pompadour, and Madame du Barry dominated the pleasures of the king, and how wars and alliances were made, provinces devastated, thousands of people killed, because of the vanities and spites of these creatures, and how all the public life of France and Europe was tainted with intrigue and prostitution and imposture because of them, the reader must learn from the memoirs of the time. The spirited foreign policy went on steadily under Louis XV towards its final smash. In 1774 this Louis, Louis the Well-Beloved, as his flatterers called him, died of smallpox, and was succeeded by his grandson, Louis XVI (1774—93), a dull, well-meaning man, an excellent shot, and an amateur locksmith of some ingenuity. Of how he came to follow Charles I to the scaffold we shall tell in a later section. Our present concern is with Grand Monarchy in the days of its glory.

Among the chief practitioners of Grand Monarchy outside France we may note first the Prussian kings, Frederick William I (1713—40), and his son and successor, Frederick II, Frederick the Great (1740—86). The story of the slow rise of the Hohenzollern family, which ruled the kingdom of Prussia, from inconspicuous beginnings, is too tedious and unimportant for us to follow here. It is a story of luck and violence, of bold claims and sudden betrayals. It is told with great appreciation in Carlyle's *Frederick the Great*. By the eighteenth century the Prussian kingdom was important enough to threaten the empire ; it had a strong, well-drilled army, and its king was an attentive and worthy student of Machiavelli. Frederick the Great perfected his Versailles at Potsdam. There the park of Sans Souci, with its fountains, avenues, statuary, aped its model ; there also was the New Palace, a vast brick building erected at enormous expense, the Orangery in the Italian style, with a collection of pictures, a Marble Palace, and so on. Frederick carried culture to the pitch of authorship, and corresponded with and entertained Voltaire, to their mutual exasperation. The Austrian dominions were kept too busy between the hammer of the French and the anvil of the Turks to develop the real Grand Monarch style until the reign of Maria-Theresa (who, being a woman, did not bear the title of Empress) (1740—80). Joseph II, who was Emperor from 1765—92, succeeded to her palaces in 1780. With Peter the Great (1682—1725) the empire of Muscovy broke away from her Tartar traditions and entered the sphere of French attraction. Peter shaved the Oriental beards of his nobles and introduced Western costume. These were but the outward and visible symbols of his westering tendencies. To release himself from the Asiatic feeling and traditions of Moscow, which, like Pekin, has a sacred inner city, the Kremlin, he built himself a new capital, Petrograd, upon the swamp of the Neva. And of

Photo : Rischgitz Collection.
FREDERICK THE GREAT.

course he built his Versailles, the Peterhof, about eighteen miles from this new Paris, employing a French architect and having a terrace, fountains, cascades, picture gallery, park, and all the recognized features. His more distinguished successors were Elizabeth (1741—62) and Catherine the Great, a German princess, who, after obtaining the crown in sound Oriental fashion through the murder of her husband, the legitimate Tsar, reverted to advanced Western ideals and ruled with great vigour from 1762 to 1796. She set up an academy, and corresponded with Voltaire. And she lived to witness the end of the system of Grand Monarchy in Europe and the execution of Louis XVI.

We cannot even catalogue here the minor Grand Monarchs of the time in Florence (Tuscany) and Savoy and Saxony and Denmark and Sweden. Versailles, under a score of names, is starred in every volume of Bædeker, and the

Photo : James's Press Agency.

THE KREMLIN, MOSCOW.

tourist gapes in their palaces. Nor can we deal with the war of the Spanish Succession. Spain, overstrained by the imperial enterprizes of Charles V and Philip II, and enfeebled by a bigoted persecution of Protestants, Moslems, and Jews, was throughout the seventeenth and eighteenth centuries sinking down from her temporary importance in European affairs to the level of a secondary power again.

These European monarchs ruled their kingdoms as their noblemen ruled their estates: they plotted against one another, they were politic and far-seeing in an unreal fashion, they made wars, they spent the substance of Europe upon absurd " policies " of aggression and resistance. At last there burst upon

Photo : Rischgitz Collection.

CATHERINE THE GREAT.

them a great storm out of the depths. That storm, the First French Revolution, the indignation of the common man in Europe, took their system unawares. It was but the opening outbreak of a great cycle of political and social storms that still continue, that will perhaps continue until every vestige of nationalist monarchy has been swept out of the world and the skies clear again for the great peace of the federation of mankind.

§ 6

We have seen how the idea of a world-rule and a community of mankind first came into human affairs, and we have traced how the failure of the Christian church to sustain and establish those conceptions of its Founder, led to a moral collapse in political affairs and a reversion to egotism and want of faith. We have seen how Machiavellian monarchy set itself up against the spirit of brotherhood in Christendom, and how Machiavellian monarchy developed throughout a large part of Europe into the Grand Monarchies and Parliamentary

The Growth of the Idea of Great Powers.

Monarchies of the seventeenth and eighteenth centuries. But the mind and imagination of man is incessantly active, and beneath the sway of the grand monarchs, a complex of notions and traditions was being woven as a net is woven, to catch and entangle men's minds, the conception of international politics not as a matter of dealings between princes, but as a matter of dealings between a kind of immortal Beings, the Powers. The Princes came and went ; a Louis XIV would be followed by a petticoat-hunting Louis XV, and he again by that dull-witted amateur locksmith, Louis XVI. Peter the Great gave place to a succession of empresses ; the chief continuity of the Habsburgs after Charles V, either in Austria or Spain, was a continuity of thick lips, clumsy chins, and superstition ; the amiable scoundrelism of a Charles II would make a mock of his own pretensions. But what remained much more steadfast were the secretariats of the foreign ministries and the ideas of people who wrote of state concerns. The ministers maintained a continuity of policy during the " off days " of their monarchs, and between one monarch and another.

So we find that the prince gradually became less important in men's minds than the " Power " of which he was the head. We begin to read less and less of the schemes and ambitions of King This or That, and more of the " Designs of France " or the " Ambitions of Prussia." In an age when religious faith was declining, we find men displaying a new and vivid belief in the reality of these personifications. These vast vague phantoms, the " Powers," crept insensibly into European political thought, until in the later eighteenth and in the nineteenth centuries they dominated it entirely. To this day they dominate it. European life remained nominally Christian, but to worship one God in spirit and in truth is to belong to one community with all one's fellow worshippers. In practical reality Europe does not do this, she has given herself up altogether to the worship of this strange state mythology. To these sovereign deities, to the unity of "Italy," to the hegemony of "Prussia," to the glory of "France," and the destinies of "Russia," she has sacrificed many generations of possible unity, peace, and prosperity and the lives of millions of men.

To regard a tribe or a state as a sort of personality is a very old disposition of the human mind. The Bible abounds in such personifications. Judah, Edom, Moab, Assyria, figure in the Hebrew Scriptures as if they were individuals; it is sometimes impossible to say whether the Hebrew writer is dealing with a person or with a nation. It is manifestly a primitive and natural tendency. But in the case of modern Europe it is a retrocession. Europe, under the idea of Christendom, had gone far towards unification. And while such tribal persons as "Israel" or "Tyre" did represent a certain community of blood, a certain uniformity of type, and a homogeneity of interest, the European powers which arose in the seventeenth and eighteenth centuries were entirely fictitious unities. Russia was in truth an assembly of the most incongruous elements, Cossacks, Tartars, Ukrainians, Muscovites, and, after the time of Peter, Esthonians and Lithuanians; the France of Louis XV comprehended German Alsace and freshly assimilated regions of Burgundy; it was a prison of suppressed Huguenots and a sweating-house for peasants. In "Britain," England carried on her back the Hanoverian dominions in Germany, Scotland, the profoundly alien Welsh and the hostile and Catholic Irish. Such powers as Sweden, Prussia, and still more so Poland and Austria, if we watch them in a series of historical maps, contract, expand, thrust out extensions, and wander over the map of Europe like amœbæ under the microscope. . . .

If we consider the psychology of international relationship as we see it manifested in the world about us, and as it is shown by the development of the "Power" idea in modern Europe, we shall realize certain historically very important facts about the nature of man. Aristotle said that man is a political animal, but in our modern sense of the word politics, which now covers world-politics, he is nothing of the sort. He has still the instincts of the family tribe, and beyond that he has a disposition to attach himself and his family to something larger, to a tribe, a city, a nation, or a state. But that disposition, left to itself, is a vague and very uncritical disposition. If anything, he is inclined to fear and dislike criticism of this something larger that encloses his life and to which he has given himself, and to avoid such criticism. Perhaps he has a subconscious fear of the isolation that may ensue if the system is broken or discredited. He takes the *milieu* in which he finds himself for granted; he accepts his city or his government, just as he accepts the nose or the digestion which fortune has bestowed upon him. But men's loyalties, the sides they take in political things, are not innate, they are educational results. For most men their education in these matters is the silent, continuous education of things about them. Men find themselves a part of Merry England or Holy Russia; they grow up into these devotions; they accept them as a part of their nature.

It is only slowly that the world is beginning to realize how profoundly the tacit education of circumstances can be supplemented, modified, or corrected by positive teaching, by literature, discussion, and properly criticized experience. The real life of the ordinary man is his everyday life, his little circle of affections, fears, hungers, lusts, and imaginative impulses. It is only when his attention is directed to political affairs as something vitally affecting this personal circle, that he brings his reluctant mind to bear upon them. It is scarcely too much to say that the ordinary man thinks as little about political matters as he can, and stops thinking about them as soon as possible. It is still only very curious and exceptional minds, or minds that have by example or good education acquired the scientific habit of wanting to know *why*, or minds shocked and distressed by some public catastrophe and roused to wide apprehensions of danger, that will not accept governments and institutions, however preposterous, that do not directly annoy them, as satisfactory. The ordinary human being, until he is so aroused, will acquiesce in any collective activities that are going on in this world in which he finds himself, and any phrasing or symbolization that meets his vague need for something greater to which his personal affairs, his individual circle, can be anchored.

If we keep these manifest limitations of our nature in mind, it no longer becomes a mystery how, as the idea of Christianity as a world brotherhood of men sank into discredit because of its fatal entanglement with priestcraft and the Papacy on the one hand and with the authority of princes on the other, and the age of faith passed into our present age of doubt and disbelief, men shifted the reference of their lives from the kingdom of God and the brotherhood of mankind to these apparently more living realities, France and England, Holy Russia, Spain, Prussia, which were at least embodied in active courts, which maintained laws, exerted power through armies and navies, waved flags with a compelling solemnity, and were self-assertive and insatiably greedy in an entirely human and understandable fashion. Certainly such men as Cardinal Richelieu and Cardinal Mazarin thought of themselves as serving greater ends than their own or their monarch's; they served the quasi-divine France of their imaginations. And as certainly these habits of mind percolated down from them to their subordinates and to the general body of the population. In the thirteenth and fourteenth centuries the general population of Europe was religious and only vaguely patriotic; by the nineteenth it had become wholly patriotic. In a crowded English or French or German railway carriage of the later nineteenth century it would have aroused far less hostility to have jeered at God than to have jeered at one of those strange beings, England or France or Germany. To these things men's minds clung, and they clung to them because in all the world there appeared nothing else so satisfying to cling to. They were the real and living gods of Europe.

(Yet in the background of the consciousness of the world, waiting as the silence and moonlight wait above the flares and shouts, the hurdy-gurdies and quarrels of a village fair, is the knowledge that all mankind is one brotherhood, that God is the universal and impartial Father of mankind, and that only in that universal service can mankind find peace, or peace be found for the troubles of the individual soul. . . .)

This idealization of governments and foreign offices, this mythology of " Powers " and their loves and hates and conflicts, has so obsessed the imaginations of Europe and Western Asia as to provide it with its " forms of thought." Nearly all the histories, nearly all the political literature of the last two centuries in Europe, have been written in its phraseology. Yet a time is coming when a clearer-sighted generation will read with perplexity how in the community of Western Europe, consisting everywhere of very slight variations of a common racial mixture of Nordic and Iberian peoples and immigrant Semitic and Mongolian elements, speaking nearly everywhere modifications of the same Aryan speech, having a common past in the Roman Empire, common religious forms, common social usages, and a common art and science, and intermarrying so freely that no one could tell with certainty the " nationality " of any of his great-grandchildren, men could be moved to the wildest excitement upon the question of the ascendancy of " France," the rise and unification of " Germany," the rival claims of " Russia " and " Greece " to possess Constantinople. These conflicts will seem then as reasonless and insane as those dead, now incomprehensible feuds of the " greens " and " blues " that once filled the streets of Byzantium with shouting and bloodshed.

Tremendously as these phantoms, the Powers, rule our minds and lives to-day, they are, as this history shows clearly, things only of the last few centuries, a mere hour, an incidental phase, in the vast deliberate history of our kind. They mark a phase of relapse, a backwater, as the rise of Machiavellian monarchy marks a backwater, they are part of the same eddy of faltering faith, in a process altogether greater and altogether different in its general tendency, the process of the moral and intellectual reunion of mankind. For a time men have relapsed upon these national or imperial gods of theirs; it is but for a time. The idea of the world state, the universal kingdom of righteousness of which every living soul shall be a citizen, was already in the world two thousand years ago, never more to leave it. Men know that it is present even when they refuse to recognize it. In the writings and talk of men about international affairs to-day, in the current discussions of historians and political journalists, there is an effect of drunken men growing sober, and terribly afraid of growing sober. They still talk loudly of their " love " for France, of their " hatred " of Germany, of the " traditional ascendancy of Britain at sea," and so on and so on, like those who sing of their cups in spite of the steadfast onset of sobriety and a headache. These are dead gods they serve. By sea or land men want no powers ascendant, but only law and service. That silent unavoidable challenge is in all our minds like dawn breaking slowly, shining between the shutters of a disordered room.

§ 7

The seventeenth century in Europe was the century of Louis XIV; he and French ascendancy and Versailles are the central motif of the story. The eighteenth century was equally the century of the " rise of Prussia as a great power," and the chief figure in the story is Frederick II, Frederick the Great. Interwoven with his history is the story of Poland.

The Crowned Republic of Poland and its Fate.

The condition of affairs in Poland was peculiar. Unlike its three neighbours, Prussia, Russia, and the Austro-Hungarian monarchy of the Habsburgs, Poland had not developed a Grand Monarchy. Its system of government may be best described as republican with a king, an elected life-president. Each king was separately elected. It was in fact rather more republican than Britain, but its republicanism was more aristocratic in form. Poland had little trade and few manufactures; she was agricultural and still with great areas of grazing, forest, and waste; she was a poor country, and her landowners were poor aristocrats. The mass of her population was a downtrodden and savagely ignorant peasantry, and she also harboured great masses of very poor Jews. She had remained Catholic. She was, so to speak, a poor Catholic inland Britain, entirely surrounded by enemies instead of by the sea. She had no definite boundaries at all, neither sea nor mountain. And it added to her misfortunes that some of her elected kings had been brilliant and aggressive rulers. Eastward her power extended weakly into regions inhabited almost entirely by Russians; westward she overlapped a German subject population.

Because she had no great trade, she had no great towns to compare with those of Western Europe, and no vigorous universities to hold her mind together. Her noble class lived on their estates, without much intellectual intercourse. They were patriotic, they had an aristocratic sense of freedom—which was entirely compatible with the systematic impoverishment of their serfs—but their patriotism and freedom were incapable of effective co-operation. While warfare was a matter of levies of men and horses, Poland was a comparatively strong power; but it was quite unable to keep pace with the development of military art that was making standing forces of professional soldiers the necessary weapon in warfare. Yet divided and disabled as she was, she could yet count some notable victories to her credit. The last Turkish attack upon Vienna (1683) was defeated by the Polish cavalry under King John Sobiesky, King John III. (This same Sobiesky, before he was elected king, had been in the pay of Louis XIV, and had also fought for the Swedes against his native country.) Needless to say, this weak aristocratic republic, with its recurrent royal elections, invited aggression from all three of its neighbours. " Foreign money," and every sort of exterior interference, came into the country at each election. And like the Greeks of old, every disgruntled Polish patriot flew off to some foreign enemy to wreak his indignation upon his ungrateful country.

Even when the King of Poland was elected, he had very little power because of the mutual jealousy of the nobles. Like the English peers, they preferred a foreigner, and for much the same reason, because he had no roots of power in the land; but, unlike the British, their own government had not the solidarity which the periodic assembling of Parliament in London,

The PARTITIONS of POLAND

POLAND before 1772

after 1772

after 1793

after 1795

J.F.H.

the "coming up to town," gave the British peers. In London there was "Society," a continuous intermingling of influential persons and ideas. Poland had no London and no "Society." So practically Poland had no central government at all. The King of Poland could not make war nor peace, levy a tax or alter the law, without the consent of the Diet, and *any single member of the Diet had the power of putting a veto upon any proposal before it.* He had merely to rise and say, "I disapprove," and the matter dropped. He could even carry his free veto, his *liberum veto,* further. He could object to the assembly of the Diet, and the Diet was thereby dissolved. Poland was not simply a crowned aristocratic republic like the British, it was a paralysed crowned aristocratic republic.

To Frederick the Great the existence of Poland was particularly provocative because of the way in which an arm of Poland reached out to the Baltic at Dantzig and separated his ancestral dominions in East Prussia from his territories within the empire. It was he who incited Catherine the Second of Russia and Maria Theresa of Austria, whose respect he had earned by depriving her of Silesia, to a joint attack upon Poland.

Let four maps of Poland tell the tale.

After this first outrage of 1772 Poland underwent a great change of heart. Poland was indeed born as a nation on the eve of

LOUIS XIV.

(From Rigaud's painting in the Louvre.)

dream. And they received this glorious legacy like ill-bred heirs ; it meant no more to them than a fresh occasion for atrocious disputes. But what community of human beings has ever yet preferred creation to conspiracy ? What nation in all our story has ever worked with another when, at any cost to itself, it could contrive to do that other an injury ? The Powers of Europe began by a frantic " claiming " of the new realms. They went on to exhausting conflicts. Spain, who claimed first and most, and who was for a time " mistress " of two-thirds of America, made no better use of her possession than to bleed herself nearly to death therein.

We have told how the Papacy in its last assertion of world dominion, instead of maintaining the common duty of all Christendom to make a great common civilization in the new lands, divided the American continent between Spain and Portugal. This naturally roused the hostility of the excluded nations. The seamen of England showed no respect for either claim, and set themselves particularly against the Spanish ; the Swedes turned their Protestantism to a similar account. The Hollanders, so soon as they had shaken off their Spanish masters, also set their sails westward to flout the Pope and share in the good things of the New World. His Most Catholic Majesty of France hesitated as little as any Protestant. All these powers were soon busy pegging out claims in North America and the West Indies.

Neither the Danish kingdom (which at that time included Norway and Iceland) nor the Swedes secured very much in the scramble. The Danes annexed some of the West Indian islands. Sweden got nothing. Both Denmark and Sweden at this time were deep in the affairs of Germany. We have already named Gustavus Adolphus, the Protestant " Lion of the North," and mentioned his campaigns in Germany, Poland, and Russia. These Eastern European regions are great absorbents of energy, and the strength that might have given Sweden a large share in the New World reaped a barren harvest of glory in Europe. Such small settlements as the Swedes made in America presently fell to the Dutch.

The Hollanders too, with the French monarchy under Cardinal Richelieu and under Louis XIV eating its way across the Spanish Netherlands towards their frontier, had not the undistracted resources that Britain, behind her " silver streak " of sea, could put into overseas adventures.

Moreover, the absolutist efforts of James I and Charles I, and the restoration of Charles II, had the effect of driving out from England a great number of sturdy-minded, republican-spirited Protestants, men of substance and character, who set up in America, and particularly in New England, out of reach, as they supposed, of the king and his taxes. The *Mayflower* was only one of the pioneer vessels of a stream of emigrants. It was the luck of Britain that they remained, though dissentient in spirit, under the British flag. The Dutch never sent out settlers of the same quantity and quality, first because their Spanish rulers would not let them, and then because they had got possession of their own country. And though there was a great emigration of Protestant Huguenots from the dragonnades and persecution of Louis XIV, they had Holland and England close at hand as refuges, and their industry, skill, and sobriety went mainly to strengthen those countries, and particularly England. A few of them founded settlements in Carolina, but these did not remain French ; they fell first to the Spanish and finally to the English.

The Dutch settlements, with the Swedish, also succumbed to Britain ; Nieuw Amsterdam became British in 1674, and its name was changed to New York, as the reader may learn very cheerfully in Washington Irving's *Knickerbocker's History of New York*. The state of affairs in North America in 1750 is indicated very clearly by a map we have adapted from one in Robinson's *Medieval and Modern Times*. The British power was established along the east coast from Savannah to the St. Lawrence River ; and Newfoundland and considerable northern areas, the Hudson Bay Company territories, had been acquired by treaty from the French. The British occupied Barbados (almost our oldest possession) in 1605, and acquired Jamaica, the Bahamas, and British Honduras from the Spaniards. But France was pursuing a very dangerous and alarming game, a game even more dangerous and alarming on the map than in reality. She had made real settlements in Quebec and Montreal to the north and at New Orleans in the south, and her explorers and agents had pushed south and north, making treaties with the American Indians of the great plains and setting up claims—without setting up towns—right across the continent behind the British. But the realities of the case are not adequately represented in this way. The British colonies were being very solidly settled by a good class of people ; they already numbered a population of over a million ; the French at that time hardly counted a tenth of that. They had a number of brilliant travellers and missionaries at work, but no substance of population behind them.

Many old maps of America in this period are still to be found, maps designed to scare and " rouse " the British to a sense of the " designs of France " in America. War broke out in 1754, and in 1759 the British and Colonial forces under General Wolfe took Quebec and completed the conquest of Canada in the next year. In 1763 Canada was finally ceded to Britain. (But the western part of the rather indefinite region of Louisiana in the south, named after Louis XIV, remained outside the British sphere. It was taken over by Spain ; and in 1800 it was recovered by France. Finally, in 1803, it was bought from France by the United States government.) In this Canadian war the American colonists gained a considerable experience of the military art, and a knowledge of British military organization that was to be of great use to them a little later.

§ 9

It was not only in America that the French and British powers clashed. The condition of India at this time was one very interesting and attractive to European adventurers. The great Mongol Empire of Baber, Akbar, and Aurangzebe was now far gone in decay. What had happened to India was very parallel to what had happened to Germany. The Great Mogul at Delhi in India, like the Holy Roman Emperor in Germany, was still nominally overlord, but

Britain dominates India.

after the death of Aurangzebe he exerted only a nominal authority except in the immediate neighbourhood of his capital. In the southwest a Hindu people, the Mahrattas, had risen against Islam, restored Brahmanism as the ruling religion, and for a time extended their power over the whole southern triangle of India. In Rajputana also the rule of Islam was replaced by Brahmanism, and at Bhurtpur and Jaipur there ruled powerful Rajput princes. In Oudh there was a Shiite kingdom, with its capital at Lucknow, and Bengal was also a separate (Moslem) kingdom. Away in the Punjab to the north had arisen a very interesting religious body, the Sikhs, proclaiming the universal rule of one God and assailing both the Hindu Vedas and the Moslem Koran. Originally a pacific sect, the Sikhs presently followed the example of Islam, and sought—at first very disastrously to themselves—to establish the kingdom of God by the sword. And into this confused and disordered India there presently (1738) came an invader from the north, Nadir Shah (1736—47), the Turcoman ruler of Persia, who swept down through the Khyber pass, broke every army that stood in his way, and captured and sacked Delhi, carrying off an enormous booty. He left the north of India so utterly broken, that in the next twenty years there were no less than six other successful plundering raids into North India from Afghanistan, which had become an independent state at the death of Nadir Shah. For a time Mahrattas fought with Afghans for the rule of North India ; then the Mahratta power broke up into a series of principalities, Indore, Gwalior, Baroda, and others. . . .

This was the India into which the French and English were thrusting during the eighteenth century. A succession of other European powers had been struggling for a commercial and political footing in India and the east ever since Vasco da Gama had made his memorable voyage round the Cape to Calicut. The sea trade of India had previously been in the hands of the Red Sea Arabs, and the Portuguese won it from them in a series of sea fights. The Portuguese ships were the bigger, and carried a heavier armament. For a time the Portuguese held the Indian trade as their own, and Lisbon outshone Venice as a mart for Oriental spices; the seventeenth century, however, saw the Dutch grasping at this monopoly. At the crest of their power the Dutch had settlements at the Cape of Good Hope, they held Mauritius, they had two establishments in Persia, twelve in India, six in Ceylon, and all over the East Indies they had dotted their fortified stations. But their selfish resolution to exclude traders of any other European nationality forced the Swedes,

INDIA
in
1750
✠

Danes, French, and English into hostile competition. The first effectual blows at their overseas monopoly were struck in European waters by the victories of Blake, the English republican admiral; and by the opening of the eighteenth century both the English and French were in vigorous competition with the Dutch for trade and privileges throughout India. At Madras, Bombay, and Calcutta the English established their headquarters; Pondicherry and Chandernagore were the chief French settlements.

At first all these European powers came merely as traders, and the only establishments they attempted were warehouses; but the unsettled state of the country, and the unscrupulous methods of their rivals, made it natural for them to fortify and arm their settlements, and this armament made them attractive allies of the various warring princes who now divided India. And it was entirely in the spirit of the new European nationalist politics that when the French took one side, the British should take another. The great leader upon the English side was Robert Clive, who was born in 1725, and went to India in 1743. His chief antagonist was Dupleix. The story of this struggle throughout the first half of the eighteenth century is too long and intricate to be told here. By 1761 the British found themselves completely dominant in the Indian peninsula. At Plassey (1757) and at Buxar (1764) their armies gained striking and conclusive victories over the army of Bengal and the army of Oudh. The Great Mogul, nominally their overlord, became in effect their puppet. They levied taxes over great areas; they exacted indemnities for real or fancied opposition.

These successes were not gained directly by the forces of the King of England; they were gained by the East India Trading Company, which had been originally at the time of its incorporation under Queen Elizabeth no more than a company of sea adventurers. Step by step they had been forced to raise troops and arm their ships. And now this trading company, with its tradition of gain, found itself dealing not merely in spices and dyes and tea and jewels, but in the revenues and territories of princes and the destinies of India. It had come to buy and sell, and it found itself achieving a tremendous piracy. There was no one to challenge its proceedings. Is it any wonder that its captains and commanders and officials, nay, even its clerks and common soldiers, came back to England loaded with spoils? Men under such circumstances, with a great and wealthy land at their mercy, could not determine what they might or might not do. It was a strange land to them, with a strange sunlight; its brown people were a different race, outside their range of sympathy; its temples and buildings seemed to sustain fantastic standards of behaviour. Englishmen at home were perplexed when presently these generals and officials came back to make dark accusations against each other of extortions and cruelties. Upon Clive Parliament passed a vote of censure. He committed suicide in 1774. In 1788 Warren Hastings, a second great Indian administrator, was impeached and acquitted (1792). It was a strange and unprecedented situation in the world's history. The English Parliament found itself ruling over a London trading company, which in its turn was dominating an empire far greater and more populous than all the domains of the British crown. To the bulk of the English people India was a remote, fantastic, almost inaccessible land, to which adventurous poor young men went out, to return after many years very rich and very choleric old gentlemen. It was difficult for the English to conceive what the life of these countless brown millions in the eastern sunshine could be. Their imaginations declined the task. India remained romantically unreal. It was impossible for the English, therefore, to exert any effective supervision and control over the company's proceedings.

chapter we have told of Peter the Great joining the circle of Grand Monarchs and, as it were, dragging Russia into Europe. The rise of this great central power of the Old World, which is neither altogether of the East nor altogether of the West, is one of the utmost importance to our human destiny. We have also told in the same chapter of the appearance of a Christian steppe people, the Cossacks, who formed a barrier between the feudal agriculture of Poland and Hungary to the west and the

The chief Foreign Settlements in INDIA at the end of the 17th Century

§ 10

And while the great peninsula of the south of Asia was thus falling under the dominion of the English sea traders, an equally remarkable reaction of Europe upon Asia was going on in the north. We have told in chap. xxxiv, § 5c, how the Christian states of Russia recovered their independence from the Golden Horde, and how the Tsar of Moscow became master of the republic of Novgorod; and in § 5 of this

Russia's Ride to the Pacific.

Tartar to the east. The Cossacks were the wild east of Europe, and in many ways not unlike the wild west of the United States in the middle nineteenth century. All who had made Russia too hot to hold them, criminals as well as the persecuted innocent, rebellious serfs, religious sectaries, thieves, vagabonds, murderers, sought asylum in the southern steppes, and there made a fresh start and fought for life and freedom against Pole, Russian, and Tartar alike. Doubtless fugitives from the Tartars to the east also contributed to the Cossack mixture. Chief among these new nomad tribes were the Ukraine Cossacks on the Dnieper and the Don Cossacks on the Don. Slowly these border folk were incorporated in the Russian imperial service, much as the Highland clans of Scotland were converted into regiments by the British government. New lands were offered them in Asia. They became a weapon against the dwindling power of the Mongolian nomads, first in Turkestan and then across Siberia as far as the Amur.

The decay of Mongol energy in the seventeenth and eighteenth centuries is very difficult to explain. Within two or three centuries from the days of Jengis and Timurlane, Central Asia had relapsed from a period of world ascendancy to extreme political impotence. Changes of climate, unrecorded pestilences, infections of a malarial type, may have played their part in this recession—which may be only a temporary recession measured by the scale of universal history—of the Central Asian peoples. Some authorities think that the spread of Buddhist teaching from China also had a pacifying influence upon them. At any rate, by the sixteenth century the Mongol Tartar and Turkish peoples were no longer pressing outward, but were being invaded, subjugated, and pushed back both by Christian Russia in the west and by China in the east.

All through the seventeenth century the Cossacks were spreading eastward from European Russia, and settling wherever they found agricultural conditions. Cordons of forts and stations formed a moving frontier to these settlements to the south, where the Turkomans were still strong and active ; to the north-east, however, Russia had no frontier until she reached right to the Pacific. . . .

At the same time China was in a phase of expansion. In 1644 the Ming Dynasty, in a state of artistic decay and greatly weakened by a Japanese invasion, fell to Manchu conquerors, a people apparently identical with the former Kin Dynasty, which had ruled at Pekin over North China until the days of Jengis. It was the Manchus who imposed their pigtail as a mark of political loyalty upon the Chinese population. They brought a new energy into Chinese affairs, and their northern interests led to a considerable northward expansion of the Chinese civilization and influence into Manchuria and Mongolia. So it was that by the middle of the eighteenth century the Russians and Chinese were in contact in Mongolia. At this period China ruled Eastern Turkestan, Tibet, Nepal, Burmah, and Annam. . . .

We have mentioned a Japanese invasion of China (or rather of Korea). Except for this aggression upon China, Japan plays no part in our history before the nineteenth century. Like China under the Mings, Japan had set her face resolutely against the interference of foreigners in her affairs. She was a country leading her own civilized life, magically sealed against intruders. We have told little of her hitherto because there was little to tell. Her picturesque and romantic history stands apart from the general drama of human affairs. Her population was chiefly a Mongolian population, with some very interesting white people of a Nordic type, the Hairy Ainu, in the northern islands. Her civilization seems to have been derived almost entirely from Korea and China ; her art is a special development of Chinese art, her writing an adaptation of the Chinese script.

§ 11

In these preceding ten sections we have been dealing with an age of division, of separated nationalities. We have already
What Gibbon thought of the World. described this period of the seventeenth and eighteenth centuries as an interregnum in the progress of mankind towards a world-wide unity. Throughout this period there was no ruling unifying idea in men's minds. The impulse of the empire had failed until the Emperor was no more than one of a number of competing princes, and the dream of Christendom also was a fading dream. The developing "powers" jostled one another throughout the world ; but for a time it seemed that they might jostle one another indefinitely without any great catastrophe to mankind. The great geographical discoveries of the sixteenth century had so enlarged human resources that, for all their divisions, for all the waste of their wars and

policies, the people of Europe enjoyed a considerable and increasing prosperity. Central Europe recovered steadily from the devastation of the Thirty Years' War.

Looking back upon this period, which came to its climax in the eighteenth century, looking back, as we can begin to do nowadays, and seeing its events in relation to the centuries that came before it and to the great movements of the present time, we are able to realize how transitory and provisional were its political forms and how unstable its securities. Provisional it was as no other age has been provisional, an age of assimilation and recuperation, a political pause, a gathering up of the ideas of men and the resources of science for a wider human effort. But the contemporary mind did not see it in that light. The failure of the great creative ideas as they had been formulated in the Middle Ages, had left human thought for a time destitute of the guidance of creative ideas; even educated and imaginative men saw the world undramatically; no longer as an interplay of effort and destiny, but as the scene in which a trite happiness was sought and the milder virtues were rewarded. It was not simply the contented and conservative-minded who, in a world of rapid changes, were under the sway of this assurance of an achieved fixity of human conditions. Even highly critical and insurgent intelligences, in default of any sustaining movements in the soul of the community, betrayed the same disposition. Political life, they felt, had ceased to be the urgent and tragic thing it had once been; it had become a polite comedy. The eighteenth was a century of comedy—which at the end grew grim. It is inconceivable that that world of the middle eighteenth century could have produced a Jesus of Nazareth, a Gautama, a Francis of Assisi, an Ignatius of Loyola.

Photo: Rischgitz Collection.

VOLTAIRE.

If one may imagine an eighteenth-century John Huss, it is impossible to imagine anyone with sufficient passion to burn him. Until the stirrings of conscience in Britain that developed into the Methodist revival began, we can detect scarcely a suspicion that there still remained great tasks in hand for our race to do, that enormous disturbances were close at hand, or that the path of man through space and time was dark with countless dangers, and must to the end remain a high and terrible enterprise.

We have quoted again and again in this history from Gibbon's *Decline and Fall of the Roman Empire*. Now we shall quote from it for the last time and bid it farewell, for we have come to the age in which it was written. Gibbon was born in 1737,[1] and the last volume of his history was published in 1787, but the passage we shall quote was probably written in the year 1780. Gibbon was a young man of delicate health and fairly good fortune; he had a partial and interrupted education at Oxford, and then he completed his studies in Geneva; on the whole his outlook was French and cosmopolitan rather than British, and he was much under the intellectual influence of that great Frenchman who is best known under the name of Voltaire (François Marie Arouet de Voltaire, 1694—1778). Voltaire was an author of enormous industry; seventy volumes of him adorn the present writer's shelves, and another edition of Voltaire's works runs to ninety-four; he dealt largely with history and public affairs, and he corresponded with Catherine the Great of Russia, Frederick the Great of Prussia, Louis XV, and most of the prominent people of the time. Both Voltaire and Gibbon had the sense of history strong in them; both have set out very plainly and

[1] See his fragment of autobiography (*The Autobiography of Edward Gibbon*, edited by John Murray).

fully their visions of human life; and it is clear that to both of them the system in which they lived, the system of monarchy, of leisurely and privileged gentlefolks, of rather despised industrial and trading people and of down-trodden and negligible labourers and poor and common people, seemed the most stably established way of living that the world had ever seen. They postured a little as republicans, and sneered at the divine pretensions of monarchy; but the republicanism that appealed to Voltaire was the crowned republicanism of the Britain of those days, in which the king was simply the official head, the first and greatest of the gentlemen.

The ideal they sustained was the ideal of a polite and polished world in which men—men of quality that is, for no others counted—would be ashamed to be cruel or gross or enthusiastic, in which the appointments of life would be spacious and elegant, and the fear of ridicule the potent auxiliary of the law in maintaining the decorum and harmonies of life. Voltaire had in him the possibility of a passionate hatred of injustice, and his interventions on behalf of persecuted or ill-used men are the high lights of his long and complicated life-story. And this being the mental disposition of Gibbon and Voltaire, and of the age in which they lived, it is natural that they should find the existence of religion in the world, and in particular the existence of Christianity, a perplexing and rather unaccountable phenomenon. The whole of that side of life seemed to them a kind of craziness in the human make-up. Gibbon's great history is essentially an attack upon Christianity as the operating cause of the decline and fall. He idealized the crude and gross plutocracy of Rome into a world of fine gentlemen upon the eighteenth-century model, and told how it fell before the Barbarian from without because of the decay through Christianity within. In our history here we have tried to set that story in a better light. To Voltaire official Christianity was "*l'infâme*"; something that limited people's lives, interfered with their thoughts, persecuted harmless dissentients. And indeed in that period of the interregnum there was very little life or light in either the orthodox Christianity of Rome or in the orthodox tame churches of Russia and of the Protestant princes. In an interregnum incommoded with an abundance of sleek parsons and sly priests it was hard to realize what fires had once blazed in the heart of Christianity, and what fires of political and religious passion might still blaze in the hearts of men.

At the end of his third volume Gibbon completed his account of the breaking up of the Western Empire. He then raised the question whether civilization might ever undergo again a similar collapse. This led him to review the existing state of affairs (1780) and to compare it with the state of affairs during the decline of imperial Rome. It will be very convenient to our general design to quote some passages from that comparison here, for nothing could better illustrate the state of mind of the liberal thinkers of Europe at the crest of the political interregnum of the age of the Great Powers, before the first intimations of those profound political and social forces of disintegration that have produced at length the dramatic interrogations of our own times.

"This awful revolution," wrote Gibbon of the Western collapse, "may be usefully applied to the instruction of the present age. It is the duty of a patriot to prefer and promote the exclusive interest and glory of his native country; but a philosopher may be permitted to enlarge his views, and to consider Europe as one great republic, whose various inhabitants have attained almost the same level of politeness and cultivation. The balance of power will continue to fluctuate, and the prosperity of our own or the neighbouring kingdoms may be alternately exalted or depressed; but these partial events cannot essentially injure our general state of happiness, the system of arts, and laws, and manners, which so advantageously distinguish, above the rest of mankind, the Europeans and their colonies. The savage nations of the globe are the common enemies of civilized society; and we may enquire with anxious curiosity whether Europe is still threatened with a repetition of those calamities which formerly oppressed the arms and institutions of Rome. Perhaps the same reflections will illustrate the fall of that mighty empire and explain the probable causes of our actual security.

"The Romans were ignorant of the extent of their danger, and the number of their enemies. Beyond the Rhine and Danube, the northern countries of Europe and Asia were filled with innumerable tribes of hunters and shepherds, poor, voracious, and turbulent; bold in arms, and impatient to ravish the fruits of industry. The Barbarian world was agitated by the rapid impulse of war; and the peace of Gaul or Italy was shaken by the distant revolutions of China. The Huns, who fled before a victorious enemy, directed their march towards the west; and the torrent was swelled by the gradual accession of captives and allies. The flying tribes who yielded to the Huns assumed in *their* turn the spirit of conquest; the endless column of barbarians pressed on the Roman Empire with accumulated weight; and, if the foremost were destroyed, the vacant space was instantly replenished by new assailants. Such formidable emigrations can no longer issue from the North; and the long repose, which has been imputed to the decrease of population, is the happy consequence of the progress of arts and agriculture. Instead of some rude villages, thinly scattered among its woods and morasses, Germany now produces a list of two thousand three hundred walled towns; the Christian kingdoms of Denmark, Sweden, and Poland have been successively established; and the Hanse merchants, with the Teutonic knights, have extended their colonies along the coast of the Baltic, as far as the Gulf of Finland. From the Gulf of Finland to the Eastern Ocean, Russia now assumes the form of a powerful and civilized empire. The plough, the loom, and the forge are introduced on the banks of the Volga, the Oby, and the Lena; and the fiercest of the Tartar hordes have been taught to tremble and obey. . . .

"The Empire of Rome was firmly established by the singular and perfect coalition of its members. . . . But this union was purchased by the loss of national freedom and military spirit; and the servile provinces, destitute of life and motion, expected their safety from the mercenary troops and governors, who were directed by the orders of a distant court. The happiness of a hundred millions depended on the personal merit of one or two men, perhaps children, whose minds were corrupted by education, luxury, and despotic power. Europe is now divided into twelve powerful, though unequal kingdoms, three respectable commonwealths, and a variety of smaller, though independent, states; the chances of royal and ministerial talents are multiplied, at least with the number of its rulers; and a Julian[1] or Semiramis[2] may reign in the north, while Arcadius and Honorius[3] again slumber on the thrones of the House of Bourbon. The abuses of tyranny are restrained by the mutual influence of fear and shame; republics have acquired order and stability; monarchies have imbibed the principles of freedom, or, at least, of moderation; and some sense of honour and justice is introduced into the most defective constitutions by the general manners of the times. In peace, the progress of knowledge and industry is accelerated by the emulation of so many active rivals: in war, the European forces are exercised by temperate and undecisive contests. If a savage conqueror should issue from the deserts of Tartary, he must repeatedly vanquish the robust peasants of Russia, the numerous armies of Germany, the gallant nobles of France, and the intrepid freemen of Britain; who, perhaps, might confederate for their common defence. Should the victorious Barbarians carry slavery and desolation as far as the Atlantic Ocean, ten thousand vessels would transport beyond their pursuit the remains of civilized society; and Europe would revive and flourish in the American world which is already filled with her colonies and institutions.

"Cold, poverty, and a life of danger and fatigue fortify the strength and courage of Barbarians. In every age they have oppressed the polite and peaceful nations of China, India, and Persia, who neglected, and still neglect, to counterbalance these natural powers by the resources of military art. The warlike states of antiquity, Greece, Macedonia, and Rome, educated a race of soldiers; exer-

[1] Frederick the Great of Prussia.
[2] Catherine the Great of Russia.
[3] Louis XVI of France and Charles III of Spain.

cised their bodies, disciplined their courage, multiplied their forces by regular evolutions, and converted the iron which they possessed into strong and serviceable weapons. But this superiority insensibly declined with their laws and manners ; and the feeble policy of Constantine and his successors armed and instructed, for the ruin of the empire, the rude valour of the Barbarian mercenaries. The military art has been changed by the invention of gunpowder ; which enables man to command the two most powerful agents of nature, air and fire. Mathematics, chemistry, mechanics, architecture, have been applied to the service of war ; and the adverse parties oppose to each other the most elaborate modes of attack and of defence. Historians may indignantly observe that the preparations of a siege would found and maintain a flourishing colony ; yet we cannot be displeased that the subversion of a city should be a work of cost and difficulty, or that an industrious people should be protected by those arts, which survive and supply the decay of military virtue. Cannon and fortifications now form an impregnable barrier against the Tartar horse[1] ; and Europe is secure from any future irruption of Barbarians ; since, before they can conquer, they must cease to be barbarous. . . .

" Should these speculations be found doubtful or fallacious, there still remains a more humble source of comfort and hope. The discoveries of ancient and modern navigators, and the domestic history, or tradition, of the most enlightened nations, represent the *human savage*, naked both in mind and body, and destitute of laws, of arts, of ideas, and almost of language. From this abject condition, perhaps the primitive and universal state of man, he has gradually arisen to command the animals, to fertilize the earth, to traverse the ocean, and to measure the heavens. His progress in the improvement and exercise of his mental and corporeal faculties has been irregular and various, infinitely slow in the beginning, and increasing by degrees with redoubled velocity ; ages of laborious ascent have been followed by a moment of rapid downfall ; and the several

climates of the globe have felt the vicissitudes of light and darkness. Yet the experience of four thousand years should enlarge our hopes, and diminish our apprehensions ; we cannot determine to what height the human species may aspire in their advances towards perfection ; but it may safely be presumed that no people, unless the face of nature is changed, will relapse into their original barbarism.

" Since the first discovery of the arts, war, commerce, and religious zeal have diffused, among the savages of the Old and New World, those inestimable gifts, they have been successively propagated ; they can never be lost. We may therefore acquiesce in the pleasing conclusion that every age of the world has increased, and still increases, the real wealth, the happiness, the knowledge, and perhaps the virtue, of the human race."

§ 12 [2]

One of the most interesting aspects of this story of Europe in the seventeenth and earlier eighteenth centuries during the phase of the Grand and Parliamentary Monarchies, is the comparative quiescence of the peasants and workers. The insurrectionary fires of the fourteenth and fifteenth and sixteenth centuries seem to have died down. The acute economic clashes of the earlier period had been mitigated by rough adjustments. The discovery of America had revolutionized and changed the scale of business and industry, had brought a vast volume of precious metal for money into Europe, had increased and varied employment. For a time life and work ceased to be intolerable to the masses of the poor. This did not, of course, prevent much individual misery and discontent ; the poor we have always had with us, but this misery and discontent was divided and scattered. It became inaudible.

In the earlier period the common people had had an idea to crystallize upon, the idea of Christian communism. They had found an educated leadership in the dissentient priests

The Social Truce draws to an End.

---

[1] Gibbon forgets here that cannon and the fundamentals of modern military method came to Europe with the Mongols.

[2] See for the expansion of the topics of this section, Hammond's *Town Labourer, Village Labourer,* and *Skilled Labourer.* These three books are too little known to the general reader. They are not dry-as-dust compilations of statistics, but full of interesting matter and delightfully well written.

and doctors of the Wycliffe type. As the movement for a revival in Christianity spent its force, as Lutheranism fell back for leadership from Jesus upon the Protestant Princes, this contact and reaction of the fresher minds of the educated class upon the illiterate mass was interrupted. However numerous a downtrodden class may be, and however extreme its miseries, it will never be able to make an effective protest until it achieves solidarity by the development of some common general idea. Educated men and men of ideas are more necessary to a popular political movement than to any other political process. A monarchy learns by ruling, and an oligarchy of any type has the education of affairs; but the common man, the peasant or toiler, has no experience in large matters, and can exist politically only through the services, devotion, and guidance of educated men. The Reformation, the Reformation that succeeded, the Reformation that is of the Princes, by breaking up educational facilities, largely destroyed the poor scholar and priest class whose persuasion of the crowd had rendered the Reformation possible.

The Princes of the Protestant countries, when they seized upon the national churches, early apprehended the necessity of gripping the universities also. Their idea of education was the idea of capturing young clever people for the service of their betters. Beyond that they were disposed to regard education as a mischievous thing. The only way to an education, therefore, for a poor man was through patronage. Of course there was a parade of encouragement towards learning in all the Grand Monarchies, a setting up of Academies and Royal Societies, but these benefited only a small class of subservient scholars. The church also had learnt to distrust the educated poor man. In the great aristocratic " crowned republic " of Britain there was the same shrinkage of educational opportunity. " Both the ancient universities," says Hammond, in his account of the eighteenth century, " were the universities of the rich. There is a passage in Macaulay describing the state and pomp of Oxford at the end of the seventeenth century, ' when her Chancellor, the Venerable Duke of Ormonde, sat in his embroidered mantle on his throne under the painted ceiling of the Sheldonian theatre, surrounded by hundreds of graduates robed according to their rank, while the noblest youths of England were solemnly presented to him as candidates for academical honours.' The university was a power, not in the sense in which that could be said of a university like the old university of Paris, whose learning could make Popes tremble, but in the sense that the university was part of the recognized machinery of aristocracy. What was true of the universities was true of the public schools. Education in England was the nursery not of a society, but of an order ; not of a state, but of a race of owner-rulers." The missionary spirit had departed from education throughout Europe. To that quite as much as to the amelioration of things by a diffused prosperity, this phase of quiescence among the lower classes is to be ascribed. They had lost brains and speech, and they were fed. The community was like a pithed animal in the hands of the governing class.[1]

Moreover, there had been considerable changes in the proportions of class to class. One of the most difficult things for the historian to trace is the relative amount of the total property of the community held at any time by any particular class in that community. These things fluctuate very rapidly. The peasant wars of Europe indicate a phase of comparatively concentrated property when large masses of people could feel themselves expropriated and at a common disadvantage, and so take mass action. This was the time of the rise and prosperity of the Fuggers and their like, a time of international finance. Then with the vast importation of silver and gold and commodities into Europe from America, there seems to have been a restoration of a more diffused state of wealth. The poor were just as miserable as ever, but there were perhaps not so many poor relatively, and they were

[1] " Our present public school system is candidly based on training a dominant master class. But the uprising of the workers and modern conditions are rapidly making the *dominant method* unworkable. . . . The change in the aim of schools will transform all the organizations and methods of schools, and my belief is that this change will make the new era."—F. W. Sanderson, Head Master of Oundle, in an address at Leeds, February 16, 1920.

broken up into a variety of types without any ideas in common. In Great Britain the agricultural life which had been dislocated by the confiscations of the Reformation had settled down again into a system of tenant farming under great landowners. Side by side with the large estates there was still, however, much common land for pasturing the beasts of the poorer villagers, and much land cultivated in strips upon communal lines. The middling sort of man, and even the poorer sort of man upon the land, were leading an endurable existence in 1700. The standard of life, the idea, that is, of what is an endurable existence, was, however, rising during the opening phase of Grand Monarchy ; after a time the process of the upward concentration of wealth seems to have been resumed, the larger landowners began to acquire and crowd out the poorer free cultivators, and the proportion of poor people and of people who felt they were leading impoverished lives increased again. The bigger men were unchallenged rulers of Great Britain, and they set themselves to enact laws, the Enclosure Acts, that practically confiscated the unenclosed and common lands, mainly for the benefit of the larger landowners. The smaller men sank to the level of wage workers upon the land over which they had once possessed rights of cultivation and pasture.

The peasant in France and upon the continent generally was not so expropriated ; his enemy was not the landlord, but the tax gatherer ; he was squeezed on his land instead of being squeezed off it.

As the eighteenth century progressed, it is apparent in the literature of the time that what to do with " the poor " was again exercising men's thoughts. We find such active-minded English writers as Defoe (1659—1731) and Fielding (1707—54) deeply exercised by this problem. But as yet there is no such revival of the communistic and equalitarian ideas of primitive Christianity as distinguished the time of Wycliffe and John Huss. Protestantism in breaking up the universal church had for a time broken up the idea of a universal human solidarity. Even if the universal church of the Middle Ages had failed altogether to realize that idea, it had at any rate been the symbol of that idea.

Defoe and Fielding were men of a livelier practical imagination than Gibbon, and they realized something of the economic processes that were afoot in their time. So did Oliver Goldsmith (1728—74) ; his *Deserted Village* (1770) is a pamphlet on enclosures disguised as a poem.[1] But Gibbon's circumstances had never brought economic facts very vividly before his eyes ; he saw the world as a struggle between barbarism and civilization, but he perceived nothing of that other struggle over which he floated, the mute, unconscious struggle of the commonalty against able, powerful, rich, and selfish men. He did not perceive the accumulation of stresses that were presently to strain and break up all the balance of his " twelve powerful, though unequal, kingdoms," his " three respectable commonwealths," and their rag, tag, and bobtail of independent minor princes, reigning dukes, and so forth. Even the civil war that had begun in the British colonies in America did not rouse him to the nearness of what we now call " Democracy."

From what we have been saying hitherto, the reader may suppose that the squeezing of the small farmer and the peasant off the land by the great landowners, the mere grabbing of commons and the concentration of property in the hands of a powerful privileged and greedy class, was all that was happening to the English land in the eighteenth century. So we do but state the worse side of the change. Concurrently with this change of ownership there was going on a great improvement in agriculture. There can be little doubt that the methods of cultivation pursued by the peasants, squatters, and small farmers were antiquated, wasteful, and comparatively unproductive, and that the larger private holdings and estates created by the Enclosure Acts were much more productive (one authority says twenty times more productive) than the old ways. The change was perhaps a necessary one, and the evil of it was not that it was brought about, but that it was brought about

---

[1] The student who looks up the *Encyclopædia Britannica*, article " Goldsmith," instead of going to the poem itself, will find some hostile comments thereon which are themselves now literature and history ; they were written by Lord Macaulay (1800—59).

so as to increase both wealth and the numbers of the poor. Its benefits were intercepted by the bigger private owners. The community was injured to the great profit of this class.

And here we come upon one of the chief problems of our lives at the present time, the problem of the deflection of the profits of progress. For two hundred years there has been, mainly under the influence of the spirit of science and enquiry, a steady improvement in the methods of production of almost everything that humanity requires. If our sense of community and our social science were equal to the tasks required of them, there can be little question that this great increment in production would have benefited the whole community, would have given everyone an amount of education, leisure, and freedom such as mankind had never dreamt of before. But though the common standard of living has risen, the rise has been on a scale disproportionately small. The rich have developed a freedom and luxury unknown in the world hitherto, and there has been an increase in the proportion of rich people and stagnantly prosperous and unproductive people in the community; but that also fails to account for the full benefit. There has been much sheer waste. Vast accumulations of material and energy have gone into warlike preparations and warfare. Much has been devoted to the futile efforts of unsuccessful business competition. Huge possibilities have remained undeveloped because of the opposition of owners, forestallers, and speculators to their economical exploitation. The good things that science and organization have been bringing within the reach of mankind have not been taken methodically and used to their utmost, but they have been scrambled for, snatched at, seized upon by gambling adventurers and employed upon selfish and vain ends. The eighteenth century in Europe, and more particularly in Great Britain and Poland, was the age of private ownership. " Private enterprise," which meant in practice that everyone was entitled to get everything he could out of the business of the community, reigned supreme. No sense of obligation to the state in business matters is to be found in the ordinary novels, plays, and such like representative literature of the time. Everyone is out "to make his fortune," there is no recognition that it is wrong to be an unproductive parasite on the community, and still less that a financier or merchant or manufacturer can ever be overpaid for his services to mankind. This was the moral atmosphere of the time, and those lords and gentlemen who grabbed the people's commons, assumed possession of the mines under their lands, and crushed down the yeoman farmers and peasants to the status of pauper labourers, had no idea that they were living anything but highly meritorious lives.

Concurrently with this change in Great Britain from traditional patch agriculture and common pasture to large and more scientific agriculture, very great changes were going on in the manufacture of commodities. In these changes Great Britain was, in the eighteenth century, leading the world. Hitherto, throughout the whole course of history from the beginnings of civilization, manufactures, building, and industries generally had been in the hands of craftsmen and small masters who worked in their own houses. They had been organized in guilds, and were mostly their own employers. They formed an essential and permanent middle class. There were capitalists among them, who let out looms and the like, supplied material, and took the finished product, but they were not big capitalists. There had been no rich manufacturers. The rich men of the world before this time had been great landowners or money-lenders and money manipulators or merchants. But in the eighteenth century, workers in certain industries began to be collected together into factories in order to produce things in larger quantities through a systematic division of labour, and the employer, as distinguished from the master worker, began to be a person of importance. Moreover, mechanical invention was producing machines that simplified the manual work of production, and were capable of being driven by water power and presently by steam. In 1765 Watts' steam engine was constructed, a very important date in the history of industrialism.

The cotton industry was one of the first to pass into factory production (originally with water-driven machinery). The woollen industry followed. At the same time iron smelting, which had been restrained hitherto to small methods by the use of charcoal, resorted to coke made from coal, and the coal and iron industries also began to expand. The iron industry shifted from the wooded country of Sussex and Surrey to the coal districts. By 1800 this change-over of industry from a small scale business with small employers to a large scale production under big employers was well in progress. Everywhere there sprang up factories using first water, then steam power. It was a change of fundamental importance in

WATTS' "LAP" STEAM ENGINE, BUILT AT SOHO IN 1788, AND NOW IN THE
SOUTH KENSINGTON MUSEUM.

human economy. From the dawn of history the manufacturer and craftsman had been, as we have said, a sort of middle-class townsman. The machine and the employer now superseded his skill, and he either became an employer of his fellows, and grew towards wealth and equality with the other rich classes, or he remained a worker and sank very rapidly to the level of a mere labourer. This great change in human affairs is known as the Industrial Revolution. Beginning in Great Britain, it spread during the nineteenth century throughout the world.

As the Industrial Revolution went on, a great gulf opened between employer and employed. In the past every manufacturing worker had the hope of becoming an independent master. Even the slave craftsmen of Babylon and Rome were protected by laws that enabled them to save and buy their freedom and to set up for themselves. But now a factory and its engines and machines became a vast and costly thing measured by the scale of a worker's pocket. Wealthy men had to come together to create an enterprise ; credit and plant, that is to say, "Capital," were required. "Setting up for oneself" ceased to be a normal hope for an artisan. The worker was henceforth a worker from the cradle to the grave. Besides the landlords and merchants and the money-dealers who financed trading companies and lent their money to the merchants and the state, there arose now this new wealth of industrial capital—a new sort of power in the state.

Of the working out of these beginnings we shall tell later. The immediate effect of the industrial revolution upon the countries to which it came, was to cause a vast, distressful shifting and stirring of the mute, uneducated, leaderless, and now more and more propertyless common population. The small cultivators and peasants, ruined and dislodged by the Enclosure Acts, drifted towards the new manufacturing regions, and there they joined the families of the impoverished and degraded craftsmen in the factories. Great towns of squalid houses came into existence. Nobody seems to have noted clearly what was going on at the time. It is the keynote of "private enterprise" to mind one's own business, secure the utmost profit, and disregard any other consequences. Ugly great factories grew up, built as cheaply as possible, to hold as many machines and workers as possible. Around them gathered the streets of workers' homes, built at the cheapest rate, without space, without privacy, barely decent, and let at the utmost rent that could be exacted. These new industrial centres were at first without schools, without churches. . . . The English gentleman of the closing decades of the eigh-

teenth century read Gibbon's third volume and congratulated himself that there was henceforth no serious fear of the Barbarians, with this new barbarism growing up, with this metamorphosis of his countrymen into something dark and desperate, in full progress, within an easy walk perhaps of his door.

XXXVII

THE NEW DEMOCRATIC REPUBLICS OF AMERICA AND FRANCE

§ 1 [1]

WHEN Gibbon, nearly a century and a half ago, was congratulating the world of refined and educated people that the age of great political and social catastrophes was past, he was neglecting many signs which we—in the wisdom of accomplished facts—could have told him portended far heavier jolts and dislocations than any he foresaw. We have told how the struggle of the sixteenth and seventeenth-century princes for ascendances and advantages developed into a more cunning and complicated struggle of foreign offices, masquerading as idealized " Great Powers," as the eighteenth century wore on. The intricate and pretentious art of diplomacy developed. The " Prince " ceased to be a single and secretive Machiavellian schemer, and became merely the crowned symbol of a Machiavellian scheme. Prussia, Russia, and Austria fell upon and divided Poland. France was baffled in profound schemes against Spain. Britain circumvented the " designs of France " in America and acquired Canada, and got the better of France in India. And then a remarkable thing occurred, a thing very shocking to European diplomacy. The British colonies in America flatly refused to have further part or lot in this game of " Great Powers." They objected that they had no voice and no great interest in these European schemes and conflicts, and they

Inconveniences of the Great Power System.

refused to bear any portion of the burthen of taxation these foreign policies entailed.

Of course this decision did not flash out complete and finished from the American mind at the beginning of these troubles. In America in the eighteenth century, just as in England in the seventeenth, there was an entire willingness, indeed a desire on the part of ordinary men, to leave foreign affairs in the hands of the king and his ministers. But there was an equally strong desire on the part of ordinary men to be neither taxed nor interfered with in their ordinary pursuits. These are incompatible wishes. Common men cannot shirk world politics and at the same time enjoy private freedom ; but it has taken them countless generations to learn this. The first impulse in the American revolt against the government in Great Britain was therefore simply a resentment against the taxation and interference that followed necessarily from " foreign policy " without any clear recognition of what was involved in that objection. It was only when the revolt was consummated that the people of the American colonies recognized at all clearly that they had repudiated the Great Power view of life. The sentence in which that repudiation was expressed was Washington's injunction to " avoid entangling alliances." From his time until the year 1917 the united colonies of Great Britain in North America, liberated and independent as the United States of America, stood apart altogether from the blood-stained intrigues and conflicts of the

[1] Channing's excellent new *History of the United States* to vol. iv. has been our handbook here.

European foreign offices. Soon after (1810 to 1823) they were able to extend their principle of detachment to the rest of the continent, and to make all the New World "out of bounds" for the scheming expansionists of the Old. When at length, in 1917, they were obliged to re-enter

at this story in §8 of the preceding chapter. We will now tell a little more fully—though still in the barest outline—what these colonies were, whose recalcitrance was so disconcerting to the king and ministers of Great Britain in their diplomatic game against the rest of mankind.[1]

§ 2

The extent of the British colonies in America in the early half of the eighteenth century is shown in the accompanying map.[2] The darker shading represents the districts settled in 1700, the lighter the growth of the settlements up to 1760. It will be seen that the colonies were a mere fringe of population along the coast, spreading gradually inland and finding in the Alleghany and Blue Mountains a very serious barrier. Among the oldest of these settlements was the colony of Virginia, the name of which commemorates Queen Elizabeth, the Virgin Queen of England. The first expedition to found a colony in Virginia was made by Sir Walter Raleigh in 1584, but there was no permanent settlement at that time; and the

The Thirteen Colonies before their Revolt.

the arena of world politics, it was to bring the new spirit and new aims their aloofness had enabled them to develop into the tangle of international relationships. They were not, however, the first to stand aloof. Since the Treaty of Westphalia (1648), the confederated states of Switzerland, in their mountain fastnesses, had sustained their right to exclusion from the schemes of kings and empires.

But since the North American peoples are now to play an increasingly important part in our history, it will be well to devote a little more attention than we have hitherto given to their development. We have already glanced

[1] You are, I think, unjust to Great Britain and her "great power game." She was not playing that game —or, so far as she was, she was acting against "France" to liberate the colonies from the French menace in the hinterland which alarmed them. Once liberated, they broke loose, somewhat selfishly, refusing to pay the piper, though they had enjoyed, and done much to call, the tune. Great Britain was indeed to blame, not on the "great power" ground, but on the "sovereignty" ground, which made her stickle for the "sovereignty" of the British parliament over colonial legislature. It wasn't diplomatists, it was lawyers in both countries, who precipitated the struggle of 1776.—E. B.

But see §§ 2 and 3.—H. G. W.

[2] See Channing's *History of the United States*, vol. ii.

GEORGE WASHINGTON.

From the portrait by Gilbert Stuart at Boston, U.S.A.

real beginnings of Virginia date from the foundation of the Virginia Company in 1606 in the reign of James I (1603-25). The story of John Smith and the early founders of Virginia, and of how the Indian " princess " Pocahontas married one of his gentlemen, is an English classic.[1] In growing tobacco the Virginians found the beginning of prosperity. At the same time that the Virginian Company was founded, the Plymouth Company obtained a charter for the settlement of the country to the north of Long Island Sound, to which the English laid claim. But it was only in 1620 that the northern region began to be settled, and that under fresh charters. The settlers of the northern region (New England), which became Connecticut, New Hampshire, Rhode Island, and Massachusetts, were men of

-Photo: Rischgitz Collection.
WILLIAM PENN.

a different stamp to the Virginia people. They were Protestants discontented with the Anglican Church compromise, and republican-spirited men hopeless of resistance to the Grand Monarchy of James I and Charles I. Their pioneer ship was the *Mayflower*, which founded New Plymouth in 1620. The dominant northern colony was Massachusetts. Differences in religious method and in ideas of toleration led to the separation of the three other Puritan colonies from Massachusetts. It illustrates the scale upon which things were done in those days that the whole state of New Hampshire was claimed as belonging to a certain Captain John Mason, and that he offered to sell it to the king (King Charles II) in 1671 in exchange for the right to import 300 tons of French wine free of duty—an offer which was refused. The present state of Maine was bought by Massachusetts from its alleged owner for twelve hundred and fifty pounds.

In the Civil War that ended with the decapitation of Charles I the sympathies of New

[1] *John Smith's Travels.*

England were for the Parliament, and Virginia was Cavalier ; but two hundred and fifty miles separated these settlements, and there were no serious hostilities. With the return of the monarchy in 1660, there was a vigorous development of British colonization in America. Charles II and his associates were greedy for gain, and the British crown had no wish to make any further experiments in illegal taxation at home. But the undefined relations of the colonies to the crown and the British government seemed to afford promise of financial adventure across the Atlantic. There was a rapid development of plantations and proprietary colonies. Lord Baltimore had already, in 1632, set up a colony that was to be a home of religious freedom for Catholics under the attractive name of Maryland, to the north and east of Virginia ; and now the Quaker Penn (who was nevertheless a very good friend of Charles II) established himself to the north at Philadelphia and founded the colony of Pennsylvania. Its main boundary with Maryland and Virginia was delimited by two men, Mason and Dixon, whose " Mason and Dixon line " was destined to become a very important line indeed in the later affairs of the United States. Carolina, which was originally an unsuccessful French Protestant establishment, and which owed its name not to Charles (Carolus) II of England, but to Charles IX of France, had fallen into English hands and was settled at several points.[2] Between Maryland and New

[2] There is doubt about the name Carolina. Channing, in his short history, says it was named in honour of Charles II. Bassett says it was named originally Carolana, in honour of Charles I, in 1629, and kept the name, under the new form of Carolina, in honour of Charles II. Fisk, *Old Virginia and her Neighbours*, vol. i. p. 265, speaks of Carolina, in 1629, as named " either in honour of Charles I or because the name had been given by Huguenots in 1562 in honour of Charles IX of France." Another authority speaks

England stretched a number of small Dutch and Swedish settlements, of which the chief town was New Amsterdam. These settlements were captured from the Dutch by the British in 1664, lost again in 1673, and restored by treaty when Holland and England made peace in 1674. Thereby the whole coast from Maine to Carolina became in some form or other a British possession. To the south the Spanish were established ; their headquarters were at Fort St. Augustine in Florida, and in 1732 the town of Savannah [1] was settled by a philanthropist, Oglethorpe, from England, who had taken pity on the miserable people imprisoned for debt in England, and rescued a number of them from prison to become the founders of a new colony, Georgia, which was to be a bulwark against the Spanish. So by the middle of the eighteenth century we have these settlements along the American coastline : the New England group of Puritans and free Protestants, Maine (belonging to Massachusetts), New Hampshire, Connecticut, Rhode Island, and Massachusetts ; the captured Dutch group, which was now divided up into New York (New Amsterdam rechristened), New Jersey, and Delaware (Swedish before it was Dutch, and in its earliest British phase attached to Pennsylvania) ; then came Catholic Maryland ; Cavalier Virginia ; Carolina (which was presently divided into North and South) and Oglethorpe's Georgia. Later on a number of Tyrolese Protestants took refuge in Georgia, and there was a considerable immigration of a good class of German cultivators into Pennsylvania.

Such were the miscellaneous origins of the citizens of the Thirteen Colonies.[2] The possibility of their ever becoming closely united would have struck an impartial observer in 1760 as being very slight. Superadded to the initial differences of origin, fresh differences were created by climate. North of the Mason and Dixon line farming was practised mainly upon British or Central European lines by free white cultivators. The settled country of New England took on a likeness to the English country-side ; considerable areas of Pennsylvania developed fields and farmhouses like those of South Germany. The distinctive conditions in the north had, socially, important effects. Masters and men had to labour together as backwoodsmen, and were equalized in the process. They did not start equally ; many " servants " are mentioned in the roster of the *Mayflower*. But they rapidly became equal under colonial conditions ; there was, for instance, a vast tract of land to be had for the taking, and the " servant " went off and took land like his master. The English class system disappeared. Under colonial conditions there arose equality " in the faculties both of body and mind," and an individual independence of judgment impatient of interference from England. But south of the Mason and Dixon line tobacco growing began, and the warmer climate encouraged the establishment of plantations with gang labour. Red Indian captives were employed ; Cromwell sent Irish prisoners of war to Virginia, which did much to reconcile the Royalist planters to republicanism ; convicts were sent out, and there was a considerable trade in kidnapped children, who were " spirited away " to America to become apprentices or bond slaves. But the most convenient form of gang labour proved to be that of negro slaves. The first negro slaves were brought to Jamestown in Virginia by a Dutch ship as early as 1620. By 1700 negro slaves were scattered all over the states, but Virginia, Maryland, and the Carolinas were their chief regions of employment, and while the communities to the north were communities of not very rich and not very poor farming men, the south developed a type of large proprietor and a white community of overseers and professional men subsisting on slave labour. Slave labour was a necessity to the social and economic system that had grown up in the south ; in the north the presence of slaves was unnecessary and in some respects inconvenient. Conscientious scruples about slavery were more free, therefore, to de-

of the name as used before, and now no doubt retained in honour of the English king ; but, according to him, the name had not been used for the country (called, by the French, Florida), but for a fort in it, the arx Carolana. He adds that in 1629 the name Carolana is used, but Carolina appears afterwards, and becomes normal after 1662.—E. B.

[1] From the Spanish word Sabaña = " meadow."— H. H. J.

[2] See for the fundamental differences of north and south, W. Wilson, *The State*, the historical sections at the beginning of the chapter on the United States Government.—E. B.

Photo: Rischgitz Collection.

WILLIAM PENN'S TREATY WITH THE INDIANS.
(After Benjamin West, 1682.)

velop and flourish in the northern atmosphere. To this question of the revival of slavery in the world we must return when we come to consider the perplexities of American Democracy. Here we note it simply as an added factor in the heterogeneous mixture of the British Colonies.[1]

But if the inhabitants of the Thirteen Colonies were miscellaneous in their origins and various in their habits and sympathies, they had three very strong antagonisms in common. They had a common interest against the Red Indians. For a time they shared a common dread of French conquest and dominion. And thirdly, they were all in conflict with the claims of the British crown and the commercial selfishness of the narrow oligarchy who dominated the British Parliament and British affairs.

So far as the first danger went, the Indians were a constant evil, but never more than a threat of disaster. They remained divided against themselves. Yet they had shown possibilities of combination upon a larger scale. The Five Nations of the Iroquois (see map) was a very important league of tribes. But

[1] An admirable account of negro slavery is to be found in Sir H. H. Johnston's *The Negro in the New World*.

it never succeeded in playing off the French against the English to secure itself, and no Red Indian Jengis Khan ever arose among these nomads of the New World. The French aggression was a more serious threat. The French never made settlements in America on a scale to compete with the English, but their government set about the encirclement of the colonies and their subjugation in a terrifyingly systematic manner. The English in America were colonists; the French were explorers, adventurers, agents, missionaries, merchants, and soldiers. Only in Canada did they strike root. French statesmen sat over maps and dreamt dreams, and their dreams are to be seen in our map in the chain of forts creeping southward from the great Lakes and northward up the Mississippi and Ohio rivers. The struggle of France and Britain was a world-wide struggle. It was decided in India, in Germany, and on the high seas. In the Peace of Paris (1763) the French gave England Canada, and relinquished Louisiana to the inert hands of declining Spain. It was the complete abandonment of America by France. The lifting of the French danger left the colonists unencumbered to face their third common antagonist—the crown and government of their mother land.

§ 3

We have noted in the previous chapter how the governing class of Great Britain steadily

Civil War is forced upon the Colonies. acquired the land and destroyed the liberty of the common people throughout the eighteenth century, and how greedily and blindly the new industrial revolution was brought about. We have noted also how the British Parliament, through the decay of the representative methods of the House of Commons, had become both in its upper and lower houses merely the instrument of government through the big landowners. Both these big property-holders and the crown were deeply interested in America; the former as private adventurers, the latter partly as representing the speculative exploitations of the Stuart kings, and partly as representing the state in search of funds for the expenses of foreign policy, and neither lords nor crown were disposed to regard the traders, planters, and common people of the colonies with any more consideration than they did the yeomen and small cultivators at home. At bottom the interests of the common man in Great Britain, Ireland, and America were the same. Each was being squeezed by the same system. But while in Britain oppressor and oppressed were closely tangled up in one intimate social system, in America the crown and the exploiter were far away, and men could get together and develop a sense of community against their common enemy.

Moreover, the American colonist had the important advantage of possessing a separate and legal organ of resistance to the British government in the assembly or legislature of his colony that was necessary for the management of local affairs. The common man in Britain, cheated out of his proper representation in the Commons, had no organ, no centre of expression and action for his discontents.

It will be evident to the reader, bearing in mind the variety of the colonies, that here was the possibility of an endless series of disputes, aggressions, and counter-aggressions. The story of the development of irritations between the colonies and Britain is a story far too intricate, subtle, and lengthy for the scheme of this Outline. Suffice it that the grievances fell under three main heads : attempts to secure for British adventurers or the British government the profits of the exploitation of new lands ; systematic restrictions upon trade designed to keep the foreign trade of the colonies entirely in British hands, so that the colonial exports all went through Britain and only British-made goods were used in America ; [1] and finally attempts at taxation through the British Parliament as the supreme taxing authority of the empire. Under the pressure of this triple system of annoyances, the American colonists were forced to do a very considerable amount of hard political thinking. Such men as Patrick Henry and James Otis began to discuss the fundamental ideas of government and political association very much as they had been discussed in England in the great days of Cromwell's Commonweal. They began to deny both the divine origin of kingship and the supremacy of the British Parliament, and (James Otis, 1762 [2]) to say such things as :—

" God made all men naturally equal.

" Ideas of earthly superiority are educational, not innate.

" Kings were made for the good of the people, and not the people for them.

" No government has a right to make slaves of its subjects.

" Though most governments are *de facto* arbitrary, and consequently the curse and

---

[1] I disbelieve in this " commercial selfishness " emphasized in the text. Modern American historians, such as Beer, themselves rebut the charge. On the whole, English commercial policy was fair. (1) If the colonists could only export certain " enumerated " commodities to England, the English market was the best, and they were given privileges there ; while non-enumerated commodities could be exported anywhere, and even " enumerated " articles were in practice smuggled everywhere. (2) If the colonists had to import from England, it was their best market, and they got " drawbacks " on dutiable goods imported into England from the Continent when they took them out of England ; while again in practice they freely smuggled goods from any country to America. (3) The English navigation laws, in the long run, encouraged American shipbuilding ; and if some colonial manufactures were stopped in order that they might not complete with English manufactures, the amount of such restriction was slight. On all this, see Sir William Ashley, *Surveys Historic and Economic*, pp. 300 *seqq.*—E. B.

[2] See Tudor's *Life of James Otis*.

scandal of human nature, yet none are *de jure* arbitrary."

Some of which propositions reach far.

This ferment in the political ideas of the Americans was started by English leaven. One very influential English writer was John Locke (1632–1704), whose *Two Treatises on Civil Government* may be taken, as much as any one single book can be taken in such cases, as the point of departure for modern democratic ideas. He was the son of a Cromwellian soldier, he was educated at Christ Church, Oxford, during the republican ascendancy, he spent some years in Holland in exile, and his writings form a bridge between the bold political thinking of those earlier republican days and the revolutionary movement both in America and France.

But men do not begin to act upon theories. It is always some real danger, some practical necessity, that produces action ; and it is only after action has destroyed old relationships and produced a new and perplexing state of affairs that theory comes to its own. Then it is that theory is put to the test. The discord in interests and ideas between the colonists was brought to a fighting issue by the obstinate resolve of the British Parliament after the peace of 1763 to impose taxation upon the American colonies. Britain was at peace and flushed with successes ; it seemed an admirable opportunity for settling accounts with these recalcitrant settlers. But the great British property-owners found a power beside their own, of much the same mind with them, but a little divergent in its ends—the reviving crown. King George III, who had begun his reign in 1760, was resolved to be much more of a king than his two German predecessors. He could speak English ; he claimed to " glory in the name of Briton "—and indeed it is not a bad name for a man without a perceptible drop of English, Welsh, or Scotch blood in his veins. In the American colonies and the overseas possessions generally, with their indefinite charters or no charters at all, it seemed to him that the crown might claim authority and obtain resources and powers absolutely denied to it by the strong and jealous aristocracy in Britain. This inclined many of the Whig noblemen to a sympathy with the colonists that they might not otherwise have shown. They had no

objection to the exploitation of the colonies in the interests of British " private enterprise," but they had very strong objections to the strengthening of the crown by that exploitation so as to make it presently independent of themselves.[1]

The war that broke out was therefore in reality not a war between Britain and the colonists, it was a war between the British government and the colonists, with a body of Whig noblemen and a considerable amount of public feeling in England on the side of the latter. An early move after 1763 was an attempt to raise revenue for Britain in the colonies

Photo : Rischgitz Collection.

KING GEORGE III.

by requiring that newspapers and documents of various sorts should be stamped. This was stiffly resisted, the British crown was intimidated, and the Stamp Acts were repealed (1766). Their repeal was greeted by riotous rejoicings in London, more hearty even than those in the colonies.

But the Stamp Act affair was only one eddy in a turbulent stream flowing towards civil war.

[1] I disagree entirely with this. George, with the bulk of Parliament behind him, was out to insist on the sovereignty of the British Parliament (not of himself) over the colonists. Nor was it the Whig noblemen who opposed him, but Burke (conservatively inclined, and therefore up in arms for the traditional rights of the colonial legislatures) and Chatham (liberally inclined, and therefore up in arms for the principle of " no representation, no taxation ").—E. B.

Upon a score of pretexts, and up and down the coast, the representatives of the British government were busy asserting their authority and making British government intolerable. The quartering of soldiers upon the colonists was a great nuisance. Rhode Island was particularly active in defying the trade restrictions; the Rhode Islanders were " free traders,"—that is to say, smugglers; a government schooner, the *Gaspee*, ran aground off Providence; she was surprised, boarded, and captured by armed men in boats, and burnt. In 1773, with a total disregard of the existing colonial tea trade, special advantages for the importation of tea into America[1] were given by the British Parliament to the East India Company. It was resolved by the colonists to refuse and

Sketch map to show BOSTON & neighbourhood 1775

boycott this tea. When the tea importers at Boston showed themselves resolute to land their cargoes, a band of men disguised as Indians, in the presence of a great crowd of people, boarded the three tea ships and threw the tea overboard (December 16th, 1773).

All 1774 was occupied in the gathering up of resources on either side for the coming conflict. It was decided by the British Parliament in the spring of 1774 to punish Boston by closing her port. Her trade was to be destroyed unless she accepted that tea. This is the sort of silly " firmness " of the governing class that shatters empires. In order to enforce this measure, British troops were concentrated at Boston

---

[1] This again in my view is wrong. The system proposed, I read in an American writer, meant cheaper tea in the colonies. The objection taken by the colonists was legal.—E. B.

under General Gage. The colonists took counter-measures. The first colonial Congress met at Philadelphia in September, at which twelve colonies were represented: Massachusetts, Connecticut, New Hampshire, Rhode Island, New York, New Jersey, Pennsylvania, Maryland, Delaware, Virginia, and North and South Carolina. Georgia was not present. True to the best English traditions, the Congress documented its attitude by a " Declaration of Rights." Practically this Congress was an insurrectionary government, but no blow was struck until the spring of 1775. Then came the first shedding of blood.

Two of the American leaders, Hancock and Samuel Adams, had been marked down by the British Government for arrest and trial for treason; they were known to be at Lexington, about eleven miles from Boston; and in the night of April 18th, 1775, Gage set his forces in motion for their arrest.

That night was a momentous one in history. The movement of Gage's troops had been observed, signal lanterns were shown from a church tower in Boston, and two men, Dawes and Paul Revere, stole away in boats across the Back Bay to take horse and warn the country-side. The British were also ferried over the water, and as they marched through the night towards Lexington, the firing of signal cannon and the ringing of church bells went before them. As they entered Lexington at dawn, they saw a little company of men drawn up in military fashion. It seems that the British fired first. There was a single shot and then a volley, and the little handful decamped, apparently without any answering shots, leaving eight dead and nine wounded upon the village green.

The British then marched on to Concord, ten miles further, occupied the village, and stationed a party on the bridge at that place. The expedition had failed in its purpose of arresting Hancock and Adams, and the British commander seems to have been at a loss what to do next. Meanwhile the colonial levies were coming up from all directions, and presently the picket upon the bridge found itself subjected to an increasing fire from a gathering number of assailants firing from behind trees and fences. A retreat to Boston was decided upon. It was a disastrous retreat. The country had risen behind the British; all the morning the colonials had been gathering. Both sides of the road were now swarming with sharpshooters firing from behind rock and fence and building; the soldiers were in conspicuous scarlet uniforms, with yellow facings and white gaiters and cravats; this must have stood out very vividly against the cold sharp colours of the late New England spring; the day was bright, hot, and dusty, and they were already exhausted by a night march. Every few yards a man fell, wounded or killed. The rest tramped on, or halted to fire an ineffectual volley. No counter-attack was possible. Their assailants lurked everywhere. At Lexington there were British reinforcements and two guns, and after a brief rest the retreat was resumed in better order. But the sharpshooting and pursuit were pressed to the river, and after the British had crossed back into Boston, the colonial levies took up their quarters in Cambridge and prepared to blockade the city.

§ 4

So the war began. It was not a war that promised a conclusive end. The colonists had

The War of Independence. no one vulnerable capital; they were dispersed over a great country, with a limitless wilderness behind it, and so they had great powers of resistance. They had learnt their tactics largely from the Indians; they could fight well in open order, and harry and destroy troops in movement. But they had no disciplined army that could meet the British in a pitched battle, and little military equipment; and their levies grew impatient at a long campaign, and tended to go home to their farms. The British, on the other hand, had a well-drilled army, and their command of the sea gave them the power of shifting their attack up and down the long Atlantic seaboard. They were at peace with all the world. But the king was stupid and greedy to interfere in the conduct of affairs; the generals he favoured were stupid " strong men " or flighty men of birth and fashion; and the heart of England was not in the business. He trusted rather to being able to block-

ade, raid, and annoy the colonists into submission than to a conclusive conquest and occupation of the land. But the methods employed, and particularly the use of hired German troops, who still retained the cruel traditions of the Thirty Years' War, and of Indian auxiliaries, who raped and scalped the outlying settlers, did not so much weary the Americans of the war as of the British. The Congress, meeting for the second time in 1775, endorsed the actions of the New England colonists, and appointed George Washington the American commander-in-chief. In 1777, General Burgoyne, in an attempt to get down to New York from Canada, was defeated at Freeman's Farm on the Upper Hudson, and surrounded and obliged to capitulate at Saratoga with his whole army. This disaster encouraged the French and Spanish to come into the struggle on the side of the colonists. The French sent an army to the States under General Lafayette, and their fleet did much to minimise the advantage of the British at sea. General Cornwallis was caught in the Yorktown peninsula in Virginia in 1781, and capitulated with his army. The British Government, now heavily engaged with France and Spain in Europe, was at the end of its resources.

At the outset of the war the colonists in general seem to have been as little disposed to repudiate monarchy and claim complete independence as were the Hollanders in the opening phase of Philip II's persecutions and follies. The separatists were called radicals; they were mostly extremely democratic, as we should say in England to-day, and their advanced views frightened many of the steadier and wealthier colonists, for whom class privileges and distinctions had considerable charm. But early in 1776 an able and persuasive Englishman, Tom Paine, published a pamphlet at Philadelphia with the title of *Common Sense*, which had an enormous effect on public opinion. Its style was rhetorical by modern standards. " The blood of the slain, the weeping voice of Nature cries, ' 'Tis time to part,' " and so forth. But its effects were very great. It converted thousands to the necessity of separation. The turn-over of opinion, once it had begun, was rapid.

Only in the summer of 1776 did Congress

take the irrevocable step of declaring for separation. "The Declaration of Independence," another of those exemplary documents which it has been the peculiar service of the English to produce for mankind, was drawn up by Thomas Jefferson; and after various amendments and modifications it was made the fundamental document of the United States of America. There were two noteworthy amendments to Jefferson's draft. He had denounced the slave trade fiercely, and blamed the home government for interfering with colonial attempts to end it. This was thrown out, and so too was a sentence about the British: "we must endeavour to forget our former love for them . . . we might have been a free and a great people together."

(But for the British crown and great proprietors and the mutual ignorance of the common men in the two countries.)[1]

Towards the end of 1782, the preliminary articles of the treaty in which Britain recognized the complete independence of the United States were signed at Paris. The end of the war was proclaimed on April 19th, 1783, exactly eight years after Paul Revere's ride and the retreat of Gage's men from Concord to Boston. The

Photo: Rischgitz Collection.
THOMAS PAINE.
(After Romney.)

[1] I think this gives an erroneous impression that there was no real chance of reconciliation in 1776. There was. And indeed the whole separation was far from inevitable. If the British had (1) recognized the autonomy in each colony of its legislature, and (2) granted to the colonies cabinet government in place of government by governors sent from England, there would have been no schism. By 1839, the time of Lord Durham's report, the British had learned to make the recognition and the grant; and with greater wisdom they could have made both in 1776. A great statesman in 1776 could have stopped the separation, and made history different. I am inclined to say that nothing is inevitable in history—except that when you don't have good men, you don't get good results. And that was the position under George III and Lord North.—E. B.

Treaty of Peace was finally signed at Paris in September.

§ 5

From the point of view of human history, the way in which the Thirteen States became independent is of far less importance than the fact that they did become independent. And with the establishment of their independence came a new sort of community into the world. It was like something coming out of an egg. It was a Western European civilization that had broken free from the last traces of Empire and Christendom; it had not a vestige of monarchy left and no state religion. It had no dukes, princes, counts, nor any sort of title-bearers claiming to ascendancy or respect as a right. Even its unity was as yet a mere unity for defence and freedom. It was in these respects such a clean start in political organization as the world had not seen before. The absence of any binding religious tie is especially noteworthy. It had a number of forms of Christianity, its spirit was indubitably Christian; but as a state document of 1796 explicitly declared, "The government of the United States is not in any sense founded on the Christian religion." [2] The new community had in fact gone right down to the bare and stripped fundamentals of human association, and it was building up a new sort of society and a new sort of state upon those foundations.

Here were about four million people scattered over vast areas with very slow and difficult means of intercommunication, poor as yet, but with the potentialities of limitless wealth, setting out to do in reality on a huge scale

The Constitution of the United States.

[2] The Tripoli Treaty, see Channing, vol. iii. chap. xviii.

such a feat of construction as the Athenian philosophers twenty-two centuries before had done in imagination and theory.

This situation marks a definite stage in the release of man from precedent and usage, and a definite step forward towards the conscious and deliberate reconstruction of his circumstances to suit his needs and aims. It was a new method becoming practical in human affairs. The modern states of Europe have been evolved institution by institution slowly and planlessly out of preceding things. The United States were planned and made.

In one respect, however, the creative freedom of the new nation was very seriously restricted. This new sort of community and state was not built upon a cleared site. It was not even so frankly an artificiality as some of the later Athenian colonies, which went out from the mother city to plan and build brand new city states with brand new constitutions. The thirteen colonies by the end of the war had all of them constitutions either like that of Connecticut and Rhode Island dating from their original charters (1662) or, as in the case of the rest of the states, where a British governor had played a large part in the administration, remade during the conflict. But we may well consider these reconstructions as contributary essays and experiments in the general constructive effort.

Upon the effort certain ideas stood out very prominently. One is the idea of political and social equality. This idea, which we saw coming into the world as an extreme and almost incredible idea in the age between Buddha and Jesus of Nazareth, is now asserted in the later eighteenth century as a practicable standard of human relationship. Says the fundamental statement of Virginia : " All men are by nature equally free and independent," and it proceeds to rehearse their " rights," and to assert that all magistrates and governors are but " trustees and servants " of the commonweal. All men are equally entitled to the free exercise of religion. The king by right, the aristocrat, the " natural slave," the god king, and the god have all vanished from this political scheme—so far as these declarations go. Most of the states produced similar preludes to government. The

Photo : Rischgitz Collection

SIGNING THE DECLARATION OF INDEPENDENCE.
(After the painting by Trumbull.)

Declaration of Independence said that "all men are born equal." It is everywhere asserted in eighteenth-century terms that the new community is to be—to use the phraseology we have introduced in an earlier chapter—a community of will and not a community of obedience. But the thinkers of that time had a rather clumsier way of putting the thing, they imagined a sort of individual choice of and assent to citizenship that never in fact occurred—the so-called Social Contract. The Massachusetts preamble, for instance, asserts that the state is a voluntary association, "by which the whole people covenants with each citizen and each citizen with the whole people that all shall be governed by certain laws for the common good."

Now it will be evident that most of these fundamental statements are very questionable statements. Men are not born equal, they are not born free; they are born a most various multitude enmeshed in an ancient and complex social net. Nor is any man invited to sign the social contract or, failing that, to depart into solitude. These statements, literally interpreted, are so manifestly false that it is impossible to believe that the men who made them intended them to be literally interpreted. They made them in order to express certain elusive but profoundly important ideas—ideas that after another century and a half of thinking the world is in a better position to express. Civilization, as this Outline has shown, arose as a community of obedience, and was essentially a community of obedience. But generation after generation the spirit was abused by priests and rulers. There was a continual influx of masterful will from the forests, parklands, and steppes. The human spirit had at last rebelled

altogether against the blind obediences of the common life; it was seeking—and at first it was seeking very clumsily—to achieve a new and better sort of civilization that should also be a community of will. To that end it was necessary that every man should be treated as the sovereign of himself; his standing was to be one of fellowship and not of servility. His real use, his real importance depended upon his individual quality.

The method by which these creators of political America sought to secure this community of will was an extremely simple and crude one. They gave what was for the time, and in view of American conditions, a very wide franchise. Conditions varied in the different states; the widest franchise was in Pennsylvania, where every adult male taxpayer voted, but, compared with Britain, all the United States were well within sight of manhood suffrage by the end of the eighteenth century. These makers of America also made efforts, considerable for their times, but puny by more modern standards, to secure a widely diffused common education. The information of the citizens as to what was going on at home and abroad, they left, apparently without any qualms of misgiving, to public meetings and the privately owned printing press.

The story of the various state constitutions, and of the constitution of the United States as a whole, is a very intricate one, and we can only deal with it here in the broadest way.

ultra-democratic state of affairs. Apart from the argument that legislation should be slow as well as sure, it is difficult to establish any necessity for this " bi-cameral " arrangement. It seems to have been a fashion with constitution planners in the eighteenth century rather than a reasonable necessity. The British division was an old one ; the Lords, the original parliament, was an assembly of " notables," the leading men of the kingdom ; the House of Commons came in as a new factor, as the elected spokesmen of the burghers and the small landed

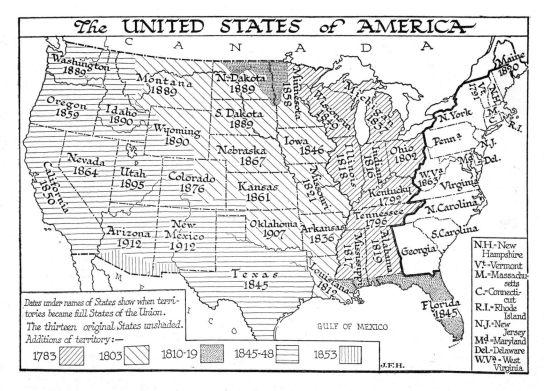

men. It was a little too hastily assumed in the eighteenth century that the commonalty would be given to wild impulses and would need checking ; opinion was for democracy, but for democracy with powerful brakes always on, whether it was going up hill or down. About all the upper houses there was therefore a flavour of selectness ; they were elected on a more limited franchise. This idea of making an upper chamber which shall be a stronghold for the substantial man does not appeal to modern thinkers so strongly as it did to the men of the eighteenth century, but the bi-cameral idea in another form still has its advocates. They

The most noteworthy point in a modern view is the disregard of women as citizens. The American community was a simple, largely agricultural community, and most women were married ; it seemed natural that they should be represented by their men folk. But New Jersey admitted a few women to vote on a property qualification. Another point of great interest is the almost universal decision to have two governing assemblies, confirming or checking each other, on the model of the Lords and Commons of Britain. Only Pennsylvania had a single representative chamber, and that was felt to be a very dangerous and suggest that a community may with advantage cousider its affairs from two points of view—through the eyes of a body elected to represent trades, industries, professions, public services, and the like, a body representing *function*, and through the eyes of a second body elected by localities to represent *communities*. For the members of the former a man would vote by his calling, for the latter by his district of residence. They point out that the British House of Lords is in effect a body representing function, in which the land, the law, and the church are no doubt disproportionately represented, but in which industrialism, finance, the great public services, art, science, and medicine, also find places ; and that the British House of Commons is purely geographical in its reference. It has even been suggested in Britain that there should be " labour peers," selected from among the leaders of the great industrial trade unions. But these are speculations beyond our present scope.

The Central Government of the United States was at first a very feeble body, a congress of representatives of the thirteen governments, held together by certain Articles of Confederation. This Congress was little more than a conference of sovereign representatives ; it had no control, for instance, over the foreign trade of each state, it could not coin money or levy taxes by its own authority. When John Adams, the first minister from the United States to England, went to discuss a commercial treaty with the British Foreign Secretary, he was met by a request for thirteen representatives, one from each of the states concerned. He had to confess his inadequacy to make binding arrangements. The British presently began dealing with each state separately over the head of Congress, and they retained possession of a number of posts in the American territory about the great lakes because of the inability of Congress to hold these regions effectually. In another urgent matter Congress proved equally feeble. To the west of the thirteen states stretched limitless lands into which settlers were now pushing in ever-increasing numbers. Each of the states had indefinable claims to expansion westward. It was evident to every clear-sighted man that the jostling of these claims must lead in the long run to war,

unless the Central Government could take on their apportionment. The feebleness of the Central Government, its lack of concentration, became so much of an inconvenience and so manifest a danger that there was some secret discussion of a monarchy, and Nathaniel Gorham of Massachusetts, the president of Congress, caused Prince Henry of Prussia, the brother of Frederick the Great, to be approached on the subject. Finally a constitutional convention was called in 1787 at Philadelphia, and there it was that the present constitution of the United States was in its broad lines hammered out. A great change of spirit had gone on during the intervening years, a widespread realization of the need of unity.

When the Articles of Confederation were drawn up, men had thought of the people of Virginia, the people of Massachusetts, the people of Rhode Island, and the like ; but now there appears a new conception, " the people of the United States." The new government, with the executive President, the senators, congressmen, and the Supreme Court that were now created, was declared to be the government of " the people of the United States " ; it was a synthesis and not a mere assembly. It said " we the people," and not " we the states," as Lee of Virginia bitterly complained. It was to be a " federal " and not a confederate government.

State by state the new constitution was ratified, and in the spring of 1788 the first congress upon the new lines assembled at New York, under the presidency of George Washington, who had been the national commander-in-chief throughout the War of Independence. The constitution then underwent considerable revision, and Washington upon the Potomac was selected as the Federal capital.

§ 6

In an earlier chapter we have described the Roman republic, and its mixture of modern features with dark superstition and primordial savagery, as the Neanderthal anticipation of the modern democratic state. A time may come when people will regard the contrivances and machinery of the American constitution as the political equivalents of the imple-

Primitive Features of the United States Constitution.

ments and contrivances of Neolithic man. They have served their purpose well, and under their protection the people of the States have grown into one of the greatest, most powerful, and most civilized communities that the world has yet seen ; but there is no reason in that for regarding the American constitution as a thing more final and unalterable than the pattern of street railway that overshadows many New York thoroughfares, or the excellent and homely type of house architecture that still prevails in Philadelphia. These things also have served a purpose well, they have their faults, and they can be improved. Our political contrivances, just as much as our domestic and mechanical contrivances, need to undergo constant revision as knowledge and understanding grow.

Photo : Rischgitz Collection.
PATRICK HENRY SPEAKING IN THE HOUSE OF BURGESSES.

Since the American constitution was planned, our conception of history and our knowledge of collective psychology have undergone very considerable development. We are beginning to see many things in the problem of government to which the men of the eighteenth century were blind ; and, courageous as their constructive disposition was in relation to whatever political creation had gone before, it fell far short of the boldness which we in these days realize to be needful if this great human problem of establishing a civilized community of will on the earth is to be solved. They took many things for granted that now we know need to be made the subject of the most exacting scientific study and the most careful adjustment. They thought it was only necessary to set up schools and colleges, with a grant of land for maintenance, and that they might then be left to themselves. But education is not a weed that will grow lustily in any soil ; it is a necessary and delicate crop that may easily wilt and degenerate. We learn nowadays that the underdevelopment of universities and educational machinery is like some underdevelopment of the brain and nerves, which hampers the whole growth of the social body. By European standards, by the standard of any state that has existed hitherto, the level of the common education of America is high ; but by the standard of what it might be, America is an uneducated country. And those fathers of America thought also that they had but to leave the press free, and everyone would live in the light. They did not realize that a free press could develop a sort of constitutional venality due to its relations with advertisers, and that large newspaper proprietors could become buccaneers of opinion and insensate wreckers of good beginnings. And, finally, the makers of America had no knowledge of the complexities of vote manipulation. The whole science of elections was beyond their ken, they knew nothing of the need of the transferable vote to prevent the "working" of elections by specialized organizations, and the crude and rigid methods they adopted left their political system the certain prey of the great party machines that have robbed American democracy of half its freedom and most of its political soul. Politics became a trade, and a very base trade; decent and able men, after the first great period, drifted out of politics and attended to "business," and what I have called elsewhere the "sense of the state"[1] declined. Private enterprise ruled in many matters of common concern, because political corruption made collective enterprise impossible.

Yet the defects of the great political system created by the Americans of the revolutionary period did not appear at

Photo: Rischgitz Collection.
BENJAMIN FRANKLIN.

once. For several generations the history of the United States was one of rapid expansion and of an amount of freedom, homely happiness, and energetic work unparalleled in the world's history. And the record of America for the whole last century and a half, in spite of many reversions towards inequality, in spite of much rawness and much blundering, is nevertheless as bright and honourable a story as that of any other contemporary people.

In this brief account of the creation of the United States of America we have been able to do little more than mention the names of some of the group of great men who made this new departure in human history. We have named casually or we have not even named such men as Tom Paine, Benjamin Franklin, Patrick Henry, Thomas Jefferson, the Adam brothers, Madison, Alexander Hamilton, and George Washington. It is hard to measure the men of one period of history with those in another. Some writers, even American writers, impressed by the artificial splendours of the European courts and by the tawdry and destructive exploits of a Frederick the Great or a Great Catherine, display a snobbish shame of something homespun about these makers of America. They feel that Benjamin Franklin at the court of Louis XVI, with his long hair, his plain clothes, and his pawky humour, was sadly lacking in aristocratic distinction. But stripped to their personalities, Louis XVI was hardly

gifted enough or noble-minded enough to be Franklin's valet. If human greatness is a matter of scale and glitter, then no doubt Alexander the Great is at the apex of human greatness. But is greatness that? Is not a great man rather one who, in a great position or amidst great opportunities—and great gifts are no more than great opportunities—serves God and his fellows with a humble heart? And a great number of these Americans of the revolutionary time do seem to have displayed much disinterestedness and devotion. They were limited men, fallible men—Washington was, for example, a conspicuously indolent man—but on the whole they seem to have cared more for the commonweal they were creating than for any personal end or personal vanity.

They were all limited men. They were limited in knowledge and outlook; they were limited by the limitations of the time. And there was no perfect man among them. They were, like all of us, men of mixed motive; good impulses arose in their minds, great ideas swept through them, and also they could be jealous, lazy, obstinate, greedy, vicious. If one were to write a true, full, and particular history of the making of the United States, it would have to be written with charity and high spirits as a splendid comedy. And in no other regard do we find the rich tortuous humanity of the American story so finely displayed as in regard to slavery. Slavery, having regard to the general question of labour, is the test of this new soul in the world's history, the American soul.

Slavery began very early in the European history of America, and no European people who went to America can be held altogether innocent in the matter. At a time when the German is still the moral whipping-boy of Europe, it is well to note that the German record is in this respect the best of all. Almost the

[1] Wells, *The Future in America.*

first outspoken utterances against negro slavery came from German settlers in Pennsylvania. But the German settler was working with free labour upon a temperate country-side, well north of the plantation zone ; he was not under serious temptation in this matter. American slavery began with the enslavement of Indians for gang work in mines and upon plantations, and it is curious to note that it was a very good and humane man indeed, Las Casas, who urged that negroes should be brought to America to relieve his tormented Indian protegés. The need for labour upon the plantations of the West Indies and the south was imperative. When the supply of Indian captives proved inadequate, the planters turned not only to the negro, but to the jails and poor-houses of Europe for a supply of toilers. The reader of Defoe's *Moll Flanders* will learn how the business of Virginian white slavery looked to an intelligent Englishman in the early eighteenth century. But the negro came very early. The year (1620) that saw the Pilgrim Fathers landing at Plymouth in New England, saw a Dutch sloop disembarking the first cargo of negroes at Jamestown in Virginia. Negro slavery was as old as New England ; it had been an American institution for over a century and a half before the War of Independence. It was to struggle on for the better part of a century more.

But the conscience of thoughtful men in the colonies was never quite easy upon this score, and it was one of the accusations of Thomas Jefferson against the crown and lords of Great Britain that every attempt to ameliorate or restrain the slave trade on the part of the colonists had been checked by the great proprietary interests in the mother country.[1] With the moral and intellectual ferment of the revolution, the question of negro slavery came right into the foreground of the public conscience. The contrast and the challenge glared upon the mind. "All men are by nature free and equal," said the Virginia Bill of Rights, and outside in the sunshine, under the whip of the overseer, toiled the negro slave.

[1] In 1776 Lord Dartmouth wrote that the colonists could not be allowed " to check or discourage a traffic so beneficent to the nation."

It witnesses to the great change in human ideas since the Roman Imperial system dissolved under the barbarian inrush, that there could be this heart-searching. Conditions of industry, production, and land tenure had long prevented any recrudescence of gang slavery ; but now the cycle had come round again, and there were enormous immediate advantages to be reaped by the owning and ruling classes in the revival of that ancient institution in mines, upon plantations, and upon great public works. It was revived—but against great opposition. From the beginning of the revival there were protests, and they grew. The revival was counter to the new conscience of mankind. In some respects the new gang slavery was worse than anything in the ancient world. Peculiarly horrible was the provocation by the trade of slave wars and man hunts in Western Africa, and the cruelties of the long transatlantic voyage. The poor creatures were packed on the ships often with insufficient provision of food and water, without proper sanitation, without medicines. Many who could tolerate slavery upon the plantations found the slave trade too much for their moral digestions. Three European nations were chiefly concerned in this dark business, Britain, Spain and Portugal, because they were the chief owners of the new lands in America. The comparative innocence of the other European powers is to be ascribed largely to their lesser temptations. They were similar communities ; in parallel circumstances they would have behaved similarly.

Throughout the middle part of the eighteenth century there was an active agitation against negro slavery in Great Britain as well as in the States. It was estimated that in 1770 there were fifteen thousand slaves in Britain, mostly brought over by their owners from the West Indies and Virginia. In 1771 the issue came to a conclusive test in Britain before Lord Mansfield. A negro named James Somersett had been brought to England from Virginia by his owner. He ran away, was captured, and violently taken on a ship to be returned to Virginia. From the ship he was extracted by a writ of *habeas corpus*. Lord Mansfield declared that slavery was a condition unknown to English law, an " odious " condition, and

Somersett walked out of the court a free man.

The Massachusetts constitution of 1780 had declared that " all men are born free and equal." A certain negro, Quaco, put this to the test in 1783, and in that year the soil of Massachusetts became like the soil of Britain, intolerant of slavery; to tread upon it was to become free. At that time no other state in the Union followed this example. At the census of 1790, Massachusetts, alone of all the states, returned " no slaves."

The state of opinion in Virginia is remarkable, because it brings to light the peculiar difficulties of the Southern states. The great Virginian statesmen, such as Washington and Jefferson, condemned the institution, yet because there was no other form of domestic service, Washington owned slaves. There was in Virginia a strong party in favour of emancipating slaves. But they demanded that the emancipated slaves should leave the state within a year or be outlawed! They were naturally alarmed at the possibility that a free barbaric black community, many of its members African-born and reeking with traditions of cannibalism and secret and dreadful religious rites, should arise beside them upon Virginian soil. When we consider that point of view, we can understand why it was that a large number of Virginians should be disposed to retain the mass of blacks in the country under control as slaves, while at the same time they were bitterly opposed to the slave trade and the importation of any fresh blood from Africa. The free blacks, one sees, might easily become a nuisance; indeed the free state of Massachusetts presently closed its borders to their entry. . . . The question of slavery, which in the ancient world was usually no more than a question of status between individuals racially akin, merged in America with the different and profounder question of relationship between two races at opposite extremes of the human species and of the most contrasted types of tradition and culture. If the black man had been white, there can be little doubt that negro slavery, like white servitude, would have vanished from the United States within a generation of the Declaration of Independence as a natural consequence of the statements in that declaration.

§ 7[1]

We have told of the War of Independence in America as the first great break away from the Revolutionary Ideas in France. system of European monarchies and foreign offices, as the repudiation by a new community of Machiavellian statescraft as the directive form of human affairs. Within a decade there came a second and much more portentous revolt against this strange game of Great Powers, this tangled interaction of courts and policies which obsessed Europe. But this time it was no breaking away at the outskirts. In France, the nest and home of Grand Monarchy, the heart and centre of Europe, came this second upheaval. And, unlike the American colonists, who simply repudiated a king, the French, following in the footsteps of the English revolution, beheaded one.

Like the British revolution and like the revolution in the United States, the French revolution can be traced back to the ambitious absurdities of the French monarchy. The schemes of aggrandisement, the aims and designs of the Grand Monarch, necessitated an expenditure upon war equipment throughout Europe out of all proportion to the taxable capacity of the age. And even the splendours of monarchy were enormously costly, measured by the productivity of the time. In France, just as in Britain and in America, the first resistance was made not to the monarch as such and to his foreign policy as such, nor with any clear recognition of these things as the roots of the trouble, but merely to the inconveniences and charges upon the individual life caused by them. The practical taxable capacity of France must have been relatively much less than that of England because of the various exemptions of the nobility and clergy. The burthen resting directly upon the common people was heavier. That made the upper classes the confederates of the court instead of the antagonists of the court as they were in England, and so prolonged the period of waste further; but when at last the bursting-

[1] A very readable and remarkably well-illustrated book for the general reader upon the French Revolution is Wheeler's *French Revolution.* Carlyle's *French Revolution* has some splendid passages, but it is often unjust and evil-spirited. Madelin's *French Revolution* is a good recent book.

Photo: Rischgitz Collection.

THE TAKING OF THE BASTILLE.
(From a contemporary aquatint.)

the Grand Monarchy that had ruled France since the days of Louis XIV, was bankrupt. No more money could be raised. There must be a gathering of the Notables of the kingdom to consider the situation.

To the gathering of notables, a summoned assembly of leading men, Calonne propounded a scheme for a subsidy to be levied upon all landed property. This roused the aristocrats to a pitch of great indignation. They demanded the summoning of a body roughly equivalent to the British parliament, the States General, which had not met since 1610. Regardless of the organ of opinion they were creating for the discontents below them, excited only by the proposal that they should bear part of the weight of the financial burthens of the country, the French notables insisted. And in May, 1789, the States General met.

It was an assembly of the representatives of three orders, the nobles, the clergy, and the Third Estate, the commons. For the Third Estate the franchise was very wide, nearly every tax-payer of twenty-five having a vote. (The parish priests voted as clergy, the small noblesse as nobles.) The States General was a body without any tradition of procedure. Enquiries were sent to the antiquarians of the Academy of Inscriptions in that matter. Its opening deliberations turned on the question whether it was to meet as one body or as three, each estate having an equal vote. Since the clergy numbered 308, the nobles 285, and the deputies 621, the former arrangement would put the commons in an absolute majority, the latter gave them one vote in three. Nor had the States General any meeting-place. Should it meet in Paris or in some provincial city? Versailles was chosen, " because of the hunting."

It is clear that the king and queen meant to treat this fuss about the national finance as a terrible bore, and to allow it to interfere with their social routine as little as possible. We find the meeting going on in salons that were not wanted, in orangeries and tennis-courts, and so forth.

The question whether the voting was to be by the estates or by head was clearly a vital one. It was wrangled over for six weeks. The Third Estate, taking a leaf from the book of the English House of Commons, then declared that it alone represented the nation, and that no taxation must be levied henceforth without its consent. Whereupon the king closed the hall in which it was sitting, and intimated that the deputies had better go home. Instead, the deputies met in a convenient tennis-court, and there took oath, the Oath of the Tennis Court, not to separate until they had established a constitution in France.

The king took a high line, and attempted to disperse the Third Estate by force. The soldiers refused to act. On that the king gave in with a dangerous suddenness, and accepted the principle that the Three Estates should all deliberate and vote together as one National Assembly. Meanwhile, apparently at the queen's instigation, foreign regiments in the French service, who could be trusted to act against the people, were brought up from the provinces under the Marshal de Broglie, and the king prepared to go back upon his concessions. Whereupon Paris and France revolted. Broglie hesitated to fire on the crowds. A provisional city government was set up in Paris and in most of the other large cities, and a new armed force, the National Guard, a force designed primarily and plainly to resist the forces of the crown, was brought into existence by these municipal bodies.

The revolt of July 1789 was really the

Photo: Rischgitz Collection.
THE PEOPLE PATROLLING THE STREETS OF PARIS ON THE NIGHT OF THE FALL OF THE BASTILLE, JULY 12, 1789.
(From a contemporary print.)

effective French revolution. The grim-looking prison of the Bastille was stormed by the people of Paris, and the insurrection spread rapidly throughout France. Everywhere châteaux belonging to the nobility were burnt by the peasants, their title-deeds carefully destroyed, and the nobles murdered or driven away. In a month the ancient and decayed system of the aristocratic order had collapsed. Many of the leading princes and courtiers of the queen's party fled abroad. The National Assembly found itself called upon to create a new political and social system for a new age.[1]

§ 9

The French National Assembly was far less fortunate in the circumstances of its task than the American Congress. The latter had half a continent to itself, with no possible antagonist but the British Government. Its religious and educational organizations were various, collectively not very powerful, and on the whole friendly. King George was far away in England, and sinking slowly towards an imbecile condition. Nevertheless, it took the United States several years to hammer out a working constitution. The French, on the other hand, were surrounded by aggressive neighbours with Machiavellian ideas, they were encumbered by a king and court resolved to make mischief, and the church was one single great organization inextricably bound up with the ancient order. The queen

The French "Crowned Republic" of '89-'91.

[1] There is a very picturesque account of the storming of the Bastille in Carlyle's *French Revolution*, book v. chap. vi.

was in close correspondence with the Count of Artois, the Duke of Bourbon, and the other exiled princes who were trying to induce Austria and Prussia to attack the new French nation. Moreover, France was already a bankrupt country, while the United States had limitless undeveloped resources; and the revolution, by altering the conditions of land tenure and marketing, had produced an economic disorganization that has no parallel in the case of America.

These were the unavoidable difficulties of the situation. But in addition the Assembly made difficulties for itself. There was no orderly procedure. The English House of Commons had had more than five centuries of experience in its work, and Mirabeau, one of the great leaders of the early Revolution, tried in vain to have the English rules adopted. But the feeling of the times was all in favour of outcries, dramatic interruptions, and such-like manifestations of Natural Virtue. And the disorder did not come merely from the assembly. There was a great gallery, much too great a gallery, for strangers; but who would restrain the free citizens from having a voice in the national control? This gallery swarmed with people eager for a "scene," ready to applaud or shout down the speakers below. The abler speakers were obliged to play to the gallery, and take a sentimental and sensational line. It was easy at a crisis to bring in a mob to kill debate.

So encumbered, the Assembly set about its constructive task. On the Fourth of August it achieved a great dramatic success. Led by several of the nobles, it made a clean sweep, in a series of resolutions, of serfdom, privileges, tax exemptions, tithes, feudal courts. Titles followed. Long before France was a republic it was an offence for a nobleman to sign his name with his title. For six weeks the Assembly devoted itself, with endless opportunities for rhetoric, to the formulation of a Declaration of the Rights of Man—on the lines of the Bills of Rights that were the English preliminaries to organized change. Meanwhile the court plotted for reaction, and the people felt that the court was plotting. The story is complicated here by the scoundrelly schemes of the king's cousin, Philip of Orleans, who hoped to use the discords of the time to replace Louis on the French throne. His gardens at the Palais Royal were thrown open to the public, and became a great centre of advanced discussion. His agents did much to intensify the popular suspicion of the king. And things were exacerbated by a shortage of provisions—for which the king's government was held guilty.

Presently the loyal Flanders regiment appeared at Versailles. The royal family was scheming to get farther away from Paris—in order to undo all that had been done, to restore tyranny and extravagance. Such constitutional monarchists as General Lafayette were seriously alarmed. And just at this time occurred an outbreak of popular indignation at the scarcity of food, that passed by an easy transition into indignation against the threat of royalist reaction. It was believed that there was an abundance of provisions at Versailles; that food was being kept there away from the people. The public mind had been much disturbed by reports, possibly by exaggerated reports, of a recent banquet at Versailles, hostile to the nation. Here are some extracts from Carlyle, descriptive of that unfortunate feast.

"The Hall of the Opera is granted; the Salon d'Hercule shall be drawing-room. Not only the Officers of Flandre, but of the Swiss, of the Hundred Swiss; nay of the Versailles National Guard, such of them as have any loyalty, shall feast; it will be a Repast like few.

"And now suppose this Repast, the solid part of it, transacted; and the first bottle over. Suppose the customary loyal toasts drunk; the King's health, the Queen's with deafening vivats; that of the Nation 'omitted,' or even 'rejected.' Suppose champagne flowing; with pot-valorous speech, with instrumental music; empty featherheads growing ever the noisier, in their own emptiness, in each other's noise. Her Majesty, who looks unusually sad to-night (His Majesty sitting dulled with the day's hunting), is told that the sight of it would cheer her. Behold! She enters there, issuing from her State-rooms, like the Moon from clouds, this fairest unhappy Queen of Hearts; royal Husband by her side, young Dauphin in her arms! She descends from the Boxes, amid splendour and acclaim; walks queen-like round the Tables; gracefully escorted, gracefully nodding ; her looks full of sorrow, yet of gratitude and daring, with the hope of France on her mother-bosom ! And now, the band striking up, *O Richard, O mon Roi, l'univers t'abandonne* (O Richard, O my king, the world is all forsaking thee), could man do other than rise to height of pity, of loyal valour ? Could feather-headed young ensigns do other than, by white Bourbon Cockades, handed them from fair fingers ; by waving of swords, drawn to pledge the Queen's health ; by trampling of National Cockades ; by scaling the Boxes, whence intrusive murmurs may come ; by bread. Maternity must forth to the streets, to the herb-markets and bakers'-queues ; meets there with hunger-stricken Maternity, sympathetic, exasperative. O we unhappy women ! But, instead of bakers'-queues, why not to Aristocrats' palaces, the root of the matter ? *Allons !* Let us assemble. To the Hôtel-de-Ville ; to Versailles. . . ."

There was much shouting and coming and going in Paris before this latter idea realized itself. One Maillard appeared with organizing power, and assumed a certain leadership. There can be little doubt that the revolutionary

Photo : Rischgitz Collection.

"À VERSAILLES, À VERSAILLES !" THE WOMEN'S MARCH, OCTOBER 5, 1789.
(From a contemporary print.)

vociferation, sound, fury and distraction, within doors and without—testify what tempest-tost state of vacuity they are in ? . . .

" A natural Repast ; in ordinary times, a harmless one : now fatal. . . . Poor ill-advised Marie Antoinette ; with a woman's vehemence, not with a sovereign's foresight ! It was so natural, yet so unwise. Next day, in public speech of ceremony, her Majesty declares herself ' delighted with Thursday.' "

And here to set against this is Carlyle's picture of the mood of the people.

" In squalid garret, on Monday morning Maternity awakes, to hear children weeping for leaders, and particularly General Lafayette, used and organized this outbreak to secure the king, before he could slip away—as Charles I did to Oxford—to begin a civil war. As the afternoon wore on, the procession started on its eleven-mile tramp. . . ."

Again we quote Carlyle :

" Maillard has halted his draggled Menads on the last hill-top ; and now Versailles, and the Château of Versailles, and far and wide the inheritance of Royalty opens to the wondering eye. From far on the right, over Marly and Saint-Germain-en-Laye ; round towards Rambouillet, on the left, beautiful all ; softly em bosomed ; as if in sadness, in the dim moist weather !   And near before us is Versailles, New and Old ; with that broad frondent *Avenue de Versailles* between—stately frondent, broad, three hundred feet as men reckon, with its four rows of elms ; and then the Château de Versailles, ending in royal parks and pleasances, gleaming lakelets, arbours, labyrinths, the *Ménagerie*, and Great and Little Trianon. High-towered dwellings, leafy pleasant places ; where the gods of this lower world abide : whence, nevertheless, black care cannot be excluded : whither Menadic hunger is even now advancing, armed with pike-thyrsi ! "

Rain fell as the evening closed.

" Behold the Esplanade, over all its spacious expanse, is covered with groups of squalid dripping women ; of lank-haired male rascality, armed with axes, rusty pikes, old muskets, iron-shod clubs (*bâtons ferrés*, which end in knives or swordblades, a kind of extempore billhook) ; looking nothing but hungry revolt. The rain pours : Gardes-du-Corps go caracoling through the groups ' amid hisses ' ; irritating and agitating what is but dispersed here to reunite there. . . .

" Innumerable squalid women beleaguer the President and Deputation ; insist on going with him : has not his Majesty himself, looking from the window, sent out to ask, What we wanted ? ' Bread, and speech with the King,' that was the answer. Twelve women are clamourously added to the deputation ; and march with it, across the Esplanade ; through dissipated groups, caracoling bodyguards and the pouring rain.

"Bread and not too much talking! Natural demands.

" One learns also that the royal Carriages are getting yoked, as if for Metz. Carriages, royal or not, have verily showed themselves at the back gates. They even produced, or quoted, a written order from our Versailles Municipality —which is a monarchic not a democratic one. However, Versailles patrols drove them in again ; as the vigilant Lecointre had strictly charged them to do. . . .

" So sink the shadows of night, blustering, rainy ; and all paths grow dark. Strangest night ever seen in these regions ; perhaps since the Bartholomew Night, when Versailles, as Bassompierre writes of it, was a *chétif château·* O for the lyre of some Orpheus, to constrain, with touch of melodious strings, these mad masses into Order ! For here all seems fallen asunder, in wide-yawning dislocation. The highest, as in down-rushing of a world, is come in contact with the lowest : the rascality of France beleaguering the royalty of France ; ' iron-shod batons ' lifted round the diadem, not to guard it ! With denunciations of blood-thirsty anti-national bodyguards, are heard dark growlings against a queenly name.

" The Court sits tremulous, powerless : varies with the varying temper of the Esplanade, with the varying colour of the rumours from Paris. Thick-coming rumours ; now of peace, now of war. Necker and all the Ministers consult ; with a blank issue. The Œil-de-Bœuf is one tempest of whispers : We will fly to Metz ; we will not fly. The royal carriages again attempt egress—though for trial merely ; they are again driven in by Lecointre's patrols."

But we must send the reader to Carlyle to learn of the coming of the National Guard in the night under General Lafayette himself, the bargaining between the Assembly and the King, the outbreak of fighting in the morning between the bodyguard and the hungry besiegers, and how the latter stormed into the palace and came near to a massacre of the royal family. Lafayette and his troops turned out in time to prevent that, and timely cartloads of loaves arrived from Paris for the crowd.

At last it was decided that the king should come to Paris.

" Processional marches not a few our world has seen ; Roman triumphs and ovations, Cabiric cymbal-beatings, Royal progresses, Irish funerals ; but this of the French Monarchy marching to its bed remained to be seen. Miles long, and of breadth losing itself in vagueness, for all the neighbouring country crowds to see. Slow : stagnating along, like shoreless Lake, yet with a noise like Niagara, like Babel and Bedlam. A splashing and a tramping ; a hurrahing, uproaring, musket-volleying ; the truest segment of Chaos seen in these latter Ages ! Till slowly it disembogue itself, in the thickening dusk, into expectant Paris, through a double row of faces all the way from Passy to the Hôtel-de-Ville.

" Consider this : Vanguard of National troops ; with trains of artillery ; of pikemen and pikewomen, mounted on cannons, on carts, hackney-coaches, or on foot. . . . Loaves stuck on the points of bayonets, green boughs stuck in gun-barrels. Next, as main-march, ' fifty cart-loads of corn,' which have been lent, for peace, from the stores of Versailles. Behind which follow stragglers of the Garde-du-Corps ; all humiliated, in Grenadier bonnets. Close on these comes the royal carriage ; come royal carriages : for there are a hundred national deputies too, among whom sits Mirabeau—his remarks not given. Then finally, pellmell, as rear-guard, Flandre, Swiss, Hundred Swiss, other bodyguards, brigands, whosoever cannot get before. Between and among all which masses flows without limit Saint-Antoine and the Menadic cohort. Menadic especially about the royal carriage. . . . Covered with tricolor ; singing ' allusive songs ' ; pointing with one hand to the royal carriage, which the allusions hit, and pointing to the provision-wagons with the other hand, and these words : ' Courage, Friends ! We shall not want bread now ; we are bringing you the Baker, the Bakeress and Baker's boy.' . . .

" The wet day draggles the tricolor, but the joy is unextinguishable. Is not all well now ? ' Ah Madame, notre bonne Reine,' said some of these Strong-women some days hence, ' Ah, Madame, our good Queen, don't be a traitor any more and we will all love you ! ' . . ."

This was October the sixth, 1789. For nearly two years the royal family dwelt unmolested in the Tuileries. Had the court kept common faith with the people, the king might have died there, a king.

From 1789 to 1791 the early Revolution held its own ; France was a limited monarchy, the king kept a diminished state in the Tuileries, and the National Assembly ruled a country at peace. The reader who will glance back to the maps of Poland we have given in the previous chapter will realize what occupied Russia, Prussia, and Austria at this time. While France experimented with a crowned republic in the west, the last division of the crowned republic of the east was in progress. France could wait.

When we consider its inexperience, the con-

ditions under which it worked, and the complexities of its problems, one must concede that the Assembly did a very remarkable amount of constructive work. Much of that work was sound and still endures, much was experimental and has been undone. Some was disastrous. There was a clearing up of the penal code ; torture, arbitrary imprisonment, and persecutions for heresy were abolished ; and the ancient provinces of France, Normandy, Burgundy, and the like gave place to eighty departments. Promotion to the highest ranks in the army was laid open to men of every class. An excellent and simple system of law courts was set up, but its value was much vitiated by having the judges appointed by popular election for short periods of time. This made the crowd a sort of final court of appeal, and the judges, like the members of the Assembly, were forced to play to the gallery. And the whole vast property of the church was seized and administered by the state ; religious establishments not engaged in education or works of charity were broken up, and the salaries of the clergy made a charge upon the nation. This in itself was not a bad thing for the lower clergy in France, who were often scandalously underpaid in comparison with the richer dignitaries. But in addition the choice of priests and bishops was made elective, which struck at the very root idea of the Roman church, which centred everything upon the Pope, and in which all authority is from above downward. · Practically the National Assembly wanted at one blow to make the church in France Protestant, in organization if not in doctrine. Everywhere there were disputes and conflicts between the state priests of the republic and the recalcitrant (non-juring) priests who were loyal to Rome. . . .

One curious thing the National Assembly did which greatly weakened its grip on affairs. It decreed that no member of the Assembly should be an executive minister. This was in imitation of the American constitution, where also ministers are separated from the legislature. The British method has been to have all ministers in the legislative body, ready to answer questions and account for their interpretation of the laws and their conduct of the nation's business. If the legislature represents the

Map to illustrate the FLIGHT to VARENNES

sovereign people, then it is surely necessary for the ministers to be in the closest touch with their sovereign. This severance of the legislature and executive in France caused misunderstandings and mistrust ; the legislature lacked control and the executive lacked moral force. This led to such an ineffectiveness in the central government that in many districts at this time, communes and towns were to be found that were practically self-governing communities ; they accepted or rejected the commands of Paris as they thought fit, declined the payment of taxes, and divided up the church lands according to their local appetites.

§ 10

It is quite possible that with the loyal support of the crown and a reasonable patriotism on **The Revolution of the Jacobins.** the part of the nobility, the National Assembly, in spite of its noisy galleries, its Rousseauism, and its inexperience, might have blundered through to a stable form of parliamentary government for France. In Mirabeau it had a statesman with clear ideas of the needs of the time ; he knew the strength and the defects of the British system, and apparently he had set himself to establish in France a parallel political organization upon a wider, more honest franchise. He had, it is true, indulged in a sort of Ruritanian flirtation with the queen, seen her secretly, pronounced her very solemnly the " only *man* " about the king, and made rather a fool of himself in that matter, but his schemes were drawn upon a much larger scale than the scale of the back stairs of the Tuileries. By his death in 1791 France certainly lost one of her most constructive statesmen, and the National

Assembly its last chance of any co-operation with the king. Where there is a court there is usually a conspiracy, and royalist schemes and royalist mischief-making were the last straw in the balance against the National Assembly. The royalists did not care for Mirabeau, they did not care for France ; they wanted to be back in their lost paradise of privilege, haughtiness, and limitless expenditure, and it seemed to them that if only they could make the government of the National Assembly impossible, then by a sort of miracle the dry bones of the ancient regime would live again. They had no sense of the other possibility, the gulf of the republican extremists, that yawned at their feet.

One June night in 1791, between eleven o'clock and midnight, the king and queen and their two children slipped out of the Tuileries disguised, threaded their palpitating way through Paris, circled round from the north of the city to the east, and got at last into a travelling-carriage that was waiting upon the road to Chalons. They were flying to the army of the east.[1] The army of the east was " loyal," that is to say, its general and officers at least were prepared to betray France to the king and court. Here was adventure at last after the queen's heart, and one can understand the pleasurable excitement of the little party as the miles lengthened between themselves and Paris. Away over the hills were reverence, deep bows, and the kissing of hands. Then back to Versailles. A little shooting of the mob in Paris—artillery, if need be. A few executions—but not of the sort of people who

[1] Carlyle is at his best on this flight, *French Revolution,* book iv., chaps. iv. and v.

matter. A White Terror for a few months. Then all would be well again. Perhaps Calonne might return too, with fresh financial expedients. He was busy just then gathering support among the German princes. There were a lot of châteaux to rebuild, but the people who burnt them down could hardly complain if the task of rebuilding them pressed rather heavily upon their grimy necks. . . .

All such bright anticipations were cruelly dashed that night at Varennes. The king had been recognized at Sainte Menehould by the landlord of the post-house, and as the night fell, the eastward roads clattered with galloping messengers rousing the country, and trying to intercept the fugitives. There were fresh horses waiting in the upper village of Varennes —the young officer in charge had given the king up for the night and gone to bed—while for half an hour in the lower village the poor king, disguised as a valet, disputed with his postillions, who had expected reliefs in the lower village and refused to go further. Finally they consented to go on. They consented too late. The little party found the postmaster from Sainte Menehould, who had ridden past while the postillions wrangled, and a number of worthy republicans of Varennes whom he had gathered together, awaiting them at the bridge between the two parts of the town. The bridge was barricaded. Muskets were thrust into the carriage : " Your passports ? "

The king surrendered without a struggle. The little party was taken into the house of some village functionary. " Well," said the king, " here you have me ! " Also he remarked that he was hungry. At dinner he commended the wine, " quite excellent wine." What the queen said is not recorded. There were royalist troops at hand, but they attempted no rescue. The tocsin began to ring, and the village " illuminated itself," to guard against surprise. . . .

A very crestfallen coachload of royalty returned to Paris, and was received by vast crowds—*in silence.* The word had gone forth that whoever insulted the king should be thrashed, and whoever applauded him should be killed. . . .

It was only after this foolish exploit that the idea of a republic took hold of the French mind.

Before this flight to Varennes there was no doubt much abstract republican sentiment, but there was scarcely any expressed disposition to abolish monarchy in France. Even in July, a month after the flight, a great meeting in the Champ de Mars, supporting a petition for the dethronement of the king, was dispersed by the authorities, and many people were killed. But such displays of firmness could not prevent the lesson of that flight soaking into men's minds. Just as in England in the days of Charles I, so now in France men realized that the king could not be trusted—he was dangerous. The Jacobins, the extreme republican party, grew rapidly in strength. Their leaders, Robespierre, Danton, Marat, who had hitherto been a group of impossibles on the extreme left, began to dominate the National Assembly.

These Jacobins were the equivalents of the American radicals, men with untrammelled advanced ideas. Their strength lay in the fact that they were unencumbered and downright. They were poor men with nothing to lose. The party of moderation, of compromise with the relics of the old order, was led by such men of established position as General Lafayette, the general who had commanded the French troops in America, and Mirabeau, an aristocrat who was ready to model himself on the rich and influential aristocrats of England. But Robespierre was a needy but clever young lawyer from Arras, whose most precious possession was his faith in Rousseau ; Danton was a scarcely more wealthy barrister in Paris, one of those big, roaring, gesticulating Frenchmen who are in normal times the heroic loudtalkers of provincial cafés ; Marat was an older man, a Swiss of very great scientific distinction, but equally unembarrassed by possessions. On Marat's scientific standing it is necessary to lay stress because there is a sort of fashion among English writers to misrepresent the leaders of great revolutionary movements as ignorant men. This gives a false view of the mental processes of revolution ; and it is the task of the historian to correct it. Marat, we find, was conversant with English, Spanish, German, and Italian ; he had spent several years in England, he was made an honorary M.D. of St. Andrew's, and had published some valuable contributions to medical science in English. Both Benjamin Franklin and Goethe were greatly interested in his work in physics. This is the man who is called by Carlyle " rabid d o g ," " atrocious," " squalid," and " Dog-leech "—this last by way of tribute to his science.

The revolution called Marat to politics, and his earliest contributions to the great discussion were fine and sane. There was a prevalent delusion in France that England was a land of liberty. His *Tableau des vices de la constitution d' Angleterre* showed the realities of the English position. His last years were maddened by an almost intolerable skin disease which he caught while hiding in the sewers of Paris to escape the consequences of his denunciation of the king as a traitor after the flight to Varennes. Only by sitting in a hot bath could he collect his mind to write. He had been treated hardly and suffered, and he became hard ; nevertheless he stands out in history as a man of rare, unblemished honesty. His poverty seems particularly to have provoked the scorn of Carlyle.

" What a road he has travelled ; and sits now, about half-past seven of the clock, stewing in slipper-bath ; sore afflicted ; ill of Revolution Fever. . . . Excessively sick and worn, poor man : with precisely eleven-pence halfpenny of ready-money, in paper ; with slipper-bath ; strong three-footed stool for writing on, the while : and a squalid Washerwoman for his sole household . . . that is his civic establishment in Medical-School Street ; thither and not elsewhere has his road led him. . . . Hark, a rap again ! A musical woman's voice, refusing to be rejected : it is the Citoyenne who would do France a service. Marat, recognizing from within, cries, Admit her. Charlotte Corday is admitted."

Photo : *Rischgitz Collection.*

MARAT.

(From the portrait now in the Carnavalet Museum.

The young heroine—for republican leaders are fair game, and their assassins are necessarily heroines and their voices " musical "—offered to give him some necessary information about the counter-revolution at Caen, and as he was occupied in making a note of her facts, she stabbed him with a large sheath knife (1792). . . .

Such was the quality of most of the leaders of the Jacobin party. They were men of no property — untethered men. They were more dissociated and more elemental, therefore, than any other party : and they were ready to push the ideas of freedom and equality to a logical extremity. Their standards of patriotic virtue were high and harsh. There was something inhuman even in their humanitarian zeal. They saw without humour the disposition of the moderates to ease things down, to keep the common folk just a little needy and respectful, and royalty (and men of substance) just a little respected. They were blinded by the formulæ of Rousseauism to the historical truth that man is by nature oppressor and oppressed, and that it is only slowly by law, education, and the spirit of love in the world that men can be made happy and free.

And while in America the formulæ of eighteenth-century democracy were on the whole stimulating and helpful because it was already a land of open-air practical equality so far as white men were concerned, in France these formulæ made a very heady and dangerous mixture for the town populations, because considerable parts of the towns of France were slums full of dispossessed, demoralized, degraded, and bitter-spirited people. The Parisian crowd was in a particularly desperate and dangerous state, because the industries of Paris had been largely luxury industries, and much of her employment parasitic on the weaknesses and vices of fashionable life. Now the fashionable world had gone over the frontier, travellers were restricted, business disordered, and the city full of unemployed and angry people.

But the royalists, instead of realizing the significance of these Jacobins with their dangerous integrity and their dangerous grip upon the imagination of the mob, had the conceit to think they could make tools of them. The time for the replacement of the National Assembly under the new-made constitution by the " Legislative Assembly " was drawing near; and when the Jacobins, with the idea of breaking

wife of her need of him. There stood another body ready at hand with which these royalists did not reckon, far better equipped than the court to step in and take the place of an ineffective Legislative Assembly, and that was the strongly Jacobin Commune of Paris installed at the Hôtel de Ville.

So far France had been at peace. None of her neighbours had attacked her, because she appeared to be weakening herself by her internal dissensions. It was Poland that suffered by the distraction of France. But there seemed no reason why they should not insult and threaten her, and prepare the way for a later partition at their convenience. At Pillnitz, in 1791, the King of Prussia and the Emperor of Austria met, and issued a declaration [2] that the restoration of order and monarchy in France was a matter of interest to all sovereigns. And an army of emigrés, French nobles and gentlemen, an army largely of officers, was allowed to accumulate close to the frontier.

It was France that declared war against Austria. The motives of those who supported this step were conflicting. Many republicans wanted it because they wished to see the kindred people of Belgium liberated from the Austrian yoke. Many royalists wanted it because they saw in war a possibility of restoring the prestige of the crown. Marat opposed it bitterly in his paper L'Ami du Peuple, because he did not want to see republican enthusiasm

Photo: Rischgitz Collection.
DAVID'S FAMOUS PAINTING OF "THE DEATH OF MARAT."

up the moderates, proposed to make the members of the National Assembly ineligible for the Legislative Assembly, the royalists supported them with great glee, and carried the proposal. They perceived that the Legislative Assembly, so clipped of all experience, must certainly be a politically incompetent body. They would " extract good from the excess of evil," [1] and presently France would fall back helpless into the hands of her legitimate masters. So they thought. And the royalists did more than this. They backed the election of a Jacobin as Mayor of Paris. It was about as clever as if a man brought home a hungry tiger to convince his

[1] Wiriath.

[2] The Declaration of Pillnitz was a diplomatic démarche that failed. Great Britain had definitely refused to intervene in favour of the French monarchy, and Austrian statesmanship proposed to save the collective face of European monarchy by a sounding announcement of sympathy with the French Bourbons, followed by a proviso that unanimity should be secured before intervention was attempted. French opinion (and most historians) concentrated on the announcement and overlooked the proviso.—P. G.

turned into war fever. His instinct warned him of Napoleon. On April 20th, 1792, the king came down to the Assembly and proposed war amidst great applause.

The war began disastrously. Three French armies entered Belgium, two were badly beaten, and the third, under Lafayette, retreated. Then Prussia declared war in support of Austria, and the allied forces, under the Duke of Brunswick, prepared to invade France. The duke issued one of the most foolish proclamations in history; he was, he said, invading France to restore the royal authority. Any further indignity shown the king he threatened to visit upon the Assembly and Paris with "military execution." This was surely enough to make the most royalist Frenchman a republican—at least for the duration of the war.

The new phase of revolution, the Jacobin revolution, was the direct outcome of this proclamation. It made the Legislative Assembly, in which orderly republicans (Girondins) and royalists prevailed, it made the government which had put down that republican meeting in the Champ de Mars and hunted Marat into the sewers, impossible. The insurgents gathered at the Hôtel de Ville, and on the tenth of August the Commune launched an attack on the palace of the Tuileries.

The king behaved with a clumsy stupidity, and with that disregard for others which is the prerogative of kings. He had with him a Swiss guard of nearly a thousand men as well as National Guards of uncertain loyalty. He held out vaguely until firing began, and then he went off to the adjacent Assembly to place himself and his family under its protection, leaving his Swiss fighting. No doubt he hoped to antagonize Assembly and Commune, but the Assembly had none of the fighting spirit of the Hôtel de Ville. The royal refugees were placed in a box reserved for journalists (out of which a small room opened), and there they remained for sixteen hours while the Assembly debated their fate. Outside there were the sounds of a considerable battle; every now and then a window would break. The unfortunate Swiss were fighting with their backs to the wall because there was now nothing else for them to do. . . .

The Assembly had no stomach to back the government's action of July in the Champ de Mars. The fierce vigour of the Commune dominated it. The king found no comfort whatever in the Assembly. It scolded him and discussed his "suspension." The Swiss fought until they received a message from the king to desist, and then—the crowd being savagely angry at the needless bloodshed and out of control—they were for the most part massacred.

The long and tedious attempt to "Merovingianize" Louis, to make an honest crowned republican out of a dull and inadaptable absolute monarch, was now drawing to its tragic close. The Commune of Paris was practically in control of France. The Legislative Assembly—which had apparently undergone a change of heart—decreed that the king was suspended from his office, confined him in the Temple, replaced him by an executive commission, and summoned a National Convention to frame a new constitution.

The tension of patriotic and republican France was now becoming intolerable. Such armies as she had were rolling back helplessly towards Paris. Longwy had fallen, the great fortress of Verdun followed, and nothing seemed likely to stop the march of the allies upon the capital. The sense of royalist treachery rose to panic cruelty. At any rate the royalists had to be silenced and stilled and scared out of sight. The Commune set itself to hunt out every royalist that could be found, until the prisons of Paris were full. Danton incited the crowd against the prisoners, Marat saw the danger of a massacre. Before it was too late Marat tried to secure the establishment of emergency tribunals to filter the innocent from the guilty in this miscellaneous collection of schemers, suspects, and harmless gentlefolk. He was disregarded, and early in September the inevitable massacre occurred.

Suddenly, first at one prison and then at others, bands of insurgents took possession. A sort of rough court was constituted, and outside gathered a wild mob armed with sabres, pikes, and axes. One by one the prisoners, men and women alike, were led out from their cells, questioned briefly, pardoned with the cry of "Vive la Nation," or thrust out to the mob at the gates. There the crowd jostled and fought to get a slash or thrust at a victim. The condemned were stabbed, hacked, and beaten to death, their heads hewn off, stuck on pikes, and carried about the town, their torn bodies thrust aside. Among others, the Princesse de Lamballe, whom the king and queen had left behind in the Tuileries, perished. Her head was carried on a pike to the Temple for the queen to see.

In the queen's cell were two National Guards. One would have had her look out and see this grisly sight. The other, in pity, would not let her do so.

Even as this red tragedy was going on in Paris, the French general Dumouriez, who had rushed an army from Flanders into the forests of the Argonne, was holding up the advance of the allies beyond Verdun. On September 20th occurred a battle, mainly an artillery encounter, at Valmy. A not very resolute Prussian advance was checked,[1] the French infantry stood firm, their artillery was better than the allied artillery. For ten days after this repulse the Duke of Brunswick hesitated, and then he began

[1] The sour grapes of Champagne spread dysentery in the Prussian army.—P. G.

to fall back towards the Rhine. This battle at Valmy—it was little more than a cannonade—was one of the decisive battles in the world's history. The Revolution was saved.

The National Convention met on September 21st, 1792, and immediately proclaimed a republic. The trial and execution of the king followed with a sort of logical necessity upon these things. He died rather as a symbol than as a man. There was nothing else to be done with him; poor man, he cumbered the earth. France could not let him go to hearten the emigrants, could not keep him harmless at home; his existence threatened her. Marat had urged this trial relentlessly, yet with that acid clearness of his he would not have the king charged with any offence committed before he signed the constitution, because before then he was a real monarch, superlegal, and so incapable of being illegal. Nor would Marat permit attacks upon the king's counsel. . . . Throughout Marat played a bitter and yet often a just part; he was a great man, a fine intelligence, in a skin of fire; wrung with that organic hate in the blood that is not a product of the mind but of the body.

Louis was beheaded in January, 1793. He was guillotined—for since the previous August the guillotine had been in use as the official instrument in French executions.

Danton, in his leonine rôle, was very fine upon this occasion. "The kings of Europe would challenge us," he roared. "We throw them the head of a king!"

§ 11

And now followed a strange phase in the history of the French people. There arose a great flame of enthusiasm for France and the Republic. There was to be an end to compromise at home and abroad; at home royalists and every form of disloyalty were to be stamped out; abroad France was to be the protector and helper of all revolutionaries. All Europe, all the world, was to become republican. The youth of France poured into the Republican armies; a new and wonderful song spread through the land, a song that still warms the blood like wine, the Marseillaise. Before that chant and the leaping columns of French bayonets and their enthusiastically served guns the foreign armies rolled back; before the end of 1792 the French armies had gone far beyond the utmost achievements of Louis XIV; everywhere they stood on foreign soil. They were in Brussels, they had overrun Savoy, they had raided to Mayence; they had seized the Scheldt from Holland. Then the French Government did an unwise thing. It had been exasperated by the expulsion of its representative from England upon the execution of Louis, and it declared war against England. It was an unwise thing to do, because the revolution which had given France a new enthusiastic infantry and a brilliant artillery, released from its aristocratic officers and many cramping traditions,[1] had destroyed the discipline of its navy, and the English were supreme upon the sea. And this provocation united all England against France, whereas there had been at first a very considerable liberal movement in Great Britain in sympathy with the revolution.

The Jacobin Republic, 1792–94.

Photo: Rischgitz Collection.
MARIE ANTOINETTE IN PRISON.

It robbed France of her one prospective ally.[2]

Of the fight that France made in the next few years against a European coalition we cannot tell in any detail. She drove the Austrians for ever out of Belgium, and made Holland a republic. The Dutch fleet, frozen in the Texel, surrendered to a handful of cavalry without firing its guns. For some time the French thrust towards Italy was hung up, and it was only in 1796 that a new general, Napoleon Bonaparte, led the ragged and hungry republican armies in triumph across Piedmont to Mantua and Verona. An *Outline of History* cannot map out campaigns; but of the new quality that had come into war, it is bound to take note. The old professional armies had fought for the fighting, as slack as workers paid by the hour; these wonderful new armies fought hungry and thirsty, for victory. Their enemies called them the "New French." Says C. F. Atkinson,[3] "What astonished the Allies most of all was the number and the velocity of the Republicans. These improvised armies had in fact nothing to delay them. Tents were unprocurable for want of money, untransportable for want of the enormous number of wagons that would have been required, and also unnecessary, for the discomfort that would have caused wholesale desertion in professional armies was cheerfully borne by the men of 1793–94. Supplies for armies of then unheard-of size could not be carried in convoys, and the French soon became

---

[1] The intelligence of the French army of the Revolution was largely due to a period of intelligent military thinking and writing which set in among French soldiers after the defeats of the army of Louis XV in the Seven Years' War. Napoleon himself was full of traces of this inspiration.—P. G.

[2] I cannot agree that England was ever, at any moment, "a prospective ally" of France. There was a deep divergence of interests; and it is impossible to think of Pitt and the Whig nobles being in any way the allies of the France of 1793.—E. B.

[3] In his article, "French Revolutionary Wars," in the *Encyclopædia Britannica*.

familiar with "living on the country." Thus 1793 saw the birth of the modern system of war—rapidity of movement, full development of national strength, bivouacs, requisitions and force as against cautious manœuvring, small professional armies, tents and full rations, and chicane. The first represented the decision-compelling spirit, the second the spirit of risking little to gain a little. . . ."

And while these ragged hosts of enthusiasts were chanting the Marseillaise and fighting for *la France*, manifestly never quite clear in their minds whether they were looting or liberating the countries into which they poured, the republican enthusiasm in Paris was spending itself in a far less glorious fashion. Marat, the one man of commanding intelligence among the Jacobins, was now frantic with an incurable disease, and presently he was murdered ; Danton was a series of patriotic thunderstorms ; the steadfast fanaticism of Robespierre dominated the situation. This man is difficult to judge ; he was a man of poor physique, naturally timid, and a prig. But he had that most necessary gift for power, faith. He believed not in a god familiar to men, but in a certain Supreme Being, and that Rousseau was his prophet. He set himself to save the Republic as he conceived it, and he imagined it could be saved by no other man than he. So that to keep in power was to save the republic. The living spirit of the republic, it seemed, had sprung from a slaughter of royalists and the execution of the king. There were insurrections : one in the west, in the district of La Vendée, where the people rose against the conscription and against the dispossession of the orthodox clergy and were led by noblemen and priests ; one in the south, where Lyons and Marseilles had risen and the royalists of Toulon had admitted an English and Spanish garrison. To which there seemed no more effectual reply than to go on killing royalists.

Nothing could have better pleased the fierce heart of the Paris slums. The Revolutionary Tribunal went to work, and a steady slaughtering began.[1] The invention of the guillotine was opportune to this mood. The queen was

[1] In the thirteen months before June, 1794, there were 1,220 executions ; in the following seven weeks there were 1,376.—P. G.

guillotined, most of Robespierre's antagonists were guillotined, atheists who argued that there was no Supreme Being were guillotined, Danton was guillotined because he thought there was too much guillotine ; day by day, week by week, this infernal new machine chopped off heads and more heads and more. The reign of Robespierre lived, it seemed, on blood, and needed more and more, as an opium-taker needs more and more opium.

Danton was still Danton, leonine and exemplary upon the guillotine. "Danton," he said, "no weakness ! "

And the grotesque thing about the story is that Robespierre was indubitably honest. He was far more honest than any of the group of men who succeeded him. He was inspired by a consuming passion for a new order of human life. So far as he could contrive it, the Committee of Public Safety, the emergency government of twelve which had now thrust aside the Convention, *constructed*. The scale on which it sought to construct was stupendous. All the intricate problems with which we still struggle to-day were met by swift and shallow solutions. Attempts were made to equalize property. "Opulence," said St. Just, "is infamous." The property of the rich was taxed or confiscated in order that it should be divided among the poor. Every man was to have a secure house, a living, a wife and children. The labourer was worthy of his hire, but not entitled to an advantage. There was an attempt to abolish *profit* altogether, the rude incentive of most human commerce since the beginning of society. Profit is the economic riddle that still puzzles us to-day. There were harsh laws against "profiteering" in France in 1793—England in 1919 found it necessary to make quite similar laws. And the Jacobin government not only replanned—in eloquent outline—the economic, but also the social system. Divorce was made as easy as marriage ; the distinction of legitimate and illegitimate children was abolished. . . . A new calendar was devised, with new names for the months, a week of ten days, and the like—that has long since been swept away ; but also the clumsy coinage and the tangled weights and measures of old France gave place to the simple and lucid decimal system that still endures. . . . There

CORONATION OF NAPOLEON I. AND THE EMPRESS JOSEPHINE IN NOTRE DAME, DEC. 2, 1804,
IN THE PRESENCE OF POPE PIUS VIII.

was a proposal from one extremist group to abolish God among other institutions altogether, and to substitute the worship of Reason. There was, indeed, a Feast of Reason in the cathedral of Notre-Dame, with a pretty actress as the goddess of Reason. But against this Robespierre set his face; he was no atheist. "Atheism," he said, "is aristocratic. The idea of a Supreme Being who watches over oppressed innocence and punishes triumphant crime is essentially the idea of the people."

So he guillotined Hébert, who had celebrated the Feast of Reason, and all his party.

A certain mental disorder became perceptible in Robespierre as the summer of 1794 drew on. He was deeply concerned with his religion. (The arrests and executions of suspects were going on now as briskly as ever.

Photo: Rischgitz Collection.
ROBESPIERRE.

Through the streets of Paris every day rumbled the Terror with its carts full of condemned people.) He induced the Convention to decree that France believed in a Supreme Being, and in that comforting doctrine, the immortality of the soul. In June he celebrated a great festival, the festival of his Supreme Being. There was a procession to the Champ de Mars, which he headed, brilliantly arrayed, bearing a great bunch of flowers and wheat-ears. Figures of inflammatory material, representing Atheism and Vice, were solemnly burnt; then, by an ingenious mechanism, and with some slight creakings, an incombustible statue of Wisdom rose in their place. There were discourses—Robespierre delivered the chief one—but apparently no worship. . . .

Thereafter Robespierre displayed a disposition to brood aloof from affairs. For a month he kept away from the Convention.

One day in July he reappeared and delivered a strange speech that clearly foreshadowed fresh prosecutions. "Gazing on the multitude of vices which the torrent of Revolution has rolled down," he cried, in his last great speech in the Convention, "I have sometimes trembled lest I should be soiled by the impure neighbourhood of wicked men. . . . I know that it is easy for the leagued tyrants of the world to overwhelm a single individual; but I know also what is the duty of a man who can die in the defence of humanity." . . .

And so on to vague utterances that seemed to threaten everyone.

The Convention heard this speech in silence; then, when a proposal was made to print and circulate it, broke into a resentful uproar and refused permission. Robespierre went off in bitter resentment to the club of his supporters, and *reread his speech to them!*

That night was full of talk and meetings and preparations for the morrow, and the next morning the Convention turned upon Robespierre. One Tallien threatened him with a dagger. When he tried to speak, he was shouted down, and the President jingled the bell at him. "President of Assassins," cried Robespierre, "I demand speech!" It was refused him. His voice deserted him; he coughed and spluttered. "The blood of Danton chokes him," cried someone.

He was accused and arrested there and then, with his chief supporters.

Whereupon the Hôtel de Ville, still stoutly Jacobin, rose against the Convention, and Robespierre and his companions were snatched out of the hands of their captors. There was a night of gathering, marching, counter-marching; and at last, about three in the morning, the forces of the Convention faced the forces of the Commune outside the Hôtel de Ville. Henriot, the Jacobin commander, after a busy day was drunk upstairs; a parley ensued, and then, after some indecision, the soldiers of the Commune went over to the Government. There was a shouting of patriotic sentiments, and someone looked out from the Hôtel de Ville. Robespierre and his last companions found themselves betrayed and trapped.

Two or three of these men threw themselves out of a window, and injured themselves frightfully on the railings below without killing themselves. Others attempted suicide. Robespierre, it seems, was shot in the lower jaw by a gendarme. He was found, his eyes staring from a pale face whose lower part was blood.

Followed seventeen hours of agony before his end. He spoke never a word during that time; his jaw being bound up roughly in dirty linen. He and his companions, and the broken, dying bodies of those who had jumped from the windows, twenty-two men altogether, were taken to the guillotine instead of the condemned appointed for that day. Mostly his eyes were closed, but, says Carlyle, he opened them to see the great knife rising above him, and struggled. Also it would seem he screamed when the executioner removed his bandages. Then the knife came down, swift and merciful.

The Terror was at an end. From first to last there had been condemned and executed about four thousand people.

Photo : Rischgitz Collection.

DANTON.

(From a painting in the Carnavalet Museum.)

§ 12

It witnesses to the immense vitality and the profound rightness of the flood of new ideals and intentions that the French Revolution had released into the world of practical endeavour, that it could still flow in a creative torrent after it had been caricatured and mocked in the grotesque personality and career of Robespierre. He had shown its deepest thoughts, he had displayed anticipations of its methods and conclusions, through the green and distorting

The Directory.

lenses of his preposterous vanity and egotism, he had smeared and blackened all its hope and promise with blood and horror, and the power of these ideas was not destroyed. They stood the extreme tests of ridiculous and horrible presentation. After his downfall, the Republic still ruled unassailable. Leaderless, for his successors were a group of crafty or commonplace men, the European republic struggled on, and presently fell and rose again, and fell and rose and still struggled, entangled but invincible.

And it is well to remind the reader here of the real dimensions of this phase of the Terror, which strikes so vividly upon the imagination and which has therefore been enormously exaggerated relatively to the rest of the revolution. From 1789 to late in 1791 the French Revolution was an orderly process, and from the summer of 1794 the Republic was an orderly and victorious state. The Terror was not the work of the whole country, but of the town mob which owed its existence and its savagery to the misrule and social injustice of the ancient regime; and the explosion of the Terror could have happened only through the persistent treacherous disloyalty of the royalists which, while it raised the extremists to frenzy, disinclined the mass of moderate republicans from any intervention. The best men were busy fighting the Austrians and royalists on the frontier. Altogether, we must remember, the total of the killed in the Terror amounted to a few thousands, and among those thousands there were certainly a great number of active antagonists whom the Republic, by all the standards of that time, was entitled to kill. It included such traitors and mischief-makers as Philip, Duke of Orleans of the Palais Royal, who had voted for the death of Louis XVI.

More lives were wasted by the British generals alone on the opening day of what is known as the Somme offensive of July, 1916, than in the whole French revolution from start to finish. We hear so much about the martyrs of the French Terror because they were notable, well-connected people, and because there has been a sort of propaganda of their sufferings. But let us balance against them in our minds what was going on in the prisons of the world generally at that time. In Britain and America, while the Terror ruled in France, far more people were slaughtered for offences—very often quite trivial offences—against property than were condemned by the Revolutionary Tribunal for treason against the State. Of course, they were very common people indeed, but in their rough way they suffered. A girl was hung in Massachusetts in 1789 for forcibly taking the hat, shoes, and buckles of another girl she had met in the street.[1] Again, Howard the philanthropist (about 1773) found a number of perfectly innocent people detained in the English prisons who had been tried and acquitted, but were unable to pay the gaoler's fees. And these prisons were filthy places under no effective control. Torture was still in use in the Hanoverian dominions of His Britannic Majesty King George III. It had been in use in France up to the time of the National Assembly. These things mark the level of the times. It is not on record that anyone was deliberately tortured by the French revolutionaries during the Terror. Those few hundreds of French gentlefolk fell into a pit that most of them had been well content should exist for others. It was tragic, but not, by the scale of universal history, a great tragedy. The common man in France was more free, better off, and happier during the " Terror " than he had been in 1787.

The story of the Republic after the summer of 1794 becomes a tangled story of political groups aiming at everything from a radical

[1] Channing, vol. iii. chap. xviii.

republic to a royalist reaction, but pervaded by a general desire for some definite working arrangement even at the price of considerable concessions. There was a series of insurrections of the Jacobins and of the royalists ; there seems to have been what we should call nowadays a hooligan class in Paris which was quite ready to turn out to fight and loot on either side ; nevertheless the Convention produced a government, the Directory of five members, which held France together for five years. The last, most threatening revolt of all, in October, 1795, was suppressed with great skill and decision by a rising young general, Napoleon Bonaparte.

"THE WHIFF OF GRAPE SHOT."

The Directory was victorious abroad, but uncreative at home ; its members were far too anxious to stick to the sweets and glories of office to prepare a constitution that would supersede them, and far too dishonest to handle the task of financial and economic reconstruction demanded by the condition of France. We need only note two of their names, Carnot, who was an honest republican, and Barras, who was conspicuously a rogue. Their reign of five years formed a curious interlude in this history of great changes. They took things as they found them. The propagandist zeal of the revolution carried the French armies into Holland, Belgium, Switzerland, South Germany, and North Italy. Everywhere kings were expelled and republics set up. But such propagandist zeal as animated the Directorate did not prevent the looting of the treasures of the liberated peoples to relieve the financial embarrassment of the French Government. Their wars became less and less the holy war of freedom, and more and more like the aggressive wars of the ancient régime. The last feature of Grand Monarchy that France was disposed to discard was her tradition of foreign policy, grasping, aggressive, restless, French-centred. One discovers it still as vigorous under the Directorate as if there had been no revolution.

§ 13

The ebb of this tide of Revolution in the world, this tide which had created the great Republic of America and threatened to submerge all European monarchies, was now at hand. It is as if something had thrust up from beneath the surface of human affairs, made a gigantic effort, and spent itself. It swept many obsolescent and evil things away, but many evil and unjust things remained. It solved many problems, and it left the desire for fellowship and order face to face with much vaster problems that it seemed only to have revealed. Privilege of certain types had gone, many tyrannies, much religious persecution. When these things of the ancient régime had vanished, it seemed as if they had never mattered. What did matter was that for all their votes and enfranchisement, and in spite of all their passion and effort, common men were still not free and not enjoying an equal happiness ; that the immense promise and air of a new world with which the Revolution had come, remained unfulfilled.

The Pause in Reconstruction and the Dawn of Modern Socialism.

Yet, after all, this wave of revolution had realized nearly everything that had been clearly thought out before it came. It was not failing now for want of impetus, but for want of finished ideas. Many things that had oppressed mankind were swept away for ever. Now that they were swept away it became apparent how unprepared men were for the creative opportunities this clearance gave them. And periods of revolution are periods of action ; in them men reap the harvests of ideas that have grown during phases of interlude, and they leave the fields cleared for a new season of growth, but

they cannot suddenly produce ripened new ideas to meet an unanticipated riddle.

The sweeping away of king and lord, of priest and inquisitor, of landlord and tax-gatherer and task-master, left the mass of men face to face for the first time with certain very fundamental aspects of the social structure ; relationships they had taken for granted, and had never realized the need of thinking hard and continuously about before. Institutions that had seemed to be in the nature of things, and matters that had seemed to happen by the same sort of necessity that brought round the dawn and springtime, were discovered to be artificial, controllable, were they not so perplexingly intricate, and—now that the old routines were abolished and done away with—in urgent need of control. The New Order found itself confronted with three riddles which it was quite unprepared to solve : Property, Currency, and International Affairs.

Let us take these three problems in order, and ask what they are and how they arose in human affairs. Every human life is deeply entangled in them, and concerned in their solution. The rest of this history becomes more and more clearly the development of the effort to solve these problems ; that is to say, so to interpret property, so to establish currency, and so to control international reactions as to render possible a world-wide, progressive and happy community of will. They are the three riddles of the sphinx of fate, to which the human commonweal must find an answer or perish.

The idea of property arises out of the combative instincts of the species. Long before men were men, the ancestral ape was a proprietor. Primitive property is what a beast will fight for. The dog and his bone, the tigress and her lair, the roaring stag and his herd, these are proprietorship blazing. No more nonsensical expression is conceivable in sociology than the term " primitive communism." The old man of the family tribe of early palæolithic times insisted upon his proprietorship in his wives and daughters, in his tools, in his visible universe. If any other man wandered into his visible universe he fought him, and if he could he slew him. The tribe grew in the course of ages, as Atkinson showed convincingly in his *Primal Law*, by the gradual toleration by the Old Man of the existence of the younger men, and of their proprietorship in the wives they captured from outside the tribe, and in the tools and ornaments they made and the game they slew. Human society grew by a compromise between this one's property and that. It was largely a compromise and an alliance forced upon men by the necessity of driving some other tribe out of its visible universe. If the hills and forests and streams were not *your* land or *my* land, it was because they had to be *our* land. Each of us would have preferred to have it *my* land, but that would not work. In that case the other fellows would have destroyed us. Society, therefore, is from its beginnings the mitigation of ownership. Ownership in the beast and in the primitive savage was far more intense a thing than it is in the civilized world to-day. It is rooted more strongly in our instincts than in our reason.

In the natural savage and in the untutored man to-day—for it is well to keep in mind that no man to-day is more than four hundred generations from the primordial savage—there is no limitation to the sphere of ownership. Whatever you can fight for, you can own ; women-folk, spared captive, captured beast, forest glade, stone pit or what not. As the community grew and a sort of law came to restrain internecine fighting, men developed rough and ready methods of settling proprietorship. Men could own what they were the first to make or capture or claim. It seemed natural that a debtor who could not pay up should become the property of his creditor. Equally natural was it that, after claiming a patch of land ("Bags I," as the schoolboy says), a man should exact payments and tribute from anyone else who wanted to use it. It was only slowly, as the possibilities of organized life dawned on men, that this unlimited property in anything whatever began to be recognized as a nuisance. Men found themselves born into a universe all owned and claimed, nay ! they found themselves born, owned and claimed. The social struggles of the earlier civilization are difficult to trace now, but the history we have told of the Roman republic shows a community waking up to the idea that debt may become a public inconvenience and should then be repudiated, and that the unlimited ownership of land is also an inconvenience. We find that later Babylonia severely limited the rights of property in slaves. Finally, we find in the teaching of that great revolutionist, Jesus of Nazareth, such an attack upon property as had never been before. Easier it was, he said, for a camel to go through the eye of a needle than for the owner of great possessions to enter the kingdom of heaven. A steady, continuous criticism of the permissible scope of property seems to have been going on in the world for the last twenty-five or thirty centuries. Eighteen hundred years after Jesus of Nazareth we find all the world that has come under the Christian teaching persuaded that there could be no property in persons. There has been a turn over in the common conscience in that matter. And also the idea that " a man may do what he likes with his own " was clearly very much shaken in relation to other sorts of property. But this world of the closing eighteenth century was still only in the interrogative stage in this matter. It had got nothing clear enough, much less settled enough, to act upon. One of its primary impulses was to protect property against the greed and waste of kings and the exploitation of noble adventurers. It was to protect private property that the Revolution began. But its equalitarian formulæ carried it into a criticism of the very property it had risen to protect. How can men be free and equal when numbers of them have no ground to stand upon and nothing to eat, and the owners will neither feed nor lodge them unless they toil ? Excessively—the poor complained.

To which riddle the Jacobin reply was to set about " dividing up." They wanted to intensify and universalize property. Aiming at the same end by another route, there were already in the eighteenth century certain primitive socialists—or, to be more exact, communists —who wanted to " abolish " private property altogether. The state (a democratic state was of course understood) was to own all property. It was only as the nineteenth century developed that men began to realize that property was not one simple thing, but a great complex of ownerships of different values and consequences, that many things (such as human beings, the air, the high seas, and perhaps undeveloped land) must be held out of the reach of private ownership ; that many things (such as the implements of an artist, clothing, tooth-brushes) are very profoundly and incurably personal property, and that there is a very great range of things, railways, machinery of various sorts, homes, cultivated gardens, pleasure-boats, for example, which need each to be considered very particularly to determine how far and under what limitations it may come under private ownership, and how far it falls into the public domain and may be administered and let out by the State in the collective interest. On the practical side these questions pass into politics, and the problem of making and sustaining efficient state administration. They open up issues in social psychology, and interact with the enquiries of educational science. We have to-day the advantage of a hundred and thirty years of discussion over the first revolutionary generation, but even now this criticism of property is still a vast and passionate ferment rather than a science. Under the circumstances it was impossible that eighteenth-century France should present any other spectacle than that of vague and confused popular movements seeking to dispossess owners, and classes of small and large owners holding on grimly, demanding, before everything else, law, order, and security, and seeking to increase their individual share of anything whatever that could be legally possessed.

Closely connected with the vagueness of men's ideas about property was the vagueness of their ideas about currency. Both the American and the French republics fell into serious trouble upon this score. Here, again, we deal with something that is not simple, a tangle of usages, conventions, laws, and prevalent mental habits, out of which arise problems which admit of no solution in simple terms, and which yet are of vital importance to the everyday life of the community. The validity of the acknowledgment a man is given for a day's work is manifestly of quite primary importance to the working of the social machine. The growth of confidence in the precious metals and of coins, until the assurance became practically universal that good money could be trusted to have its purchasing power anywhere, must have been a very slow one in human history. And being fairly established, this assurance was subjected to very considerable strains and perplexities by the action of governments in debasing currency and in substituting paper promises to pay for the actual metallic coins. Every age produced a number of clever people intelligent enough to realize the opportunities for smart operations afforded by the complex of faiths and fictions upon which the money system rested, and sufficiently unsound morally to give their best energies to growing rich and so getting people to work for them, through tricks and tampering with gold, coinage, and credit. So soon as serious political and social dislocation occurred, the money mechanism began to work stiffly and inaccurately. The United States and the French Republic both started their careers in a phase of financial difficulty. Everywhere governments had been borrowing and issuing paper promises to pay interest, more interest than they could conveniently raise. Both revolutions led to much desperate public spending and borrowing, and at the same time to an interruption of cultivation and production that further diminished real taxable wealth. Both governments, being unable to pay their way in gold, resorted to the issue of paper money, promising to pay upon the security of undeveloped land (in America) or recently confiscated church lands (France). In both cases the amount of issue went far beyond the confidence of men in the new security. Gold was called in, hidden by the cunning ones, or went abroad to pay for imports ; and people found themselves with various sorts of bills and notes in the place of coins, all of uncertain and diminishing value.

However complicated the origins of currency, its practical effect and the end it has to serve in the community may be stated roughly in simple terms. The money a man receives for his work (mental or bodily) or for relinquishing his property in some consumable good, must ultimately be able to purchase for him for his use a fairly equivalent amount of consumable goods. (" Consumable goods " is a phrase we would have understood in the widest sense to represent even such things as a journey, a lecture or theatrical entertainment, housing medical advice, and so forth.) When everyone in a community is assured of this, and assured that the money will not deteriorate in purchasing power, then currency—and the distribution of goods by trade—is in a healthy and satisfactory state. Then men will work cheerfully, and only then. The imperative need for that steadfastness and security of currency is the fixed datum from which the scientific study and control of currency must begin. But under the most stable conditions there will always be fluctuations in currency value. The sum total of saleable consumable goods in the world and in various countries varies from year to year and from season to season; autumn is probably a time of plenty in comparison with spring; with an increase the purchasing power of currency will increase, unless there is also an increase in the amount of currency. On the other hand, if there is a diminution in the production of consumable goods or a great and unprofitable destruction of consumable goods, such as occurs in a war, the share of the total of consumable goods represented by a sum of money will diminish and prices and wages will rise. In modern war the explosion of a single big shell, even if it hits nothing, destroys labour and material roughly equivalent to a comfortable cottage or a year's holiday for a man. If the shell hits anything, then that further destruction has to be added to the diminution of consumable goods. Every shell that burst in the recent war diminished by a little fraction the purchasing value of every coin in the whole world. If there is also an increase of currency during a period when consumable goods are being used up and not fully replaced—and the necessities of revolutionary and war-making governments almost always require this—then the enhance-

Photo: Rischgitz Collection.
BONAPARTE AS LIEUTENANT-COLONEL OF THE CORSICAN VOLUNTEERS.

ment of prices and the fall in the value of the currency paid in wages is still greater. Usually also governments under these stresses borrow money, that is to say, they issue interest-bearing paper, secured on the willingness and ability of the general community to endure taxation. Such operations would be difficult enough if they were carried out frankly by perfectly honest men, in the full light of publicity and scientific knowledge. But hitherto this has never been the case; at every point the clever egotist, the bad rich man, is trying to deflect things a little to his own advantage. Everywhere too one finds the stupid egotist ready to take fright and break into panic. Consequently we presently discover the state encumbered by an excess of currency, which is in effect a non-interest-paying debt, and also with a great burthen of interest upon loans. Both credit and currency begin to fluctuate wildly with the evaporation of public confidence. They are, we say, demoralized.

The ultimate consequence of an entirely demoralized currency would be to end all work and all trade that could not be carried on by payment in kind and barter. Men would refuse to work except for food, clothing, housing, and payment in kind. The immediate consequence of a partially demoralized currency is to drive up prices and make trading feverishly adventurous and workers suspicious and irritable. A sharp man wants under such conditions to hold money for as brief a period as possible; he demands the utmost for his realty, and buys a realty again as soon as possible in order to get this perishable stuff, the currency paper, off his hands. All who have fixed incomes and saved accumulations suffer by the rise in prices, and the wage-earners find, with a gathering fury, that the real value of their wages is continually less. Here is a state of affairs where the duty of every clever person is evidently to help adjust and reassure. But all the traditions of private enterprise, all the ideas of the later eighteenth century, went to justify the action of acute-minded and dexterous people who set themselves to accumulate claims, titles, and tangible property in the storms and dislocations of this currency breakdown. The number of understanding people in the world who were setting themselves sincerely and simply to restore honest and workable currency and credit conditions were few and ineffectual. Most of the financial and speculative people of the time were playing the part of Cornish wreckers— not apparently with any conscious dishonesty, but with the completest self-approval and the applause of their fellow-men. The aim of every clever person was to accumulate as much as he could of really negotiable wealth, and then, and only then, to bring about some sort of stabilizing political process that would leave him in advantageous possession of his accumulation. Here were the factors of a bad economic atmosphere, suspicious, feverish, greedy, and speculative. . . .

In the third direction in which the Revolution had been unprepared with clear ideas, the problem of international relationships, developments were to occur that interacted disastrously with this state of financial and economic adventure, this scramble and confusion, this preoccupation of men's minds with the perplexing slipperiness of their private property and their monetary position at home. The Republic at its birth found itself at war. For a time that war was waged by the new levies with a patriotism and a zeal unparalleled in the world's history. But that could not go on. The Directory found itself at the head of a conquering country, intolerably needy and embarrassed at home, and in occupation of rich foreign lands, full of seizable wealth and material and financial opportunity. We have all double natures, and the French in particular seem to be developed logically and symmetrically on both sides. Into these conquered regions France came as a liberator, the teacher of Republicanism to mankind. Holland and Belgium became the Batavian Republic, Genoa and its Riviera the Ligurian Republic, North Italy the Cisalpine Republic, Switzerland was rechristened the Helvetian Republic, Mülhausen, Rome, and Naples were designated republics. Grouped about France, these republics were to be a constellation of freedom leading the world. That was the ideal side. At the same time the French government, and French private individuals in concert with the government, proceeded to a complete and exhaustive exploitation of the resources of these liberated lands.

So within ten years of the meeting of the States General, New France begins to take on a singular likeness to the Old. It is more flushed, more vigorous ; it wears a cap of liberty instead of a crown ; it has a new army—but a damaged fleet ; it has new rich people instead of the old rich people, a new peasantry working even harder than the old and yielding more taxes, a new foreign policy curiously like the old foreign policy disrobed, and—there is no Millennium.

XXXVIII

THE CAREER OF NAPOLEON BONAPARTE[1]

§ 1

AND now we come to one of the most illuminating figures in modern history, the figure of an adventurer and a wrecker, whose story seems to display with an extraordinary vividness the universal subtle

The Bonaparte Family in Corsica. conflict of egotism, vanity and personality with the weaker, wider claims of the common good. Against this background of confusion and stress and hope, this strained and heaving France and Europe, this stormy and tremendous dawn, appears this dark little archaic personage, hard,

[1] Two very useful books have been Holland Rose's *Personality of Napoleon* and his *Life of Napoleon I*. A compact and convenient biography, with good battle maps, is R. M. Johnston's *Napoleon*. Thomas Hardy's great epic-drama, *The Dynasts*, is a magnificent picture of Napoleon's career, historically very exact. It is one of the greater stars of English literature, too little known as yet to the general public.

compact, capable, unscrupulous, imitative, and neatly vulgar. He was born (1769) in the still half-barbaric island of Corsica, the son of a rather prosaic father, a lawyer who had been first a patriotic Corsican against the French monarchy which was trying to subjugate Corsica, and who had then gone over to the side of the invader. His mother was of sturdier stuff, passionately patriotic and a strong and managing woman. (She birched her sons; on one occasion she birched Napoleon when he was sixteen.) There were numerous brothers and sisters, and the family pursued the French authorities with importunities for rewards and jobs. Except for Napoleon it seems to have been a thoroughly commonplace, "hungry" family. He was clever, bad-tempered, and overbearing. From his mother he had acquired a romantic Corsican patriotism.

Through the patronage of the French governor of Corsica he got an education first at the military school of Brienne and then at the military school of Paris, from which he passed into the artillery in 1785. He was an industrious student both of mathematics and history, his memory was prodigiously good, and he made copious note-books which still exist. These note-books show no very exceptional intelligence, and they contain short pieces of original composition—upon suicide and similar adolescent topics. He fell early under the spell of Rousseau; he developed sensibility and a scorn for the corruptions of civilization. In 1786 he wrote a pamphlet against a Swiss pastor who had attacked Rousseau. It was a very ordinary adolescent production, rhetorical and imitative. He dreamt of an independent Corsica, freed from the French. With the revolution, he became an ardent republican and a supporter of the new French régime in Corsica. For some years, until the fall of Robespierre, he remained a Jacobin.

§ 2

He soon gained the reputation of a useful and capable officer, and it was through Robespierre's younger brother that he got his first chance of distinction at Toulon. Toulon had been handed over to the British and Spanish by the royalists, and an allied fleet occupied its

Bonaparte as a Republican General.

harbour. Bonaparte was given the command of the artillery, and under his direction the French forced the allies to abandon the port and town.

He was next appointed commander of the artillery in Italy, but he had not taken up his duties when the death of Robespierre seemed likely to involve his own; he was put under arrest as a Jacobin, and for a time he was in danger of the guillotine. That danger passed. He was employed as artillery commander in an abortive raid upon Corsica, and then went to Paris (1795) rather down at heel. Madame Junot in her Memoirs describes his lean face and slovenly appearance at this time, "his ill-combed, ill-powdered hair hanging down over his grey overcoat," his gloveless hands and badly blacked boots. It was a time of exhaustion and reaction after the severities of the Jacobin republic. "In Paris," says Holland Rose, "the star of Liberty was paling before Mercury, Mars, and Venus"—finance, uniforms, and social charm. The best of the common men were in the armies, away beyond the frontiers. We have already noted the last rising of the royalists in this year (1795). Napoleon had the luck to be in Paris, and found his second opportunity in this affair. He saved the Republic—of the Directory.

His abilities greatly impressed Carnot, the most upright of the Directors. Moreover, he married a charming young widow, Madame Josephine de Beauharnais, who had great influence with Barras. Both these things probably helped him to secure the command in Italy.

We have no space here for the story of his brilliant campaigns in Italy (1796–97), but of the spirit in which that invasion of Italy was conducted we must say a word or two, because it illustrates so vividly the double soul of France and of Napoleon, and how revolutionary idealism was paling before practical urgencies. He proclaimed to the Italians that the French were coming to break their chains—*and they were!* He wrote to the Directory: "We will levy 20,000,000 francs in exactions in this country; it is one of the richest in the world." To his soldiers he said, "You are famished and nearly naked. . . . I lead you into the most fertile plain in the world. There you will find great towns, rich provinces, honour, glory, riches. . . ."

We are all such mixed stuff as this ; in all of us the intimations of a new world and a finer duty struggle to veil and control the ancient greeds and lusts of our inherited past ; but these passages, written by a young man of twenty-seven, seem to show the gilt of honourable idealism rubbed off at an unusually early age. These are the bribes of an adventurer who has brought whatever impulse of devotion to a great cause once stirred within him, well under the control of his self-love.

His successes in Italy were brilliant and complete ; they enormously stimulated his self-confidence and his contempt for the energy and ability of his fellow creatures. He had wanted to go into Italy because there lay the most attractive task—he had risked his position in the army by refusing to take up the irksome duties of a command against the rebels in La Vendée—and there are clear signs of a vast expansion of his vanity with his victories. He had been a great reader of Plutarch's Lives and of Roman history, and his extremely active but totally uncreative imagination was now busy with dreams of a revival of the eastern conquests of the Roman Empire. He got the republic of Venice out of his way by cutting it up between the French and Austria, securing the Ionian Islands and the Venetian fleet for France. This peace, the Peace of Campo Formio, was for both sides a thoroughly scoundrelly and ultimately a disastrous bargain. The new republic of France assisted in the

murder of an ancient republic—Napoleon carried his point against a considerable outcry in France—and Austria got Venetia, in which land in 1918 she was destined to bleed to death. There were also secret clauses by which both France and Austria were later to acquire South German territory. And it was not only the Roman push eastward that was now exciting Napoleon's brain. This was the land of Cæsar —and Cæsar was a bad example for the successful general of a not very stable republic.

Cæsar had come back to Rome from Gaul a hero and conqueror. His new imitator would come back from Egypt and India— Egypt and India were to be his Gaul. There was really none of the genius about which historians write so glibly in this decision. It was a tawdry and ill-conceived imitation. The elements of failure stared him in the face. The way to Egypt and India was by sea, and the British, in spite of two recent naval mutinies, whose importance Napoleon exaggerated, were stronger than the French at sea. Moreover, Egypt was a part of the Turkish empire, by no means a contemptible power in those days. Nevertheless he persuaded the Directory, which was dazzled by his Italian exploits, to let him go. An armada started from Toulon in May, 1798, captured Malta, and had the good luck to evade the British fleet and arrive at Alexandria. He landed his troops hurriedly, and the battle of the Pyramids made him master of Egypt.

The main British fleet at that time was in the Atlantic outside Cadiz, but the admiral had detached a force of his best ships, under Vice-Admiral Nelson—a man certainly as great a genius in naval affairs as was Napoleon in things military—to chase and engage the French flotilla.[1] For a time Nelson sought the French fleet in vain ; finally, on the evening of the first of August, he found it at anchor in Aboukir Bay. He had caught it unawares ; many of the men were ashore and a council was being held in the flagship. He had no charts, and it was a hazardous thing to sail into the shallow water in a bad light. The French admiral concluded, therefore, that he would

[1] See Mahan's *Life of Nelson*.

not attack before morning, and so made no haste in recalling his men aboard until it was too late to do so. Nelson struck at once—against the advice of some of his captains. One ship only went aground. She marked the shoal for the rest of the fleet. He sailed to the attack in a double line about sundown, putting the French between two fires. Night fell as the battle was joined ; the fight thundered and crashed in the darkness, until it was lit presently by the flames of burning French ships, and then by the flare of the French flag-ship, the *Orient*, blowing up. . . . Before midnight the Battle of the Nile was over, and Napoleon's fleet was destroyed. Napoleon was cut off from France.

Says Holland Rose, quoting Thiers, this Egyptian expedition was " the rashest attempt history records." Napoleon was left in Egypt with the Turks gathering against him and his army infected with the plague. Nevertheless, with a stupid sort of persistence, he went on for a time with this Eastern scheme. He gained a victory at Jaffa, and, being short of provisions, *massacred all his prisoners*. Then he tried to take Acre, where his own siege artillery, just captured at sea by the English, was used against him. Returning baffled to Egypt, he gained a brilliant victory over a Turkish force at Aboukir, and then, deserting the army of Egypt —it held on until 1801, when it capitulated to a British force—made his escape back to France (1799), narrowly missing capture by a British cruiser off Sicily.

Here was muddle and failure enough to discredit any general—had it been known. But the very British cruisers which came so near to catching him, helped him by preventing any real understanding of the Egyptian situation from reaching the French people. He could make a great flourish over the battle of Aboukir and conceal the shame and loss of Acre. Things were not going well with France just then. There had been military failures at several points ; much of Italy had been lost, Bonaparte's Italy, and this turned men's minds to him as the natural saviour of that situation ; moreover, there had been much peculation, and some of it was coming to light ; France was in one of her phases of financial scandal, and Napoleon had not filched ; the public was in that state of moral fatigue when a strong and honest man is called for, a wonderful, impossible healing man who will do everything for everybody. People, poor lazy souls, persuaded themselves that this specious young man with the hard face, so providentially back from Egypt, was the strong and honest man required—another Washington.

With Julius Cæsar rather than Washington at the back of his mind, Napoleon responded to the demand of his time. A conspiracy was carefully engineered to replace the Directory by three " Consuls "—everybody seems to have been reading far too much Roman history just then—of whom Napoleon was to be the chief. The working of that conspiracy is too intricate a story for our space ; it involved a Cromwell-like dispersal of the Lower House (the Council of Five Hundred), and in this affair Napoleon lost his nerve. The deputies shouted at him and hustled him, and he seems to have been very much frightened. He nearly fainted, stuttered, and could say nothing, but the situation was saved by his brother Lucien, who brought in the soldiers and dispersed the council. This little hitch did not affect the final success of the scheme. The three consuls were installed at the Luxembourg Palace, with two commissioners, to reconstruct the constitution.

With all his confidence restored and sure of the support of the people, who supposed him to be honest, patriotic, republican, and able to bring about a good peace, Napoleon took a high hand with his colleagues and the commissioners. A constitution was produced in which the chief executive officer was to be called the First Consul, with enormous powers. He was to be Napoleon ; this was part of the constitution. He was to be re-elected or replaced at the end of ten years. He was to be assisted by a Council of State, appointed by himself, which was to initiate legislation and send its proposals to two bodies, the Legislative Body (which could vote, but not discuss) and the Tribunate (which could discuss, but not vote), which were *selected* by an appointed Senate from a special class, the " notabilities of France," who were elected by the " notabilities of the departments," who were elected by the " notabilities of the commune," who were elected by the common voters. The suffrage for the election of the notabilities of the commune was universal. This was the sole vestige of democracy in the astounding pyramid. This constitution was chiefly the joint production of a worthy philosopher Sieyès, who was one of the three consuls, and Bonaparte. But so weary was France with her troubles and efforts, and so confident were men in the virtue and ability of this adventurer from Corsica, that when, at the birth of the nineteenth century, this constitution was submitted to the country, it was carried by 3,011,007 votes to 1,562. France put herself absolutely in Bonaparte's hands, and prepared to be peaceful, happy, and glorious.

§ 3

Now surely here was opportunity such as never came to man before. Here was a position *Napoleon First Consul 1799-1804.* in which a man might well bow himself in fear of himself, and search his heart and serve God and man to the utmost. The old order of things was dead or dying; strange new forces drove through the world seeking form and direction; the promise of a world republic and an enduring world peace whispered in a multitude of startled minds. Had this man had any profundity of vision, any power of creative imagination, had he been accessible to any disinterested ambition, he might have done work for mankind that would have made him the very sun of history. All Europe and America, stirred by the first promise of a new age, was waiting for him. Not France alone. France was in his hand, his instrument, to do with as he pleased, willing for peace, but tempered for war like an exquisite sword. There lacked nothing to this great occasion but a noble imagination. And failing that, Napoleon could do no more than strut upon the crest of this great mountain of opportunity like a cockerel on a dunghill. The figure he makes in history is one of almost incredible self-conceit, of vanity, greed, and cunning, of callous contempt and disregard of all who trusted him, and of a grandiose aping of Cæsar, Alexander, and Charlemagne which would be purely comic if it were not caked over with human blood. Until, as Victor Hugo said in his tremendous way, " God was bored by him," and he was kicked aside into a corner to end his days, explaining and explaining how very clever his worst blunders had been, prowling about his dismal hot island shooting birds

and squabbling meanly with an underbred gaoler who failed to show him " proper respect."

His career as First Consul was perhaps the least dishonourable phase in his career. He took the crumbling military affairs of the Directory in hand, and after a complicated campaign in North Italy brought matters to a head in the victory of Marengo, near Alessandria (1800). It was a victory that at some moments came very near disaster. In the December of the same year General Moreau, in the midst of snow, mud, and altogether abominable weather, inflicted an overwhelming defeat upon the Austrian army at Hohenlinden. If Napoleon had gained this battle, it would have counted among his most characteristic and brilliant exploits. These things made the hoped-for peace possible. In 1801 the preliminaries of peace with England and Austria were signed. Peace with England, the Treaty of Amiens, was concluded in 1802, and Napoleon was free to give himself to the creative statescraft of which France, and Europe through France, stood in need. The war had given the country extended boundaries; the treaty with England restored the colonial empire of France and left her in a position of security beyond the utmost dreams of Louis XIV. It was open to Napoleon to work out and consolidate the new order of things, to make a modern state that should become a beacon and inspiration to Europe and all the world.

He attempted nothing of the sort. He did not realize that there were such things as modern states in the scheme of possibility. His little imitative imagination was full of a deep cunning dream of being Cæsar over again—as if this universe would ever tolerate anything of that sort over again! He was scheming to make himself a real emperor, with a crown upon his head and all his rivals and school-fellows and friends at his feet. This could give him no fresh power that he did not already exercise, but it would be more splendid—it would astonish his mother. What response was there in a head of that sort for the splendid creative challenge of the time? But first France must be prosperous. France hungry would certainly not endure an emperor. He set himself to carry out an old scheme of roads that

Louis XV had approved ; he developed canals in imitation of the English canals ; he re-organized the police and made the country safe ; and, preparing the scene for his personal drama, he set himself to make Paris look like Rome, with classical arches, with classical columns. Admirable schemes for banking development were available, and he made use of them. In all these things he moved with the times, they would have happened—with less auto-cracy, with less centralization, if he had never been born. And he set himself to weaken the republicans whose fundamental convictions he was planning to outrage. He recalled the émigrés, provided they gave satisfactory assur-ances to respect the new régime. Many were very willing to come back on such terms, and let Bourbons be bygones. And he worked out a great reconciliation, a Concordat, with Rome. Rome was to support him, and he was to restore the authority of Rome in the parishes. France would never be obedient and manage-able, he thought ; she would never stand a new monarchy, without religion. " How can you have order in a state," he said, " without religion ? Society cannot exist without in-equality of fortunes, which cannot endure apart from religion. When one man is dying of hunger near another who is ill of surfeit, he cannot resign himself to this difference, unless there is an authority which declares—' God wills it thus : there must be poor and rich in the world : but hereafter and during all eternity the division of things will take place differently.' " Religion—especially of the later Roman brand—was, in fact, excellent stuff for keeping the common people quiet. In his early honest Jacobin days he had de-nounced it for that very reason.

Another great achievement which marks his imaginative scope and his estimate of human nature was the institution of the Legion of Honour, a scheme for decorating Frenchmen with bits of ribbon which was admirably cal-culated to divert ambitious men from subversive proceedings. (Washington, when he became President of the United States, abolished the only order that has ever adorned any citizen of the American republic, the Order of Cin-cinnatus, because he had no use for the snob in his fellow-man.)

And also Napoleon interested himself in Christian propaganda. Here is the Napoleonic view of the political uses of Christ, a view that has tainted all French missions from that time forth. " It is my wish to re-establish the institution for foreign missions ; for the religious missionaries may be very useful to me in Asia, Africa, and America, as I shall make them reconnoitre all the lands they visit. The sanctity of their dress will not only protect them, but serve to conceal their political and com-mercial investigations. The head of the missionary establishment shall reside no longer at Rome, but in Paris."

These are the ideas of a roguish merchant rather than a statesman. His treatment of education shows the same narrow vision, the same blindness to the realities of the dawn about him. Elementary education he neglected almost completely ; he left it to the conscience of the local authorities, and he provided that the teachers should be paid out of the fees of the scholars ; it is clear he did not want the common people to be educated ; he had no glimmering of any understanding why they should be ; but he interested himself in the provision of technical and higher schools because his state needed the services of clever, self-seeking, well-informed men. This was an astounding retro-gression from the great scheme, drafted by Condorcet for the Republic in 1792, for a com-plete system of free education for the entire nation. Slowly but steadfastly the project of Condorcet comes true ; the great nations of the world are being compelled to bring it nearer and nearer to realization, and the cheap devices of Napoleon pass out of our interest. As for the education of the mothers and wives of our race, this was the quality of Napoleon's wisdom : " I do not think that we need trouble ourselves with any plan of instruc-tion for young females, they cannot be better brought up than by their mothers. Public education is not suitable for them, because they are never called upon to act in public. Manners are all in all to them, and marriage is all they look to."

The First Consul was no kinder to women in the Code Napoléon. A wife, for example, had no control over her own property ; she was in her husband's hands. This code was the work very largely of the Council of State. Napoleon seems rather to have hindered than helped its deliberations. He would invade the session without notice, and favour its members with lengthy and egotistical monologues, frequently quite irrelevant to the matter in hand. The Council listened with profound respect ; it was all the Council could do. He would keep his councillors up to unearthly hours, and betray a simple pride in his superior wakefulness. He recalled these discussions with peculiar satisfaction in his later years, and remarked on one occasion that his glory consisted not in having won forty battles, but in having created the Code Napoléon. . . . So far as it substituted plain statements for inaccessible legal mysteries his Code was a good thing ; it gathered together, revised and made clear a vast disorderly accumulation of laws, old and new. Like all his constructive work, it made for immediate efficiency, it defined things and relations so that men could get to work upon them without further discussion. It was of less immediate practical importance that it frequently defined them wrongly. There was no intellectual power, as distinguished from intellectual energy, behind this codification. It took everything that existed for granted. ("Sa Majesté ne croit que ce qui est."[1]) The fundamental ideas of the civilized community and of the terms of human co-operation were in process of reconstruction all about Napoleon— and he never perceived it. He accepted a phase of change, and tried to fix it for ever. To this day France is cramped by this early nineteenth-century strait-waistcoat into which he clapped her. He fixed the status of women, the status of labourers, the status of the peasant ; they all struggle to this day in the net of his hard definitions.

So briskly and forcibly Napoleon set his mind, hard, clear, narrow, and base, to brace up France. That bracing up was only a part of the large egotistical schemes that dominated him. His imagination was set upon a new Cæsarism. In 1802 he got himself made First Consul for life, with the power of appointing a successor, and his clear intention of annexing Holland and Italy, in spite of his treaty obligations to keep them separate, made the Peace of Amiens totter

[1] Gourgaud, quoted by Holland Rose.

crazily from the very beginning. Since his schemes were bound to provoke a war with England, he should, at any cost, have kept quiet until he had brought his navy to a superiority over the British navy. He had the control of great resources for ship-building, the British government was a weak one, and three or four years would have sufficed to shift that balance. But in spite of his rough experiences in Egypt, he had never mastered the importance of sea power, and he had not the mental steadfastness for a waiting game and long preparation. In 1803 his occupation of Switzerland precipitated a crisis,[2] and war broke out again with England. The weak Addington in England gave place to the greater Pitt. The rest of Napoleon's story turns upon that war.

During the period of the Consulate, the First Consul was very active in advancing the fortunes of his brothers and sisters. This was quite human, very clannish and Corsican, and it helps us to understand just how he valued his position and the opportunities before him. Few of us can live without an audience, and the first audience of our childhood is our family ; most of us to the end of our days are swayed by the desire to impress our parents and brothers and sisters. Few "letters home" of successful men or women display the graces of modesty and self-forgetfulness. Only souls uplifted, as the soul of Jesus of Nazareth was uplifted, can say of all the world, " Behold my mother and my brethren ! " A large factor in the making of Napoleon was the desire to amaze, astonish, and subdue the minds of the Bonaparte family and their neighbours. He promoted his brothers ridiculously—for they were the most ordinary of men. The hungry Bonapartes were in luck. Surely all Corsica was open-mouthed ! But one person who knew him well was neither amazed nor subdued. This was his mother. He sent her money to spend and astonish the neighbours ; he exhorted her to make a display, to live as became the mother of so marvellous,

[2] The resumption of war was more directly due to the publication in France of the Sebastiani Report, a full account by a staff officer of the ports and strong places of Egypt and Syria. The alarm occasioned by this document hardened the determination of the British government to retain a garrison at Malta in spite of the obligation to evacuate it imposed by the Peace of Amiens.—P. G.

so world-shaking, a son. But the good lady, who had birched the Man of Destiny at the age of sixteen for grimacing at his grandmother, was neither dazzled nor deceived by him at the age of thirty-two. All France might worship him, but she had no illusions. She put by the money he sent her; she continued her customary economies. "When it is all over," she said, "you will be glad of my savings."

with the iron crown of Lombardy in the cathedral of Milan. All this mummery was to have a wonderful effect upon the imagination of western Germany, which was to remember that it too had been a part of the empire of Charlemagne.

The four daughter republics of France were now to become kingdoms; in 1806 he set up brother Louis in Holland and brother Joseph

Photo : Rischgitz Collection.

A CONTEMPORARY BRITISH IDEA OF THE VAST RAFT DESIGNED FOR THE CONVEYANCE OF NAPOLEON'S ARMY ACROSS THE CHANNEL, 1798.

§ 4

We will not detail the steps by which Napoleon became Emperor. His coronation was the most extraordinary revival of stale history that it is possible to imagine. Cæsar was no longer the model; Napoleon was playing now at being Charlemagne. He was crowned emperor, not indeed at Rome, but in the cathedral of Notre-Dame in Paris; the Pope (Pius VII) had been brought from Rome to perform the ceremony; and at the climax Napoleon I seized the crown, waved the Pope aside, and crowned himself. The attentive reader of this *Outline* will know that a thousand years before this would have had considerable significance; in 1804 it was just a ridiculous scene. In 1806 Napoleon revived another venerable antiquity, and, following still the footsteps of Charlemagne, crowned himself

Napoleon I Emperor, 1804-14.

in Naples. But the story of the subordinate kingdoms he created in Europe, helpful though this free handling of frontiers was towards the subsequent unification of Italy and Germany, is too complex and evanescent for this *Outline*.

The pact between the new Charlemagne and the new Leo did not hold good for very long. In 1807 he began to bully the Pope, and in 1811 he made him a close prisoner at Fontainebleau. There does not seem to have been much reason in these proceedings. They estranged all Catholic opinion, as his coronation had estranged all liberal opinion. He ceased to stand either for the old or the new. The new he had betrayed; the old he had failed to win. He stood at last for nothing but himself.

There seems to have been as little reason in the foreign policy that now plunged Europe into a fresh cycle of wars. Having quarrelled with Great Britain too soon, he (1804) assembled a vast army at Boulogne for the conquest of England, regardless of the naval situation. He even struck a medal and erected a column at Boulogne to commemorate the triumph of this projected invasion. In some " Napoleonic " way the British fleet was to be decoyed away, this army of Boulogne was to be smuggled across the Channel on a flotilla of rafts and boats, and London was to be captured before the fleet returned. At the same time his aggressions in South Germany forced Austria and Russia steadily into a coalition with Britain against him. In 1805 two fatal blows were struck at any hope he may have entertained of ultimate victory, by the British Admirals Calder and Nelson. In July the former inflicted a serious reverse upon the French fleet in the Bay of Biscay ; in October the latter destroyed the joint fleets of France and Spain at the Battle of Trafalgar. Nelson died splendidly upon the *Victory*, victorious. Thereafter Napoleon was left with Britain in pitiless opposition, unattainable and unconquerable, able to strike here or there against him along all the coasts of Europe.

But for awhile the mortal wound of Trafalgar was hidden from the French mind altogether. They heard merely that " storms have caused us to lose some ships of the line after an imprudent fight." After Calder's victory he had snatched his army from Boulogne, rushed it across half Europe, and defeated the Austrian and Russian armies at Ulm and Austerlitz. Under these inauspicious circumstances Prussia came into the war against him, and was utterly defeated and broken at the battle of Jena (1806). Although Austria and Prussia were broken, Russia was still a fighting power, and the next

ALEXANDER THE FIRST.

year was devoted to this unnecessary antagonist of the French, against whom an abler and saner ruler would never have fought at all. We cannot trace in any detail the difficulties of the Polish campaign against Russia ; Napoleon was roughly handled at Pultusk—which he announced in Paris as a brilliant victory—and again at Eylau. Then the Russians were defeated at Friedland (1807). As yet he had never touched Russian soil, the Russians were still as unbeaten as the British ; but now came an extraordinary piece of good fortune for Napoleon. By a mixture of boasting, subtlety, and flattery he won over the young and ambitious Tsar, Alexander I—he was just thirty years old— to an alliance. The two emperors met on a raft in the middle of the Niemen at Tilsit, and there came to an understanding.

This meeting was an occasion for sublime foolishness on the part of both of the principal actors. Alexander had imbibed much liberalism during his education at the court of Catherine II, and was all for freedom, education, and the new order of the world—subject to his own preeminence. " He would gladly have everyone free," said one of his early associates, " provided that everyone was prepared to do freely exactly what he wished." And he declared that he would have abolished serfdom if it had cost him his head—if only civilization had been more advanced. He made war against France, he said, because Napoleon was a tyrant, to free the French people. After Friedland he saw Napoleon in a different light. These two men met eleven days after that rout ; Alexander no doubt in the state of explanatory exaltation natural to his type during a mood of change.

To Napoleon the meeting must have been extremely gratifying. This was his first meeting with an emperor upon terms of equality. Like

Photo: *Rischgitz Collection.*
A REVIEW DAY UNDER THE EMPIRE: TROOPS PASSING THROUGH THE ARC DE TRIOMPHE DU CARROUSEL,
ONE OF NAPOLEON'S PSEUDO-CLASSICAL MONUMENTS.
(By Bellange, Versailles.)

victories; but now he was in the net again, and this time he was not to escape. Perhaps he would have wintered in Moscow, but the Russians smoked him out; they set fire to and burnt most of the city.[1]

It was late in October, too late altogether, before he decided to return. He made an ineffectual attempt to break through to a fresh line of retreat to the south-west, and then turned the faces of the survivors of his Grand Army towards the country they had devastated in their advance. Immense distances separated them from any friendly country. The winter was in no hurry. For a week the Grand Army struggled through mud; then came sharp frosts, and then the first flakes of snow, and then snow and snow. . . .

Slowly discipline dissolved. The hungry army spread itself out in search of supplies until it broke up into mere bands of marauders. The peasants, if only in self-defence, rose against them, waylaid them, and murdered them; a cloud of light cavalry—Scythians still —hunted them down. That retreat is one of the great tragedies of history.

[1] All this is admirably told in Tolstoy's wonderful *War and Peace.*

At last Napoleon and his staff and a handful of guards and attendants reappeared in Germany, bringing no army with him, followed only by straggling and demoralized bands. The Grand Army, retreating under Murat, reached Königsberg in a disciplined state, but only about a thousand strong out of six hundred thousand. From Königsberg Murat fell back to Posen. The Prussian contingent had surrendered to the Russians; the Austrians had gone homeward to the south. Everywhere scattered fugitives, ragged, lean, and frost-bitten, spread the news of the disaster.

Napoleon's magic was nearly exhausted. He did not dare to stay with his troops in Germany; he fled post haste to Paris. He began to order new levies and gather fresh armies amidst the wreckage of his world empire. Austria turned against him (1813); all Europe was eager to rise against this defaulting trustee of freedom, this mere usurper. He had betrayed the new order; the old order he had saved and revived now turned against him. Prussia rose, and the German "War of Liberation" began. Sweden came in against him. Later Holland revolted. Murat had rallied about 14,000 Frenchmen round his disciplined nucleus in Posen, and this force retreated through Germany, as a man might retreat who had ventured into a cageful of drugged lions and found that the effects of the drug were evaporating. Napoleon, with fresh forces, took up the chief command in the spring, won a great battle at Dresden, and then for a time he seems to have gone to pieces intellectually and morally. He became insanely irritable, with moods of inaction. He did little or nothing to follow up the Battle of Dresden. In September the "Battle of the Nations" was fought round and about Leipzig, after which the Saxons, who had hitherto followed his star, went over to the allies. The end of the year saw the French beaten back into France.

1814 was the closing campaign. France was invaded from the east and the south ; Swedes, Germans, Austrians, Russians, crossed the Rhine; British and Spanish came through the Pyrenees. Once more Napoleon fought brilliantly, but now he fought ineffectually. The eastern armies did not so much defeat him as push past him, and Paris capitulated in March. A little later at Fontainebleau the emperor abdicated.

In Provence, on his way out of the country, his life was endangered by a royalist mob.

§ 5

This was the natural and proper end of Napoleon's career. So this raid of an intolerable egotist across the disordered beginnings of a new time should have closed. At last he was suppressed. And had there been any real wisdom in the conduct of human affairs, we should now have to tell of the concentration of human science and will upon the task his treachery and vanity had interrupted, the task of building up a world system of justice and free effort in the place of the bankrupt ancient order. But we have to tell of nothing of the sort. Science and wisdom were conspicuously absent from the great council of the Allies. Came the vague humanitarianism and dreamy vanity of the Tsar Alexander, came the shaken Habsburgs of Austria, the resentful Hohenzollerns of Prussia, the aristocratic traditions of Britain, still badly frightened by the revolution and its conscience all awry with stolen commons and sweated factory children. No

The Hundred Days.

peoples came to the Congress, but only monarchs and foreign ministers ; and though you bray a foreign office in the bloodiest of war mortars, yet will its diplomatic habits not depart from it. The Congress had hardly assembled before the diplomatists set to work making secret bargains and treaties behind each other's back. Nothing could exceed the pompous triviality of the Congress which gathered at Vienna after a magnificent ceremonial visit of the allied sovereigns to London. The social side of the Congress was very strong, pretty ladies abounded, there was a galaxy of stars and uniforms, endless dinners and balls, a mighty flow of bright anecdotes and sparkling wit. Whether the two million dead men upon the battlefields laughed at the jokes, admired the assemblies, and marvelled at the diplomatists is beyond our knowledge. It is to be hoped their poor wraiths got something out of the display. The brightest spirit of the gathering was a certain Talleyrand, one of Napoleon's princes, a very brilliant man indeed, who had been a pre-revolutionary cleric, who had proposed the revolutionary confiscation of the church estates, and who was now for bringing back the Bourbons.

The allies, after the fashion of Peace Congresses, frittered away precious time in more and more rapacious disputes ; the Bourbons returned to France. Back came all the remainder of the émigrés with them, eager for restitution and revenge. One great egotism had been swept aside—only to reveal a crowd of meaner egotists. The new king was the brother of Louis XVI ; he had taken the title of Louis XVIII very eagerly so soon as he learnt that his little nephew (Louis XVII) was dead in the Temple. He was gouty and clumsy, not perhaps ill-disposed, but the symbol of the ancient system ; all that was new in France felt the heavy threat of reaction that came with him. This was no liberation, only a new tyranny, a heavy and inglorious tyranny instead of an active and splendid one. Was there no hope for France but this ? The Bourbons showed particular malice against the veterans of the Grand Army, and France was now full of returned prisoners of war, who found themselves under a cloud. Napoleon had been packed off to a little consolation empire of his own, upon the island of Elba. He was still to be called

Emperor and keep a certain state. The chivalry or whim of Alexander had insisted upon this treatment of his fallen rival. The Habsburgs, who had toadied to his success, had taken away his Habsburg empress—she went willingly enough—to Vienna, and he never saw her again.

After eleven months at Elba Napoleon judged that France had had enough of the Bourbons; he contrived to evade the British ships that watched his island, and reappeared at Cannes in France for his last gamble against Fate. His progress to Paris was a triumphal procession; he walked on white Bourbon cockades. For a hundred days, " the Hundred Days," he was master of France again.

His return created a perplexing position for any honest Frenchman. On the one hand there was this adventurer who had betrayed the republic; on the other the dull weight of old kingship restored. The allies would not hear of any further experiments in republicanism; it was the Bourbons or Napoleon. Is it any wonder that on the whole France was with

Napoleon? And he came back professing to be a changed man; there was to be no more despotism; he would respect the constitutional régime. . . .

He gathered an army, he made some attempts at peace with the allies; when he found these efforts ineffectual, he struck swiftly at the British, Dutch, and Prussians in Belgium, hoping to defeat them before the Austrians and Russians could come up. He did very nearly manage this. He beat the Prussians at Ligny, but not sufficiently; and then he was hopelessly defeated by the tenacity of the British under Wellington at Waterloo (1815); the Prussians, under Blücher, coming in on his right flank as the day wore on. Waterloo ended in a rout; it left Napoleon without support and without hope. France fell away from him again. Everyone who had joined him was eager now to attack him, and so efface that error. A provisional government in Paris ordered him to leave the country; was for giving him twenty-four hours to do it in.

He tried to get to America, but Rochefort,

The TRAIL of NAPOLEON

Showing the chief places of importance in his life

Note.— The map does not attempt to show precise routes. Nor does it cover in detail all Napoleon's movements (e.g. various returns to Paris.)

which he reached, was watched by British cruisers. France, now disillusioned and uncomfortably royalist again, was hot in pursuit of him. He went aboard a British frigate, the *Bellerophon*, asking to be received as a refugee, but being treated as a prisoner. He was taken to Plymouth, and from Plymouth straight to the lonely tropical island of St. Helena.

There he remained until his death from cancer in 1821, devoting himself chiefly to the preparation of his memoirs, which were designed to exhibit the chief events of his life in a misleading and attractive light and to minimise his worst blunders. One or two of the men with him recorded his conversations and set down their impressions of him.

These works had a great vogue in France and Europe. The Holy Alliance of the monarchs of Russia, Austria, and Prussia (to which other monarchs were invited to adhere) laboured under the delusion that in defeating Napoleon they had defeated the Revolution, turned back the clock of Fate, and restored Grand Monarchy —on a sanctified basis—for evermore. The cardinal document of the scheme of the Holy Alliance is said to have been drawn up under the inspiration of the Baroness von Krüdener, who seems to have been a sort of spiritual director to the Russian emperor. It opened, " In the name of the Most Holy and Indivisible Trinity," and it bound the participating monarchs " regarding themselves towards their subjects and armies as fathers of families," and " considering each other as fellow-countrymen," to sustain each other, protect true religion, and urge their subjects to strengthen and exercise themselves in Christian duties. Christ, it was declared, was the real King of all Christian peoples, a very Merovingian king, one may remark, with these reigning sovereigns as his mayors of the palace. The British King had no power to sign this document, the Pope and the Sultan were not asked ; the rest of the European monarchs, including the King of France, adhered. But the King of Poland did not sign because there was no king in Poland ; Alexander, in a mood of pious abstraction, was sitting on the greater part of Poland. The Holy Alliance never became an actual legal alliance of states ; it gave place to a real league of nations, the Concert of Europe, which

France joined in 1818, and from which Britain withdrew in 1822.

There followed a period of peace and dull oppression in Europe over which Alexander brooded in attitudes of orthodoxy, piety, and unquenchable self-satisfaction. Many people in those hopeless days were disposed to regard even Napoleon with charity, and to accept his claim that in some inexplicable way he had, in asserting himself, been asserting the revolution and France. A cult of him as of something mystically heroic grew up after his death.[1]

§ 6

In the long perspectives of history the cult of Napoleon, and his peculiar effect upon certain types of mind, is of far more interest and far more importance than his actual adventures. The world has largely recovered from the mischief he did ; perhaps that amount of mischief had to be done by some agency ; perhaps his career, or some such career, was a necessary consequence of the world's mental unpreparedness for the crisis of the revolution. But that his peculiar personality should dominate the imaginations of great numbers of people, throws a light upon factors of enduring significance in our human problem.

The Cult of the Napoleonic.

It would be difficult to find a human being less likely to arouse affection. One reads in vain through the monstrous accumulations of Napoleonic literature for a single record of self-forgetfulness. Laughter is one great difference between man and the lower animals, one method of our brotherhood, and there is no evidence that Napoleon ever laughed. Nor can we imagine another of the most beautiful of human expressions upon the face of this saturnine egotist, that expression of disinterested interest that one sees in the face of an artist or artisan " lost," as we say, in his work. Out of his portraits he looks at us with a thin scorn upon his lips, the scorn of the criminal who believes that he can certainly cheat such fools as we are, and withal with a certain uneasiness in his eyes. That uneasiness haunts all his portraits. Are we really convinced he is quite right ? Are his laurels straight ? He

[1] The best textbook to follow in expanding this chapter is W. A. Phillips' *Confederation of Europe*.

trouble to us all. Our uneasiness grows. Napoleon was free from it. The cultivation of the Napoleonic legend seems to offer a kind of refuge. From salvation.

In that antithesis lies the essential historical importance of Napoleon. His career marks the beginning of a new phase in the relations of strong and able and energetic and advantageously placed men to the main mass of mankind. They are robbed of self-deception ; they must either serve or openly defy the idea of service. They must be humble or Napoleonic ; there is no more service with privilege and pride. Napoleon adorned himself with ancient titles and antiquated robes, but the more he brought himself into contact with tradition, the more manifestly he displayed himself as something new. In the Tsar Alexander I, who was never direct, this direct new imperialism met the old.

Photo: Rischgitz Collection.
NAPOLEON AT ST. HELENA: A...
AN ENGLISH OFFICE...

Hitherto the kings and potentates of the world had taken themselves in good faith, had had the support of religion in their consciences, had believed they were serving God in their kingship, and that they were necessary to mankind and beneficial to mankind. In many cases they were no doubt swayed by very mixed motives, his majesty had " weaknesses," his majesty almost always had a sensitive personal vanity. Sometimes, indeed, some born rascal like Charles II of England would have the grace or the gracelessness to laugh at himself, but the generality of kings and tyrants had the profoundest faith in themselves, and were sustained by the sincere faith of their loyal supporters. The Emperor Charles V and his son Philip II, Charles I of England, Louis XIV, and the Tsar Alexander were all inspired by a complete assurance of

their ow...
oppositi...
wickedn...
punishe...
Napoleo...
individu...
men. H...

delusi...
not ...
Pruss...
but f...
uncha...
" Wh...
mona...

So...
apolo...
we sh...
But s...
any ...
ancie...
tradi...
and ...
more...
affai...
whic...

had a vast contempt for man in general and men in particular, a contempt that took him at last to St. Helena, that same contempt that fills our jails with forgers, poisoners, and the like victims of self-conceit. There is no proof that this unbrotherly, unhumorous egotist was ever sincerely loved by any human being. The Empress Josephine was unfaithful to him as he to her. His young Austrian wife would not accompany him to Elba. A certain Polish countess followed him thither, but not, it would seem, for love, but on account of the son she

fostered legend of an incredibly clever, recklessly brave little man, a little pet of a man, who was devoted to France and them.

Why, then, is there an enormous cult of Napoleon, an endless writing of books about him, an insatiable collecting of relics and documents, a kind of worship of his memory ? Marat was a far more noble, persistent, subtle, and pathetic figure ; Talleyrand a greater statesman and a much more amusing personality ; Moreau and Hoche abler leaders of armies ; his rival, the Tsar Alexander, as egotistical, more success-

Photo: Rischgitz Collection.
NAPOLEON DISTRIBUTING EAGLE STANDARDS TO THE ARMY, CHAMP DE MARS.
By David (Versailles.)

had borne him. She wanted settlements. She stayed only two days with him. He had never even a dog to love him. He estranged most of his colleagues and fellow-generals. He had no familiar friend. No one who knew him felt safe with him. In his intimacy, his unflinching self-concentration must have been a terrible bore. His personal habits were unpleasant ; the moodiness of bad health came to him early. True it is that his soldiers, who, save for a few rare melodramatic encounters, saw nothing of him, idolized their " Little Corporal." But it was not him they idolized, but a carefully

ful, more emotional, and with a finer imagination. Are men dazzled simply by the scale of his flounderings, by the mere vastness of his notoriety ?

No doubt scale has something to do with the matter ; he was a " record," the record plunger ; but there is something more in it than that. There is an appeal in Napoleon to something deeper and more fundamental in human nature than mere astonishment at bigness. His very deficiencies bring out starkly certain qualities that lurk suppressed and hidden in us all. He was unhampered. He had never a gleam of

religion or affection or the sense of duty. H
was, as few men are or dare to be, a scoundre
bright and complete. Most of us are co
strained more or less and now and then to serv
God or our fellow-men, to do things disi
terestedly, to behave decently when no one
watching us. He was not so constraine
Most men do a little regret and resent the
good deeds, and find a secret satisfaction
their unpunished bad ones. The early pala
lithic strain is still strong in us; we a
being made over, slowly and reluctantly, ir

EUROPE after the Congress

Boundary of the German
Confederation ————

J.F.H.

social and fraternal creatures. Few of
thoroughly enjoy being good citizens.
moral conflicts, therefore, are intricate and co
the constant effort to explain to ourselves
others that there is a fine moral purpose in
shirking of our duty or in that self-seeking
We are all regretfully of the race of
Alexander, who destroyed the freedom of Pol
annexed Finland, and secured his imp
predominance piously, "in the name of
Most Holy and Indivisible Trinity"—whe
would have been far more agreeable to
done it in the name of the most Holy
Magnificent Alexander. There was non

§ 7[1]

For nearly forty years the idea of the Holy
Alliance, the Concert of Europe which arose out
The Map of Europe in 1815. of it, and the series of congresses
and conferences that succeeded the
concert, kept an insecure peace in
war-exhausted Europe. Two main things
prevented that period from being a complete
social and inter-
national peace, and
prepared the way
for the cycle of
wars between 1854
and 1871. The
first of these was
the tendency of
the royal courts
concerned, towards
the restoration of
unfair privilege
and interference
with freedom of
thought and writ-
ing and teaching.
The second was the
impossible system
of boundaries
drawn by the dip-
lomatists of
Vienna.

The obstinate
disposition of mon-
archy to march
back towards past
conditions was
first and most par-

Photo: Rischgitz Collection.
THE TOMB OF NAPOLEON AT THE HÔTEL DES INVALIDES.
Note the battle names round the base of the Sarcophagus, and the banners
in the background.

ticularly manifest in Spain. Here even the
Inquisition was restored. Across the Atlantic
the Spanish colonies had followed the example
of the United States and revolted against
the European Great Power system, when
Napoleon set up his brother Joseph upon the
Spanish throne in 1810. The Washington of
South America was General Bolivar. Spain
was unable to suppress this revolt, it dragged

[1] W. A. Phillips' *Confederation of Europe* is the
leading textbook here. H. E. Egerton's *British Foreign Policy in the Nineteenth Century* and L. S. Woolf's
International Government are very illuminating. See
also Thatcher and Schwill's convenient *General History
of Europe* and Philip Guedalla's *Partition of Europe :
1715-1815*.

on much as the United States War of Independence had dragged on, and at last the suggestion
was made by Austria in accordance with the
spirit of the Holy Alliance, that the European
monarchs should assist Spain in this struggle.
This was opposed by Britain in Europe, but it
was the prompt action of President Monroe of
the United States in 1823 which conclusively
warned off this
projected monar-
chist restoration.
He announced that
the United States
would regard any
extension of the
European system
in the Western
Hemisphere as a
hostile act. Thus
arose the Monroe
Doctrine, which
has kept the Great
Power System out
of America for
nearly a hundred
years, and per-
mitted the new
states of Spanish
America to work
out their destinies
along their own
lines. But if Spa-
nish monarchism
lost its colonies, it
could at least,
under the protec-
tion of the Concert of Europe, do what it
chose in Europe. A popular insurrection in
Spain was crushed by a French army in 1823,
with a mandate from a European congress,
and simultaneously Austria suppressed a revolution in Naples. The moving spirit in this
conspiracy of governments against peoples was
the Austrian statesman, Metternich.

In 1824 Louis XVIII died, and was succeeded
by that Count d'Artois whom we have seen
hovering as an émigré on the French frontiers
in 1789 ; he took the title of Charles X. Charles
set himself to destroy the liberty of the press
and universities, and to restore absolute government ; the sum of a billion francs was voted to

compensate the nobles for the château burnings and sequestrations of 1789. In 1830 Paris rose against this embodiment of the ancient régime, and replaced him by the son of that sinister Philip, Duke of Orleans, whose execution was one of the brightest achievements of the Terror. The other Continental monarchies, in face of the open approval of the revolution by Great Britain and a strong liberal ferment in Germany and Austria, did not interfere in this affair. After all, France was still a monarchy. This young man, Louis Philippe (1830–48), remained the constitutional king of France for eighteen years. He went down in 1848, a very eventful year for Europe, of which we shall tell in the next chapter.

Such were the uneasy swayings of the peace of the Congress of Vienna, which were provoked by the reactionary proceedings to which, sooner or later, all monarchist courts seem by their very nature to gravitate. The stresses that arose from the unscientific map-making of the diplomatists gathered force more deliberately, but they were even more dangerous to the peace of mankind. It is extraordinarily inconvenient to administer together the affairs of peoples speaking different languages and so reading different literatures and having different general ideas, especially if those differences are exacerbated by religious disputes. Only some strong mutual interest, such as the common defensive needs of the Swiss mountaineers, can justify a close linking of peoples of dissimilar languages and faiths ; and even in Switzerland there is the utmost local autonomy. Ultimately, when the Great Power tradition is certainly dead and buried, those Swiss populations may gravitate towards their natural affinities in Germany, France, and Italy. When, as in Macedonia, populations are mixed in a patchwork of villages and districts, the cantonal system is imperatively needed. But if the reader will look at the map of Europe as the Congress of Vienna drew it, he will see that this gathering seems almost as if it had planned the maximum of local exasperation. It destroyed the Dutch Republic, quite needlessly, it lumped together the Protestant Dutch with the French-speaking Catholics of the old Spanish (Austrian) Netherlands, and set up a kingdom of the Netherlands. It handed over not merely the old republic of Venice, but all of North Italy as far as Milan to the German-speaking Austrians. French-speaking Savoy it combined with pieces of Italy to restore the kingdom of Sardinia.[1] Austria and Hungary, already a sufficiently explosive mixture of discordant nationalities, Germans, Hungarians, Czecho-Slovaks, Jugo-Slavs, Roumanians, and now Italians, was made still more impossible by confirming Austria's Polish acquisitions of 1772 and 1795. The Polish people, being catholic and republican-spirited, were chiefly given over to the less civilized rule of the Greek-orthodox Tsar, but important districts went to Protestant Prussia. The Tsar was also confirmed in his acquisition of the entirely alien Finns. The very dissimilar Norwegian and Swedish peoples were bound together under one king. Germany, the reader will see, was left in a particularly dangerous state of muddle. Prussia and Austria were both partly in and partly out of a German confederation, which included a multitude of minor states. The King of Denmark came into the German confederation by virtue of certain German-speaking possessions in Holstein. Luxembourg was included in the German Confederation, though its ruler was also King of the Netherlands, and though many of its people talked French. Here was a crazy tangle, an outrage on the common sense of mankind, a preposterous disregard of the fact that the people who talk German and base their ideas on German literature, the people who talk Italian and base their ideas on Italian literature, and the people who talk Polish and base their ideas on Polish literature, will all be far better off and most helpful and least obnoxious to the rest of mankind if they conduct their own affairs in their own idiom within the ring-fence of their own speech. Is it any wonder that one of the most popular songs in Germany during this period declared that wherever the German tongue was spoken, there was the German Fatherland ?

[1] The Dukes of Savoy (ancestors of the present Italian kings) had been astride the Alps, ruling in France and Italy, for centuries ; and their strategic position had long given them a European importance. The Dukes of Savoy had been kings since 1713, first as Kings of Sicily, 1713–20, and then (when Sicily was exchanged for Sardinia in 1720) as Kings of Sardinia.—E. B.

The NATURAL POLITICAL MAP of EUROPE

Latins
{
French (and Walloons) ....
Spanish ....
Italians ....
Rumanians ....
}

Teutons
{
Germans ....
Dutch (and Flemish) ....
English ....
Scandinavian ....
}

Slavs
{
Russians ....
Poles ....
Ukrainians (Ruthenes) ....
Czechs & Slovaks ....
South Slavs (Serbs, Croats, Slovenes, Monteneg.) ....
Bulgars ....
}

Greeks ....
Albanians ....
Magyars ....
Turks ....

In certain areas the mixture of peoples necessitates a cantonal system. Some of the more obvious of these are shown thus:—

[MACEDONIA] Bulgarians, Serbs, Turks, &c.

Even to-day men are still reluctant to recognize that areas of government are not matters for the bargaining and interplay of tsars and kings and foreign offices. There is *a natural and necessary political map of the world* which transcends these things. There is *a best way possible* of dividing any part of the world into administrative areas, and a best sort of possible government for every area, having regard to the speech and race of its inhabitants, and it is the common concern of all men of intelligence to secure those divisions and establish those forms of government quite irrespective of diplomacies and flags, "claims" and melo-dramatic "loyalties" and the existing political map of the world. The natural political map of the world insists upon itself. It heaves and frets beneath the artificial political map like some misfitted giant. In 1830 French-speaking Belgium, stirred up by the current revolution in France, revolted against its Dutch association in the kingdom of the Netherlands.[1] The Powers, terrified at the possibility of a republic and of annexation to France, hurried in to pacify this situation, and gave the Belgians a monarch from that rich breeding-ground of monarchs, Germany, Leopold I of Saxe-Coburg Gotha. There were also ineffectual revolts in Italy and Germany in 1830, and a much more serious one in Russian Poland. A republican government held out in Warsaw for a year against Nicholas I (who succeeded Alexander in 1825), and was then stamped out of existence with great violence and cruelty. The Polish language was banned, and the Greek Orthodox church was substituted for the Roman Catholic as the State religion. . . .

An outbreak of the natural political map of the world, which occurred in 1821, ultimately secured the support of England, France, and Russia. This was the insurrection of the Greeks against the Turks. For six years they fought a desperate war, while the governments of Europe looked on. Liberal opinion protested against this inactivity; volunteers from every European country joined the insurgents, and at last Britain, France, and Russia took joint action. The Turkish fleet was destroyed by the French and English at the Battle of Navarino (1827), and the Tsar invaded Turkey. By the Treaty of Adrianople (1829) Greece was declared free, but she was not permitted to resume her ancient republican traditions. There is a sort of historical indecency in a Greek monarchy. But a Greek republic would have been dangerous to all monarchy in a Europe that fretted under the ideas of the Holy Alliance. One monarch makes many. A German king was found for Greece, one Prince Otto of Bavaria, slightly demented, but quite royal—he gave way to delusions about his divine right, and was ejected in 1862—and Christian governors were set up in the Danubian provinces (which are now Roumania) and Serbia (a part of the Jugo-Slav region). This was a partial concession to the natural political map, but much blood had still to run before the Turk was altogether expelled from these lands. A little later the natural political map was to assert itself in Italy and Germany.

---

[1] Also Holland was Protestant and Belgium Catholic. —P. G.

XXXIX

THE REALITIES AND IMAGINATIONS OF THE NINETEENTH CENTURY[1]

§ 1

THE career and personality of Napoleon I bulks disproportionately in the nineteenth-century histories. He was of little significance to the broad onward movement of human affairs; he was an interruption, a reminder of latent evils, a thing like the bacterium of some pestilence. Even regarded as a pestilence, he was not of supreme rank; he killed far fewer people than the influenza epidemic of 1918, and produced less political and social disruption than the plague of Justinian. Some such interlude had to happen, and some such patched-up settlement of Europe as the Concert of Europe, because there was no worked-out system of ideas upon which a new world could be constructed. And even the Concert of Europe had in it an element of progress. It did at least set aside the individualism of Machiavellian monarchy and declare that there was a human, or at any rate a European, commonweal. If it divided the world among the kings, it made respectful gestures towards human unity and the service of God and man.

The Mechanical Revolution.

The permanently effective task before mankind which had to be done before any new and enduring social and political edifice was possible, the task upon which the human intelligence is, with many interruptions and amidst much anger and turmoil, still engaged, was, and is, the task of working out and applying a Science of Property as a basis for freedom and social justice, a Science of Currency to ensure and preserve an efficient economic medium, a Science of Government and Collective Operations whereby in every community men may learn to pursue their common interests in harmony, a Science of World Politics, through which the stark waste and cruelty of warfare between races, peoples, and nations may be brought to an end and the common interests of mankind brought under a common control, and, above all, a worldwide System of Education to sustain the will and interest of men in their common human adventure. The real makers of history in the nineteenth century, the people whose consequences will be determining human life a century ahead, were those who advanced and contributed to this fivefold constructive effort. Compared to them, the foreign ministers and " statesmen " and politicians of this period were no more than a number of troublesome and occasionally incendiary schoolboys—and a few metal thieves —playing about and doing transitory mischief amidst the accumulating materials upon the site of a great building whose nature they did not understand.

And while throughout the nineteenth century the mind of Western civilization, which the Renascence had released, gathered itself to the task of creative social and political reconstruction that still lies before it, there swept across the world a wave of universal change in human power and the material conditions of life that the first scientific efforts of that liberated mind had made possible. The prophecies of Roger Bacon began to live in reality. The accumulating knowledge and confidence of the little succession of men who had been carrying on the development of science, now began to bear fruit that common men could understand. The most obvious firstfruit was the steam-engine. The first steam-engines in the eighteenth century were pumping engines, used to keep water out of the newly opened coal mines. These coal mines were being worked to supply coke for iron smelting, for which wood-charcoal had previously been employed. It was James Watt, a mathematical instrument maker of Glasgow, who improved this steam-pumping engine and made it available

[1] An excellent book on the substance of this chapter is F. S. Marvin's *Century of Hope*. Another is R. A. Gregory's *Discovery*. See also Seignobos' *Political History of Contemporary Europe*.

for the driving of machinery. The first engine so employed was installed in a cotton mill in Nottingham in 1785. In 1804 Trevithick adapted the Watt engine to transport, and made the first locomotive. In 1830 the first railway, between Liverpool and Manchester, was opened, and Stephenson's "Rocket," with a thirteen-ton train, got up to a speed of forty-four miles per hour. From 1830 onward railways multiplied. By the middle of the century a network of railways had spread all over Europe.

Here was a sudden change in what had long been a fixed condition of human life, the maxi-

made it possible to carry out administrative work in areas ten times as great as any that had hitherto been workable under one administration. The full significance of that possibility in Europe still remains to be realized. Europe is still netted in boundaries drawn in the horse and road era. In America the effects were immediate. To the United States of America, sprawling westward, it meant the possibility of a continuous access to Washington, however far the frontier travelled across the continent. It meant unity, sustained on a scale that would otherwise have been impossible.

The steamboat was, if anything, a little ahead

Photo: Rischgitz Collection.

OPENING OF THE GLASGOW AND GARNKIRK RAILWAY, 1831.

mum rate of land transport. After the Russian disaster, Napoleon travelled from near Vilna to Paris in 312 hours. This was a journey of about 1,400 miles. He was travelling with every conceivable advantage, and he averaged under five miles an hour. An ordinary traveller could not have done this distance in twice the time. These were about the same maximum rates of travel as held good between Rome and Gaul in the first century A.D., or between Sardis and Susa in the fourth century B.C. Then suddenly came a tremendous change. The railways reduced this journey for any ordinary traveller to less than forty-eight hours. That is to say, they reduced the chief European distances to about a tenth of what they had been. They

of the steam-engine in its earlier phases. There was a steamboat, the *Charlotte Dundas*, on the Firth of Clyde Canal in 1802, and in 1807 an American named Fulton had a paying steamer, *The Clermont*, with British-built engines, upon the Hudson river above New York. The first steamship to put to sea was also an American, the *Phœnix*, which went from New York (Hoboken) to Philadelphia. So, too, was the first ship using steam (she also had sails) to cross the Atlantic, the *Savannah* (1819). All these were paddle-wheel boats, and paddle-wheel boats are not adapted to work in heavy seas. The paddles smash too easily, and the boat is then disabled. The screw steamship followed rather slowly. Many difficulties had to be surmounted before the screw was a practicable thing. Not until the middle of the century did the tonnage of steamships upon the sea begin to overhaul that of sailing-ships. After that the evolution in sea transport was rapid. For the first time men began to cross the seas and oceans with some certainty as to the date of their arrival. The transatlantic crossing, which had been an uncertain adventure of several weeks—which might stretch to months—was accelerated, until in 1910 it was brought down, in the case of the fastest boats, to under five days, with a practically notifiable hour of arrival.

Photo : Rischgitz Collection.
THE "SAVANNAH," THE FIRST STEAMER TO CROSS THE ATLANTIC FROM AMERICA.

All over the oceans there was the same reduction in the time and the same increase in the certainty of human communications.

Concurrently with the development of steam transport upon land and sea a new and striking addition to the facilities of human intercourse arose out of the investigations of Volta, Galvani, and Faraday into various electrical phenomena. The electric telegraph came into existence in 1835. The first underseas cable was laid in 1851 between France and England. In a few years the telegraph system had spread over the civilized world, and news which had hitherto travelled slowly from point to point became practically simultaneous throughout the earth.

These things, the steam railway and the electric telegraph, were to the popular imagination of the middle nineteenth century the most striking and revolutionary of inventions, but they were only the most conspicuous and clumsy firstfruits of a far more extensive process. Technical knowledge and skill were developing with an extraordinary rapidity, and to an extraordinary extent measured by the progress of any previous age. Far less conspicuous at first in everyday life, but finally far more important, was the extension of man's power over various structural materials. Before the middle of the eighteenth century iron was reduced from its ores by means of wood-charcoal, was handled in small pieces, and hammered and wrought into shape. It was material for a craftsman. Quality and treatment were enormously dependent upon the experience and sagacity of the individual iron-worker. The largest masses of iron that could be dealt with under those conditions amounted at most (in the sixteenth century) to two or three tons. (There was a very definite upward limit, therefore, to the size of cannon.) The blast furnace arose in the eighteenth century, and developed with the use of coke. Not before the eighteenth century do we find rolled sheet iron (1728) and rolled rods and bars (1783). Nasmyth's steam hammer came as late as 1838. The ancient world could not use steam because of its metallurgical inferiority. The steam-engine, even the primitive pumping engine, could not develop before sheet iron was available. The early engines seem to the modern eye very pitiful and clumsy bits of ironmongery, but they were the utmost that the metallurgical science of the time could do. As late as 1856 came the Bessemer process, and presently (1864) the open-hearth process, in which steel and every sort of iron could be melted, purified, and cast in a manner and upon a scale hitherto unheard of. To-day in the electric furnace one may see tons of incandescent steel swirling about like boiling milk in a saucepan. Nothing in the previous practical advances of mankind is comparable in its consequences to the complete mastery over enormous masses of steel and iron and over their texture and quality which man has now achieved. The railways and early engines of

NINETEENTH-CENTURY PATRIOTIC IMPERIALISM: THE GERMANIA MONUMENT
AT BINGEN.

all sorts were the mere first triumphs of the new metallurgical methods. Presently came ships of iron and steel, vast bridges, and a new way of building with steel upon a gigantic scale. Men realized too late that they had planned their railways with far too timid a gauge, that they could have organized their travelling with far more steadiness and comfort upon a much bigger scale.

Before the nineteenth century there were no ships in the world much over 2,000 tons burthen; now there is nothing wonderful about a 50,000-ton liner. There are people who sneer at this kind of progress as being a progress in "mere size," but that sort of sneering merely marks the intellectual limitations of those who indulge in it. The great ship or the steel-frame building is not, as they imagine, a magnified version of the small ship or building of the past; it is a thing different in kind, more lightly and strongly built, of finer and stronger materials; instead of being a thing of precedent and rule-of-thumb, it is a thing of subtle and intricate calculation. In the old house or ship, matter was dominant—the material and its needs had to be slavishly obeyed; in the new, matter has been captured, changed, coerced. Think of the coal and iron and sand dragged out of the banks and pits, wrenched, wrought, molten and cast, to be flung at last, a slender, glittering pinnacle of steel and glass, six hundred feet above the crowded city!

We have given these particulars of the advance in man's knowledge of the metallurgy of steel and its results by way of illustration. A parallel story could be told of the metallurgy of copper and tin, and of a multitude of metals, nickel and aluminium to name but two, unknown before the nineteenth century dawned. It is in this great and growing mastery over substances, over different sorts of glass, over rocks and plasters and the like, over colours and textures, that the main triumphs of the mechanical revolution have thus far been achieved. Yet we are still in the stage of the firstfruits in the matter. We have the power, but we have still to learn how to use our power. Many of the first employments of these gifts of science have been vulgar, tawdry, stupid or horrible. The artist and the adaptor have still hardly begun to work with the end-less variety of substances now at their disposal.

Concurrently with this extension of mechanical possibilities the new science of electricity grew up. It was only in the eighties of the nineteenth century that this body of inquiry began to yield results to impress the vulgar mind. Then suddenly came electric light and electric traction; and the transmutation of forces, the possibility of sending *power*, that could be changed into mechanical motion or light or heat as one chose, along a copper wire, as water is sent along a pipe, began to come through to the ideas of ordinary people. . . .

The British and the French were at first the leading peoples in this great proliferation of knowledge; but presently the Germans, who had learnt humility under Napoleon, showed such zeal and pertinacity in scientific inquiry as to overhaul these leaders. British science was largely the creation of Englishmen and Scotchmen[1] working outside the ordinary centres of erudition.[2] We have told how in England the universities after the reformation ceased to have a wide popular appeal, how they became the educational preserve of the nobility and gentry, and the strongholds of the established church. A pompous and unintelligent classical pretentiousness dominated them, and they dominated the schools of the middle and upper classes. The only knowledge recognized was an uncritical textual knowledge of a selection of Latin and Greek classics, and the test of a good style was its abundance of quotations, allusions, and stereotyped expressions. The early development of British science went on, therefore, in spite of the formal educational organization, and in the teeth of the bitter hostility of the teaching and clerical professions. French education, too, was dominated by the classical tradition of the Jesuits, and consequently it was not difficult for the Germans to organize a body of investigators, small indeed in relation to the possibilities of the case, but

[1] But note Boyle and Sir Wm. Hamilton as conspicuous scientific men who were Irishmen.

[2] It is worth noting that nearly all the great inventors in England during the eighteenth century were working men, that inventions proceeded from the workshop, and not from the laboratory. It is also worth noting that only two of these inventors accumulated fortunes and founded families.—E. B.

large in proportion to the little band of British and French inventors and experimentalists. And though this work of research and experiment was making Britain and France the most rich and powerful countries in the world, it was not making scientific and inventive men rich and powerful. There is a necessary unworldliness about a sincere scientific man; he is too preoccupied with his research to plan and scheme how to make money out of it. The economic exploitation of his discoveries falls very easily and naturally, therefore, into the hands of a more acquisitive type; and so we find that the crops of rich men which every fresh phase of scientific and technical progress has produced in Great Britain, though they have not displayed quite the same passionate desire to insult and kill the goose that laid the national golden eggs as the scholastic and clerical professions, have been quite content to let that profitable creature starve. Inventors and discoverers came by nature, they thought, for cleverer people to profit by.

In this matter the Germans were a little wiser. The German " learned " did not display the same vehement hatred of the new learning. They permitted its development. The German business man and manufacturer again had not quite the same contempt for the man of science as had his British competitor. Knowledge, these Germans believed, might be a cultivated crop, responsive to fertilizers. They did concede, therefore, a certain amount of opportunity to the scientific mind; their public expenditure on scientific work was relatively greater, and this expenditure was abundantly rewarded. By the latter half of the nineteenth century the German scientific worker had made German a necessary language for every science student who wished to keep abreast with the latest work in his department, and in certain branches, and particularly in chemistry, Germany acquired a very great superiority over her Western neighbours. The scientific effort of the sixties and seventies in Germany began to tell after the eighties, and the Germans gained steadily upon Britain and France in technical and industrial prosperity.

In an Outline of History such as this it is impossible to trace the network of complex mental processes that led to the incessant extension of knowledge and power that is now going on; all we can do here is to call the reader's attention to the most salient turning-points that finally led the toboggan of human affairs into its present swift ice-run of progress. We have told of the first release of human curiosity and of the beginnings of systematic inquiry and experiment. We have told, too, how, when the plutocratic Roman system and its resultant imperialism had come and gone again, this process of inquiry was renewed. We have told of the escape of investigation from ideas of secrecy and personal advantage to the idea of publication and a brotherhood of knowledge, and we have noted the foundation of the British Royal Society, the Florentine Society, and their like as a consequence of this socializing of thought. These things were the roots of the mechanical revolution, and so long as the root of pure scientific inquiry lives, that revolution will progress. The mechanical revolution itself began, we may say, with the exhaustion of the wood supply for the ironworks of England. This led to the use of coal, the coal mine led to the simple pumping engine; the development of the pumping engine by Watt into a machine-driving engine led on to the locomotive and the steamship. This was the first phase of a great expansion in the use of steam. A second phase in the mechanical revolution began with the application of electrical science to practical problems and the development of electric lighting, power-transmission, and traction.

A third phase is to be distinguished when in the eighties a new type of engine came into use, an engine in which the expansive force of an explosive mixture replaced the expansive force of steam. The light, highly efficient engines that were thus made possible were applied to the automobile, and developed at last to reach such a pitch of lightness and efficiency as to render flight—long known to be possible—a practical achievement. A successful flying-machine—but not a machine large enough to take up a human body—was made by Professor Langley of the Smithsonian Institute of Washington as early as 1897. By 1909 the aeroplane was available for human locomotion. There had seemed to be a pause in the increase of more clearly. Human beings were no longer wanted as a source of mere indiscriminated power. What could be done mechanically by a human being could be done faster and better by a machine. The human being was needed now only where choice and intelligence had to be exercised. Human beings were wanted only as human beings. The *drudge*, on whom all the previous civilizations had rested, the creature of mere obedience, the man whose brains were superfluous, had become unnecessary to the welfare of mankind.

This was as true of such ancient industries as agriculture and mining as it was of the newest metallurgical processes. For ploughing, sowing, and harvesting, swift machines came forward to do the work of scores of men.[1] The Roman civilization was built upon cheap and degraded human beings; modern civilization is being rebuilt upon cheap mechanical power. For a hundred years power has been getting cheaper and labour dearer. If for a generation or so machinery has had to wait its turn in the mine, it is simply because for a time men were cheaper than machinery.[2]

Now here was a change-over of quite primary importance in human affairs. The chief solicitude of the rich and of the ruler in the old civilization had been to keep up a supply of drudges. As the nineteenth century went on, it became more and more plain to the intelligent

directive people that the common man had now to be something better than a drudge. He had to be educated—if only to secure "industrial efficiency." He had to understand what he was about. From the days of the first Christian propaganda, popular education had been

EDGAR THOMSON STEEL WORKS, PITTSBURGH.
Seen and drawn by Joseph Pennell.

smouldering in Europe, just as it has smouldered in Asia wherever Islam has set its foot, because of the necessity of making the believer understand a little of the belief by which he is saved, and of enabling him to read a little in the sacred books by which his belief is conveyed. Christian controversies, with their competition for adherents, ploughed the ground for the harvest of

[1] Here America led the Old World.
[2] In Northumberland and Durham in the early days of coal mining they were so cheaply esteemed that it was unusual to hold inquests on the bodies of men killed in mine disasters.

popular education. In England, for instance, by the thirties and forties of the nineteenth century, the disputes of the sects and the necessity of catching adherents young had produced an abundance of night schools, Sunday schools, and a series of competing educational organizations for children, the dissenting British schools, the church National Schools, and even Roman Catholic elementary schools. The earlier, less enlightened manufacturers, unable to take a broad view of their own interests, hated and opposed these schools. But here again needy Germany led her richer neighbours. The religious teacher found the profit-seeker at his side, unexpectedly eager to get the commonalty, if not educated, at least " trained." The student of the English magazines of the middle and later Victorian period may trace the steadily spreading recognition of the new necessity for popular education. The upper and middle classes of England, themselves by no means well educated, regarded popular education for a generation or so with a sort of tittering hostility. In the middle Victorian period it was thought to be extraordinarily funny that a shop assistant should lean across the counter and ask two lady customers not to speak French, as he " understood the langwidge." This was a " joke " in that monumental record of British humour, *Punch*. It was almost as amusing to the Victorian English as the story of Balaam's ass. The German competitor later on robbed that joke of its fun. Before the death of Queen Victoria, English shop assistants were being badgered to attend evening classes to learn French.

The second half of the nineteenth century was a period of rapid advance in popular education throughout all the Westernized world. There was no parallel advance in the education of the upper classes, some advance no doubt, but nothing to correspond, and so the great gulf that had divided that world hitherto into the readers and the non-reading mass became little more than a slightly perceptible difference in educational level. At the back of this process was the mechanical revolution, apparently regardless of social conditions, but really insisting inexorably upon the complete abolition of a totally illiterate class throughout the world.

The economic revolution of the Roman republic had never been clearly apprehended by the common people of Rome. The ordinary Roman citizen never saw the changes through which he lived, clearly and comprehensively as we see them. But the industrial revolution, as it went on towards the end of the nineteenth century, was more and more distinctly *seen* as one whole process by the common people it was affecting, because presently they could read and discuss and communicate, and because they went about and saw things as no commonalty had ever done before.

In this Outline of History we have been careful to indicate the gradual appearance of the ordinary people as a class with a will and ideas in common. It is the writer's belief that massive movements of the " ordinary people " over considerable areas only became possible as a result of the propagandist religions, Christianity and Islam, and their insistence upon individual self-respect. We have cited the enthusiasm of the commonalty for the First Crusade as marking a new phase in social history. But before the nineteenth century even these massive movements were comparatively restricted. The equalitarian insurrections of the peasantry, from the Wycliffe period onward, were confined to the peasant communities of definite localities, they spread only slowly into districts affected by similar forces. The town artisan rioted indeed, but only locally. The château-burning of the French revolution was not the act of a peasantry who had overthrown a government, it was the act of a peasantry released by the overthrow of a government. The Commune of Paris was the first effective appearance of the town artisan as a political power, and the Parisian crowd of the First Revolution was a very mixed, primitive-thinking, and savage crowd compared with any Western European crowd after 1830.

But the mechanical revolution was not only pressing education upon the whole population, it was leading to a big-capitalism and to a large-scale reorganization of industry that was to produce a new and distinctive system of ideas in the common people in the place of the mere uncomfortable recalcitrance and elemental rebellions of an illiterate commonalty. We have already noted how the industrial revolution had split the manufacturing class, which had hitherto been a middling and various sort of class, into two sections, the employers, who became rich enough to mingle with the financial, merchandizing, and landowning classes, and the employees, who drifted to a status closer and closer to that of mere gang and agricultural labour. As the manufacturing employee sank, the agricultural labourer, by the introduction of agricultural machinery and the increase in his individual productivity, rose. By the middle of the nineteenth century, Karl Marx (1818–83), a German Jew of great scholarly attainments, who did much of his work in the British Museum library in London, was pointing out that the organization of the working

Photo : Rischgitz Collection.

KARL MARX.

classes by the steadily concentrating group of capitalist owners, was developing a new social classification to replace the more complex class systems of the past (see Chap. XX, §§ 4, 5, and 6). Property, so far as it was power, was being gathered together into relatively few hands, the hands of the big rich men, the capitalist class ; while there was a great mingling of workers with little or no property, whom he called the " expropriated," or " proletariat "— a misuse of this word (see Chap. XXVII, § 2)— who were bound to develop a common " class consciousness " of the conflict of their interests with those of the rich men. Differences of education and tradition between the various older social elements which were in process of being fused up into the new class of the expropriated, seemed for a time to contradict this sweeping generalization ; the traditions of the professions, the small employers, the farmer peasant and the like were all different from one another and from the various craftsman traditions of the workers ; but with the spread of education and the cheapening of litera-

ture, this " Marxian " generalization becomes now more and more acceptable. These classes, who were linked at first by nothing but a common impoverishment, were and are being reduced or raised to the same standard of life, forced to read the same books and share the same inconveniences. A sense of solidarity between all sorts of poor and propertyless men, as against the profit-amassing and wealth-concentrating class, is growing more and more evident in our world. Old differences fade away, the difference between craftsman and open-air worker, between black coat and overall, between poor clergyman and elementary school-master, between policeman and bus-driver. They must all buy the same cheap furnishings and live in similar cheap houses ; their sons and daughters will all mingle and marry ; success at the upper levels becomes more and more hopeless for the rank and file. Marx, who did not so much advocate the class-war, the war of the expropriated mass against the appropriating few, as foretell it, is being more and more justified by events.[1]

§ 3

To trace any broad outlines in the fermentation of ideas that went on during the mechanical and industrial revolution of the nineteenth century is a very difficult task. But we must

[1] It is sometimes argued against Marx that the proportion of people who have savings invested has increased in many modern communities. These savings are technically " capital " and their owners " capitalists " to that extent, and this is supposed to contradict the statement of Marx that property concentrates into few and fewer hands. Marx used many of his terms carelessly and chose them ill, and his ideas were better than his words. When he wrote property he meant " property so far as it is power." The small investor has remarkably little power over his invested capital.

attempt it if we are to link what has gone before in this history with the condition of our world to-day.

The Fermentation of Ideas, 1848. It will be convenient to distinguish two main periods in the hundred years between 1814 and 1914. First came the period 1814–48, in which there was a very considerable amount of liberal thinking and writing *in limited circles*, but during which there were no great changes or development of thought in the general mass of the people. Throughout this period the world's affairs were living, so to speak, on their old intellectual capital, they were going on in accordance with the leading ideas of the revolution and the counter-revolution. The dominant liberal ideas were freedom and a certain vague equalitarianism ; the conservative ideas were monarchy, organized religion, social privilege, and obedience.

Until 1848 the spirit of the Holy Alliance, the spirit of Metternich, struggled to prevent a revival of the European revolution that Napoleon had betrayed and set back. In America, both North and South, on the other hand, the revolution had triumphed, and nineteenth-century liberalism ruled unchallenged. Britain was an uneasy country, never quite loyally reactionary nor quite loyally progressive, neither truly monarchist nor truly republican, the land of Cromwell and also of the Merry Monarch, Charles ; anti-Austrian, anti-Bourbon, anti-papal, yet weakly repressive. We have told of the first series of liberal storms in Europe in and about the year 1830 ; in Britain in 1832 a Reform Bill, greatly extending the franchise and restoring something of its representative character to the House of Commons, relieved the situation. Round and about 1848 came a second and much more serious system of outbreaks, that overthrew the Orleans monarchy and established a second Republic in France (1848–52), raised North Italy and Hungary against Austria, and the Poles in Posen against the Germans, and sent the Pope in flight from the republicans of Rome. A very interesting Pan-Slavic conference held at Prague foreshadowed many of the territorial readjustments of 1919. It dispersed after an insurrection at Prague had been suppressed by Austrian troops.

Ultimately all these insurrections failed ; the current system staggered, but kept its feet. There were no doubt serious social discontents beneath these revolts, but as yet, except in the case of Paris, these had no very clear form ; and this 1848 storm, so far as the rest of Europe was concerned, may be best described, in a phrase, as a revolt of the natural political map against the artificial arrangements of the Vienna diplomatists, and the system of suppressions those arrangements entailed.

The history of Europe, then, from 1815 to 1848 was, generally speaking, a sequel to the history of Europe from 1789 to 1814. There were no really new *motifs* in the composition. The main trouble was still the struggle, though often a blind and misdirected struggle, of the interests of ordinary men against the Great Power system which cramped and oppressed the life of mankind.

But after 1848, from 1848 to 1914, though the readjustment of the map still went on towards a free and unified Italy and a unified Germany, there began a fresh phase in the process of mental and political adaptation to the new knowledge and the new material powers of mankind. Came a great irruption of new social, religious, and political ideas into the general European mind. In the next three sections we will consider the origin and quality of these irruptions. They laid the foundations upon which we base our political thought to-day, but for a long time they had no very great effect on contemporary politics. Contemporary politics continued to run on in the old lines, but with a steadily diminishing support in the intellectual convictions and consciences of men. We have already described the way in which a strong intellectual process undermined the system of Grand Monarchy in France before 1789. A similar undermining process was going on throughout Europe during the Great Power period of 1848–1914. Profound doubts of the system of government and of the liberties of many forms of property in the economic system spread throughout the social body. Then came the greatest and most disorganizing war in history, so that it is still impossible to estimate the power and range of the accumulated new ideas of those sixty-six years. We have been through a greater catastrophe even than the Napoleonic catastrophe, and we are in a slack-water period, corresponding to the period 1815–30. Our 1830 and our 1848 are still to come and show us where we stand.

§ 4

We have traced throughout this history the gradual restriction of the idea of property from the first unlimited claim of the strong man to possess everything and the gradual realization of brotherhood as something transcending personal self-seeking (see especially Chap. XXXVII, § 13). Men were first subjugated into more than tribal societies by the fear of monarch and deity. It is only within the last three or at most four thousand years that we have any clear evidence that voluntary self-abandonment to some greater end, without fee or reward, was an acceptable idea to men, or that anyone had propounded it. Then we find spreading over the surface of human affairs, as patches of sunshine spread and pass over the hillsides upon a windy day in spring, the idea that there is a happiness in self-devotion greater than any personal gratification or triumph, and a life of mankind different and greater and more important than the sum of all the individual lives within it. We have seen that idea become vivid as a beacon, vivid as sunshine caught and reflected dazzlingly by some window in the landscape, in the teachings of Buddha, Lao Tse, and, most clearly of all, of Jesus of Nazareth. Through all its variations and corruptions Christianity has never completely lost the suggestion of a devotion to God's commonweal that makes the personal pomps of monarchs and rulers seem like the insolence of an overdressed servant and the splendours and gratifications of wealth like the waste of robbers. No man living in a community which such a religion as Christianity or Islam has touched can be altogether a slave ; there is an ineradicable quality in these religions that compels men to judge their masters and to realize their own responsibility for the world.

As men have felt their way towards this new state of mind from the fierce self-centred greed and instinctive combativeness of the early palæolithic family group, they have sought to express the drift of their thoughts and necessities very variously. They have found themselves in disagreement and conflict with old-established ideas, and there has been a natural tendency to contradict these ideas flatly, to fly over to the absolute contrary. Faced by a world in which rule and classes and order seem to do little but give opportunity for personal selfishness and unrighteous oppression, the first impatient movement was to declare for a universal equality and a practical anarchy. Faced by a world in which property seemed little more than a protection for selfishness and a method of enslavement, it was as natural to repudiate all property. Our history shows an increasing impulse to revolt against rulers and against ownership. We have traced it in the middle ages burning the rich man's châteaux and experimenting in theocracy and communism. In the French revolutions this double revolt is clear and plain. In France we find side by side, inspired by the same spirit and as natural parts of the same revolutionary movement, men who, with their eyes on the ruler's taxes, declared that property should be inviolable, and others who, with their eyes on the employer's hard bargains, declared that property should be abolished. But what they are really revolting against in each case is that the ruler and the employer, instead of becoming servants of the community, still remain, like most of mankind, self-seeking, oppressive individuals.

Throughout the ages we find this belief growing in men's minds that there can be such a rearrangement of laws and powers as to give rule and order while still restraining the egotism of any ruler and of any ruling class that may be necessary, and such a definition of property as will give freedom without oppressive power. We begin to realize nowadays that these ends are only to be attained by a complex constructive effort ; they arise through the conflict of new human needs against ignorance and old human nature ; but throughout the nineteenth century there was a persistent disposition to solve the problem by some simple formula. (And be happy ever afterwards, regardless of the fact that all human life, all life, is throughout the ages nothing but the continuing solution of a continuous synthetic problem.)

The earlier half of the nineteenth century

The Development of the Idea of Socialism.

saw a number of experiments in the formation of trial human societies of a new kind. One of these, the Oneida Community (1845–79), under the leadership of a man of very considerable genius and learning, John Humphry Noyes, did for a number of decades succeed in realizing many of the most striking proposals of Plato's *Republic*; it became wealthy and respected; but it broke up in 1879 largely because of the disposition of the younger generation to leave its peculiar limitations in order to play a part in the larger community of the world outside. A powerful business corporation still preserves its industrial tradition.[1] But the Oneida experiment was too bold and strange a departure to influence the general development of modern civilization. Far more important historically were the experiments and ideas of Robert Owen (1771–1858), a Manchester cotton-spinner. He is very generally regarded as the founder of modern Socialism; it was in connection with his work that the word "socialism" first arose (about 1835.)

Photo : Rischgitz Collection.

ROBERT OWEN.

He seems to have been a thoroughly competent business man; he made a number of innovations in the cotton-spinning industry, and acquired a fair fortune at an early age. He was distressed by the waste of human possibilities among his workers, and he set himself to improve their condition and the relations of employer and employed. This he sought to do first at his Manchester factory and afterwards at New Lanark, where he found himself in practical control of works employing about two thousand people. Between 1800 and 1828 he achieved very considerable things : he reduced the hours of labour, made his factory sanitary and agreeable, abolished the employment of very young children, improved the training of his workers, provided unemployment pay during a period of trade depression, established a system of schools, and made New Lanark a model of a better industrialism, while at the same time sustaining its commercial prosperity. He wrote vigorously to defend the mass of mankind against the charges of intemperance and improvidence which were held to justify the economic iniquities of the time.[2] He held that men and women are largely the product of their educational environment, a thesis that needs no advocacy to-day. And he set himself to a propaganda of the views that New Lanark had justified. He attacked the selfish indolence of his fellow-manufacturers, and in 1819, largely under his urgency, the first Factory Act was passed, the first attempt to restrain employers from taking the most stupid and intolerable advantages of their workers' poverty. Some of the restrictions of that Act amaze us to-day. It seems incredible now that it should ever have been necessary to protect little children of *nine* (!) from work in factories, or to limit the nominal working day of such employees to *twelve hours* !

People are perhaps too apt to write of the industrial revolution as though it led to the enslavement and overworking of poor children who had hitherto been happy and free. But this misinterprets history. From the very beginnings of civilization the little children of the poor had always been obliged to do whatever work they could do. But the factory system gathered up all this infantile toil and made it systematic, conspicuous, and scandalous. The factory system challenged the quickening human conscience on that issue. The British

---

[1] See J. H. Noyes, *History of American Socialisms*, and Eastlake, *The Oneida Community*.

[2] See his *A New View of Society, or Essays on the Principles of the Formation of the Human Character*.

Factory Act of 1819, weak and feeble though it seems to us, was the Magna Charta of childhood; thereafter the protection of the children of the poor, first from toil and then from bodily starvation and ignorance, began.

We cannot tell here in any detail the full story of Owen's life and thought.[1] His work at New Lanark had been, he felt, only a trial upon a small working model. What could be done for one industrial community could be done, he held, for every industrial community in the country; he advocated a resettlement of the industrial population in townships on the New Lanark plan. For a time he seemed to have captured the imagination of the world. The *Times* and *Morning Post* supported his proposals; among the visitors to New Lanark was the Grand Duke Nicholas, who succeeded Alexander I as Tsar; a fast friend was the Duke of Kent, son of George III and father of Queen Victoria. But all the haters of change, and all—and there are always many such—who were jealous of the poor, and all the employers who were likely to be troubled by his projects, were waiting for an excuse to counter-attack him, and they found it in the expression of his religious opinions, which were hostile to official Christianity, and through those he was success-

[1] See F. Podmore, *Life of Robert Owen*, or his own *Life of Robert Owen, Written by Himself*.

fully discredited. But he continued to develop his projects and experiments, of which the chief was a community at New Harmony in Indiana (U.S.A.), in which he sank most of his capital. His partners bought him out of the New Lanark business in 1828.

Owen's experiments and suggestions ranged very widely, and do not fall under any single formula. There was nothing doctrinaire about him. His New Lanark experiment was the first of a number of " benevolent businesses " in the world; Lord Leverhulme's Port Sunlight, the Cadburys' Bournville, and the Ford businesses in America are contemporary instances; it was not really a socialist experiment at all; it was a " paternal " experiment. But his proposals for state settlements were what we should call state socialism to-day. His American experiment and his later writings point to a completer form of socialism, a much wider departure from the existing state of affairs. It is clear that the riddle of currency exercised Owen. He understood that we can no more hope for real economic justice while we pay for work with money of fluctuating value than we could hope for a punctual world if there was a continual inconstant variability in the length of an hour. One of his experiments was an attempt at a circulation of labour notes representing one hour, five hours, or twenty hours

ONE OF OWEN'S LABOUR NOTES.

of work. The co-operative societies of to-day, societies of poor men which combine for the collective buying and distribution of commodities or for collective manufacture or dairying or other forms of agriculture, arose directly out of his initiatives, though the pioneer co-operative societies of his own time ended in failure. Their successors have spread throughout the whole world, and number to-day some thirty or forty million of adherents.

A point to note about this early socialism of Owen's is that it was not at first at all "democratic." Its initiative was benevolent, its early form patriarchal; it was something up to which the workers were to be educated by liberally disposed employers and leaders. The first socialism was not a worker's movement; it was a master's movement.

Concurrently with this work of Owen's, another and quite independent series of developments was going on in America and Britain which was destined to come at last into reaction with his socialistic ideas. The English law had long prohibited combinations in restraint of trade, combinations to raise prices or wages by concerted action. There had been no great hardship in these prohibitions before the agrarian and industrial changes of the eighteenth century let loose a great swarm of workers living from hand to mouth and competing for insufficient employment. Under these new conditions, the workers in many industries found themselves intolerably squeezed. They were played off one against another; day by day and hour by hour none knew what concession his fellow might not have made, and what further reduction of pay or increase of toil might not ensue. It became vitally necessary for the workers to make agreements —illegal though they were—against such underselling. At first these agreements had to be made and sustained by secret societies. Or clubs, established ostensibly for quite other purposes, social clubs, funeral societies, and the like, served to mask the wage-protecting combination. The fact that these associations were illegal disposed them to violence; they were savage against "blacklegs" and "rats" who would not join them, and still more savage with traitors. In 1824 the House of Commons recognized the desirability of relieving tension

in these matters by conceding the right of workmen to form combinations for "collective bargaining" with the masters. This enabled Trade Unions to develop with a large measure of freedom. At first very clumsy and primitive organizations and with very restricted freedoms, the Trade Unions have risen gradually to be a real Fourth Estate in the country, a great system of bodies representing the mass of industrial workers.

Arising at first in Britain and America, they have, with various national modifications, and under varying legal conditions, spread to France, Germany, and all the Westernized communities.

Organized originally to sustain wages and restrict intolerable hours, the Trade Union movement was at first something altogether distinct from socialism. The Trade Unionist tried to make the best for himself of the existing capitalism and the existing conditions of employment; the socialist proposed to change the system. It was the imagination and generalizing power of Karl Marx which brought these two movements into relationship. He was a man with the sense of history very strong in him; he was the first to perceive that the old social classes that had endured since the beginning of civilization were in process of dissolution and regrouping. His racial Jewish commercialism made the antagonism of property and labour very plain to him. And his upbringing in Germany—where, as we have pointed out, the tendency of class to harden into caste was more evident than in any other European country—made him conceive of labour as presently becoming "class conscious" and collectively antagonistic to the property-concentrating classes. In the Trade Union movement which was spreading over the world, he believed he saw this development of class-conscious labour.

What, he asked, would be the outcome of the "class war" of the capitalist and proletariat? The capitalist adventurers, he alleged, because of their inherent greed and combativeness, would gather power over capital into fewer and fewer hands,[1] until at last they would con-

[1] Increases or diminutions of the passive shareholding class would not affect this concentration very materially. A shareholder has very little power over his property.

centrate all the means of production, transit, and the like into a form seizable by the workers, whose class consciousness and solidarity would be developed *pari passu* by the process of organizing and concentrating industry. They would seize this capital and work it for themselves. This would be the social revolution. Then individual property and freedom would be restored, based upon the common ownership of the earth and the management by the community as a whole of the great productive services which the private capitalist had organized and concentrated. This would be the end of the "*capitalist*" system, but not the end of the system of capitalism. State capitalism would replace private owner capitalism.

This marks a great stride away from the socialism of Owen. Owen (like Plato) looked to the commonsense of men of any or every class to reorganize the casual and faulty political, economic, and social structure. Marx found something more in the nature of a driving force in his class hostility based on expropriation and injustice. And he was not simply a prophetic theorist; he was also a propagandist of the revolt of labour, the revolt of the so-called "proletariat." Labour, he perceived, had a common interest against the capitalist everywhere, though under the test of the Great Power wars of the time, and particularly of the liberation of Italy, he showed that he failed to grasp the fact that labour everywhere has a common interest in the peace of the world. But with the social revolution in view he did succeed in inspiring the formation of an international league of workers, the First International.

The subsequent history of socialism is chequered between the British tradition of Owen and the German class feeling of Marx. What is called Fabian Socialism, the exposition of socialism by the London Fabian Society, makes its appeal to reasonable men of all classes. What are called "Revisionists" in German Socialism incline in the same direction. But on the whole, it is Marx who has carried the day against Owen, and the general disposition of socialists throughout the world is to look to the organization of labour and labour only to supply the fighting forces that will disentangle the political and economic organization of human affairs from the hands of the more or less irresponsible private owners and adventurers who now control it.

These are the broad features of the project which is called Socialism. We will discuss its incompletenesses and inadequacies in our next section. It was perhaps inevitable that socialism should be greatly distraught and subdivided by doubts and disputes and sects and schools; they are growth symptoms like the spots on a youth's face. Here we can but glance at the difference between state socialism, which would run the economic business of the country through its political government, and the newer schools of syndicalism and guild socialism which would entrust a large measure in the government of each industry to the workers of every grade—including the directors and managers—engaged in that industry. This "guild socialism" is really a new sort of capitalism with a committee of workers and officials in each industry taking the place of the free private capitalists of that industry. The *personnel* becomes the collective capitalist. Nor can we discuss the undemocratic idea of the Russian leader Lenin, that a population cannot judge of socialism before it has experienced it, and that a group of socialists are therefore justified in seizing and socializing, if they can, the life of a country without at first setting up any democratic form of general government at all, for which sort of seizure he uses the Marxian phrase, a very incompetent phrase, the "dictatorship of the proletariat." All Russia now is a huge experiment in that dictatorship (February 1920).[1] The "pro-

[1] I find in a book of essays and addresses by Professor Soddy an interesting and compact statement of certain resemblances in spirit between scientific research and modern socialism. I venture to quote a passage here because of its great significance at the present time:

"The immense acquisition," he says, "to the wealth and resources of mankind which has been the result of the past century of science, should have been the golden opportunity of statesmen and humanitarians and the raw material out of which the sum total of human happiness could have been augmented. Instead, it has but revealed a growing incapacity and failure on the part of the altruist to appreciate the nature and power of the new weapon that science has placed in his hands, and an everincreasing rapacity and far-sightedness on the part of the egotist to secure it for his own ends.

"For many a decade now, owing primarily and indisputably to the intellectual achievements of a comparative handful of men of communistic and cloisteral habit of thought, a steady shower of material benefits letariat " is supposed to be dictating through committees of workmen and soldiers, the Soviets, but at present we have no means of ascertaining how far Russian affairs are under the direction of a genuine mass intelligence and will, and how far the activities of the Soviets are restrained and directed by the group of vigorous personalities which leads the revolution. Nor do we know if the methods of election used for the Soviets are any improvement upon the unsatisfactory methods in use in the Atlantic democracies. Non-workers have no representation in this new Russian state.

§ 5

We are all socialists nowadays, said Sir William Harcourt years ago, and that is loosely true to-day. There can be few people who fail to realize the provisional nature and the dangerous instability of our present political and economic

has been raining down upon humanity, and for these benefits men have fought in the traditional manner of the struggle when the fickle sunlight was the sole hazardous income of the world. The strong have fed and grown fat upon a larger and ever larger share of the manna. Initial slight differences of strength and sagacity have become so emphasized by the virile stream that the more successful are becoming monstrously so, and the unsuccessful less and less able to secure a full meal than before the shower began.

" Already it savours of indelicacy and tactlessness to recall that the exploiters of all this wealth are not its creators ; that the spirit of acquisitiveness which has ensured success to them, rather than to their immediate neighbours, is the antithesis of the spirit by which the wealth was won.

" Amid all the sneers at the impracticability and visionary character of communist schemes, let it not be forgotten that science is a communism, neither theoretical nor on paper, but actual and in practice. The results of those who labour in the fields of knowledge for its own sake are published freely and pooled in the general stock for the benefit of all. Common ownership of all its acquisitions is the breath of its life. Secrecy or individualism of any kind would destroy its fertility."

So far Professor Soddy, but let the writer add that there is this point about the scientific world not to be overlooked. Every worker in the latter is a specially educated man, and he is free to leave the communism of science if he thinks fit. This is very different from a communism imposed upon an unprepared mass of people containing large recalcitrant minorities or majorities. A communism sustained by a community of will based on education—an extension, that is, of the communism of scientific research to human affairs generally—is the ideal underlying the political ideas of most intelligent modern men.

system, and still fewer who believe with the doctrinaire individualists that profit-hunting " go as you please " will guide mankind to any haven of prosperity and happiness. Great rearrangements are necessary, and a systematic legal subordination of personal self-seeking to the public good. So far most reasonable men are socialists. But these are only preliminary propositions. How far has socialism and modern thought generally gone towards *working out* the conception of this new political and social order, of which our world admittedly stands in need ? We are obliged to answer that there is no clear conception of the new state towards which we vaguely struggle, that our science of human relationships is still so crude and speculative as to leave us without definite guidance upon a score of primarily important issues. In 1920 we are no more in a position to set up a scientifically conceived political system in the world than were men to set up an electric power station in 1820. They could not have done that then to save their lives.

Shortcomings of Socialism as a Scheme of Human Society.

The Marxist system points us to an accumulation of revolutionary forces in the modern world. These forces will continually tend towards revolution. But Marx assumed too hastily that a revolutionary impulse would necessarily produce an ordered state of a new and better kind. A revolution may stop half way in mere destruction. No socialist sect has yet defined its projected government clearly ; the Bolsheviks in their Russian experiment seem to have been guided by a phrase, the dictatorship of the proletariat, and in practice, we are told, Trotsky and Lenin have proved as autocratic as the less intelligent but equally well-meaning Tsar, Alexander I. We have been at some pains to show from our brief study of the French revolution that a revolution can establish nothing permanent that has not already been thought out beforehand and apprehended by the general mind. The French republic, confronted with unexpected difficulties in economics, currency, and international relationships, collapsed to the egotisms of the newly rich people of the Directory, and finally to the egotism of Napoleon. Law and a plan, steadily upheld, are more necessary in revoluas a natural consequence of his projected social revolution. At most that is a vague aspiration. But if there is any logic about the Marxist, it should be his declared political end for which he should work without ceasing. Put to the test of the war of 1914, the socialists of almost all the European countries showed that their class-conscious internationalism was veneered very thinly indeed over their patriotic feelings, and had to no degree replaced them. Everywhere during the German war socialists denounced that war as made by capitalist governments, but it produces little or no permanent effect to denounce a government or a world system unless you have a working idea of a better government and a better system to replace it.

We state these things here because they are facts, and a living and necessary part of a contemporary survey of human history. It is not our task either to advocate or controvert socialism. But it is in our picture to note that political and social life are, and must remain, chaotic and disastrous without the development of some such constructive scheme as socialism *sketches*, and to point out clearly how far away the world is at present from any such scheme. An enormous amount of intellectual toil and discussion and education and many years—whether decades or centuries, no man can tell—must intervene before a new order, planned as ships and railways are planned, runs, as the cables and the postal deliveries run, over the whole surface of our earth. And until such a new order draws mankind together with its net, human life, as we shall presently show by the story of the European wars since 1854, must become more and more casual, dangerous, miserable, anxious, and disastrous because of the continually more powerful and destructive war methods the continuing mechanical revolution produces.

§ 6[1]

While the mechanical revolution which the growth of physical science had brought about was destroying the ancient social classification of the civilized state which had been evolved

---

[1] For a closely parallel view of religion to that given here, see that admirable book, *Outspoken Essays*, by Dean Inge, Essays VIII and IX on *St. Paul* and on *Institutionalism and Mysticism*.

42

MODERN INDUSTRIALISM: SHEFFIELD AT WORK.

at this distance of time, to clash or interfere with any discovery or expansion of the history of the world and mankind. But it is equally a fact in history that St. Paul and his successors added to or completed or imposed upon or substituted another doctrine for—as you may prefer to think—the plain and profoundly revolutionary teachings of Jesus by expounding a subtle and complex theory of salvation, a salvation which could be attained very largely by belief and formalities, without any serious disturbance of the believer's ordinary habits and occupations, and that this Pauline teaching *did* involve very definite beliefs about the history of the world and man. It is not the business of the historian to controvert or explain these matters; the question of their ultimate significance depends upon the theologian; the historian's concern is merely with the fact that official Christianity throughout the world adopted St. Paul's view so plainly expressed in his epistles and so untraceable in the gospels, that the meaning of religion lay not in the future, but in the past, and that Jesus was not so much a teacher of wonderful new things, as a predestinate divine blood sacrifice of deep mystery and sacredness made in atonement of a particular historical act of disobedience to the Creator committed by our first parents, Adam and Eve, in reponse to the temptation of a serpent in the Garden of Eden. Upon the belief in that Fall as a fact, and not upon the personality of Jesus of Nazareth, upon the theories of Paul, and not upon the injunctions of Jesus, doctrinal Christianity built itself.

We have already noted that this story of the special creation of the world and of Adam and Eve and the serpent was also an ancient Babylonian story, and probably a still more ancient Sumerian story, and that the Jewish sacred books were the medium by which this very ancient and primitive " heliolithic " serpent legend entered Christianity. Wherever official Christianity has gone, it has taken this story with it. It has tied itself up to that story. Until a century and less ago the whole Christianized world felt bound to believe, and did believe, that the universe had been specially created in the course of six days by the word of God a few thousand years before—according to Bishop Ussher, 4004 B.C. (The *Universal*

History, in forty-two volumes, published in 1779 by a group of London booksellers, discusses whether the precise date of the first day of Creation was March 21st or September 21st, 4004 B.C., and inclines to the view that the latter was the more probable season.)

Upon this historial assumption rested the religious fabric of the Western and Westernized civilization, and yet the whole world was littered, the hills, mountains, deltas, and seas were bursting with evidence of its utter absurdity. The religious life of the leading nations, still a very intense and sincere religious life, was going on in a house of history built upon sand.

There is frequent recognition in classical literature of a sounder cosmogony. Aristotle was aware of the broad principles of modern geology, they shine through the speculations of Lucretius, and we have noted also Leonardo da Vinci's (1452–1519) lucid interpretation of fossils. A Frenchman, Descartes (1596–1650), speculated boldly upon the incandescent beginnings of our globe, and an Italian, Steno, (1631–87) began the collection of fossils and the description of strata. But it was only as the eighteenth century drew to its close that the systematic study of geology assumed such proportions as to affect the general authority of the Bible version of that ancient Sumerian narrative. Contemporaneously with the *Universal History* quoted above, a great French naturalist, Buffon, was writing upon the Epochs of Nature (1778), and boldly extending the age of the world to 70,000 or 75,000 years. He divided his story into six epochs to square with the six days of the Creation story. These days, it was argued, were figurative days; they were really ages. There was a general disposition to do this on the part of the new science of geology. By that accommodating device, geology contrived to make a peace with orthodox religious teaching that lasted until the middle of the nineteenth century.

We cannot trace here the contributions of such men as Hutton and Playfair and Sir Charles Lyell, and the Frenchmen Lamarck and Cuvier, in unfolding and developing the record of the rocks. It was only slowly that the general intelligence of the Western world was awakened to two disconcerting facts: firstly, that the succession of life in the geological record did not correspond to the acts of the six days of creation; and, secondly, that the record, in harmony with a mass of biological facts, pointed away from the Bible assertion of a separate creation of each species straight towards a genetic relation between all forms of life, *in which even man was included*! The importance of this last issue to the existing doctrinal system was manifest. If all the animals and man had been evolved in this ascendant manner, then there had been no first parents, no Eden, and no Fall. And if there had been no Fall, then the entire historical fabric of Christianity, the story of the first sin and the reason for an atonement, upon which the current teaching based Christian emotion and morality, collapsed like a house of cards.

Photo: Rischgitz Collection.
CHARLES DARWIN.
(After W. W. Ouless, R.A.)

It was with something like horror, therefore, that great numbers of honest and religious-spirited men followed the work of the great English naturalist, Charles Darwin (1809–82); in 1859 he published his *Origin of Species by Means of Natural Selection*, a powerful and permanently valuable exposition of that conception of the change and development of species which we have sketched briefly in Chapter III ; and in 1871 he completed the outline of his work with the *Descent of Man*, which brought man definitely into the same scheme of development with the rest of life.

Many men and women are still living who can remember the dismay and distress among ordinary intelligent people in the Western communities as the invincible case of the biologists and geologists against the orthodox Christian cosmogony unfolded itself. The minds of many quite honest men resisted the new knowledge instinctively and irrationally. Their whole moral edifice was built upon false history ; they were too old and set to rebuild it ; they felt the practical truth of their moral convictions, and this new truth seemed to them to be incompatible with that. They believed that to assent to it would be to prepare a moral collapse for the world. And so they produced a moral collapse by not assenting to it. The universities in England particularly, being primarily clerical in their constitution, resisted the new learning very bitterly. Throughout the seventies and eighties a stormy controversy raged throughout the civilized world. The quality of the discussions and the fatal ignorance of the church may be gauged by a description in Hackett's *Commonplace Book* of a meeting of the British Association in 1860, at which Bishop Wilberforce assailed Huxley, the great champion of the Darwinian views, in this fashion.

Facing "Huxley with a smiling insolence, he begged to know, *was it through his grandfather or grandmother that he claimed his descent from a monkey*? Huxley turned to his neighbour, and said, 'The Lord hath delivered him into my hands.' Then he stood before us and spoke these tremendous words, 'He was not ashamed to have a monkey for his ancestor ; but he would be ashamed to be connected with a man who used great gifts to obscure the truth.'" (Another version has it : "I have certainly said that a man has no reason to be ashamed of having an ape for his grandfather. If there were an ancestor whom I should feel ashamed in recalling, it would rather be a man of restless and versatile intellect who plunges into scientific questions with which he has no real acquaintance, only to obscure them by an aimless rhetoric and distract the attention of his audience from the real point at issue by eloquent digressions and skilled appeals to prejudice.") These words were certainly spoken with passion.

The scene was one of great excitement. A lady fainted, says Hackett. . . . Such was the temper of this controversy.

The Darwinian movement took formal Christianity unawares, suddenly. Formal Christianity was confronted with a clearly demonstrable error in her theological statements. The Christian theologians were neither wise enough nor mentally nimble enough to accept the new truth, modify their formulæ, and insist upon the living and undiminished vitality of the religious reality those formulæ had hitherto sufficed to express. For the discovery of man's descent from sub-human forms does not even remotely touch the teaching of the Kingdom of Heaven. Yet priests and bishops raged at Darwin ; foolish attempts were made to suppress Darwinian literature and to insult and discredit the exponents of the new views. There was much wild talk of the " antagonism " of religion and science. Now in all ages there have been sceptics in Christendom. The Emperor Frederick II was certainly a sceptic ; in the eighteenth century Gibbon and Voltaire were openly anti-Christian, and their writings influenced a number of scattered readers. But these were exceptional people. . . . Now the whole of Christendom became as a whole sceptical. This new controversy touched everybody who read a book or heard intelligent conversation. A new generation of young people grew up, and they found the defenders of Christianity in an evil temper, fighting their cause without dignity or fairness. It was the orthodox theology that the new scientific advances had compromised, but the angry theologians declared that it was religion.

In the end men may discover that religion shines all the brighter for the loss of its doctrinal wrappings, but to the young it seemed as if indeed there had been a conflict of science and religion, and that in that conflict science had won.

The immediate effect of this great dispute upon the ideas and methods of people in the prosperous and influential classes throughout the westernized world was very detrimental indeed. The new biological science was bringing nothing constructive as yet to replace the old moral stand-bys. A real demoralization ensued. The general level of social life in those classes was far higher in the early twentieth than in the early seventeenth century, but in one respect, in respect to disinterestedness and conscientiousness in these classes, it is probable that the tone of the earlier age was better than the latter. In the owning and active classes of the seventeenth century, in spite of a few definite " infidels," there was probably a much higher percentage of men and women who prayed sincerely, who searched their souls to find if they had done evil, and who were prepared to suffer and make great sacrifices for what they conceived to be right, than in the opening years of the twentieth century. There was a real loss of faith after 1859. The true gold of religion was in many cases thrown away with the worn-out purse that had contained it for so long, and it was not recovered. Towards the close of the nineteenth century a crude misunderstanding of Darwinism had become the fundamental mindstuff of great masses of the " educated " everywhere. The seventeenth-century kings and owners and rulers and leaders had had the idea at the back of their minds that they prevailed by the will of God ; they really feared Him, they got priests to put things right for them with Him ; when they were wicked, they tried not to think of Him. But the old faith of the kings, owners, and rulers of the opening twentieth century had faded under the actinic light of scientific criticism. Prevalent peoples at the close of the nineteenth century believed that they prevailed by virtue of the Struggle for Existence, in which the strong and cunning get the better of the weak and confiding. And they believed further that they had to be strong, energetic, ruthless, " practical," egotistical, because God was dead, and had always, it seemed, been dead—which was going altogether further than the new knowledge justified.

They soon got beyond the first crude popular misconception of Darwinism, the idea that every man is for himself alone. But they stuck at the next level. Man, they decided, is a social animal like the Indian hunting dog. He is much more than a dog—but this they did not see. And just as in a pack it is necessary to bully and subdue the younger and weaker for the general good, so it seemed right to them that the big dogs of the human pack should bully and subdue. Hence a new scorn for the ideas of democracy that had ruled the earlier nineteenth century, and a revived admiration for the overbearing and the cruel. It was quite characteristic of the times that Mr. Kipling should lead the children of the middle and upper-class British public back to the Jungle, to learn " the law," and that in his book *Stalky and Co.* he should give an appreciative description of the torture of two boys by three others, who have by a subterfuge tied up their victims helplessly before revealing their hostile intentions.

It is worth while to give a little attention to this incident in *Stalky and Co.*, because it lights up the political psychology of the British Empire at the close of the nineteenth century very vividly. The history of the last half century is not to be understood without an understanding of the mental twist which this story exemplifies. The two boys who are tortured are " bullies," that is the excuse of their tormentors, and these latter have further been incited to the orgy by a clergyman. Nothing can restrain the gusto with which they (and Mr. Kipling) set about the job. Before resorting to torture, the teaching seems to be, see that you pump up a little justifiable moral indignation, and all will be well. If you have the authorities on your side, then you cannot be to blame. Such, apparently, is the simple doctrine of this typical imperialist. But every bully has to the best of his ability followed that doctrine since the human animal developed sufficient intelligence to be consciously cruel.

Another point in the story is very significant indeed. The head master and his clerical assistant are both represented as being privy to the affair. They want this bullying to occur. Instead of exercising their own authority, they use these boys, who are Mr. Kipling's heroes, to punish the two victims. Head master and clergyman turn a deaf ear to the complaints of an indignant mother. All this Mr. Kipling represents as a most desirable state of affairs. In this we have the key to the ugliest, most retrogressive, and finally fatal idea of modern imperialism; the idea of a *tacit conspiracy between the law and illegal violence.* Just as the Tsardom wrecked itself at last by a furtive encouragement of the ruffians of the Black Hundred, who massacred Jews and other people supposed to be inimical to the Tsar, so the good name of British Imperial Government has been tainted—and is still tainted—by an illegal raid made by Doctor Jameson into the Transvaal before the Boer War, and by the adventures, which we shall presently describe, of Sir Edward Carson and Mr. F. E. Smith (now Lord Birkenhead) in Ireland. By such treasons against their subjects, empires destroy themselves. The true strength of rulers and empires lies not in armies and emotions, but in the belief of men that they are inflexibly open and truthful and legal. So soon as a government departs from that standard, it ceases to be anything more than " the gang in possession," and its days are numbered.

It was just this dignity of government which the crude Darwinism and the Kiplingism of the later Victorian years was destroying. Competition and survival were accepted as the basal facts of life. " War is the natural state of nations," said a popular London men's weekly [1] the other day, with an air of repeating something universally known. " Peace is only the interval of rest and preparation between wars." In accordance with such ideas the growing boy was exhorted to be " loyal " to his school and contemptuous of other schools, " loyal " to his class against other classes, " loyal " to his nation and contemptuous and fierce towards other nations, " loyal " to the English-speaking peoples and contemptuous and hostile to the German or French-speaking. His instinct for brotherhood was narrowed and debased. The universal brotherhood of mankind was laughed to scorn. All life was bickering, he was taught; and yet the whole course of history has shown that the bickering nations perish, and that the alliances and coalescences of peoples and nations ensure the life they comprehend.

So the Darwinian crisis continued that destruction of Christian prestige which the narrowness of priestcraft and the consequent division of Christendom among the monarchist and national Protestant churches of the Reformation had begun, and at a time when man's need for pacifying and unifying ideas was greater than it had ever been. Just when men of different races and languages and political ideas were being brought by the mechanical revolution

[1] *Town Topics*, November 26th, 1919.

to a closeness of contact and a power of mutual injury undreamt of before, the authority of the doctrines by which men had hitherto transcended tribal and local limitations was undermined. Just when different classes were being aroused to a fierce realization of mutual economic antagonism, the fundamental teaching of brotherhood was discredited and a pseudo-scientific sanction given to self-seeking and oppression.[1] From this stage onward the historian can tell no longer of ordinary clerical Christianity as a power in men's affairs. In politics and social questions the appeal to its standards ceased. Yet never was there so imperative a demand in the world of men for a common basis upon which they could work together, a common conception of aim in which they could lose themselves. We shall find great masses of people inspired to passionate devotion, by ideas of nationalism, of imperialism, of class-conscious socialism. But official and orthodox Christianity no longer inspired. Men would no longer live by it or die for it.

This paradoxical final decline of a universal faith in the Westernized world, just when men were being drawn together by the mechanical revolution into one inseparable political and economic system, may have been due entirely to the coincidence of that revolution with destructive scientific discovery, or it may also have been accelerated by the irritations produced by the sudden close clashing with unfamiliar peoples and races. It may have been a merely temporary decline due to the need for a sloughing-off of the outworn theology and antique sacerdotalism which confined its appeal to the Western world, preparatory to a reconstruction of religious statement upon simpler world-wide lines. It may have been merely a cleansing of the teachings of Jesus of Nazareth from theological and ceremonial accretions. Upon such "may have beens" we can speculate here, but we cannot decide. History can deal with the small beginnings in the past of the great things of the present, but in the present only with what is plain and obvious. We cannot tell what seeds of the future may not be germinating already amidst our present confusions.

[1] Kropotkin's *Mutual Aid* is worth noting here as one of the earliest correctives to these popular misconceptions of Darwinism.—G. M.

§ 7

The vast changes we have been recording in the range of human power and intercourse constitute the fundamental realities of nineteenth-century history. But the atlas and political history of a time do not show what is being made, but what has been made, and what is still going on. The formal history of the latter half of the nineteenth century is not so much concerned with these permanent changes in human affairs, as with the schemes of Foreign Offices and the continuing exploits of the Great Powers. The men who were discovering, inventing, developing inventions and working out ideas were far too busy and far too few for effective interference in public affairs. The diplomatists, politicians, and statesmen, on the other hand, were far too occupied with their established interplay of nations and parties to heed what the contemporary mind was doing. The Earl of Beaconsfield (1804–81), a leading British statesman, remarked (of the Darwinian controversy) that it seemed to be a dispute whether men were descended from apes or angels, and that for his part, he was "on the side of the angels" —a sprightly saying which added greatly to his reputation. His rival, Gladstone (1809–98), was of a more serious quality, and in the habit of plunging during his vacations heavily and conspicuously into intellectual affairs; among other such exploits he joined in public controversy with Huxley upon Huxley's own subject. He revealed ideas derived from Buffon (died 1788) uncontaminated by any later influence. The whole field of modern discovery, says Lecky in his *Democracy and Liberty*, was outside his range.

When this Mr. Gladstone was taken by Sir John Lubbock to see Charles Darwin,[2] he talked all the time of Bulgarian politics, and was evidently quite unaware of the real importance of the man he was visiting. Darwin, Lord Morley records, expressed himself as deeply sensible of the honour done him by the visit of "such a great man," but he offered no comments on the Bulgarian discourse. Faraday, the English electrician, whose work lives wherever a dynamo spins, who is in the aeroplane, the deep-sea cable, the lights that light the ways

Mr. Gladstone and the idea of Nationalism.

[2] Morley's *Life of Gladstone*.

of the world, and wherever electricity serves our kind, was also visited by Gladstone when the latter was Chancellor of the Exchequer. The man of science tried in vain to explain some simple piece of apparatus to this fine flower of the parliamentary world. " But," said Mr. Gladstone, " after all, what *good* is it ? " " Why, sir," said Faraday, doing his best to bring things home to him, " presently you will be able to tax it." [1]

Mr. Gladstone was one of the most central and representative politician statesmen of the later nineteenth century, and it will be worth while to devote a paragraph or so to his ideas and intellectual limitations. They will help us to understand better the astonishing irrelevance of the political life of this period to the realities that rose about it. He was a person of exceptional intellectual vigour ; he had flashes of real insight ; but his circumstances and temperament conspired against his ever attaining any real vision of the world in which he lived.

He was the son of Sir John Gladstone, a West Indian slave-holder, the mortality among whose slaves was a matter of debate in the House of Commons ; he was educated at Eton College, and at Christ Church, Oxford, and his mind never recovered from the process. We have already told how after the Reformation the English universities ceased to be the organs of the general intellectual life, and shrank to be merely the educational preserves of the aristocracy and the church. Jews, Roman Catholics, dissenters, sceptics, and all forms of intellectual activity were carefully barred out from those almost extinguished lamps of learning. Their mathematical work was poor, a series of exercises in the mere patience-games and formulæ-writing of lower mathematics ; science they despised and excluded, and their staple training was the study, without any archæology or historical perspective, of the more rhetorical and " poetic " of the Latin and Greek classics.[2] Such a training prepared

men not so much to tackle and solve the problems of life, as to plaster them over with more or less apt quotations. It turned the mind away from living contemporary things ; it showed the world reflected in a distorting mirror of bad historical analogies ; all the fated convergencies of history were refracted into false parallels. The British Parliament was thought of as a Senate, statesmen postured as patricians and equestrians ; the new industrial population, now learning to read and think for itself, was transfigured into the likeness of the illiterate savage and privileged citizen mob of later republican Rome.[3] It was natural, there-

take *two* schools, and to offer Mathematics as well as *Literæ Humaniores*. Both Peel (about 1810) and Gladstone (about 1830) took these two schools, and both gained Firsts in both. (This, by the way, is the only true and genuine " double first.") Men with such a training were genuinely and nobly trained for statesmanship.—E. B.

With no knowledge of ethnology, no vision of history as a whole, misconceiving the record of geology, ignorant of the elementary ideas of biological science, of modern political, social, and economic science and modern thought and literature !—H. G. W.

[3] The old classical training had great faults, but not quite those which are here imputed to it. It was the education of an aristocratic leisured class who had not to earn their living. Hence it was (1) entirely idealist and non-utilitarian. It aimed not at fitting people for a paid profession, but at culture and inner development. (2) It depended enormously on *leisure*. The work done in compulsory work-hours was small in range, but severe, almost entirely classics and mathematics. These were intended as a training of the mind and a test of ability, but were not the real field of ambition. That lay in the large amount of time allotted to *free study*. Peel, Gladstone, Macaulay, Hallam, etc., show what was expected of the best men. Literature, modern history, French and Italian, theology and philosophy, and even a good deal of generalized science, were things you read in your free time. Think what Macaulay's " schoolboy " was supposed to know, and reflect that practically none of it was taught in school hours ! Some of the best papers on English literature that I ever read were done by a certain sixth form which had, I was told, no time at all given to the subject in the time-table. As the Head Master told me, " A good man was rather laughed at if he did not know Shakespeare and Milton."

This conception of a small hard nucleus of compulsory work, combined with a wide margin of leisure, was very good for the best men, who used their free time in the right way, but left the weak men thoroughly uneducated. The reaction against it came with long hours, wide curriculum, and compulsory games, leaving no leisure either for study or for mischief.

The modern idea that school should teach *all* that a boy ought to know, is educationally disastrous ; but it

[1] R. A. Gregory's *Discovery*.

[2] The great Oxford school of *Literæ Humaniores*, which means a serious study of Ancient Philosophy and Ancient History, was already thirty years old in Gladstone's time, and was a really serious training in solid philosophy and solid history. It was all the more serious, as every candidate for Honours had to

is the natural result of boys coming from uneducated homes. The home, not the school, is the real key to the wider and higher side of education. But this raises large questions.—G. M.

G. M., I submit, has not grasped the modern idea in education. The modern idea of a public school as exemplified in such a case as Oundle does not fill up the time of the boy with prescribed work and games; it leaves large spaces for self-development; but also it provides museums, a good collection of pictures, libraries, and an abundance of good music instead of the mere " playing fields " of the old type of public school. And it inquires into the use a boy is making of his free energies. The phase of " cram " is over, but the new schools do provide good pasture, show the way thither, and " vet " a boy who displays no appetite. G. M. ignores entirely the clear statement in the text that Gladstone was a grossly *ignorant* man, and the instances given of the feebleness and worthlessness of the " generalized science " these boys of the old persuasion picked up. So far from the old classical training being the education of an aristocratic class, it was, as G. M. admits within a line or so, the education of a few individuals, the rest of the class remaining barbarians. It may have aimed at culture and inner development, but it missed its aim. Consequently, the bright lads of the Gladstone-Macaulay-Peel type who did not pick up a few enlightened ideas by accident or at home, were quite unable to carry their own class with them; it remained politically boorish. They had to' appeal for understanding to classes whose education had been free from " classical " pretentiousness. . . .

These notes submitted to E. B. at this stage provoked him to a warm protest. His sympathies were " heart and soul with G. M.," and Mr. Gladstone, he declared with emphasis, was not an ignorant man. A little more must be said on this question. If the reader realize, what we have been trying to make clear in this history, that human progress is largely mental progress, a clearing and an enlargement of ideas, then he will understand why it is that the compiler of this *Outline* has given so much space here to these controversial notes upon the education of Mr. Gladstone. For the education of Mr. Gladstone was typical of that ruling-class education which has dominated British and European affairs, so far as they have been dominated by ideas, up to the present time. It is most significant of the differences and difficulties of our age that the statement, which seemed to the writer a simple statement of an obvious fact, that Mr. Gladstone was a profoundly ignorant man, should have so scandalized two of the editors of this work. No doubt Mr. Gladstone knew much and knew many things, and it is just because he did so and was in many respects the fine flower of the education of his period, that his ignorance is so interesting to us. Many Chinese mandarins knew much and many things —beautifully. And were ignorant men. Mr. Gladstone's was not the ignorance of deficiency, but the ignorance of excess, a copious ignorance; it was not a failure to know this or that particular fact, an ignorance excusable enough, but a profound and sought-after and established ignorance of reality, so

that he did not grasp the bearing of definite facts presented to him or of far-reaching ideas put before him, upon the great issues with which he was concerned. He lived, as it were, in a luminous and blinding cloud. That cloud, which I call his ignorance, my two editors call his wonderful and abounding culture. It was a culture that wrapped about and adorned the great goddess Reality. But, indeed, she is not to be adorned but stripped. She ceases to be herself or to bless her votary unless she is faced stark and fearlessly.--H. G. W.

fore, that at the Oxford Union Society young Gladstone should distinguish himself by an eloquent speech against the threatened reform of the worst electoral abuses (see Chap. XXXVI, § 2), should contest the immediate emancipation of the parental slaves—slavery, he said, was " sanctioned by Holy Scripture "—and should oppose on religious grounds the removal of the disabilities of the Jews. He was returned to Parliament as Tory member for Newark in 1832, promising to resist " that growing desire for change " which threatened to produce, " along with partial good, a melancholy preponderance of mischief." In his first Parliament he distinguished himself by his opposition to the admission of religious dissenters to the universities.

Here we have a mind manifestly of a tradition and make-up akin to that of the framers of the Holy Alliance, a mind set steadfastly against all the vast creative tendencies of the nineteenth-century world, as though they were no more than a mere mischievous restlessness of slaves and lower-class persons that would presently be allayed. But because of the streak of insight in his composition, Gladstone did not remain set in a course of pure conservatism, he presently began to realize the strength of the stream upon which things were being carried forward; his intelligence, in spite of its perversion, set itself to grasp the real forms of the torrent of change about him. He was a man of great ambitions and immense energy; his animosity against his brilliant and flippant Jewish rival Disraeli (afterwards Lord Beaconsfield), who was becoming the leader amid the shifting of groups and parties, swung this man who had been the " rising hope of the stern unbending Tories " more and more into a liberal attitude. He began to express belief in the people, to support extensions of the franchise, to cultivate the esteem of the dissenters, and, as Chancellor of the Exchequer, to shift the burthen of taxation from off the food and comforts of the new classes of needy voters that the franchise extensions were bringing into the political world. It is clear that for some years he was profoundly perplexed by the deep forces that evidently lay beneath the stir and thrust of international politics; then he became a great exponent of a half-true theory, the theory of Nationalism, that has played and still plays an intensely mischievous part in the world.

We have already pointed out that there must be a natural political map of the world which gives the best possible geographical divisions for human administrations. Any other political division of the world than this natural political map will necessarily be a misfit, and must produce stresses of hostility and insurrection tending to shift boundaries in the direction indicated by the natural political map. These would seem to be self-evident propositions were it not that the diplomatists at Vienna evidently neither believed nor understood anything of the sort, and thought themselves as free to carve up the world as one is free to carve up such a boneless structure as a cheese, Nor were these propositions evident to Mr. Gladstone. Most of the upheavals and conflicts that began in Europe as the world recovered from the exhaustion of the Napoleonic wars were quite obviously attempts of the ordinary common men to get rid of governments that were such misfits as to be in many cases intolerable. Generally the existing governments were misfits throughout Europe because they were not socially representative, and so they were hampering production and wasting

Photo : Rischgitz Collection.
GLADSTONE AS CHANCELLOR OF THE EXCHEQUER, 1854.
(From the painting by P. Westcott, at the National Liberal Club.)

human possibilities; but when there were added to these universal annoyances differences of religion and racial culture between rulers and ruled (as in most of Ireland), differences in race and language (as in Austrian North Italy and throughout most of the Austrian Empire), or differences in all these respects (as in Poland and the Turkish Empire in Europe), the exasperation drove towards bloodshed. Europe was a system of governing machines abominably adjusted. But Mr. Gladstone was no patient mechanic set upon easing and righting the clumsy injuries of those stupid adjustments. He was a white-faced, black-haired man of incredible energy, with eyes like an eagle's, wrath almost divine, and the "finest baritone voice in Europe." He apprehended these things romantically, therefore, in a manner suitable for passionate treatment in large halls.

He was blind to the pitiful and wonderful reality of mankind, to these millions and millions of ill-informed, ill-equipped, inexpressive, and divided human beings, mostly very willing, could they but do it, to live rightly and well. He fixed his eagle eye on a fantastic vision of "nations rightly struggling to be free."[1]

[1] The impression made on me, an old Gladstonian, by Gladstone's politics, was mainly twofold. (1) A strong assertion that politics were (as Aristotle said) a development of ethics, and concerned with discovering and doing what is Right, not what is convenient or profitable to any particular class or nation. (2) A strong sub-conscious suggestion that the highest education and culture and knowledge were useful for politics, which was in fact a very high practical art, demanding the highest qualities. Hence largely the horror we had of Dizzy. (3) A general sanguine conviction that Honesty was the best policy; that what was right would also prove to be ultimately the most profitable, so that there was no real conflict.

What is a nation? What is nationality? He never paused to ask. No one under the spell of that fine baritone paused to ask. But historians must stand to the questions a politician can evade. If our story of the world has demonstrated anything, it has demonstrated the mingling of races and peoples, the instability of human divisions, the swirling variety of human groups and human ideas of association. A nation, it has been said, is an accumulation of human beings who think they are one people; but we are told that Ireland is a nation, and Protestant Ulster certainly does not share that idea; and Italy did not think it was one people until long after its unity was accomplished. When the writer was in Italy in 1916, people were saying: "This war will make us one nation." Again, are the English a nation or have they merged into a "British nationality?" Scotchmen do not seem to believe very much in this British nationality. It cannot be a community of race or language that constitutes a nation, because the Gaels and the Lowlanders make up the Scotch "nation"; it cannot be a common religion, for England has scores; nor a common literature, or why is Britain separated from the United States, and the Argentine Republic from Spain? We may suggest that a nation is in effect any assembly, mixture, or confusion of people which is either afflicted by or wishes to be afflicted by a foreign office of its own, in order that it should behave collectively as if it alone constituted humanity. We have al-

I do not say that Mr. G. acted consistently up to these principles, or that they could be acted up to; but they formed the milk of the word for most of us.
G. M.

I cannot agree that Gladstone was a prophet of nationalism. He was a prophet of Liberalism, and, as such, a hater of oppression. He protested against Bourbon oppression in Naples or Turkish oppression in Bulgaria or Armenia; but to protest against oppression is not to champion nationalism. Gladstone championed not nationalism, but internationalism; he emphasized the idea that "public right" should control the relations of states. The fine words which Mr. Asquith used to state the British cause in August 1914 were (unless I am mistaken) an echo of Gladstone's own words. A noble objection to oppression; a noble championing of the rule of public right—these were the staples of Gladstone's prophecy. The pity was that, when it came to the actual handling of foreign affairs (e.g. in Egypt about 1884), Gladstone could not translate his ideals into practice.—E. B.

ready in Chap. XXXVI, § 6, traced the development of the Machiavellian monarchies into the rule of their foreign offices, playing the part of "Powers." The "nationality" which Mr. Gladstone made his guiding political principle, is really no more than the romantic and emotional exaggeration of the stresses produced by the discord of the natural political map with unsuitable political arrangements. These stresses could be used for the benefit of this power or the detriment of that.

Throughout the nineteenth century, and particularly throughout its latter half, there had been a great working up of this nationalism in the world. All men are by nature partizans and patriots, but the natural tribalism of men in the nineteenth century was unnaturally exaggerated, it was fretted and over-stimulated and inflamed and forced into the nationalist mould. Nationalism was taught in schools, emphasized by newspapers, preached and mocked and sung into men. Men were brought to feel that they were as improper without a nationality as without their clothes in a crowded assembly. Oriental peoples who had never heard of nationality before, took to it as they took to the cigarettes and bowler hats of the West. India, a galaxy of contrasted races, religions, and cultures, Dravidian, Mongolian, and Aryan, became a "nation." There were perplexing cases, of course, as when a young Whitechapel Jew had to decide whether he belonged to the British or the Jewish nation.[1] Caricature and political cartoons played a large part in this elevation of the cult of these newer and bigger tribal gods—for such indeed the modern "nations" are—to their ascendancy over the imagination of the nineteenth century. If one turns over the pages of *Punch*, that queer contemporary record of the British soul, which has lasted now since 1841, one finds the figures of Britannia, Hibernia, France, and Germania embracing, disputing, reproving, rejoicing, grieving. It greatly helped the diplomatists to carry on their game of Great Powers to convey politics in this form to the doubting general intelligence. To the common man, resentful that his son should be sent abroad to

[1] G. B. Stern's *Children of No Man's Land* is a novel of this topic of British nationality in relation to German Jews written with great insight.

be shot, it was made clear that instead of this being merely the result of the obstinacy and greed of two foreign offices, it was really a necessary part of a righteous inevitable gigantic struggle between two of these dim vast divinities. France had been wronged by Germania, or Italia was showing a proper spirit to Austria. The boy's death ceased to appear an outrage on common sense ; it assumed a sort of mythological dignity. And insurrection could clothe itself in the same romantic habiliments as diplomacy. Ireland became a Cinderella goddess, Cathleen ni Houlihan, full of heartrending and unforgivable wrongs, and Young India

a world of perpetual injuries, a world of states constantly preparing for or waging war. But concurrently and discordantly with the preaching of this nationalism of which Gladstone was the outstanding exponent,[1] there was, among the stronger nationalities, a vigorous propagation of another set of ideas, the ideas of imperialism, in which a powerful and advanced nation was conceded the right to dominate a group of other less advanced nations or less politically developed nations or peoples whose nationality was still undeveloped, who were expected by the dominating nation to be grateful for its protection and dominance. This use

Tribal Gods — *national symbols* for which men would die — of the 19th Century

John Bull — Britannia — Germania — France — Cathleen ni Houlihan

transcended its realities in the worship of Bande Mataram.

The essential idea of nineteenth-century nationalism was the "legitimate claim" of every nation to complete sovereignty, the claim of every nation to manage all its affairs within its own territory, regardless of any other nation. The flaw in this idea is that the affairs and interests of every modern community extend to the uttermost parts of the earth. The assassination at Serajevo in 1914, for example, which caused the Great War, produced the utmost distress among the Indian tribes of Labrador because that war interrupted the marketing of the furs upon which they relied for such necessities as ammunition, without which they could not get sufficient food. A world of independent sovereign nations means, therefore,

of the word empire was evidently a different one from its former universal significance. The new empires did not even pretend to be a continuation of the world empire of Rome. The leading spirit in British imperialism was Lord Beaconsfield, Gladstone's antagonist. These two ideas of nationality and, as the crown of

[1] The doctrine of nationalities was in reality a legacy of French revolutionary theory. From the men of the First Republic, who found it a useful excuse for a forward foreign policy in the best Richelieu tradition, it passed into the possession of Napoleon, who gave more attention to it at St. Helena than he had ever done at the Tuileries. Thence it came naturally into the political inheritance of Napoleon III, who sacrificed France to his belief in it. Gladstone only got it by a side wind, the theory having drifted into the British tradition by reason of the accident of Canning's anti-interventionist foreign policy during the Spanish American War of Independence.—P. G.

national success, "empire," ruled European political thought, ruled indeed the political thought of the world, throughout the latter half of the nineteenth century, and ruled it to the practical exclusion of any wider conception of a common human welfare. They were plausible and dangerously unsound working ideas. They represented nothing fundamental and unalterable in human nature, and they failed to meet the new needs of world controls and world security that the mechanical revolution was every day making more imperative. They were accepted because people in general had neither the sweeping views that a scientific study of history can give, nor had they any longer the comprehensive charity of a world religion. Their danger to all the routines of ordinary life was not realized until it was too late.

§ 8

After the middle of the nineteenth century, this world of new powers and old ideas, this *Europe be-* fermenting new wine in the old *tween 1848* bottles of diplomacy, broke out *and 1878.* through the flimsy restraints of the Treaty of Vienna into a series of wars. By an ironical accident the new system of disturbances was preceded by a peace festival in London, the Great Exhibition of 1851.

The moving spirit in this exhibition was Prince Albert of Saxe-Coburg-Gotha, the nephew of Leopold I, the German king who had been placed upon the Belgian throne in 1831, and who was also the maternal uncle of the young Queen Victoria of England. She had become queen in 1837 at the age of eighteen. The two young cousins—they were of the same age— had married in 1840 under their uncle's auspices, and Prince Albert was known to the British as the "Prince Consort." He was a young man of sound intelligence and exceptional education, and he seems to have been greatly shocked by the mental stagnation into which England had sunken. Oxford and Cambridge, those once starry centres, were still recovering but slowly from the intellectual ebb of the later eighteenth century. At neither university did the annual matriculations number more than four hundred. The examinations were for the most part mere *viva voce* ceremonies. Except for two colleges in London (the University of London) and one

in Durham, this was all the education on a university footing that England had to offer. It was very largely the initiative of this scandalized young German who had married the British queen which produced the university commission of 1850, and it was with a view to waking up England further that he promoted the first International Exhibition which was to afford some opportunity for a comparison of the artistic and industrial products of the various European nations.

The project was bitterly opposed. In the House of Commons it was prophesied that England would be overrun by foreign rogues and revolutionaries who would corrupt the morals of the people and destroy all faith and loyalty in the country.

The exhibition was held in Hyde Park in a great building of glass and iron—which afterwards was re-erected as the Crystal Palace. Financially it was a great success. It made many English people realize for the first time that theirs was not the only industrial country in the world, and that commercial prosperity was not a divinely appointed British monopoly. There was the clearest evidence of a Europe recovering steadily from the devastation of the Napoleonic wars, and rapidly overtaking the British lead in trade and manufacture. It was followed directly by the organization of a Science and Art Department (1853), to recover, if possible, the educational leeway that Britain had lost.

The exhibition released a considerable amount of international talk and sentiment. It had already found expression in the work of such young poets as Tennyson, who had glanced down the vista of the future.

" Till the war-drum throb'd no longer, and the battle-
　　flags were furl'd
　In the Parliament of man, the Federation of the
　　world."

There was much shallow optimism on the part of comfortable people just then. Peace seemed to be more secure than it had been for a long time. The social gales of 1848 had blown, and, it seemed, blown themselves out. Nowhere had the revolution succeeded. In France it had been betrayed a second time by a Bonaparte, a nephew of the first Napoleon, but a much more supple and intelligent man.[1] He had posed as a revolutionary while availing himself of the glamour of his name ; he had twice attempted raids on France during the Orleans monarchy. He had written a manual of artillery to link himself to his uncle's prestige, and he had also published an account of what he alleged to be Napoleonic views, *Des Idées Napoléoniennes* in which he jumbled up socialism, socialistic reform, and pacificism with the Napoleonic legend. The republic of 1848 was soon in difficulties with crude labour experiments, and in October he was able to re-enter the country and stand for election as President. He took an oath as President to be faithful to the democratic republic, and to regard as enemies all who attempted to change the form of government. In two years' time (December 1852) he was Emperor of the French.

At first he was regarded with considerable suspicion by Queen Victoria, or rather by Baron Stockmar, the friend and servant of King Leopold of Belgium, and the keeper of the international conscience of the British queen and her consort. All this group of Saxe-Coburg-Gotha people had a reasonable and generous enthusiasm for the unity and well-being of Germany—upon liberal lines—and they were disposed to be alarmed at this Bonapartist revival. Lord Palmerston, the British foreign minister, was, on the other hand, friendly with the usurper from the outset ; he offended the queen by sending amiable dispatches to the French President without submitting them for her examination, and so giving her sufficient time to consult Stockmar upon them, and he was obliged to resign. But subsequently the British Court veered round to a more cordial attitude to the new adventurer. The opening years of his reign promised a liberal monarchy rather than a Napoleonic career ; a government of " cheap bread, great public works, and holidays,"[2] and he expressed himself warmly in favour of the idea of nationalism, which was naturally a very acceptable idea to any liberal German intelligence. There had been a brief all-German parliament at Frankfort in 1848,

[1] This is a paradox to which I cannot subscribe. Please put me down as convinced of the opposite. —E. B.

[2] Albert Thomas in the *Encyclopædia Britannica*.

which was overthrown in 1849 by the Prussian monarchy.

(This conflict between Palmerston and the Crown is interesting because it shows the way in which the aristocratic ruling class of the crowned republic of the Britain of the early Georges was now, with an uneasy democracy below it, an educated royal consort above, and an education which had not kept pace with the times, losing power to the renascent energy of the Crown. A Stockmar would have been impossible in the reigns of George I or George II., or in a nineteenth-century Great Britain with a reasonably well-educated peerage.)

Before 1848 all the great European courts of the Vienna settlement had been kept in a kind of alliance by the fear of a second and more universal democratic revolution. After the revolutionary failures of 1848 this fear was lifted, and they were free to resume the scheming and counter-scheming of the days before 1789— with the vastly more powerful armies and fleets the first Napoleonic phase had given them. The game of Great Powers was resumed with zest, after an interval of sixty years, and it continued until it produced the catastrophe of 1914.

The Tsar of Russia, Nicholas I, was the first to move towards war. He resumed the traditional thrust of Peter the Great towards Constantinople. Nicholas invented the phrase of the " sick man of Europe " for the Sultan, and, finding an excuse in the misgovernment of the Christian population of the Turkish empire, he occupied the Danubian principalities in 1853. European diplomatists found themselves with a question of quite the eighteenth-century pattern. The designs of Russia were understood to clash with the designs of France in Syria, and to threaten the Mediterranean route to India of Great Britain, and the outcome was an alliance of France and England to bolster up Turkey and a war, the Crimean War, which ended in the repulse of Russia. One might have thought that the restraint of Russia was rather the business of Austria and Germany, but the passion of the foreign offices of France and England for burning their fingers in Russian affairs has always been very difficult to control.

The next phase of interest in this revival of

the Great Power drama was the exploitation by the Emperor Napoleon III and the King of the small kingdom of Sardinia in North Italy, of the inconveniences and miseries of the divided state of Italy, and particularly of the Austrian rule in the north. The King of Sardinia, Victor Emmanuel, made an old-time bargain for Napoleon's help in return for the provinces of Nice and Savoy. The war between France and Sardinia on the one hand, and Austria on the other, broke out in 1859, and was over in a few weeks. The Austrians were badly beaten at Magenta and Solferino. Then, being threatened by Prussia on the Rhine, Napoleon made peace, leaving Sardinia the richer for Lombardy.

Photo : Rischgitz Collection.

GARIBALDI.

The next move in the game of Victor Emmanuel, and of his chief minister Cavour, was an insurrectionary movement in Sicily led by the great Italian patriot Garibaldi. Sicily and Naples were liberated, and all Italy, except only Rome (which remained loyal to the Pope) and Venetia, which was held by the Austrians, fell to the King of Sardinia. A general Italian parliament met at Turin in 1861, and Victor Emmanuel became the first King of Italy.

But now the interest in this game of European diplomacy shifted to Germany. Already the common sense of the natural political map had asserted itself. In 1848 all Germany, including, of course, German Austria, was for a time united under the Frankfurt parliament. But that sort of union was particularly offensive to all the German courts and foreign offices ; they did not want a Germany united by the will of its people, they wanted Germany united by regal and diplomatic action—as Italy was being united. In 1848 the German parliament had insisted that the largely German provinces of Schleswig-Holstein, which had been in the

German Bund, must belong to Germany. It had ordered the Prussian army to occupy them, and the King of Prussia had refused to take his orders from the German parliament, and so had precipitated the downfall of that body. Now the King of Denmark, Christian IX, for no conceivable motive except the natural folly of kings, embarked upon a campaign of annoyance against the Germans in these two duchies. Prussian affairs were then very much in the hands of a minister of the seventeenth-century type, von Bismarck (count in 1865, prince in 1871), and he saw brilliant opportunities in this trouble. He became the champion of the German nationality in these duchies—it must be remembered that the King of Prussia had refused to undertake this rôle for democratic Germany in 1848—and he persuaded Austria to side with Prussia in a military intervention. Denmark had no chance against these Great Powers; she was easily beaten and obliged to relinquish the duchies. Then Bismarck picked a quarrel with Austria for the possession of these two small states. So he brought about a needless and fratricidal war of Germans for the greater glory of Prussia and the ascendancy of the Hohenzollern dynasty in Germany. German writers of a romantic turn of mind represent Bismarck as a great statesman planning the unity of Germany; but indeed he was doing nothing of the kind. The unity of Germany was a reality in 1848. It was and is in the nature of things. The Prussian monarchy was simply delaying the inevitable in order to seem to achieve it in Prussian fashion. That is why, when at last Germany was unified, instead of bearing the likeness of a modern civilized people, it presented itself to the world with the face of this archaic Bismarck, with a fierce moustache,

The KINGDOM of ITALY, 1861.

J.F.H.

(born 1809, died 1865, president from 1861) rose to greatness, how the republic was cleansed from the stain of slavery, and how the federal government of the union was preserved.

For four long years (1861–65) this war swung to and fro, through the rich woods and over the hills of Virginia between Washington and Richmond, until at last the secessionist left was thrust back and broken, and Sherman, the unionist general, swept across Georgia to the sea in the rear of the main confederate (secessionist) armies. All the elements of reaction in Europe rejoiced during the four years of republican dissension; the British aristocracy openly sided with the confederate states, and the British Government permitted several privateers, and particularly the *Alabama*, to be launched in England to attack the federal shipping. Napoleon III was even more rash in his assumption that after all the New World had fallen before the Old. The sure shield of

huge jack boots, a spiked helmet, and a sword.

In this war between Prussia and Austria, Prussia had for an ally Italy; most of the smaller German states, who dreaded the schemes of Prussia, fought on the side of Austria. The reader will naturally want to know why Napoleon III did not grasp this admirable occasion for statecraft and come into the war to his own advantage. All the rules of the Great Power game required that he should. But Napoleon, unhappily for himself, had got his fingers in a trap on the other side of the Atlantic, and was in no position to intervene.

In order to understand the entanglement of this shifty gentleman, it is necessary to explain that the discord in interests between the northern and southern states of the American union, due to the economic differences based on slavery, had at last led to open civil war. The federal system established in 1789 had to fight the secessionist efforts of the confederated slave-holding states. We have traced the causes of that great struggle in Chapter XXXVII, § 6; its course we cannot relate here, nor tell how President Lincoln

BISMARCK.

the Monroe doctrine, it seemed to him, was thrust aside for good, the Great Powers might meddle again in America, and the blessings of an adventurous monarchy be restored there. A pretext for interference was found in certain liberties taken with the property of foreigners by the Mexican president. A joint expedition of French, British, and Spanish occupied Vera group of eager Europeans in possession of Mexico found themselves faced by the victorious federal government in a thoroughly grim mood, with a large, dangerous-looking army in hand. The French imperialists were bluntly given the alternative of war with the United States or clearing out of America. In effect this was an instruction to go. This was the entanglement which prevented Napoleon III from interference between Prussia and Austria in 1866, and this was the reason why Bismarck precipitated his struggle with Austria.

Map of EUROPE, 1848–1871

Prussia to 1866..........
territory seized 1866-7..........
N. German Confederation, 1866..
German Empire, 1871..........
France..territory acquired (Savoy & Nice, 1860)..
territory lost (Alsace-Lorraine, 1871)..
Austria. territory lost (Lombardy, 1859, Venetia, 1866)
[For Italy see also separate map]

While Prussia was fighting Austria, Napoleon III was trying to escape with dignity from the briars of Mexico. He invented a shabby quarrel upon financial grounds with Maximilian and withdrew the French troops. Then, by all the rules of kingship, Maximilian should have abdicated. But instead he made a fight for his empire;

Cruz, but Napoleon's projects were too bold for his allies, and they withdrew when it became clear that he contemplated nothing less than the establishment of a Mexican empire. This he did, after much stiff fighting, making the Archduke Maximilian of Austria Emperor of Mexico in 1864. The French forces, however, remained in effectual possession of the country, and a crowd of French speculators poured into Mexico to exploit its mines and resources.

But in April 1865, the civil war in the United States was brought to an end by the surrender of the great Southern commander, General Lee, at Appomattox Court House, and the little he was defeated by his recalcitrant subjects, caught, and shot as a public nuisance in 1867. So the peace of President Monroe was restored in the New World. There remained only one monarchy in America, the empire of Brazil, where a branch of the Portuguese royal family continued to reign until 1889. In that year the emperor was quietly packed off to Paris, and Brazil came into line with the rest of the continent.

But while Napoleon was busy with his American adventure, Prussia and Italy were snatching victory over the Austrians (1866). Italy was badly beaten at Custozza and in the naval

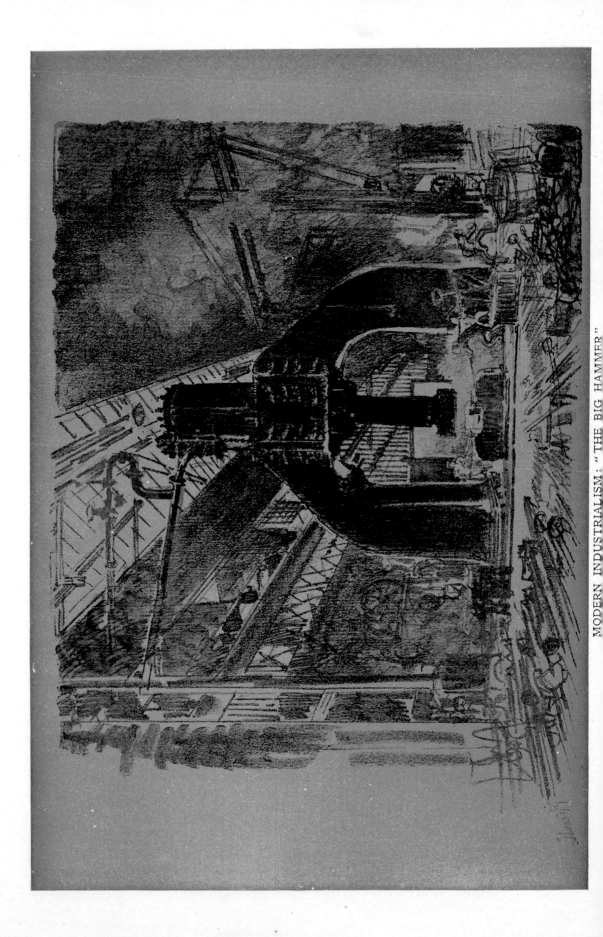

MODERN INDUSTRIALISM: "THE BIG HAMMER"

battle of Lissa, but the Austrian army was so crushed by the Prussian at the battle of Sadowa, that Austria made an abject surrender. Italy gained the province of Venetia, so making one more step towards unity—only Rome and Trieste and a few small towns on the north and north-western frontiers remained—and Prussia became the head of a North German Confederation, from which Bavaria, Württemberg, Baden, Hesse, and Austria were excluded.

Four years later came the next step towards the natural political map of Europe, when Napoleon III plunged into war against Prussia. A kind of self-destroying foolishness urged him to this. He came near to this war in 1867 so soon as he was free from Mexico, by demanding Luxembourg for France; he embarked upon it in 1870, when a cousin of the King of Prussia became a candidate for the vacant throne of Spain. Napoleon had some theory in his mind that Austria, Bavaria, Württemberg, and the other states outside the North German Confederation would side with him against Prussia.[1] He probably thought this would happen, because he wanted it to happen. But since 1848 the Germans, so far as foreign meddling was concerned, had been in spirit a united people; Bismarck was merely imposing the Hohenzollern monarchy, with pomp, ceremony, and bloodshed, upon accomplished facts. All Germany sided with Prussia.

Early in August 1870 the united German forces invaded France. After the battles of Wörth and Gravelotte, one French army under Bazaine was forced into Metz and surrounded there; and, on September 1st, a second, with

which was Napoleon, was defeated and obliged to capitulate at Sedan. Paris found herself bare to the invader. For a second time the promises of Napoleonism had failed France disastrously. On September 4th, France declared herself a republic again, and thus regenerated, prepared to fight for existence against triumphant Prussianism. For though it was a united Germany that had overcome French imperialism, it had Prussia in the saddle. The army in Metz capitulated in October; Paris, after a siege and a bombardment, surrendered in January 1871.

With pomp and ceremony, in the Hall of Mirrors at Versailles, amidst a great array of military uniforms, the King of Prussia was declared German Emperor, and Bismarck and the sword of the Hohenzollerns claimed the credit for that German unity which a common language and literature had long since assured.

The Peace of Frankfort was a Hohenzollern peace. Bismarck had availed himself of the national feeling of Germany to secure the aid of the South German states, but he had no grasp of the essential forces that had given victory to him and to his royal master. The power that had driven Prussia to victory was the power of the natural political map of Europe insisting upon the unity of the German-speaking peoples. In the east, Germany was already sinning against that natural map by her administration of Posen and other Polish districts. Now, greedy for territory, and particularly for iron mines, she annexed a considerable area of French-speaking Lorraine, including Metz, and Alsace, which, in spite of its German speech, was largely French in sympathy. Inevitably there was a clash between German rulers and French subjects in these annexed provinces; inevitably the wrongs and bitterness of the subjugated France of Lorraine echoed in Paris

Photo: Rischgitz Collection.
NAPOLEON III.

[1] There were also hopes of an Italian alliance for France, and these, combined with the anti-Prussian direction of Austrian policy, and the Franco-Russian *rapprochement* which had followed the Crimean War almost justified Napoleon in believing that he would not be left entirely alone.—P. G.

and kept alive the passionate resentment of the French. . . .

The natural map had already secured political recognition in the Austrian Empire after Sadowa (1866). Hungary, which had been subordinated to Austria, was erected into a kingdom on an equal footing with Austria, and the Empire of Austria had become the "dual monarchy" of Austria-Hungary. But in the south-east of this empire, and over the Turkish empire, the boundaries and subjugations of the conquest period still remained.

A fresh upthrust of the natural map began in 1875, when the Christian races in the Balkans, and particularly the Bulgarians, became restless and insurgent. The Turks adopted violent repressive measures, and embarked upon massacres of Bulgarians on an enormous scale. Thereupon Russia intervened (1877), and after a year of costly warfare obliged the Turks to sign the Treaty of San Stefano, which was, on the whole, a sensible treaty, breaking up the artificial Turkish Empire, and to a large extent establishing the natural map. But it had become the tradition of British policy to thwart "the designs of Russia"—heaven knows why!—whenever Russia appeared to have a

design; and the British Foreign Office, under the premiership of Lord Beaconsfield, intervened with a threat of war if a considerable restoration of the Turks' facilities for exaction, persecution, and massacre was not made. For a time war seemed very probable. The British music-halls, those lamps to British foreign policy, were lit with patriotic fire, and the London errand-boy on his rounds was inspired to chant, with the simple dignity of a great people conscious of its high destinies, a song declaring that :

> "We don't want to fight, but, by Jingo,[1] if we do,
> We got the ships, we got the men, we got
> the munn-aye too " . . .

and so on to a climax :

> "The Russ'ns shall not 'ave Con-stan-te-
> no - - - ple."

In consequence of this British opposition, a conference was assembled in 1878 at Berlin to revise the Treaty of San Stefano, chiefly in the interests of the Turkish and Austrian monarchies; the British acquired the island of Cyprus, to which they had no sort of right whatever, and which has never been of the slightest use to them, and Lord Beaconsfield returned triumphantly from the Berlin Conference, to the extreme exasperation of Mr. Gladstone, with what the British were given to understand at the time was "Peace with Honour."

This Treaty of Berlin was the second main factor, the Peace of Frankfort being the first, in bringing about the great war of 1914–18.

These thirty years after 1848 are years of very great interest to the student of international political methods. Released from their terror of a world-wide insurrection of the common people, the governments of Europe were doing their best to resume the game of Great Powers that had been so rudely interrupted by the American and French revolutions. But it looked much more like the old game than it was in reality. The mechanical revolution was making war a far more complete disturbance of the general life than it had ever been before,

[1] Hence " Jingo " for any rabid patriot.

Comparative Maps of ASIA
(a) as part of hemisphere
(b) on Mercator's projection
to show relative sizes of Asiatic Russia and India in the two cases

and the proceedings of the diplomatists were ruled, in spite of their efforts to disregard the fact, by imperatives that Charles V and Louis XIV had never known. Irritation with misgovernment was capable of far better organization and far more effective expression than it had ever been before. Statesmen dressed this up as the work of the spirit of Nationalism, but there were times and occasions when that costume wore very thin. The grand monarchs of the seventeenth and eighteenth centuries had seemed to be free to do this or that, to make war or to keep the peace, to conquer this province or cede that as they willed; but such a ruler as Napoleon III went from one proceeding to another with something of the effect of a man who feels his way among things unseen.

None of these European governments in the nineteenth century was in fact a free agent. We look to-day at the maps of Europe since 1814, we compare them with the natural map, and we see that the game the Great Powers played was indeed a game of foregone conclusions. Whatever arrangements they made that were in accordance with the natural political map of the world, and the trend towards educational democracy, held, and whatever arrangements they made contrary to these things, collapsed. We are forced, therefore, to the conclusion that all the diplomatic fussing, posturing, and scheming, all the intrigue and bloodshed of these years, all the monstrous

turmoil and waste of kings and armies, all the wonderful attitudes, deeds, and schemes of the Cavours, Bismarcks, Disraelis, Bonapartes, and the like "great men," might very well have been avoided altogether had Europe but had the sense to instruct a small body of ordinarily honest ethnologists, geographers, and sociologists to draw out its proper boundaries and prescribe suitable forms of government in a reasonable manner. The romantic phase in history had come to an end. A new age was beginning with new and greater imperatives, and these nineteenth-century statesmen were but pretending to control events.

§ 9

We have suggested that in the political history of Europe between 1848 and 1878, the mechanical revolution was not yet producing any very revolutionary changes. The post-revolutionary Great Powers were still going on within boundaries of practically the same size and with much the same formalities as they had done in pre-revolutionary times. But where the increased speed and certainty of transport and telegraphic communications were already producing very considerable changes of condition and method, was in the overseas enterprises of Britain and the other European Powers, and in the relation of Asia and Africa to Europe.

The (Second) Scramble for Overseas Empires.

The end of the eighteenth century was a period of disrupting empires and disillusioned expansionists. The long and tedious journey between Britain and Spain and their colonies in America prevented any really free coming and going between the home land and the daughter lands, and so the colonies separated into new and distinct communities, with distinctive ideas and interests and even modes of speech. As they grew they strained more and more at the feeble and uncertain link of shipping that joined them. Weak trading-posts in the wilderness, like those of France in Canada,

The British Empire in 1815 consisted of the thinly populated coastal river and lake regions of Canada, and a great hinterland of wilderness in which the only settlements as yet were the fur-trading stations of the Hudson Bay Company, about a third of the Indian peninsula, under the rule of the East India Company, the coast districts of the Cape of Good Hope inhabited by blacks and rebellious-spirited Dutch settlers; a few trading stations on the coast of West Africa, the rock of Gibraltar, the island of Malta, Jamaica, a few minor slave-labour possessions in the West Indies, British

The BRITISH EMPIRE in 1815 [Mercator's Projection]

or trading establishments in great alien communities, like those of Britain in India, might well cling for bare existence to the nation which gave them support and a reason for their existence. That much and no more seemed to many thinkers in the early part of the nineteenth century to be the limit set to overseas rule. In 1820 the sketchy great European " empires " outside of Europe that had figured so bravely in the maps of the middle eighteenth century, had shrunken to very small dimensions. Only the Russian sprawled as large as ever across Asia. It sprawled much larger in the imaginations of many Europeans than in reality, because of their habit of studying the geography of the world upon Mercator's projection, which enormously exaggerated the size of Siberia.

Guiana in South America, and, on the other side of the world, two dumps for convicts at Botany Bay in Australia and in Tasmania. Spain retained Cuba and a few settlements in the Philippine Islands. Portugal had in Africa some vestiges of her ancient claims. Holland had various islands and possessions in the East Indies and Dutch Guiana, and Denmark an island or so in the West Indies. France had one or two West Indian Islands and French Guiana. This seemed to be as much as the European Powers needed, or were likely to acquire of the rest of the world. Only the East India Company showed any spirit of expansion.

In India, as we have already told, a peculiar empire was being built up, not by the British peoples, nor by the British Government, but by this company of private adventurers with their monopoly and royal charter. The company had been forced to become a military and political power during the years of Indian division and insecurity that followed the break up of India after the death of Aurangzeb in 1707. It had learnt to trade in states and peoples during the eighteenth century. Clive founded, Warren Hastings organized, this strange new sort of empire; French rivalry was defeated, as we have already told; and by 1798, Lord Mornington, afterwards the Marquis Wellesley, the elder brother of that General Wellesley who became the Duke of Wellington, became Governor-General of India, and set the policy of the company definitely upon the line of replacing the fading empire of the Grand Mogul by its own rule. Napoleon's expedition to Egypt was a direct attack upon the empire of this British company. While Europe was busy with the Napoleonic wars, the East India Company, under a succession of governor-generals, was playing much the same rôle in India that had been played before by Turkoman and such-like invaders from the north. And after the Peace of Vienna it went on, levying its revenues, making wars, sending ambassadors to Asiatic powers, a quasi-independent state, a state, however, with a marked disposition to send wealth westward.

In Chapter XXXVI, § 9, we have sketched the break-up of the empire of the Great Mogul and the appearance of the Mahratta states, the Rajput principalities, the Moslem kingdoms of Oudh and Bengal, and the Sikhs. We cannot tell here in any detail how the British company made its way to supremacy sometimes as the ally of this power, sometimes of that, and finally as the conqueror of all. Its power spread to Assam, Sind, Oudh. The map of India began to take on the outlines familiar to the English schoolboy of to-day, a patchwork of native states embraced and held together by the great provinces under direct British rule. . . .

Now as this strange unprecedented empire of the company grew in the period between 1800 and 1858, the mechanical revolution was quietly abolishing the great distance that had once separated India and Britain. In the old days the rule of the company had interfered little in the domestic life of the Indian states; it had given India foreign overlords, but India was used to foreign overlords, and had hitherto assimilated them; these Englishmen came into the country young, lived there most of their lives, and became a part of its system. But now the mechanical revolution began to alter this state of affairs. It became easier for the British officials to go home and to have holidays in Europe, easier for them to bring out wives and families; they ceased to be Indianized; they remained more conspicuously foreign and western—and there were more of them. And they began to interfere more vigorously with Indian customs. Magical and terrible things like the telegraph and the railway arrived. Christian missions became offensively busy. If they did not make very many converts, at least they made sceptics among the adherents of the older faiths. The young men in the towns began to be "Europeanized" to the great dismay of their elders.

India had endured many changes of rulers before, but never the sort of changes in her ways that these things portended. The Moslem teachers and the Brahmins were alike alarmed, and the British were blamed for the progress of mankind. Conflicts of economic interests grew more acute with the increasing nearness of Europe; Indian industries, and particularly the ancient cotton industry, suffered from legislation that favoured the British manufacturer.[1] A piece of incredible folly on the part of the company precipitated an outbreak. To the Brahmin a cow is sacred; to the Moslem the pig is unclean. A new rifle, needing greased cartridges—which the men had to bite—was served out to the company's Indian soldiers; the troops discovered that their cartridges were greased with the fat of cows and swine. This discovery precipitated a revolt of the company's Indian army, the Indian Mutiny (1857). First the troops mutinied at Meerut. Then Delhi rose to restore the empire of the Great Mogul. . . .

The British public suddenly discovered India. They became aware of that little garrison of British people, far away in that strange land

[1] See *England's Debt to India* by Lajpat Rai for a good statement of India's economic grievance.

of fiery dust and weary sunshine, fighting for life against dark multitudes of assailants. How they had got there and what right they had there, the British public did not ask. The love of one's kin in danger overrides such questions; 1857 was a year of passionate anxiety in Great Britain. With mere handfuls of troops the British leaders, and notably Lawrence and Nicholson, did amazing things. They did not sit down to be besieged while the mutineers organized and gathered prestige ; that would have lost them India for ever. They attacked, often against overwhelming odds. " Clubs, not spades, are trumps," said Lawrence. The Sikhs, the Gurkhas, the Punjab troops stuck to the British. The South remained tranquil. Of the massacres of Cawnpore and Lucknow in Oudh, and how a greatly outnumbered force of British troops besieged and stormed Delhi, other histories must tell. By April, 1859, the last embers of the blaze had been stamped out, and the British were masters of India again. In no sense had the mutiny been a popular insurrection ; it was a mutiny merely of the Bengal Army, due largely to the unimaginative rule of the company officials. Its story abounds in instances of Indian help and kindness to British fugitives. But it was a warning.

The direct result of the mutiny was the annexation of the Indian Empire to the British Crown. By the Act entitled *An Act for the Better Government of India*, the Governor-General became a Viceroy representing the Sovereign, and the place of the company was taken by a Secretary of State for India responsible to the British Parliament. In 1877, Lord Beaconsfield, to complete this work, caused Queen Victoria to be proclaimed Empress of India.

Upon these extraordinary lines India and Britain are linked at the present time. India is still the empire of the Great Mogul, but the Great Mogul has been replaced by the " crowned republic " of Great Britain. India is an autocracy without an autocrat. Its rule combines the disadvantage of absolute monarchy with the impersonality and irresponsibility of democratic officialdom. The Indian with a complaint to make has no visible monarch to go to ; his Emperor is a golden symbol ; he must circulate pamphlets in England or inspire a question in the British House of Commons. The more occupied Parliament is with British affairs, the less attention India will receive, and the more she will be at the mercy of her small group of higher officials.

This is manifestly impossible as a permanent state of affairs. Indian life, whatever its restraints, is moving forward with the rest of the world ; India has an increasing service of newspapers, an increasing number of educated people affected by Western ideas, and an increasing sense of a common grievance against her government. There had been little or no corresponding advance in the education and quality of the British official in India during the century. His tradition is a high one ; he is often a man of exceptional quality, but the system is unimaginative and inflexible. Moreover, the military power that stands behind these officials has developed neither in character nor intelligence during the last century. No other class has been so stagnant intellectually as the British military caste. Confronted with a more educated India, the British military man, uneasily aware of his educational defects and constantly apprehensive of ridicule, has in the last few years displayed a disposition towards spasmodic violence that has had some very lamentable results. For a time the Great War diverted what small amount of British public attention was previously given to India altogether, and drew away the more intelligent military men from her service. During those years, and the feverish years of unsettlement that followed, things occurred in India; the massacre of an unarmed political gathering at Amritzar in which nearly two thousand people were killed or wounded, floggings and humiliating outrages, a sort of Officials' Terror, that produced a profound moral shock when at last the Hunter Commission of 1919 brought them before the home public. In liberal-minded Englishmen, who had been wont to regard their empire as an incipient league of free peoples, this revelation of the barbaric quality in its administrators produced a very understandable dismay. . . .

But the time has not yet come for writing the chapter of history that India is opening for herself. . . . We cannot discuss here in detail the still unsettled problems of the new India that struggles into being. Already in the Government of India Act of 1919 we may have the opening of a new and happier era that may culminate in a free and willing group of Indian peoples taking an equal place among the confederated states of the world. . . .

The growth of the British Empire in directions other than that of India was by no means so rapid during the earlier half of the nineteenth century. A considerable school of political thinkers in Britain was disposed to regard overseas possessions as a source of weakness to the kingdom. The Australian settlements developed slowly until in 1842 the discovery of valuable copper mines, and in 1851 of gold, gave them a new importance. Improvements in transport were also making Australian wool an increasingly marketable commodity in Europe. Canada too was not remarkably progressive until 1849 ; it was troubled by dissensions between its French and British inhabitants, there were several serious revolts, and it was only in 1867 that a new constitution creating a Federal Dominion of Canada relieved its internal strains. It was the railway that altered the Canadian outlook. It enabled Canada, just as it enabled the United States, to expand westward, to market its corn and other produce in Europe, and in spite of its swift and extensive growth, to remain in language and sympathy and interests one community. The railway, the steamship, and the telegraphic cable were indeed changing all the conditions of colonial development.

Before 1840, English settlements had already begun in New Zealand, and a New Zealand Land Company had been formed to exploit the possibilities of the island. In 1840 New

Zealand also was added to the colonial possessions of the British Crown.

Canada, as we have noted, was the first of the British possessions to respond richly to the new economic possibilities the new methods of transport were opening. Presently the republics of South America, and particularly the Argentine Republic, began to feel, in their cattle trade and coffee growing, the increased nearness of the European market. Hitherto the chief commodities that had attracted the

AFRICA
about the middle
of the 19th Century

European Powers into unsettled and barbaric regions had been gold or other metals, spices, ivory, or slaves. But in the last quarter of the nineteenth century the increase of the European populations was obliging their governments to look abroad for staple foods ; and the growth of scientific industrialism was creating a demand for new raw materials, fats and greases of every kind, rubber, and other hitherto disregarded substances. It was plain that Great Britain and Holland and Portugal were reaping a great and growing commercial advantage from their very considerable control of tropical

AFRICA
1914

British.....
French......
German....
Portuguese..
Belgian.....
Spanish....
Italian....

and sub-tropical products. After 1871 Germany, and presently France and later Italy, began to look for unannexed raw-material areas, or for Oriental countries capable of profitable modernization.

So began a fresh scramble all over the world, except in the American region where the Monroe Doctrine now barred such adventures, for politically unprotected lands. Close to Europe was the continent of Africa, full of vaguely known possibilities. In 1850 it was a continent of black mystery; only Egypt and the coast were known. A map must show the greatness of the European ignorance at that time. It would need a book as long as this *Outline* to do justice to the amazing story of the explorers and adventurers who first pierced this cloud of darkness, and to the political agents, administrators, traders, settlers, and scientific men who followed in their track. Wonderful races of men like the pigmies, strange beasts like the okapi, marvellous fruits and flowers and insects, terrible diseases, astounding scenery of forest and mountain, enormous inland seas and gigantic rivers and cascades were revealed;

a whole new world. Even remains (at Zimbabwe) of some unrecorded and vanished civilization, the southward enterprise of an early people, were discovered. Into this new world came the Europeans, and found the rifle already there in the hands of the Arab slave-traders, and negro life in disorder. By 1900, as our second map must show, all Africa was mapped, explored, estimated, and divided between the European Powers, divided with much snarling and disputation into portions that left each Power uneasy or discontented. Little heed was given to the welfare of the natives in this scramble. The Arab slaver was indeed curbed rather than expelled, but the greed for rubber, which was a wild product collected under compulsion by the natives in the Belgian Congo, a greed exacerbated by the pitiless avarice of the King of the Belgians, and the clash of inexperienced European administrators with the native population in many other annexations, led to horrible atrocities. No European Power has perfectly clean hands in this matter.

We cannot tell here in any detail how Great Britain got possession of Egypt in 1883, and remained there in spite of the fact that Egypt was technically a part of the Turkish Empire, nor how nearly this scramble led to war between France and Great Britain in 1898, when a certain Major Marchand, crossing Central Africa from the West coast, tried at Fashoda to seize the Upper Nile. In Uganda the French Catholic and the British Anglican missionaries disseminated a form of Christianity so heavily charged with the spirit of Napoleon, and so finely insistent upon the nuances of doctrine, that a few years after its first glimpse of European civilization, Mengo, the capital of Uganda, was littered with dead " Protestants " and

"Catholics" extremely difficult to distinguish from the entirely unspiritual warriors of the old régime.

Nor can we tell how the British Government first let the Boers, or Dutch settlers, of the Orange River district and the Transvaal set up independent republics in the inland parts of South Africa, and then repented and annexed the Transvaal Republic in 1877; nor how the Transvaal Boers fought for freedom and won it after the Battle of Majuba Hill (1881). Majuba Hill was made to rankle in the memory of the English people by a persistent press campaign. A war with both republics broke out in 1899, a three years' war enormously costly to the British people, which ended at last in the surrender of the two republics.

Their period of subjugation was a brief one. In 1907, after the downfall of the imperialist government which had conquered them, the Liberals took the South African problem in hand, and these former republics became free and fairly willing associates with Cape Colony and Natal in a confederation of all the states of South Africa as one self-governing republic under the British Crown.

In a quarter of a century the partition of Africa was completed. There remained unannexed three comparatively small countries: Liberia, a settlement of liberated negro slaves on the west coast; Morocco, under a Moslem Sultan [1]; and Abyssinia, a barbaric country, with an ancient and peculiar form of Christianity, which had successfully maintained its independence against Italy at the Battle of Adowa in 1896.

§ 10

It is difficult to believe that any large number of people really accepted this headlong painting **The Indian Precedent in Asia.** of the map of Africa in European colours as a permanent new settlement of the world's affairs, but it is the duty of the historian to record that it was so accepted. There was but a shallow historical background to the European mind in the nineteenth century, hardly any sense of what constitutes an enduring political system, and no habit of penetrating criticism. The quite temporary advantages that the onset of the

[1] Now a French protectorate.—P. G.

mechanical revolution in the West had given the European Great Powers over the rest of the Old World were regarded by people, blankly ignorant of the great Mongol conquests of the thirteenth and following centuries, as evidences of a permanent and assured leadership. They had no sense of the transferability of science and its fruits. They did not realize that Chinamen and Indians could carry on the work of research as ably as Frenchmen or Englishmen. They believed that there was some innate intellectual drive in the West, and some innate indolence and conservatism in the East, that assured the Europeans a world predominance for ever.

The consequence of this infatuation was that the various European foreign offices set themselves not merely to scramble with the British for the savage and undeveloped regions of the world's surface, but also to carve up the populous and civilized countries of Asia as though these peoples also were no more than raw material for European exploitation. The inwardly precarious but outwardly splendid imperialism of the British ruling class in India, and the extensive and profitable possessions of the Dutch in the East Indies, filled the ruling and mercantile classes of the rival Great Powers with dreams of similar glories in Persia, in the disintegrating Ottoman Empire, and in Further India, China, and Japan. In the closing years of the nineteenth century it was assumed, as the reader may verify by an examination of the current literature of the period, to be a natural and inevitable thing that all the world should fall under European dominion. With a hypocritical pretence of reluctant benevolent effort the European mind prepared itself to take up what Mr. Rudyard Kipling called "the White Man's Burthen"—that is to say, the loot and lordship of the earth. The Powers set themselves to this enterprise in a mood of jostling rivalry, with half-educated or illiterate populations at home, with a mere handful of men, a few thousand at most, engaged in scientific research, with their internal political systems in a state of tension or convulsive change, with a creaking economic system of the most provisional sort, and with their religions far gone in decay. They really believed that the vast populations of Eastern Asia could be permanently subordinated to such a Europe.

Even to-day there are many people who fail to grasp the essential facts of this situation. They do not realize that in Asia the average brain is not one whit inferior in quality to the average European brain ; that history shows Asiatics to be as bold, as vigorous, as generous, as self-sacrificing, and as capable of strong collective action as Europeans, and that there are and must continue to be a great many more Asiatics than Europeans in the world. It has always been difficult to restrain the leakage of know-ledge from one population to another, and now it becomes impossible. Under modern conditions world-wide economic and educational equaliza-tion is in the long run inevitable. An intellec-tual and moral rally of the Asiatics is going on at the present time. The slight leeway of a century or so, a few decades may recover. At the present time, for example, for one Englishman who knows Chinese thoroughly, or has any intimate knowledge of Chinese life and thought, there are hundreds of Chinamen conversant with everything the English know. The balance of knowledge in favour of India may be even greater. To Britain, India sends students ; to India, Britain sends officials. There is no organization whatever for the sending of European students, as students, to examine and inquire into Indian history, archæology, and current affairs.

Since the year 1898, the year of the seizure of Kiau-Chau by Germany and of Wei-hai-wei by Britain, and the year after the Russian taking of Port Arthur, events in China have moved more rapidly than in any other country except Japan. A great hatred of Europeans swept like a flame over China, and a political society for the expulsion of Europeans, the Boxers, grew up and broke out into violence in 1900. This was an outbreak of rage and mis-chief on quite old-fashioned lines. In 1900 the Boxers murdered 250 Europeans and, it is said, nearly 30,000 Christians. China, not for the first time in history, was under the sway of a dowager empress, who, like the Empress Theo-dora of Constantinople, had once, it is said, been a woman of no repute. She was an ignor-ant woman, but of great force of character and in close sympathy with the Boxers. She

supported them, and protected those who perpetrated outrages on the Europeans. All that again is what might have happened in 500 B.C. or thereabouts against the Huns.

Things came to a crisis in 1900. The Boxers became more and more threatening to the Europeans in China. Attempts were made to send up additional European guards to the Pekin legations, but this only precipitated matters. The German Ambassador was shot down in the streets of Pekin by a soldier of the imperial guard. The rest of the foreign ambassadors gathered together and made a fortification of the more favourably situated embassies and stood a siege of two months. A combined allied force of 20,000 under a German general then marched up to Pekin and relieved the legations, and the old Empress fled north-westward. Some of the European troops com-mitted grave atrocities upon the Chinese civil population.[1] That brings one up to about the level of 1850, let us say.

There followed the practical annexation of Manchuria by Russia, a squabble among the Powers, and in 1904 a British invasion of Tibet, hitherto a forbidden country. But what did not appear on the surface of these events, and what made all these events fundamentally different, was that China now contained a considerable number of able people who had a European education and European knowledge. The Boxer Insurrection subsided, and then the influence of this new factor began to appear in talk of a constitution (1906), in the suppres-sion of opium-smoking, and in educational re-forms. A constitution of the Japanese type came into existence in 1909, making China a limited monarchy. But China is not to be moulded to the Japanese pattern, and the revolutionary stir continued. Japan, in her own reorganization, and in accordance with her temperament, had turned her eyes to the Monarchist West, but China was looking across the Pacific. In 1911 the essential Chinese revolution began. In 1912 the Emperor ab-dicated, and the greatest community in the world became a republic. The overthrow of the Emperor was also the overthrow of the Manchus, and the Mongolian pigtail, which had

---

[1] See Putnam Weale's *Indiscreet Letters from Pekin*, a partly fictitious book, but true and vivid in its effects.

been compulsory throughout China since 1644, vanished from the land.

At the present time it is probable that there are more good brain matter and more devoted men working out the modernization and the reorganization of the Chinese civilization than we should find directed to the welfare of any single European people. China will presently have a modernized practicable script, a press, new and vigorous modern universities, a re-organized industrial system, and a growing body of scientific and economic inquiry. The natural industry and ingenuity of her vast population will be released to co-operate upon terms of equality with the Western world. She may have great internal difficulties ahead of her yet; of that no man can judge. Never-theless, the time may not be very distant when the Federated States of China may be at one with the United States of America and a pacified and reconciled Europe in upholding the organized peace of the world.

§ 11

The pioneer country, however, in the recovery of the Asiatic peoples was not China, but **The History** Japan. We have outrun our story **of Japan.** in telling of China. Hitherto Japan has played but a small part in this history; her secluded civilization has not contributed very largely to the general shaping of human des-tinies; she has received much, but she has given little. The original inhabitants of the Japanese Islands were probably a northern people with remote Nordic affinities, the Hairy Ainu. But the Japanese proper are of the Mongolian race. Physically they resemble the Amerindians, and there are many curious resemblances be-tween the prehistoric pottery and so forth of Japan and similar Peruvian products. It is not impossible that they are a back-flow from the trans-Pacific drift of the early heliolithic culture, but they may also have absorbed from the south a Malay and even a Negrito element.

Whatever the origin of the Japanese, there can be no doubt that their civilization, their writing, and their literary and artistic traditions, are derived from the Chinese. They were emerging from barbarism in the second and third centuries of the Christian Era, and one of their earliest acts as a people outside their own country was an invasion of Korea under a queen Jingo, who seems to have played a large part in establishing their civilization. Their history is an interesting and romantic one; they developed a feudal system and a tradition of chivalry; their attacks upon Korea and China are an Eastern equivalent of the English wars in France. Japan was first brought into con-tact with Europe in the sixteenth century; in 1542 some Portuguese reached it in a Chinese junk, and in 1549 a Jesuit missionary, Francis Xavier, began his teaching there. The Jesuit accounts describe a country greatly devastated by perpetual feudal war. For a time Japan welcomed European intercourse, and the Chris-tian missionaries made a great number of converts. A certain William Adams, of Gilling-ham, in Kent, became the most trusted European adviser of the Japanese, and showed them how to build big ships. There were voyages in Japanese-built ships to India and Peru. Then arose complicated quarrels between the Spanish Dominicans, the Portuguese Jesuits, and the English and Dutch Protestants, each warning the Japanese against the evil political designs of the others. The Jesuits, in a phase of as-cendancy, persecuted and insulted the Budd-hists with great acrimony. These troubles interwove with the feudal conflicts of the time. In the end the Japanese came to the conclusion that the Europeans and their Christianity were an intolerable nuisance, and that Catholic Christianity in particular was a mere cloak for the political dreams of the Pope and the Spanish monarchy—already in possession of the Philip-pine Islands; there was a great and conclusive persecution of the Christians, and in 1638 Japan was absolutely closed to Europeans,[1] and remained closed for over 200 years. During those two centuries the Japanese remained as completely cut off from the rest of the world as though they lived upon another planet. It was forbidden to build any ship larger than a mere coasting boat. No Japanese could go abroad, and no European enter the country.

For two centuries Japan remained outside

[1] With the exception of one wretched Dutch factory on the minute island of Deshima in the harbour of Nagasaki. The Dutch were exposed to almost un-endurable indignities. They had no intercourse with any Japanese except the special officials appointed to deal with them.

the main current of history. She lived on in a state of picturesque feudalism enlivened by blood feuds, in which about five per cent. of the population, the *samurai*, or fighting men, and the nobles and their families, tyrannized without restraint over the rest of the population. All common men knelt when a noble passed ; to betray the slightest disrespect was to risk being slashed to death by his *samurai*. The elect classes lived lives of romantic adventure without one redeeming gleam of novelty ; they loved, murdered, and pursued fine points of honour—which probably bored the intelligent ones extremely. We can imagine the wretchedness of a curious mind, tormented by the craving for travel and knowledge, cooped up in these islands.

Meanwhile the great world outside went on to wider visions and new powers. Strange shipping became more frequent, passing the Japanese headlands ; sometimes ships were wrecked and sailors brought ashore. Through the Dutch settlement at Deshima, their one link with the outer universe, came warnings that Japan was not keeping pace with the power of the Western world. In 1837 a ship sailed into Yedo Bay flying a strange flag of stripes and stars, and carrying some Japanese sailors she had picked up far adrift in the Pacific. She was driven off by a cannon shot. This flag presently reappeared on other ships. One in 1849 came to demand the liberation of eighteen shipwrecked American sailors. Then in 1853 came four American warships under Commodore Perry, who refused to be driven away. He lay at anchor in forbidden waters, and sent messages to the two rulers who at that time shared the control of Japan. In 1854 he returned with ten ships, amazing ships propelled by steam, and equipped with big guns, and he made proposals for trade and intercourse that the Japanese had no power to resist. He landed

with a guard of 500 men to sign the treaty. Incredulous crowds watched this visitation from the outer world, marching through the streets.

Russia, Holland, and Britain followed in the wake of America. Foreigners entered the country, and conflicts between them and Japanese gentlemen of spirit ensued. A

British subject was killed in a street brawl, and a Japanese town was bombarded by the British (1863). A great nobleman whose estates commanded the Straits of Shimonoseki saw fit to fire on foreign vessels, and a second bombardment by a fleet of British, French, Dutch, and American warships destroyed his batteries and scattered his swordsmen. Finally an allied squadron (1865), at anchor off Kioto, imposed

A STREET IN OSAKA.

a ratification of the treaties which opened Japan to the world.

The humiliation of the Japanese by these events was intense, and it would seem that the salvation of peoples lies largely in such humiliations. With astonishing energy and intelligence they set themselves to bring their culture and organization up to the level of the European Powers. Never in all the history of mankind did a nation make such a stride as Japan then did. In 1866 she was a mediæval people, a fantastic caricature of the extremest romantic feudalism; in 1899 hers was a completely Westernized people, on a level with the most advanced European Powers, and well in advance of Russia. She completely dispelled the persuasion that Asia was in some irrevocable way hopelessly behind Europe. She made all European progress seem sluggish and tentative by comparison.

We cannot tell here in any detail of Japan's war with China in 1894–95. It demonstrated the extent of her Westernization. She had an efficient Westernized army and a small but sound fleet. But the significance of her renascence, though it was appreciated by Britain and the United States, who were already treating her as if she were a European state, was not understood by the other Great Powers engaged in the pursuit of new Indias in Asia. Russia was pushing down through Manchuria to Korea,

France was already established far to the south in Tonkin and Annam, Germany was prowling hungrily on the look-out for some settlement. The three powers combined to prevent Japan reaping any fruits from the Chinese war, and particularly from establishing herself on the mainland at the points commanding the Japan Sea. She was exhausted by her war with China, and they threatened her with war.

In 1898 Germany descended upon China, and, making the murder of two missionaries her excuse, annexed a portion of the province of Shang-tung. Thereupon Russia seized the Liao-tung Peninsula, and extorted the consent of China to an extension of her trans-Siberian railway to Port Arthur; and in 1900 she occupied

A SAMURAI IN ARMOUR.

Manchuria. Britain was unable to resist the imitative impulse, and seized the port of Wei-hai-wei (1898). How alarming these movements must have been to every intelligent Japanese a glance at the map will show. They led to a war with Russia which marks an epoch in the history of Asia, the close of the period of European arrogance. The Russian people were, of course, innocent and ignorant of this trouble that was being made for them half-way round the world, and the wiser Russian statesmen were against these foolish thrusts; but a gang of financial adventurers surrounded the

A FARMER IN THE FIELDS.

Tsar, including the Grand Dukes, his cousins. They had gambled deeply in the prospective looting of Manchuria and China, and they would suffer no withdrawal. So there began a transportation of great armies of Japanese soldiers across the sea to Port Arthur and Korea, and the sending of endless trainloads of Russian peasants along the Siberian railway to die in those distant battlefields.

The Russians, badly led and dishonestly provided, were beaten on sea and land alike. The Russian Baltic Fleet sailed round Africa to be utterly destroyed in the Straits of Tshushima. A revolutionary movement among the common people of Russia, infuriated by this remote and reasonless slaughter, obliged the Tsar to end the war (1905); he returned the southern half of Saghalien, which had been seized by Russia in 1875, evacuated Manchuria, resigned Korea to Japan. The White Man was beginning to drop his " Burthen " in Eastern Asia. For some years, however, Germany remained in uneasy possession of Kiau-Chau.

§ 12

We have already noted how the enterprise of Italy in Abyssinia had been checked at the terrible battle of Adowa (1896), in which over 3,000 Italians were killed and more than 4,000 taken prisoner. The phase of imperial expansion at the expense of organized non-European states was manifestly drawing to a close. It had entangled the quite sufficiently difficult political and social problems of Great Britain, France, Spain, Italy, Germany, and Russia with the affairs of considerable alien, unassimilable, and resentful populations; Great Britain had Egypt (not formally annexed as yet), India, Burmah, and a variety of such minor problems as Malta and Shanghai; France had cumbered herself with Tonkin and Annam in addition to Algiers and Tunis; Spain was newly entangled in Morocco; Italy had found trouble for herself in Tripoli; and German overseas imperialism, though its " place in the sun " seemed a poor one, derived what satisfaction it could from the thought of a prospective war with Japan over Kiau-Chau. All these " subject " lands had populations at a level of intelligence and education very little lower than those of the possessing country; the development of a native press, of a collective self-consciousness, and of demands for self-government was in each case inevitable, and the statesmen of Europe had been far too busy achieving these empires to have any clear ideas of what they would do with them when they got them.

Close of the Period of Overseas Expansion.

OVERSEAS EMPIRES of EUROPEAN POWERS, *January 1914.*

Greenland
Arctic Circle
Newfoundland
Canada
United States
British Isles
Mexico
British Honduras

F U R O P E
France
Italy
Spain
Portugal
Azores (P.)
Madeira (P.)
Canary Is. (Sp.)
C. Verde Is. (P.)
Bermudas (Br.)
Bahamas (Br.)
West Indian Is.
(Br. & Fr.)
Jamaica (Br.)

A T L A N T I C

South America
British Guiana
Dutch Guiana
French Guiana

Falkland Is.
(Br.)

(Br.)

P A C I F I C

[Other Pacific
Islands (not
shown in this
map – Brit.,
French and
German.]

(Br.)

[Mercator's Projection]

Norway
Sweden
Germany
Austria

R u s s i a

S i b e r i a

Arabia
Persia
Russ. Sphere
Brit. Sphere

Mongolia
Manchuria
China
Tibet
India

P A C I F I C

Philippines
(U.S.A.)

Dutch
East Indies

I N D I A N
O C E A N

New Zealand

Australia

Tasmania

(Fr.)

(Br.)

(Gr.)

(Fr.)

(Br.)

(Br.)

(Br.)

[See separate
map of Africa
for details]

(Fr.)

(Br.)

(Fr.)

(Br.)

(Fr.)

(Br.)

(Ital.)

Aden

(Ital.)

(Fr.)

Br.

Br.

Br.

Br.

Belgian

P.

P.

G.

Br.

Br.

J.F.H.

British
French
German
Dutch
Belgian
Spanish
Italian
Portuguese
Russian

687

The Western democracies, as they woke up to freedom, discovered themselves "imperial," and were considerably embarrassed by the discovery. The East came to the Western capitals with perplexing demands. In London the common Englishman, much preoccupied by strikes, by economic riddles, by questions of nationalization, municipalization, and the like, found that his path was crossed and his public meetings attended by a large and increasing number of swarthy gentlemen in turbans, fezes, and other strange headgear, all saying in effect : "You have got us. The people who represent your government have destroyed our own government, and prevent us from making a new one. What are you going to do with us ? "

(A question whose answer still lies beyond the frontiers of history.)

§ 13

We may note here briefly the very various
The British nature of the constituents of the
Empire in British Empire in 1914. It was and
1914. is a quite unique political combination ; nothing of the sort has ever existed before.

First and central to the whole system was the " crowned republic " of the United British Kingdoms, including (against the will of a considerable part of the Irish people) Ireland. The majority of the British Parliament, made up of the three united parliaments of England, Scotland, and Ireland, determines the headship, the quality and policy of the ministry, and determines it largely on considerations arising out of British domestic politics. It is this ministry which is the effective supreme government, with powers of peace and war, over all the rest of the empire.

Next in order of political importance to the British States were the " crowned republics " of Australia, Canada, Newfoundland (the oldest British possession, 1583), New Zealand, and South Africa, all practically independent and self-governing states in alliance with Great Britain, but each with a representative of the Crown appointed by the Government in office.

Next the Indian Empire, an extension of the empire of the Great Mogul, with its dependent and " protected " states reaching now from Beluchistan to Burmah, and including

Aden, in all of which empire the British Crown *and* the Indian Office (under Parliamentary control) played the rôle of the original Turkoman dynasty.

Then the ambiguous possession of Egypt, still nominally a part of the Turkish Empire and still retaining its own monarch, the Khedive, but under almost despotic British official rule.

Then the still more ambiguous " Anglo-Egyptian " Sudan province, occupied and administered jointly by the British and by the (British controlled) Egyptian Government.

Then a number of partially self-governing communities, some British in origin and some not, with elected legislatures and an appointed executive, such as Malta,[1] Jamaica, the Bahamas, and Bermuda.

Then the Crown colonies in which the rule of the British Home Government (through the Colonial Office) verged on autocracy, as in Ceylon, Trinidad, and Fiji (where there was an appointed council), and Gibraltar and St. Helena (where there was a governor).

Then great areas of (chiefly) tropical lands, raw-product areas, with politically weak and under-civilized native communities, which were nominally protectorates, and administered either by a High Commissioner set over native chiefs (as in Basutoland) or over a chartered company (as in Rhodesia). In some cases the Foreign Office, in some cases the Colonial Office, and in some cases the India Office had been concerned in acquiring the possessions that fell into this last and least definite class of all, but for the most part the Colonial Office was now responsible for them.

It will be manifest, therefore, that no single office and no single brain had ever comprehended the British Empire as a whole. It was a mixture of growths and accumulations entirely different from anything that had ever been called an empire before. It guaranteed a wide peace and security ; that is why it was endured and sustained by many men of the " subject " races—in spite of official tyrannies and insufficiencies, and of much negligence on the part of the " home " public. Like the " Athenian " empire," it was an overseas empire ; its

[1] A new and much more liberal Maltese constitution was promulgated in June 1920, practically putting Malta on the footing of a self-governing colony.

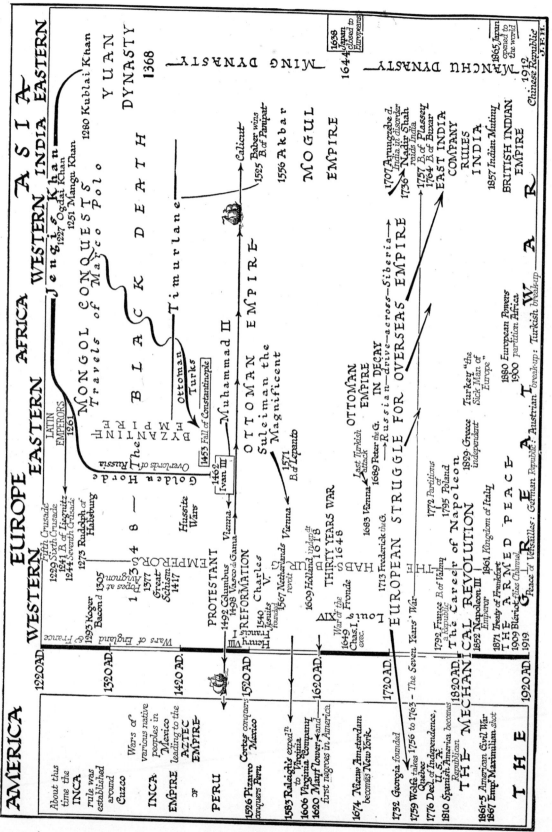

ways were sea ways, and its common link was the British Navy. Like all empires, its cohesion was dependent physically upon a method of communication; the development of seamanship, ship-building, and steamships between the sixteenth and nineteenth centuries had made it a possible and convenient Pax—the "Pax Britannica," and fresh developments of air or swift land transport might at any time make it inconvenient.

Air transport may indeed be already opening the way to a still more extensive and universal "Pax," in which the British system may of its own accord merge. It is impossible to say whether this unprecedented imperialism will obstruct or help forward that final unification of the world's affairs towards which all history is pointing. A system so various in its structure has many contradictory aspects, some very attractive and some very repellent to a liberal intelligence. The conversion of Canada, Australia, New Zealand, and South Africa from mere administered dependencies into quasi-independent allies, has been a very fine feat of statescraft. But in these cases the British Government had to deal with largely kindred and sympathetic populations, very ready to renew the methods of the old country upon a distant soil. In the case of mainly alien peoples the record is not so good, and, for reasons we have already partly analysed (§ 9), it has been worse during the last few decades than it was before. There has been a deterioration in the quality of British imperialism in relation to "subject peoples." Whether that is a temporary deterioration or whether it is a fated drift towards disruption is a question of the profoundest moment to an English writer, but it is one that it is impossible to discuss properly within the limits of this Outline. But even at its worst it is open to question whether the British rule in India does not compare favourably with any other domination of one entirely remote and alien civilization by another. What is wrong is not so much that Britain rules India and Egypt, but that any civilized country should be ruled by the legislature of another, and that there should be no impartial court of appeal in the world yet to readjust this arrangement.[1]

[1] All intelligent Englishmen or Englishwomen with a vote owe it to the Empire and themselves to read at least one book dealing with India or Egypt from the native point of view. For India, Lajpat Rai's *Political Future of India* is to be recommended. A compact book running counter to the views in this text, and giving the Church missionary point of view, is the Rev. W. E. S. Holland's *Goal of India*. William Archer's *India and the Future* is an interesting display of the temperamental clash of a Nordic writer with things Dravidian. It sustains the argument that even the most high-minded Nordic type cannot be trusted to govern other races sympathetically. (See also in that matter Archer's *In Afro-America*). The Aga Khan's *India in Transition* gives very admirably the views of a liberal Indian gentleman. Sidney Low's *A Vision of India* is still not superseded as a picture of India in 1905-6, when the present stir was still only brewing.

XL

THE INTERNATIONAL CATASTROPHE OF 1914[1]

§ 1

The Armed Peace before the Great War.

FOR thirty-six years after the Treaty of San Stefano and the Berlin Conference, Europe maintained an uneasy peace within its borders; there was no war between any of the leading states during this period. They jostled, browbeat, and threatened one another, but they did not come to actual hostilities. There was a general realization after 1871 that modern war was a much more serious thing than the professional warfare of the eighteenth century, an effort of peoples as a whole that might strain the social fabric very severely, an adventure not to be rashly embarked upon. The mechanical revolution was giving constantly more powerful (and expensive) weapons by land and sea, and more rapid methods of transport; and making it more and more impossible to carry on warfare without a complete dislocation of the economic life of the community. Even the foreign offices felt the fear of war.

But though war was dreaded as it had never been dreaded in the world before, nothing was done in the way of setting up a federal control to prevent human affairs drifting towards war. In 1898, it is true, the young Tsar Nicholas II (1894–1917) issued a rescript inviting the other Great Powers to a conference of states " seeking to make the great idea of universal peace triumph over the elements of trouble and dis-

[1] A very good book for the expansion of this chapter is Stearns Davis' (with Anderson and Tyler) *Armed Peace*, a history of Europe from 1870 to 1914. Even more illuminating is G. P. Gooch's *History of Our Time* (1885–1911). This is quite a tiny book, but very clear and thorough. It was revised in its present form in February, 1914, so that its title is misleading; it comes up to 1914. It contains an excellent student's bibliography.

THE PALACE OF PEACE: THE HAGUE.

cord." His rescript recalls the declaration of his predecessor, Alexander I, which gave its tone to the Holy Alliance, and it is vitiated by the same assumption that peace can be established between sovereign governments rather than by a broad appeal to the needs and rights of the one people of mankind. The lesson of the United States of America, which showed that there could be neither unity of action nor peace until the thought of the " people of Virginia " and the " people of Massachusetts " had been swept aside by the thought of the " people of the United States," went entirely disregarded in the European attempts at pacification. Two conferences were held at The Hague in Holland, one in 1899 and another in 1907, and at the second nearly all the sovereign states of the world were represented. They were represented diplomatically, there was no direction of the general intelligence of the world to their deliberations, the ordinary common man did not even know that these conferences were sitting, and for the most part the assembled representatives haggled cunningly upon points of international law affecting war, leaving aside the abolition of war as a chimera. These Hague Conferences did nothing to dispel the idea that international life is necessarily competitive. They accepted that idea. They did nothing to develop the consciousness of a world commonweal overriding sovereigns and foreign offices. The international lawyers and statesmen who attended these gatherings were as little disposed to hasten on a world commonweal on such a basis as were the Prussian statesmen of 1848 to welcome an all-German parliament overriding the rights and " policy " of the King of Prussia.

In America a series of three Pan-American conferences in 1889, 1901, and 1906 went some way towards the development of a scheme of international arbitration for the whole American continent.

The character and good faith of Nicholas II, who initiated these Hague gatherings, we will not discuss at any length here. He may have thought that time was on the side of Russia. But of the general unwillingness of the Great Powers to face the prospect of a merger of sovereign powers, without which permanent peace projects are absurd, there can be no sort of doubt whatever. It was no cessation of international competition with its acute phase of war that they desired, but rather a cheapening of war, which was becoming too costly. Each wanted to economize the wastage of minor disputes and conflicts, and to establish international laws that would embarrass its more formidable opponents in war-time without incommoding itself. These were the practical ends they sought at the Hague Conference. It was a gathering they attended to please Nicholas II, just as the monarchs of Europe had subscribed to the evangelical propositions of the Holy Alliance to please Alexander I; and as they had attended it, they tried to make what they conceived to be some use of it.

§ 2

The Peace of Frankfort had left Germany Prussianized and united, the most formidable of all the Great Powers of Europe. France was humiliated and crippled. Her lapse into republicanism seemed likely to leave her without friends in any European court. Italy was as yet a mere stripling. Austria sank now rapidly to the position of a confederate in German policy. Russia was vast, but undeveloped; and the British Empire was mighty only on the sea. Beyond Europe the only power to be reckoned with by Germany was the United States of America, growing now into a great industrial nation, but with no army nor navy worth considering by European standards.

Imperial Germany.

The new Germany which was embodied in the empire that had been created at Versailles was a complex and astonishing mixture of the fresh intellectual and material forces of the world, with the narrowest political traditions of the European system. She was vigorously educational; she was by far the most educational state in the world; she made the educational pace for all her neighbours and rivals. In this time of reckoning for Germany, it may help the British reader to a balanced attitude to recall the educational stimulation for which his country has to thank first the German Prince Consort and then German competition. That mean jealousy of the educated common man on the part of the British church and ruling class, which no patriotic pride or generous impulse had ever sufficed to overcome, went down before a growing fear of German efficiency. And Germany took up the organization of scientific research and of the application of scientific method to industrial and social development with such a faith and energy as no other community had ever shown before. Throughout all this period of the armed peace she was reaping and sowing afresh and reaping again the harvests, the unfailing harvests, of freely disseminated knowledge. She grew swiftly to become a great manufacturing and trading power; her steel output outran the British; in a hundred new fields of production and commerce, where intelligence and system were of more account than mere trader's cunning, in the manufacture of optical glass, of dyes and of a multitude of chemical products and in endless novel processes, she led the world.

To the British manufacturer who was accustomed to see inventions come into his works, he knew not whence nor why, begging to be adopted, this new German method of keeping and paying scientific men seemed abominably unfair. It was compelling fortune, he felt. It was packing the cards. It was encouraging a nasty class of intellectuals to interfere in the affairs of sound business men. Science went abroad from its first home like an unloved child. The splendid chemical industry of Germany was built on the work of the Englishman Perkins, who could find no "practical" English business man to back him. And Germany also led the way in many forms of social legislation. Germany realized that labour is a national asset, that it deteriorates through unemployment, and that, for the common good, it has to be taken care of outside the works. The British employer was still under the delusion that labour had no business to exist outside the works, and that the worse such exterior existence was, the better somehow for him. Moreover, because of his general illiteracy, he was an intense individualist: his was the insensate rivalry of the vulgar mind; he hated his fellow manufacturers about as much as he hated his labour and his customers. German producers, on the other hand, were persuaded of the great advantages of combination and civility; their enterprises tended to flow together and assume more and more the character of national undertakings.

This educating, scientific, and organizing Germany was the natural development of the liberal Germany of 1848; it had its roots far back in the recuperative effort after the shame of the Napoleonic conquest. All that was good, all that was great in this modern Germany, she owed indeed to her schoolmasters. But this scientific organizing spirit was only one of the two factors that made up the new German Empire. The other factor was the Hohenzollern monarchy which had survived Jena, which had tricked and bested the revolution of 1848, and which, under the guidance of Bismarck, had now clambered to the legal headship of all Germany outside Austria. Except the Tsardom, no other European state had so preserved the tradition of the Grand Monarchy of the eighteenth century as the Prussian. Through the tradition of Frederick the Great, Machiavelli now reigned in Germany. In the head of this fine new modern state, therefore, there sat no fine modern brain to guide it to a world predominance in world service, but an old spider lusting for power. Prussianized Germany was at once the newest and the most antiquated thing in Western Europe. She was the best and the wickedest state of her time.

The psychology of nations is still but a rudimentary science. Psychologists have scarcely begun to study the citizen side of the individual man. But it is of the utmost importance to our subject that the student of universal history should give some thought to the mental growth of the generations of Germans educated since the victories of 1871. They were naturally inflated by their sweeping unqualified successes in war, and by their rapid progress from comparative poverty to wealth. It would have been more than human in them if they had not given way to some excesses of patriotic vanity. But this reaction was deliberately seized upon and fostered and developed by a systematic exploitation and control of school and college, literature and press, in the interests of the Hohenzollern dynasty. A teacher, a professor, who did not teach and preach, in and out of season, the racial, moral, intellectual, and physical superiority of the Germans to all other peoples, their extraordinary devotion to war and their dynasty, and their inevitable destiny under that dynasty to lead the world, was a marked man, doomed to failure and obscurity.[1] German historical teaching became an immense systematic falsification of the human past, with a view to the Hohenzollern future. All other nations were represented as incompetent and decadent; the Prussians were the leaders and regenerators of mankind. The young German read this in his school-books, heard it in church, found it in his literature, had it poured into him with passionate conviction by his professor. It was poured into him by all his professors; Hueffer (*op. cit.*) says that lectures in biology or mathematics would break off from their proper subject to indulge in long passages of royalist patriotic rant. Only minds of extraordinary toughness and originality could resist such a torrent of suggestion. Insensibly there was built up in the German mind a conception of Germany and its emperor as of something splendid and predominant as nothing else had ever been before, a godlike nation in "shining armour" brandishing the "good German sword" in a world of inferior—and very badly disposed—peoples. We have told our story of Europe; the reader may judge whether the glitter of the German sword is exceptionally blinding. Germania was deliberately intoxicated, she was systematically kept drunk, with this sort of patriotic rhetoric. It is the greatest of the Hohenzollern crimes that the Crown constantly and persistently tampered with education, and particularly with historical teaching. No other modern state has so sinned against education. The oligarchy of the crowned republic of Great Britain may have crippled and starved education, but the Hohenzollern monarchy corrupted and prostituted it.

It cannot be too clearly stated, it is the most important fact in the history of the last half century, that the German people was methodically indoctrinated with the idea of a German world-predominance based on might, and with the theory that war was a necessary thing in life. The key to German historical teaching is to be found in Count Moltke's dictum: "Perpetual peace is a dream, and it is not even a beautiful dream. War is an element in the order of the world ordained by God." (Gladstone, we have noted, in his Tory days showed the same pious acquiescence in the family slaveholding.) "Without war the world would stagnate and lose itself in materialism." And the anti-Christian German philosopher, Nietzsche, found himself quite at one with the pious fieldmarshal. "It is mere illusion and pretty sentiment," he observes, "to expect much (even anything at all) from mankind if it forgets how to make war. As yet no means are known which call so much into action as a great war that rough energy born of the camp, that deep impersonality born of hatred, that conscience born of murder and cold-bloodedness, that fervour born of effort in the annihilation of the enemy, that proud indifference to loss, to one's own existence, to that of one's fellows, that earthquake-like soul-shaking which a people needs when it is losing its vitality."[2]

This sort of teaching, which pervaded the German Empire from end to end, was bound to be noted abroad, bound to alarm every other power and people in the world, bound to provoke an anti-German confederation. And it was accompanied by a parade of military, and presently of naval preparation, that threatened France, Russia, and Britain alike. It affected the thoughts, the manners, and morals of the entire German people—for they are a plastic people, and not refractory under instruction like the Irish and English. After 1871, the German abroad thrust out his chest and raised his voice. He threw a sort of trampling quality even into the operations of commerce. His machinery came on the markets of the world, his shipping took the seas with a splash of patriotic challenge. His very merits he used as a means of offence. (And probably most other peoples, if they had had the same experiences and undergone the same training, would have behaved in a similar manner.)

By one of those accidents in history that personify and precipitate catastrophes, the ruler of Germany, the Emperor William II, embodied the new education of his people and the Hohen-

[1] See F. M. Hueffer's able but badly named book, *When Blood is their Argument*. It gives an admirable account of just how the pressure was applied to the teaching organization.

[2] These quotations are from Sir Thomas Barclay's article "Peace" in *The Encyclopædia Britannica*.

zollern tradition in the completest form. He came to the throne in 1888 at the age of twenty-nine; his father, Frederick III, had succeeded his grandfather, William I, in the March, to die in the June of that year. William II was the grandson of Queen Victoria on his mother's side, but his temperament showed no traces of the liberal German tradition that distinguished the Saxe-Coburg-Gotha family. His head was full of the frothy stuff of the new imperialism. He signalized his accession by an address to his army and navy; his address to his people followed three days later. A high note of contempt for democracy was sounded: " The soldier and the army, not parliamentary majorities, have welded together the German Empire. My trust is placed in the army." So the patient work of the German schoolmasters was disowned, and the Hohenzollern declared himself triumphant.

The next exploit of the young monarch was to quarrel with the old Chancellor, Bismarck, who had made the new German Empire, and to dismiss him (1890). There were no profound differences of opinion between them, but, as Bismarck said, the Emperor intended to be his own chancellor.

These were the opening acts of an active and aggressive career. This William II meant to make a noise in the world, a louder noise than any other monarch had ever made. The whole of Europe was soon familiar with the figure of the new monarch, invariably in military uniform of the most glittering sort, staring valiantly, fiercely moustached, and with a withered left arm ingeniously minimized. He affected silver shining breastplates and long white cloaks. A great restlessness was manifest. It was clear he conceived himself destined for great things, but for a time it was not manifest what particular great things these were. There was no oracle at Delphi now to tell him that he was destined to destroy a great empire.

The note of theatricality about him and the dismissal of Bismarck alarmed many of his subjects, but they were presently reassured by the idea that he was using his influence in the cause of peace and to consolidate Germany. He travelled much, to London, Vienna, Rome— where he had private conversations with the Pope—to Athens, where his sister married the King in 1889, and to Constantinople. He was the first Christian sovereign to be a Sultan's guest. He also went to Palestine. A special gate was knocked through the ancient wall of Jerusalem so that he could ride into that place; it was beneath his dignity to walk in. He induced the Sultan to commence the reorganization of the Turkish Army upon German lines and under German officers. In 1895 he announced that Germany was a " world power," and that " the future of Germany lay upon the water "—regardless of the fact that the British considered that they were there already— and he began to interest himself more and more in the building up of a great navy. He also took German art and literature under his care; he used his influence to retain the distinctive and blinding German blackletter against the Roman type used by the rest of Western Europe, and he supported the Pan-German movement, which claimed the Dutch, the Scandinavians, the Flemish Belgians, and the German Swiss as members of a great German brotherhood—as in fact good assimilable stuff for a hungry young empire which meant to grow. All other monarchs in Europe paled before him.

He used the general hostility against Britain aroused throughout Europe by the war against the Boer Republics to press forward his schemes for a great navy, and this, together with the rapid and challenging extension of the German colonial empire in Africa and the Pacific Ocean, alarmed and irritated the British extremely. British liberal opinion in particular found itself under the exasperating necessity of supporting an ever-increasing British Navy. " I will not rest," he said, " until I have brought my navy to the same height at which my army stands." The most peace-loving of the islanders could not ignore that threat.

In 1890 he had acquired the small island of Heligoland from Britain. This he made into a great naval fortress.

As his navy grew, his enterprise increased. He proclaimed the Germans " the salt of the earth." They must not " weary in the work of civilization; Germany, like the spirit of Imperial Rome, must expand and impose itself." This he said on Polish soil, in support of the steady efforts the Germans were making to suppress the Polish language and culture, and to Germanize their share of Poland. God he described as his "Divine Ally." In the old absolutisms the monarch was either God himself or the adopted agent of God; the Kaiser took God for his trusty henchman. "Our old God," he said affectionately. When the Germans seized Kiau-chau, he spoke of the German "mailed fist." When he backed Austria against Russia, he talked of Germany in her "shining armour."

The disasters of Russia in Manchuria in 1905 released the spirit of German imperialism to bolder aggressions. The fear of a joint attack from France and Russia seemed lifting. The Emperor made a kind of regal progress through the Holy Land, landed at Tangier to assure the Sultan of Morocco of his support against the French, and inflicted upon France the crowning indignity of compelling her by a threat of war to dismiss Delcassé, her Foreign Minister. He drew tighter the links between Austria and Germany, and in 1908, Austria, with his support, defied the rest of Europe by annexing from the Turk the Yugo-Slav provinces of Bosnia and Herzegovina. So by his naval challenge to Britain and these aggressions upon France and the Slavs he forced Britain, France, and Russia into a defensive understanding against him. The Bosnian annexation had the further effect of estranging Italy, which had hitherto been his ally.

Such was the personality that the evil fate of Germany set over her to stimulate, organize, and render intolerable to the rest of the world

THE EMPEROR WILLIAM II.

the natural pride and self-assertion of a great people who had at last, after long centuries of division and weakness, escaped from a jungle of princes to unity and the world's respect. It was natural that the commercial and industrial leaders of this new Germany who were now getting rich, the financiers intent upon overseas exploits, the officials and the vulgar, should find this leader very much to their taste. Many Germans who thought him rash or tawdry in their secret hearts, supported him publicly because he had so taking an air of success. *Hoch der Kaiser!*

Yet Germany did not yield itself without a struggle to the strong-flowing tide of imperialism. Important elements in German life struggled against this swaggering new autocracy. The old German nations, and particularly the Bavarians, refused to be swallowed up in Prussianism. And with the spread of education and the rapid industrialization of Germany, organized labour developed its ideas and a steady antagonism to the military and patriotic clattering of its ruler. A new political party was growing up in the state, the Social Democrats, professing the doctrines of Marx. In the teeth of the utmost opposition from the official and clerical organizations, and of violently repressive laws against its propaganda and against combinations, this party grew. The Kaiser denounced it again and again; its leaders were sent to prison or driven abroad. Still it grew. When he came to the throne it polled not half a million votes;

in 1907 it polled over three million. He attempted to concede many things, old age and sickness insurance, for example, as a condescending gift, things which it claimed for the workers as their right. His conversion to socialism was noted, but it gained no converts to imperialism. His naval ambitions were ably and bitterly denounced; the colonial adventures of the new German capitalists were incessantly attacked by this party of the common sense of the common man. But to the army, the Social Democrats accorded a moderate support, because, much as they detested their home-grown autocrat, they hated and dreaded the barbaric and retrogressive autocracy of Russia on their eastern frontier more.

The danger plainly before Germany was that this swaggering imperialism would compel Britain, Russia, and France into a combined attack upon her, an offensive-defensive. The Kaiser wavered between a stiff attitude towards Britain and clumsy attempts to propitiate her, while his fleet grew and while he prepared for a preliminary struggle with Russia and France. When in 1913 the British Government proposed a cessation on either hand of naval construction for a year, it was refused. The Kaiser was afflicted with a son and heir more Hohenzollern, more imperialistic, more Pan-Germanic than his father. He had been nurtured upon imperialist propaganda. His toys had been soldiers and guns. He snatched at a premature popularity by outdoing his father's patriotic and aggressive attitudes. His father, it was felt, was growing middle-aged and over-careful. The Crown Prince renewed him. Germany had never been so strong, never so ready for a new great adventure and another harvest of victories. The Russians, he was instructed, were decayed, the French degenerate, the British on the verge of civil war. This young Crown Prince was but a sample of the abounding upper-class youth of Germany in the spring of 1914. They had all drunken from the same cup. Their professors and teachers, their speakers and leaders, their mothers and sweethearts, had been preparing them for the great occasion that was now very nearly at hand. They were full of the tremulous sense of imminent conflict, of a trumpet call to stupendous achievements, of victory over mankind abroad, triumph over the recalcitrant workers at home. The country was taut and excited like an athletic competitor at the end of his training.

§ 3

Throughout the period of the armed peace Germany was making the pace and setting the tone for the rest of Europe. The influence of her new doctrines of aggressive imperialism was particularly strong upon the British mind, which was ill-equipped to resist a strong intellectual thrust from abroad. The educational impulse the Prince Consort had given had died away after his death; the universities of Oxford and Cambridge were hindered in their task of effective revision of upper-class education by the fears and prejudices the so-called "conflict of science and religion" had roused in the clergy who dominated them through Convocation; popular education was crippled by religious squabbling, by the extreme parsimony of the public authorities, by the desire of employers for child labour, and by individualistic objection to "educating other people's children." The old tradition of the English, the tradition of plain statement, legality, fair play, and a certain measure of republican freedom had faded considerably during the stresses of the Napoleonic Wars; romanticism, of which Sir Walter Scott, the great novelist, was the chief promoter, had infected the national imagination with a craving for the florid and picturesque. "Mr. Briggs," the comic Englishman of *Punch* in the fifties and sixties, getting himself into highland costume and stalking deer, was fairly representative of the spirit of the new movement. It presently dawned upon Mr. Briggs as a richly coloured and creditable fact he had hitherto not observed, that the sun never set on his dominions. The country which had once put Clive and Warren Hastings on trial for their unrighteous treatment of Indians, was now persuaded to regard them as entirely chivalrous and devoted figures. They were "empire builders." Under the spell of Disraeli's Oriental imagination, which had made Queen Victoria an "empress," the Englishman turned readily enough towards the vague exaltations of modern imperialism.

The perverted ethnology and distorted history

The Spirit of Imperialism in Britain and Ireland.

which was persuading the mixed Slavic, Keltic, and Teutonic Germans that they were a wonderful race apart, was imitated by English writers who began to exalt a new ethnological invention, the " Anglo-Saxon." This remarkable compound was presented as the culmination of humanity, the crown and reward of the accumulated effort of Greek and Roman, Egyptian, Assyrian, Jew, Mongol, and such-like lowly precursors of its white splendour. The senseless legend of German superiority did much to exacerbate the irritations of the Poles in Posen and the French in Lorraine. The even more ridiculous legend of the superior Anglo-Saxon did not merely increase the irritations of English rule in Ireland, but it lowered the tone of British dealings with " subject " peoples throughout the entire world. For the cessation of respect and the cultivation of " superior " ideas are the cessation of civility and justice. In the early days of British rule in India, British officials went out modestly as to a wonderful country to learn and live ; now they went out absurdly, as samples of a wonderful people, as lights to a great darkness, to profit and prevail.

The imitation of German patriotic misconceptions did not end with this " Anglo-Saxon " fabrication. The clever young men at the British universities in the eighties and nineties, bored by the flatness and insincerities of domestic politics, were moved to imitation and rivalry by this new teaching of an arrogant, subtle, and forceful nationalist imperialism, this combination of Machiavelli and Attila, which was being imposed upon the thought and activities of young Germany. Britain too, they thought, must have her shining armour and wave her good sword. The new British imperialism found its poet in Mr. Kipling and its practical support in a number of financial and business interests whose way to monopolies and exploitations was lighted by its glow. These Prussianizing Englishmen carried their imitation of Germany to the most extraordinary lengths. Central Europe is one continuous economic system, best worked as one ; and the new Germany had achieved a great customs union, a Zollverein of all its constitutents. It became naturally one compact system, like a clenched fist. The British Empire sprawled like an open hand throughout the world, its members different in nature, need, and relationship, with no common interest except the common guarantee of safety. But the new Imperialists were blind to that difference. If new Germany had a Zollverein, then the British Empire must be in the fashion ; and the natural development of its various elements must be hampered everywhere by " imperial preferences " and the like. . . .

Yet the imperialist movement in Great Britain never had the authority nor the unanimity it had in Germany. It was not a natural product of any of the three united but diverse British peoples. It was not congenial to them. Queen Victoria and her successors, Edward VII and George V, were indisposed either by temperament or tradition to wear shining armour, shake mailed fists, and flourish " good swords " in the Hohenzollern fashion. They had the wisdom to refrain from any overt meddling with public ideas. And this " British " imperialist movement had from the first aroused the hostility of the large number of English, Welsh, Irish, and Scotch writers who refused to recognize this new " British " nationality or to accept the theory that they were these " Anglo-Saxon " supermen. And many great interests in Britain, and notably the shipping interest, had been built up upon free trade, and regarded the fiscal proposals of the new imperialists, and the new financial and mercantile adventurers with whom they were associated, with a justifiable suspicion. On the other hand, these ideas ran like wildfire through the military class, through Indian officialdom and the like. Hitherto there had always been something apologetic about the army man in England. He was not native to that soil. Here was a movement that promised to make him as splendidly important as his Prussian brother in arms. And the imperialist idea also found support in the cheap popular press that was now coming into existence to cater for the new stratum of readers created by elementary education. This press wanted plain, bright, simple ideas adapted to the needs of readers who had scarcely begun to think.

In spite of such support, and its strong appeal to national vanity, British imperialism never saturated the mass of the British peoples. The English are not a mentally docile people, and the noisy and rather forced enthusiasm for imperialism and higher tariffs of the old Tory Party, the army class, the country clergy, the music-halls, the assimilated alien, the vulgar rich and the new large employers, inclined the commoner sort, and particularly organized labour, to a suspicious attitude. If the continually irritated sore of the Majuba defeat permitted the country to be rushed into the needless, toilsome, and costly conquest of the Boer republics in South Africa, the strain of that adventure produced a sufficient reaction towards decency and justice to reinstate the Liberal Party in power, and to undo the worst of that mischief by the creation of a South African confederation. Considerable advances continued to be made in popular education, and in the recovery of public interests and the general wealth from the possession of the few. And in these years of the armed peace, the three British peoples came very near to a settlement, on fairly just and reasonable lines, of their long-standing misunderstanding with Ireland. The Great War, unluckily for them, overtook them in the very crisis of this effort.

Like Japan, Ireland has figured but little in this *Outline of History,* and for the same reason, because she is an extreme island country, receiving much, but hitherto giving but little back into the general drama. Her population is a very mixed one, its basis, and probably its main substance, being of the dark " Mediterranean " strain, pre-Nordic and pre-Aryan, like the Basques and the people of Portugal and South Italy. These people reached the island in neolithic times ; no paleolithic remains have been found in Ireland. Over this original basis there flowed, about the sixth century B.C.—we do not know to what degree of submergence— a wave of Keltic peoples, in at least sufficient strength to establish a Keltic language, the Irish Gaelic. There were comings and goings, invasions and counter-invasions of this and that Keltic or Kelticized people between Ireland, Scotland, Wales, and England. The island was Christianized in the fifth century. Later on the east coast was raided and settled by Northmen, but we do not know to what extent they altered the racial quality. The Norman-English came in 1169, in the time of Henry II and onward. The Teutonic strain may be as strong or stronger than the Keltic in modern Ireland.

Hitherto Ireland had been a tribal and barbaric country, with a few centres of security wherein the artistic tendencies of the more ancient race found scope in metal-work and the illumination of holy books. Now, in the twelfth century, there was an imperfect conquest by the English Crown, and scattered settlements by Normans and English in various parts of the country. From the outset profound temperamental differences between the Irish and English were manifest, differences exacerbated by a difference of language, and these became much more evident after the Protestant reformation. The English were naturally a non-sacerdotal people ; they had the Northman's dislike for and disbelief in priests ; the share of Englishmen in the European reformation was a leading one. The Irish found the priest congenial, and resisted the reformation obstinately and bitterly.

The English rule in Ireland had been from the first an intermittent civil war due to the clash of languages and the different laws of land tenure and inheritance of the two peoples. It was further embittered at the Reformation by this religious incompatability. The rebellions, massacres, and subjugations of the unhappy island during the reigns of Elizabeth and James I we cannot tell of here ; but under James came a new discord with the confiscation of large areas of Ulster and their settlement with Presbyterian Scotch colonists. They formed a Protestant community in necessary permanent conflict with the Catholic remainder of Ireland.

In the political conflicts during the reign of Charles I and the Commonwealth, and of James II and William and Mary, the two sides in English affairs found sympathizers and allies in the Irish parties. There is a saying in Ireland that England's misfortune is Ireland's opportunity, and the English civil trouble that led to the execution of Strafford, enabled the Irish Catholics to perpetrate a ferocious massacre of the English in Ireland (1641)—a very cruel and barbaric massacre in which neither women nor little children were spared. Later on Cromwell was to avenge the massacre by giving no quarter to any men actually found under arms, a severity remembered by the Irish Catholics with extravagant bitterness. Between 1689 and 1691 Ireland was again torn by civil war. James II sought the support of the Irish

Catholics against William III, and his adherents were badly beaten at the Battles of the Boyne (1690) and Aughrim (1691).

There was a settlement, the Treaty of Limerick, a disputed settlement in which the English Government promised much in the way of tolerance for Catholics and the like, and failed to keep its promises. Limerick is still a cardinal memory in the long story of Irish embitterment. Comparatively few English people have even heard of this Treaty of Limerick; in Ireland it rankles to this day.

The eighteenth century was a century of accumulating grievance. English commercial jealousy put heavy restraints upon Irish trade, and the development of a wool industry was destroyed in the south and west. The Ulster Protestants were treated little better than the Catholics in these matters, and they were the chief of the rebels. There was more agrarian revolt in the north than in the south; the Steel Boys, and later the Peep-o'-Day Boys, were Ulster terrorists. There was a parliament in Ireland, but it was a Protestant parliament, even more limited and corrupt than the contemporary British Parliament; there was a

considerable civilization in and about Dublin, and much literary and scientific activity, conducted in English and centring upon the Protestant university of Trinity College. This was the Ireland of Swift, Goldsmith, Burke, Berkeley, and Boyle. It was essentially a part of the English culture. The Catholic religion and the Irish language were outcast and persecuted things in the darkness.

It was from this Ireland of the darkness that the recalcitrant Ireland of the twentieth century arose. The Irish Parliament, its fine literature, its science, all its culture, gravitated naturally enough to London, because they were inseparably a part of that world. The more prosperous landlords went to England to live, and had their children educated there. The increasing facilities of communication enhanced this tendency and depleted Dublin. The Act of Union (January 1st, 1801) was a natural coalescence of two entirely kindred systems, of the Anglo-Irish Parliament with the British Parliament, both oligarchic, both politically corrupt in the same fashion. There was a vigorous opposition on the part not so much of the outer Irish as of Protestants settled in Ireland, and a futile insurrection under Robert Emmet in 1803. Dublin, which had been a fine Anglo-Irish city in the middle eighteenth century, was gradually deserted by its intellectual and political life, and invaded by the outer Irish of Ireland. Its fashionable life became more and more official, centring upon the Lord Lieutenant in Dublin Castle; its chief social occasion is now a horse show. But, while the Ireland of Swift and Goldsmith was part and lot with the England of Pope, Dr. Johnson, and Sir Joshua Reynolds, while there has never been and is not now any real definable difference except one of geography between the "governing class" in Ireland and in Britain, the Irish underworld and the English underworld were essentially dissimilar. The upward struggle of the English "democracy" to education, to political recognition, had no Irish counterpart. Britain was producing a great industrial population, Protestant or sceptical; she had agricultural labourers indeed, but no peasants. Ireland had become a land of peasants, blankly ignorant and helplessly priest-ridden. Their cultivation degenerated more and more into a growing of potatoes and a feeding of pigs. The people married and bred; except for the consumption of whisky when it could be got, and a little fighting, family life was their only amusement. This was the direct result of orthodox Catholic teaching; the priests were all-powerful with the people, and they taught them nothing; not even washing or drainage; they forbade them to seek any Protestant learning, they allowed their agricultural science to sink to mere potato-growing, and they preyed upon their poverty. Here are the appalling consequences. The population of Ireland

> in 1785 was 2,845,932,
> in 1803 was 5,536,594,
> in 1845 was 8,295,061,

at which date the weary potato gave way under its ever-growing burthen and there was a frightful famine. Many died, many emigrated, especially to the United States; an outflow of emigration began that made Ireland for a time a land of old people and empty nests.

Now because of the Union of the Parliaments, the enfranchisement of the English and Irish populations went on simultaneously. Catholic enfranchisement in England meant Catholic enfranchisement in Ireland. The British got votes because they wanted them; the Irish commonalty got votes because the English did. Ireland was over-represented in the Union Parliament, because originally Irish seats had been easier for the governing class to manipulate than English; and so it came about that this Irish and Catholic Ireland, which had never before had any political instrument at all, and which had never sought a political instrument, found itself with the power to thrust a solid body of members into the legislature of Great Britain. After the general election of 1874, the newly enfranchised "democracy" of Britain found itself confronted by a strange and perplexing Irish "democracy," different in its religion, its traditions, and its needs, telling a tale of wrongs of which the common English had never heard, clamouring passionately for a separation which they could not understand and which impressed them chiefly as being needlessly unfriendly. The national egotism of the Irish is intense;

their circumstances have made it intense; they were incapable of considering the state of affairs in England; the new Irish party came into the British Parliament to obstruct and disorder English business until Ireland became free, and to make themselves a nuisance to the English. This spirit was only too welcome to the oligarchy which still ruled the British Empire; they allied themselves with the "loyal" Protestants in the north of Ireland—loyal that is to the Imperial Government because of their dread of a Catholic predominance in Ireland—and they watched and assisted the gradual exasperation of the British common people by this indiscriminate hostility of the common people of Ireland.

The story of the relation of Ireland to Britain for the last half-century is one that reflects the utmost discredit upon the governing class of the British Empire, but it is not one of which the English commons need be ashamed. Again and again they have given evidences of goodwill. British legislation in relation to Ireland for nearly half a century shows a series of clumsy attempts on the part of liberal England, made in the face of a strenuous opposition from the Conservative Party and the Ulster Irish, to satisfy Irish complaints and get to a footing of fellowship. In 1886 Gladstone, in pursuit of his idea of nationality, brought political disaster upon himself by introducing the first Irish Home Rule Bill, a genuine attempt to give over Irish affairs *for the first time in history* to the Irish people. In many respects it was a faulty and dangerous proposal, and it provided no satisfactory assurance to the Protestant Irish, and especially the Ulster Protestants, of protection against possible injuries from the priest-ridden illiterates of the south. This may have been a fancied danger, but these fears should have been respected. The bill broke the Liberal Party asunder; and a coalition government, the Unionist Government, replaced that of Mr. Gladstone.

This digression into the history of Ireland now comes up to the time of infectious imperialism in Europe. The Unionist Government, which ousted Mr. Gladstone, had a predominantly Tory element, and was in spirit "imperialist" as no previous British Government had been. The British political history of the subsequent years is largely a history of the conflict of the new imperialism, through which an arrogant "British" nationalism sought to override the rest of the empire against the temperamental liberalism and reasonableness of the English, which tended to develop the empire into a confederation of free and willing allies. Naturally the "British" imperialists wanted a subjugated Irish; naturally the English Liberals wanted a free, participating Irish. In 1892 Gladstone struggled back to power with a small Home Rule majority; and in 1893 his second Home Rule Bill passed the Commons, and was rejected by the Lords. It was not, however, until 1895 that

This was a very fundamental struggle in British affairs. On the one hand were the Liberal majority of the people of Great Britain honestly and wisely anxious to put this Irish affair upon a new and more hopeful footing, and, if possible, to change the vindictive animosity of the Irish into friendship; on the other were all the factors of this new British Imperialism resolved at any cost, and in spite of every electoral verdict, legally, if possible, but, if not, illegally, to maintain their ascendancy over the affairs of the English, Scotch, and Irish and all the rest of the empire alike. It was, under new names, the age-long internal struggle of the English community;

Photo: Topical Press Agency.

THE IRISH PARLIAMENT HOUSE (NOW THE BANK OF IRELAND), DUBLIN.

an imperialist government took office. The party which sustained it was called not Imperialist, but "Unionist"—an odd name when we consider how steadily and strenuously it has worked to destroy any possibility of an Empire commonweal. These Imperialists remained in power for ten years. We have already noted their conquest of South Africa. They were defeated in 1905 in an attempt to establish a tariff wall on the Teutonic model. The ensuing Liberal Government then turned the conquered South African Dutch into contented fellow-subjects by creating the self-governing Dominion of South Africa. After which it embarked upon a long-impending struggle with the persistently imperialist House of Lords.

that same conflict of a free and liberal-spirited commonalty against powerful "big men" and big adventurers and authoritative persons which we have already dealt with in our account of the liberation of America. Ireland was merely a battleground as America had been. In India, in Ireland, in England, the governing class and their associated adventurers were all of one mind; but the Irish people, thanks to their religious difference, had little sense of solidarity with the English. Yet such Irish statesmen as Redmond, the leader of the Irish Party in the House of Commons, transcended this national narrowness for a time, and gave a generous response to English good intentions. Slowly yet steadily the barrier of the House of Lords was broken down, and a third Irish Home Rule Bill was brought in by Mr. Asquith, the Prime Minister, in 1912. Throughout 1913 and the early part of 1914 this bill was fought and re-fought through Parliament. At first it gave Home Rule to all Ireland ; but an Amending Act, excluding Ulster on certain conditions, was promised. This struggle lasted right up to the outbreak of the Great War. The Royal Assent was given to this bill after the actual outbreak of war, and also to a bill suspending the coming into force of Irish Home Rule until after the end of the war. These bills were put upon the Statute Book.

But from the introduction of the third Home Rule Bill onward, the opposition to it had assumed a violent and extravagant form. Sir Edward Carson, a Dublin lawyer who had be-come a member of the English Bar, and who had held a legal position in the ministry of Mr. Gladstone (before the Home Rule split) and in the subsequent imperialist government, was the organizer and leader of this resistance to a reconciliation of the two peoples. In spite of his Dublin origin, he set up to be a leader of the Ulster Protestants; and he brought to the conflict that contempt for law which is all too common a characteristic of the successful barrister, and those gifts of persistent, unqualified, and un-compromising hostility which distinguish a certain type of Irishman. He was the most " un-English " of men, dark, romantic, and violent ; and from the opening of the struggle he talked with gusto of armed resistance to this freer reunion of the English and Irish which the third Home Rule Bill contemplated. The excitement intensified throughout 1913. A body of volunteers was organized in Ulster, arms were smuggled into the country, and Sir Edward Carson and a rising lawyer named F. E. Smith, trapped up in semi-military style, toured Ulster, inspecting these volunteers and inflaming local passion. The arms of these prospective rebels were obtained from Germany, and various utter-ances of Sir Edward Carson's associates hinted at support from " a great Protestant monarch." The first bloodshed occurred at Londonderry in August, 1913. Contrasted with Ulster, the rest of Ireland was at that time a land of order and decency, relying upon its great leader Redmond and the good faith of the three British peoples.

Now these threats of civil war from Ireland were not in themselves anything very excep-tional in the record of that unhappy island ; what makes them exceptional and significant in the world's history is the vehement support they found among the English military and governing classes, and the immunity from punishment and restraint of Sir Edward Carson and his friends. The virus of reaction which came from the success and splendour of German imperialism had spread widely, as we have explained, throughout the prevalent and prosperous classes in Great Britain. A generation had grown up forgetful of the mighty traditions of their fore-fathers, and ready to exchange the greatness of English freedom for the tawdriest of imperialisms. A fund of a million pounds was raised, chiefly in England, to support the Ulster Rebellion, an Ulster Provisional Government was formed, prominent English people mingled in the fray and careered about Ulster in automobiles, assist-ing in the gun-running, and there is evidence that a number of British officers and generals were prepared for a pronunciamento upon South American lines rather than obedience to the law. The natural result of all this upper-class dis-orderliness was to alarm the main part of Ireland, never a ready friend to England. That Ireland also began in its turn to organize " National Volunteers " and to smuggle arms. The mili-tary authorities showed themselves much keener in the suppression of the Nationalist than of the Ulster gun importation, and in July, 1914, an attempt to run guns at Howth, near Dublin, led to fighting and bloodshed in the Dublin streets. The British Isles were on the verge of civil war.

Such in outline is the story of the imperialist revolutionary movement in Great Britain up to the eve of the Great War. For revolutionary this movement of Sir Edward Carson and his associates was. It was plainly an attempt to set aside parliamentary government and the slow-grown, imperfect liberties of the British peoples, and, with the assistance of the army, to substitute a more Prussianized type of rule, using the Irish conflict as the point of departure. It was the reactionary effort of a few score thousand people to arrest the world movement towards democratic law and social justice, strictly parallel to and closely sympathetic with the new imperialism of the German junkers and rich men. But in one very important respect British and German imperialism differed. In Germany it centred upon the crown; its noisiest, most conspicuous advocate was the Heir Apparent. In Great Britain the king stood aloof. By no single public act did King George V betray the slightest approval of the new movement, and the behaviour of the Prince of Wales, his son and heir, has been equally correct.

In August, 1914, the storm of the great war burst upon the world. In September, Sir Edward Carson was denouncing the placing of the Home Rule Bill upon the Statute Book. On the same day, Mr. John Redmond was calling upon the Irish people to take their equal part in the burthen and effort of the war. For a time Ireland played her part in the war side by side with England faithfully and well, until in 1915 the Liberal Government was replaced by a coalition, in which this Sir Edward Carson, with the bloodshed at Londonderry and Howth upon his head, figured as Attorney-General (with a salary of £7,000 and fees), to be replaced presently by his associate in the Ulster sedition, Sir F. E. Smith.

Grosser insult was never offered to a friendly people. The work of reconciliation, begun by Gladstone in 1886, and brought so near to completion in 1914, was wrecked.[1]

In the spring of 1916 Dublin revolted unsuccessfully against this new government. The ringleaders of this insurrection, many of them mere boys, were shot with a deliberate and clumsy sternness that, in view of the treatment of the Ulster rebel leaders, impressed all Ireland as atrociously unjust. A traitor, Sir Roger Casement, who had been knighted for previous services to the empire, was tried and executed, no doubt deservedly, but his prosecutor was Sir F. E. Smith of the Ulster insurrection, a shocking conjunction. The Dublin revolt had had little support in Ireland generally, but thereafter the movement for an independent republic grew rapidly to great proportions. Against this strong emotional drive there struggled the more moderate ideas of such Irish statesmen as Sir Horace Plunkett, who wished to see Ireland become a Dominion, a "crowned

republic" that is, within the empire, on an equal footing with Canada and Australia.[2]

When in December, 1919, Mr. Lloyd George introduced his Home Rule Bill into the Imperial Parliament there were no Irish members, except Sir Edward Carson and his followers, to receive it. The rest of Ireland was away. It refused to begin again that old dreary round of hope and disappointment. Let the British and their pet Ulstermen do as they would, said the Irish. . . .

§ 4

Our studies of modern imperialism in Germany and Britain bring out certain forces common to the two countries, and we shall find these same forces at work in variable degrees and with various modifications in the case of the other great modern communities at which we shall now glance. This modern imperialism is not a synthetic uniting movement like the older imperialism; it is essentially a *megalomaniac nationalism*, a nationalism made aggressive by prosperity; and always it finds its strongest support in the military and official castes, and in the enterprising and acquisitive strata of society, in new money, that is, and big business; its chief critics in the educated poor, and its chief opponents in the peasantry and the labour masses. It accepts monarchy where it finds it, but it is not necessarily a monarchist movement. It does, however, need a foreign office of the traditional type for its full development. Its origin, which we have traced very carefully in this book of our history, makes this clear. Modern imperialism is the natural development of the Great Power system which arose, with the foreign office method of policy, out of the Machiavellian monarchies after the break up of Christendom. It will only come to an end when the intercourse of nations and peoples through embassies and foreign offices is replaced by an assembly of elected representatives in direct touch with their peoples.

French imperialism during the period of the Armed Peace in Europe was naturally of a less

Imperialism in France, Italy, and the Balkans.

---

[1] St. John Ervine's novel, *Changing Winds*, gives a good account of the mentality of this time.

[2] See the various publications of the Irish Dominion League, St. Stephen's Green, Dublin. A good recent account of Irish ideas is to be found in Lynd's *Ireland a Nation* (1919).

divided states of Central and South America would long since have been subjugated and placed under the disciplinary control of United States officials of the "governing class." There would have been a perpetual campaign to Americanize Australia and New Zealand, and yet another claimant for a share in tropical Africa.

And by an odd accident America had produced in President Roosevelt (President 1901–1908) a man of an energy as restless as the German Kaiser's, as eager for large achievements, as florid and eloquent, an adventurous man with a turn for world politics and an instinct for armaments, the very man, we might imagine, to have involved his country in the scramble for overseas possession.

There does not appear to be any other explanation of this general restraint and abstinence on the part of the United States except in their fundamentally different institutions and traditions. In the first place the United States Government has no foreign office and no diplomatic corps of the European type, no body of "experts" to maintain the tradition of an aggressive policy. The president has great powers, but they are subject to the control of the senate, which again is responsible to the state legislatures and the people. The foreign relations of the country are thus under open and public control. Secret treaties are impossible under such a system, and foreign Powers complain of the difficulty and uncertainty of "understandings" with the United States, a very excellent state of affairs. The United States are constitutionally incapacitated, therefore, from the kind of foreign policy that has kept Europe for so long constantly on the verge of war.

And, secondly, there has hitherto existed in the States no organization for and no tradition

of what one may call non-assimilable possessions. Where there is no crown there cannot be crown colonies. In spreading across the American continent, the United States had developed a quite distinctive method of dealing with new territories, admirably adapted for unsettled lands, but very inconvenient if applied too freely to areas already containing an alien population. This method was based on the idea that there cannot be in the United States system a permanently subject people. The

Photo: Brown Bros., New York.

42ND STREET WEST, NEW YORK.

first stage of the ordinary process of assimilation had been the creation of a "territory" under the federal government, having a considerable measure of self-government, sending a delegate (who could not vote) to congress, and destined, in the natural course of things, as the country became settled and population increased, to flower at last into full statehood. This had been the process of development of all the latter states of the Union; the latest territories to become states being Arizona and New Mexico in 1910. The frozen wilderness of Alaska, bought from Russia, remained politically undeveloped simply because it had an insufficient population for state organization. As the annexations of Germany and Great Britain in the Pacific threatened to deprive the United States navy of coaling stations in that ocean, a part of the Samoan Islands (1889) and the Sandwich Islands (Hawaii) were annexed (1898). Here for the first time the United States had real subject populations to deal with. But in the absence of any class comparable to the Anglo-Indian officials who sway British opinion, the American procedure followed the territorial method. Every effort was made to bring the educational standards of Hawaii up to the American level, and a domestic legislature on the territorial pattern was organized so that these dusky islanders seem destined ultimately to obtain full United States citizenship. (The small Samoan Islands are taken care of by a United States naval administrator.)

In 1895 occurred a quarrel between the United States and Britain upon the subject of Venezuela, and the Monroe doctrine was upheld stoutly by President Cleveland. Then Mr. Olney made this remarkable declaration : " To-day the United States is practically sovereign on this continent, and its fiat is law upon the subjects to which it confines its interposition." This, together with the various Pan-American congresses that have been held, point to a real open " foreign policy " of alliance and mutual help throughout America. Treaties of arbitration hold good over all that continent, and the future seems to point to a gradual development of inter-state organization, a Pax Americana, of the English-speaking and Spanish-speaking

peoples, the former in the rôle of elder brother. Here is something we cannot even call an empire, something going far beyond the great alliance of the British Empire in the open equality of its constituent parts.

Consistently with this idea of a common American welfare, the United States in 1898 intervened in the affairs of Cuba, which had been in a state of chronic insurrection against Spain for many years. A brief war ended in the acquisition of Cuba, Porto Rico, and the Philippine Islands. Cuba is now an independent self-governing republic. Porto Rico and the Philippines have, however, a special sort of government, with a popularly elected lower house and an upper body containing members appointed by the United States senate. It is improbable that either Porto Rico or the Philippines will become states in the Union. They are much more likely to become free states in some comprehensive alliance with both English-speaking and Latin America.

Both Cuba and Porto Rico welcomed the American intervention in their affairs, but in the Philippine Islands there was a demand for complete and immediate freedom after the Spanish war, and a considerable resistance to the American military administration. There it was that the United States came nearest to imperialism of the Great Power type, and that her record is most questionable. There was much sympathy with the insurgents in the States. Here is the point of view of ex-President Roosevelt as he wrote it in his *Autobiography* (1913) :

" As regards the Philippines, my belief was that we should train them for self-government

SKY-LINE OF NEW YORK, FROM JERSEY CITY, N.J.

as rapidly as possible, and then leave them free to decide their own fate. I did not believe in setting the time-limit within which we would give them independence, because I did not believe it wise to try to forecast how soon they would be fit for self-government ; and once having made the promise, I would have felt that it was imperative to keep it. Within a few months of my assuming office we had stamped out the last armed resistance in the Philippines that was not of merely sporadic character ; and as soon as peace was secured, we turned our energies to developing the islands in the interests of the natives. We established schools everywhere ; we built roads ; we administered an even-handed justice ; we did everything possible to encourage agriculture and industry ; and in constantly increasing measure we employed natives to do their own governing, and finally provided a legislative chamber. . . . We are governing, and have been governing the islands in the interests of the Filipinos themselves. If, after due time the Filipinos themselves decide that they do not wish to be thus governed, then I trust that we will leave ; but when we do leave, it must be distinctly understood that we retain no protectorate—and above all that we take part in no joint protectorate—over the islands, and give them no guarantee, of neutrality or otherwise ; that in short, we are absolutely quit of responsibility for them, of every kind and description."[1]

This is an entirely different outlook from that of a British or French foreign office or colonial office official. But it is not very widely different from the spirit that created the Dominions of Canada, South Africa, and Australia, and brought forward the three Home Rule Bills for Ireland. It is in the older and more characteristic English tradition from which the Declaration of Independence derives. It sets aside, without discussion, the detestable idea of " subject peoples."

Here we will not enter into political complications attendant upon the making of the Panama Canal, for they introduce no fresh light upon this interesting question of the American method in world politics. The history of Panama is American history purely. But manifestly just as the political structure of the Union was a new thing in the world, so too were its relations with the world beyond its borders.[2]

§ 7

We have been at some pains to examine the state of mind of Europe and of America in regard to international relations in the years that led up to the world tragedy of 1914; because, as more and more people are coming to recognize, that great war or some such war was a necessary consequence of the mentality of the period. All the things that men and nations do are the outcome of instinctive motives re-acting upon the ideas which talk and books and newspapers and schoolmasters and so forth have put into people's heads. Physical necessities, pestilences, changes of climate, and the like outer things may deflect and distort the growth of human history, but its living root is thought.

The Immediate Causes of the Great War.

All human history is fundamentally a history of ideas. Between the man of to-day and the Cro-Magnard the physical and mental differences

---

[1] One very good reason for the provisional retention of the Philippines under American control is the certainty that the " Moros," the Muhammadan peoples of Palawan, and the southern islands of the main groups would proceed to conquer the " Christian " Filipinos, and that after a welter of civil war and destruction, Japan or some other outside Power would be appealed to to intervene.   H. H. J.

[2] An unfriendly critic might denounce the treaty-making power of the United States, and the machinery by which it operates, as complicated and cumbersome, ill adapted to the complex demands of international intercourse, slow in action and uncertain in outcome. The requirement of a two-thirds rather than a majority vote in the Senate he might criticize not unjustly as a dubious excess of caution. . . . Believe me, the American people are like for many years to accomplish through this means their compacts with mankind. The checks and balances by which it is surrounded, the free and full debate which it allows, are in their eyes virtues rather than defects. They rejoice in the fact that all engagements which affect their destinies must be spread upon the public records, and that there is not, and there never can be, a secret treaty binding them either in law or in morals. Looking back upon a diplomatic history which is not without its chapters of success, they feel that on the whole the scheme the fathers builded has served the children well. With a conservatism in matters of government as great perhaps as that of any people in the world, they will suffer much inconvenience and run the risk of occasional misunderstanding before they make a change.—J. W. Davis (U.S.A. Ambassador to Britain), *The Treaty Making Power of the United States.* (Oxf. Univ. Brit. Am. Club. Paper No. 1.)

are very slight ; their essential difference lies in the extent and content of the mental background which we have acquired in the five or six hundred generations that intervene.

We are too close to the events of the Great War to pretend that this *Outline* can record the verdict of history thereupon, but we may hazard the guess that when the passions of the conflict have faded, it will be Germany that will be most blamed for bringing it about, and she will be blamed not because she was morally and intellectually very different from her neighbours, but because she had the common disease of imperialism in its most complete and energetic form. No self-respecting historian, however

German dreams were those of Russia, which was scheming for an extension of the Slav ascendancy to Constantinople and through Serbia to the Adriatic. These lines of ambition lay across one another and were mutually incompatible. The feverish state of affairs in the Balkans was largely the outcome of the intrigues and propagandas sustained by the German and Slav schemes. Turkey turned for support to Germany, Serbia to Russia. Roumania and Italy, both Latin in tradition, both nominally allies of Germany, pursued remoter and deeper schemes in common. Ferdinand, the Tsar of Bulgaria, was following still darker ends ; and the squalid mysteries of the Greek court, whose

Photo : Imperial War Museum.

HEAVY ARTILLERY IN ACTION.

superficial and popular his aims may be, can countenance the legend, produced by the stresses of the war, that the German is a sort of human being more cruel and abominable than any other variety of men. All the great states of Europe before 1914 were in a condition of aggressive nationalism and drifting towards war ; the government of Germany did but lead the general movement. She fell into the pit first, and she floundered deepest. She became the dreadful example at which all her fellow sinners could cry out.

For long Germany and Austria had been plotting an extension of German influence eastward through Asia Minor to the East. The German idea was crystallized in the phrase " Berlin to Bagdad." Antagonized to the

king was the German Kaiser's brother-in-law, are beyond our present powers of inquiry.

But the tangle did not end with Germany on the one hand and Russia on the other. The greed of Germany in 1871 had made France her inveterate enemy. The French people, aware of their inability to recover their lost provinces by their own strength, had conceived exaggerated ideas of the power and helpfulness of Russia. The French people had subscribed enormously to Russian loans. France was the ally of Russia. If the German Powers made war upon Russia, France would certainly attack them.

Now the short Eastern French frontier was very strongly defended. There was little prospect of Germany repeating the successes of

1870–71 against that barrier. But the Belgian frontier of France was longer and less strongly defended. An attack in overwhelming force on France through Belgium might repeat 1870 on a larger scale. The French left might be swung back south-eastwardly on Verdun as a pivot, and crowded back upon its right, as one shuts an open razor. This scheme the German strategists had worked out with great care and elaboration. Its execution involved an outrage upon the law of nations because Prussia had undertaken to guarantee the neutrality of Belgium and had no quarrel with her, and it involved the risk of bringing in Great Britain (which power was also pledged to protect Belgium) against Germany. Yet the Germans believed that their fleet had grown strong enough to make Great Britain hesitate to interfere, and with a view to possibilities they had constructed a great system of strategic railways to the Belgian frontier, and made every preparation for the execution of this scheme. So they might hope to strike down France at one blow, and deal at their leisure with Russia.

In 1914 all things seemed moving together in favour of the two Central Powers. Russia, it is true, had been recovering since 1906, but only very slowly ; France was distracted by financial scandals. The astounding murder of M. Calmette, the editor of the *Figaro*, by the wife of M. Caillaux, the Minister of Finance, brought these to a climax in March ; Britain, all Germany was assured, was on the verge of a civil war in Ireland. Repeated efforts were made both by foreign and English people to get some definite statement of what Britain would do if Germany and Austria assailed France and Russia ; but the British Foreign Secretary maintained a front of heavy ambiguity up to the very day of the British entry into the war.[1] As a consequence, there was a feeling on the Continent that Britain would either not fight or delay fighting, and this may have encouraged

Germany to go on threatening France. Events were precipitated on June 28th by the assassination of the Archduke Francis Ferdinand, the heir to the Austrian Empire, when on a state visit to Sarajevo, the capital of Bosnia. Here was a timely excuse to set the armies marching. "It is now or never," said the German Emperor.[2] Serbia was accused of instigating the murderers, and notwithstanding the fact that Austrian commissioners reported that there was no evidence to implicate the Serbian government, the Austro-Hungarian government contrived to press this grievance towards war. On July 23rd Austria discharged an ultimatum at Serbia, and, in spite of a practical submission on the part of Serbia, and of the efforts of Sir Edward Grey, the British Foreign Secretary, to call a conference of the Powers, declared war against Serbia on July 28th.

Russia mobilized her army on July 30th, and on August 1st Germany declared war upon her. German troops crossed into French territory next day, and, simultaneously with the delivery of an ultimatum to the unfortunate Belgians, the big flanking movement through Luxembourg and Belgium began. Westward rode the scouts and advance guards. Westward rushed a multitude of automobiles packed with soldiers. Enormous columns of grey-clad infantry followed ; round-eyed, fair young Germans they were for the most part—law-abiding, educated youngsters who had never yet seen a shot fired in anger. "This was war," they were told. They had to be bold and ruthless. Some of them did their best to carry out these militarist instructions at the expense of the ill-fated Belgians.

A disproportionate fuss has been made over the detailed atrocities in Belgium, disproportionate, that is, in relation to the fundamental atrocity of August 1914, which was the invasion of Belgium. Given that, the casual shootings and lootings, the wanton destruction of property, the plundering of inns and of food and drink shops by hungry and weary men, and the consequent rapes and incendiarism follow naturally enough. Only very simple people believe that an army in the field can maintain as high a level of honesty, decency, and justice as a settled community at home. And the tradition of

[1] I think his policy was quite clear. He said to Germany, "If you bring on war, you must expect England to support France and Russia." To France and Russia he said : "If you are unreasonable, do not expect England to support you." He thus brought pressure to bear on both sides.   G. M.

An illuminating book on the causes of the war is Lord Loreburn's *How the War Came.*

H. H. J.

[2] Kautsky's report on the origin of the war.

Photo: Imperial War Museum.
THE FLANDERS MUD—A TYPICAL SCENE IN THE YPRES SALIENT. IN THE FOREGROUND ARE THE RIBS OF A
GERMAN PILL-BOX.

the Thirty Years War still influenced the Prussian army. It has been customary in the countries allied against Germany to treat all this vileness and bloodshed of the Belgian months as though nothing of the sort had ever happened before, and as if it were due to some distinctively evil strain in the German character. They were nicknamed " Huns." But nothing could be less like the systematic destructions of the nomads (who once proposed to exterminate the entire Chinese population in order to restore China to pasture) than the German crimes in Belgium. Much of that crime was the drunken brutality of men who for the first time in their lives were free to use lethal weapons, much of it was the hysterical violence of men shocked at their own proceedings and in deadly fear of the revenge of the people whose country they had outraged, and much of it was done under duress because of the theory that men should be terrible in warfare and that populations are best subdued by fear. The German common people were bundled from an orderly obedience into this war in such a manner that atrocities were bound to ensue. They certainly did horrible and disgusting things. But any people

who had been worked up for war and led into war as the Germans were, would have behaved in a similar manner.

On the night of August 2nd, while most of Europe, still under the tranquil inertias of half a century of peace, still in the habitual enjoyment of such a widely diffused plenty and cheapness and freedom as no man living will ever see again, was thinking about its summer holidays, the little Belgian village of Visé was ablaze, and stupefied rustics were being led out and shot because it was alleged someone had fired on the invaders. The officers who ordered these acts, the men who obeyed, must surely have felt scared at the strangeness of the things they did. Most of them had never yet seen a violent death. And they had set light not to a village, but a world. It was the beginning of the end of an age of comfort, confidence, and gentle and seemly behaviour in Europe.

So soon as it was clear that Belgium was to be invaded, Great Britain ceased to hesitate, and (at eleven at night on August 4th) declared war upon Germany. The following day a German mine-laying vessel was caught off the Thames mouth by the cruiser *Amphion* and sunk,—the first time that the British and Germans had ever met in conflict under their own national flags upon land or water. . . .

All Europe still remembers the strange atmosphere of those eventful sunny August days, the end of the Armed Peace. For nearly half a century the Western world had been tranquil and had seemed *safe*. Only a few middle-aged and ageing people in France had had any practical experience of warfare. The newspapers spoke of a world catastrophe, but that conveyed very little meaning to those for whom the world had always seemed secure, who were indeed almost incapable of thinking of it as otherwise than secure. In Britain particularly for some weeks the peace-time routine continued in a slightly dazed fashion. It was like a man still walking about the world unaware that he has contracted a fatal disease which will alter every routine and habit in his life. People went on with their summer holidays; shops reassured their customers with the announcement " business as usual." There was much talk and excitement when the newspapers came, but it was the talk and excitement of spectators who have no vivid sense of participation in the catastrophe that was presently to involve them all.

§ 8[1]

We will now review very briefly the main phases of the world struggle which had thus commenced. Planned by Germany, it began with a swift attack designed to " knock out " France while Russia was still getting her forces together in the East. For a time all went well. Military science is never up to date under modern conditions, because military men are as a class unimaginative; there are always at any date undeveloped inventions capable of disturbing current tactical and strategic practice which the military intelligence has declined. The

A Summary of the Great War up to 1917.

German plan had been made for some years; it was a stale plan ; it could probably have been foiled at the outset by a proper use of entrenchments and barbed wire and machine guns, but the French were by no means as advanced in their military science as the Germans, and they trusted to methods of open warfare that were at least fourteen years behind the tines. They had a proper equipment neither of barbed wire nor machine guns, and there was a ridiculous tradition that the Frenchman did not fight well behind earthworks. The Belgian frontier was defended by the fortress of Liége, ten or twelve years out of date, with forts whose armament had been furnished and fitted in many cases by German contractors ; and the French northeastern frontier was very badly equipped. Naturally the German armament firm of Krupp had provided nutcrackers for these nuts in the form of exceptionally heavy guns firing high explosive shell. These defences proved therefore to be mere traps for their garrisons. The French attacked and failed in the Southern Ardennes. The German hosts swung round the French left with an effect of being irresistible ; Liége fell on August 9th, Brussels was reached on August 20th, and the small British army of about 70,000, which had arrived in Belgium, was struck at Mons (August 22nd) in overwhelming force, and driven backward in spite of the very deadly rifle tactics it had learnt during the South African War. (The German troops could not believe that the British were using rifles and not machine guns against them). The little British force was pushed aside westward, and the German right swept down so as to leave Paris to the west and crumple the entire French army back upon itself.

So confident was the German higher command at this stage of having won the war, that by the end of August German troops were already being withdrawn for the Eastern front, where the Russians were playing havoc in East and West Prussia. And then came the French counter-attack, strategically a very swift and brilliant counter-attack. The French struck back on their centre, they produced an unexpected army on their left, and the small British army, shaken but reinforced, was still fit to play a worthy part in the counter-stroke. The German right overran itself, lost its cohesion,

[1] For the common soldier's view of this last war there is no book better than *Le Feu* by Barbusse. An illustrated book of great quaintness, beauty, and veracity is André Hellé's *Le Livre des Heures*. No other book recalls so completely the *feel* and effect of the phases of the war. An admirably written and very wise book is Philip Gibbs' *Realities of War*. Some light on the peculiar difference of the fighting of the Great War from any previous warfare will be found in McCurdy's *War Neuroses* and Eder's book on the same subject

Map to illustrate the Original GERMAN Plan, 1914

French-British line before the fall of Namur ━ ━ ━
"   "   " a fortnight later (before the Battle of the Marne) ━━━━
Advance of the German right wing ➤➤➤
Ground over 1000 ft. ‖‖‖   over 3000 ft. ▓▓

J. F. H.

and was driven back from the Marne to the Aisne (Battle of the Marne, September 6th to 10th). It would have been driven back further had it not had the art of entrenchment in reserve. Upon the Aisne it stood and dug itself in. The heavy guns, the high explosive shell, the tanks, needed by the Allies to smash up these entrenchments, did not yet exist.

The Battle of the Marne shattered the original German plan. For a time France was saved. But the German was not defeated; he had still a great offensive superiority in men and equipment. His fear of the Russian in the East had been relieved by a tremendous victory at Tannenberg. His next phase was a headlong, less elaborately planned campaign to outflank the left of the allied armies and to seize the Channel ports and cut off supplies coming from Britain to France. Both armies extended to the west in a sort of race to the coast. Then the Germans, with a great superiority of guns and equipment, struck at the British round and about

Ypres. They came very near to a break through, but the British held them.

The war on the Western front settled down to trench warfare. Neither side had the science and equipment needed to solve the problem of breaking through modern entrenchments and entanglements, and both sides were now compelled to resort to scientific men, inventors, and such-like unmilitary persons for counsel and help in their difficulty. At that time the essential problem of trench warfare had already been solved; there existed in England, for instance, the model of a tank, which would have given the Allies a swift and easy victory before 1916; but the professional military mind is by necessity an inferior and unimaginative mind; no man of high intellectual quality would willingly imprison his gifts in such a calling; nearly all supremely great soldiers have been either inexperienced fresh-minded young men like Alexander, Napoleon, and Hoche, politicians turned soldiers like Julius Cæsar, nomads like the Hun and Mongol captains, or amateurs like Cromwell and Washington ; whereas this war, after fifty years of militarism, was a hopelessly professional war ; from first to last it was impossible to get it out of the hands of the regular generals, and neither the German nor Allied headquarters were disposed to regard an invention with toleration that would destroy their traditional methods.[1] The tank was not only disagreeably strange to these military gentlemen, but it gave an unprofessional protection to the common soldiers within it. The Germans, however, did make some innovations. In February (28th) they produced a rather futile novelty, the flame projector, the user of which was in constant danger of being burnt alive, and in April, in the midst of a second great offensive upon the British (Second Battle of Ypres, April 17th to May 17th), they employed a cloud of poison gas. This horrible device was used against Algerian and Canadian troops ; it shook them by the physical torture it inflicted, and by the anguish of those who died, but it failed to break through them. For some weeks chemists were of more importance than soldiers on the allied front, and within six weeks the defensive troops were already in possession of protective methods and devices.

For a year and a half, until July 1916, the Western front remained in a state of indecisive tension. There were heavy attacks on either side that ended in bloody repulses. The French made costly but glorious thrusts at Arras and in Champagne in 1915, the British at Loos. From Switzerland to the North Sea there ran two continuous lines of entrenchment, sometimes at a distance of a mile or more, sometimes at a distance of a few feet (at Arras *e.g.*), and in

and behind these lines of trenches millions of men toiled, raided their enemies, and prepared for sanguinary and foredoomed offensives. In any preceding age these stagnant masses of men would have engendered a pestilence inevitably, but here again modern science had altered the conditions of warfare. Certain novel diseases appeared, trench feet, for instance, caused by prolonged standing in cold water, new forms of dysentery, and the like, but none developed to an extent to disable either combatant force. Behind this front the whole life of the belligerent nations was being turned more and more to the task of maintaining supplies of food, munitions, and, above all, men to supply the places of those who day by day were killed or mangled.[2] The Germans had had the luck to possess a considerable number of big siege guns intended for the frontier fortresses ; these were now available for trench smashing with high explosive, a use no one had foreseen for them. The Allies throughout the first years were markedly inferior in their supply of big guns and ammunition, and their losses were steadily greater than the German. Mr. Asquith, the British Prime Minister, though a very fine practitioner in all the arts of Parliament, was wanting in creative ability ; and it is probably due to the push and hustle of Mr. Lloyd George (who presently ousted him in December 1916) and the clamour of the British press that this inferiority of supplies was eventually rectified.[3]

There was a tremendous German onslaught upon the French throughout the first half of 1916 round and about Verdun. The Germans

---

[1] " What mainly was wrong with our generalship was the system which put the High Command into the hands of a group of men belonging to the old school of war, unable by reason of their age and traditions to get away from rigid methods, and to become elastic in face of new conditions. Our Staff College had been hopelessly inefficient in its system of training, if I am justified in forming such an opinion from specimens produced by it, who had the brains of canaries and the manners of Potsdam. There was also a close corporation among the officers of the Regular Army, so that they took the lion's share of Staff appointments, thus keeping out brilliant young men of the New Armies, whose brain power, to say the least of it, was on a higher level than that of the Sandhurst standard."
Philip Gibbs, *Realities of War.*

[2] " The smart society of G.H.Q. was best seen at the Officers' Club at dinner-time. It was as much like musical comedy as any stage setting of war at the Gaiety. The band played rag-time and light music while the warriors fed, and all these generals and staff officers, with their decorations and Army bands, and polished buttons and crossed swords, were waited upon by little W.A.A.C.S., with the G.H.Q. colours tied up in bows on their hair, and khaki stockings under their short skirts, and fancy aprons. Such a chatter ! Such bursts of light-hearted laughter ! Such whisperings of secrets, of intrigues, and scandals in high places ! Such callous-hearted courage when British soldiers were being blown to bits, gassed, blinded, maimed, and shell-shocked in places that were far, so very far, from G.H.Q."—Philip Gibbs, *The Realities of War.*

[3] But see Roch, *Mr. Lloyd George and the War,* and Arthur's *Life of Lord Kitchener.*

suffered enormous losses and were held, after pushing in the French lines for some miles. The French losses were as great or greater. " *Ils ne passeront pas*," said and sang the French infantry—and kept their word.

The Eastern German front was more extended and less systematically entrenched than the Western. For a time the Russian armies continued to press westward in spite of the Tannenberg disaster. They conquered nearly the whole of Galicia from the Austrians, took Lemberg on September 2nd, 1914, and the great fortress of Przemysl on March 22nd, 1915. But after the Germans had failed to break the Western

Goritzia (which fell in the summer of 1916), but her intervention was of little use at that time to either Russia or the two Western Powers. She merely established another line of trench warfare among the high mountains of her picturesque north-eastern frontier.

While the main fronts of the chief combatants were in this state of exhaustive deadlock, both sides were attempting to strike round behind the front of their adversaries. The Germans made a series of Zeppelin, and later of aeroplane raids upon Paris and the east of England. Ostensibly these aimed at depôts, munition works, and the like targets of military importance, but

Photo : *Imperial War Museum.*

A BIG RAILWAY GUN FIRING.

front of the Allies, and after an ineffective Allied offensive made without proper material,[1] they turned to Russia, and a series of heavy blows, with a novel use of massed artillery, were struck first in the south and then at the north of the Russian front. On June 22nd, Przemysl was retaken, and the whole Russian line was driven back until Vilna (September 2nd) was in German hands.

In May 1915 (23rd) Italy joined the Allies, and declared war upon Austria. (Not until a year later did she declare war on Germany.) She pushed over her eastern boundary towards

practically they bombed promiscuously at inhabited places. At first these raiders dropped not very effective bombs, but later the size and quality of these missiles increased, considerable numbers of people were killed and injured, and very much damage was done. The English people were roused to a pitch of extreme indignation by these outrages.[2] Although the Germans had possessed Zeppelins for some years, no one in authority in Great Britain had thought out the proper methods of dealing with them, and it was not until late in

[1] " The want of an unlimited quantity of high explosive was a fatal bar to our success."—*The Times.* May 14th, 1915.

[2] But compare the British bombardment of Japanese towns noted in Chap. XXXIX, § 11. And aeroplane bombs and machine-gun fire have since been used by the British military authorities against Indian village crowds *suspected* of sedition.

1916 that an adequate supply of anti-aircraft guns was brought into play and that these raiders were systematically attacked by aeroplanes. Then came a series of Zeppelin disasters, and after the spring of 1917 they ceased to be used for any purpose but sea scouting, and their place as raiders was taken by large aeroplanes (the Gothas). The visits of these latter machines to London and the east of England became systematic after the summer of 1917. All through the winter of 1917-18, London on every moonlight night became familiar with the banging of warning maroons, the shrill whistles of the police alarm, the hasty clearance of the streets, the distant rumbling of scores and hundreds of anti-aircraft guns growing steadily to a wild uproar of thuds and crashes, the swish of flying shrapnel, and at last, if any of the raiders got through the barrage, with the dull heavy bang of the bursting bombs. Then presently, amidst the diminuendo of the gun fire would come the inimitable rushing sound of the fire brigade engines and the hurry of the ambulances. . . . War was brought home to every Londoner by these experiences.

While the Germans were thus assailing the nerve of their enemy home population through the air, they were also attacking the overseas trade of the British by every means in their power. At the outset of the war they had various trade destroyers scattered over the world, and a squadron of powerful modern cruisers in the Pacific, namely, the *Scharnhorst*, the *Gneisenau*, the *Leipzig*, the *Nürnberg*, and the *Dresden*. Some of the detached cruisers, and particularly the *Emden*, did a considerable amount of commerce destroying before they

were hunted down, and the main squadron caught an inferior British force off the coast of Chile and sank the *Good Hope* and the *Monmouth* on November 1st, 1914. A month later these German ships were themselves pounced upon by a British force, and all (except the *Dresden*) sunk by Admiral Sturdee in the Battle of the Falkland Isles. After this conflict the Allies remained in undisputed possession of the surface of the sea, a supremacy which the great naval Battle of Jutland (May 1st, 1916) did nothing to shake. The Germans concentrated their attention more and more upon submarine warfare. From the beginning of the war they had had considerable submarine successes. On one day, September 22nd, 1914, they sank three powerful cruisers, the *Aboukir*, the *Hogue*, and the *Cressy*, with 1,473 men. They continued to levy a toll upon British shipping throughout the war; at first they hailed and examined passenger and mercantile shipping, but this practice they discontinued for fear of traps, and in the spring of 1915 they began to sink ships without notice. In May 1915 they sank the great passenger liner, the *Lusitania*, without any warning, drowning a number of American citizens. This embittered American feeling against them, but the possibility of injuring and perhaps reducing Britain by a submarine blockade was so great, that they persisted in a more and more intensified submarine campaign, regardless of the danger of dragging the United States unto the circle of their enemies.

Meanwhile, Turkish forces, very ill-equipped, were making threatening gestures at Egypt across the Desert of Sinai.

And while the Germans were thus striking at

Photo: Imperial War Museum.

A CAMOUFLAGED SHIP—H.M.S. AIRCRAFT CARRIER "FURIOUS."

Britain, their least accessible and most formidable antagonist, through the air and under the sea, the French and British were also embarking upon a disastrous flank attack in the east upon the Central Powers through Turkey. The Gallipoli campaign was finely imagined, but disgracefully executed. Had it succeeded, the Allies would have captured Constantinople in 1915. But the Turks were given two months' notice of the project by a premature bombardment of the Dardanelles in February, the scheme was also probably betrayed through the Greek Court, and when at last British and French forces were landed upon the Gallipoli peninsula in April, they found the Turks well entrenched and better equipped for trench warfare [1] than themselves. The Allies trusted for heavy artillery to the great guns of the ships, which were comparatively useless for battering down entrenchments, and among every other sort of thing that they had failed to foresee, they had not foreseen hostile submarines. Several great battleships were lost; they went down in the same clear waters over which the ships of Xerxes had once sailed to their fate at Salamis. The story of the Gallipoli campaign from the side of the Allies is at once heroic and pitiful, a story of courage and incompetence, and of life, material, and prestige wasted, culminating in a withdrawal in January 1916.[2]

This failure was due in part to the refusal of the Greeks to co-operate in the adventure. For a year and a half the Greek king, the brother-in-law of the Kaiser, being protected by friends in high quarters on the Allied side, tricked and misled the Allies, and wasted the lives of great numbers of common British and French soldiers. In June 1917 he was forced to abdicate, but instead of permitting the Greeks, under their proper leader Venizelos, to follow their natural and traditional republican disposition, his son, Alexander, the Kaiser's nephew, was made king in his place—*by the Allies*! This Greek chapter in the story of the Great War still awaits

[1] *E.g.* in hand grenades.
[2] For the flighty incapacity of the British military authorities in this adventure, see Sir Ian Hamilton's *Gallipoli Diary.* H. G. W.
It is only fair to the British Commander to add that the incapacity was that of the home authorities to understand his demands for men and material.
P. G.

the investigations of the historian. It is at present a quite inexplicable story, and we give these preposterous facts with no attempt to rationalize them.

Linked up closely with this Greek vacillation was the entry of Bulgaria into the war (October 12th, 1915). The King of Bulgaria had hesitated for more than a year to make any decision between the two sides. Now the manifest failure of the British at Gallipoli, coupled with a strong Austro-German attack in Serbia, swung him over to the Central Powers. While the Serbs were hotly engaged with the Austro-German invaders upon the Danube, he attacked Serbia in the rear, and in a few weeks the country had been completely overrun. The Serbian army made a terrible retreat through the mountains of Albania to the coast, where its remains were rescued by an Allied fleet.

An Allied force landed at Salonika in Greece, and pushed inland towards Monastir, but was unable to render any effectual assistance to the Serbians. It was the Salonika plan which sealed the fate of the Gallipoli expedition.

To the east, in Mesopotamia, the British, using Indian troops chiefly, made a still remoter flank attack upon the Central Powers. An army, very ill provided for the campaign, was landed at Basra in the November of 1914, and pushed up towards Bagdad in the following year. It gained a victory at Ctesiphon, the ancient Arsacid and Sassanid capital within twenty-five miles of Bagdad, but the Turks were heavily reinforced, there was a retreat to Kut, and there the British army, under General Townshend, was surrounded and starved into surrender on April 29th, 1916.

All these campaigns in the air, under the seas, in Russia, Turkey, and Asia, were subsidiary to the main front, the front of decision, between Switzerland and the sea; and there the main millions lay entrenched, slowly learning the necessary methods of modern scientific warfare. There was a rapid progress in the use of the aeroplane. At the outset of the war this had been used chiefly for scouting, and by the Germans for the dropping of marks for the artillery. Such a thing as aerial fighting was unheard of. In 1916 the aeroplanes carried machine guns and fought in the air; their bombing work was increasingly important, they

A TANK IN ACTION

The WESTERN FRONT 1915-18

Allied line, March 1915 ——————
"   " April 1917 ------------
German line, July 1918 —·—·—·—
Allied line, Nov. 11th 1918 ——————

0   25   50 Miles

J.F.H.

mon soldiers, the Soviet; and this body clamoured for an international conference of socialists at Stockholm. Food riots were occurring in Berlin at this time, war weariness in Austria and Germany was profound, and there can be little doubt, in the light of subsequent events, that such a conference would have precipitated a reasonable peace on democratic lines in 1917 and a German revolution. Kerensky implored his Western allies to allow this conference to take place, but, fearful of a worldwide outbreak of socialism and republicanism, they refused, in spite of the favourable response of a small majority of the British Labour Party. Without either moral or physical help from the Allies the "moderate" Russian republic still fought on and made a last desperate offensive effort in July. It failed after some preliminary successes and another great slaughtering of Russians.

The limit of Russian endurance was reached. Mutinies broke out in the Russian armies, and particularly upon the northern front, and upon November 7th, 1917, Kerensky's government was overthrown and power was seized by the Soviet Government, dominated by the Bolshevik socialists under Lenin, and pledged to make peace regardless of the Western Powers. Russia passed definitely "out of the war."

In the spring of 1917 there had been a costly and ineffective French attack upon the Champagne front which had failed to break through and sustained enormous losses. Here, then, by the end of 1917, was a phase of events altogether favourable to Germany, had her government been fighting for security and well-being rather than for pride and victory. But to the very end, to the pitch of final exhaustion, the people

position to embarrass the new government as much as possible. At the head of the Russian republican government was an eloquent and picturesque leader Kerensky, who found himself assailed by the deep forces of a profounder revolutionary movement, the "social revolution," at home and cold-shouldered by the Allied governments abroad. His allies would let him give the Russian people neither land nor peace beyond their frontiers. The French and the British press pestered their exhausted ally for a fresh offensive, but when presently the Germans made a strong attack by sea and land upon Riga, the British Admiralty quailed before the prospect of a Baltic expedition in relief. The new Russian republic had to fight unsupported. In spite of their great naval predominance, it is to be noted that the Allies, except for some submarine attacks, left the Germans the complete mastery of the Baltic throughout the war.

The Russian masses were resolute to end the war. There had come into existence in Petrograd a body representing the workers and com-

Reproduced by permission of Sir W. G. Armstrong, Whitworth & Co., Ltd.

WAR INDUSTRY: THE ARMSTRONG SHIPYARD AT NEWCASTLE-ON-TYNE, OF SIR W. G. ARMSTRONG, WHITWORTH
& CO., LTD. "AQUITANIA" BEING RECONDITIONED ALONGSIDE QUAY.

Walker Shipyard in background.

of the Central Powers were held to the effort to realize an impossible world imperialism.

To that end it was necessary that Britain should be not merely resisted, but subjugated, and in order to do that Germany had already dragged America into the circle of her enemies. Throughout 1916 the submarine campaign had been growing in intensity, but hitherto it had respected neutral shipping. In January 1917, a completer " blockade " of Great Britain and France was proclaimed, and all neutral Powers were warned to withdraw their shipping from the British seas. An indiscriminate sinking of the world's shipping began which compelled the United States to enter the war in April (6th) 1917. Throughout 1917, while Russia was breaking up and becoming impotent, the American people was changing swiftly and steadily into a great military nation. And the unrestricted submarine campaign, for which the

German imperialists had accepted the risk of this fresh antagonist, was far less successful than had been hoped. The British navy proved itself much more inventive and resourceful than the British army ; there was a rapid development of anti-submarine devices under water, upon the surface, and in the air ; and after a month or so of serious destruction, the tale of submarine sinkings declined. The British found it necessary to put themselves upon food rations ; but the regulations were well framed and ably administered, the public showed an excellent spirit and intelligence, and the danger of famine and social disorder was kept at arm's length.

Yet the German imperial government persisted in its course. If the submarine was not doing all that had been expected, and if the armies of America gathered like a thundercloud, yet Russia was definitely down ; and in

October the same sort of autumn offensive that had overthrown Serbia in 1915 and Rumania in 1916 was now turned with crushing effect against Italy. The Italian front collapsed after the Battle of Caporetto, and the Austro-German armies poured down into Venetia and came almost within gunfire of Venice. Germany felt justified, therefore, in taking a high line with the Russian peace proposals, and the peace of Brest-Litovsk (March 2nd, 1918) gave the Western allies some intimation of what a German victory would mean to them. It was a crushing and exorbitant peace, dictated with the utmost arrogance of confident victors.

All through the winter German troops had been shifting from the Eastern to the Western front, and now, in the spring of 1918, the jaded enthusiasm of hungry, weary, and bleeding Germany was lashed up for the one supreme effort that was really and truly to end the war. For some months American troops had been in France, but the bulk of the American army was still across the Atlantic. It was high time for the final conclusive blow upon the Western front, if such a blow was ever to be delivered. The first attack was upon the British in the Somme region. The not very brilliant cavalry generals who were still in command of a front upon which cavalry was a useless encumbrance, were caught napping ; and on March 21st, in "Gough's Disaster," a British army was driven back in such disorder as no British army had ever known before. Thousands of guns were lost, and scores of thousands of prisoners. Many of these losses were due to the utter incompetence of the higher command. No less than a hundred tanks were abandoned *because they ran out of petrol* ! The British were driven back almost to Amiens.[1] Throughout April and May the Germans rained offensives on the Allied front. They came near to a break through in the north, and they made a great drive back to the Marne, which they reached again on May 30th, 1918.

This was the climax of the German effort. Behind it was nothing but an exhausted homeland. Fresh troops were hurrying from Britain across the Channel, and America was now pouring men into France by the hundred thousand. In June the weary Austrians made a last effort in Italy, and collapsed before an Italian counter-attack. Early in June the French began to develop a counter-attack in the Marne angle. By July the tide was turning, and the Germans were reeling back. The Battle of Château Thierry (July 18th) proved the quality of the new American armies. In August the British opened a great and successful thrust into Belgium, and the bulge of the German lines towards Amiens wilted and collapsed. Germany had finished. The fighting spirit passed out of her army, and October was a story of defeat and retreat along the entire Western front. Early in November British troops were in Valenciennes and Americans in Sedan. In Italy also the Austrian armies were in a state of disorderly retreat. But everywhere now the Hohenzollern and Habsburg forces were collapsing. The smash at the end was amazingly swift. Frenchmen and Englishmen could not believe their newspapers as day after day they announced the capture of more hundreds of guns and more thousands of prisoners.

In September a great Allied offensive against Bulgaria had produced a revolution in that country and peace proposals. Turkey had followed with a capitulation at the end of October, and Austro-Hungary on November 4th. There was an attempt to bring out the German Fleet for a last fight, but the sailors mutinied (November 7th).

The Kaiser and the Crown Prince bolted hastily, and without a scrap of dignity, into Holland. It was like welshers bolting from a racecourse to escape a ducking. On November 11th an armistice was signed, and the war was at an end. . . .

[1] " I found a general opinion among officers and men under the command of the Fifth Army that they had been victims of atrocious staff work, tragic in its consequence. From what I saw of some of the Fifth Army staff officers, I was of the same opinion. Some of these young gentlemen, and some of the elderly officers, were arrogant and supercilious, without revealing any sign of intelligence. If they had wisdom, it was deeply camouflaged by an air of inefficiency. If they had knowledge, they hid it as a secret of their own. General Gough in Flanders, though personally responsible for many tragic happenings, was badly served by some of his subordinates, and battalion officers and divisional staffs raged against the whole of the Fifth Army organization, or lack of organization, with an extreme passion of speech."—Philip Gibbs, *Realities of War.*

For four years and a quarter the war had lasted, and gradually it had drawn nearly everyone, in the Western world at least, into its vortex. Upwards of ten millions of people had been actually killed through the fighting, another twenty or twenty-five million had died through the hardships and disorders entailed. Scores of millions were suffering and enfeebled by under-nourishment and misery. A vast proportion of the living were now engaged in war work, in drilling and armament, in making munitions, in hospitals, in working as substitutes for men who had gone into the armies and the like. Business men had been adapting themselves to the more hectic methods necessary for profit in a world in a state of crisis. The

Main EASTERN FRONT RUSSIA | SERBIA | TURKEY | AFRICA | CHINA & PACIFIC

Main EASTERN FRONT RUSSIA

Aug. 2 Russia invades Germany
Aug. 28 B. of TANNENBERG
RUSSIAN OFFENSIVES RELIEVE WESTERN FRONT
Russians over-run Galicia
Sept. 3 Russians take Lemberg
Oct. 23-Lodz

Mch. 22 Russians take Przemysl
Germans make massed artillery offensive
June- Przemysl retaken
GREAT RUSSIAN RETREAT
Sept. 18 Vilna falls

GRADUAL EXHAUSTION OF RUSSIA

POLAND under GERMAN rule

Mch. 15 Tsar abdicates
FIRST REVOLUTION

July Last Russian offensive in Galicia

Nov. 7 The BOLSHEVIK Revolution
Dec. 15 Armistice of BREST-LITOVSK

BOLSHEVIK I

March 2 Peace of B-LITOVSK
Germans in Ukraine Mch. 13 take Odessa

SERBIA

Successful resistance to Austrian attacks

Sept. 18- Great Austro-German attack begun
Oct. 5- Allies land at Salonika
BULGARIA
Oct. 12- war on Serbia
Serbia completely crushed between Bulgaria & Central Powers

RUMANIA
Aug. 27 declares war

Austro-Germans under Falkenhayn and Mackensen crush Rumania

Rumania occupied by Austro-Germans

SERBIA under GERMAN rule

May 7 Rumania signs peace with Central Powers

Sept. Allied offensive against Bulgaria
Sept. 30 B. capitulates.

TURKEY

MESOPOTAMIA
British occupy
Nov. 21- Basra

Feb. 5 Turks repulsed from Suez Canal
Feb. 19 Allied fleets bombard Dardanelles
Ap. 26 Allies land on Gallipoli Peninsula

Nov. 22 Battle of Ctesiphon
Dec. 1 British retreat to Kut
Siege of KUT

Jan. 8 Gallipoli evacuated

Apr. 29 Townshend surrenders

Gen. Maude's advance   Kut
Feb. 24 British retake
Mch. 11- Bagdad

June Abdicatⁿ of K.Constantine of Greece

Nov. 7 British take Gaza
Dec. 9- Jerusalem

French forces join British

Allies occupy
Oct. 1 Damascus
" 26 Aleppo
Oct. 30 Turkey capitulates

AFRICA

Sept. 27 Union of S.A. invades German S.W. Africa
Oct. De Wet rebels, &
Dec. 1- is captured

July 15 Gen. Botha conquers German S.W.

Conquest of German E. Africa under Gen. Smuts

Ger. East A. clear of Germans

CHINA & PACIFIC

Aug. 15 Japanese take Kiau-Chau
Nov. 7
Aug. 29 N. Zealand takes Samoa
Sept. 11 Australia takes Ger. N. Guinea

1915

1916

1917

Aug. 14 CHINA declares war

1918

J.F.H.

---

war had become, indeed, an atmosphere, a habit of life, a new social order. Then suddenly it ended.

In London the armistice was proclaimed about midday on November 11th. It produced a strange cessation of every ordinary routine. Clerks poured out of their offices and would not return, assistants deserted their shops, omnibus drivers and the drivers of military lorries set out upon journeys of their own devising, with picked-up loads of astounded and cheering passengers going nowhere in particular and careless whither they went. Vast vacant crowds presently choked the streets, and every house and shop that possessed such adornments hung out flags. When night came, many of the main streets, which had been kept in darkness for many months because of the air raids, were brightly lit. It was very strange to see thronging multitudes assembled in an artificial light again. Everyone felt aimless, with a kind of strained and aching relief. It was over at last. There would be no more killing in France, no more air raids—and things would get better. People wanted to laugh, and weep—and could do neither. Youths of spirit and young soldiers on leave formed thin noisy processions that shoved their way through the general drift, and did their best to make a jollification. A captured German gun was hauled from the Mall, where a vast array of such trophies had been set out, into Trafalgar Square, and its carriage burnt. Squibs and crackers were thrown about. But there was little concerted rejoicing. Nearly everyone had lost too much and suffered too much to rejoice with any fervour.[1]

§ 10

The world in the year after the Great War was like a man who has had some vital surgical

The Political, Economic, and Social Disorganization caused by the War.

operation very roughly performed, and who is not yet sure whether he can now go on living or whether he has not been so profoundly shocked and injured that he will presently fall down and die. It was a world dazed and stunned. German militarist imperialism had been defeated, but at an overwhelming cost. It had come very near to victory. Everything went on, now that the strain of the conflict had ceased, rather laxly, rather weakly, and with a gusty and uncertain temper. There was a universal hunger for peace, a universal desire for the lost safety and liberty and prosperity of pre-war times, without any power of will to achieve and secure these things.

Just as with the Roman Republic under the long strain of the Punic War, so now there had been a great release of violence and cruelty, and a profound deterioration in financial and economic morality. Generous spirits had sacrificed themselves freely to the urgent demands

of the war, but the sly and base of the worlds of business and money had watched the convulsive opportunities of the time and secured a firm grip upon the resources and political power of their countries. Everywhere men who would have been regarded as shady adventurers before 1914 had acquired power and influence while better men toiled unprofitably. Such men as Lord Rhondda, the British food controller, killed themselves with hard work, while the war profiteer waxed rich and secured his grip upon press and party organization.

In the course of the war there had been extraordinary experiments in collective management in nearly all the belligerent countries. It was realized that the common expedients of peace-time commerce, the higgling of the market, the holding out for a favourable bargain, were incompatible with the swift needs of warfare. Transport, fuel, food supply, and the distribution of the raw materials not only of clothing, housing, and the like, but of everything needed for war munitions, had been brought under public control. No longer had farmers been allowed to under-farm ; cattle had been put upon deer-parks and grass-lands ploughed up, with or without the owner's approval. Luxury building and speculative company promotion had been restrained. In effect, a sort of emergency socialist state had been established throughout belligerent Europe. It was rough-and-ready and wasteful, but it was more effective than the tangled incessant profit-seeking, the cornering and forestalling and incoherent productiveness of "private enterprise."

In the earlier years of the war there was a very widespread feeling of brotherhood and the common interest in all the belligerent states. The common men were everywhere sacrificing life and health for what they believed to be the common good of the state. In return, it was promised, there was to be less social injustice after the war, a more universal devotion to the common welfare. In Great Britain, for instance, Mr. Lloyd George was particularly insistent upon his intention to make the after-war Britain "a land fit for heroes." He foreshadowed the continuation of this new war communism into the peace period in discourses of great fire and beauty. In Great Britain,

[1] A very good account of the state of mind of Paris during and after the war is in W. P. Adams' *Paris Sees it Through*.

there was created a Ministry of Reconstruction, which was understood to be planning a new and more generous social order, better labour conditions, better housing, extended education, a complete and scientific revision of the economic system. Similar hopes of a better world sustained the common soldiers of France and Germany and Italy. It was premature disillusionment that caused the Russian collapse. So that two mutually dangerous streams of anticipation were running through the minds of men in Western Europe towards the end of the war. The rich and adventurous men, and particularly the new war profiteers, were making their plans to prevent such developments as that air transport should become a state property, and to snatch back manufactures, shipping, land transport, the public services generally, and the trade in staples from the hands of the commonweal into the grip of private profit ; they were securing possession of newspapers and busying themselves with party caucuses and the like to that end ; while the masses of common men were looking forward naïvely to a new state of society planned almost entirely in their interest and according to generous general ideas. The history of 1919 is largely the clash of these two streams of anticipation. There was a hasty selling off by the " business " government in control, of every remunerative public enterprise to private speculators. . . . By the middle of 1919 the labour masses throughout the world were manifestly disappointed and in a thoroughly bad temper. The British " Ministry of Reconstruction " and its foreign equivalents were exposed as a soothing sham. The common man felt he had been cheated. There was to be no reconstruction, but only a restoration of the old order—in the harsher form necessitated by the poverty of the new time.

For four years the drama of the war had obscured the social question which had been developing in the Western civilizations throughout the nineteenth century. Now that the war was over, this question reappeared gaunt and bare, as it had never been seen before.

And the irritations and hardships and the general insecurity of the new time were exacerbated by a profound disturbance of currency and credit. Money, a complicated growth of conventions rather than a system of values, had been deprived within the belligerent countries of the support of a gold standard. Gold had been retained only for international trade, and every government had produced excessive quantities of paper money for domestic use. With the breaking down of the war-time barriers the international exchange became a wildly fluctuating confusion, a source of distress to everyone except a few gamblers and wily speculators. Prices rose and rose—with an infuriating effect upon the wage-earner. On the one hand was the employer resisting his demands for more pay ; on the other hand, food, house-room, and clothing were being steadily cornered against him. And, which was the essential danger of the situation, *he had lost any confidence he had ever possessed that any patience or industrial willingness he displayed would really alleviate the shortages and inconveniences by which he suffered.*

In the speeches of politicians towards the close of 1919 and the spring of 1920, there was manifest an increasing recognition of the fact that what is called the capitalist system—the private ownership system that is, in which private profit is the working incentive—was on its trial. It had to produce general prosperity, they admitted, or it had to be revised. It is interesting to note such a speech as that of Mr. Lloyd George, the British Premier, delivered on Saturday, December 6th, 1919. Mr. Lloyd George had had the education and training of a Welsh solicitor ; he entered politics early, and in the course of a brilliant parliamentary career he had had few later opportunities for reading and thought. But being a man of great natural shrewdness, he was expressing here very accurately the ideas of the more intelligent of the business men and wealthy men and ordinary citizens who supported him.

" There is a new challenge to civilization," he said. " What is it ? It is fundamental. It affects the whole fabric of society as we know it ; its commerce, its trade, its industry, its finance, its social order—all are involved in it. There are those who maintain that the prosperity and strength of the country have been built up by the stimulating and invigorating appeal to individual impulse, to individual action. That is one view. The State must educate ; the

State must assist where necessary ; the State must control where necessary ; the State must shield the weak against the arrogance of the strong ; but the life springs from individual impulse and energy. (Cheers.) That is one view. What is the other ? That private enterprise is a failure, tried, and found wanting —a complete failure, a cruel failure. It must be rooted out, and the community must take charge as a community, to produce, to distribute, as well as to control.

" Those are great challenges for us to decide. *We* say that the ills of private enterprise can be averted. *They* say, ' No, they cannot. No ameliorative, no palliative, no restrictive, no remedial measure will avail. These evils are inherent in the system. They are the fruit of the tree, and you must cut it down.' That is the challenge we hear ringing through the civilized world to-day, from ocean to ocean, through valley and plain. You hear it in the whining and maniacal shrieking of the Bolshevists. You hear it in the loud, clear, but more restrained tones of Congresses and Conferences. The Bolshevists would blow up the fabric with high explosive, with horror. Others would pull it down with the crowbars and with cranks—especially cranks. (Laughter.)

" Unemployment, with its injustice for the man who seeks and thirsts for employment, who begs for labour and cannot get it, and who is punished for failure he is not responsible for by the starvation of his children—that torture is *something that private enterprise ought to remedy for its own sake.* (Cheers.) Sweating, slums, the sense of semi-slavery in labour, must go. We must cultivate a sense of manhood by treating men as men. If I—and I say this deliberately—if I had to choose between this fabric I believe in, and allowing millions of men and women and children to rot in its cellars, I would not hesitate one hour. That is not the choice. Thank God it is not the choice. Private enterprise can produce more, so that all men get a fair share of it. . . ."[1]

Here, put into quasi-eloquent phrasing, and with a jest adapted to the mental habits of the audience, we have the common-sense view of the ordinary prosperous man not only of Great Britain, but of America or France or Italy or

[1] *The Times*, December 8th, 1919.

Germany. In quality and tone it is a fair sample of British political thought in 1919. The prevailing economic system has made us what we are, is the underlying idea ; and we do not want any process of social destruction to precede a renascence of society, we do not want to experiment with the fundamentals of our social order. Let us accept that. Adaptation, Mr. Lloyd George admitted, there had to be. Now this occasion of his speaking was a year and a month after the Armistice, and for all that period private enterprise had been failing to do all that Mr. Lloyd George was so cheerfully promising it would do. The community was in urgent need of houses. Throughout the war there had been a cessation not only of building, but of repairs. The shortage of houses in the last months of 1919 amounted to scores of thousands in Britain alone.[2] Multitudes of people were living in a state of exasperating congestion, and the most shameless profiteering in apartments and houses was going on. It was a difficult, but not an impossible situation. Given the same enthusiasm and energy and self-sacrifice that had tided over the monstrous crisis of 1916, the far easier task of providing a million houses could have been performed in a year or so. But there had been corners in building materials, transport was in a disordered state, and it did not *pay* private enterprise to build houses at any rents within the means of the people who needed them. Private enterprise, therefore, so far from bothering about the public need of housing, did nothing but corner and speculate in rents and sub-letting. It now demanded grants in aid from the State—in order to build at a profit. And there was a great crowding and dislocation of goods at the depôts because there was insufficient road transport. There was an urgent want of cheap automobiles to move about goods and workers. But private enterprise in the automobile industry found it far more profitable to produce splendid and costly cars for those whom the war had made rich. The munition factories built with public money could have been converted very readily into factories for the mass production of cheap automobiles, but private enterprise had in-

[2] Authorities vary between 250,000 and a million houses.

Photo : Imperial War Museum.

IN THE WAR ZONE. THE RUINS OF THE HÔTEL DE VILLE, ARRAS.

sisted upon these factories being sold by the State, and would neither meet the public need itself nor let the State do so. So, too, with the world in the direst discomfort for need of shipping, private enterprise insisted upon the shutting down of the newly constructed State shipyards. Currency was dislocated everywhere, but private enterprise was busy buying and selling francs or marks and intensifying the trouble. While Mr. Lloyd George was making the very characteristic speech we have quoted, the discontent of the common man was gathering everywhere, and little or nothing was being done to satisfy his needs. It was becoming very evident that unless there was to be some profound change in the spirit of business, under an unrestrained private enterprise system there was little or no hope, in Europe at any rate, of decent housing, clothing, or education for the workers for two or three generations.

These are facts that the historian of mankind is obliged to note with as little comment as possible. Private enterprise in Europe in 1919 displayed neither will nor capacity for meeting the crying needs of the time. So soon as it was released from control, it ran naturally into speculation, cornering, and luxury production. It followed the line of maximum profit. It displayed no sense of its own dangers ; and it resisted any attempt to restrain and moderate its profits and make itself serviceable, even in its own interest. And this went on in the face of the most striking manifestations of the extreme recalcitrance on the part of the European masses to the prolonged continuance of the privations and inconveniences they suffered. In 1913 these masses were living as they had lived since birth ; they were habituated to the life they led. The masses of 1919, on the other hand, had been uprooted everywhere, to go into the armies, to go into munition factories, and so on. They had lost their habits of acquiescence, and they were hardier and more capable of desperate action. Great multitudes of men had gone through such brutalizing training as, for instance, bayonet drill ; they had learnt to be ferocious, and to think less either of killing or being killed. Social unrest had become, therefore, much more dangerous. Everything seemed to point to a refusal to tolerate the current state of affairs for many years. Unless the educated and prosperous and comfortable people of Europe could speedily get their private enterprise under sufficient restraint to make it work well and rapidly for the common good, unless they could develop the idea of business as primarily a form of public service and not primarily a method of profit-making, unless they could in their own interest achieve a security of peace that would admit of a cessation not only of war preparation, but of international commercial warfare, strike and insurrection promised to follow strike and insurrection up to a complete social and political collapse. It was not that the masses had or imagined that they had the plan of a new social, political, and economic system. They had not, and they did not believe they had. The defects we have pointed out in the socialist scheme (Chapter XXXIX, § 5) were no secret to them. It was a much more dangerous state of affairs than that. It was that they were becoming so disgusted with the current system, with its silly luxury, its universal waste, and its general misery, that they did not care what happened afterwards so long as they could destroy it. It was a return to a state of mind comparable to that which had rendered possible the debacle of the Roman Empire.

Already in 1917 the world had seen one great community go that way, the Russian people. The Russians overturned the old order and submitted to the autocratic rule of a small group of doctrinaire Bolshevik socialists, because these men seemed to have something new to try. They wrecked the old system, and at any cost they would not have it back. The information available from Russia at the time of writing this summary is still too conflicting and too obviously tainted by propagandist aims for us to form any judgment upon the proceedings and methods of the Soviet Government, but it is very plain that from November 1917, Russia has not only endured that government and its mainly socialistic methods, but has fought for it successfully against anything that seemed to threaten a return to the old regime.

We have already (§ 5) pointed out the very broad differences between the Russian and the Western communities, and the strong reasons there are for doubting that they will move upon parallel lines and act in similar ways. The Russian masses were cut off by want of education and sympathy from the small civilized community of prosperous and educated people which lived upon them. These latter were a little separate nation. The masses below have thrown that separate nation off and destroyed it and begun again, so to speak, upon a new sort of society which, whether it succeed or collapse, cannot fail to be of intense interest to all mankind. But there is much more unity of thought and feeling between class and class in the West than in Russia, and particularly in the Atlantic communities. Even if they wrangle, classes can talk together and understand each other. There is no unbroken stratum of illiterates. The groups of rich and speculative men, the " bad men " in business and affairs, whose freedoms are making the very name of " private enterprise " stink in the nostrils of the ordinary man, are only the more active section of very much larger classes, guilty perhaps of indolence and self-indulgence, but capable of being roused to a sense not merely of the wickedness but of the danger of systematic self-seeking in a strained, impoverished, and sorely tried world. Many of these more reasonable and moral people have shown themselves clearly aware of the nature of the present situation, and some of them have made speeches and delivered sermons and written books— often addressed to the working classes—expressing very generous and unselfish views. Speeches and sermons and books will in themselves do little to allay the gathering wrath of classes ill housed, ill fed and unhealthy, and angry because they believe things are so through the reckless greed of others ; but such utterances are valuable as admissions, and if these good intentions, encouraged perhaps and aided by a certain pressure from below, presently develop into a resolute combining and direction of the energies of private enterprise—for a time at least—towards socially necessary work and a restriction of speculation and luxury, and if there begin a rapid provision, even at some cost to the hoards and satisfactions of the successful classes, of the decent homes and gardens, of the pleasant public surroundings, the health services and the education and leisure needed to tranquillize the fiercer discontents, it is still possible that readjustment rather than revolution will be the method of the Atlantic communities. But that adjustment cannot be indefinitely delayed ; it must come soon.

In one way or another it seems inevitable now that the new standard of well-being which the mechanical revolution of the last century has rendered possible, should become the general standard of life. Revolution is conditional upon public discomfort. Social peace is impossible without a rapid amelioration of the needless discomforts of the present time. A rapid resort to willing service and social reconstruction on the part of those who own and rule, or else a world-wide social revolution leading towards an equalization of conditions and an attempt to secure comfort on new and untried lines, seem now to be the only alternatives before mankind. The choice which route shall be taken lies, we believe, in Western Europe, and still more so in America, with the educated, possessing, and influential classes. The former route demands much sacrifice, for prosperous people in particular, a voluntary assumption of public duties and a voluntary acceptance of class discipline and self-denial ; the latter may take an indefinite time to traverse, it will certainly be a very destructive and bloody process, and whether it will lead to a new and better state of affairs at last is questionable. A social revolution, if ultimately the Western European States blunder into it, may prove to be a process extending over centuries : it may involve a social breakdown as complete as that of the Roman Empire, and it may necessitate as slow a recuperation.

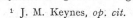

Photo : Imperial War Museum.

TWENTIETH-CENTURY WARRIORS : TWO TYPICAL BRITISH "TOMMIES" IN FIGHTING KIT.

Let us add to what has been written above a short passage from an abler and far more authoritative pen.[1] It approaches this question of economic disorganization from a different angle, but the drift of its implications is the same. It says as plainly to the private capitalist system : " Mend, show more understanding, and a better and a stronger will for the common welfare, or go.

" In the latter stages of the war all the belligerent governments practised, from necessity or incompetence, what a Bolshevist might have done from design.[2] Even now, when the war is over, most of them continue out of weakness the same malpractices. But further, the Governments of Europe, being many of them at this moment reckless in their methods as well as weak, seek to direct on to a class known as ' profiteers ' the popular indignation against the more obvious consequences of their vicious methods. These ' profiteers ' are, broadly speaking, the *entrepreneur* class of capitalists, that is to say, the active and constructive element in the whole capitalist society, who in a period of rapidly rising prices cannot but get rich quick whether they wish it or desire it or not.[3] If prices are continually rising, every trader who has purchased for stock or owns property and plant inevitably makes profits. By directing hatred against this class, there-

[1] J. M. Keynes, *op. cit.*
[2] They debauched the currency, and wasted money recklessly.
[3] Mr. Keynes ignores the fortunes made by deliberately cornering and withholding commodities in a time of shortage.

fore, the European Governments are carrying a step further the fatal process which the subtle mind of Lenin had consciously conceived. The profiteers are a consequence and not a cause of rising prices. By combining a popular hatred of the class of *entrepreneurs* with the blow already given to social security by the violent and arbitrary disturbance of contract and of the established equilibrium of wealth which is the inevitable result of inflation, these governments are fast rendering impossible a continuance of the social and economic order of the nineteenth century. But they have no plan for replacing it.

" We are thus faced in Europe with the spectacle of an extraordinary weakness on the part of the great capitalist class, which has emerged from the industrial triumphs of the nineteenth century, and seemed a very few years ago our all-powerful master. The terror and personal timidity of the individuals of this class is now so great, their confidence in their place in society and in their necessity to the social organism so diminished, that they are the easy victims of intimidation. This was not so in England twenty-five years ago, any more than it is now in the United States. Then the capitalists believed in themselves, in their value to society, in the propriety of their continued existence in the full enjoyment of their riches and the unlimited exercise of their power. Now they tremble before every insult. Call them pro-Germans, international financiers, or profiteers, and they will give you any ransom you choose to ask not to speak of them so harshly. They allow themselves to be ruined and altogether undone by their own instruments, governments of their own making, and a press of which they are the proprietors. Perhaps it is historically true that no order of society ever perished save by its own hand."

§ 11 [1]

We have dealt with the social and economic disorder of the European communities, and the

rapid return of the " class-war " to the foreground of attention, before giving any account

President Wilson and the Problems of Versailles. of the work of world settlement that centred on the Peace Conference at Paris, because the worried and pre-occupied state of everyone concerned with private problems of income, prices, employment, and the like goes far to explain the jaded atmosphere in which that Conference addressed itself to the vast task before it.

The story of the Conference turns very largely upon the adventure of one particular man, one of those men whom accident or personal quality picks out as a type to lighten the task of the historian. We have in the course of this history found it very helpful at times to focus our attention upon some individual, Buddha, Alexander the Great, Yuan Chwang, the Emperors Frederick II and Charles V and Napoleon I, for example, and to let him by reflection illuminate the period in which he lived. The conclusion of the Great War can be seen most easily as the rise of the American President, President Wilson, to predominant importance in the world's hopes and attention, and his failure to justify that predominance.

President Wilson (born 1856) had previously been a prominent student and teacher of history, constitutional law, and the political sciences generally. He had held various professorial chairs, and had been President of Princeton University (New Jersey). There is a long list of books to his credit, and they show a mind rather exclusively directed to American history and American politics. There is no evidence that he had at any time in his life made a general study of the world problem outside the very peculiar and exceptional American case. He was mentally the new thing in history, negligent of and rather ignorant of the older things out of which his new world had arisen. He retired from academic life, and was elected Democratic Governor of New Jersey in 1910. In 1913 he became the Democratic presidential

[1] Among the books consulted here, for this and the two following sections, were Dr. Dillon's *Peace Conference* ; H. Wilson Harris's *The Peace in the Making* and *President Wilson, his Problems and his Policy* ; J. M. Keynes's *Economic Consequences of the Peace* ; Weyl's *The End of the War* ; Stallybrass's *Society of* States ; Brailsford's *A League of Nations* ; F. C. Howe's *Why War ?* L. S. Woolf's *International Government* ; J. A. Hobson's *Towards International Government* ; Lowes Dickinson's *The Choice before Us* ; Sir Walter Phillimore's *Three Centuries of Treaties*, and C. E. Fayle's *Great Settlement*.

candidate, and as a consequence of a violent quarrel between ex-President Roosevelt and President Taft, which split the dominant Republican party, he became President of the United States.

The events of August, 1914, seem to have taken President Wilson, like the rest of his fellow-countrymen, by surprise. We find him cabling an offer of his services as a mediator on August 3rd. Then, for a time, he and America watched the conflict. At first neither the American people nor their President seem to have had a very clear or profound understanding of that long-gathered catastrophe. Their tradition for a century had been to disregard the problems of the Old World, and it was not to be lightly changed. The imperialistic arrogance of the German Court and the stupid inclination of the German military authorities towards melodramatic "frightfulness," their invasion of Belgium, their cruelties there, their use of poison gas, and the nuisance of their submarine campaign, created a deepening hostility to Germany in the States as the war proceeded; but the tradition of political abstinence and the deep-rooted persuasion that America possessed a political morality altogether superior to European conflicts, restrained the President from active intervention. He adopted a lofty tone. He professed to be unable to judge the causes and justice of the great war. It was largely his high pacific attitude that secured his re-election as President for a second term. But the world is not to be mended by merely regarding evil-doers with an expression of rather undiscriminating disapproval. By the end of 1916 the Germans had been encouraged to believe that under no circumstances whatever would the United States fight, and in 1917 they began their unrestricted submarine warfare and the sinking of American ships without notice. President Wilson and the American people were dragged into the war by this supreme folly. And also they were dragged into a reluctant attempt to define their relations to Old-World politics in some other terms than those of mere aloofness. Their thoughts and temper changed very rapidly. They came into the war side by side with the Allies, but not in any pact with the Allies. They came into the war, in the name of their own modern civilization, to punish and end

an intolerable political and military situation.

Slow and belated judgments are sometimes the best judgments. In a series of "Notes," too long and various for detailed treatment in this Outline, thinking aloud, as it were, in the hearing of all mankind, President Wilson sought to state the essential differences of the American State from the Great Powers of the Old World. We have been at some pains in this history to make plain the development of these differences. He unfolded a conception of international relationships that came like a gospel, like the hope of a better world, to the whole Eastern hemisphere. Secret agreements were to cease, "nations" were to determine their own destinies, militarist aggression was to cease, the sea-ways were to be free to all mankind. These commonplaces of American thought, these secret desires of every sane man, came like a great light upon the darkness of anger and conflict in Europe. At last, men felt, the ranks of diplomacy were broken, the veils of Great Power "policy" were rent in twain. Here with authority, with the strength of a powerful new nation behind it, was the desire of the common man throughout the world, plainly said.

Manifestly there was needed some overriding instrument of government to establish world law and maintain these broad and liberal generalizations upon human intercourse. A number of schemes had floated in men's minds for the attainment of that end. In particular there was a movement for some sort of world league, a "League of Nations." The American President adopted this phrase and sought to realize it. An essential condition of the peace he sought through the overthrow of German imperialism was, he declared, to be this federal organ. This League of Nations was to be the final court of appeal in international affairs. It was to be the substantial realization of the peace. Here again he awakened a tremendous echo.

President Wilson was the spokesman of a new age. Throughout the war, and for some little time after it had ended, he held, so far as the Old World was concerned, that exalted position. But in America, where they knew him better, there were doubts. And writing as we do now with the wisdom of subsequent events, we can understand these doubts. America, throughout a century and more of detachment and security, had developed new ideals and formulæ of political thought, without realizing with any intensity that, under conditions of stress and danger, these ideals and formulæ might have to be passionately sustained. To her community many things were platitudes that had to the Old-World communities, entangled still in ancient political complications, the quality of a saving gospel. President Wilson was responding to the thought and conditions of his own people and his own country, based on a liberal tradition that had first found its full expression in English speech ; but to Europe and Asia he seemed to be thinking and saying, for the first time in history, things hitherto undeveloped and altogether secret. And that misconception he may have shared.

We are dealing here with an able and successful professor of political science, who did not fully realize what he owed to his contemporaries and the literary and political atmosphere he had breathed throughout his life ; and who passed very rapidly after his re-election as President, from the mental attitudes of a political leader to those of a Messiah. His " Notes " are a series of explorations of the elements of the world situation. When at last, in his Address to Congress of January 8th, 1918, he produced his Fourteen Points as a definite statement of the American peace intentions, they were, as a statement, far better in their spirit than in their arrangement and matter.

Yet, since the Fourteen Points certainly mark a new epoch in human affairs, and since it was in the belief that they would determine and limit the pains and penalties of the peace treaty that Germany capitulated,[1] it may be well to summarize them here, with a word or so of explanation.

[1] " The Allied Governments," the effective passage ran, " have given careful consideration to the correspondence which has passed between the President of the United States and the German Government. Subject to the qualifications which follow, they declare their readiness to make peace with the Government of Germany on the terms of peace laid down in the President's Address to Congress of January 8th, 1918, and the principles of settlement enunciated in his subsequent Addresses."

(Note transmitted to the German Government by the Allies through the Swiss Minister on November 5th, 1918.)

(I) The First Point was the most vital of all. It summarizes and dismisses the essential evils of the Great Power system. It demands : " Open covenants of peace openly arrived at, after which there shall be no private international understandings of any kind, but diplomacy shall proceed always frankly and in the public view."

(II) " Absolute freedom of navigation upon the seas outside territorial waters alike in peace and in war, except as the seas may be closed in whole or in part by international action for the enforcement of international covenants."

(III) " The removal, so far as possible, of all economic barriers and the establishment of an equality of trade conditions among all the nations consenting to the peace and associating themselves for its maintenance."

(IV) " Adequate guarantees given and taken that national armaments will be reduced to the lowest point consistent with domestic safety."

There are four points of universal importance, admirably stated. But II is insufficient. Why should the sea-ways alone be free ? What of the air-ways above three thousand feet ? What of the great international land routes ? Why, if Switzerland is at war with Germany and Italy, should those Powers be able to stop air and land transit and the passage of peaceful people between France and Constantinople ?

After IV, the Fourteen Points embark upon the consideration of particular cases, for which one general statement should have provided.

(V) provides for " A free, open-minded and absolutely impartial adjustment of all colonial claims based upon a strict observance of the principle that in determining all such questions of sovereignty, the interests of the populations concerned must have equal weight with the equitable claims of the government whose title is to be determined." . . . This is hopelessly vague. What, for instance, is this about claims and title ? There is no definition, no standard here.

The drop towards particular current issues continues in the next eight points, which betray clearly how limited and accidental was the President's vision of European affairs.

(VI) is a vague demand for the evacuation of Russian territory (then occupied by Germany), and the "assistance" (undefined) of the Russian people.

(VII) Evacuation and restoration of Belgium.

(VIII) Evacuation and restoration of all French territory, and the "righting" of the wrong done to France by Prussia in the matter of Alsace-Lorraine.

(IX) The readjustment of the Italian frontier "on the lines of nationality."

(X) "Autonomy" of the Austrian "subject nations."

(XI) The Balkans to be evacuated, Serbia to be granted an outlet to the sea, and the independence of the Balkan States to be guaranteed.

(XII) Turkish subject nations to be assured of "undoubted security of life and unmolested opportunity of autonomous development." The Dardanelles to be internationalized, and Ottoman sovereignty to be recognized only in Turkish districts.

(XIII) Poland to be independent.

Finally the Fourteenth Point arises again to the Great Charter level out of this peddling with special cases.

(XIV) "A general association of nations must be formed under specific covenants for the purpose of affording mutual guarantees of political and territorial independence for great and small States alike."

So far the Fourteen Points. But some of the things that President Wilson said after this epoch-making address went much further and much higher than this first statement. On September 27th, 1918, at New York, he said some very important things:

"As I see it, the constitution of that League of Nations and the clear definition of its objects must be a part, in a sense the most essential part, of the peace settlement itself. It cannot be formed now. If formed now, it would be merely a new alliance confined to the nations associated against a common enemy. . . .

"But these general terms do not disclose the whole matter. Some details are needed to make them sound less like a thesis and more like a practical programme. These, then, are some of the particulars, and I state them with the greater confidence because I can state them authoritatively as representing this Government's interpretation of its own duty with regard to peace.

"First, the impartial justice meted out must involve no discrimination between those to whom we wish to be just and those to whom we do not wish to be just. It must be a justice that has no favourites and knows no standards but the equal rights of the several peoples concerned.

"Second, no special or separate interest of any single nation or any group of nations can be made the basis of any part of the settlement which is not consistent with the common interest of all.

"Third, there can be no leagues or alliances or special covenants and understandings within the general and common family of the League of Nations.

"Fourth, and more specifically, there can be no special selfish economic combinations within the League, and no employment of any form of economic boycott or exclusion, except as the power of economic penalty, by exclusion from the markets of the world, may be vested in the League of Nations itself as a means of discipline and control.

"Fifth, all international agreements and treaties of every kind must be made known in their entirety to the rest of the world. . . .

"In the same sentence in which I say that the United States will enter into no special arrangements or understandings with particular nations, let me say also that the United States is prepared to assume its full share of responsibility for the maintenance of the common covenants and understandings upon which peace must henceforth rest.

"We still read Washington's immortal warning against "entangling alliances" with full comprehension and an answering purpose. But only special and limited alliances entangle; and we recognize and accept the duty of a new day in which we are permitted to hope for a general alliance, which will avoid entanglements and clear the air of the world for common understandings and the maintenance of common rights."

These Fourteen Points and their significant later addenda had an immense reception throughout the world. Here at last seemed a peace for reasonable men everywhere, as good and acceptable to honest and decent Germans and Russians, as to honest and decent French-the dictatorship of the group of Premiers, Mr. Wilson being excepted. . . ."[1]

The restriction upon our space in this *Outline* will not allow us to tell here how the Peace Conference shrank from a Council of Ten to a Council of Four (Wilson, Clemenceau, Lloyd George, and Orlando), and how it became a conference less and less like a frank and open discussion of the future of mankind, and more and more like some old-fashioned diplomatic conspiracy. Great and wonderful had been the hopes that had gathered to Paris. " The Paris of the Conference," says Dr. Dillon, " ceased to be the capital of France. It became a vast cosmopolitan caravanserai teeming with unwonted aspects of life and turmoil, filled with curious samples of the races, tribes, and tongues of four continents who came to watch and wait for the mysterious to-morrow.

" An Arabian Nights' touch was imparted to the dissolving panorama by strange visitants from Tartary and Kurdistan, Corea and Aderbeijan, Armenia, Persia, and the Hedjaz —men with patriarchal beards and scimitar-shaped noses, and others from desert and oasis, from Samarkand and Bokhara. Turbans and fezes, sugar-loaf hats and head-gear resembling episcopal mitres, old military uniforms devised for the embryonic armies of new states on the eve of perpetual peace, snowy-white burnouses, flowing mantles, and graceful garments like the Roman toga, contributed to create an atmosphere of dreamy unreality in the city where the grimmest of realities were being faced and coped with.

" Then came the men of wealth, of intellect, of industrial enterprise, and the seed-bearers of the ethical new ordering, members of economic committees from the United States, Britain, Italy, Poland, Russia, India, and Japan, representatives of naphtha industries and far-off coal mines, pilgrims, fanatics and charlatans from all climes, priests of all religions, preachers of every doctrine, who mingled with princes, field-marshals, statesmen, anarchists, builders-up and pullers-down. All of them burned with desire to be near to the crucible in which the political and social systems of the world

were to be melted and recast. Every day, in my walks, in my apartment, or at restaurants, I met emissaries from lands and peoples whose very names had seldom been heard of before in the West. A delegation from the Pont-Euxine Greeks called on me, and discoursed of their ancient cities of Trebizond, Samsoun, Tripoli, Kerassund, in which I resided many years ago, and informed me that they, too, desired to become welded into an independent Greek Republic, and had come to have their claims allowed. The Albanians were represented by my old friend Turkhan Pasha, on the one hand, and by my friend Essad Pasha on the other—the former desirous of Italy's protection, the latter demanding complete independence. Chinamen, Japanese, Coreans, Hindus, Kirghizes, Lesghiens, Circassians, Mingrelians, Buryats, Malays, and Negroes and Negroids from Africa and America were among the tribes and tongues foregathered in Paris to watch the rebuilding of the political world system and to see where they ' came in.' . . ."

To this thronging, amazing Paris, agape for a new world, came President Wilson, and found its gathering forces dominated by a personality narrower, in every way more limited and beyond comparison more forcible than himself: the French Premier, M. Clemenceau. At the instance of President Wilson, M. Clemenceau was elected President of the Conference. " It was," said President Wilson, " a special tribute to the sufferings and sacrifices of France." And that, unhappily, sounded the keynote of the Conference, whose sole business should have been with the future of mankind.

Georges Benjamin Clemenceau[2] was an old journalist politician, a great denouncer of abuses, a great upsetter of governments, a doctor who had, while a municipal councillor, kept a free clinic, and a fierce, experienced duellist. None of his duels ended fatally, but he faced them with great intrepidity. He had passed from the medical school to republican journalism in the days of the Empire. In those days he was an extremist of the left. He was for a time a teacher in America, and he married and divorced an American wife. He was thirty in the eventful

---

[1] Dillon. And see his *The Peace Conference*, Chapter III, for instances of the amazing ignorance of various delegates.

[2] See *Clemenceau*, by C. Ducray.

year 1871. He returned to France after Sedan, and flung himself into the stormy politics of the defeated nation with great fire and vigour. Thereafter France was his world, the France of vigorous journalism, high-spirited personal quarrels, challenges, confrontations, scenes, dramatic effects, and witticisms at any cost. He was what people call "fierce stuff," he was nicknamed the "Tiger," and he seems to have been rather proud of the nickname. Professional patriot rather than statesman and thinker, this was the man whom the war had flung up to misrepresent the fine mind and the generous spirit of France.[1] His limitations had a profound effect upon the conference, which was

Photo: Henri Manuel.

M. CLEMENCEAU

further coloured by the dramatic resort for the purposes of signature to the very Hall of Mirrors at Versailles in which Germany had triumphed and proclaimed her unity. There the Germans were to sign. To M. Clemenceau and to France, in that atmosphere, the war ceased to seem a world war; it was merely the sequel of the previous conflict of the Terrible Year, the downfall and punishment of offending Germany. "The world had to be made safe for democracy," said President Wilson. That from M. Clemenceau's expressed point of view was "talking like Jesus Christ." The world had to be made safe for Paris. "Talking like Jesus Christ" seemed a very ridiculous thing to many of those brilliant rather than sound diplomatists and politicians who made the year 1919 supreme in the history of human insufficiency.

[1] He wrote several novels. They are not very good novels; they incline to sentimental melodrama. In some respects they resemble the work of the well-known English writer Miss Marie Corelli. *Le Plus Fort* is now available to English readers in a translation under the title of "The Stronger." A cinematograph version has been shown.

(Another flash of the "Tiger's" wit, it may be noted, was that President Wilson with his fourteen points was "worse" than God Almighty. "Le bon Dieu" only had ten. . . .)

M. Clemenceau sat with Signor Orlando in the more central chairs of a semicircle of four in front of the fire, says Keynes. He wore a black frock-coat and grey suede gloves, which he never removed during these sessions. He was, it is to be noted, the only one of these four reconstructors of the world who could understand and speak both French and English.

The aims of M. Clemenceau were simple and in a manner attainable. He wanted all the settlement of 1871 undone. He wanted Germany punished as though she was a uniquely sinful nation and France a sinless martyr land. He wanted Germany so crippled and devastated as never more to be able to stand up to France. He wanted to hurt and humiliate Germany more than France had been hurt and humiliated in 1871. He did not care if in breaking Germany Europe was broken; his mind did not go far enough beyond the Rhine to understand that possibility. He accepted President Wilson's League of Nations as an excellent proposal if it would guarantee the security of France whatever she did, but he preferred a binding alliance of the United States and England to maintain, uphold, and glorify France under practically any circumstances. He wanted wider opportunities for the exploitation of Syria, North Africa, and so forth by Parisian financial groups. He wanted indemnities to recuperate France, loans, gifts, and tributes to France, glory and homage to France. France had suffered, and France had to be rewarded. Belgium, Russia, Serbia, Poland, Armenia, Britain, Germany, and Austria had all suffered too, all mankind had suffered, but what would you? that was not *his* affair. These were the supers of a drama in which France was for him the star. . . . In much the same spirit Signor Orlando seems to have sought the welfare of Italy.

Mr. Lloyd George brought to the Council of Four the subtlety of a Welshman, the intricacy of a European, and an urgent necessity for respecting the nationalist egotism of the British imperialists and capitalists who had returned him to power. Into the secrecy of that council went President Wilson (leaving Point I at the door) with the very noblest aims for his newly discovered American world policy, his rather hastily compiled Fourteen (now reduced to Thirteen) Points, and a project rather than a scheme for a League of Nations.

Photo: *Henri Manuel.*
MR. LLOYD GEORGE.

The Second Point was presently observed to be missing. It may have fallen into the Atlantic on the way over. It may have been thrown into the sea as an offering to the British Admiralty.

"There can seldom have been a statesman of the first rank more incompetent than the President in the agilities of the Council Chamber."[1] From the whispering darknesses and fireside disputes of that council, and after various comings and goings we cannot here describe, he emerged at last with his Fourteen Points pitifully torn and dishevelled, but with a little puling infant of a League of Nations, which might die or which might live and grow—no one could tell. This history cannot tell. We are at the end of our term. But that much, at least, he had saved. . . .

Let us now consider briefly this Covenant of the League of Nations, and recapitulate the terms of the quasi-settlement of the world's

[1] Keynes.

affairs of 1919–20; and let us indicate here and there where the latter departs from the promised standard of the Fourteen Points, and where it is most dangerous to the future peace and most manifestly contrary to the welfare of mankind. Because just as the history of Europe in the nineteenth century was largely the undoing of the Treaty of Vienna, and as the Great War was the necessary outcome of the Treaty of Frankfort and the Treaty of Berlin, so the general history of the twentieth century henceforth will be largely the amendment or reversal of the more ungenerous and unscientific arrangements of the Treaty of 1919, and a struggle to establish those necessary impartial world controls of which the League of Nations is the first insufficient and unsatisfactory sketch.

§ 12

This homunculus in a bottle which it was hoped might become at last Man ruling the Earth, this League of Nations as *Summary of the First Covenant of the League of Nations.* it was embodied in the Covenant of April 28th, 1919, was not a league of peoples at all; it was a league of "states, dominions, or colonies." It was stipulated that these should be "fully self-governing," but there was no definition whatever of this phrase. There was no bar to a limited franchise and no provision for any direct control by the people of any state. India figured—presumably as a "fully self-governing state!" An autocracy would no doubt have been admissible as a "fully self-governing" democracy with a franchise limited to one person. The League of the Covenant of 1919 was, in fact, a league of "representatives" of foreign offices, and it did not even abolish the nonsense of embassies at every capital. The British Empire appeared once as a whole, and then India (!) and the four dominions of Canada, Australia, South Africa, and New Zealand appeared as separate sovereign states. The Indian representative was, of course, sure to be merely a British nominee; the other four would be colonial politicians. But if the British Empire was to be thus dissected, a representative of Great Britain should have been substituted for the Imperial representative, and Ireland and Egypt should also have been given representation. Moreover, either New York State or Virginia was historically and legally almost as much a sovereign state as New Zealand or Canada. The inclusion of India raised logical claims for French Africa and French Asia. One French representative did propose a separate vote for the little principality of Monaco.

There was to be an Assembly of the League in which every member state was to be represented and to have an equal voice, but the working directorate of the league was to vest in a Council, which was to consist of the representatives of the United States, Britain, France, Italy, and Japan, with four other members elected by the Assembly. The Council was to meet once a year; the gatherings of the Assembly were to be at "stated intervals," not stated.

Except in certain specified instances the league of this Covenant could make only unanimous decisions. One dissentient on the council could bar any proposal—on the lines of the old Polish *liberum veto* (Chapter XXXVI, § 7). This was a quite disastrous provision. To many minds it made the Covenant League rather less desirable than no league at all. It was a complete recognition of the unalienable sovereignty of states, and a repudiation of the idea of an overriding commonweal of mankind. This provision practically barred the way to all amendments to the league constitution in future except by the clumsy expedient of a simultaneous withdrawal of the majority of member states desiring a change, to form the league again on new lines. The covenant made inevitable such a final winding-up of the league it created, and that was perhaps the best thing about it.

The following Powers, it was proposed, should be excluded from the original league: Germany, Austria, Russia, and whatever remains there were of the Turkish Empire. But any of these might subsequently be included with the assent of two-thirds of the Assembly. The original membership of the league as specified in the projected Covenant was: the United States of America, Belgium, Bolivia, Brazil, the British Empire (Canada, Australia, South Africa, New Zealand, and India), China, Cuba, Ecuador, France, Greece, Guatemala, Haiti, the Hedjaz, Honduras, Italy, Japan, Liberia, Nicaragua, Panama, Peru, Poland, Portugal, Rumania, the Serb-Croat-Slovene State, Siam, Czecho-Slovakia, and Uruguay. To which were to be added by invitation the following Powers which had been neutral in the war: the Argentine Republic, Chile, Colombia, Denmark, Holland, Norway, Paraguay, Persia, Salvador, Spain, Sweden, Switzerland, and Venezuela.

Such being the constitution of the league, it is scarcely to be wondered at that its powers were special and limited. It was given a seat at Geneva and a secretariat. It had no powers even to inspect the military preparations of its constituent states, or to instruct a military and naval staff to plan out the armed co-operation needed to keep the peace of the world. The French representative in the League of Nations Commission, M. Leon Bourgeois, insisted lucidly and repeatedly on the logical necessity of such powers. As a speaker he was rather copious and lacking in "spice" of the Clemenceau quality. The final scene in the plenary session of April 28th, before the adoption of the Covenant, is described compactly by Mr. Wilson Harris, the crowded Banqueting Hall at the Quai d'Orsay, with its " E " of tables for the delegates, with secretaries and officials lining the walls and a solid mass of journalists at the lower end of the room. " At the head of the room the ' Big Three ' *diverted themselves in undertones* at the expense of the worthy M. Bourgeois, now launched, with the help of what must have been an entirely superfluous sheaf of notes, on the fifth rendering of his speech in support of his famous amendments."

They were so often " diverting themselves in undertones," those three men whom God had mocked with the most tremendous opportunity in history. Keynes (*op. cit*) gives other instances of the levities, disregards, inattentions and inadequacies of these meetings.

This poor Covenant arrived at in this fashion returned with President Wilson to America, and there it was subjected to an amount of opposition, criticism, and revision which showed, among other things, how relatively unimpaired was the mental energy of the United States. It was manifest that the people of America had no mind to a compact that was virtually little more than a league of allied imperialisms for mutual insurance. The Senate refused to ratify the covenant, and the first meeting of the League Council was held therefore without American representatives. The close of 1919 and the opening months of 1920 saw a very curious change come over American feeling after the pro-French and pro-British enthusiasms of the war period. The peace negotiations reminded the Americans, in a confused and very irritating way, of their profound differences in international outlook from any European Power that the war had for a time helped them to forget. They felt they had been " rushed " into many things without due consideration. They experienced a violent revulsion towards that policy of isolation that had broken down in 1917. The close of 1919 saw a phase, a very understandable phase, of passionate and even violent " Americanism," in which European imperialism and European socialism were equally anathema. There may have been a sordid element in the American disposition to " cut " the moral responsibilities the United States had incurred in the affairs of the Old World, and to realize the enormous financial and political advantages the war had given the New World; but the broad instinct of the American people seems to have been sound in its distrust of the proposed settlement.

§ 13

The main terms of the Treaties of 1919-20 with which the Conference of Paris concluded

A General Outline of the Treaties of 1919 and 1920.

its labours can be stated much more vividly by a few maps than by a written abstract. We need scarcely point out how much those treaties left unsettled, but we may point perhaps to some of the more salient breaches

of the Twelve that survived out of the Fourteen Points at the opening of the Conference.

One initial cause of nearly all those breaches lay, we believe, in the complete unpreparedness and unwillingness of that pre-existing league of nations, subjected states and exploited areas, the British Empire, to submit to any dissection and adaptation of its system or to any control of its naval and aerial armament. A kindred contributory cause was the equal unpreparedness of the American mind for any interference with the ascendancy of the United States in the New World (compare Secretary Olney's declaration in this chapter, § 6). Neither of those Great Powers, who were necessarily dominant and leading Powers at Paris, had properly thought out the implications of a League of Nations in relation to these older arrangements, and so their support of that project had to most European observers a curiously hypocritical air ; it was as if they wished to retain and ensure their own vast predominance and security while at the same time restraining any other Power from such expansions, annexations, and alliances as might create a rival and competitive imperialism. Their failure to set an example of international confidence destroyed all possibility of international confidence in the other nations represented at Paris.

Even more unfortunate was the refusal of the Americans to assent to the Japanese demand for a recognition of racial equality.

Moreover, the foreign offices of the British, the French, and the Italians were haunted by traditional schemes of aggression entirely incompatible with the new ideas. A League of Nations that is to be of any appreciable value to mankind must supersede imperialisms ; it is either a super-imperialism, a liberal world-empire of united states, participant or in tutelage, or it is nothing ; but few of the people at the Paris Conference had the mental vigour even to assert this obvious consequence of the League proposal. They wanted to be at the same time bound and free, to ensure peace for ever, but to keep their weapons in their hands. Accordingly the old annexation projects of the Great Power period were hastily and thinly camouflaged as proposed acts of this poor little birth of April 28th. The newly born and barely animate League was represented to be

GERMANY after the PEACE TREATY of 1919

(Rivers Rhine, Danube, Elbe, Oder and Vistula internationalised.)

1914 frontiers of Germany	
Territory lost by Germany...	
"Free territory" of Danzig....	
Plebiscite areas..........	

distributing, with all the reckless munificence of a captive pope, "mandates" to the old imperialisms that, had it been the young Hercules we desired, it would certainly have strangled in its cradle. Britain was to have extensive "mandates" in Mesopotamia and East Africa; France was to have the same in Syria; Italy was to have all her holdings to the west and south-east of Egypt consolidated as mandatory territory. Clearly, if the weak thing that was being nursed by its Secretary in its cradle at Geneva into some semblance of life, did presently succumb to the infantile weakness of all institutions born without passion, all these "mandates" would become frank annexations. Moreover, all the Powers fought tooth and nail at the Conference for "strategic" frontiers—the ugliest symptom of all. Why should a state want a strategic frontier unless it contemplates war? If on that plea Italy insisted upon a subject population of Germans in the Southern Tyrol and a subject population of Jugo-Slavs in Dalmatia, and if little Greece began landing troops in Asia Minor, neither France nor Britain was in a position to rebuke these outbreaks of pre-millennial method.

We will not enter here into any detailed account of how President Wilson gave way to the Japanese and consented to their replacing the Germans at Kiau Chau, which is Chinese property; how the almost purely German city of Danzig was practically, if not legally, annexed to Poland; and how the Powers disputed over the claim of the Italian imperialists, a claim strengthened by these instances, to seize the Jugo-Slav port of Fiume and deprive the Jugo-Slavs of a good Adriatic outlet. Nor will we do more than note the complex arrangements and justifications that put the French in possession of the Saar valley, which is German territory, or the entirely iniquitous breach of the right of "self-determination" which practically forbade German Austria to unite—as it is natural and proper that she should unite—with the rest of Germany. These burning questions of 1919-20 which occupied the newspapers and the minds of statesmen and politicians, and filled all our wastepaper baskets with propaganda literature, may seem presently very incidental things in the larger movement of these times. All these disputes, like the suspicions and tetchy injustices of a weary and irritated man, may lose their importance as the tone of the world improves, and the still inadequately apprehended lessons of the Great War and the Petty Peace that followed it, begin to be digested by the general intelligence of mankind.

It is worth while for the reader to compare the treaty maps we give with what we have called the natural political map of Europe. The new arrangements do approach this latter more closely than any previous system of boundaries. It may be a necessary preliminary to any satisfactory league of peoples, that each people should first be in something like complete possession of its own household.

It is absurd to despair of mankind because of these treaties, or to regard them as anything more than feeble first sketches of a world settlement. To do so would be to suppose that there is nothing in France—that land of fine imaginations—better than M. Clemenceau, nothing in America stronger and wiser than President Wilson, and nothing in Britain to steady the Keltic traits of Mr. Lloyd George. The attention we have given to these three personalities in this *Outline* is intended less to enhance their importance than to emphasize their unimportance, and to make it clear to the reader how provisional and incidental all that they did must be in the world's affairs. On no statesmen, on no particular men or groups of men, on no state or organization indeed, and on no Covenant or Treaty, does the future of our race now depend. The year 1919 was not a year of creation and decision, it was just the first cheerless dawn of a long day of creative effort. The conferences of the Ten, of the Four, of the Big Three, had no trace of creative power ; there was no light in the men of Versailles ; the dawn was manifest rather as a grey light of critical disapproval that broke through the shutters and staled the guttering candles of the old diplomacy as the conference yawned and drawled to its end. Creation was not there. But a great process of thought spreads throughout the world ; many thousands of men and women, in every country, for the most part undistinguished and unknown people, are awakening to their responsibility, are studying, thinking, writing, and teaching, getting together, correcting false impressions, challenging foolish ideas, trying to find out and tell the truth ; and upon them it is that we must rest our hope, such hope as we can

Map to illustrate the TURKISH TREATY, 1920

Territory remaining Turkish...
Turkish territory acquired by Greece...
Bulgarian territory to Greece (by Bulgar'ⁿ Treaty)

entertain, of a saner plan to take the place of this first flimsy League and this patched and discomforting garment of treaties that has been flung for awhile over the naked distresses of our world.

§ 14

The failure to produce a more satisfactory world settlement in 1919-20 was, we have **A Forecast of the "Next War."** suggested, a symptom of an almost universal intellectual and moral lassitude resulting from the over-strain of the Great War. A lack of fresh initiative is characteristic of a fatigue phase ; everyone, for sheer inability to change, drifts on for a time along the lines of mental habit and precedent.

Nothing could be more illustrative of this fatigue inertia than the expressed ideas of military men at this time. It will round off this chapter in an entirely significant way, and complete our picture of the immense world interrogation on which our history must end, if we give here the briefest summary of a lecture that was delivered to a gathering of field-marshals, generals, major-generals, and the like by Major-General Sir Louis Jackson at the Royal United Service Institution in London

one day in December 1919. Lord Peel, the British Under-Secretary for War, presided ; and the reader must picture to himself the not too large and quite dignified room of assembly in that building and all these fine grave soldierly figures quietly intent upon the lecturer's words. He is describing, with a certain subdued enthusiasm, the probable technical developments of military method in the "next war."

Outside, through the evening twilight of Whitehall, flows the London traffic, not quite so abundant as in 1914, but still fairly abundant ; the omnibuses all overcrowded because there are now not nearly enough of them, and the clothing of people generally shabbier. Some little way down Whitehall is a temporary erection, the Cenotaph, with its base smothered with a vast, pathetic heap of decaying wreaths, bunches of flowers, and the like, a cenotaph to commemorate the eight hundred thousand young men of the Empire who have been killed in the recent struggle. A few people are putting fresh flowers and such-like little offerings there. One or two are crying.

The prospect stretches out beyond this gathering into the grey vastness of London, where people are now crowded as they have never been crowded before, whose food is dear and employment more uncertain than it has ever been. But let not the spectacle be one of unrelieved gloom ; Regent Street, Oxford Street, and Bond Street are bright with shoppers and congested with new automobiles, because we must remember that everybody does not lose by a war. Beyond London the country sinks into night, and across the narrow sea are North France and Belgium devastated, Germany with scores of thousands of her infants dwindling and dying for want of milk, all Austria starving. Half the population of Vienna, it is believed, unless American relief comes quickly, is doomed to die of hardship before the spring. Beyond that bleak twilight stretches the darkness of Russia. There, at least, no rich people are buying anything, and no military men are reading essays on the next war. But in icy Petrograd is little food, little wood, and no coal. All the towns of Russia southward as far as the snow reaches are in a similar plight, and in the Ukraine and to the south a ragged and dingy war drags to its end. Europe is bankrupt, and people's pockets rustle with paper money, whose purchasing power dwindles as they walk about with it.

But now we will return to Sir Louis in the well-lit room at the United Service Institution.

He was of opinion—we follow the report in next morning's *Times* [1]—that we were merely on the eve of the most extensive modifica- tions of the art of war known to history. It behoved us, therefore—us being, of course, the British and not the whole of mankind—to get on with our armaments and to keep ahead ; a fine opening generalization. " It was neces- sary to develop new arms. . . . The nation which best did so would have a great advantage in the next war. There were people who were crying aloud for a reduction of armaments——"

(But there the Director of Trench Warfare and Supplies was wrong. They were just crying at the Cenotaph, poor, soft, and stupid souls, because a son or a brother or a father was dead !)

Sir Louis believed that one of the greatest developments in the art of warfare would be brought about in mechanical transport. The

tank he treated with ingratitude. These military gentlemen are ungrateful to an in- vention which shoved and butted them into victory almost in spite of themselves. The tank, said Sir Louis, was " a freak. . . . The outstanding feature " of the tank, he said, was that it made mechanical transport independent of the roads. Hitherto armies on the march had only been able to spoil the roads ; now their transport on caterpillar wheels would advance in open order on a broad front carrying guns, munitions, supplies, bridging equipment, rafts, and men—and incidentally ploughing up and destroying hedges, ditches, fields, and cultivation generally. Armies would wallow across the country, leaving nothing behind but dust and mud.

So our imaginations are led up to the actual hostilities.

Sir Louis was in favour of gas. For punitive expeditions particularly, gas was to be recom- mended. And here he startled and disconcerted his hearers by a gleam of something approach- ing sentimentality. " It *might* be possible," he said, " to come to some agreement that no gas should be used which caused unnecessary suffering." But there his heart spoke rather than his head ; it should have been clear to him that if law can so far override warfare as to prohibit any sort of evil device whatever, it can overrride warfare to the extent of pro- hibiting it altogether. And where would Sir Louis Jackson and his audience be then ? War is war ; its only law is the law that the maximum destruction of the forces of the enemy is necessary. To that law in warfare all con- siderations of humanity and justice are sub- ordinate.

From gas Sir Louis passed to the air. Here he predicted " most important advances. . . . We need not trouble ourselves yet with flying destroyers or flying concrete forts, but in twenty years' time the Air Force Estimates might be the most important part of our preparations for war." He discussed the conversion of com- mercial flying machines to bombing and re- connaissance uses, and the need for special types of fighting machine in considerable numbers and always ready. He gave reasons for supposing that the bombers in the next war would not have the same targets near

---

[1] Checked by subsequent comparison with the pub- lished article in the *Jour. of the Roy. United Service Institution*, vol. lxv., No. 457, February 1920.

the front of the armies, and would secure better results by going further afield and bombing the centres "where stores are being manufactured and troops trained." As everyone who stayed in London or the east of England in 1917-18 knows, this means the promiscuous bombing of any and every centre of population. But, of course, the bombing of those 'prentice days would be child's play to the bombing of the "next war." There would be countless more aeroplanes, bigger and much nastier bombs. . . .

Sir Louis, proceeding with his sketch, mentioned the " destruction of the greater part of London " as a possible incident in the coming struggle. And so on to the culminating moral,

and camouflaged G.H.Q. would be reasonably safe, in which countless bombers would bomb the belligerent lands incessantly, and great armies with lines of caterpillar transport roll to and fro, churning the fields of the earth into blood-streaked mud. There is not energy enough and no will whatever left in the world for such things. Generals who cannot foresee tanks cannot be expected to foresee or understand world bankruptcy ; still less are they likely to understand the limits imposed upon military operations by the fluctuating temper of the common man. Apparently these military authorities of the United Service Institution did not even know that warfare aims at the

Photo : Imperial War Museum.

A LANDSCAPE IN THE SOMME AREA. MAKING A ROAD THROUGH CAPTURED GROUND. GUILLEMONT-MONTAUBAN ROAD.

that the highest pay, the utmost importance, the freest expenditure, must be allowed to military gentlemen. " The expense entailed is in the nature of an absolutely necessary insurance." With which his particular audience warmly agreed. And a certain Major-General Stone, a little forgetful of the source of his phrases,[1] said he hoped that this lecture " may be the beginning not of trusting in the League of Nations, but in *our own* right hand and *our* stretched-out arm ! "

But we will not go on with the details of this dream. For indeed no Utopia was ever so impossible as this forecast of a world in which scarcely anything but very carefully sandbagged

[1] Cp. Psalm cxxxvi.

production of states of mind in the enemy, and is sustained by states of mind. The chief neglected factor in the calculations of Sir Louis is the fact that no people whatever will stand such warfare as he contemplates, not even the people on the winning side. For as Northern France, South-eastern Britain, and North Italy now understand, the victor in the " next war " may be bombed and starved almost as badly as the loser. A phase is possible in which a war-tormented population may cease to discriminate between military gentlemen on this side or that, and may be moved to destroy them as the common enemies of the race. The Great War of 1914-18 was the culmination of the military energy of the begins. This chapter of history which tells of the Great Powers into which Christendom broke up and of the unbridled national and individual self-seeking which ensued, has culminated in a world catastrophe and is at its end. What will be the next stage in history?

BOOK IX
THE NEXT STAGE IN HISTORY

XLI

THE POSSIBLE UNIFICATION OF THE WORLD INTO ONE COMMUNITY OF KNOWLEDGE AND WILL

§ 1

WE have brought this Outline of History up to our own times, but we have brought it to no conclusion. It breaks off at a dramatic phase of expectation. The story of life **The Possible** which began inestimable millions of **Unification** **of Men's** years ago, the adventure of mankind **Wills in** which was already afoot half a **Political** million years ago, rises to a crisis **Matters.** in the immense interrogation of to-day. The drama becomes ourselves. It is you, it is I, it is all that is happening to us and all that we are doing which will supply the next chapter of this continually expanding adventure.

Our history has traced a steady growth of the social and political units into which men have combined. In the brief period of ten thousand years these units have grown from the small family tribe of the early neolithic culture to the vast united realms—vast, yet still too small and partial—of the present time. And this change in size of the state—a change manifestly incomplete—has been accompanied by profound changes in its nature. Compulsion and servitude have given way to ideas of associated freedom, and the sovereignty that was once concentrated in an autocratic king and god, has been widely diffused throughout the community. Until the Roman republic extended itself to all Italy, there had been no free community larger than a city state; all

great communities were communities of obedience under a monarch. The great united republic of the United States would have been impossible before the printing press and the railway. The telegraph and telephone, the aeroplane, the continual progress of land and sea transit, are now insisting upon a still larger political organization.

If our Outline has been faithfully drawn, and if these brief conclusions are sound, it follows that we are engaged upon an immense task of adjustment to these great lines upon which our affairs are moving. Our wars, our social conflict, our enormous economic stresses, are all aspects of that adjustment. The loyalties and allegiances to-day are at best provisional loyalties and allegiances. Our true State, this state that is already beginning, this state to which every man owes his utmost political effort, must be now this nascent Federal World State to which human necessities point. Our true God now is the God of all men. Nationalism as a God must follow the tribal gods to limbo. Our true nationality is mankind.

How far will modern men lay hold upon and identify themselves with this necessity and set themselves to revise their ideas, remake their institutions, and educate the coming generations to this final extension of citizenship? How far will they remain dark, obdurate, habitual, and traditional, resisting the convergent forces that offer them either unity or misery? Sooner or later that unity must come or else plainly men must perish by their own inventions. We, because we believe in the power of reason and in the increasing good-will in men, find ourselves compelled to reject the latter possibility. But the way to the former may be very long and tedious, very tragic and wearisome, a martyrdom of many generations, or it may be travelled over almost swiftly in the course of a generation or so. That depends upon forces whose nature we understand to some extent now, but not their power. There has to be a great process of education, by precept and by information and by experience, but there are as yet no quantitative measures of education to tell us *how much* has to be learnt or *how soon* that learning can be done. Our estimates vary with our moods ; the time may be much longer than our hopes and much shorter than our fears.

The terrible experiences of the Great War have made very many men who once took political things lightly take them now very gravely. To a certain small number of men and women the attainment of a world peace has become the supreme work in life, has become a religious self-devotion. To a much greater number it has become at least a ruling motive. Many such people now are seeking ways of working for this great end, or they are already working for this great end, by pen and persuasion, in schools and colleges and books, and in the highways and byways of public life. Perhaps now most human beings in the world are well-disposed towards such efforts, but rather confusedly disposed ; they are without any clear sense of what must be done and what ought to be prevented, that human solidarity may be advanced. The world-wide outbreak of faith and hope in President Wilson, before he began to wilt and fail us, was a very significant thing indeed for the future of mankind. Set against these motives of unity indeed are other motives entirely antagonistic, the fear and hatred of strange things and peoples, love of and trust in the old traditional thing, patriotisms, race prejudices, suspicions, distrusts—and the elements of spite, scoundrelism, and utter selfishness that are so strong still in every human soul.

The overriding powers that hitherto in the individual soul and in the community have struggled and prevailed against the ferocious, base, and individual impulses that divide us from one another, have been the powers of religion and education. Religion and education, those closely interwoven influences, have made possible the greater human societies whose growth we have traced in this *Outline :* they have been the chief synthetic forces throughout this great story of enlarging human co-operations that we have traced from its beginnings. We have found in the intellectual and theological conflicts of the nineteenth century the explanation of that curious exceptional disentanglement of religious teaching from formal education which is a distinctive feature of our age, and we have traced the consequences of this phase of religious disputation and confusion in the reversion of international politics towards a brutal nationalism and in the backward drift of industrial and business life towards harsh, selfish, and uncreative profit-seeking. There has been a slipping off of ancient restraints ; a real *de-civilization* of men's minds. We would lay stress here on the suggestion that this divorce of religious teaching from organized education is necessarily a temporary one, a transitory dislocation, and that presently education must become again in intention and spirit religious, and that the impulse to devotion, to universal service and to a complete escape from self, which has been the common underlying force in all the great religions of the last five and twenty centuries, an impulse which ebbed so perceptibly during the prosperity, laxity, disillusionment and scepticism of the past seventy or eighty years, will reappear again, stripped and plain, as the recognized fundamental structural impulse in human society.

Education is the preparation of the individual for the community, and his religious training is the core of that preparation. With the great intellectual restatements and expansions of the nineteenth century, an educational break-up, a confusion and loss of aim in education, was inevitable. We can no longer prepare the individual for a community when our ideas of a community are shattered and undergoing reconstruction. The old loyalties, the old too limited and narrow political and social assumptions, the old too elaborate religious formulæ, have lost their power of conviction, and the greater ideas of a world state and of an economic commonweal have been winning their way only very slowly to recognition. So far they have swayed only a minority of exceptional people. But out of the trouble and tragedy of this present time there may emerge a moral and intellectual revival, a religious revival, of a simplicity and scope to draw together men of alien races and now discrete traditions into one common and sustained way of living for the world's service. We cannot foretell the scope and power of such a revival; we cannot even produce evidence of its onset. The beginnings of such things are never conspicuous. Great movements of the racial soul come at first " like a thief in the night," and then suddenly are discovered to be powerful and world-wide. Religious emotion—stripped of corruptions and freed from its last priestly entanglements—may presently blow through life again like a great wind, bursting the doors and flinging open the shutters of the individual life, and making many things possible and easy that in these present days of exhaustion seem almost too difficult to desire.[1]

§ 2

If we suppose a sufficient righteousness and intelligence in men to produce presently, from the tremendous lessons of history, an effective will for a world peace—that is to say an effective will *for a world law under a world government*—for in no other fashion is a secure world peace conceivable—in what manner may we expect things to move towards this end? That movement will certainly not go on equally in every country, nor is it likely to take at first one uniform mode of expression. Here it will find a congenial and stimulating atmosphere; here it will find itself antagonistic to deep tradition or racial idiosyncrasy or well-organized base oppositions. In some cases those to whom the call of the new order has come will be living in a state almost ready to serve the ends of the greater political synthesis; in others they will have to fight like conspirators

How a Feder-
al World
Government
may come
about.

[1] A suggestive book here containing a good account of the drift of modern religious thought is G. W. Cooke's *Social Evolution of Religion.*

against the rule of evil laws. There is little in the political constitution of such countries as the United States or Switzerland that would impede their coalescence upon terms of frank give and take with other equally civilized confederations; political systems involving dependent areas and " subject peoples " such as the Turkish Empire was before the Great War, seem to require something in the nature of a breaking up before they can be adapted to a federal world system. Any state obsessed by traditions of an aggressive foreign policy will be difficult to assimilate into a world combination. But though here the government may be helpful, and here dark and hostile, the essential task of men of goodwill in all states and countries remains the same, it is an educational task, and its very essence is to bring to the minds of all men everywhere, as a necessary basis for world co-operation, *a new telling and interpretation, a common interpretation, of history.*

Does this League of Nations which has been created by the covenant of 1919 contain within it the germ of any permanent federation of human effort? Will it grow into something for which, as Stallybrass says, men will be ready to " work wholeheartedly and, if necessary, *fight* "—as hitherto they have been willing to fight for their country and their own people? There are few intimations of any such enthusiasm for the League at the present time. The League does not even seem to know how to talk to common men. It has gone into official buildings, and comparatively few people in the world understand or care what it is doing there. It may be that the League is no more than a first project of union, exemplary only in its insufficiencies and dangers, destined to be superseded by something closer and completer as were the United States Articles of Confederation by the Federal Constitution (see Chapter XXXVII, § 5). The League is at present a mere partial league of governments and states. It emphasizes nationality; it defers to sovereignty. What the world needs is no such league of nations as this nor even a mere league of peoples, but *a world league of men.* The world perishes unless sovereignty is merged and nationality subordinated. And for that the minds of men must first be prepared by experience and knowledge and thought. The supreme task before

The
United States
of the
World

EUROPE
ASIA
AFRICA
AUSTRALIA

J.F.H.

THE
OLD WORLD
IN THE
FUTURE

men at the present time is political education.

It may be that several partial leagues may precede any world league. The common misfortunes and urgent common needs of Europe and Asia may be more efficacious in bringing the European and Asiatic states to reason and a sort of unity, than the mere intellectual and sentimental ties of the United States and Great Britain and France. A United States of the Old World is a possibility to set against the possibility of an Atlantic union. Moreover, there is much to be said for an American experiment, a Pan-American league, in which the New World European colonies would play an in-and-out part as Luxembourg did for a time in the German Confederation.

We will not attempt to weigh here what share may be taken in the recasting and consolidation of human affairs by the teachings and propaganda of labour internationalism, by the studies and needs of international finance, or by such boundary-destroying powers as science and art and historical teaching. All these things may exert a combined pressure, in which it may never be possible to apportion the exact shares. Opposition may dissolve, antagonistic cults flatten out to a common culture, almost imperceptibly. The bold idealism of to-day may seem mere commonsense to-morrow. And the problem of a forecast is complicated by the possibilities of interludes and backwaters. History has never gone simply forward. More particularly are the years after a great war apt to be years of apparent retrocession ; men are too weary to see what has been done, what has been cleared away, and what has been made possible.

Among the things that seem to move commandingly towards an adequate world control at the present time are these :

(1) The increasing destructiveness and intolerableness of war waged with the new powers of science.

(2) The inevitable fusion of the world's economic affairs into one system, leading necessarily, it would seem, to some common control of currency, and demanding safe and uninterrupted communications, and a free movement of goods and people by sea and land throughout the whole world. The satisfaction of these needs will require a world control of very considerable authority and powers of enforcement.

(3) The need, because of the increasing mobility of peoples, of effectual controls of health everywhere.

(4) The urgent need of some equalization of labour conditions, and of the minimum standard of life throughout the world. This seems to carry with it, as a necessary corollary, the establishment of some minimum standard of education for everyone.

(5) The impossibility of developing the enormous benefits of flying without a world control of the air-ways.

The necessity and logic of such diverse considerations as these push the mind irresistibly, in spite of the clashes of race and tradition and the huge difficulties created by differences in language, towards the belief that a conscious struggle to establish or prevent a political world community will be the next stage in human history. The things that require that world community are permanent *needs* ; one or other of these needs appeals to nearly everyone, and against their continuing persistence are only mortal difficulties, great no doubt, but mortal ; prejudices, passions, animosities, delusions about race and country, egotisms, and such-like fluctuating and evanescent things, set up in men's minds by education and suggestion ; none of them things that make now for the welfare and survival of the individuals who are under their sway nor of the states and towns and associations in which they prevail.

§ 3

Our *Outline of History* has been ill written if it has failed to convey our conviction of the character of the state towards Some Fundamental which the world is moving. Let us Characteristics of a summarize here, very briefly, the tics of a main lines to which the developments Modern of history seem to point as the necessary lines of that world organization. The attainment of this world state may be impeded and may be opposed to-day by many apparently vast forces ; but it has, urging it on, a much more powerful force, that of the free and growing common intelligence of mankind. To-day there is in the world a small but increasing number of men, historians, archæologists, ethnologists, economists, sociologists, psychologists, educationists, and the like, who are doing for human institutions that same task of creative analysis which the scientific men of the seventeenth and eighteenth centuries did for the materials and mechanism of human life ; and just as these latter, almost unaware of what they were doing, made telegraphy, swift transit on sea and land, flying and a thousand hitherto impossible things possible, so the former may be doing more than the world suspects, or than they themselves suspect, to clear up and make plain the thing to do and the way to do it, in the greater and more urgent human affairs.

Let us ape Roger Bacon in regard to these matters, and set down what we believe will be the broad fundamentals of the coming world state.

(i) It will be based upon a common world religion, very much simplified and universalized and better understood. This will not be Christianity nor Islam nor Buddhism nor any such specialized form of religion, but religion itself pure and undefiled ; the Eightfold Way, the Kingdom of Heaven, brotherhood, creative service, and self-forgetfulness. Throughout the world men's thoughts and motives will be turned by education, example, and the circle of ideas about them, from the obsession of self to the cheerful service of human knowledge, human power, and human unity.

(ii) And this world state will be sustained by a universal education, organized upon a scale and of a penetration and quality beyond all present experience. The whole race, and not simply classes and peoples, will be *educated*. Most parents will have a technical knowledge of teaching. Quite apart from the duties of parentage, perhaps ten per cent. or more of the adult population will, at some time or other in their lives, be workers in the world's educational organization. And education, as the new age will conceive it, will go on throughout life ; it will not cease at any particular age. Men and women will simply become self-educators and individual students and student teachers as they grow older.

(iii) There will be no armies, no navies, and no classes of unemployed people, wealthy or poor.

(iv) The world-state's organization of scientific research and record compared with that of to-day will be like an ocean liner beside the dug-out canoe of some early heliolithic wanderer.

(v) There will be a vast free literature of criticism and discussion.

(vi) The world's political organization will be democratic, that is to say, the government and direction of affairs will be in immediate touch with and responsive to the general thought of the educated whole population.

(vii) Its economic organization will be an exploitation of all natural wealth and every fresh possibility science reveals, by the agents and servants of the common government for the common good. Private enterprise will be the servant—a useful, valued, and well-rewarded servant—and no longer the robber master of the commonweal.

(viii) And this implies two achievements that seem very difficult to us to-day. They are matters of mechanism, but they are as essential to the world's well-being as it is to a soldier's, no matter how brave he may be, that his machine gun should not jam, and to an aeronaut's that his steering-gear should not fail him in mid-air. Political well-being demands that electoral methods shall be used, and economic well-being requires that a currency shall be used, safeguarded or proof against the contrivances and manipulations of clever, dishonest men.

§ 4

There can be little question that the attainment of a federation of all humanity, together with a sufficient measure of social justice, to ensure health, education, and a rough equality of opportunity to most of the children born into the world, would mean such a release and increase of human energy as to open a new phase in human history. The enormous waste caused by military preparation and the mutual annoyance of competing Great Powers, and the still more enormous waste due to the under-productiveness of great masses of people, either because they are too wealthy for stimulus or too poor for efficiency, would cease. There would be a vast increase in the supply of human necessities, a rise in the standard

What this World might be were it under one Law and Justice.

day the power of tradition is destroyed.[1] The body of our state is civilization still, but its spirit is the spirit of the nomadic world. It is the spirit of the great plains and the high seas.

So that it is difficult to resist the persuasion that so soon as one law runs in the earth and the fierceness of frontiers ceases to distress us, that urgency in our nature that stirs us in spring and autumn to be up and travelling, will have its way with us. We shall obey the call of the summer pastures and the winter pastures in our blood, the call of the mountains, the desert, and the sea. For some of us also, who may be of a different lineage, there is the call of the forest, and there are those who would hunt in the summer and return to the fields for the harvest and the plough. But this does not mean that men will have become homeless and all adrift. The normal nomadic life is not a homeless one, but a movement between homes. The Kalmucks to-day, like the swallows, go yearly a thousand miles from one home to another. The beautiful and convenient cities of the coming age, we conclude, will have their seasons when they will be full of life, and seasons when they will seem asleep. Life will ebb and flow to and from every region seasonally as the interest of that region rises or declines.

There will be little drudgery in this better-ordered world. Natural power harnessed in machines will be the general drudge. What drudgery is inevitable will be done as a service and duty for a few years or months out of each life; it will not consume nor degrade the whole life of anyone. And not only drudges, but many other sorts of men and ways of living which loom large in the current social scheme will necessarily have dwindled in importance or passed away altogether. There will be few professional fighting men or none at all, no custom-house officers; the increased multitude of teachers will have abolished large police forces and large jail staffs, mad-houses will be rare or non-existent; a world-wide sanitation will have diminished the proportion of hospitals, nurses, sick-room attendants, and the like; a world-wide economic justice, the floating

[1] Compare Basil Thompson, *The Fijians, a Study of the Decay of Custom*; Introduction and opening chapters. This is a fine study of an ancient "heliolithic" culture breaking up under modernization.

population
stallers, p
But there
romance i
Sea fisheri
the sea, f
stalwart ty
for manho
places of
renewed i
disordered
sacre of
angles of
than hu
century
them ver
but one
state wo
are now
human
since the
and app
that me
to-day,
educate
of the
in this
in the
and lea
and b
pathet
fear as
And a
mean
institu
mount
and gi
and p
before
will n
so de
and b
Th
gath
the F
for "
civil
men
and
diffe
The

of life and in what is considered a necessity, a development of transport and every kind of convenience; and a multitude of people would be transferred from low-grade production to such higher work as art of all kinds, teaching, scientific research, and the like. All over the world there would be a setting free of human capacity, such as has occurred hitherto only in small places and through precious limited phases of prosperity and security. Unless we are to suppose that spontaneous outbreaks of super-men have occurred in the past, it is reasonable to conclude that the Athens of Pericles, the Florence of the Medici, Elizabethan England, the great deeds of Asoka, the Tang and Ming periods in art, are but samples of what a whole world of sustained security would yield continuously and cumulatively. Without supposing any change in human quality, but merely its release from the present system of inordinate waste, history justifies this expectation.

We have seen how, since the liberation of human thought in the fifteenth and sixteenth centuries, a comparatively few curious and intelligent men, chiefly in Western Europe, have produced a vision of the world and a body of science that is now, on the material side, revolutionizing life. Mostly these men have worked against great discouragement, with insufficient funds and small help or support from the mass of mankind. It is impossible to believe that these men were the maximum intellectual harvest of their generation. England alone in the last three centuries must have produced scores of Newtons who never learnt to read, hundreds of Daltons, Darwins, Bacons, and Huxleys who died stunted in hovels, or never got a chance of proving their quality. All the world over, there must have been myriads of potential first-class investigators, splendid artists, creative minds, who never caught a gleam of inspiration or opportunity, for every one of that kind who has left his mark upon the world. In the trenches of the Western Front alone during the late war thousands of potential great men died unfulfilled. But a world with something like a secure international peace and something like social justice, will fish for capacity with the fine net of universal education, and may expect a yield beyond comparison greater than

any yield of able and brilliant men that the world has known hitherto.

It is such considerations as this indeed which justify the concentration of effort in the near future upon the making of a new world state of righteousness out of our present confusions. War is a horrible thing, and constantly more horrible and dreadful, so that unless it is ended it will certainly end human society; social injustice, and the sight of the limited and cramped human beings it produces, torment the soul; but the strongest incentive to constructive political and social work for an imaginative spirit lies not so much in the mere hope of escaping evils as in the opportunity for great adventures that their suppression will open to our race. We want to get rid of the militarist not simply because he hurts and kills, but because he is an intolerable thick-voiced blockhead who stands hectoring and blustering in our way to achievement. We want to abolish many extravagancies of private ownership just as we should want to abolish some idiot guardian who refused us admission to a studio in which there were fine things to do.

There are people who seem to imagine that a world order and one universal law of justice would end human adventure. It would but begin it. But instead of the adventure of the past, the "romance" of the cinematograph world, the perpetual reiterated harping upon the trite reactions of sex and combat and the hunt for gold, it would be an unending exploration upon the edge of experience. Hitherto man has been living in a slum, amidst quarrels, revenges, vanities, shames and taints, hot desires and urgent appetites. He has scarcely tasted sweet air yet and the great freedoms of the world that science has enlarged for him.

To picture to ourselves something of the wider life that world unity would open to men is a very attractive speculation. Life will certainly go with a stronger pulse, it will breathe a deeper breath, because it will have dispelled and conquered a hundred infections of body and mind that now reduce it to invalidism and squalor. We have already laid stress on the vast elimination of drudgery from human life through the creation of a new race of slaves, the machines. This—and the disappearance of

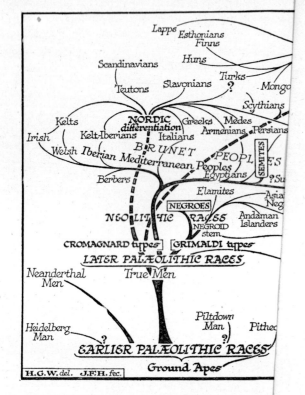

Lapps Esthonians Finns Huns Scandinavians Turks? Teutons Slavonians Mongo Scythians Kelts NORDIC differentiation Greeks Medes Armenians Persians Irish Kelt-Iberians Italians Welsh Iberian Mediterranean Peoples BRUNET PEOPLES SEMITES Berbers Egyptians ?Su Elamites Asia Neg NEGROES NEOLITHIC RACES NEGROID stem Andaman Islanders CROMAGNARD types GRIMALDI types LATER PALÆOLITHIC RACES Neanderthal Men True Men Heidelberg Man Piltdown Man Pithec EARLIER PALÆOLITHIC RACES Ground Apes H.G.W.del. J.F.H.fec.

war and the smoothing out of endless restraints and contentions by juster social and economic arrangements—will lift the burthen of toilsome work and routine work, that has been the price of human security since the dawn of the first civilizations, from the shoulders of our children. Which does not mean that they will cease to work, but that they will cease to do irksome work under pressure, and will work freely, planning, making, creating, according to their gifts and instincts. They will fight nature no longer as dull conscripts of the pick and plough, but for a splendid conquest. Only the spiritlessness of our present depression blinds us to the clear intimations of our reason that in the course of a few generations every little country town could become an Athens, every human being could be gentle in breeding and healthy in body and mind, the whole solid earth man's mine and its uttermost regions his playground.

In this *Outline* we have sought to show two great systems of development interacting in the story of human society. We have seen growing out of that later special neolithic culture, the heliolithic culture, and arising

does not imply the creation of a homogeneous community, but rather the reverse; the welcome and the adequate utilization of diverse gifts in an atmosphere of understanding. It is the almost universal bad manners of the present age which make race intolerable to race. The community to which we may be moving will be more mixed—which does not necessarily mean more interbred—more various and more interesting than any existing community. Communities all to one pattern, like boxes of toy soldiers, are things of the past rather than of the future.

But one of the hardest, most impossible tasks a writer can set himself, is to picture the life of people better educated, happier in their circumstances, more free and more healthy than he is himself. We know enough to-day to know that there is infinite room for betterment in every human concern. Nothing is needed but collective effort. Our poverty, our restraints, our infections and indigestions, our quarrels and misunderstandings, are all things controllable and removable by concerted human action, but we know as little how life would feel without them as some poor dirty ill-treated, fierce-souled creature born and bred amidst the cruel and dingy surroundings of a European back street can know what it is to bathe every day, always to be clad beautifully, to climb mountains for pleasure, to fly, to meet none but agreeable, well-mannered people, to conduct researches or make delightful things. Yet a time when all such good things will be for all men may be coming more nearly than we think. Each one who believes that brings the good time nearer; each heart that fails delays it.

One cannot foretell the surprises or disappointments the future has in store. Before this chapter of the World State can begin fairly in our histories, other chapters as yet unsuspected may still need to be written, as long and as full of conflict as our account of the dismal rivalries of the Great Powers. There may be tragic economic struggles, grim grapplings of race with race and class with class. We do not know; we cannot tell. These are unnecessary disasters, but they may be unavoidable disasters. Human history becomes more and more a race between education and catastrophe. Against the unifying effort of Christen-

dom and against the unifying influence of the mechanical revolution, catastrophe won. New falsities may arise and hold men in some unrighteous and fated scheme of order for a time, before they collapse amidst the misery and slaughter of generations. Yet, clumsily or smoothly, the world progresses and will progress. In this *Outline*, in our account of palæolithic men, we have borrowed a description from Mr. Worthington Smith of the very highest life in the world some fifty thousand years ago. It was a bestial life. We have sketched too the gathering for a human sacrifice, some fifteen thousand years ago. That scene again is almost incredibly cruel to a modern civilized reader. Yet it is not more than five hundred years since the great empire of the Aztecs still believed that it could live only by the shedding of blood. Every year in Mexico hundreds of human victims died in this fashion: the body was bent like a bow over the curved stone of sacrifice, the breast was slashed open with a knife of obsidian, and the priest tore out the beating heart of the still living victim. The day may be close at hand when we shall no longer tear out the hearts of men, even for the sake of our national gods. Let the reader but go back to the earlier time charts we have given in this history, and he will see the true measure and transitoriness of all the conflicts, deprivations, and miseries of this present period of painful and yet hopeful change.

§ 5

History is and must always be no more than an account of beginnings. We can venture to prophesy that the next chapters to *The Stages Beyond.* be written will tell, though perhaps with long interludes of setback and disaster, of the final achievement of world-wide political and social unity. But when that is attained, it will mean no resting stage, nor even a breathing stage, before the development of a new struggle and of new and vaster efforts. Men will unify only to intensify the search for knowledge and power, and live as ever for new occasions. Animal and vegetable life, the obscure processes of psychology, the intimate processes of matter and the interior of our earth, will yield their secrets and endow their conqueror. Life begins perpetually. Gathered together at last under the leadership of man, the student-teacher of the universe, unified, disciplined, armed with the secret powers of the atom and with knowledge as yet beyond dreaming, Life, for ever dying to be born afresh, for ever young and eager, will presently stand upon this earth as upon a footstool, and stretch out its realm amidst the stars.

CHRONOLOGICAL TABLE

In conclusion it will round off this *Outline* to give one more chronological table in continuation of those already given.

1563. End of the Council of Trent and the reform of the Catholic Church.
1564. Galileo born.
1566. Suleiman the Magnificent died.
1567. Revolt of the Netherlands.
1568. Execution of Counts Egmont and Horn.
1571. Kepler born.
1573. Siege of Alkmaar.
1578. Harvey born.
1583. Sir Walter Raleigh's expedition to Virginia.
1603. James I King of England and Scotland.
1605. Jehangir Great Mogul.
1606. Virginia Company founded.
1609. Holland independent.
1618. Thirty Years War began.
1620. *Mayflower* expedition founded New Plymouth. First negro slaves landed at Jamestown (Va.)
1625. Charles I of England.
1628. Shah Jehan Great Mogul. The English *Petition of Right*.
1629. Charles I of England began his eleven years of rule without a parliament.
1632. Leeuwenhoek born. Gustavus Adolphus killed at the Battle of Lützen.
1634. Wallenstein murdered.
1638. Japan closed to Europeans (until 1865).
1640. Charles I of England summoned the Long Parliament.
1641. Massacre of the English in Ireland.
1643. Louis XIV began his reign of seventy-two years.
1644. The Manchus ended the Ming dynasty.
1645. Swine pens in the inner town of Leipzig pulled down.

1648. Treaty of Westphalia. Thereby Holland and Switzerland were recognized as free republics and Prussia became important. The treaty gave a complete victory neither to the Imperial Crown nor to the Princes.
    War of the Fronde; it ended in the complete victory of the French Crown.
1649. Execution of Charles I of England.
1658. Aurungzeb Great Mogul.
1674. Nieuw Amsterdam finally became British by treaty and was renamed New York.
1683. The last Turkish attack on Vienna defeated by John III of Poland.
1688. The British Revolution. William and Mary began to reign.
1689. Peter the Great of Russia. (To 1725.)
1690. Battle of the Boyne in Ireland.
1694. Voltaire born.
1701. Frederick I first King of Prussia.
1704. John Locke, the father of modern democratic theory, died.
1707. Death of Aurungzeb. The empire of the Great Mogul disintegrated.
1713. Frederick the Great of Prussia born.
1714. George I of Britain.
1715. Louis XV of France.
1727. Newton died. George II of Britain.
1732. Oglethorpe founded Georgia.
1736. Nadir Shah raided India. (The beginning of twenty years of raiding and disorder in India.)
1740. Maria-Theresa began to reign. (Being a woman, she could not be empress. Her husband, Francis I, was emperor until his death in 1765, when her son, Joseph II, succeeded him.)
1740. Accession of Frederick the Great, King of Prussia.
1741. The Empress Elizabeth of Russia began to reign.
1755–63. Britain and France struggled for America and India. France in alliance with Austria and Russia against Prussia and Britain (1756–63); the Seven Years War.
1757. Battle of Plassey.
1759. The British general, Wolfe, took Quebec.
1760. George III of Britain.

NOTES AND ERRATA

The following points should be noted for correction by the readers of the OUTLINE OF HISTORY:—

PAGE

4. The figures in the second column are inaccurate. The moon's distance should be 30, not 20, inches. 850 should be 1,850.

18, line 3, col. 1. "Palæolithic" should be "Palæozoic."

24, footnote. Dr. Mary Stopes should be Dr. Marie Stopes.

29, col. 2, line 10. Some monitors in the East Indies are larger than any iguana.

38. In the diagram there should be a query against Eoanthropus, which may have lived as early as the Pliocene. Compare what E. R. L. says on p. 46, col. 2.

39, 40, 41. There is too much stress upon the lemur in the account of the ancestry of man. The ancestor of man and the higher apes was probably a ground monkey and not a lemur.

54, col. 1. "Palæozoic" should be "Palæolithic."

71, col. 2. "A.D. 10,000" should of course be "10,000 B.C."

84. There is no swastika in any known Palæolithic drawings. The statement that there is, is flatly wrong.

103, col. 1. Add: The existence of a real wild wheat in Palestine has been settled once for all by Mr. Aaron Aaronson (*Bul.* 274, Plant. Indus. Bureau, U.S. Dept. of Agriculture).

111, diagram. The date of Shi-Hwang-ti is incorrect. See Note to p. 324 (below).

165, col. 2. "Judges I and II" should be "the Book of Judges."

189. The illustration represents the temple of the Olympian Zeus at Athens, and not the temple of Zeus at Olympia, which has long since disappeared.

265, col. 2, illus. The iron pillar at Delhi figured is incorrectly described. It is of wrought, not cast, iron; and its inscription is several centuries later than the time of Asoka. Sir Robert Hadfield has shown that this column was made of discs of wrought iron hammered together. The power to cast so great a mass of iron was only attained by mankind in the nineteenth century.

266, col. 2, and 267, fig. "Kwannon" is the Japanese name of this goddess. The Chinese name is Kuan-yin.

274, col. 2. Wolves are still found near Rome.

295. Calabria is the heel of Italy, not the toe.

296. Scipio Africanus Minor was the grandson (by adoption), not the son, of Sc. Africanus Major.

298. For "sestertii" read "sestertia." A *sestertium* (plur. *sestertia*) was worth a thousand *sestertii* (sing. *sestertius*).

323, diagram. "Sassenid" should be "Sassanid," and "Pau Chau" should be "Pan Chau."

324, and diagram p. 323. See also diagram p. 111. The dates for Shi-Hwang-ti are too early. He was a provincial king of Ch'in in 247 B.C. He became emperor of China only in 220 B.C., ten years before his death.

357, col. 1. The massacre of the innocents throughout Judea is an invention of the Middle Ages. The New Testament says merely that the male children in the district of Bethlehem were killed. They may not have numbered a score. This would have been far too small a tragedy to leave any record in history.

388. Battle of Nineveh was 627, not 617, A.D.

392, footnote. Muhammad means "the praised one," not "the praiser." The form used in the *Encyclopædia Brit.* is Mahomet, not Mohammed.

393, col. 1, line 16. "Second" should be "third," and "Medean" should be "Median."

404, and following pages. Yuan Chwang is several times spelt incorrectly as Yung Chwang.

408. "Galba" should begin a new line.

413, footnote. Abu Bakr means "Father of the Camel."

415. The second footnote is quite wrong. The Moslem year contains only 354 days, and the Moslem count of years is thus steadily overtaking the Christian, at the rate of a year in every thirty-three years.

433, col. 2, line 39. "Potash," not "potassium," which element was not discovered until the nineteenth century. Alcohol (spirits of wine) was known to Pliny.

485, and diagram on p. 489. Ivan III took the Byzantine eagle and the claim to be Cæsar's heir, but did not assume the title of Tsar. This was done by Ivan the Terrible (Ivan IV) in 1547. (In a number of copies this was corrected in the press.)

513, col. 1. Copernicus was a Pole, not a Dane. Tycho Brahe was a Dane who studied at Prague.

520. Columbus sailed on his second voyage with 1,500, not 15,000, men.

524, col. 2. For "Alexander Borgia" read "Rodrigo Borgia" (who took the title of Pope Alexander VI).

530, col. 2, bottom. Henry VIII was anxious to have a son and heir, and there was no prospect of this unless he divorced Catherine of Aragon. England had been recently devastated by a series of bitter dynastic wars, the Wars of the Roses, and the desire to secure the succession was a reasonable one.

544, col. 1. It was Worcester, not Dunbar, which Cromwell called his "crowning mercy."

544. Blake destroyed the pirate fleet in Tunis harbour, not in the harbour of Algiers.

566. "Their pigtail" should be "the pigtail." The pigtail was only obligatory on the Chinese.

611. For "while the terror ruled in France" read "while the Revolution was in progress in France." The terror lasted only a few months.

635. Louis Philippe was not "young," but at the end of his middle age.

639. Before the Liverpool and Manchester line came the Stockton and Darlington in 1825.

KEY TO PRONUNCIATION

VOWELS

a as in far (far), father (fa'thèr), mikado (mi ka' dō).
ă „ „ fat (făt), ample (ămpl), abstinence (ăb' stin ĕns).
ā „ „ fate (fāt), wait (wāt), deign (dān), jade (jād).
aw „ „ fall (fawl), appal (a pawl'), broad (brawd).
ä „ „ fair (fär), bear (bär), where (hwär).

e „ „ bell (bel), bury (ber' i).
ĕ „ „ her (hĕr), search (sĕrch), word (wĕrd), bird (bĕrd).
ē „ „ beef (bēf), thief (thēf), idea (ī dē' à), beer (bēr), casino (kà sē' nō).

i „ „ bit (bit), lily (lil' i), nymph (nimf), build (bild).
ī „ „ bite (bīt), analyse (ăn' a līz), light (līt).

o „ „ not (not), watch (woch), cough (kof), sorry (sor' i).
o „ „ no (nō), blow (blō), brooch (brōch).
ö „ „ north (nörth), absorb (ab sörb').
oo „ „ food (food), do (doo), prove (proov), blue (bloo), strew (stroo).

u „ „ bull (bul), good (gud), would (wud).
ŭ „ „ sun (sŭn), love (lŭv), enough (è nŭf').
ū „ „ muse (mūz), stew (stū), cure (kūr).

ou „ „ bout (bout), bough (bou), crowd (kroud).
oi „ „ join (join), joy (joi), buoy (boi).

A dot placed over **a, e, o,** or **u** (à, è, ò, ù,) signifies that the vowel has an obscure, indeterminate, or slurred sound, as in:

advice (àd vīs'), sailor (sā' lòr),
breakable (brā' kàbl), notion (nō' shùn),
current (kŭr' ènt), pleasure (plezh' ùr).

CONSONANTS

"s" is used only for the sibilant "s" (as in "toast," tōst, "place," plās); the sonant "s" (as in "toes," "plays") is printed "z" (tōz, plāz).

"c" (except in the combinations "ch" and "*ch*"), "q" and "x" are not used.

b, d, f, h (but see the combinations below), k, l, m, n (see *n* below), p, r, t, v, z, and w and y when used as consonants have their usual values.

ch as in church (chĕrch), batch (băch), capriccio (ka prē' chō).

c' „ „ loch (lo*ch*), coronach (kor' o na*ch*), clachan (klă*ch*' an).

g „ „ get (get), finger (fing' gér).
j „ „ join (join), judge (jŭj), germ (jĕrm), ginger (jin' jér).

gh (in List of Proper Names only) as in Ludwig (lut' vigh).
hl („ „ „ „) „ „ l lanċilo (hlăn di' lō).
hw as in white (hwīt), nowhere (nō' hwär).

n „ „ cabochon (ka bō shon'), congé (kon' zhā).

sh „ „ shawl (shawl), mention (men' shùn).
zh „ „ measure (mezh' ùr), vision (vizh' òn).

th „ „ thin (thin), breath (breth).
th „ „ thine (*th*īn), breathe (brē*th*).

The accent (') *follows* the syllable to be stressed.

(CASSELL'S *New English Dictionary*. Ed. by DR. BAKER.)

INDEX